Lecture Notes in Computer Science   11064

Commenced Publication in 1973
Founding and Former Series Editors:
Gerhard Goos, Juris Hartmanis, and Jan van Leeuwen

Xingming Sun · Zhaoqing Pan
Elisa Bertino (Eds.)

Cloud Computing and Security

4th International Conference, ICCCS 2018
Haikou, China, June 8–10, 2018
Revised Selected Papers, Part II

Springer

Editors
Xingming Sun 🄳
Nanjing University of Information Science
  and Technology
Nanjing
China

Elisa Bertino 🄳
Department of Computer Science
Purdue University
West Lafayette, IN
USA

Zhaoqing Pan 🄳
Nanjing University of Information Science
  and Technology
Nanjing
China

ISSN 0302-9743   ISSN 1611-3349 (electronic)
Lecture Notes in Computer Science
ISBN 978-3-030-00008-0   ISBN 978-3-030-00009-7 (eBook)
https://doi.org/10.1007/978-3-030-00009-7

Library of Congress Control Number: 2018952646

LNCS Sublibrary: SL3 – Information Systems and Applications, incl. Internet/Web, and HCI

This Springer imprint is published by the registered company Springer Nature Switzerland AG
The registered company address is: Gewerbestrasse 11, 6330 Cham, Switzerland

Preface

The 4th International Conference on Cloud Computing and Security (ICCCS 2018) was held in Haikou, China, during June 8–10, 2018, and hosted by the School of Computer and Software at the Nanjing University of Information Science and Technology. ICCCS is a leading conference for researchers and engineers to share their latest results of research, development, and applications in the field of cloud computing and information security.

We made use of the excellent Tech Science Press (TSP) submission and reviewing software. ICCCS 2018 received 1743 submissions from 20 countries and regions, including USA, Canada, UK, Italy, Ireland, Japan, Russia, France, Australia, South Korea, South Africa, India, Iraq, Kazakhstan, Indonesia, Vietnam, Ghana, China, Taiwan, and Macao. The submissions covered the areas of cloud computing, cloud security, information hiding, IOT security, multimedia forensics, and encryption, etc. We thank our Technical Program Committee members and external reviewers for their efforts in reviewing papers and providing valuable comments to the authors. From the total of 1743 submissions, and based on at least two reviews per submission, the Program Chairs decided to accept 386 papers, yielding an acceptance rate of 22.15%. The volume of the conference proceedings contains all the regular, poster, and workshop papers.

The conference program was enriched by six keynote presentations, and the keynote speakers were Mauro Barni, University of Siena, Italy; Charles Ling, University of Western Ontario, Canada; Yunbiao Guo, Beijing Institute of Electronics Technology and Application, China; Yunhao Liu, Michigan State University, USA; Nei Kato, Tokyo University, Japan; and Jianfeng Ma, Xidian University, China. We thank them very much for their wonderful talks.

There were 42 workshops organized in conjunction with ICCCS 2018, covering all the hot topics in cloud computing and security. We would like to take this moment to express our sincere appreciation for the contribution of all the workshop chairs and their participants. In addition, we would like to extend our sincere thanks to all authors who submitted papers to ICCCS 2018 and to all PC members. It was a truly great experience to work with such talented and hard-working researchers. We also appreciate the work of the external reviewers, who assisted the PC members in their particular areas of expertise. Moreover, we would like to thank our sponsors: Nanjing University of Information Science and Technology, Springer, Hainan University, IEEE Nanjing Chapter, ACM China, Michigan State University, Taiwan Cheng Kung University, Taiwan Dong Hwa University, Providence University, Nanjing University of Aeronautics and Astronautics, State Key Laboratory of Integrated Services Networks, Tech Science Press, and the National Nature Science Foundation of China. Finally, we would like to thank all attendees for their active participation and the organizing team, who nicely managed this conference. Next year, ICCCS will be renamed as the International Conference on Artificial Intelligence and Security (ICAIS). We look forward to seeing you again at the ICAIS.

July 2018

Xingming Sun
Zhaoqing Pan
Elisa Bertino

Organization

General Chairs

Xingming Sun   Nanjing University of Information Science
and Technology, China

Han-Chieh Chao   Taiwan Dong Hwa University, Taiwan, China

Xingang You   China Information Technology Security Evaluation
Center, China

Elisa Bertino   Purdue University, USA

Technical Program Committee Chairs

Aniello Castiglione   University of Salerno, Italy

Yunbiao Guo   China Information Technology Security Evaluation
Center, China

Zhangjie Fu   Nanjing University of Information Science
and Technology, China

Xinpeng Zhang   Fudan University, China

Jian Weng   Jinan University, China

Mengxing Huang   Hainan University, China

Alex Liu   Michigan State University, USA

Workshop Chair

Baowei Wang   Nanjing University of Information Science
and Technology, China

Publication Chair

Zhaoqing Pan   Nanjing University of Information Science
and Technology, China

Publicity Chair

Chuanyou Ju   Nanjing University of Information Science
and Technology, China

Local Arrangement Chair

Jieren Cheng   Hainan University, China

Website Chair

Wei Gu   Nanjing University of Information Science
                                and Technology, China

Technical Program Committee Members

Saeed Arif	University of Algeria, Algeria
Zhifeng Bao	Royal Melbourne Institute of Technology University, Australia
Lianhua Chi	IBM Research Center, Australia
Bing Chen	Nanjing University of Aeronautics and Astronautics, China
Hanhua Chen	Huazhong University of Science and Technology, China
Jie Chen	East China Normal University, China
Xiaofeng Chen	Xidian University, China
Ilyong Chung	Chosun University, South Korea
Jieren Cheng	Hainan University, China
Kim-Kwang Raymond Choo	University of Texas at San Antonio, USA
Chin-chen Chang	Feng Chia University, Taiwan, China
Robert H. Deng	Singapore Management University, Singapore
Jintai Ding	University of Cincinnati, USA
Shaojing Fu	National University of Defense Technology, China
Xinwen Fu	University of Central Florida, USA
Song Guo	Hong Kong Polytechnic University, Hong Kong, China
Ruili Geng	Spectral MD, USA
Russell Higgs	University College Dublin, Ireland
Dinh Thai Hoang	University of Technology Sydney, Australia
Robert Hsu	Chung Hua University, Taiwan, China
Chih-Hsien Hsia	Chinese Culture University, Taiwan, China
Jinguang Han	Nanjing University of Finance & Economics, China
Debiao He	Wuhan University, China
Wien Hong	Nanfang College of Sun Yat-Sen University, China
Qiong Huang	South China Agricultural University, China
Xinyi Huang	Fujian Normal University, China
Yongfeng Huang	Tsinghua University, China
Zhiqiu Huang	Nanjing University of Aeronautics and Astronautics, China
Mohammad Mehedi Hassan	King Saud University, Saudi Arabia
Farookh Hussain	University of Technology Sydney, Australia
Hai Jin	Huazhong University of Science and Technology, China
Sam Tak Wu Kwong	City University of Hong Kong, China
Patrick C. K. Hung	University of Ontario Institute of Technology, Canada

Krzysztof Szczypiorski	Warsaw University of Technology, Poland
Frank Y. Shih	New Jersey Institute of Technology, USA
Arun Kumar Sangaiah	VIT University, India
Jing Tian	National University of Singapore, Singapore
Cezhong Tong	Washington University in St. Louis, USA
Shanyu Tang	University of West London, UK
Tsuyoshi Takagi	Kyushu University, Japan
Xianping Tao	Nanjing University, China
Yoshito Tobe	Aoyang University, Japan
Cai-Zhuang Wang	Ames Laboratory, USA
Xiaokang Wang	St. Francis Xavier University, Canada
Jie Wang	University of Massachusetts Lowell, USA
Guiling Wang	New Jersey Institute of Technology, USA
Ruili Wang	Massey University, New Zealand
Sheng Wen	Swinburne University of Technology, Australia
Jinwei Wang	Nanjing University of Information Science and Technology, China
Ding Wang	Peking University, China
Eric Wong	University of Texas at Dallas, USA
Pengjun Wan	Illinois Institute of Technology, USA
Jian Wang	Nanjing University of Aeronautics and Astronautics, China
Honggang Wang	University of Massachusetts-Dartmouth, USA
Liangmin Wang	Jiangsu University, China
Xiaojun Wang	Dublin City University, Ireland
Q. M. Jonathan Wu	University of Windsor, Canada
Shaoen Wu	Ball State University, USA
Yang Xiao	The University of Alabama, USA
Haoran Xie	The Education University of Hong Kong, China
Zhihua Xia	Nanjing University of Information Science and Technology, China
Yang Xiang	Deakin University, Australia
Naixue Xiong	Northeastern State University, USA
Shuangkui Xia	Beijing Institute of Electronics Technology and Application, China
Fan Yang	University of Maryland, USA
Kun-Ming Yu	Chung Hua University, Taiwan, China
Xiaoli Yue	Donghua University, China
Ming Yin	Harvard University, USA
Aimin Yang	Guangdong University of Foreign Studies, China
Qing Yang	University of North Texas, USA
Ching-Nung Yang	Taiwan Dong Hwa University, Taiwan, China
Ming Yang	Southeast University, China
Qing Yang	Montana State University, USA
Xinchun Yin	Yangzhou University, China

Yong Yu	University of Electronic Science and Technology of China, China
Guomin Yang	University of Wollongong, Australia
Wei Qi Yan	Auckland University of Technology, New Zealand
Shaodi You	Australian National University, Australia
Yanchun Zhang	Victoria University, Australia
Mingwu Zhang	Hubei University of Technology, China
Wei Zhang	Nanjing University of Posts and Telecommunications, China
Weiming Zhang	University of Science and Technology of China, China
Yan Zhang	Simula Research Laboratory, Norway
Yao Zhao	Beijing Jiaotong University, China
Linna Zhou	University of International Relations, China

Organization Committee Members

Xianyi Chen	Nanjing University of Information Science and Technology, China
Yadang Chen	Nanjing University of Information Science and Technology, China
Beijing Chen	Nanjing University of Information Science and Technology, China
Chunjie Cao	Hainan University, China
Xianyi Chen	Hainan University, China
Xianmei Chen	Hainan University, China
Fa Fu	Hainan University, China
Xiangdang Huang	Hainan University, China
Zhuhua Hu	Hainan University, China
Jielin Jiang	Nanjing University of Information Science and Technology, China
Zilong Jin	Nanjing University of Information Science and Technology, China
Yan Kong	Nanjing University of Information Science and Technology, China
Jingbing Li	Hainan University, China
Jinlian Peng	Hainan University, China
Zhiguo Qu	Nanjing University of Information Science and Technology, China
Le Sun	Nanjing University of Information Science and Technology, China
Jian Su	Nanjing University of Information Science and Technology, China
Qing Tian	Nanjing University of Information Science and Technology, China
Tao Wen	Hainan University, China
Xianpeng Wang	Hainan University, China

Lizhi Xiong   Nanjing University of Information Science
                       and Technology, China
Chunyang Ye   Hainan University, China
Jiangyuan Yao   Hainan University, China
Leiming Yan   Nanjing University of Information Science
                       and Technology, China
Yu Zhang   Hainan University, China
Zhili Zhou   Nanjing University of Information Science
                       and Technology, China

Contents – Part II

Cloud Security

Cloud Computing

Quality-Aware Query Based on Relative Source Quality

Mohan Li, Yanbin Sun, Le Wang$^{(\boxtimes)}$, and Hui Lu

Cyberspace Institute of Advanced Technology, Guangzhou University,
Guangzhou 510006, China
limohan.hit@gmail.com, yanbin_hit@foxmail.com,
{wangle,luhui}@gzhu.edu.cn

Abstract. In many circumstances, such as internet of things or data fusion, a common scenario is that more than one sources provide the data of the same object, but the data quality of the sources are different. Therefore, when querying the sources which may provide low quality data, the query results should include high quality data. In this paper, we define quality-aware query, and build a model to describe the quality-aware query scenario, which aims to get high quality results from multi-sources which may have different data quality scores. Uncertain graph is used to simulate the relative source quality, and a method to compute the quality of the query results is provided.

Keywords: Data quality · Quality-aware query · Uncertain graph

1 Introduction

Low quality of data arouses a lot of attentions in recent years, since these data may severely impacted on the usability of data and led to huge losses [6,11]. In many circumstances, such as internet of things or data fusion, a common scenario is that more than one sources provide the data of the same object, but the data quality of the sources are different. The following example illustrates the scenario.

Example 1. Consider the three data sources in Fig. 1, each of them provides a data set about the weather conditions of the same place at the same time. Different sources provide different observations about the same object. Some domain knowledge, such as the type of sensor of each source, can help us to infer the relative quality of an observations. For instance, Source 1 claims that the temperature is 16 °C, but Source 2 and Source 3 claim that the temperature are 16.7 °C and 15 °C, respectively. The sensors used by Source 2 might be newer versions of the sensors used by Source 1, thus the values provided by Source 2 is likely to be more accurate than the values from Source 1. Assume

---

The first two authors have the same contributions to this paper.

© Springer Nature Switzerland AG 2018
X. Sun et al. (Eds.): ICCCS 2018, LNCS 11064, pp. 3–8, 2018.
https://doi.org/10.1007/978-3-030-00009-7_1

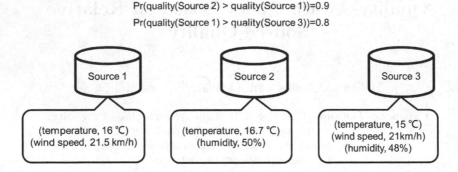

Fig. 1. Data sources with different data quality.

that the probability that sensors used by Source 2 are newer than Source 1 is 0.9. Then we can assume that the probability that Source 2 is more accurate than Source 1 is 0.9. Similarly, Source 1 is accurate than Source 3 with the probability of 0.8. Therefore, although Source 3 provide all the three attributes, i.e., temperature, wind speed and humidity, the quality of the source cannot be ensured. It means that if we only visit Source 3, we might get wrong values.

When querying multi-sources which may provide low quality data, three conditions of the query results need to be guaranteed. First, the query results must include all required data. Second, to avoid of low quality data, the query must access high quality data sources as much as possible. Third, the cost of accessing multiple data sources must be controlled.

In this paper, we build a model to describe this type of query, namely Quality-aware Query. The contribution of this paper is as follows.

1. We formally define quality-aware query.
2. We build a model to describe the quality-aware query scenario, which aims to get high quality results from multi-sources which may provide low quality data.
3. We use uncertain graph to simulate the relative source quality, and give a method to compute the quality of the query results.

The rest of this paper is organized as follows. Section 2 discusses the related work. Section 3 builds the model of Quality-aware Query on multiple data sources. Section 4 studies the method to compute the quality of the query results, and Sect. 5 concludes the paper.

2   Related Work

There is currently a lot of work on constraint-based data quality [2,3,7,8,12]. These work studies the data quality evaluation and data repairing based on conditional functional dependencies and denial constraints. Based on the models and algorithm provided by these work, the relative data quality can be determined. Most of these methods focus on single data source, and the algorithms are more inclined to repair the entire data set rather than answering a query.

Data fusion and truth discovering study how to find high quality data from multi-sources [4,5,9,10,13]. These methods focus on how to estimate the quality of data sources based on the observations. However, they do not consider how to guarantee the data quality of query results.

3 A Model of Multiple Sources and Quality-Aware Query

3.1 Preliminaries

Data Sources. Let $\mathbb{S} = \{S_1, ..., S_n\}$ be a set of data sources, where S_i is the ith data source. $S_i = ((o_1, v_1), ..., (o_{m_i}, v_{m_i}))$ means that a set of observations is provided by S_i, where an observation (o_j, v_j) is a pair of an object and a corresponding value. For instance, $(humidity, 50\%) \in S_2$ in Fig. 1 means that Source 2 claims that the monitored area humidity should be 50%.

Data Quality Constraints. We use relative source quality as data quality constraints. Relative source quality is in the form of $qua(S_i, S_j)$, where qua is the relative accuracy function, the value of $qua(S_i, S_j)$ is the probability that the data quality of S_i is higher than S_j. For example, $qua(S_2, S_1) = 0.9$ means that the data quality of S_i is higher than S_j with the probability 0.9. Ideally, we want to query the source with highest data quality.

Access Cost. Each data source S_i in $\mathbb{S}$ has a access cost $cost(S_i) \in R^+$, indicating the cost of querying S_i. High data quality often means high access cost, thus how to balance the cost and quality is worth studying.

3.2 Definition of Quality-Aware Query

A quality-aware query Q is a query with data quality requirements. Q corresponds to an object set O and a quality lower bound θ. The object set Q consists of the objects queried by Q. For example, if $O = windspeed, humidty$ means that the query asks to return the value of wind speed and humidity. The quality lower bound θ means that Q must return a result with data quality no less than θ. Based on the above two concepts, a quality-aware query is defined as follows.

Definition 1. *A quality-aware query is in the form of $Q = (O, \theta)$, where*

1. *O is the object set corresponding to the query, and*
2. *θ is the quality lower bound corresponding to Q.*

Please note that, for a given object set O and a quality lower bound θ, there could be more than one query plans can return the values of O and satisfy the quality requirement θ. As we discussed above, each data source S_i in $\mathbb{S}$ has a access cost $cost(S_i) \in R^+$. Under the condition of satisfying the lower bound of quality, we naturally want to find the quality-aware query with the minimum cost. The min-cost quality-aware query problem is defined as follows.

Input: a quality-aware query $Q = (O, \theta)$,
Output: a source set $\mathbb{S}' \subseteq \mathbb{S}$ satisfying the following two conditions:

(1) $\mathbb{S}'$ can return the values of all queried objects and satisfy the quality lower bound θ,
(2) $\nexists \mathbb{S}''$ such that $\mathbb{S}''$ satisfies condition (1) and $\sum_{S \in \mathbb{S}''} cost(S) < \sum_{S \in \mathbb{S}'} cost(S)$.

As of now, we have not discussed how to calculate the data quality of query results. In the next subsection we will present a model to describe multi-source data queries and calculate the data quality of the query results.

4   Computing the Quality Score of the Query Results

As defined before, $qua(S_i, S_j)$ is the probability that the data quality of S_i is higher than S_j. In the model, we consider each source as a node, and $qua(S_i, S_j)$ as a weighted arc from S_j to S_i. For instance, Source 1 to 3 in Fig. 1 can be modeled as a direct graph shown by Fig. 2.

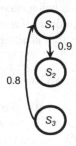

Fig. 2. The direct graph of Source 1 to 3 in Fig. 1

We try to use uncertain graph [14,15] to simulate the relative source quality. Given source set $\mathbb{S}$ and quality constraints set $\mathbb{C}$, the corresponding uncertain graph (namely quality graph) $G_q = (V, A)$ can be obtained as follows.

1. For each $S \in \mathbb{S}$, create a node v_S for S into V.
2. For each constraint $qua(S_i, S_j) \in \mathbb{C}$, add an arc from S_j to S_i to A, and the weight of arc (S_j, S_i) is the value of $qua(S_i, S_j)$.

The semantics of the weight of an arc is the probability of the arc's existence. For example, for the arc (S_1, S_2) in Fig. 2, the probability of (S_1, S_2)'s existence is 0.9, and the probability of non-existence is $1 - 0.9 = 0.1$.

Based on the above semantics, we can use the possible worlds [1] to describe the relative quality constraints between data sources. For example, the possible worlds corresponding to Fig. 2 are shown in Fig. 3. The probabilities of each possible world are 0.18, 0.72, 0.02, and 0.08, respectively.

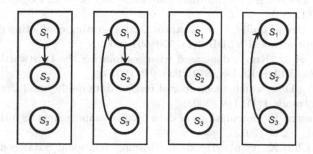

Fig. 3. The possible worlds.

Data Quality Scores of Sources. We define the data quality score of a source S_i (denoted by $dq(S_i)$) is the probability that the quality of S_i is NOT lower than other data sources. In any possible world, the quality of S_i is lower than S_j if there exists an arc from S_i to S_j. Therefore, $dq(S_i)$ is the probability that the node v_{S_i} has an out-degree of 0. It can be verified that $qua(S_i, S_j)$ can be easily changed into other similar definitions.

Data Quality Score of an Query Results. Given a quality-aware query $Q = (O, \theta)$, we can run Q on a subset $\mathbb{S}'$ of sources to get a query result. Let $res(Q, \mathbb{S}')$ be the result of executing the query Q on $\mathbb{S}'$, then the quality score of $res(Q, \mathbb{S}')$ is $\sum_{S \in \mathbb{S}'} dq(S)$.

5 Conclusions

In this paper, we formally define quality-aware query, and build a model to describe the quality-aware query scenario, which aims to get results from multi-sources which may provide low quality data. The relative source quality is simulated by uncertain graph, and a method to compute the quality of the query results is proposed based on the uncertain graph. In future work, we will analyze the computational complexity of the problem of minimum cost quality-aware query, and try to design efficient algorithms to solve the problem.

Acknowledgments. This work is supported by the National Natural Science Foundation of China (No.61572153, No. 61702220, No. 61702223).

References

1. Abiteboul, S., Kanellakis, P., Grahne, G.: On the representation and querying of sets of possible worlds. Theor. Comput. Sci. **78**(1), 159–187 (1991)
2. Cao, Y., Fan, W., Yu, W.: Determining the relative accuracy of attributes. In: Proceedings of the 2013 ACM SIGMOD International Conference on Management of Data, pp. 565–576. ACM (2013)
3. Chu, X., Ilyas, I.F., Papotti, P.: Holistic data cleaning: putting violations into context. In: The IEEE 29th International Conference on Data Engineering (ICDE), pp. 458–469 (2013)
4. Dong, X.L., Berti-Equille, L., Srivastava, D.: Integrating conflicting data: the role of source dependence. PVLDB **2**(1), 550–561 (2009)
5. Dong, X.L., et al.: Knowledge-based trust: estimating the trustworthiness of web sources. Proc. VLDB Endow. **8**(9), 938–949 (2015)
6. Eckerson, W.: Data warehousing special report: data quality and the bottom line. Appl. Dev. Trends **1**(1), 1–9 (2002)
7. Fan, W., Geerts, F.: Foundations of data quality management. Synth. Lect. Data Manag. **4**(5), 1–217 (2012)
8. Ilyas, I.F., Chu, X., et al.: Trends in cleaning relational data: consistency and deduplication. Found. Trends® Databases **5**(4), 281–393 (2015)
9. Li, Q., et al.: A confidence-aware approach for truth discovery on long-tail data. Proc. VLDB Endow. **8**(4), 425–436 (2014)
10. Li, Q., Li, Y., Gao, J., Zhao, B., Fan, W., Han, J.: Resolving conflicts in heterogeneous data by truth discovery and source reliability estimation. In: Proceedings of the 2014 ACM SIGMOD International Conference on Management of Data, pp. 1187–1198. ACM (2014)
11. Pipino, L.L., Lee, Y.W., Wang, R.Y.: Data quality assessment. Commun. ACM **45**(4), 211–218 (2002)
12. Rammelaere, J., Geerts, F., Goethals, B.: Cleaning data with forbidden itemsets. In: 2017 IEEE 33rd International Conference on Data Engineering (ICDE), pp. 897–908 (2017)
13. Rekatsinas, T., Joglekar, M., Garcia-Molina, H., Parameswaran, A., Ré, C.: Slimfast: guaranteed results for data fusion and source reliability. In: Proceedings of the 2017 ACM International Conference on Management of Data, pp. 1399–1414. ACM (2017)
14. Zou, Z., Gao, H., Li, J.: Discovering frequent subgraphs over uncertain graph databases under probabilistic semantics. In: Proceedings of the 16th ACM SIGKDD International Conference on Knowledge Discovery and Data Mining, KDD 2010, pp. 633–642 (2010)
15. Zou, Z., Li, J., Gao, H., Zhang, S.: Frequent subgraph pattern mining on uncertain graph data. In: Proceedings of the 18th ACM Conference on Information and Knowledge Management, CIKM 2009, pp. 583–592 (2009)

Railway Passenger Volume Forecast Based on Web Search Terms and Adversarial Nets

Wan Li and Fenling Feng[✉]

School of Traffic and Transportation Engineering, Central South University,
Changsha, China
FFL0731@163.com

Abstract. Accurate forecast of railway passenger volume makes policy formulation effective and transportation resource allocation reasonable. With the popularity of the Internet, more and more people choose to use Internet to get information related to travel. Therefore, this paper puts forward to taking web search as training data to predict railway passenger volume. In addition, adversarial nets (AN) are proposed to predict railway passenger volume. The AN training consists of two steps in which the first is adversarial training and the second is fine tuning. Through the unsupervised adversarial training, the initial parameters of the neural network are optimized and its generalization ability is increased. Then supervised fine tuning makes AN have ability to predict railway passenger volume. Besides, in order to optimize the parameters of AN, an improved particle swarm optimization algorithm is proposed. The experimental results show that the proposed model has better performance.

Keywords: Railway passenger volume · Forecast · Web search
Adversarial nets

1 Introduction

As the highlight of China railway reformation, passenger traffic reformation will focus on strengthening the ability to respond to market change in the short term, obtaining passenger demand information timely and real-timely adjusting serving passenger strategies.

There were many methods used to forecast the transportation demand, such as autoregressive integrated moving average (ARIMA) [1], neural network [2], nonparametric regression [3], Kalman filtering model [4] and gray model. Among these techniques, the neural networks have been frequently adopted as the modeling approach because they possess characteristics of adaptability, non-linearity and arbitrary function mapping capability [5].

With the development of neural networks, generative adversarial nets (GAN) [6] were proposed, which was used to generate image originally. But this model still had many drawbacks, which concluded parameters being too liberal, training difficultly, the value function of G and D being unable to indicate training process, samples generated being lack of diversity and so on. Given these disadvantages, new methods were put

© Springer Nature Switzerland AG 2018
X. Sun et al. (Eds.): ICCCS 2018, LNCS 11064, pp. 9–20, 2018.
https://doi.org/10.1007/978-3-030-00009-7_2

forward to solve these problems. Conditional GAN [7] (CGAN) was proposed to solve the problem that the model was too liberal. Finally, Wasserstein GAN [8] (WGAN) addressed these problems. WGAN used Wasserstein distance, which was also called earth mover distance [9]. Given these, this paper attempts to use the framework of WGAN to train AN for predicting railway passenger volume.

With the popularity of the Internet, Internet technology is widely used in the transportation industry. Currently, Internet has been applied by almost all of the transportation companies, which publish product information and provide tickets booking and accommodation. The majority of travelers also get these relevant information through the Internet. Before getting these information, travelers will use search engines, such as Google and Baidu, to find them. The study of web search data began in Ginsberg [10] by studying the main public health problem of seasonal influenza and the method of tracking the disease by analyzing a large number of Google search queries was obtained. In addition, search engine data had been widely used in ranking universities [11], and gathering public opinions [12], predicting stock market volumes [13], predicting academic fame [14], forecasting Chinese tourist volume [15]. Search engine data were also used for forecasting general economic indicators such as unemployment rates [16] and general consumer consumptions [17]. Furthermore, search engine data had also been applied to other specific consumption categories, like box-office revenue [18]. These studies indicated that the web search terms had relationships with social behavior and they led to the actual social behavior, including travel behavior. In order to promote the study of web search behavior, Baidu company and Google company have launched the Baidu index and the Google trends, respectively. Both of them provide scholars with convenience. Baidu index performs better due to its larger market share in China than Google trends [19]. The previous studies were divided into two directions, in which one direction was the analysis of the time series of railway passenger traffic volume and another direction was to forecast the passenger volume using the economic or industrial indexes, such as the amount of people, the number of tourists and railway operating mileage. The disadvantage of the first direction is that when the actual situation changes, it is no longer applicable. The disadvantage of the second direction is that its information collection is cumbersome and not timely. Thus it is not timely to predict railway passenger volume using traditional data. In summary, this paper attempts to use web search terms to predict the railway passenger volume.

There are mainly three innovations in this paper: (i) web search terms data are used to predict railway passenger volume; (ii) the AN is proposed to forecast railway passenger volume; (iii) an improved PSO is put forward to optimize parameters of AN.

2 Model and Experiment Procedure

2.1 Improved Particle Swarm Optimization Algorithm

According to [20] the PSO algorithm is introduced briefly as follows. Firstly, PSO algorithm randomly initializes the position and velocity of a random population of particles. Each particle i is defined by its position vectors X_i^t and a random velocity V_i^t.

At the following iteration, the particle moves according to its velocity and is evaluated according to the fitness function $f(X_i^t)$. The value of the fitness function is compared with the best value attained before. The best value ever obtained for each particle is stored as $pbest_i$ which actually is the personal optimum searching, and the best value among all $pbest_i$ is stored as $gbest$ which actually is the global optimum searching. Velocity of the particle is then updated by:

$$V_i^{t+1} = \lambda * V_i^t + c_1 * rand * (pbest_i - X_i^t) + c_2 * rand * (gbest - X_i^t) \qquad (1)$$

$$X_i^{t+1} = X_i^t + V_i^{t+1} \qquad (2)$$

where λ is the inertia weight, $rand$ generates a random number ranging from 0 to 1, c_1 and c_2 are the velocity coefficient.

It is well-founded that λ controls the convergence and exploration ability effectively on the basis of Eq. (1). Equation (1) indicates that the particle velocity is changed linearly. Linear change of particle velocity has two drawbacks: (i) if particle swarm searches optimum value at the beginning, it is hoped to converge to global optimum quickly, but invariant λ decreases the convergence speed of the algorithm; (ii) in late operation of algorithm, invariant λ leads to the decline of local search ability and decrease of particle diversity. Therefore, two improvements are proposed to overcome them:

(i) Nonlinear velocity changing

$$w = \lambda_{\max} - (\lambda_{\max} - \lambda_{\min}) * e^{\frac{t}{t_{\max}} - 1} \qquad (3)$$

Where $\lambda_{\max}$ is the maximum inertia weight and $\lambda_{\min}$ is the minimum inertia weight; $t_{\max}$ is the maximum iteration time. At the beginning of operation, λ close to $\lambda_{\max}$ guarantees the global search capability of algorithm. The closer t is to $t_{\max}$, the more rapidly λ decreases. At the end of operation, λ close to $\lambda_{\min}$ guarantees the local search capability of algorithm. This nonlinear decrease of λ guarantees the convergence speed and local search ability. Then the balance between global search and local search capability can be adjusted flexibly.

(ii) Particle crossover and mutation

In order to make the PSO expand search space that is constantly narrow with iteration and help particles jump out of the best position that has been searched, mutation method of genetic algorithm is used here for maintaining the particle diversity. Besides, the crossover operation with global optimum, which originates from genetic algorithm, is applied for particle to obtain part of best position and converge rapidly. The detailed procedure is as follows. After velocity and position of particle $P_i^t(p_i^1, p_i^2, \ldots p_I^n)$ is updated, it may be initialized according to probability $prob_1$. And then it may be crossed and recombined with the $gbest(p_g^1, p_g^2, \ldots p_g^n)$ based on possibility $prob_2$, i.e., $P_i^t(p_i^1, p_i^2, \ldots p_I^n)$ may be replaced by $P_i^t(p_i^1, p_g^2, p_i^3, p_g^4, \ldots p_I^n)$.

2.2 The Adversarial Nets

Before discussing the proposed AN, it is necessary to introduce WGAN. According to [6, 8], the WGAN is described as follows. The training procedure of WGAN corresponds to a minimax two-player game. WGAN is a framework for improving generative models through an adversarial process, in which two models are trained simultaneously: a generator G that captures the data distribution, and a discriminator D estimates that a sample comes from the training data rather than generator. The training procedure for G is to maximize the probability of D making a mistake. In the case where G and D are defined by multilayer perceptrons (MLP), the entire system can be trained with back propagation (BP) algorithm.

The purpose of G is to output data that have same distribution with real data. A input noise variable z is defined, then a mapping to data space as $x' = g_\theta(z)$ is represented, where g_θ is a differentiable function represented by G with parameters θ. At present, the data distribution of x' is far away from that of x. The goal of D is to discriminate that the input data come from the real data rather than the generated data. Then $f_w(x)$ and $f_w(x')$ are defined, where f_w represents by D with parameters w.

The closer data distribution of x' to that of x is, the smaller value of L_{AN} (Eq. (4)) is. The more different data distribution of x' from that of x is, the larger value of L_{AN} (Eq. (4)) is.

$$L_{AN} = E[f_w(x)] - E[f_w(x')] \tag{4}$$

Where L_{AN} is Wasserstein distance between $f_w(x')$ and $f_w(x)$, and $E[\cdot]$ represents expectation value. Equation (4) is also the loss function of whole AN, which can indicate the training process.

The D is aim at discriminating input data being real data rather than generated data. Based on this, D tries its best to make L_{AN} bigger. So the loss function of D is as follows.

$$L_D = E[f_w(x')] - E[f_w(x)] \tag{5}$$

The Eq. (5) is the inverse of Eq. (4).

G makes every effort to bring L_D down. Considering that $E[f_w(x)]$ in Eq. (5) is not related to G, the loss function of G is as follows.

$$L_G = -E[f_w(x')] \tag{6}$$

The parameters of D and G are updated by BP algorithm and standard gradient decrease algorithm. The sigmoid function is used as activation function. In order to make Eq. (4) satisfy the Wasserstein distance, the parameters of G will be limited to range $[-\beta, \beta]$.

If only use real data as train samples and the number of data is not enough, this will result in limited generalization ability of neural network. Through the adversarial process between G and D, the distribution of data generated by G is close to that of real data, which is equivalent to doubling the number of training samples for D. Therefore, the parameters in D are optimized by more training samples and the generalization ability of D is improved. The adversarial process is unsupervised training.

But at this time the D can not be directly used as a predictor, and this is because that the output dimension of D is the same as the dimension of the input data and it has not been supervised trained. We add a regression layer to the last layer of D, so the output dimension becomes 1. The regression layer also uses sigmoid function as activation function. Then the D with added regression layer will be fine tuned using real data with labels, which is a supervised training. At the end, we can get a predictor P.

The detailed steps of training AN are as follows:

Algorithm 1

α_D,the learning rate of D. α_G,the learning rate of G. α_F,the learning rate of fine tuning. n, the number of iterations of adversarial procedure. n_D, the number of iterations of D. n_G, the number of iterations of G. w_0,initial D's parameters. θ_0,initial G's parameters. m, the number of training samples. β,the upper limit of parameters of D.

Step 1 Adversarial training

Sample $x^{(i)}$ from the real data.

Sample $z^{(i)}$ from noise data.

for n do

    for n_D do

$$g_w \leftarrow \nabla_w[f_w(g_\theta(z^{(i)})) - f_w(x^{(i)})]$$
$$w \leftarrow w - \alpha_D * g_w$$
$$w \leftarrow \text{limit}(w, -\beta, \beta)$$

    end

    for n_G do

$$g_\theta \leftarrow \nabla_\theta[f_w(g_\theta(z^{(i)}))]$$
$$\theta \leftarrow \theta - \alpha_G * g_\theta$$

    end

end

Step 2 Fine tuning

Add regression layer to the end of trained D,i.e., $f_\varepsilon \leftarrow f_w$.

Label $l^{(i)}$ from the real data.

while $j < n_F$ or ε do not converge do

$$g_\varepsilon \leftarrow \nabla_\varepsilon[l^{(i)} - f_\varepsilon(x^{(i)})]$$
$$\varepsilon \leftarrow \varepsilon - \alpha_F * g_\varepsilon$$
$$j \leftarrow j + 1$$

end

2.3   Experiment Process

Before executing the adversarial process, it is necessary to determine the structures of nets and the corresponding parameters. Too many network layers will result in great computational cost, so D and G are 3 layers MLP. Because many parameters affect the performance of AN, it is essential to optimize these parameters using the proposed IPSO. These parameters include neurons h_D and h_G in hidden layers of D and G, the learning rates α_D and α_G of D and G, the learning rates α_F for fine tuning, the number of iterations n_D and n_G of D and G, the upper limit of parameters of D β and the initial weights of the last regression layers $(w_r^1, w_r^1, \ldots, w_r^N)$. Then a particle is designed to be a multiple dimensions vector $X_i(h_D, h_G, \alpha_D, \alpha_G, \alpha_F, n_D, n_G, \beta, w_r^1, w_r^2, \ldots, w_r^N)$. In order to avoid over fitting of P, the all samples are divided into training samples, validating samples and test samples. The training samples are used for training AN, and validating samples are used for validating the performance of P, and test samples are used for predicting railway passenger volume. In this article, the fitness function of IPSO is the sum of fitting error of training samples and error of validating samples, where the error is mean square error (MSE).

The proposed IPSO algorithm used to decide parameters of AN is given as following:

Step 1. Decide the population size of particles P and limitation of iteration number I.
Step 2. Initialize the start position X_i^0 and the start velocity V_i^0 of each particle.
Step 3. Evaluate each particle using the fitness function having been mentioned above, and find the best position of a particle $pbest_i$ from its history, and the best particle position of the swarm $gbest$.
Step 4. Renew positions and velocities of particles by Eqs. (1) and (2), respectively.
Step 5. If the fitness function converged, or $t = I$, finish the algorithm. Otherwise, return to Step 3.

3   Experiments and Results

3.1   Selection of Web Search Terms

Through Spearman rank correlation analysis, the relational degrees between search terms and railway passenger volume can be obtained.

In this paper, the search terms related to railway passenger volume can be found via Baidu Index. The web search volumes are sum of web search volumes on computer and on mobile phone. The web search terms in this paper are divided into 5 types: (i) related to railway; (ii) booking software; (iii) scenic spot; (iv) city; (v) province. And the search terms related to the railway are: 12306, tielu (railway), dingpiao (booking), huoche (train), huochepiao (train ticket), gaotie (high speed rail). These are the terms that people often search for when they travel by railway, and the 12306 is the official railway booking website of China. The search terms related to the booking software are: xiecheng (Ctrip), qvnaer (Qunar). Since the two booking softwares have high market share in China, they are chosen as the search key words. The search terms related to the tourist attractions are: Lijiang, Sanya, huangshan (Mount Huangshan), Jiuzhaigou, and Guilin. These five scenic spots are popular in China. The search terms that belong to the city type are: Beijing, Shanghai, Guangzhou, Shenzhen, Chengdu, Hangzhou, Chongqing, Nanjing, Xi'an, Kunming, Xiamen. As tourist cites, these 11 cities attract a large number of tourists to play every year, which promotes the generation of passenger flow. The search terms related to province are: Zhejiang, Guangdong, Jiangsu. These three provinces, as the provinces with more passengers trip, contribute more to the railway passenger traffic volume. These terms are used in Chinese when people use search engine to search.

We need to analyze the time difference (TD) between the web search terms volumes and the railway passenger volume. From January 2014 to January 2017, railway tickets are scheduled for a period of 20 to 60 days in China. Thus TD between the railway passenger volume and search terms is not more than 60 days, i.e., two months. For the sake of calculating convenience, the TD is set to 1 month or 2 months. The Spearman correlation degrees between monthly search times of terms from January 2014 to January 2017 and the monthly railway passenger volume from February 2014 to February 2017 are shown in the Table 1. When TD is one month, the correlation degrees between terms and railway passenger volume are greater than that of two months TD (Table 1). Therefore, we choose 1 month TD for railway passenger volume forecasting. Finally, the data of search terms range from January 2014 to January 2017, railway passenger volume ranges from February 2014 to February 2017.

Table 1. Results of Spearman rank correlation analysis.

Types	Search terms	Correlation degrees (TD is 1 month)	Correlation degrees (TD is 2 months)
Booking software	Xiecheng	0.34	0.15
Scenic spot	Lijiang	0.51	0.28
Cities	Chengdu	0.60	0.39
	Xi'an	0.36	0.16
	Xiamen	0.32	0.07
Provinces	Zhejiang	0.57	0.31
	Guangdong	0.33	0.21

Finally 7 search terms highly related to railway passenger volume are got (Table 1). These 7 terms are divided into 4 types, including booking software, scenic spot, cities and provinces. Xiecheng, a app having relatively high market share in China, is used to complete booking, hotel reservation and other related services. So Xiecheng has correlation with railway passenger volume. The population of cities or provinces in Table 1 is large and the flow is large, so there are high correlations between these cities and provinces and people's travel. In addition, Lijiang, a popular tourist destinations in China, is also highly correlated with the volume of passenger traffic. The search terms related to the railway (including 12306, railway, booking, train, train ticket, high speed rail) should be highly correlated to railway passenger volume, but the correlation degrees are low actually. This is probably because that there are many channels for booking train tickets and people don't search for these search terms.

3.2 Railway Passenger Volume Forecast

Data Normalization. The data, concluding railway passenger volume and search terms, are normalized by the following formula,

$$x' = \frac{x - x_{min}}{x_{max} - x_{min}} \tag{8}$$

Where, x' is the normalized value, x_{max} represents the maximum value of original data series, x_{min} represents the minimum value of original data series. x represents no normalized value.

Forecast Experiments of Railway Passenger Volume. The training samples are search terms data from January 2014 to July 2016 and railway passenger volume from February 2014 to August 2016, total 31 months. The validating samples are search terms data from August 2016 to October 2016 and railway passenger volume from September 2016 to November 2016, total 3 months. The test samples are search terms data from November 2016 to January 2017 and railway passenger volume from December 2016 to February 2017, total 3 months. The generated data in this paper accord with the standard normal distribution, i.e. the expectation value is 0, and the variance is 1.

In order to compare the performance of the proposed IPSO-AN, BP neural networks having 3 layers (3 layers BPNN) and 4 layers (4 layers BPNN), Elman neural networks having 3 layers (3 layers ELM) and 4 layers (4 layers ELM), radial basis function neural network (RBF), support vector machine (SVM) and auto-regressive integrated moving average model (ARIMA) are also used for predicting railway passenger volume. BPNN, ELM and RBF are implemented through the built-in toolkit of matlab software. SVM and ARIMA are implemented through the toolkit of R software. The maximum iteration times, learning rate, convergence error of BPNN are 5000, 0.1 and 0.0001, respectively. The maximum iteration times, learning rate, convergence error of ELM are 5000, 0.5 and 0.0001, respectively. The error goal and spread of RBF are 0 and 0.2, respectively. Kernel function of SVM is Gaussian radial basis function. The parameters of AN are shown in Table 2.

The predicting results are shown in Table 3. The unit of MSE is the square of ten thousand people. The proposed IPSO-AN has achieved the best prediction performance, the MSE is 2.79 and the mean absolute percentage error (MAPE) is 2.43%. These two errors MAE and MAPE are smallest than those of other 7 models. The network structure of P is 7-70-7-1, which means that P has 4 layers and neurons in the input layer, the first hidden layer, the second hidden layer and the output layer are 7, 70, 7 and 1, respectively. Similarly, the structure of G is 7-70-7. Besides, $\alpha_D = 1$, $\alpha_G = 1$, $\alpha_F = 1$, $n_D = 10$, $n_G = 10$. The structure of 3 layers BPNN, 4 layers BPNN,

Table 2. Parameters of IPSO-AN.

Name	Abbreviation	Value
Velocity coefficient of IPSO	c_1, c_2	2
Population of IPSO	–	5
Iteration times of IPSO	t	10
The maximum inertia weight	w_{max}	0.9
The minimum inertia weight	w_{min}	0.1
The number of layers of D	–	3
The number of neurons in input layer and output layer of D	–	8
The number of neurons in hidden layer of D	$h_D(1 \leq h_D \leq 100)$	Given by IPSO
Learning rate of D	α_D	Given by IPSO
The upper limit of parameters of D	β	Given by IPSO
The number of layers of G	–	3
The number of neurons in input layer and output layer of G	–	8
The number of neurons in hidden layer of G	$h_G(1 \leq h_G \leq 100)$	Given by IPSO
Learning rate of G	α_G	Given by IPSO
Learning rate of fine tuning	α_F	Given by IPSO
Convergence error of BP algorithm	–	0.001
Iteration times of D	n_D	Given by IPSO
Iterations times of G	n_G	Given by IPSO
Iteration times of adversarial training	n	50
Iteration times of fine tuning	n_F	1000
The weights of the last regression layer	–	Given by PSO

3layers ELM, 4 layers ELM and RBF are 8-18-1, 8-65-20-1, 8-30-1, 8-10-25-1 and 8-34-1, respectively. The parameters of ARIMA are (4, 1, 4).

There are two main differences between AN and BPNN: (i) The training process of AN is divided into two stages, in which the first stage is adversarial stage and the second stage is fine-tuning stage; (ii) BPNN is trained only using training samples, but the proposed AN not only uses training samples for supervised training, but also uses generated samples having same data distribution as real data for unsupervised training, which makes AN have better generalization ability than BPNN. Therefore, the MSE and MAPE of AN are smaller than BPNN, whether it is 3 layers or 4 layers.

Table 3. Results of predicting railway passenger volume.

Predicting models	Error	
	MSE	MAPE (%)
IPSO-AN	2.79	2.43
3 layers BPNN	306.41	20.17
4 layers BPNN	107.06	14.90
3 layers ELM	28.45	5.00
4 layers ELM	29.88	8.02
RBF	355.89	24.45
SVM	697.60	27.78
ARIMA	336.45	6.53

ARIMA is different from other models in that the input data are only the time series of railway passenger volume. It only carries on the trend analysis and forecasting the time series of railway passenger volume. As a kind of dynamic time series, railway passenger volume is influenced by many external factors so it shows great volatility and high uncertainty. Therefore, it is not accurate to only use the time series of railway passenger volume to predict.

The fitting result of IPSO-AN is shown in Fig. 1, and we can see that the IPSO-AN fits the railway passenger volume well.

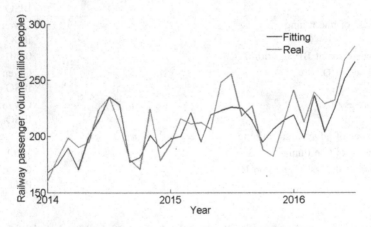

Fig. 1. The fitting results of IPSO-AN

4   Conclusion

Railway passenger volume forecast is always a hot topic for transportation professionals and transportation enterprises. Using web search terms as training data has the advantages of timely and convenient collection, so it is very suitable for short-term forecasting. Neural network is one of the generally prediction methods, but it is criticized due to falling into local minimum easily and limited generalization ability. Therefore, this paper proposes the use of AN as a prediction model to predict the volume of railway passenger traffic. Besides, the IPSO, having better ability of searching for global optimal value and faster convergence ability, is proposed to improve the parameters of AN. The results of forecast experiments show that the proposed model achieves the best performance, which indicates that it has strong generalization ability. Future research will focus on that if more relevant search terms are found, the prediction results might be better.

Acknowledgement. This research is supported by China Railway Science and Technology Research Development Program (2015F024).

References

1. Hansen, J.V., McDoald, J.B., Nelson, R.D.: Time series prediction with genetic-algorithms designed neural networks: an empirical comparison with modern statistical models. Comput. Intell. **15**(3), 171–183 (1999)
2. Tsai, T., Lee, C., Wei, C.: Neural network based temporal feature models for short-term railway passenger demand forecasting. Expert Syst. Appl. **36**(2), 3728–3736 (2009)
3. Clark, S.: Traffic prediction using multivariate nonparametric regression. J. Transp. Eng. **129**(2), 161–168 (2003)
4. Wang, Y., Papageorgiou, M.: Real-time freeway traffic state estimation based on extend Kalman filter: a case study. Transp. Sci. **42**(2), 167–181 (2007)
5. Zhang, G., Patuwo, B.E., Hu, M.Y.: Forecasting with artificial neural networks: the state of the art. Int. J. Forecast. **14**(1), 35–62 (1998)
6. Goodfellow, I.J., et al.: Generative adversarial nets (2014). https://arxiv.org/pdf/1406.2661.pdf
7. Mehdi, M., Simon, O.: Conditional Generative Adversarial Nets (2014). https://arxiv.org/pdf/1411.1784v1.pdf
8. Martin, A., Soumith, C., Leon, B.: Wasserstein GAN (2017). https://arxiv.org/pdf/1701.07875v1.pdf
9. Xia, Z., Zhu, Y., Sun, X., Qin, Z., Ren, K.: Towards privacy-preserving content-based image retrieval in cloud computing. IEEE Trans. Cloud Comput. **6**(1), 276–286 (2015)
10. Ginsberg, J., Mohebbi, M.H., Patel, R.S., Brammer, L., Smolinski, M.S., Brilliant, L.: Detecting influenza epidemics using search engine query data. Nature **457**, 1012–1014 (2009)
11. Vaughan, L., Romero Frías, E.: Web search volume as a predictor of academic fame: an exploration of Google trends. J. Am. Soc. Inf. Sci. Technol. **65**(4), 707–720 (2013)
12. Baram Tsabari, A., Segev, E.: Exploring new web-based tools to identify public interest in science. Public Underst. Sci. **20**(1), 130–143 (2011)
13. Ilaria, B., Stefano, B., Guido, C.: Web search queries can predict stock market volumes. PLoS One **7**(7), e40014 (2012)
14. Liwen, V., Esteban, R.: Web search volume as a predictor of academic fame: an exploration of Google trends. J. Assoc. Inf. Sci TECH. **65**(4), 707–720 (2014)
15. Yang, X., Pan, B., Evans, J.A., Lv, B.: Forecasting Chinese tourist volume with search engine data. Tourism Manag. **46**, 386–397 (2015)
16. Choi, H., Varian, H.: Predicting present with Google trends. Econ. Rec. **88**(S1), 2–9 (2012)

17. Dzielinski, M.: Measuring economic uncertainty and its impact on the stock markct. Finance Res. Lett. **9**(3), 167–175 (2012)
18. Hand, C., Judge, G.: Searching for the picture: forecasting UK cinema admissions using Google trends data. Appl. Econ. Lett. **19**(11), 1051–1055 (2012)
19. Xin, Y., Bing, P., James, A.E., Benfu, L.: Forecasting Chinese tourist volume with search engine data. Tourism Manag. **46**, 386–397 (2015)
20. Zhang, J., Zhang, J., Lok, T., Michael, R.L.: A hybrid particle swarm optimization-backpropagation algorithm for feedforward neural network training. Appl. Math. Comput. **185**, 1026–1037 (2007)
21. Shi, Y.H., Eberhart, R.: A modified particle swarm optimizer. In: Proceedings of the IEEE International Conference on Evolutionary Computation (1998). https://wenku.baidu.com/view/e3dd76c80508763231121275.html

RCS: Hybrid Co-scheduling Optimization in Virtualized System

Zhiqiang Zhu[1,2], Jin Wu[1(✉)], Lei Sun[1], and Ruiyu Dou[1]

[1] Zhengzhou Information Science and Technology Institute, Zhengzhou 450001, Henan, China
wujin930716@foxmail.com
[2] Zhengzhou Xinda Institute of Advanced Technology, Zhengzhou 450001, Henan, China

Abstract. As a support technology for cloud computing, virtualization enables multiple guest operating systems run on a system, which will improve utilization of resource. However, due to the semantic gap in the virtualization system, the mainstream of the current scheduling policy doesn't take the tasks' spin lock and cache misses into account, which leads to the performance degradation in virtual machine. In this paper, we propose an optimization of the hybrid co-scheduling in KVM called Regional Co-Scheduling (RCS). Our solution includes two aspects: co-scheduling the vCPUs of the concurrent VM within CPU cores in the same CPU socket, and optimizing the load balancing by adding two strategies, which include that vCPUs belonging to the same VM should not be in the same queue and cross-region migration should be avoided. The experiment results show that RCS significantly reduces the execution time and context switches, compared with the default scheduler CFS and Co-Scheduling, and suffers less overhead as well, while when the number of VMs is large, it is with fair-share feature.

Keywords: Virtualized environment · Hybrid co-scheduling · CFS
Lock Holder Preemption · Cache misses

1 Introduction

Virtualization is the supporting technology for cloud computing. Amazon's Elastic Compute Cloud (EC2) [1], for instance, uses virtualization to offer datacenter resources to applications run by different customers, safely providing different kinds of services to diverse codes running on the same underlying hardware [2]. There are some prevalent virtualization technologies, like Xen, VMWare and KVM, among which KVM [3] is becoming more and more widely used. KVM is a new virtualization solution for Linux, which is built as a kernel module in Linux Kernel. It has been designed to make full use of mature and powerful Linux kernel [4, 5]. Although virtualization enables the resource sharing, the performance in virtual machines (VM) degrades distinctly. The degradation results from the semantic gap between the hypervisor and the host. Every VM is with several virtual CPUs (vCPUs) on which the tasks in the VM is allocated to, while these vCPUs are treated as threads in the host.

© Springer Nature Switzerland AG 2018
X. Sun et al. (Eds.): ICCCS 2018, LNCS 11064, pp. 21–32, 2018.
https://doi.org/10.1007/978-3-030-00009-7_3

Due to the semantic gap, the hypervisor has little awareness of the code being executed inside each vCPU [6], which introduces many problems and leads to the performance reduction. Lock-Holder Preemption (LHP) is one of the reasons for low performance phenomenon. Spinlock is one of the main synchronization mechanism. It avoids context switch and is designed to wait for a short time. In non-virtual environment, a thread holding a spinlock cannot be preempted, which ensures that the thread will be executed and releases the lock as soon as possible. However, it is different in the virtual environment. The scheduler is imperceptive of the thread of VMs whether holds a spinlock, that means, a vCPU that holds a spinlock may be preempted, and other vCPUs waiting for this spinlock have to spin for a long time, which causes resource waste and performance decreases.

Cache miss is also another serious problem that leads to the low performance. In the non-virtual environment, it will adopt some measures to mitigate this problem, while it is inevitable in virtual environment. It is alike to the LHP. The vCPUs belonging to the same VM may be allocated or migrated to two CPU cores in different sockets because of the semantic gap, which will counteract the cache effect.

In this paper, we purpose a technique to relieve the LHP problem and cache misses in KVM. Specifically, we optimize the hybrid co-scheduling called Regional Co-Scheduling (RCS) taking Linux balancing and the cache misses into account. We set the CPU core which belongs to the same socket into a scheduling domain and vCPUs of the same VM should be co-scheduled among the cores belongs to the same domain, which can not only alleviate LHP, but also can reduce the cache misses. We also add two restrictions for the threads that be migrated when balancing happens to avoid the cache misses.

The rest of the paper is structured as follows. We first introduce previous solutions to LHP and followed by motivation in Sect. 3. The design and implement of RCS are illustrated in Sect. 4. In Sect. 5 we evaluate our technique. Finally, we conclude the paper in Sect. 6.

2 Related Work

There have been some solutions proposed to solve LHP problem. Uhlig et al. [7] proposed two schemes to relieve the LHP problem for both full-virtualization and paravirtualization, which are based on the characteristics of spinlock [8]. The two schemes are called the delayed preemption. For full-virtualization, two states are defined for virtual cores used by guest OSes, and they are safe and unsafe state. The virtualization layer changes the state of the virtual core from safe to unsafe when a trap instruction is invoked for entering to the kernel and intercepts the event. The state of virtual core is set from safe to unsafe so it cannot be preempted. Another technique for the para-virtualization is to mark a flag when the kernel enters into a critical section and clear the flag when the kernel exits it [9]. When the flag is marked, the virtual core is not allowed to be preempted.

Co-scheduling is also applied to avoid LHP [3, 10, 11], which is designed to co-schedule all or the relevant vCPUs of the same VM onto physical cores.

However, There are some problems in co-scheduling, for example, it may introduce CPU fragmentation and priority inversion. Hybrid co-scheduling allows non-concurrent domains to reside in a system to achieve higher CPU utilization by filling the co-scheduling gaps with non-concurrent vCPUs [10]. Yu etc. [10] propose two optimizations in hybrid co-scheduling called Partial Co-Scheduling (PCS) and Boost Co-Scheduling (BCS). PCS co-schedule vCPUs of domains by only raising the co-scheduling signals to the CPUs which contain the corresponding co-scheduled vCPU, while other CPUs remain untouched. BCS promotes the priority of vCPUs to be co-scheduled instead of sending co-scheduling signals. The two optimizations alleviate exclusiveness and contention among multiple concurrent domains in current versions of hybrid co-scheduling.

However, the current solutions to LHP do not take cache misses into account, for example, co-scheduling may allocate the relevant vCPU to different CPU cores that belongs to different sockets, which will increase the communication cost. To address the problem, we propose an optimization scheduling algorithm called Regional Co-Scheduling (RCS), which aim to retain the advantage of hybrid co-scheduling and as well as avoid the cache misses. Moreover, we set some restrictions for the threads migrated when balancing happens to mitigate cache misses.

3 Motivation

State-of-the-art scheduling schemes, such as CFS [12] used by KVM usually oblivious of synchronization operations inside an SMP VM. Hence, it may preempt a vCPU regardless of what it is running [13]. An example is shown in Fig. 1. The vCPU1, vCPU2 and vCPU3 are the vCPU of a VM. The spinlock holder vCPU2 is executed in pCPU1, and in non-co-scheduling scenario, the lock waiter vCPU1 may be allocated to the same pCPU queue. When vCPU2 enters the critical section, it is preempted by vCPU3 at T1, and it only can be executed until T2. The waiting time of vCPU1 is the execution time of vCPU2 plus that of vCPU3.

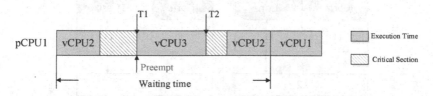

Fig. 1. Synchronization latency in non-co-scheduling

The problem can be relieved when utilizing co-scheduling, which can be shown in Fig. 2. In co-scheduling, vCPU1 is allocated to pCPU1, and vCPU3 is allocated to pCPU3 while vCPU2 is in the queue of pCPU2. Because of co-scheduling, the lock holder can be executed in its critical section and release the spinlock, so the waiting time of vCPU1 is equal to the critical section, which can reduce computing resources due to the spinning waiting of lock waiter.

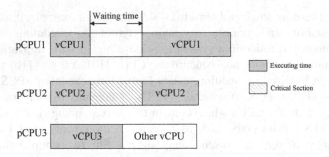

Fig. 2. Latency improvement in co-scheduling

However, there some problems in co-scheduling. Co-scheduling may cause CPU fragmentation and priority inversion [13]. Hybrid co-scheduling [10, 14] can make up for these disadvantages, which allows non-concurrent domains to reside in a system to achieve higher CPU utilization by filling the co-scheduling gaps with non-concurrent vCPUs [10]. However, they set the VM type when a VM is created, which decides whether it operate co-scheduling or other scheduling algorithm. The VM type may change at times, which will induce more waste. Partial Co-Scheduling (PCS) and Boost Co-Scheduling (BCS) make up for hybrid co-scheduling exclusiveness and contention.

Nonetheless, the solution above neglects the cache mechanism. For communication and improving the processing speed, the tasks of the same CPU core share L1 cache with each other, which the communication latency is about 1–2 processor cycles. The tasks of the different cores which are in the same socket communicate with each other through L2 cache, which will produce a 10–20 processor cycles latency. It may cause up to several hundred processor cycles delay when the tasks communicate with each other that belongs to different sockets, because they may communicate through cache coherence protocol or memory. The cache mechanism is shown in Fig. 3.

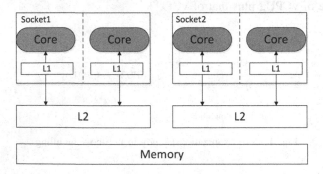

Fig. 3. Cache mechanism

When co-scheduling is employed, it does not consider cache mechanism and it may happen that vCPUs of the same VM is allocated to the CPU cores that in different socket, which will offset the improvement of co-scheduling. Hence, we should impose restrictions on co-scheduling to retain the its advantage. It is also essential to concern that when load balancing happens, the tasks to be chosen to migrate are in the same socket at best. As a result, in this paper, we propose a Reginal Co-Scheduling (RCS). Specifically, we delimitate the region of CPU cores when operating co-scheduling, and add some migrate restrictions for load balancing. We will give more details of RCS in next section.

4 Design and Implementation

4.1 Design of RCS

We propose RCS to inherit the advantage of RCS and avoid the cache misses. The framework of RCS is shown in Fig. 4.

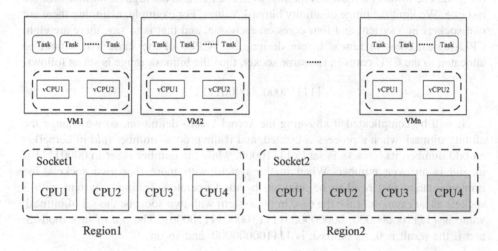

Fig. 4. Framework of RCS

In previous sections, we have analyzed that the co-scheduling can reduce the latency resulted from LHP. However, when co-scheduling is applied, the vCPUs of the same VM may be scheduled at the different CPU cores that at different sockets, causing cache misses and communication latency. To avoid the cache misses offsetting the advantage, RCS gives a delineation of a region where co-scheduling is operated in. The CPU cores in the same socket are in the same region. The concurrent vCPUs when are co-scheduled, they should be scheduled at the CPU cores belongs to the same region, which will avoid cache misses.

To strengthen the effect of avoiding cache misses, we also add two restrictions of tasks to be pick when load balancing happens. The two conditions are as follows.

(1) The vCPUs that belongs to the same VM with the one is running in the queue should not be migrated to the same queue;
(2) Do not have a cross-regional migration.

The first strategy is set for the reason that dispersed scheduling will improve the performance of VMs, which has been proved in previous work [3, 4, 15]. The strategy will benefit VM without synchronous tasks, which will be scheduled with default scheduling algorithm, for dispersed scheduling takes advantage of multi-core system and improves the processing speed of tasks in VM.

The second one aims to strengthen our RCS. RCS help to reduce the cache misses of VMs with concurrent tasks, while this strategy will avoid the cache misses of VMs with asynchronous ones.

4.2 Implementation of RCS

4.2.1 Regional Scheduling Implementation

The regional scheduling can be achieved by changing the CPU affinity. In Linux, CPU affinity uses a bitmask, where each bit represents a CPU, and the value of bit is set to 1 for bind. The lowest bit indicates the first logical CPU, and the highest bit indicates the last one. We limit the range of affinity bitmask values. For example, assuming there are two sockets in a system and four cores on each one, and that is to say, there are eight CPU logical cores in Linux. In our design, the vCPUs of the same VM should be allocated to the CPU cores in the same socket, thus the bitmask range is set as follows.

$$\{11110000, 000001111\}$$

It will be complicated if changing the kernel macro definition, so we change the affinity bitmask when a process is created, and if the process number (*pid* in kernel) is an odd number, its bitmask is set to 11110000, while the number is set to 00001111 if its *pid* is an even number. When in the system with more than two sockets, the implementation just need to be adjusted by mod operator. Taking a system with 3 sockets as an example. Like the case in the system with two sockets, the set of bitmask value is {111100000000, 0000000001111, 000011110000}. The *pid* of task mods 3, and if the result is 0, its bitmask is 111100000000, and so on.

4.2.2 Hybrid Co-scheduling Implementation

The hybrid co-scheduling is implemented by setting the VM type when it is created, and the scheduling algorithm is selected, depending on the type. It is short of flexibility. Hence in this paper, we propose a dynamic method referring to LHP Disable [4]. We add 2 variables to *task_struct* to help scheduler check the state: (1) *VMflag*. The variable indicates that the VM is a concurrent VM. (2) *LockNum*. This is an atomic variable for every vCPU in the VM, which is for recording the spinlock number the VM is holding.

When a locking action happens, the variable *LockNum* is increased. It is decreased when a lock is released. When the *LockNum* is more than 0, the VM client needs to invoke the hypercall in smp_callin() to set *VMflag* = 1 in host. A hypercall also be invoked when *LockNum* is decreased to 0 to set *VMflag* = 0, indicating it is not a concurrent VM. The VM type determination is shown in Fig. 5.

Different scheduling algorithm is adopted depending on the VM type. When the VM is set as a concurrent VM, the vCPUs of it will be co-scheduled. On the contrary,

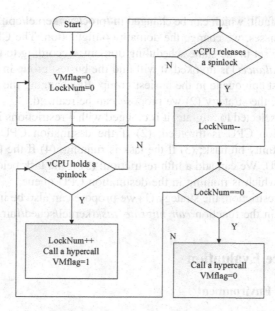

Fig. 5. Determination of VM type

they will be scheduled by default scheduling algorithm. In a CPU queue, when the scheduler picks a concurrent vCPU as the next thread to be executed, the priority of all the vCPUs that belong to the same VM will be boosted. In CFS, the priority of being executed hinges on its virtual running time (*vruntime* in kernel). The one with the minimum *vruntime* will be executed first. The *vruntime* of the vCPUs that are co-scheduled is set to minimum *vruntime (min_vruntime* in kernel*)* in the queue so they will boost up. Their *vruntime* returns to its actual value when they are picked by the scheduler. The pseudo-codes are displayed in Algorithm 1.

Algorithm 1 Hybrid Co-scheduling
1   Select next thread:
2   *actual_vruntime*= vCPU.*vruntime*
3   **if** (Next.*ParentProcess->VMflag*==1)
4   **for** all vCPUs in VM
5   vCPU.*vruntime*=rq->*min_vruntime*
6   **end for**
7   **end if**
8   vCPUs vruntime is recover their actual value:
9   vCPU.*vruntime*=*actual_vruntime* + *slice*

4.2.3   Load Balancing Strategy

It is worth noting that balancing will preferentially migrate tasks among the CPU run queues in the same scheduling domain, and all the processors in SMP system is in the same domain by default, which can be changed in /proc/sys/kernel/cpuX/domain Y [5]. To reduce cache misses, we change the domain configuration. The CPU cores that in the same socket are set in the same scheduling domain. According to the Linux kernel code, when *load_balance()* is invoked, it will find the busiest group in the domain, and then find the busiest cpu queue in the busiest group. By changing the configuration of scheduling domain, the strategy (2) we propose can be realized.

When a task is selected to migrate, it is clogged with 4 restrictions in kernel, that is: (1) If the destination CPU is throttled; (2) If the destination CPU is not allowed according to the affinity bitmask; (3) If the task is running; (4) If the task is cache-hot on their current CPU. We can add a fifth restriction: (5) If the task belongs to the same VM as the vCPU which is running in the destination CPU queue.

By adding the restriction, the strategy (1) we propose can also be implemented. We add the restriction in the function *can_migrate_task*(kernel/sched/fair.c).

5   Performance Evaluation

5.1   Experiment Environment

In this section, we first introduce our experiment environment and benchmarks that we select. We conduct the RCS in the environment and analyze the experiment result compared with CFS and Co-Scheduling.

Our experiments are conducted on Inspur server. There are 4 Inspur servers, whose model number is NF5270M4, and the motherboard is Intel C610. There are a couple of 6-core CPUs (Intel(R) Xeon(R) CPU E5-2620, 2.5 GHz) in our testbed, with 128 GB memory in total. The host is running Linux kernel 4.10 and qemu-kvm-1.5.3-126.el7. Four VMs are established in the system whose operating systems are Centos-7-x86_64-1511. All VMs are configured with 2G memory and 4 vCPUs, which simulates the common case in the cloud computing system that the total number of vCPUs are larger than physical CPU cores.

Three benchmarks to evaluate the performance of RCS.

1. Lookbusy [16]. It uses relatively simple techniques to generate active CPU, memory and disk utilization. In our experiment, we use lookbusy to keep the CPU utilization at determined levels during experiments.
2. Kernbench. This is a CPU throughput benchmark originally devised and used by Martin J. Bligh [17]. It is designed to compare kernels on the same machine, or to compare hardware. Optionally it can also run single threaded. At least 2 GB of ram is required for utilizing the benchmark to be a true throughput benchmark, which will avoid swap storms. KernBench frequently reads files or links through Linux VFS layer, thus incurring file system's inode lock contentions, which is protected by spin-lock in kernel space [18].
3. NPB. NAS parallel benchmarks consists of eight programs: EP (Embarrassingly Parallel), IS (Integer Sort), CG (Conjugate Gradient), LU (Lower Upper Triangular), MG (Multi-Grid), FT (Fast Fourier Transformation), BT (Block Tridiagonal) and SP

(Scalar Penta-diagonal). For these programs, the scale class of the problems can be specified by user, i.e., S, W, A, B, C, D, E, from the smallest to the largest (some classes are not available for some programs) [15].

5.2   Experiment Result

5.2.1   Execution Time and Context Switches Number

We run Kernbench in one VM with the other one or three VMs running lookbusy for simulating CPU-bound workload and measure the completion time of KernBench. According to requirement mentioned above, every VM is configured with 2G memory to avoid swap storms and eliminate uncertainties.

Figure 6(a) shows that, the average runtime in 4-VM case is much larger than that in 2-VM case. The result met our expectations, for the contention becomes heavier with the number of VMs increasing. The result also shows that the default CFS scheduler performs worst compared with Co-Scheduling and RCS, which both co-schedule vCPUs in the same VM to reduce the overhead of LHP. RCS achieve 13.2% performance improvement over Co-Scheduling and 29.2% over CFS. The number of context switches during Kernbench is running is shown in Fig. 6(b). From the result, it is obvious that RCS can reduce considerable number of context switches, which is 2.54% less than Co-Scheduling and 7.06% less than CFS. The less context switches are also the important reason for better performance of Kernbench execution.

(a)   **(b)**

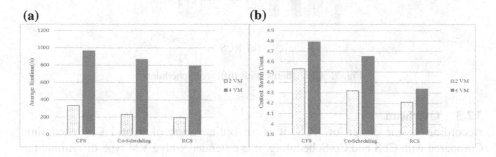

Fig. 6. (a). Average runtime of Kernbench (b). Switch count number of Kernbench

5.2.2   Fair Share

Fair capability is essential for a scheduler, and in this subsection, we will evaluate the fair share of RCS, compared with CFS and Co-Scheduling. In this subsection, seven NPB programs are running on the 4 VMs and the experiment results with different scheduling algorithms are shown in Fig. 7. From the Fig. 7(a) and (b) we can see that every VM enjoys fair share of CPU in CFS case and Co-Scheduling case, while it is different in Fig. 7(c). On the contrary, CPU resource is not allocated to every VM evenly and the VM3 occupies a large CPU share in the RCS case. We check the *pid* of each VM and found that the *pids* of VM1, VM2 and VM4 are all odd numbers which they can only share 6 CPU cores in the same socket. However, the unfair share is obvious when the VM number is small, which will be relieved with the number of VMs increasing according to the probability theory, especially in the cloud computing scenario, where there are considerable amounts of VMs and the probability of *pid* being odd and even are almost the same.

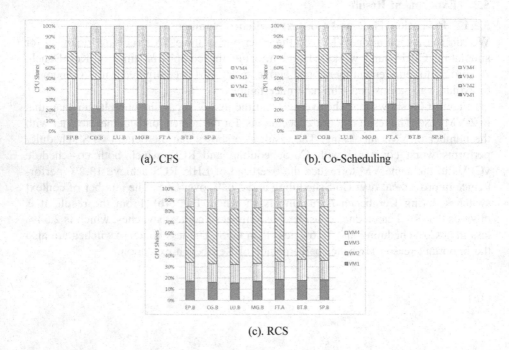

(a). CFS   (b). Co-Scheduling

(c). RCS

Fig. 7. CPU shares with different schedulers

5.2.3   Overhead

According to our design of RCS, it is an optimization of hybrid Co-Scheduling. Compared with CFS and Co-Scheduling, it is extended with a VM type discrimination and scheduling algorithm selection, which may increase the overhead of executing a task. In this subsection, we will evaluate the execution time of NPB's programs which also reflect the overhead. We run seven programs of NPB in one VM while the other three VMs are running lookbusy at the determined level. The experiment result is shown in Fig. 8. It shows the relative performance of NPB programs with CFS, Co-Scheduling and RCS, and in order to contrast the overhead, we standardize the source data of execution time, assuming the one of CFS is 100%.

The result shows that the execution time of Co-Scheduling and RCS are both less than CFS. The Co-Scheduling reduces the spinning time of waiting lock and thus it reduces the execution time by 6%. RCS inherits the advantage of Co-Scheduling and reduces the cache misses as well. The result also confirms our analysis with the execution time of RCS less than Co-Scheduling by about 5%.

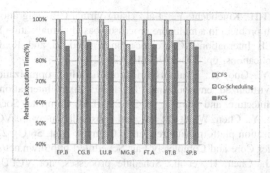

Fig. 8. The relative execution time of NPB programs of different scheduler

6 Conclusion

In this paper, in order to alleviate LHP and cache misses reduced by semantic gap between the hypervisor and the host, we propose an optimization scheduler RCS in KVM. Based on the hybrid co-scheduling, RCS co-schedules the vCPUs of the same concurrent VM by boosting their priority. within the CPU cores in a region, which belongs to the same CPU socket. We also add two strategies on load balancing, which help non-concurrent VMs avoid cache misses as well. We evaluate the performance of RCS, compared with CFS and Co-Scheduling. The experiment results show that the execution time and context switch number of RCS are less than CFS and Co-Scheduling, while when it still should be improved in fair share when the number of VMs is small. The overhead of RCS is also less than that of CFS and Co-Scheduling. The evaluation results enhance the availability of our solution.

Acknowledgment. This research was supported by National Key Research Program of China under Grant No. 2012BAH94F03.

References

1. Amazon: Amazon elastic compute cloud. http://aws.amazon.com/ecs2
2. Bai, Y., Xu, C., Li, Z.: Task-aware based co-scheduling for virtual machine system. In: ACM Symposium on Applied Computing, pp. 181–188. DBLP (2010)
3. https://amazonaws-china.com/cn/ec2/faqs/
4. Jiang, W., Zhou, Y., Cui, Y., et al.: CFS optimizations to KVM threads on multi-core environment, pp. 348–354 (2009)
5. Mauerer, W.: Professional Linux Kernel Architecture. Wiley, Hoboken (2008)
6. Arpaci-Dusseau, A.C.: Implicit Coscheduling: Coordinated Scheduling with Implicit Information. University of California, Berkeley (1999)
7. Uhlig, V., Levasseur, J., Skoglund, E., et al.: Towards scalable multiprocessor virtual machines. In: Proceedings of the Virtual Machine Research & Technology Symposium, vol. 3 (2004)
8. Friebel, T., Biemueller, S.: How to deal with lock holder preemption. In: GI OS Workshop (2013)

9. Mitake, H., Lin, T.H., Kinebuchi, Y., et al.: Using virtual CPU migration to solve the lock holder preemption problem in a multicore processor-based virtualization layer for embedded systems. In: IEEE International Conference on Embedded and Real-Time Computing Systems and Applications, pp. 270–279. IEEE (2012)

10. Yu, Y., Wang, Y., Guo, H., et al.: Hybrid co-scheduling optimizations for concurrent applications in virtualized environments. In: IEEE Sixth International Conference on Networking, Architecture, and Storage, pp. 20–29. IEEE Computer Society (2011)

11. Wang, B., Cheng, Y., Chen, W., et al.: Efficient consolidation-aware VCPU scheduling on multicore virtualization platform. Future Gener. Comput. Syst. 56(C), 229–237 (2016)

12. Modular Scheduler Core and Completely Fair Scheduler. http://lwn.net/Articles/230501/

13. Song, X., Shi, J., Chen, H., et al.: Schedule processes, not VCPUs. In: Asia-Pacific Workshop on Systems, pp. 1–7 (2013)

14. Weng, C., Wang, Z., Li, M., et al.: The hybrid scheduling framework for virtual machine systems. In: ACM SIGPLAN/SIGOPS International Conference on Virtual Execution Environments, pp. 111–120. ACM (2009)

15. Chen, H., Jin, H., et al.: Scheduling overcommitted VM: behavior monitoring and dynamic switching-frequency scaling. Future Gener. Comput. Syst. 29(1), 341–351 (2013)

16. Lookbusy-a synthetic load generator. https://www.devin.com/lookbusy/

17. NPB NASA. NAS parallel benchmarks. http://www.nas.nasa.gov/Software/NPB/

18. Wang, K., Wei, Y., Xu, C.Z., et al.: Self-boosted co-scheduling for SMP virtual machines. In: IEEE International Symposium on Modeling, Analysis and Simulation of Computer and Telecommunication Systems, pp. 154–163. IEEE (2015)

Remove-Duplicate Algorithm Based on Meta Search Result

Hongbin Wang[1] , Ming He[1,2] , Lianke Zhou[1(✉)] , Zijin Li[1] ,
Haomin Zhan[3] , and Rang Wang[1]

[1] College of Computer Science and Technology, Harbin Engineering University,
Harbin 150001, China
zhoulianke@hrbeu.edu.cn
[2] College of Computer and Information Engineering,
Heilongjiang University of Science and Technology, Harbin 150022, China
[3] Beijing General Institute of Electronic Engineering, Beijing 100854, China

Abstract. According to the characteristics of duplicate web pages in the meta search engine, a duplicate web pages detection algorithm is proposed based on a web page URL, title and abstract, and according to their different characteristics, different similarity computing method is proposed, firstly, the page URL is standardization processed in the algorithm, and then for the title detection, the algorithm improves the title string fuzzy matching algorithm and calculate the similarity based on the word frequency of each items in the query, for the abstract judgment, similarity computing is in accordance with the sentences of the abstract, for each sentence the algorithm gives three weights, and calculates the weights of similarity on base of each summary statement, the effect of the algorithm is obvious, it has been verified by experiment that the algorithm is superior to the traditional algorithm in the precision and recall rate.

Keywords: Meta search engine · Web pages remove-duplicate
Web pages similarity

1 Introduction

The high-speed development of Internet gives people more and more convenient to get information, but how to get effective information from the huge amount of data has become a big problem. The emergence of search engines solves this problem effectively. However, when people use search engines for information retrieval, they find that a lot of web pages are duplicate or very similar. Too much duplicate web pages will affect the user's query experience, reduce the efficiency of the system, and increase the query time. How to judge and remove duplicate web pages is a big problem because it is the structure and principle of meta search engine [1–3] that contribute to the higher duplication rate among the return results of meta search engine. There are many common characteristics among the duplicate web pages, such as different images with different pages, duplication caused by reprint and so on. In addition, there are redundancy. For example, a picture is uploaded to the micro blog, then it will be added the corresponding watermark and attributive site. It is necessary to do away with them.

© Springer Nature Switzerland AG 2018
X. Sun et al. (Eds.): ICCCS 2018, LNCS 11064, pp. 33–44, 2018.
https://doi.org/10.1007/978-3-030-00009-7_4

There is also a different version, which means not all the people like the same version on some social hot issues.

Meta search engine calls on a number of its members to complete the search behavior, so the results of a number of search engines returned together must be duplicate. It is calculated that duplication rate of returned results can reach about 10% to 30%. The duplicate information causes burden of browsing, affects the user's query feeling, increases storage space, and affects the user satisfaction to the results, so it is necessary to remove redundant information to improve the efficiency of the system.

2   Classic Algorithm of Remove-Duplicate Web Pages

There are many algorithms of remove-duplicate web pages of search engine nowadays. Although the structure and principle of meta search engine is different from independent search engine, remove-duplicate Web pages are based algorithms of search engines for meta search engine, as is summarized below.

Remove-Duplicate Web Pages According to the URL. This algorithm is applied in many meta search engines, for result sets returned from each independent engine. It determines whether the web pages are duplicate or not according to the URL address of the page. If the web pages are duplicate, the algorithm removes them. The advantage of this algorithm is very easy and fast [4, 5]. The disadvantage is that without the consideration of the characteristics of different web pages. There are many pages with different URLs reprinted, but some URL are just different formats, which is actually the same page. Thus the effect is not always good.

The I-Match Algorithm. The I-Match Algorithm, newly developed based on the DSC, DSC-SS algorithm by University of Birmingham, uses the method of collection statistics rather than syntactic analysis to identify string. The idea is to provide *idf* to every string. The distinguishing method is defining the log (N: the number of the documents in the collection/N: the number of the string in the documents). If the number is larger than this number, the document will be regarded as duplicated. The method is to input the document to be compared, strip the key string of the document and then apply the Hash algorithm to judge whether the document is duplicated [6, 7].

The Remove-Duplicate Algorithm Based on the Clustering Algorithm. This algorithm takes the Chinese characters (over 6000) in GB2312 as vector basis [8, 9]. The frequency of these characters appearing in the text or abstract is different. The algorithm takes the different frequency as web page vector and then figure out the cosine vector value to judge whether the document is duplicated.

The Algorithm Based on Character Code. This algorithm focuses on the punctuation marks in the text or abstract. In China, Tsinghua University is a representative university which adopts this algorithm. Their method is to choose the punctuation marks in the sentences and regard the two characters beside the marks as character codes. Harbin Industry University's method is to choose 5 characters beside the marks [10]. The details are as follows:

First, extract the text information; second, extract the character code; third, according to the sequence of the segmented sentences, express the character codes as digit feature string and then apply the fuzzy matching algorithm to match the feature string. Hence, the steps are: Extract the text information on the web pages and the feature string; Match the feature string and compare the factors matched. If the result is larger than certain threshold, the document is regarded as duplicated. Though this algorithm is effective, it only works under linear time. When it comes to BBS, post bar and reprinted web pages, the algorithm is not effective enough. The time efficiency would be affected if scale is large. The defect of the algorithm based on character code is that the information beside punctuation marks cannot represent that of the whole web pages. In addition, the information is highly affected by the position of punctuation marks. Therefore, the effectiveness of this algorithm is unsatisfactory.

The Remove-Duplicate Algorithm Based on Title and Abstract. This kind of algorithm is suitable for duplicating web pages of meta search engine. The working principle is to segment words from titles and abstract returned by search engine, then calculate similarity of two web pages in light of the fuzzy matching of string. Suppose T_1 and T_2 are titles of two web pages, A_1 and A_2 are the two abstracts. After segmenting words from the two titles and abstract, the results are marked as T_1' and T_2', A_1' and A_2'. The computing pattern is shown in formula (1).

$$TitleSim\left(T_1', T_2'\right) = t_n/t_w * 100\% \tag{1}$$

Where t_n and t_w respectively stands for the number of the same characters and the larger value of characters in the two titles. It is shown in formula (2).

$$AbstractSim\left(A_1', A_2'\right) = a_n/a_w * 100\% \tag{2}$$

Where a_n and aw respectively stands for the number of the same characters and the larger value of characters in the two abstracts. The shortcoming is that this algorithm only focuses on word frequency, however, fuzzy matching of word frequency cannot represent sentences and texts comprehensively.

3   The Design of Duplicated Web Pages Deletion Algorithm Based on Meta Search

In this paper, working principle of the duplicated web pages deletion algorithm based on meta search is judging URL returning to web pages. Firstly, format URL. If the URL is same, the web page is duplicated. If not, the URL and title will be judged whether they are redirected. When the URL and title are found redirected, the web page is duplicated; If not, further judge the abstract and title of the web page, and then figure out the similarity of the abstract and title of two web pages. At last, calculate the similarity of the two web pages. If the result meets the given threshold value, the web page is duplicated, then delete the duplicated information; if the result does not meet the given threshold value, the web page is not duplicated. The details are as follows:

3.1   Judgement Based on URL

There are two circumstances: One is direct judgement of URL's standardization. The other is judgement of URL's redirection. The two kinds of judgement are based on URL. The details are:

Direct judgement of URL is of high efficiency, however, some web pages do not follow the standard form of URL and part of some web pages' URL are missing. Thus standardization of URL is required. The standard form of every URL is: *protocol + domain* name of the *host + pathname + filename*. Firstly, standardize the URL of all web pages. If there is no filename, add '/index.html'. For the URL with suffix like '.htm', change that to 'html'. For example:

> www.hrbeu.edu.cn
> After being standardized, it will be:
> http://www.hrbeu.edu.cn/index.html

Both URL can be traced back to the same web page, thus the web page is duplicated. In this way, many situations can be tested, including default of URL.

In the case of URL redirection, some web pages are traced back for many times on the same website. The former URL changes into a new one. The domain name of the host, filename and titles are still the same, while the path is different from that of before. According to this, web pages of this circumstance can be judged based on URL.

Considering the two circumstances above, judgement of URL's redirection is more comprehensive than direct judgement based on URL. When a web page is considered as not duplicated after these two steps, further judgement is required which involves working out the similarity of titles and abstracts and then the similarity of two web pages. Finally take the result as a judgment standard.

3.2   Judgement Based on Similarity of Web Page Titles

Studies show that information in web page titles is very representative for the whole web page. Thus, it is feasible to judge whether a web page is duplicated or not in terms of web page titles. By doing so, the judgement of some reprint web pages can be done. This method is mainly used for judging approximate and reprint web pages.

The traditional duplicated web pages deletion algorithm based on judging titles is not feasible, because it depends on whether the titles of two web pages are different, but even some forum and reprint web pages use different titles, they may be duplicated. Another algorithm is based on fuzzy matching of string. It figures out the similarity of web page titles and abstracts. Its work principle mainly is:

Some web page titles contain a lot of redundant information, normally '_', '|' or blank character, which has no use for extracting titles. Firstly, delete redundant information and get the title's main part. Then segment words left. The following algorithm is used for working out the similarity between two titles:

$$similarity(A, B) = t_n/t_w * 100\% \tag{3}$$

In the formula (3), t_n is the number of the same characters; t_w is the maximum number of characters in the two titles.

The result of fuzzy matching of string is not representative enough for the similarity of two web pages. For example, search '*where is the best place in Harbin?*'. There are two results, one is '*where is the best place to play in Harbin?*'; The other is '*where is the best place to eat in Harbin?*'. The matching degree of the two titles is high, but they are different in many ways. Therefore, this paper suggests following methods.

Suppose that User Retrieval Words Contain m Feature Items. The importance of item t_i in title b_j is represented by W_{ij}. The calculating method is shown in formula (4).

$$W_{ij} = \begin{cases} \sum_{x=1}^{num(t_i,b_j)} \frac{length(q)}{length(b_j)} & num(t_i, b_j) > 0 \\ 0 & num(t_i, b_j) = 0 \end{cases} \tag{4}$$

In the formula, num(ti, bj) stands for the times item ti appears in title bj; length(q) stands for the length of the searched string q, length(bj) stands for the length of title bj. When num(ti, bj) is zero, Wij is zero.

For any two titles bp and bq, two vectors are applied to stand for the weights of feature items. $b_p = (w_{1p}, w_{2p}, \cdots, w_{mp})$ and $Borda(q, S_j, r_k)$. The formula (5) to judge the similarity of the titles are:

$$\cos(b_p, b_q) = \frac{b_p \cdot b_q}{|b_p| \cdot |b_q|} = \frac{\sum_{i=1}^{m} w_{ip} * w_{iq}}{\sqrt{\sum_{i=1}^{m} w_{ip}^2} * \sqrt{\sum_{i=1}^{m} w_{iq}^2}} \tag{5}$$

In the formula, $|b_p|$ and ω stand for the lengths of b_q and b_q, $b_p \cdot b_q$ is the inner product of the two vectors. From the formula, $0 \leq \cos(b_p, b_q) \leq 1$ can be observed.

3.3 Judgement Based on Similarity of Web Page Abstract

Studies show that web page abstract is generally passages which generalize main idea of web pages. Currently all of the main searching engines adopt the method of generating abstract dynamically based on query terms, a process in which the searching engine locates query terms, dynamically generates abstract according to the current text and finally returns web page abstract, links and titles to users.

Considering the dynamic generation of abstract, judgment based on abstract can apply method of judging duplicated abstract sentences. In this way, meanings of every sentence can be fully used and inaccuracy caused by fuzzy matching can be avoided. If there are many same sentences in abstract of two web pages, they are more likely duplicated pages. This method is more accurate in judging reprint web pages.

Suppose α stands for an abstract to be examined, the formula $s(\alpha) = \{\partial_1, \partial_2, \ldots, \partial_n\}$ stands for the set of sentences in the abstract. In the set, every sentence is parted according to punctuation marks. In accordance with Bayesian probability, the probability of several words appearing continuously is low among these sentences. Thus, the probability of the same sentence appearing in two abstracts is low. It is more likely that the two sentences are from the same web page. In addition, some web pages have too many stop words, modal particles and internet common words, thus it becomes difficult to distinguish these web pages. The weighing of this aspect should be reduced. Last, length of a sentence has some influence on the judgement. The longer the sentence is, the more representative it is. Two long sentences in different abstract are more representative than two short sentences. If two web pages have the same long sentence, one of the web pages is more likely to be duplicated. Therefore, every sentence in an abstract should be defined by three weighing factors.

$f(\partial, key)$ **stands for the occurrence frequency of retrieval words in abstract. The calculating method is.** First figure out the times for which retrieval words appear in sentence ∂ and use $fre(\partial, key)$ to stand for the result:

$$fre(\partial, key) = \sum_{i=1}^{N} num(\partial, key_i) \tag{6}$$

$num(\partial, key)$ stands for whether retrieval word key_i appears in sentence ∂ or not. If it appears, the number is one; if not, the number is zero.

After that, unify the frequency of occurrence and the calculating method is:

$$f(\partial, key) = \frac{fre(\partial, key)}{\max(fre(\partial, key))} \tag{7}$$

In the formula, $max(fre(\partial, key))$ represents the max occurrence frequency of retrieval words.

Reducing weights of unrelated sentences, which means reducing modal particles and internet common words. Sentence ∂ appears in the set of sentences for k times. The total number of sentences in the set is represented by M, the occurrence frequency of the sentence is $S(\partial)$. After reducing its weight, the inverse frequency is $NS(\partial)$. The specific formula is shown in formulas (8) and (9)

$$S(\partial) = k/M \tag{8}$$

$$NS(\partial) = \lg\left(\frac{M}{k}\right) \tag{9}$$

Length of a sentence: $length(\partial)$ **stands for the number of characters contained in sentence** ∂.

The weight $w(\partial)$ of sentence ∂ is shown in formula (10).

$$w(\partial) = fre(\partial, key) \times NS(\partial) \times length(\partial) \tag{10}$$

Suppose there are abstract a and b and sentence collection A and B. Define $S = A \cup B = \{s_1, s_2, \ldots, s_N\}$. Unify the two abstracts:

$$a = \left\langle s_1^{n_1}, s_2^{n_2}, \cdots s_N^{n_N} \right\rangle$$

$$b = \left\langle s_1^{m_1}, s_2^{m_2}, \cdots, s_N^{m_N} \right\rangle$$

The sentence weights' vectors are:

$$X = \langle x_1, x_2, \cdots, x_n \rangle \quad Y = \langle y_1, y_2, \cdots, y_n \rangle$$

The Similarity of the two abstracts are:

$$\cos(X, Y) = \frac{\sum_{i=1}^{N} x_i \cdot y_i}{|X| \times |Y|} = \frac{\sum_{i=1}^{N} m_i^2}{|X| \times |Y|} \tag{11}$$

In the formula, mi stands for the weight of the same sentence in the two abstracts.

3.4 Computing of Similarity of Web Pages

Similarity $Sim(A, B)$ of web page A and B are:

$$Sim(A, B) = \alpha * \cos(b_p, b_q) + \beta * \cos(X, Y) \tag{12}$$

In the formula, $\cos(b_p, b_q)$ stands for the similarity of titles of page A and B; $\cos(X, Y)$ stands for the similarity of abstract of page A and B. α and β are weighing factors and α plus β is one. If the result is larger than some certain threshold, one web page is regarded as duplicated. If not, the web page is not duplicated. The threshold and weighing factors are selected from experiments.

4 Experiment and Analysis

This section is the experiment and analysis to the algorithm remove-duplicate web pages according to itself. Details of the contents about the experiment and the results of the analysis are as followed.

4.1 Construction of Data Sets

To construct a prototype system NMSE on the basis of Chinese meta search engine. The test is carried according to different query topics and tested search engines are included Baidu, Yahoo, Bing and Sogou because of the non-availability of Google's Chinese service. The query topics chosen by system come from the top 100 in 2014 search ranks, which are included 10 different topics, such as "lost contact in Malaysia Airlines 370", "you from the star", "where has the time gone", "how to refer to the IP address". The first 100 results sent by each tested search engine are analyzed after obtained from artificial markers and statistical analyses. Then we get the best value of the optimal values in weighed way and the threshold of similarity. Last, the effect comparison of algorithms is made.

4.2   Evaluation Methods

In this paper, we use precision and recall ratio which are the most commonly used in research of information retrieval to evaluate the effect on the algorithm of remove-duplicate web pages:

$$Precision = \frac{numbers\ of\ eliminating\ duplicated\ webpage\ correctly}{numbers\ of\ eliminating\ webpage} * 100\% \tag{13}$$

$$Recall = \frac{numbers\ of\ eliminating\ duplicated\ webpage\ correctly}{numbers\ of\ duplicated\ webpage} * 100\% \tag{14}$$

In order to ensure the accuracy of the experimental results in this paper, we carry the successive 10 days of query according to the selected topics and calculate the mean value as the experimental basis when we evaluate each algorithm.

4.3   Results and Analysis

In this section, algorithm weakens the weights of unrelated sentences based on the similarity of the statements in the abstract. The computing source of weights is from the proportion accounted by statements in the training set of web pages sentences. The training set applies the grabbed pages from Sina to extract text and calculate the frequency of statements in text for the purpose of calculating the weight of sentences.

In addition, the experiment consists of three parts: the first is experiments in value of weighted factor and the similarity threshold; the second is the comparative experiments in effect on the algorithm finding duplicated web pages; the third is comparative experiments in precision and recall between algorithm proposed in this paper and the traditional algorithms.

The Influence of Weight Factor and Threshold Value on Algorithm. In the algorithm proposed in this paper, we use URL to determine duplication or not at first; if different, the title and abstract respectively are calculated the similarity, and then we calculate the similarity of web pages in weighted form. The performance and precision are affected by α and β. The similarity threshold value determines the two pages whether duplicate or not, and the choice of threshold value also influences the accuracy of algorithm. The results show that the titles are more valuable than abstract in the search engine. Therefore, the experiment selects the value of α from 0.5 to 0.9, and the similarity threshold value from 0.1 to 0.8. The precisions of different values are shown in Fig. 1.

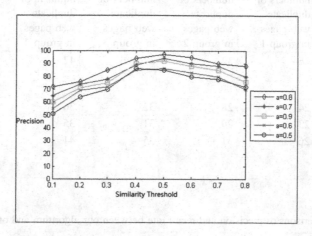

Fig. 1. The precisions of the algorithm when the value of α is different

From Fig. 1, we can see that with the increase of the threshold, precision gradually rises. When α = 0.8, that's to say, α = 0.8, β = 0.2, the precision of remove-duplicate web pages are more accurate. It is also illustrates the importance of the title indirectly. In the following experiment in evaluating the performance of the algorithm, the values of the weight factors α and β are based on it. And when the threshold value is near 0.5, the accuracy is best, so the similarity threshold value is 0.5.

Effect Analysis on Algorithms Remove-Duplicate Web Pages. Five groups of query words are selected from the data set, and each query is used to obtain the first 100 results of the tested engine, thus 400 results are obtained. Then we compare algorithm proposed in this paper with algorithm (algorithm 1) based on traditional feature codes and algorithm (algorithm 2) based on MD5 abstract according to the results contributed by artificial markers and statistical analyses. Comparison results in the effect of the number of duplicate pages can be detected by each algorithm are as shown in Table 1.

As seen from the table, the recognition rate of the algorithm proposed in this paper is close to the numbers sent by artificial markers, which is higher than the rate of traditional algorithms remove-duplicate web pages.

Comparative analysis of the algorithm proposed in this paper and the traditional algorithms. Using the precision and recall rate as the evaluation indexes of the algorithm, the algorithm selects a query word "migration of wild animals" from the data sets, and calculates the number of duplicated web pages, of distinguished duplicated web pages, of distinguished and corrects duplicated web pages from 400 web pages. According to that, we calculate the precision and recall rate. Specific effects are showed as Table 2.

Table 1. Effect comparisons of examining duplicated web pages

	The page numbers of duplicate web pages in group 1	The page numbers of duplicate web pages in group 2	The page numbers of duplicate web pages in group 3	The page numbers of duplicate web pages in group 4	The page numbers of duplicate web pages in group 5
Results by artificial markers	26	32	37	42	35
Algorithm 1	24	28	32	36	32
Algorithm 2	23	29	31	35	29
Algorithm proposed in this paper	26	31	35	41	33

Table 2. Comparisons of precision and recall rate between our algorithm and other algorithms

Algorithm	The number of duplicated web pages	The number of distinguished duplicated web pages	The number of distinguished and correct duplicated web pages	Precision	Recall
Algorithm1	63	59	53	89.8%	84.1%
Algorithm2	63	57	50	87.7%	79.3%
Algorithm proposed in this paper	63	62	59	95.1%	93.6%

Where algorithm 1 is based on codes of traditional feature and algorithm 2 is based on MD5 abstract. The precision and recall of two traditional algorithms are lower than that of the algorithm proposed in this paper.

In order to ensure the accuracy, the query words of different themes are selected from data sets. Each query that is done for 100 times is used to obtain the first 100 results of the tested engine. Then we calculate the precision and recall of each query. Taking the average value as the basis for comparison, we compare the algorithm proposed in this paper with the traditional two algorithms. The results are shown in Fig. 2.

From the Fig. 2, we can see that the precision and recall rate of the algorithm proposed in this paper are higher than that of two traditional algorithms, which means that the proposed algorithm is more effective.

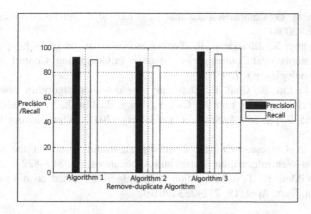

Fig. 2. Comparisons of the precision and recall rate between the algorithms proposed in this paper and the traditional algorithms

5 Conclusion

The researches at home and abroad based on the meta search engine have made a lot of achievements and put into use. As the mother of search engines, the meta search engine serves for users by integrating a number of outstanding search engines as members. Currently, algorithms of remove-duplicate web pages on meta search engine field are not too much. Using titles and abstract returned from web pages to determine whether they are duplicate is very effective. However, the algorithm proposed in this paper that uses URL, titles and abstract to determine whether they are duplicate is verified by experiments. It is better than traditional algorithms in the precision and recall rate, but it also needs to be improved in the effect of time. Improving the user's search feeling is the research focus in the future.

Acknowledgments. This work was funded by the National Natural Science Foundation of China under Grant (No. 61772152 and No. 61502037), the Basic Research Project (No. JCKY2016206B001, JCKY2014206C002 and JCKY2017604C010), and the Technical Foundation Project (No. JSQB2017206C002).

References

1. Smyth, B., Boydell, O.: Meta search engine. US (2010)
2. Lawrence, S., Giles, L.: The NECI meta search engine. In: World Wide Web Conference Series
3. Lawrence, S., Giles, C.L.: Inquirus, the NECI meta search engine. Comput. Netw. ISDN Syst. **30**, 95–105 (1998)
4. Zhao-Hui, X.U., Zhao, S.M., Yan, F.L., Qin, J.: An improved DSC removing duplicated webpages algorithm based on feature vector. Sci. Technol. Eng. (2013)
5. Guo-Rong, S.U., Yang, Y.X., Deng, J.S.: An algorithm of removing duplicate URL. J. Guangxi Normal Univ. (2010)

6. Qiang, S., Cheng, G.: Comparison and analysis of hash algorithm based on flows. J. Nanjing Normal Univ. (2008)
7. Rathinasabapathy, R., Bhaskaran, R.: Performance comparison of hashing algorithm with Apriori. In: International Conference on Advances in Computing, Control, & Telecommunication Technologies, pp. 729–733
8. Ye, F., Liu, J., Liu, B., Chai, K.: Duplicate page detection algorithm based on the field characteristic clustering. In: Luo, X., Cao, Y., Yang, B., Liu, J., Ye, F. (eds.) ICWL 2010. LNCS, vol. 6537, pp. 75–84. Springer, Heidelberg (2011). https://doi.org/10.1007/978-3-642-20539-2_9
9. Yang, J.W.: A Chinese web page clustering algorithm based on the suffix tree. In: Conference on Web Information System and Applications, pp. 817–822
10. YuJun, Y., YiMei, Y.: Text information hiding algorithm based on dot-matrix character code. Comput. Syst. Appl. **19**, 231–233 (2010)

Research into Effects of Shrimp Aquaculture by Extensible Mind Mapping

Fuli Chen[1], Rui Fan[2(✉)], Bifeng Guo[2], Fuyu Ma[2], and Weitao He[2]

[1] Faculty of Mathematics and Computer Science, Guangdong Ocean University,
Zhanjiang, China
1446730028@qq.com
[2] Faculty of Software Technology,
Guangdong Ocean University, Zhanjiang, China
fanrui@gdou.edu.cn, 1037486652@qq.com,
452388727@qq.com, 1305190319@qq.com

Abstract. Today's worldwide consumer value shrimp as a high-protein aquatic food. As the demand for shrimp increases, traditional fishing methods fall short of the ability to produce enough shrimp for demand. In consequence, shrimp aquaculture industry emerges as the demand requires. However, the troubling question is that although farmers can earn high revenues from farming shrimp, the risks of raising the shrimp are also very high. The contradictory problem is the value of shrimp versus the potential costs of producing it, that is value versus risk. This paper focuses on this contradictory problem with the method of Extenics theory and mind mapping.

Keywords: Extenics · Shrimp · Mind mapping · Aquaculture

1 Introduction

With the rapid growth of the world economy, living standards have greatly improved. Shrimp, the main aquatic products of global trade rich in protein, is more and more popular in the world. It's common to see shrimps on the table referred as a "delicacy". Needless to say, the supply of shrimp available through traditional fishing methods alone falls short of the increasing demand for shrimp. Therefore, worldwide consumer demand calls for increasing shrimp production. Consequently, shrimp aquaculture industry emerges as the demand requires.

In 2013–2017 years the annual growth rate of the global shrimp production may be around 7.7% but it isn't mean that all the farmers are profitable, still some breed shrimp successfully and profit while other fail and suffer a deficit [1]. From many different regions, it is commonly seen that people fail to raise shrimp, which has a lot to do with how they raise shrimp [2]. If those who raise shrimps just increase the density of a shrimp alone to seek high yield, they will likely to get the unwanted result that the efforts people have made in raising shrimps for a long time will be in vain [3]. Among many influencing factors, the most difficult part of raising shrimp is its basic management, including water quality and feed [4]. A series of problems will happen because of the bad basic management. Typically, White Spot Syndrome and Early

© Springer Nature Switzerland AG 2018
X. Sun et al. (Eds.): ICCCS 2018, LNCS 11064, pp. 45–58, 2018.
https://doi.org/10.1007/978-3-030-00009-7_5

Mortality Syndrome [5] are two major diseases that have occurred in the global shrimp aquaculture industry. It's necessary to provide the shrimp with healthy environment to live and resist to the virus that require the physical and chemical factors of water should be control well. [6] Due to the breeding cost is getting higher and higher, some shrimp farmers choose cut-price feed to reduce cost. Hence, they can't make sure the feed quality. For feed of poor quality, it not only leads to low utilization but also have bad impact on the intestines and stomach of shrimps. Moreover, the water could be destructively polluted. Residual baits and excretion not be disposed of in time makes dissolved oxygen (Do) inadequate in the bottom of the shrimp ponds. The inadequate Do will seriously affect the life of the shrimp. One is that inadequate Do leads anaerobic bacteria multiply rapidly causing the syndromes that the shrimps have yellow gills, black gills, red beards, red legs, difficult shelling etc.

It is the strong demand that leads to shrimp value increase and farmers can earn high revenues from farming shrimp. However, the risks of raising the shrimp are also very high. Breeding shrimp is not an easy thing, the survival rate of shrimp is very unstable. Once the living condition cannot meet shrimp need, the survival rate will decrease. And once the virus is infected, the whole pool of shrimp will suffer.

People try to solve the problem by many ways, but no one solve the problem by a new principle named Extenics [7]. What is Extenics? Extenics is a Chinese principle using some mathematical methods to solve contradictory problem [8]. Up to now according to the direction of people's minds, Extenics has solve some problems successfully. And our team has made some contributions to Extenics, too. One is Extenics innovation software in Android operating system [9], the other is a modeling software of Extenics [10]. As Extenics is useful, it is not efficient. Especially when you analyze problem at the last stage, your mind may easily become messy, because Extenics doesn't reflect the process people think. There exits another way of researching Extenics, that is the developed self-adaptive software modeling [11]. All in all, to make better use of Extenics, we try to combine Extenics with mind mapping. Through mind mapping we can clearly see the whole process we think when we solve the contradictory problem.

Here is brief introduction to Extenics with Mind mapping model. As is shown in the following picture the original problem can be divided into two sub-problems. And once the sub-problem is identified as a kernel problem, three parts are included, goal base elements, conditional base elements and dependent functions. We use base element attributes, base element attribute values and dependent function values to describe goal base elements and conditional base elements. As to dependent functions, they are comprised of three parts, including function types, function parameters and parameter values. The relationships among original problem, kernel problems and base elements can be clearly recognized from the following picture, which makes contribution to our better understanding on the conflict points of the problem. Every base element is analyzed and transformed according to Extension analysis and Extension transformation, from which the final base element is found. At last, we come up with the best solution to solving the contradictory problem through evaluating the optimal value of dependent functions by Extendable Superiority Evaluation.

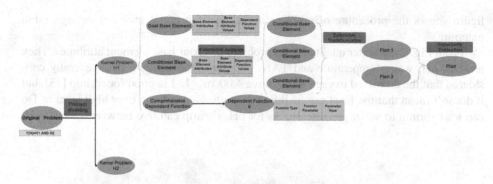

Fig. 1. Extensible procedure mind mapping made with a flexible software

2 Procedures of Solving the Problem

2.1 The Reason of Using Model in Fig. 1

Generally, people's ways of innovative thinking happen by chance. If the inspiration occurs people will consider the problem in different ways which makes a good idea arises subsequently. However, the occurrence of such an opportunity is uncertain. We cannot make sure to better use the innovative thinking when solving a contradictory problem. But Extenics do help, Extenics is a new discipline that opens up innovative methods and techniques. Therefore, we choose this model and show how it works.

2.2 Problem Modeling

What we are going to do is to divide the original problem into water quality problem and feeding problem. Here are our reasons. Water quality and feeding are most important factors that affect the life of shrimp. Water is the living environment for shrimp which quality directly affects the growth of shrimp. And what we are going talk about are the main physical and chemical factors in water, they are dissolved oxygen (Do), pH, ammonia nitrogen and water temperature.

Dissolved oxygen affects shrimp activity and feeding, lacking of which can cause severe outbreak of shrimp diseases, leading shrimp to floating head or death. The pH value of water is one of the important indicators of water quality. The lower pH is, the higher hydrogen sulphide content and toxicity will be. Low pH also influences shrimp molting, it causes the shrimp softening of the crustaceans. When pH is too high, the toxicity of ammonia will be relatively high. In addition, ammonia nitrogen affects shrimp development, immunity, metabolism and survival. Last but not least is water temperature. Excessive water temperature can cause obvious changes in DO, pH, salinity, phytoplankton, bacteria and so on which subsequently make the water quality deteriorated and cause the outbreak of shrimp disease [12].

As food is to human, so bait is to shrimp. The nutrients and content in the feed are essential to shrimp lives. The physical properties of feed itself and the frequency of feeding are also factors that affecting the good absorption of shrimp. Consequently, we divide the original problem into water quality and feeding problem. The following figure shows the procedure of problem modeling of original problem through mind mapping.

From Fig. 2 the water quality kernel problem has four base element attributes. They are Do, pH, water temperature and TAN. For dissolved oxygen, it is generally considered that the dissolved oxygen level above 4.00 mg. L-1 is good for shrimp [13], but it doesn't mean that the level can be infinitely high. Because the over high level of Do can lead shrimp to suffer gas disease. As for pH, shrimp can live between 7.0–9.0 pH,

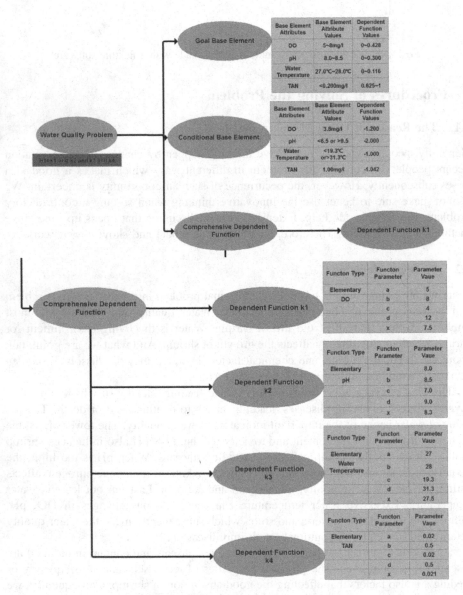

Fig. 2. Modeling of water quality problem

and 8.0–8.5 pH would be more suitable [14]. In summers and winters, the pH values rang is slightly different. In summer the shrimp can live between 6.5–9.5 pH, but 8.0–8.5 pH and the gap between 0.3 and 0.6 pH in the morning and evening would be better for the growth of shrimp [15]. Water temperature between 19.3–31.3 °C is acceptable while 27–28 °C is better. Ammonia nitrogen (TAN) level had better lower than 0.5 mg/l [16]. The following data are what we have just analyzed.

$$
L1 \begin{bmatrix} Water & Do & 3.8 \\ & pH & <6.5 or > 9.5 \\ & Temperature & <19.3 or > 31.3 \\ & TAN & 1.00 \end{bmatrix}
$$

$$
G1 \begin{bmatrix} Water & Do & 5 \sim 10 \\ & pH & 8.0 \sim 8.5 \\ & Temperature & 27.0 \sim 28.0 \\ & TAN & <0.200 \end{bmatrix}
$$

By the following formula, we calculate the dependent function values.

$$
\rho(x, X0) = \left| x - \frac{a+b}{2} \right| - \frac{b-a}{2} \qquad \rho(x, X) = \left| x - \frac{c+d}{2} \right| - \frac{d-c}{2} \qquad (1)
$$

$$
D(x, X0, X) = \begin{cases} \rho(x, X) - \rho(x, X0) & \rho(x, X) \neq \rho(x, X0) AND x \notin X0 \\ \rho(x, X) - \rho(x, X0) + a - b & \rho(x, X) \neq \rho(x, X0) AND x \in X0 \\ a - b & \rho(x, X) = \rho(x, X0) \end{cases} \qquad (2)
$$

$$
\rho(x, x0, X) = \begin{cases} a - x, & x \leq x0 \\ \frac{a-x0}{b-x0}(b-x), & x \in <x0, b> \\ x - b, & x \geq b \end{cases}
$$

$$
\rho(x, x0, X) = \begin{cases} a - x, & x \leq a \\ \frac{b-x0}{a-x0}(x-a), & x \in <a, x0> \\ x - b, & x \geq x0 \end{cases} \qquad (3)
$$

$$
k(x) = \begin{cases} \frac{\rho(x, X0)}{D(x, x0, X)} - 1 & \rho(x, x0) = \rho(x, X) AND x \notin X0 \\ \frac{\rho(x, X0)}{D(x, x0, X)} & else \\ \frac{\rho(x, x0, X)}{D(x, x0, X)} & D(x, x0, X) \neq 0, x \in X \\ -\rho(x, x0, X0) + 1 & D(x, x0, X) = 0, x \in X0 \\ 0 & D(x, x0, X) = 0, x \notin x0, x \in X \end{cases} \qquad (4)
$$

The dependent function values we calculate are k1(x) = −1.200, k2(x) < −2.000, k2(x) < −1.000, k4(x) = −1.042. They are all less than zero meaning that they are incompatibility problems.

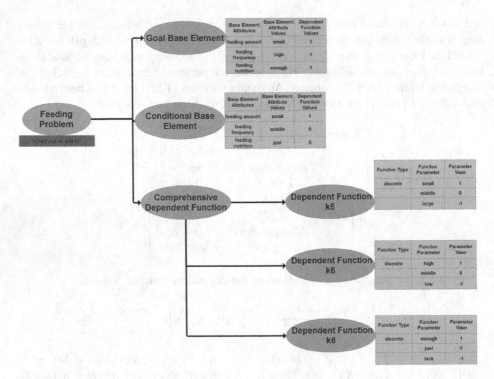

Fig. 3. Modeling of feeding problem

As is shown in Fig. 3, we divide the kernel problem 2 into three parts, they are feeding amount, feeding frequency and feed nutrition. Feeding too much would make residual feed soak in the water for a long time. As time goes by, residual feed turns spoiled and when shrimp eat the spoiling feed, shrimp would be in poor health. Besides residual feed would pollute the water. While feed shortage will result in shrimp killing each other for feed. Therefore, we choose the way that small amount of feed with enough nutrition and feed frequently. By this way we can reduce the amount of residual feed without making feed lack. To make sure the shrimp grow healthily we also need to consider the nutrient composition of the feed. That requires us to choose feed carefully when buying feed. We use three discrete dependent functions k5(x), k6(x), k7(x) to describe these three base elements shown as the following.

$$
L2\begin{bmatrix} Feeding & Amount & Small \\ & Frequency & Middle \\ & Nutrition & Just \end{bmatrix} \quad G2\begin{bmatrix} Feeding & Amount & Small \\ & Frequency & High \\ & Nutrition & Enough \end{bmatrix}
$$

$$
k5 = \begin{cases} small & 1 \\ middle & 0 \\ l\,\arg e & -1 \end{cases} \quad k6\begin{cases} high & 1 \\ middle & 0 \\ low & -1 \end{cases} \quad k7\begin{cases} enough & 1 \\ just & 0 \\ lack & -1 \end{cases} \quad (5)
$$

According to the three discrete dependent functions, we calculate the dependent function values are k(5) = 1, k(6) = 0, and k(7) = 0 respectively. Therefore, the second kernel problem is compatible.

2.3   Extensible Analysis

From mind mapping, we can clearly see the base element attributes of the contradictory problem. Then according to these elements, we divert our thinking to solve the problem by the method of Extensible analysis. According to the importance of the base elements attributes, we give different weights to calculate the comprehensive dependent function value. That is 0.30 for water temperature, 0.27 for Do, 0.23 for pH and 0.20 for TAN. And now we solve the problem according to some of the base elements attribute of kernel problem 1.

We can solve the contradictory problem by changing its conditional base elements. Here L1.for taking care of algae, L1.2 for adding stress elements, L1.3 for removing the debris, L1.4for controlling the amount of microorganism, L1.5 for adding carbon source, L1.6 for chemical neutralization reaction, L1.7 for removing some shrimps and L1.8for changing the water. The following eight are our methods.

Method 1: Take care of algae. The dissolved oxygen in water mainly comes from the photosynthesis of algae, though the oxygen increasing machine do help to a degree. Algae can also absorb some of the inorganic salts that are decomposed by bacteria, which can purify the water and control the pH value. But not all kinds of algae are useful for shrimp breeding, we have to control the species and quantity of algae, otherwise the result is counterproductive like the happen of red tide. The comprehensive dependent function value of this method is 0.12676.

Method 2: Add stress hormone. Stress hormone can be helpful to adjust the micro ecological environment of the pond. It can reduce the content of harmful substances, such as ammonia nitrite, to improve water quality. At the same time, stress hormone can help the shrimp to adapt to the intense stress response causing by the sudden changes in the environment like weather mutation or changes in the water physical and chemical factors. The comprehensive dependent function value of this method is −0.01734.

Method 3: Removing the debris. The residual bait, the corpse and other litter piled up at the bottom of the pond will produce toxic substances such as hydrogen sulfide, ammonia, etc., which would affect the pH value of water. It takes a long time to rely merely on bacterial decomposition, so it will be better to clean up the impurities manually to reduce the toxic substances. The comprehensive dependent function value of this method is 0.19605.

Method 4: Control the amount of microorganism. Except the breath of the shrimp most of the dissolved oxygen is consumed by bacteria. To let more dissolved oxygen to be used by shrimp, we can control the amount of the bacteria. However, in the actual situation, it is difficult to control the sum of microbes. Once the conditions are suitable, the germs will grow wantonly. Therefore, we take a precautionary approach to microbes, especially the harmful viruses and germs, instead of controlling the number of microorganisms after they are overflowing. The comprehensive dependent function value of this method is 0.02576.

Method 5: Add activated carbon. Carbon has the ability of absorbing, which can adsorb hydrogen sulfide to control the pH value of water. Besides it can also absorb some of the impurities and toxins to purify the water. But the ash on the surface of carbon causes water secondary pollution. And considering the carbon adsorption capacity, we need to add a lot of carbon to achieve the purification effect, which will increase the cost of breeding. The comprehensive dependent function value of this method is 0.0053.

Method 6: Chemical neutralization reaction. We can add acetic acid or hydrated lime to adjust the pH value. When pH value is too low, a proper amount of hydrated lime should be added to neutralize the acidic materials, while the pH is high, we add a proper amount of acetic acid. In addition, hydrated lime can also supplement the calcium ions in the water, which is beneficial to the shrimp molting shell. The comprehensive dependent function value of this method is 0.0738 (Fig. 4).

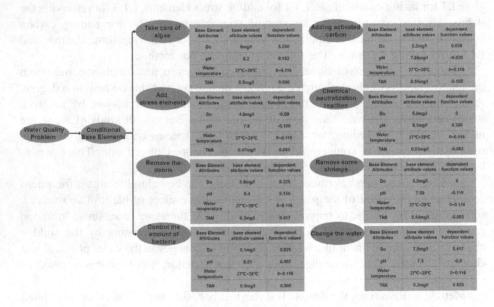

Fig. 4. Extensible analysis

Method 7: Remove some shrimps. The density of the shrimp can be reduced by fishing some from the pond. This method can increase the resources needed for the shrimp in the pond, also reduce the amount of residual bait, feces and other impurities to make the water quality stable. However, it is limited to use this method. In the early stage of raising shrimp, it is possible to take this approach, but in the middle and late stage using this will affect the profitability and will not solve the problem fundamentally. The comprehensive dependent function value of this method is −0.0245.

Method 8: Change the water. When the physical and chemical factors in the water are found to be quite abnormal, change the clean water in time. This method is most effective in dealing with the polluted water. However, the frequent large-scale change of water not only causes the stress response of the shrimp, but also reduces the utilization rate of water and raises the cost price. The comprehensive dependent function value of this method is 0.13999.

As for kernel problem 2: Feeding problem, we have proved in 2.2 that it is a compatible problem. The following picture is the specific process of our Extensible analysis.

2.4   Extensible Transformation

For kernel problem 1, through Extensible Analysis we have come out several methods. We select methods L1, L3, L6and L8 because the comprehensive dependent function value of each of them is higher than the others and their feasibility is high, too. Then we choose one more method from the others. For L4, its value is 0.02576 highest among L2, L4, L5and L7. However, just as it is said in 2.3 Extensible Analysis it's not easy to control the sum of microbes. For L5, its value is 0.0053 but it will increase the cost of breeding. For L7, its value is −0.0245 lowest among all. Then for L2, its value is −0.01734 but it is feasible, when combined with L1, L3, L6and L8, it can make the value higher. Therefore, we finally select L1, L2, L3, L6and L8 and integrate them into one method L1.12368. Shown as following.

$$L1.12368 \begin{bmatrix} Water & Do & 6.5 \\ & pH & 8.2 \\ & Temperature & 27.5 \\ & TAN & 0.3 \end{bmatrix}$$

The comprehensive dependent function values of kernel problem 1 we calculate is 0.26131.

For kernel problem 2, we add an artificial management attribute to it. In the process of raising shrimps, the manager chooses the appropriate size of feed according to the different states of the shrimp. At the early stage of the shrimp, we choose a small feed, such as the powdery feed, to help the young shrimp to absorb food. While in the middle and late stages, we choose a larger feed, such as granular feed. In the whole process of raising the shrimp, we use a small amount of feed each time with high frequency to feed them. What the manager should do is to adjust the amount of the feed feeding next time by watching the shrimp taking feed this time. If the shrimp finish the meal quickly, then the next time we can add a little amount of feed. And if there is a lot of feed left after the meal, then in the next feeding, we reduce the amount slightly. This method is helpful to reduce residual feed to prevent pathogenic vibrio from growing. The discrete dependent function of the new attribute artificial management K8 and the kernel problem 2 after adding the new attribute is shown as follow. We set weigh to each base element attribute. It is 0.15 for amount, 0.15 for frequency, 0.4 for nutrition and 0.3 for management.

$$k8 \begin{cases} well & 1 \\ just & 0 \\ poor & -1 \end{cases} \qquad L2' \begin{bmatrix} Feeding & Amount & Small \\ & Frequency & High \\ & Nutrition & Enough \\ & Management & Well \end{bmatrix}$$

The comprehensive dependent function value of kernel problem 2 we calculate is 1.

The process of Extensible Transformation of kernel problem 1 and 2 shown as follow (Fig. 5).

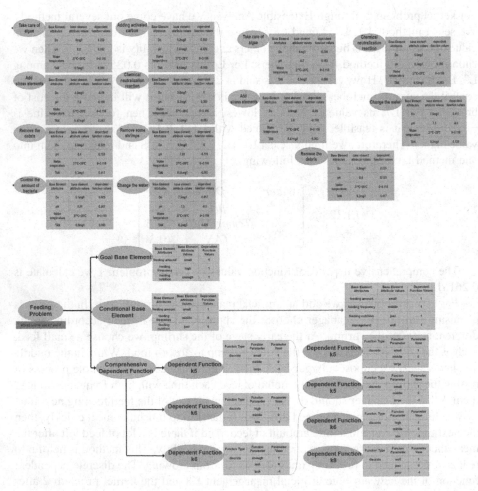

Fig. 5. Extensible Transformation

2.5 Superiority Evaluation

We find out the best solution to each of the two kernel problems. L1.12368 for kernel problem 1 while L2' for kernel problem 2. The dependent function values are shown as follow.

$$H1 = L1.12368 \begin{bmatrix} Water & Do & 6.5 & 0.375 \\ & pH & 8.2 & 0.182 \\ & Temperature & 27.5 & 0.116 \\ & TAN & 0.3 & 0.417 \end{bmatrix} \qquad H2 = L2' \begin{bmatrix} Feeding & Amount & Small & 1 \\ & Frequency & High & 1 \\ & Nutrition & Enough & 1 \\ & Management & Well & 1 \end{bmatrix}$$

$$Y(H) = H1(k) \wedge H2(k)$$
$$= k1 \wedge k2 \wedge k3 \wedge k4 \wedge k5 \wedge k6 \wedge k7 \wedge k8$$
$$= 0.116$$

The final conclusion is that the way to solve the kernel problem 1 including taking care of algae, adding stress elements, removing the debris, chemical neutralization reaction and changing the water. The way to solve the kernel problem 2 is to choose a small amount of feed with enough nutrition and feed frequently with the manager adjusting.

The process is shown as follow (Fig. 6).

The whole procedure of solving the problem is shown in Fig. 7 in a mind mapping.

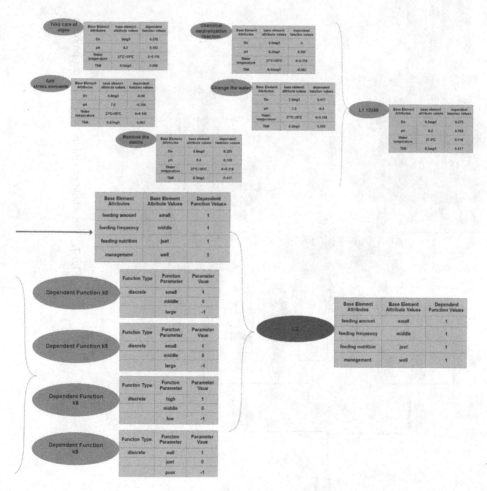

Fig. 6. Superiority Evaluation

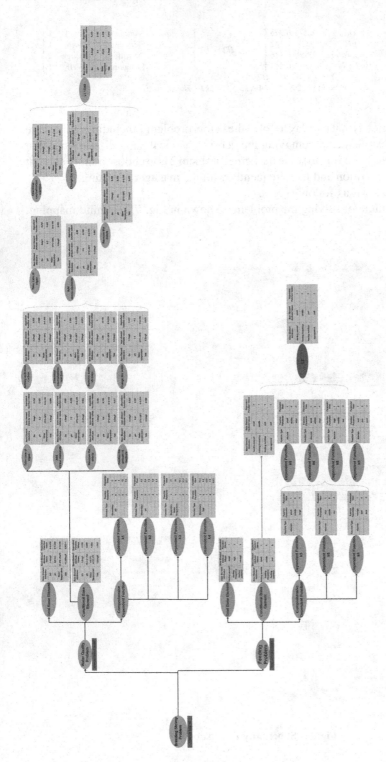

Fig. 7. The whole procedure of solving the problem

3 Conclusion

There is a problem that, for farmers, raising shrimp has both high income and high risk. We solve the problem through Extenics with mind mapping. And we come to such a conclusion. In order to reduce the risk greatly, we should maintain the good water quality. To provide dissolved oxygen in waters, enough algae should be planted in the water and make sure the algae grow well before putting out the shrimp seed. Watch the water quality in the process of breeding. If the pH value of water is too high, add a proper amount of acetic acid to it, while the pH value is too low add a proper amount of hydrated lime. Control the content of hydrogen sulfide and ammonium sulphide in water by removing the accumulated residual bait, the excreta, the corpse and other impurities at the bottom of the pond regularly. Add some stress elements to slow down the stress response of the shrimp when the physical and chemical factors of the water change greatly. If the content of physical and chemical factors such as ammonia nitrogen has been severely exceeded the standard, change the whole water. When feeding shrimp, the manager should adjust the amount of feed by observing the feeding table. Small amount of feed with enough nutrition each time and feed frequently to make sure the feed is fresh for the shrimp. Reduce the residual feed in time to prevent pathogenic vibrio from growing.

Acknowledgements. The research is supported by Guangdong Provincial Science and Technology Project (2014A040402010) and Guangdong Province Innovation and Entrepreneurship Training Program for College Students (201710566036).

References

1. Li, F.: Global shrimp industry status and future trends. J. Mar. Fish. Aquac. Front. (10) (2016)
2. Li, S.: A brief discussion on the wrong views and breeding methods of breeding penaeus vannamei. J. Sci. Fish Farming (1), 32–33 (2016)
3. Liang, J.: Environmental protection is the most effective way to prevent and control shrimp disease. J. Mar. Fish. (3), 67–68 (2016)
4. Lin, R.Q.: What is the hardest part about breeding shrimp. J. Contemp. Aquac. (9), 83(2016)
5. Li, F.: Dabioma brings the shrimp breeding solution into the China dynamic insurance market. J. Mar. Fish. Aquac. Front. (8) (2016)
6. Wu, Q., Li, J., Chen, X., et al.: Rudong greenhouse penaeus aquaculture water quality control strategy. J. Sci. Fish Farming 31(11), 33–34 (2015)
7. Yang, C., Wang, et al.: A new cross discipline—extenics. J. China Sci. Found. (Engl. Ed.) 13(1), 55–61 (2005)
8. Cai, W., Yang, C.Y., Bin, H.E.: Several problems on the research of extenics. J. Guangdong Univ. Technol. (2001)
9. Yan, S., Fan, R., Chen, Y., et al.: Research on web services-based extenics aided innovation system. J. Procedia Comput. Sci. 107, 103–110 (2017)
10. Fan, R.: Modelling extenics innovation software by intelligent service components. Open Cybern. Syst. J. 8, 1–7 (2014)

11. Fan, R., Peng, Y., Chen, Y., et al.: A method for self-adaptive software formal modeling by extenics. CAAI Trans. Intell. Syst. **10**(6), 901–911 (2015)
12. Li, L.: Study on the effects of main physical and chemical factors on the growth of penaeus vannamei in greenhouse. Zhejiang Ocean University (2015)
13. Bao, Y.: Data analysis on water quality of penaeus prawns based on visualization technology. J. Anhui Agric. Sci. Bull. **22**(20), 83–85 (2016)
14. Zhang, S.: Effects of pH value on water quality and shrimp and its control measures. J. Guid. Fish. Wealth (24), 27–28 (2015)
15. Zhang, Y., Lin, D.J., Zou, Z.H.: Analysis of meteorological conditions of shrimp culture greenhouse. J. Guangdong Meteorol. **16**(3), 45–49 (2016)
16. Zhang, J.: Study on water quality and aquatic organisms of penaeus vannamei aquaculture. Shanghai Ocean University (2016)

Research of Tool State Recognition Based on CEEMD-WPT

Runzhe Tao[1], Yonghong Zhang[1(✉)], Lihua Wang[1],
and Xiaoping Zhao[2]

[1] School of Information and Control, Nanjing University of Information Science
and Technology, Nanjing 210044, China
510877671@qq.com
[2] School of Computer and Software, Nanjing University of Information Science
and Technology, Nanjing 210044, China

Abstract. As a direct machining tool, the tool will inevitably wear out during production and processing. In order to grasp the wear state of cutting tools accurately and realize the accurate diagnosis in the cutting process, the CEMMD-WPT feature extraction method is proposed, which is based on Complementary Ensemble Empirical Mode Decomposition (CEEMD) and Wavelet Package Transform (WPT). Firstly, the CEEMD is used to decompose the Acoustic Emission (AE) signal that acquired by cutting tool. The AE signal is adaptively decomposed into several Intrinsic Mode Functions (IMFs) among with each IMF contains different time scale characteristic. Then, for less IMFs that still have mode mixing, is corrected with good local processing ability by WPT. The CEEMD-WPT combination algorithm not only can effectively solve the problem of the mode mixing after CEEMD, but also eliminate the influence of frequency mixing and illusive component after WPT treatment. Finally, this work select the first few IMFs component with large energy values, calculate the proportion of the total energy as feature vectors, and input them into the Support Vector Machine (SVM) for training and testing, to establish the tool state recognition system. Compared with CEEMD feature extraction method, the feature extracted by CEEMD-WPT method is more accurate and more representative, which lays a good foundation for later recognition.

Keywords: Tool wear · State recognition · CEEMD · WPT

1 Introduction

In practical production, the wear state of tool not only directly affects the machining quality, efficiency and cost of processing, but also may causes damage to equipment and threatens the safety of processing personnel. However, as the direct executioner of the machining process, the tool will inevitably wear out. Therefore, in order to ensure product quality and simultaneously, it is of great significance to establish an effective tool state detection system in the process of production. In the detection system, the tool monitoring signal is nonstationary and nonlinear. Meanwhile, the signal components are complex. So, how to extract the information that indicating the state of the tool has great influence on the recognition accuracy. Domestic and foreign scholars

© Springer Nature Switzerland AG 2018
X. Sun et al. (Eds.): ICCCS 2018, LNCS 11064, pp. 59–70, 2018.
https://doi.org/10.1007/978-3-030-00009-7_6

have carried out a series of research on feature extraction algorithms. Sun et al. [1] used the wavelet transform (WT) to decompose the acoustic emission (AE) signal of tool, and then realized the tool condition monitoring system. Yu et al. used the WPT to extract the feature value from AE signal power spectrum and distinguished two different tool wear states effectively [2]. However, WT and WPT are both constantly subjected to the choice of wavelet base function, which lacks self-adaptability in decomposition process, affecting the efficiency and accuracy in late state recognition. Thus, new methods need to be introduced for analyzing nonstationary and nonlinear signals.

With proposed Hilbert-Huang Transform [3], Empirical Mode Decomposition (EMD) behaves as an adaptive time-frequency signal processing method to extract features, and finally decomposes the signal into a series of intrinsic mode functions (IMFs). EMD, however, often suffers from the problem of mode mixing [4]. So the result of EMD extraction is rather poor. As a valuable aid to EMD, Ensemble Empirical Mode Decomposition (EEMD) [5] and Complementary Ensemble Empirical Mode Decomposition (CEEMD) [6] have been introduced to improve the results to some extent. But these algorithm still can't applied to extract the features accurately. After EEMD decomposing the vibration signal, the energy of the IMF component as feature vector, and the Support Vector Machine (SVM) is used to classify the wear state of tool in literature [7]. But the effect of classification is still not ideal. So, it is obvious that the quality of feature extraction directly affects the effect of classification. In order to achieve higher recognition rate, we need a better feature extraction method.

In view of the above, a feature extraction algorithm of combining CEEMD and WPT is proposed in this paper. CEEMD-WPT algorithm captures the AE signal during cutting process, which decomposed by CEEMD firstly, and then the partial IMFs are chosen to correct mode mixing problems by local analysis capability of WPT. Therefore, the mode mixing problem of each IMF can be effectively solved, which realizes the accurate extraction of characteristic components. It lays a good foundation for the tool status recognition. Finally, based on feature extraction, the energy of the corrected IMF is used to calculate the feature vector and input SVM to realize the accurate detection of the tool state in the cutting process.

2 Algorithm Description

2.1 CEEMD

CEEMD is an improved algorithm based on EMD [8]. CEEMD consists of the following steps [9]:

1. A couple of white Gaussian noises is added to the analyzed signal $x(t)$ to form two new signals. Generating two signals as follows:

$$
\begin{aligned}
x_1(t) &= x(t) + n(t) \\
x_2(t) &= x(t) - n(t)
\end{aligned}
\tag{1}
$$

2. Decompose $x_1(t)$ and $x_2(t)$ by EMD and obtain IMF_{1i} from those positive mixtures and IMF_{2i} from those negative mixture.
3. Repeat step 1&2 to n times and white noise sequence should be different added every time. Obtain two sets of ensemble IMFs as follows:

$$IMF_1 = \sum_{i=1}^{n} IMF_{1i}$$
$$IMF_2 = \sum_{i=1}^{n} IMF_{2i}$$

$$(2)$$

4. The final IMF is the ensemble of both the IMFs with positive and negative noises:

$$IMF = \frac{(IMF_1 + IMF_2)}{2n} \tag{3}$$

In addition, The effect of the added white noises can be controlled into,

$$k_n = k/\sqrt{n} \tag{4}$$

where n is the number of ensemble members, k is the standard deviation of the added noises, and k_n is the final standard deviation of errors [10].

In summary, CEEMD adaptive feature extraction algorithm can control the problem of mode mixing, but still can't realize the accurate extraction.

2.2 WPT

WPT has more accurate local analysis ability than that of wavelet transform. But, the frequency domain characteristics of the wavelet packet filter are not ideal only by using WPT to extract the characteristic frequency signals [11]. On the one hand, down sampling the signal in the decomposition process, halving the sampling frequency will often cause frequency folding. On the other hand, the zero insertion between each point will doubling the sampling frequency in the reconstruction process. Therefore, the whole decomposition and reconstruction process can lead to frequency mixing and produce illusive component [12].

3 Signal Feature Extraction Based on CEEMD-WPT

Combining CEEMD and WPT, WPT can be used to correct the mode mixing existing after CEEMD decomposition, and achieve the accurate extraction of feature signals.

The signal is adaptively decomposed into a series of IMFs by CEEMD algorithm. Because the amplitude of main frequency components in IMF is larger than the mixed frequency after the decomposition and only contains the corresponding frequency bands. Therefore, using WPT to correct mode mixing, which can effectively eliminate the influence of frequency mixing and illusive components in the sub-band during the decomposition process. To summarize, the proposed CEEMD-WPT algorithm can accurately extract the characteristic components of the signal. The specific algorithm flow is shown in Fig. 1:

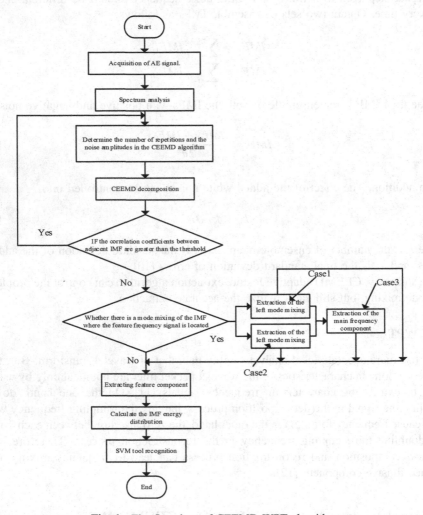

Fig. 1. The flowchart of CEEMD-WPT algorithm

- Step one: Making frequency analysis to the signal, and determining the amplitude of the noise signal and each frequency component.
- Step two: Determine two parameters in CEEMD: n and k. In this paper, the k take 0.01-0.2 and n generally choose within 50 times.
- Step three: Decompose the signal into a series of IMFs using CEEMD.
- Step four: Making frequency analysis to each IMF and calculate the correlation coefficient between adjacent IMF. If the correlation coefficient are greater than the threshold, readjust n and k and repeat Step three and four.

- Step five: Check for mode mixing in the characteristic frequency signal. If there is a little mode mixing appearance, we use WPT to extract characteristic frequency components. Suppose in a certain IMF component, the main frequency component f is in the middle, and the mode mixing parts f_1 and f_2 are distributed on both side of the f respectively. Then we use WPT for mode mixing correction, It is divided into the following three cases:

- Case 1: if the required feature component is f_1 on the left side, Since IMF only contains a component of a certain frequency band, it is only necessary to remove the frequency components above the characteristic components;
- Case 2: if the feature component that needs to be extracted is f_2 on the right side, only the component below the characteristic component should be eliminated;
- Case 3: if the essential component of the extraction is f, f_1 and f_2 are first extracted, and then subtracted the extracted f_1 and f_2 with IMF.
- In addition, the lower limit of the wavelet packet frequency segmentation needs to be lower than the eliminated frequency, and the upper limit needs to be higher than the eliminated frequency, so that the characteristic frequency components can be extracted from the mode mixing IMF effectively.

- Step six: Extract the same characteristic frequency components from different IMF and add them in time domain, so that the feature signal can be accurately extracted. When the tool condition changes, the collected signals change accordingly. Calculate the energy of each IMF, $p_k = E_k/E$ is used to represent the proportion of the energy E_k in IMF_k to the total energy. We use $[p_1 \quad p_2 \quad \cdots \quad p_k]$ as the feature vector, then input feature vector into SVM and implement feature classification determining whether the wear state of the tool.

4 Simulation Experiment and Engineering Application

4.1 Actual Signal Processing Under CEEMD-WPT

In order to verify the decomposition effect of CEEMD-WPT algorithm and illustrate the process of WPT correcting mode mixing, this experiment analyzed the specific signal as an example to show the signal for the vibration signal of rotating machinery under working condition [13]. The sampling frequency is 12.8 kHz (Fig. 2 is time domain signal and spectrum diagram). The working frequency of this signal is 55 Hz, and it contains multiple sub-frequency doubling and frequency doubling. The CEEMD-WPT algorithm is used to extract the 55 Hz component signal of the characteristic frequency [14, 15].

Due to space limitations, this paper lists the two IMF components that feature frequency of 55 Hz (IMF7 and IMF8 as show in Fig. 3) with mode mixing.

As the circle in the Fig. 3 still has mode mixing after CEEMD, we need to use WPT. First of all, we extract the left mode mixing part (55 Hz) component in IMF7.

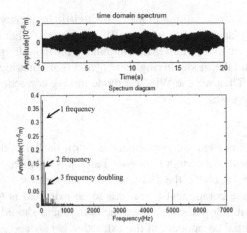

Fig. 2. Time domain and frequency spectrogram

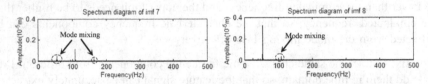

Fig. 3. IMF7, IMF8 component spectrum

According to the first case of Step five in CEEMD-WPT algorithm, do 6 layer decomposition for IMF7 by WPT. The frequency component above 100 Hz is removed, and that (M_1) between 0 Hz and 100 Hz is reserved (As shown in Fig. 4).

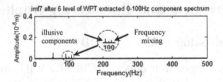

Fig. 4. The component spectrum of IMF7 after 6 layers of WPT extracted

As shown in Fig. 4, due to the existence of a double frequency (110 Hz component) near the upper limit of the frequency band division (100 Hz), the phenomenon that frequency mixing and illusive component is generated in M_1 (As the circle in Fig. 4), which needs to be eliminated. After this, do 8 layer decomposition for IMF7 and extract M_2 (75–100 Hz as shown in Fig. 5). Due to the 55 Hz component in IMF7 has less amplitude, and it is far away from the lower limit 75 Hz of the frequency band decomposed by the WPT 8-th layer decomposition. The illusive component generated by the decomposition is the same as that obtained by the 6 layer decomposition.

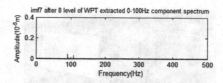

Fig. 5. The component spectrum of IMF7 after 8 layers of WPT extracted

To eliminate the illusive component and frequency mixing caused by WPT extraction, we use M_1 minus M_2. This method effectively extracts the 55 Hz components from the mode mixing of the IMF7, the spectrogram is shown in Fig. 6.

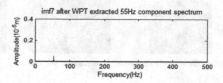

Fig. 6. The 55 Hz component spectrum is extracted by WPT

Then extract the main frequency component f (55 Hz) of the IMF8 with mode mixing, and add the components extracted from IMF7 and IMF8 in the time domain. The extracted characteristic signal time domain and spectrogram are shown in Fig. 7.

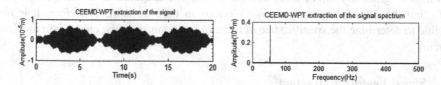

Fig. 7. Frequency spectrum signal extracted by WPT

From the Spectrum diagram in Fig. 7, it can be seen that the mode mixing is eliminated, and the characteristic frequency signal is extracted effectively.

5 Tool State Feature Extraction Based on CEEMD-WPT

5.1 Data Acquisition

In order to obtain the AE signals produced by cutting tools in different states, this experiment takes Baoji CS6140 machine tool (Fig. 8) as the research platform.

According to the average wear bandwidth VB of the main rake face, the tool wear is divided into four kinds: Initial wear (VB value less than 0.15 mm), early and middle stage wear (VB value 0.15 ~ 0.3 mm), middle and late wear (VB value 0.3 ~ 0.4 mm), late (severe) wear (VB value is greater than 0.4 mm). As shown in Fig. 9.

Fig. 8. Baoji CS6140 machine tool

(a) Initial wear   (b) middle and early stage wear   (c) middle and late wear   (d) later wear

Fig. 9. Four state of tool

The GH4169 materials were excircle turned by four cutters with different wear states, and the experimental conditions are as follows: spindle speed 260RPM, feed rate 0.08 mm/r, cutting depth 1 mm. AE sensor is used to collect the AE signals at the sampling frequency of 1 MHz. With the development of turning process, the tool wear condition is gradually aggravated, and the AE signal acquired also changes accordingly, but the waveform change is not obvious in time domain. Therefore, it is not feasible to determine the specific state of the tool by monitoring the changes in the time domain.

5.2   Signal Feature Extraction

AE signal is a high frequency signal, the main component of the signal in the high frequency segment. A series of IMFs are arranged according to the high frequency to the low frequency, so the main information of the signal is concentrated in the first several IMFs. Experiments show that the first 5 IMFs obtained by decomposition are the most appropriate ones. Because the energy of the first 5 IMFs has already occupied more than 95% of the total energy. A signal of early and middle wear is selected for concrete analysis.

The time domain diagram and spectrogram of the signal are shown in Fig. 10. The signal is decomposed by CEEMD, the n is 30, and the k is 0.01. The frequency domain diagram of the first 5 IMF components are shown in Fig. 11.

It is obvious that there are still some mode mixing problems after CEEMD decomposition as shown in Fig. 11, the same frequency components are adaptively decomposed into different IMFs, the effect of extraction is not ideal. The signal of two

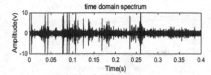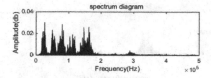

Fig. 10. Initial signal in time and frequency plots

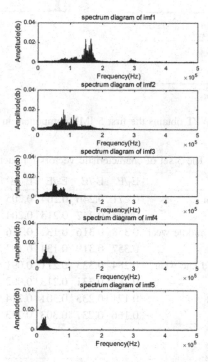

Fig. 11. CEEMD obtains the first 5 IMF component in frequency plots

wear states in early-middle and middle-late has some changes in the overall frequency distribution, but is not obvious. Therefore, the presence of mode mixing will directly result in no significant difference between the extracted features, thus greatly increasing the difficulty of pattern recognition. The spectrum of IMFs after the WPT correction is shown in Fig. 12.

In Fig. 12, the frequency bands extracted by CEEMD-WPT are more accurate, and it effectively solves the problem of mode mixing in CEEMD decomposition. Studied the energy distribution of each IMF component.

Using $[p_1 \quad p_2 \quad \cdots \quad p_k]$ as a feature vector, In Table 1, the eigenvectors of the 2 sets of signals for each state are listed.

Select a set of eigenvalues for each tool state in Table 1 for comparison, contrast results are shown in Fig. 13.

As can be seen from Fig. 13, when the tool is in the initial wear state, the first four IMFs have an evenly distributed energy value. With the change of tool state, from the

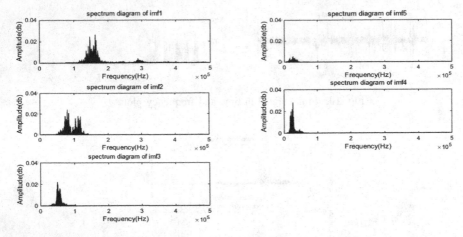

Fig. 12. CEEMD-WPT obtains the first 5 IMF component in frequency plots

Table 1. The 3 set of characteristic vectors for each state

State	E_1/E	E_2/E	E_3/E	E_4/E	E_5/E
Initial wear	0.271	0.246	0.204	0.205	0.038
	0.263	0.242	0.215	0.204	0.041
Early and middle wear	0.358	0.316	0.132	0.116	0.032
	0.357	0.319	0.134	0.113	0.038
Middle and late wear	0.284	0.333	0.211	0.091	0.038
	0.281	0.331	0.213	0.092	0.035
Later wear	0.171	0.233	0.301	0.214	0.042
	0.166	0.237	0.303	0.213	0.039

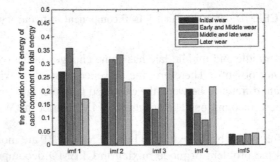

Fig. 13. Comparison of four state feature values extracted by CEEMD-WPT

early stage to the Middle and late stage wear, the frequency distribution of the signal has a regular change. The main energy of AE signals is shifted from low frequency to medium-high frequency, IMF1 and IMF2 occupy the main energy of the signal. When severe wear in the later stage, the main energy of AE signals is shifted from high frequency to medium-low frequency, The IMF1 energy ratio of the highest frequency is smaller, and the IMF2, IMF3 and IMF4 occupy the main energy in the middle frequency. Therefore, the feature extracted by CEEMD-WPT is more accurate and more characteristic, which lays a better foundation for later state recognition.

5.3 Tool Wear State Identification Based on SVM

On the MATLAB software platform, this article uses the libsvm toolbox. The SVM uses RBF as kernel function. The kernel function parameter $g = 0.15$ is proved by experiment, when the penalty coefficient of the error sample is $c = 50$, and the other parameters are the default, the SVM mode recognition is the best. Each tool status corresponds to 80 sets of signals, the 40 sets are used for training, and the remaining for testing. The test data (4 states, a total of 160 sets of feature vectors) are fed into a trained support vector machine for testing, the results of the state identification of this method and the comparison with CEEMD are shown in Table 2.

Table 2. Comparison results of CEEMD and CEEMD-WPT

Feature extraction method	Tool wear state	SVM classification accuracy
CEEMD	Initial	95%
	Middle and early	77.5%
	Middle and late	72.5%
	Later	100%
CEEMD-WPT	Initial	100%
	Middle and early	100%
	Middle and late	100%
	Later	100%

It can be seen from Table 2, when CEEMD is used as feature extraction method, the recognition rate of the initial and middle stage is low, especially in the two stages of the medium term. Because of the existence of mode mixing after CEEMD decomposition, the features obtained by each frequency band are very similar, and the recognition rate is difficult to improve. When using CEEMD-WPT to extract feature values, the recognition rate reached 100%. The CEEMD-WPT is obviously better than that of the CEEMD algorithm, the tool wear state recognition system can be established effectively.

6 Conclusion

- (1) This paper expounds the importance of setting up tool condition detection system. Aiming at the problem of mode confusion in traditional feature extraction methods, a CEEMD-WPT feature extraction method is proposed.
- (2) Although CEEMD effectively improves the problem of mode mixing, but the mode mixing is still inevitable in practical applications. WPT can realize the

extraction of local features of signals, but there is no ideal band-pass filter, it can not be accurate extraction. In this paper, the CEEMD-WPT algorithm combines the advantages of CEEMD and WPT, which realizes the accurate extraction of the characteristic frequency signal.

- (3) The CEEMD-WPT algorithm is used to extract the AE signals in the actual processing. The proportion of each component to the total energy is calculated as the characteristic input of SVM, and the tool state detection can be realized accurately and effectively.

Acknowledgements. This work was financially supported by the Natural Science Foundation of China (Grant No. 51405241, 51505234).

References

1. Sun, J.: Effective training data selection in tool condition monitoring system. Int. J. Mach. Tools Manuf. **46**(2), 218–224 (2006)
2. Yu, J.: Wavelet package analysis to picking-up characteristics of AE signal of tools. J. Data Acquis. Process. **20**(3), 346–350 (2009)
3. Huang, N.E.: The empirical mode decomposition and the Hilbert spectrum for non-linear and non-stationary time series analysis. In: Proceedings of the Royal Society A, vol. 454, pp. 903–995 (1998)
4. Ying, C.: Research and application of mode-mixing in Hilbert-Huang Transform. J. Vib. Meas. Diagn. **36**(3), 518–523 (2016)
5. Wu, Z.: Ensemble empirical mode decomposition: a noise assisted data analysis method. Adv. Adapt. Data Anal. **1**(01), 1–41 (2009)
6. Yeh, J.R.: Complementary ensemble empirical mode decomposition: a noise enhanced data analysis method. Adv. Adapt. Data Anal. **2**(2), 135–156 (2010)
7. Nie, P.: Application of EEMD method in state recognition of tool wear. Transducer Microsyst. Technol. **31**(5), 147–152 (2012)
8. Colominas, M.A.: Noise-assisted EMD methods in action. Adv. Adapt. Data Anal. **4**(04), 1250025 (2012)
9. Lei, Y.: Adaptive ensemble empirical mode decomposition and its application to fault detection of planetary gearboxes. Chin. J. Mech. Eng. **50**(3), 64–70 (2014)
10. Wang, D.: An enhanced empirical mode decomposition method for adaptive blind component separation of a single-channel vibration signal mixture. J. Vib. Control **22**(11), 1–14 (2015)
11. Gao, Y.: Wavelet packets analysis based method for hydraulic pump condition monitoring. J. Mech. Eng. **8**(49), 80–87 (2009)
12. Qin, Y.: Fundamental wave detection based on wavelet transform and empirical mode decomposition with application in mechanical system. J. Mech. Eng. **44**(3), 135–142 (2008)
13. Zhao, X.: Gabor order tracking based on viterbi algorithm. J. Mech. Eng. **45**(11), 247–252 (2009)
14. Wang, L.: Feature extraction of rolling bearing based on CEEMD-WPT. J. Vib. Meas. Diagn. **37**(1), 181–187 (2017)
15. Zhang, Y.: Research on feature extraction of rolling bearing based on decorrelation CEEMD. Manuf. Technol. Mach. Tool **11**(105), 78–84 (2016)

Research on Data Mining Method for Breast Cancer Case Data

Yanning Cao[1] and Xiaoshu Zhang[2(✉)]

[1] Network Information Center, Binzhou Medical University,
Yantai 264003, China
[2] School of Basic Medical Sciences, Binzhou Medical University,
Yantai 264003, China
xiaoshu_cz@163.com

Abstract. With the development of computer technology, medical institutions not only treat patients using advanced instruments but can also improve the collection and storage of patient medical records. We used distributed cloud data platforms to obtain case data of breast cancer patients from different medical institutions and quantified the text data based on a physician's advice. We then processed the data using a common classification algorithm, predicted each patient's survival, and compared the accuracy of different algorithms. Our experimental results show that the locally weighted learning (LWL) algorithm has high accuracy and precision, indicating that the LWL algorithm is a good way to predict breast cancer patient survival.

Keywords: Patient medical records · Locally weighted learning
Classification · Cloud computing

1 Introduction

Currently, it is a big data era where terabytes of data are produced all the time around the world. These data exist in all aspects of our work and life, but a lot of data are overlooked. Data mining and distributed collection and processing data are the act of transforming large amounts of data into a wide variety of knowledge.

In recent years, medical engineering research has rapidly developed. Improvements in instrumentation technology have resulted in a large volume of medical information being accurately recorded, leading to an explosion of medical data. With the medical information system gradually being put into use in major hospitals, the collected patient information includes medical images and various physiological indexes, as well as a large amount of detailed background information such as patients' age, gender, height, weight, and past medical history. Moreover, the data sets collected by major hospitals are combined further. The quantity of data collected in this way is huge. Although single data is very easy to collect, the questions of how to quantify different collection tools and how to find meaningful information from a large amount of data have been challenging. Medical data are affected by healthcare conditions and patient's physical condition, making them extremely complex. Analysis of potential patterns in these data has become a current focus of healthcare workers. We used distributed cloud data

© Springer Nature Switzerland AG 2018
X. Sun et al. (Eds.): ICCCS 2018, LNCS 11064, pp. 71–78, 2018.
https://doi.org/10.1007/978-3-030-00009-7_7

platform to collect and process data of breast cancer patients provided by medical institutions. Common classifier algorithms were used to predict the survival of patients.

The structure of the article is as follows: in Sect. 2, we introduce the concepts and evaluation criteria of the methods used in this paper; in Sect. 3, we summarize the features, advantages, and disadvantages of our classification algorithms and propose standards for data quantification; the experimental results are presented in Sect. 4; and the corresponding conclusions are given in Sect. 5.

2   Preliminaries

Classification is one of the most important and widely used techniques in data mining. So far, many algorithms have been proposed. Classification is based on the characteristics of a data set to construct a classifier, and is a technique for classifying samples of unknown category. The process of constructing a classifier is generally divided into two steps, training and testing. During the training phase, the characteristics of the training data set are analyzed, producing an accurate description or model of the corresponding data set. During the testing phase, the test is categorized using the description or model of the category, and its classification accuracy is tested.

Breast cancer is the most common cancer and also the primary cause of mortality due to cancer in female around the World. About 1.38 million new breast cancer cases were diagnosed in 2008 with almost 50% of all breast cancer patients and approximately 60% of deaths occurring in developing countries. There is a huge difference in breast cancer survival rates worldwide, with an estimated 5-year survival of 80% in developed countries to below 40% for developing countries [1]. Developing countries face resource and infrastructure constraints that challenge the objective of improving breast cancer outcomes by timely recognition, diagnosis and management [2]. In developed countries like the United States, about 232,340 female will be diagnosed and death of 39,620 female will occur due to breast cancer in 2013 [3].

According to the World Health Organization (WHO), enhancing breast cancer outcome and survival by early detection remains the foundation of breast cancer regulations. Different modern medicines are prescribed to treat breast cancer. Medical therapy of breast cancer with antiestrogens such as raloxifene or tamoxifen might avoid breast cancer in individuals who are at increased possibility of developing it [4]. Surgery of both breasts is an added preventative measure in some increased probability of developing cancer in female. In patients who have been identified with breast tumor, different strategies of management are used such as targeted therapy, hormonal therapy, radiation therapy, surgery and chemotherapy. In individuals with distant metastasis, managements are typically aimed at enhancing life quality and survival rate [5]. The unpleasant side effects of breast cancer treatment are one of the most motivating factors to find some alternative methods. The use of herbs for treating the patients having breast cancer is considered a natural alternative, because some plants may contain properties that naturally have the ability to treat breast cancer [6–10].

In the 1960s, the decision tree algorithm was proposed. Then, in the late 1970s, J. B. Quinlan proposed the ID3 algorithm, on the basis of which Quinlan also proposed the C4.5 algorithm [11]. In 1997, Friedman et al. proposed Bayesian Network

Classifiers [12]. Bayesian Network Classifiers have good results in biological data. In 1968, Cover first proposed the neighbor algorithm [13]. In 1980, Short and Fukunaga proposed the initial concept of kNN, which was continuously improved in the following work [14]. The kNN algorithm is most suitable for processing text data [15]. In 1997, Atkeson, Moore, and Schaal proposed locally weighted learning (LWL) algorithm [16]. In cloud computing environment, Li Qin Huang et al. designed a distributed parallel text training algorithm based on multi-class support vector machine (SVM) in the cloud computing environment [17]. In this paper, we used the C4.5 algorithm, Bayesian Network Classifiers, kNN, and locally weighted learning to test breast cancer data and compare the results.

We used accuracy, precision, recall, and F1-Measure to evaluate the classification algorithm's prediction. The TP, FP, TN, and FN in the formula are defined as follows.

TP, Positive samples predicted as True
FP, Positive samples predicted as False
TN, Negative samples predicted as True
FN, Negative samples predicted as False

The accuracy is the probability of predicting the correct sample in all samples.

$$\text{Accuracy} = \frac{TP + TN}{TP + TN + FP + FN}$$

The precision is based on our prediction, which shows how many of the positive predictions are true positives. There are two possible positive predictions: (1) predict the positive samples as in the positive category; (2) predict negative samples as in the positive category.

$$\Pr\text{ecision} = \frac{TP}{TP + FP}$$

The recall rate is for our original sample, which indicates how many positive cases in the sample were predicted correctly. There are also two possibilities: (1) predict the original positive cases as in the positive category; (2) predict the original positive cases as in the negative category.

$$\text{Recall} = \frac{TP}{TP + FN}$$

When we evaluate, of course, we hope that the higher the precision of search results, the better, and the higher the recall, the better, but in fact these two are contradictory in some cases. High precision is often accompanied by low recall, thus F1 is used to evaluate the quality of the results.

$$F1 = \frac{2 \cdot TP}{2 \cdot TP + FP + TN}$$

3 Methodology

3.1 Classification Algorithm

Decision tree is a common technique used for classification and prediction. It focuses on reasoning out classification rules in the decision tree representation form from a set of random cases. It uses a top-down recursive approach, compares attribute values in the decision tree's internal nodes, judges the node from the branch down according to different attributes, and obtains conclusion at the leaf node of decision tree. Therefore, from root node to leaf node corresponds to a reasonable rule, and the whole tree corresponds to a set of expression rules. One of the biggest advantages of the decision tree-based algorithm is that it does not require the user to know a lot of background knowledge during the learning process. Whenever a training case can be expressed in the form of attribute, namely conclusion, the algorithm can be used for learning. However, there are 5 major shortcomings of the decision tree-based algorithm: (1) It is more difficult to predict consecutive fields. (2) For chronological data, a lot of pre-processing work is required. (3) When the category is too large, the error may increase faster. (4) The general algorithm classification only classifies according to a field. (5) The performance is not very good when dealing with data that has a strong correlation with features.

Bayesian network, also known as reliability network, is an extension of Bayesian method and is one of the most effective theoretical models in the field of knowledge representation and reasoning. Based on the Bayesian formula, the formula is as follows.

$$P(B_i|A) = \frac{P(B_i)P(A|Bi)}{\sum_{j=1}^{n} P((B_j)P(A|B_j))}$$

A Bayesian network is a directed acyclic graph (DAG), consisting of nodes representing variables and directed edges connecting these nodes. The nodes represent random variables. The directed edges between the nodes represent the inter-node relationship (from the parent node to its child node), and conditional probability is used to express the strength of the relationship. For those without a parent node, the priori probability is used to express the information. Node variables can be abstractions of any problem, such as test values, observations, and opinions. A Bayesian network is suitable for the expression and analysis of uncertainties and probabilistic events, and it is applied to decisions that are conditionally dependent on multiple control factors because information can be inferred from incomplete, inaccurate or uncertain knowledge or information. The disadvantage is that the Bayesian network requires a large data set, so analysis and calculation are complicated, which is especially troubling when solving complex problems.

The kNN method is based on analogy learning and is a non-parametric classification technique that is very effective in statistical-based pattern recognition. It achieves high classification accuracy for unknown and non-normally distributed data, and has the advantages of robustness and clear concept. The basic principle is as follows: the kNN classification algorithm searches in the sample space, calculates the similarity value between the vector of an unknown category and each vector in sample set, finds K most similar text vectors in the sample set, and the classification result is the category with the largest number of similar samples. However, the shortcomings of the KNN method are prominent in large sample sets and high-dimensional sample categories (such as text classification). First, KNN is a lazy classification algorithm, and the computations required for the classification are postponed to the classification. Therefore, a large number of sample vectors are stored in the classifier. When samples of unknown category need to be classified, high-dimensional or large sample sets require great time and space complexity when calculating the distance between all stored and unknown sample sets. Second, the KNN algorithm is based on the VSM model and uses Euclidean distance for measuring sample distance. If the weights of each dimension are the same, it is considered that the contribution of each dimension to the classification is the same, which is obviously not in conformity with the actual situation. Based on the above shortcomings, some improved algorithms are also adopted: when the sample size is large, in order to reduce the calculation, the sample set can be edited by selecting the optimal reference subset from the original sample set for KNN calculation to reduce sample storage and improve computational efficiency.

LWL is also a kind of lazy learning, using an instance-based algorithm to assign instance weights, which are then used by a specified weighted instances handler. Based on kNN, a linear function is fit to k nearest neighbors and fit quadratic, thus producing a piecewise approximation function to minimize error over k nearest neighbors of XQ and minimize error of the entire set of examples, weighting by distances. Compared with kNN, LWL has higher accuracy, but when the data set is excessively large, the training time is too long.

3.2 Data Preprocessing

The data used in this article are from a subset of breast cancer case data collected by a city's medical facility. Because text descriptions were most often used for tumor location and cancer cell shape in the case data, we used the following method to normalize the data:

Survival status: 1 for survival; 2 for death;

Survival time: 1 for within 12 months, 2 for 13–36 months, 3 for 37–60 months, 4 for 61–96 months, 5 for 97–120 months, and 6 for 121–132 months;

Age: 1 for 45 years old and below, 2 for 46–60 years old, 3 for 61–70 years old, 4 for 71 years old and above;

Tissue typing: 1 for invasive ductal carcinoma, 2 for infiltrating ductal carcinoma with other cancer, 3 for infiltrating lobular carcinoma, 4 for mucinous carcinoma, 5 for intraductal carcinoma, poorly differentiated invasive carcinoma, and intracapsular papillary carcinoma;

Pathological grade: 1 for grade I–II, 2 for grade II, 3 for grade II–III, and 4 for grade III;

Number of positive lymph nodes (LNs): 1 for 0 LNs, 2 for 1–5 LNs, 3 for 6–10 LNs, 4 for 11 LNs and above;

1 for T1, 2 for T2, 3 for T3, 4 for T4;

1 for N0, 2 for N1, 3 for N2, and 4 for N3;
Clinical stage: 1 for 1, 2 for 2A, 3 for 2B, 4 for 3A, and 5 for 3C;

Tissue typing, pathological grade, number of positive lymph nodes, T, N and M are all attributes related to the severity of the disease.

4   The Experimental Results

We used c4.5, bayesnet, kNN, and LWL algorithms to classify this data set. Accuracy, precision, recall, and F1-Measure were obtained by 10-fold cross-validation method, as shown in Table 1.

Table 1. Experimental results

Function	Accuracy	Precision	Recall	F1-Measure
J48 (c4.5)	64.7%	43.9%	64.7%	52.3%
BayesNet	61.9%	49.0%	61.9%	52.8%
IBK (kNN)	56.1%	38.6%	56.1%	42.3%
LWL	66.2%	72.8%	66.2%	56.8%

It can be seen from the experimental results that the LWL algorithm had high test results in all the attributes of the test, indicating that the data were suitable for classification by the LWL algorithm, while the precision of other data sets cannot exceed 60%.

For the LWL algorithm, the experimental results of precision, recall, and F1-Measure of different survival periods are shown in Table 2.

Table 2. LWL survival test results

Rank of survival time	Survival time (mon)	Precision	Recall	F1-Measure
1	12	0	0	0
2	13–36	0	0	0
3	37–60	75.0%	27.3%	40.0%
4	61–96	56.5%	68.4%	61.9%
5	97–120	100%	3.2%	6.3%
6	121–132	72.8%	100%	81.1%

From the above experimental results, the algorithm could not classify patients survived less than 12 months or survived 13–36 months correctly because too few training samples were in these two groups; for the data of patients survived 37–60 months, 97–120 months, and 121–132 months, the algorithm achieved good accuracy. The algorithm achieved a 100% prediction rate for patients who survived 97–120 months; therefore, the model using this algorithm can predict such data well.

5   Conclusion

From the experimental results in the previous section, we can see that the LWL algorithm was most suitable for the classification prediction of breast cancer, while the accuracies of other algorithms were low. One of the reasons for the low accuracy of other algorithms is that results are affected by the data sources; if the amount of data is low, the data of cancer cells are difficult to quantify. Another reason is that it is not possible to quantify the medication, psychological status, physical condition, and other important factors of the patient during the treatment. However, the LWL algorithm still achieved a relatively high accuracy, indicating that the LWL algorithm is suitable for analyzing such problems. Future work will consider a larger volume of data, especially those with a shorter survival time, and utilize data on patients' medication, physical conditions, and other health characteristics with a view to achieve greater accuracy.

References

1. Coleman, M.P., Quaresma, M., Berrino, F., et al.: Cancer survival in five continents: a worldwide population-based study (CONCORD). Lancet Oncol. **9**(8), 730–756 (2008)
2. Anderson, B., Yip, C., Smith, R., Shyyan, R., Sener, S., Eniu, A., et al.: Guideline implementation for breast healthcare in low-income and middle-income countries: overview of the breast health global initiative global summit 2007. Cancer **113**(S8), 2221–2243 (2008)
3. Siegel, R., Naishadham, D., Jemal, A.: Cancer statistics, 2013. CA Cancer J. Clin. **63**(1), 11–30 (2010)
4. Peng, J., Sengupta, S., Jordan, V.C.: Potential of selective estrogen receptor modulators as treatments and preventives of breast cancer. Anti-Cancer Agents Med. Chem. **9**(5), 481–499 (2009)
5. Reeder, J., Vogel, V.: Breast Cancer Prevention, 2nd edn. Springer, US (2008)
6. Abdull Razis, A.F., Noor, N.M.: Cruciferous vegetables: dietary phytochemicals for cancer prevention. Asian Pac. J. Cancer Prev. **14**(3), 1565–1570 (2013)
7. Dwivedi, V., Shrivastava, R., Hussain, S.: Comparative anticancer potential of clove (Syzygium aromaticum)—an Indian spice—against cancer cell lines of various anatomical origin. Asian Pac. J. Cancer Prev. **12**(8), 1989–1993 (2011)
8. Mary, J.S., Vinotha, P., Pradeep, A.M.: Screening for in vitro cytotoxic activity of seaweed, Sargassum sp. against Hep-2 and MCF-7 cancer cell lines. Asian Pac. J. Cancer Prev. **13** (12), 6073–6076 (2012)
9. Mukherjee, P.K., Wahile, A.: Integrated approaches towards drug development from Ayurveda and other Indian system of medicines. J. Ethnopharmacol. **103**(1), 25–35 (2006)
10. Zhu, Y.Y., Zhou, L., Jiao, S.C., et al.: Relationship between soy food intake and breast cancer in China. Asian Pac. J. Cancer Prev. **12**(11), 2837–2840 (2011)
11. Quinlan, J.R.: C4.5: Programs for Machine Learning. Morgan Kaufmann Publishers, Inc., Burlington (1993)
12. Friedman, N., Dan, G., Goldszmidt, M.: Bayesian network classifiers. Mach. Learn. **29**(2–3), 131–163 (1997)
13. Cover, T.M.: Rates of convergence for nearest neighbor procedures. In: Hawaii International Conference on System Sciences, HCISS, Hawaii, p. 143 (1968)

14. Short, R.D., Fukunaga, K.: A new nearest neighbor distance measure. In: NATO Conference Series, (Series) 4: Marine Sciences, Hawaii, p. 81. IEEE (1980)
15. Cortes, C., Vapnik, V.: Support-vector networks. Mach. Learn. **20**(3), 273–297 (1995)
16. Atkeson, C.G., Moore, A.W., Schaal, S.: Locally weighted learning. Artif. Intell. Rev. **11**(1–5), 11–73 (1997)
17. Huang, L.Q., Lin, L.Q., Liu, Y.H.: Algorithm of text categorization based on cloud computing. Appl. Mech. Mater. **311**, 158–163 (2013)

Research on Flame Generation Method Based on Particle System and Texture Mapping

Fei Gui[1,2], Yao-jie Chen[1,2,3(✉)], and Ya-ting Xue[1,2]

[1] College of Computer Science and Technology,
Wuhan University of Science and Technology, Wuhan, China
850891712@qq.com
[2] Hubei Province Key Laboratory of Intelligent Information Processing and Real-Time Industrial System, Wuhan, China
[3] College of Shipping, Wuhan University of Technology, Wuhan, China

Abstract. In the three-dimensional scene simulation, the realistic sense of flame simulation is of great significance to the simulation effect. Particle systems are widely used as effective simulation methods for irregularly blurred objects. This paper combines the particle system with texture mapping and proposes a more efficient method for generating flame particles. When the initial state of the particle is set, this method introduces a random function to construct a normally distributed particle distribution model. Through a reasonable analysis of the force of the particle, the motion state variation equation of the flame particle is given. On this basis, the texture particles of the flame particles are rendered using square texture sheets in different stages. Finally, the simulation of the environmental factors of the locally attenuated wind field and the dynamic vortex force field makes the flame form more flexible. The results of the study show that while meeting real-time performance, it has a more realistic flame effect.

Keywords: Particle system · Texture rendering · Motion state Flame simulation

1 Introduction

The simulation of irregular fuzzy objects has been a hot issue in the field of computer simulation. Among them, the flame simulation process is extremely complex. Because the combustion mechanism contains many chemical properties, the flame shape is variable and unpredictable with time and space, so the more realistic flame simulation effect more intuitively reflects the rationality of a flame model, and it has a good application in visual simulation. According to the rendering effect of flame simulation, the current flame simulation methods are roughly divided into three categories: flame simulation based on particle systems, flame simulation based on textures, and flame simulation based on physical equations.

In 1983, Reeves proposed a method of particle system simulation of irregularly blurred objects for the first time [1]. The basic idea is to treat irregularly blurred objects as a group of particles consisting of a large number of particles and ignore the interaction between the particles. Each particle has its own attributes such as initial position, color

X. Sun et al. (Eds.): ICCCS 2018, LNCS 11064, pp. 79–89, 2018.
https://doi.org/10.1007/978-3-030-00009-7_8

range, transparency, life cycle, initial velocity and Acceleration [2–13] and so on. The system constantly changes its state of motion over time. However, the method requires a large number of particles, occupies more computing resources, and has low real-time performance. The flame evolution model constructed by texture drawing [14–22] uses high detailed textures to render the smooth boundary of fire. This method is difficult to obtain realistic flame change images, artificial traces are more obvious, and it is suitable for scenes with less authenticity. Flame simulation based on physical equations is mainly based on the physical evolution of the flame in nature to establish a model, through the N-S equations to represent physical quantities of flame physical characteristics [23–32], such as gas density, diffusion speed, temperature and so on. This method is more accurate for the simulation of the flame, but the computational complexity for solving the N-S equations is very large and cannot meet the requirements of real-time performance. This paper combines the custom particle system with the texture to carry out the flame simulation. Through the particle manipulation of the texture, based on the analysis of the comprehensive force of the particle, the motion equation of the particle is given and a more realistic flame simulation effect is achieved.

2   Flame Particle Modeling

2.1   Particle Properties

The initial flame particle properties include: particle number, particle position, particle size, life cycle, transparency, velocity, and acceleration. Through the analysis of the real flame, the initial values of the various properties of the particle are reasonably given, and the state change of the particle is dynamically simulated according to the combustion process of the flame.

Number of Particles
At the initial moment of flame generation, the number of particles is critical to the final simulation of the flame. If the number of particles is too small, the real effect of the flame effect is not strong, the number of particles is too large, and the occupied computing resources are excessive, which affects the real-time performance of the system. This article uses the LOD technique [33], which uses a simplified form of the object to represent it. When the viewpoint is close to the object, it is represented in detail, when the viewpoint is far from the object, it is represented by a simplified model. In the case of effectively reducing the number of particles, draw at different levels to accelerate the rendering speed, thereby increasing the frame rate. Let the average number of particles generated in the unit area on the screen be AverageNumber, the quantity offset is delta, the size of the unit area is area, and the particle size is size, then the number of particles at the initial moment is expressed by Formula (1):

$$InitialNumber = (AverageNumber + delta * rand()) * area/size \qquad (1)$$

rand() is a random number between −1 and 1.

Particle Position Distribution

The particle distribution model determines the shape of the flame [34]. In the actual combustion process of the flame, the location of the ignition point and the size of the flame are two important factors that affect the shape of the flame.In general, the center of the flame is brighter, the number of particles is larger, the edges are darker, and the number of particles is fewer. In order to improve the operating efficiency, this paper uses random numbers to construct a normally distributed particle distribution model.

$$\begin{cases} PosX = \dfrac{1}{n} \sum_{i=0}^{n} (1 - 2 * Rand()) * R \\ PosY = \dfrac{1}{n} \sum_{j=0}^{n} (1 - 2 * Rand()) * R \end{cases} \tag{2}$$

Rand() is a random number from 0 to 1, and R is the radius of the particle's area. The particles generated by this model have dense centers and sparse boundaries, which can show the clustering of real flames. This paper takes n = 4 and performs 2,000 calculations. The statistical distribution of PosX is shown in Table 1. The result of approximate normal distribution can be obtained (Fig. 1).

Table 1. PosX distribution intervals

Interval	[−3.5, −2.5]	[−2.5, −1.5]	[−1.5, −0.5]	[−0.5, 0.5]	[0.5, 1.5]	[1.5, 2.5]	[2.5, 3.5]
Group 1	11	120	488	779	467	129	6
Group 2	8	119	497	719	494	154	9
Group 3	12	139	473	748	493	122	13
Group 4	9	131	443	714	539	153	11

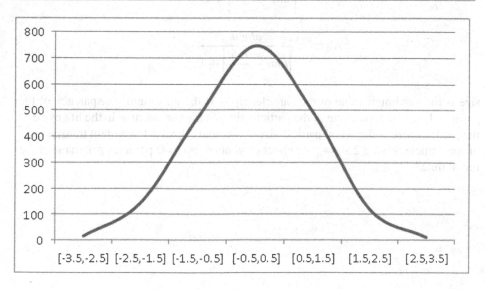

Fig. 1. Distribution of initial position

The PosX and PosY generation functions are consistent, and the value distribution interval basically conforms to the normal distribution law. This paper divides by the area radius and sets [0, 1.5], [1.5, 2.5], [2.5, 3.5] three regions, and the initial particle number ratio is about 40:9:1.

Basic State of Particles

The life cycle of particles is expressed in seconds. Under certain external conditions, the size of the life cycle is proportional to the height of the flame. Therefore, the particle life cycle near the ignition point is greater than the edge particle life cycle. This paper adds a random function to the ignition point and the life cycle of the two sides to act as an interference factor to increase the randomness of the flame combustion.

$$Life = life + Rand() \tag{3}$$

Among them, Life is the final life cycle, life is the default initial value, and Rand() is the random disturbance factor.

In the process of flame combustion, the particle size and transparency change with different combustion stages, the particles in the ignition and attenuation stages are smaller, the transparency is lower, the particles in the outbreak combustion stage are the largest, and the transparency is high. Assume that the particle reaches the explosion combustion stage when the life cycle is half, the particle size reaches the maximum, and the particle size and the transparency are represented by Formula (4) and Formula (5) respectively:

$$Size = \frac{size}{\left| time - \dfrac{Life}{2} \right| + 1} \tag{4}$$

$$Alpha = \frac{alpha}{\left| time - \dfrac{Life}{2} \right| + 1} \tag{5}$$

size is the maximum value of the particle, alpha is the maximum transparency of the particle, Life is the life cycle of the particle, time is the current time in the life cycle of the particle, Size is the actual particle size value, and Alpha is the current transparency of the particle. Figure 2 shows the effect of generating 2000 particles per frame at the initial time.

Fig. 2. Initial particle effect diagram

2.2 Particle Motion Analysis

The main forces of the flame particles are gravity, buoyancy, wind force and vortex force. For the arbitrariness of wind power, it is necessary to add a random function in the X-axis and Y-axis directions to simulate the wind. The effect of the tumbling of the flame is achieved by the vortex force. When the line of sight is in the positive direction of the Y axis, the particles flip in the XOZ plane. That is, the Y-axis value does not change and the X-axis and Z-axis values change.

$$\begin{cases} PosX' = P_{Rx} + \left(PosX - P_{Rx}\right) * cos\theta - \left(PosZ - P_{Rz}\right) * sin\theta \\ PosZ' = P_{Rz} + \left(PosZ - P_{Rz}\right) * cos\theta - \left(PosX - P_{Rx}\right) * sin\theta \end{cases} \tag{6}$$

Where PosX and PosZ are the X-axis and Z-axis coordinates of the particle before rotation. P_{Rx} and P_{Rz} are the X-axis and Z-axis coordinates of the rotation point on the XOZ plane, PosX' and PosZ' are the X-axis coordinate values and the Z-axis coordinate values after the particles are rotated respectively.

When the particles are outside the vortex, the effects of vortex forces are not considered. At this time, the force condition of the flame particles is shown in Formula (7):

$$\begin{cases} G = mg \\ F_w = \dfrac{pv_w^2 S}{2} * Rand() \\ F_f = \rho g V \end{cases} \tag{7}$$

Where m is the particle mass, g is the gravitational acceleration, p is the air pressure, v_w is the wind speed, S is the force area of the particle, Rand() is the interference factor, ρ is the air density, and V is the total volume of the flame particle object. G, F_w, and F_f are gravity, wind, and buoyancy respectively. Under acceleration, the velocity and position of the particle will change with time. Let the time interval between the i + 1-th frame and the i-th frame be ΔT, Then the velocity $V(V_x, V_y, V_z)$ and spatial position $P(P_x, P_y, P_z)$ of the i + 1-th frame are respectively expressed by Formula (8) and Formula (9):

$$
\begin{cases}
V_x = v_x + \int_0^{\Delta T} \dfrac{F_w}{m} * cos\beta dt \\[2mm]
V_y = v_y + \int_0^{\Delta T} \dfrac{F_w}{m} * sin\beta dt \\[2mm]
V_z = v_z + \int_0^{\Delta T} \dfrac{F_f - G}{m} dt
\end{cases}
\tag{8}
$$

$$
\begin{cases}
P_x = p_x + \int_0^{\Delta T} V_x dt \\
P_y = p_y + \int_0^{\Delta T} V_y dt \\
P_z = p_z + \int_0^{\Delta T} V_z dt
\end{cases}
\tag{9}
$$

Among them, $V(v_x, v_y, v_z)$ and $P(p_x, p_y, p_z)$ are the velocity and spatial position corresponding to the particles of the i-th frame, and β is the horizontal wind direction angle.

3 Texture Mapping

3.1 Flame Structure

The texture of the middle part and the edge part of the flame differ greatly, the texture brightness of the middle part is larger, the color is yellowish, and the texture of the edge

Table 2. Colors and temperatures

Colour	Approximate temperature /°C	Approximate temperature/°F	Colour
kermesinus	500-600	930-1100	
crimson	600-800	1100-1470	
jacinth	800-1000	1470-1830	
Gold orange	1000-1200	1830-2200	
pale yellow	1200-1400	2200-2550	
white	1400-1600	2550-2910	

part is generally less bright and the color is reddish. The flame texture needs to satisfy the consistency and continuity of the current texture, and also the continuity of the texture between consecutive frames [35]. The study of the color and temperature of the combustion flame is shown in Table 2:

3.2 Particle Texture Sheet

This article sets the particle shape to a quadrilateral for accepting texture images, thereby reducing the use of particle counts and enhancing the realism of the flame simulation. The choice of texture image and its quality of effect are very important for the final flame simulation. The flame combustion stage can be divided into four stages of ignition, growth, explosion, and decay. Four groups of texture images are made based on the flame burning photos taken under real conditions in the combustion stage.

Call the texture slice in the OSG custom particle system to adjust the parameters such as shape, texture, transparency, size, and quantity. The relevant parameters are set as shown in Table 3:

Table 3. Flame parameter settings

Parameter	Function name	Value
Life cycle	setLifeTime()	5 s
Texture	setDefaultAttribute()	Texture picture, fire.png
Quality	setMass()	0.1f
Size range	setSizeRange()	(0.1f, 15.0f)
Transparency	setAlphaRange()	(1.0f, 0.0f)
Number of particles	setRateRange()	(20.0f, 25.0f)
Buoyancy and gravity	setToGravity()	−0.05
Environment	setFluidToAir()	Air environment
Wind power	setWind()	Random wind vector Vec3

4   External Factors Simulation

4.1   Locally Attenuated Wind Field

In this paper, the wind field model is set as a random wind field whose direction and wind force change with time. As the wind passes through the fire, wind attenuation occurs, increasing the randomness of particle motion. The wind power at any moment can be expressed as the sum of the reference wind force and the random function.

$$V_w(t) = v * |\sin(wt + \beta)| + \alpha * rand() \tag{10}$$

Where v, w, α, β are constants, different parameter values correspond to different wind speeds, and rand() is a random function between 0 and 1. In the wind field model, the wind direction is set as the horizontal direction, that is, the wind direction vector mainly shows the changes of the x and y values, and the wind direction vector is represented by the Formula (11):

$$V_d = \left(V_w(t) * cos\theta, V_w(t) * sin\theta, 0\right) \tag{11}$$

4.2 Dynamic Vortex Field

The vortex force field is applied to the simulation of the "tumble and jump" phenomenon of real flames, making the form of flame combustion more flexible and real. It is defined as a five-dimensional vector over the real number domain:

$$\text{Vertex} = \left\{angle, Delta, P_{ver}, V_{ver}, a_{ver}\right\} \tag{12}$$

P_{ver} is the center position of the vortex space, V_{ver} is the vortex space moving velocity vector, a_{ver} is the acceleration of the vortex space, angle is the rotation angle of the affected particles in the vortex force field, and Delta is the increment of the particle rotation angle. The spatial description of the vortex force field is:

$$S_{Vertex} = \left\{(x, y, z) | x^2 + y^2 \le R_{Vertex}^2, z \in [bottom, top]\right\} \tag{13}$$

The role of the vortex force field is a cylinder, Rvertex is the radius, bottom and top are the height of the bottom of the cylinder and the height of the top. The properties of the vortex space motion will change in real time over time. Let the time interval between the i + 1-th frame and the i-th frame be ΔT, and the description of the change of the vortex force field is represented by Formula (14):

$$\begin{cases} angle' = angle + Delta * \Delta T \\ V'_{ver} = V_{ver} + a_{ver} * \Delta T \\ P'_{ver} = P_{ver} + \dfrac{V_{ver} + V'_{ver}}{2} * \Delta T \end{cases} \tag{14}$$

The rotation of particles in this rotation space is described as:

1. At time t_0, particles m_1 and m_2 are outside the vortex force field, and both particles make upward linear motion;
2. At time t_1, the vortex field moves, m_1 particles enter the vortex force field, and do a rotating upward movement; the m_2 particle motion remains unchanged;
3. At time t_2, the vortex field moves, and the particle m_1 leaves the vortex force field and makes an upward straight motion again, but the distance from the particle m_2 changes and it is on another trajectory.

Finally, the flame effect obtained by generating 100 square texture particles per frame is shown in Fig. 3.

Fig. 3. Flame effect diagram

5 Conclusion

Based on the discussion of the existing flame model, this paper proposes a flame generation method combined with particle system and texture mapping. In this method, the initial state of the flame particles is given through the reasonable setting of the particle properties. Based on this, the particle motion analysis is performed. In combination with the texture mapping, the texture is manipulated by the particles, and finally the external factors are simulated and the generated flame has a strong sense of reality. Experimental results show that this method is more flexible while meeting real-time performance. At present, this method is mainly focused on the generation of a single flame. The aggregation of multiple flames and the collision of the flame with external obstacles will be the subject of subsequent research and discussion.

Acknowledgment. This work was financially supported by national science and technology support program (2015BAG20B05) and Hubei Provincial key laboratory of open fund (2016znss09B).

References

1. Reeves, W.T.: Particle systems - a technique for modeling a class of fuzzy objects. ACM SIGGRAPH Comput. Graph. **17**(3), 359–375 (1983)
2. Michalski, M., Rieth, M., Kempf, A.: CoFlaVis: a visualization system for pulverized coal flames. Comput. Sci. Eng. **19**(6), 72–78 (2017)
3. Ren, B., Yuan, T., Li, C.: Real-time high-fidelity surface flow simulation. IEEE Trans. Vis. Comput. Graph. **PP**(99), 1 (2017)

4. Wang, J.W., Wen-Ping, H.U., Jin, Y.F.: 8-word dynamic fireworks simulation based on particle system. Comput. Simul. **27**(10), 211–214 (2010)
5. Wang, J.W., Yang, Y.U., Li, Y.-M.: Meteorite explosion simulation based on particle system. Comput. Technol. Dev. 39–41 (2010)
6. Chen, X., Liang, Y., Guo, F.: Fireworks simulation based on CUDA particle system. J. Comput. Appl. **33**(7), 2059–2062 (2013)
7. Pan, Q., Bi, S., Lu, L.: Fast 3D clouds simulation based on particle system. Int. J. Adv. Comput. Technol. **5**(3), 20–28 (2013)
8. Sun, J., Hou, J.: Realistic simulation of snow scenes. Comput. Eng. Appl. (03), 159–163 (2016)
9. Liu, C., Li, T., Huang, Z.: Ship wake simulation based on particle system in virtual test. Lect. Notes Eng. Comput. Sci. (01), 447–450 (2011)
10. Liu, F., Liu, X.: Real-time snowfall simulation based on particle system and pulverization. Microcomput. Appl. **32**(07), 1–5 (2011)
11. Zhiqiang, D., Liu, Y.: A method of snowstorm simulation and real-time rendering based on 3D particle system. Geomatics World **24**(03), 25–29 (2017)
12. Yang, F., Li, J.P., Liang, Z.W.: A real-time rendering method of flame simulation. In: International Conference on Wavelet Active Media Technology and Information Processing, pp. 177–180 (2012)
13. Wei, Z., Shi, W., Li, Z.: Dynamic flame simulation of ceramic roller kiln based on particle system. In: IEEE International Conference on Computer-Aided Design and Computer Graphics, pp. 268–273 (2009)
14. Bai, X., Lu, G., Yong, Y.: Flame image segmentation using multiscale color and wavelet-based texture features. Comput. Eng. Appl. **53**(09), 213–219 (2017)
15. Fang, T.: Seamless texture mapping algorithm for image-based three-dimensional reconstruction. J. Electron. Imaging **25**(05), 25–30 (2016)
16. Jin, B., Xu, J.: Visualization simulation in air separation based on particle system and texture mapping. Zhongguo Jixie Gongcheng/China Mech. Eng. **38**(8), 1053–1058 (2014)
17. Zhao, J.: Simulation of surface flow based on near-regular texture and triangular-patch mapping. J. Syst. Simul. **24**(9), 1954–1957 (2012)
18. Wang, X.H.: Real-time simulation of dynamic cloud based on repeating texture mapping. Comput. Sci. **38**(2), 233–257 (2011)
19. Tan, T.D., Zhao, S., Zhao, H.L.: Real-time water surface simulation based on refraction and reflection texture. J. Zhengzhou Univ. **32**(02), 88–92 (2011)
20. Kouno, A., Kobayashi, M., Toda, H.: Simulation of deformation texture evolution in aluminum alloy based on local strain obtained by synchrotron 3D measurement. J. Jpn. Inst. Light Metals **64**(11), 557–563 (2014)
21. Lin, G., Dingjun, H.: Visual simulation of explosion effects based on mathematical model and particle system. J. Netw. **9**(4), 1020–1026 (2014)
22. Cui, H., Qi, M., Li, D.: 3D cloud modeling base on fractal particle method. In: International Conference on Electrical and Control Engineering, pp. 5639–5643 (2011)
23. Lei, S., Wang, W.: Study on algorithm for fireworks simulation based on particle system. In: International Conference on Computer Science and Network Technology, pp. 231–234 (2014)
24. Lisboa, R.C., Teixeira, P.R.F., Didier, E.: Regular and irregular wave propagation analysis in a flume with numerical beach using a navier-stokes based model. In: Defect & Diffusion Forum, vol. 372, pp. 81–90 (2017)
25. Elizarova, T.G., Graur, I.A., Lengrand, J.C.: Rarefied gas flow simulation based on quasigasdynamic equations. AIAA J. **33**(12), 2316–2324 (2015)

26. Winters, K.B., Seim, H.E., Finnigan, T.D.: Simulation of non-hydrostatic, density-stratified flow in irregular domains. Int. J. Numer. Meth. Fluids **32**(3), 263–284 (2015)
27. Lu, Y., Wang, J., Wu, H.: Recognition of objects in simulated irregular phosphene maps for an epiretinal prosthesis. Artif. Organs **38**(2), E10–E20 (2014)
28. Munoz, P., Castano, B., R-Moreno, M.D.: Simulation of the hexapod robot PTinto walking on irregular surfaces. Int. J. Simul. Model. **14**(1), 5–16 (2015)
29. Richmond, P., Walker, D., Coakley, S.: High performance cellular level agent-based simulation with FLAME for the GPU. Briefings Bioinform. **11**(3), 334 (2010)
30. Han, X., Morgans, A.S.: Simulation of the flame describing function of a turbulent premixed flame using an open-source LES solver. Combust. Flame **162**(5), 1778–1792 (2015)
31. Ding, W., Zheng, L., Xu, L.: Visual simulation of plant interacting with burning flame based on the law of physics. In: IEEE International Conference on Multimedia Big Data, pp. 362–365 (2015)
32. Li, X., Wang, X., Wan, W.: Parallel simulation of large-scale universal particle systems using CUDA. In: International Conference on Dependable, Autonomic and Secure Computing, pp. 572–577 (2013)
33. Xu, M., Pan, Z., Zhang, M.: Character behavior planning and visual simulation in virtual 3D space. IEEE Multimedia **20**(1), 49–59 (2013)
34. Wang, H., Fu, X., Wang, R.: New macroparticle coalescing models that conserve particle's phase-space distribution in 3-D particle-in-cell simulations of plasmas. IEEE Trans. Plasmaence **44**(11), 2638–2643 (2016)
35. Huber, P., Kopp, P., Christmas, W.: Real-Time 3D face fitting and texture fusion on in-the-wild videos. IEEE Sig. Process. Lett. **24**(4), 437–441 (2017)

Research on Indirect Location Technology of Ground Target Based on Scene Matching

Lin Zhang[1], Ruili Zhao[2], Mengxing Huang[3,4(✉)], Zhonghua Liu[1(✉)],
Jieren Cheng[3,4], and Yu Zhang[3,4]

[1] Information Engineering College,
Henan University of Science and Technology, Luoyang, China
zlin_27@163.com, lzhua_217@163.com
[2] Luoyang Quality and Technical Supervision & Testing Center,
Luoyang, China
[3] State Key Laboratory of Marine Resource Utilization in South China Sea,
Haikou 570228, China
huangmx09@163.com
[4] College of Information Science and Technology,
Hainan University, Haikou 570228, China

Abstract. The key positions of target (key points) are usually selected as matching points (aiming points) in traditional target recognition based on image matching. However, sometimes the key points are not suitable for the aiming points. For example, when the features of key points are relatively single, they will be hard to be located, or When the key points are damaged, it is inappropriate for the key points to act as matching points (aiming points), and so on. Therefore, according to the relative position between the aiming point and key point of reference image, the indirect location technology on the key point is researched in this paper. The matching point is firstly determined by the template image which is produced by a model of geometric distortion based on attitude angle and flight altitude deviation. Secondly, the geometry relationship model between the matching point and the key point is established. The efficiency and applicability of our method is demonstrated by the experimental results.

Keywords: Scene matching · Indirect location · Distortion model
The key point

1 Introduction

The indirect location technology main idea of target key point is that the seeker axis always points to the aiming point. Based on the relative position between the key point and the aiming point of reference image and the framework angle of coordinator, the position of key point is firstly computed on the image. Then the LOS-rate of key point is output to the flight control by seeker, which always makes missile body to point to the key point. Finally, the warhead is blasting on the key point [1–10]. That is to say, the eyes look at the aiming point, and the body is flying to the key points. For example, the runway is the key part of the airport, however, it is not easy to match location for

© Springer Nature Switzerland AG 2018
X. Sun et al. (Eds.): ICCCS 2018, LNCS 11064, pp. 90–104, 2018.
https://doi.org/10.1007/978-3-030-00009-7_9

image. Therefore, the key part runway of airport should not be selected as the aiming point [11–17]. Through the evaluation technique of the aiming point, the helipad is selected for the aiming point, thus achieving accurate location of target key point based on indirect location technology.

Indirect location has the following advantages. (1) As long as the aiming point is selected to be appropriate, any position can be hit. (2) In the traditional target recognition based on matching, hitting target can destroy the target feature, which makes the variation between real time image and the reference image to be too big and goes against the subsequent matching location. Since the target point is away from the aiming point in indirect location, it is convenience to realize the second attack. (3) Pretending and concealing of objective is often camouflaged target itself. Since indirect location technology is adopted, pretending and concealing of objective is not interference effect for recognition target.

However, there are no related literature reports for the indirect location technology of the key point. Therefore, the model of image geometric distortion based on the missile attitude angle deviation and flight height deviation is firstly established. Then based on the reference image, the template image with the same imaging conditions of the real time image is generated. Finally, the matching position of template image is determined in the reference image. Meanwhile, according to the relative position $(\Delta x, \Delta y)$ between the aiming point and key point of reference image and the established model of image geometric distortion, an analytical expression from the relative position of the reference image to the distortion model is derived, namely: $(\Delta x', \Delta y') = f(\Delta x, \Delta y)$. Thus the position of target key point is located through indirect location [18–25].

2 Geometry Correction of Template Image

Assume that the reference image is captured under a certain height h and vertical ground, and the template image is obtained by selecting matching area from the reference image which is suitable for the aiming point. When the missile should be parallel to the ground and flight height is h, camera imaging regional of missile is a rectangle and has the same resolution with the reference image. The camera imaging regional of missile is called as real time image, and the template image can more accurate matching in real time image. However, because the missile in the process of flying is affected by various factors, there are some altitude deviation and attitude angle deviation. Thus the onboard camera has caused the corresponding deviation. The camera imaging regional is away from the ideal state, and the captured real time image is generated geometric distortion [26–30]. In order to make the template image match better in the real time image, the template should also carry out the corresponding geometric correction.

2.1 Coordinate System Definition

(1) Reference coordinate system oxyz

The upper left corner vertex of the reference image is selected as origin O, the direction of missile flight is taken as ox axis. Oy axis is vertical to reference image plane. Oz plane is vertical to the plane formed by ox and Oy, and the right hand rule is meeting.

(2) Camera coordinate system $ox_1y_1z_1$

The corresponding point on ground under the inferior-side aeration of camera is selected as origin O, the direction of missile flight is taken as ox_1 axis. oy_1 axis is vertical to reference image plane. oz_1 plane is vertical to the plane formed by ox_1 and oy_1, and the right hand rule is meet.

2.2 Template Image Correction

Suppose the size of the template image be $m \times m$, the coordinates of the camera in reference coordinate system is (x_0, y_0, z_0), the pitch angle, roll angle, yaw angle of missile are respectively denoted by θ, ψ and γ, where y_0 can be obtained by the missile altitude sensor, three attitude angles can be obtained by the attitude angle sensor.

(1) Imaging height h

When the selected camera is determined, the size of the image is also determined. If the image with ideal resolution is wanted to be obtained, the flight height must satisfy certain criteria. Camera image can be regarded as intersection plane of a plane and a four pyramid, and the geometric relationship between each edge of four pyramids and edge plane. If the height of missile is h in an ideal situation, we can obtain:

$$h = m/\sqrt{6} \tag{1}$$

(2) Transformation between the camera coordinate system and reference coordinate system

Assume that the coordinates of any point in reference coordinate system and camera coordinate system are respectively denoted by (x, y, z) and (x_1, y_1, z_1). The coordinate transformation relation between reference coordinate and camera coordinate is:

$$\begin{bmatrix} x \\ y \\ z \end{bmatrix} = G \begin{bmatrix} x_1 \\ y_1 \\ z_1 \end{bmatrix} + \begin{bmatrix} x_0 \\ y_0 \\ z_0 \end{bmatrix} \tag{2}$$

where the transformation matrix G is defined as follows.

$$G = \begin{bmatrix} \cos\theta\cos\psi & -\sin\theta\cos\psi\cos\gamma + \sin\psi\sin\gamma & \sin\theta\cos\psi\sin\gamma + \sin\psi\cos\gamma \\ \sin\theta & \cos\theta\cos\gamma & -\cos\theta\sin\gamma \\ -\cos\theta\sin\psi & \sin\theta\sin\psi\cos\gamma + \cos\psi\sin\gamma & -\sin\theta\sin\psi\sin\gamma + \cos\psi\cos\gamma \end{bmatrix} \tag{3}$$

(3) Correction template image

According to the literature [26], the imaging region of template image is calculated. Then the projection point corresponding to each point on template image is acquired. Lastly, the gray vale of the projection point is assigned to the corresponding imaging region.

The geometric correction algorithm of template image is as follows.

Step 1. Input: the size of template image $m \times m$, the camera coordinates in the reference coordinate system (x_0, y_0, z_0) and pitch angle θ, roll angle ψ, yaw angle γ.
Step 2. According to the formula (1) and (3), the camera height h and transformation matrix G are respectively obtained.
Step 3. The projection coordinates on xoz plane corresponding to the each point of imaging region is obtained.
Step 4. The gray value of projection point is assigned to the corresponding point on imaging region. Since the coordinate of the projection points obtained in step 3 may not all integers, three cubic spline interpolation methods are used to solve the problem.

3 Indirect Location

Suppose the coordinates of matching point in reference image be (x_0, y_0) and the coordinates of the key point be (x, y). So the relation between the matching point and the key point is as follows. $\Delta x = x_0 - x$, $\Delta y = y_0 - y$, namely:

$$\begin{aligned} x &= x_0 - \Delta x \\ y &= y_0 - \Delta y \end{aligned} \tag{4}$$

where the matching point coordinates (x_0, y_0) can be easily obtained according to the matching algorithm, and $(\Delta x, \Delta y)$ vary with altitude and angle. The value of $(\Delta x, \Delta y)$ is emphatically discussed as follows.

(1) When both the real time image and the reference image are captured under the same height h, pitching angle θ, roll angle γ and yaw angle ψ, the location relationship between the matching point and the key point will not change in the real time image. Namely: $\begin{cases} \Delta x' = \Delta x \\ \Delta y' = \Delta y \end{cases}$.

(2) When both the real time image and the reference image are captured under the same pitching angle θ, roll angle γ and yaw angle ψ and different height h, the location relationship between the matching point and the key point can be computed by $\begin{cases} \Delta x' = \Delta x/m \\ \Delta y' = \Delta y/m \end{cases}$.

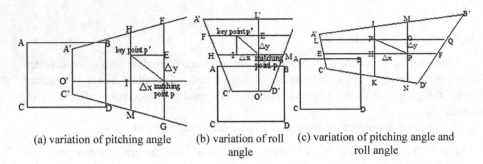

(a) variation of pitching angle   (b) variation of roll   (c) variation of pitching angle and
                                        angle   roll angle

Fig. 1. The obtained imaging region under angle variation

where $m = h'/h$, h' is the height when the real time image is captured and h is the height when the reference image is captured.

(3) When both the real time image and the reference image are captured under the same height h, pitching angle θ, roll angle γ and different yaw angle ψ, the location relationship between the matching point and the key point will not change in the real time image. Namely:

$$\begin{cases} \Delta x' = \Delta x \\ \Delta y' = \Delta y \end{cases} \qquad (5)$$

(4) When both the real time image and the reference image are captured under the same height h, yaw angle ψ, roll angle γ and different pitching angle θ, as shown in Fig. 1(a).

Assume that the boundary of reference image be $A'B'C'D'$, the boundary of real time image be $ABCD$, the coordinate of matching point P in referenec image is (aa, bb) and the coordinate of key point P' is (aa_1, bb_1). The corresponding length lxx and lyy of Δx and Δy in real time image are respectively computed by $lxx = |\Delta x/(abs(B_x - A_x)/N_2)|$ and $lyy = \Delta y/abs((G_y - F_y)/N_1)$. The location relationship between the matching point and the key point in real time image are computed by
$\begin{cases} \Delta x' = abs(tp_4 - tp_2)/kkkk \\ \Delta y' = te_4 - te_2 + lyy \end{cases}$.

Where $\begin{matrix} te_2 = te_1/abs((F_y - G_y)/N_1) & te_1 = abs(G_y - bb_1) \\ te_4 = te_3/abs((H_y - M_y)/N_1) & te_3 = abs(M_y - bb_1) \end{matrix}$, G_y, F_y, H_y and M_y are respectively ordinates of point G, F, H and M, B_x and A_x are abscissa of point B and A. $kkkk = abs(tg_4 - tg_2)/N_2$, $N_1 = \|AC\|_2$, $N_2 = \|AB\|_2$,

$$\begin{cases} tg_2 = |O'C'|/(|A'C'|/N_1) \\ tg_4 = |L'D'|/(|B'D'|/N_1) \\ tp_1 = abs(G_y - bb) \\ tp_3 = abs(M_y - bb) \end{cases}, \qquad \begin{cases} tp_2 = tp_1/abs((G_y - F_y)/N_1) \\ tp_4 = tp_3/abs((M_y - H_y)/N_1) \end{cases},$$

(5) When both the real time image and the reference image are captured under the same height h, yaw angle ψ, pitching angle θ and different roll angle γ, as shown in Fig. 1 (b). The obtained image are all trapezoidal under the variation of roll angle γ or pitching angle θ and the difference of two trapezoids is 90°. Therefore, the relationship between matching point and key point in real time image can be easily gotten on the basis of (4). $\Delta x' = |te_2 - te_4| + lxx$, $\Delta y' = |abs(tp_4 - tp_2)/kkkk|$. Where

$$\begin{cases} te_2 = te_1/abs((F_x - G_x)/N_1) \\ te_4 = te_3/abs((H_x - M_x)/N_1) \end{cases}, \qquad lxx = \Delta x/abs((H_x - M_x)/N_2),$$

$$kkkk = abs(tg_4 - tg_2)/N_1 \qquad , \qquad \begin{aligned} tg_2 &= |O'C'|/(|D'C'|/N_2) \\ tg_4 &= |L'A'|/(|B'A'|/N_2) \end{aligned},$$

$$tp_2 = tp_1/abs((G_x - F_x)/N_1) \quad tp_1 = abs(G_x - bb)$$
$$tp_4 = tp_3/abs((M_x - H_x)/N_1)' \quad tp_3 = abs(M_x - bb)$$

(6) When both the real time image and the reference image are captured under the same yaw angle ψ, roll angle γ, and different height h, pitching angle θ, and $tp_4 = tp_2$, the abscissa relationship between matching point and key point can be obtained by $\Delta x' = |lxx/m|$, where $m = h'/h$. if $tp_4 \neq tp_2$, the abscissa relationship between matching point and key point can be obtained by $\Delta x' = (|abs(tp_4 - tp_2)|/kkkk)/m$. The ordinate relationship between matching point and key point can be obtained by $\Delta y' = (|te_2 - te_4| + lyy)/m$.

(7) When both the real time image and the reference image are captured under the same yaw angle ψ, pitching angle θ, and different height h, roll angle γ, the location relationship between matching point and key point can be obtained by

$$\begin{cases} \Delta x' = (|te_4 - te_2| + lxx)/m \\ \Delta y' = |abs(tp_4 - tp_2)/kkkk| \end{cases}.$$

(8) When both the real time image and the reference image are captured under the same yaw angle ψ, height h, and different pitching angle θ, roll angle γ, as shown in Fig. 1(c), the location relationship between matching point and key point can be obtained by
$$\begin{aligned} \Delta x' &= |te_4 - te_2| + lxx \\ \Delta y' &= |te_2 - te_4| + lyy \end{aligned},$$

where $lxx = \Delta x/(abs(F_x - E_x)/N_2)$, $lyy = \Delta y/(abs(F_x - E_x)/N_2)$, $te4 = \|JP'\|_2$, $te2 = \|MG\|_2$.

Table 1. Simulink data

Image	Height h	Yaw angle ψ	Pitching angle θ	Roll angle γ
a	h	0°	0°	0°
b	0.75 h	0°	0°	0°
c	h	−15°	0°	0°
d	h	0°	−15°	0°
e	h	0°	0°	−15°
f	1.2 h	−5°	−5°	−5°

4 Experiments

4.1 The Template Image

According to the proposed geometric distortion model, the height h, pitching angle θ, roll angle γ, yaw angle ψ by height, angle sensor carried on the missile, the template image is generated. In experiment, the size of reference image is 996×916, the size of the generated template image is 64×64. The values of height and angle are as shown in Table 1, and Fig. 2 shows the generated template images.

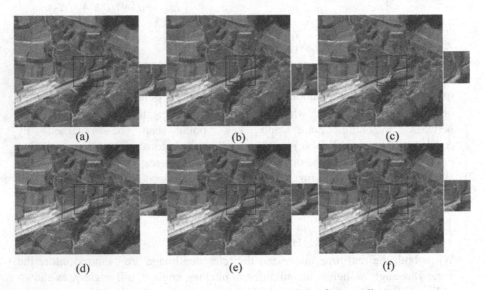

Fig. 2. The generated template image (Color figure online)

Figure 2 shows the six images set, left image each set point out the ideal imaging region (blue line) an the actual imaging region (red line), and right small image each set is generated template image according to height, angle information and the actual imaging region. where the imaging region and the generated template image on an ideal condition is shows in Fig. 2(a).

From Fig. 2, we can see five main points. First, missile altitude deviation will cause the proportion distortion of template image (such as Fig. 2(b)). Second, yaw angle deviation will cause the rotation distortion (such as Fig. 2(c)). Third, pitch angle deviation will cause the forward perspective distortion (such as Fig. 2(d)). Forth, sliding angle deviation will cause the lateral perspective distortion (such as Fig. 2(e)). Fifth, attitude and angle deviation will cause the distortion (such as Fig. 2(f)). It can be seen that the results obtained by the proposed method is consistent with the conclusion in analysis of image geometric distortion. The experiments prove the feasibility and efficiency of the method.

4.2   Indirect Location

The height sensor and the angle sensor carried by missile have no measurement error under ideal condition. However, any measuring Instrument has measurement error under actual condition. Therefore, the height and angle information measured by missile must exist measurement deviation, which results in distortion between the template image and real time image. Further, when the template image is matching on real time image, it will produce error. The error is called matching error. In addition, because the height and angle information measured by missile has measurement deviation, the position relation between the aiming point and key point can change. That is, Δx and Δy can be change, we call it position error. Therefore, the error of indirect location is the sum of matching error and position error. According to the actual situation, a height error is set to $[0 \quad 0.1h]$, The error of pitching angle, roll angle and yaw angle are respectively set to $[-1 \quad 1]$. The size of real time image is 256×320, the size of template image is 64×64.

When only one of four variables (Height, yaw angle, pitching angle, rolling angle) has a measurement error, four infrared images, such as high-speed iron tunnel, airport, bridge, and dam, are used for indirect location error test, which are shown as Fig. 3.

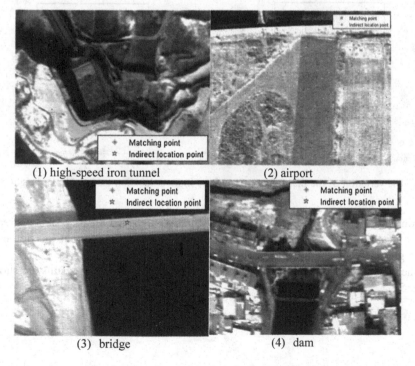

(1) high-speed iron tunnel   (2) airport

(3) bridge   (4) dam

Fig. 3. Experimental images for indirect location

When only height has a measurement error, the experimental results are shown in Fig. 4.

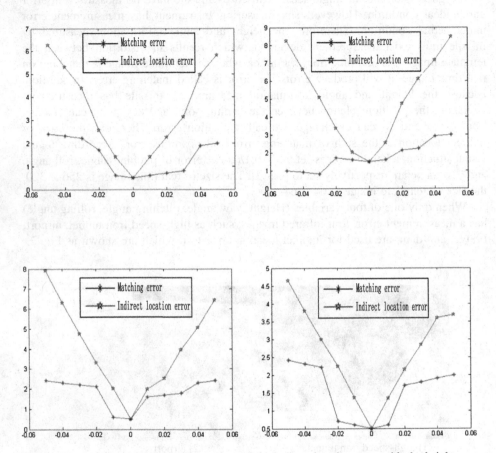

Fig. 4. The variation of the matching error and the indirect location error with the height error

From Fig. 4, we can draw two points. Firstly, high error can produce greater indirect location error. Secondly, under the same condition, the indirect location error will be greater when the height error is negative.

When only yaw angle has a measurement error, the experimental results are shown in Fig. 5.

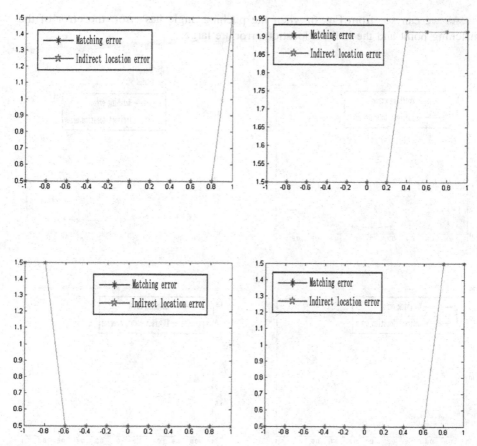

Fig. 5. The variation of the matching error and the indirect location error with the yaw angle error

As we can see from Fig. 5, when the yaw angle has error, the error of the matching point and the indirect location point are the same, and the error is relatively small.

When only pitching angle has a measurement error, the experimental results are shown in Fig. 6.

As we can see from Fig. 6, when the pitching angle has error, the error of the matching point and the indirect location error are large.

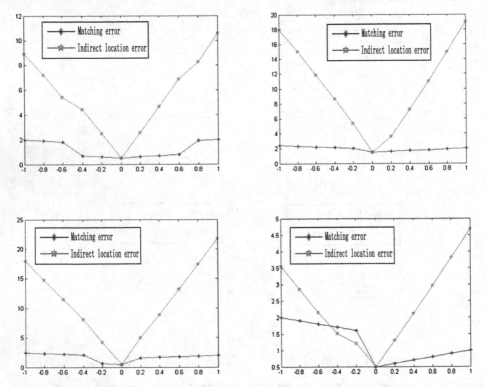

Fig. 6. The variation of the matching error and the indirect location error with the pitching angle error

When only Rolling angle has a measurement error, the experimental results are shown in Fig. 7.

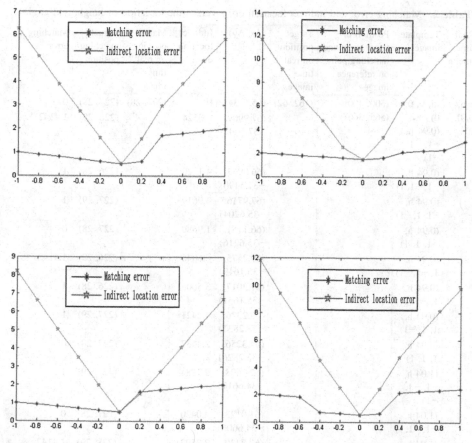

Fig. 7. The variation of the matching error and the indirect location error with the rolling angle error

As we can see from Fig. 7, when the rolling angle has error, the error of the matching point and the indirect location point are also large.

When more than one variables (Height, yaw angle, pitching angle, rolling angle) has a measurement error, we take the image in Fig. 2(a) as real time image, and some experimental results are shown in Table 2.

Table 2. Matching error and indirect location error versus the variation of height and angle

Real time image	Template image	Position of target point and matching point on reference image	Target position on real time image	$(\Delta x, \Delta y)$	Indirect location error	Match position on real time image	Actual matching position	Matching error
a(h, 0, 0, 0)	(h, 0, 0, 0) (0.94 h, −1, −1, −1)	(500, 400) (565, 366)	(162, 62)	(65, −34)	0	(227, 28)	(227, 28)	0
				(67.9909, −37.5502)	6.0524		(226, 29)	1.4142
	(0.94 h, −1, −1, 1)			(66.0967, −37.5490)	4.1220		(226, 28)	1
	(0.94 h, −1, 1, −1)			(67.9716, −35.6204)	3.9619		(227, 29)	1
	(0.94 h, −1, 1, 1)			(66.1151, −35.6216)	1.9680		(227, 28)	0
	(0.94 h, 1, −1, −1)			(69.2575, −35.1619)	5.6846		(226, 29)	1.4142
	(0.94 h, 1, −1, 1)			(67.3017, −35.1631)	3.5006		(226, 28)	1
	(0.94 h, 1, 1, −1)			(69.2326, −33.2837)	4.2421		(227, 29)	1
	(0.94 h, 1, 1, 1)			(67.3256, −33.2826)	2.4337		(227, 28)	0
	(1.04 h, −1, −1, −1)			(62.7608, −34.6617)	2.7884		(227, 29)	1
	(1.04 h, −1, −1, 1)			(61.0123, −34.6606)	4.0420		(227, 28)	0
	(1.04 h, −1, 1, −1)			(62.7430, −32.8803)	3.2592		(228, 29)	1.4142
	(1.04 h, −1, 1, 1)			(61.0293, −32.8815)	5.0950		(228, 28)	1
	(1.04 h, 1, −1, −1)			(63.9300, −32.4571)	0.5474		(226, 29)	1.4142
	(1.04 h, 1, −1, 1)			(62.1247, −32.4582)	3.8377		(227, 27)	1
	(1.04 h, 1, 1, −1)			(63.9070, −30.7234)	2.5242		(227, 29)	1
	(1.04 h, 1,1,1)			(62.1467, −30.7224)	5.0587		(228, 28)	1

From Table 2 we can draw three conclusions. First, the height measurement error is the most influential factor for final error, and then followed by roll angle, pitching angle and yaw angle.

5 Conclusion

The indirect location technology of key part is studied deeply in this paper. Firstly, based on the principle of geometric distortion in the process of capturing real-time image, a novel method of anti geometric distortion for scene matching is proposed. Secondly, a new indirect location algorithm is presented on the basis of position relation between target point and key point. Extensive experiments have demonstrated the effectiveness and practicability of our algorithm. The proposed method gives security for further planning route and effective hitting target.

Acknowledgement. This work was partly supported by NSFC of China (U1504610), Henan international cooperation project (152102410036), the Natural Science Foundations of Henan Province (14A413013, 142102210584, 18A120002), the Development Foundations of Henan University of Science and Technology (2014ZCX013).

References

1. Li, C., Jing, W.: Gain-varying guidance algorithm using differential geometric guidance command. IEEE Trans. Aerosp. Electron. Syst. **46**(2), 725–736 (2010)
2. Golestani, M., Mohammadzaman, I.: Finite-time convergent guidance law based on integral backstepping control. Aerosp. Sci. Technol. **39**, 370–376 (2014)
3. Gang, Z., Wen Shuang, W.: Research on simulation of three-dimension terminal guidance law of antiship missile. Guidance Fuze **33**(1), 6–11 (2012)
4. Le Ménec, S., Shin, H.-S.: Cooperative allocation and guidance for air defence application. Control Eng. Pract. **32**, 236–244 (2014)
5. Wu, C.-C., Wang, H.-C.: The roles of scene gist and spatial dependency among objects in the semantic guidance of attention in real-world scenes. Vis. Res. **105**, 10–20 (2014)
6. Xi, M., Tian, K., Li, H.: New trajectory simulation method for ballistic missiles. J. Air Force Radar Acad. **26**(1), 8–10 (2012)
7. Buontempo, J.T.: A trajectory for homeland ballistic missile defense. Defense Secur. Anal. **31**, 1–11 (2017)
8. Wang, X., Qin, W.: Trajectory estimation for ballistic missile in boost stage using robust filtering. IET Radar Sonar Navig. **11**(3), 513–519 (2017)
9. Zhou, Q., Dong, C.: The trajectory of anti-ship ballistic missile design and simulation. In: International Conference on Instrumentation & Measurement, pp. 373–377 (2016)
10. Kasdaglis, N., Bernard, T., Stowers, K.: Trajectory recovery system: angle of attack guidance for inflight loss of control. In: Harris, D. (ed.) EPCE 2016. LNCS (LNAI), vol. 9736, pp. 397–408. Springer, Cham (2016). https://doi.org/10.1007/978-3-319-40030-3_39
11. Wu, P., Yang, M.: Integrated guidance and control design for missile with terminal impact angle constraint based on sliding mode control. J. Syst. Eng. Electron. **21**(4), 623–628 (2010)
12. Zhi-an, Z., Zheng, J.: Guidance control law design for penetrating guided bomb based on multi-section composite guidance. In: 2014 33rd Chinese Control Conference (CCC), pp. 9070–9074 (2014)
13. Nan, W., Lincheng, S.: Robust optimization of aircraft weapon delivery trajectory using probability collectives and meta-modeling. Chin. J. Aeronaut. **26**(2), 423–434 (2013)

14. Wang, Y., Song, L., Zhang, Y.: Research on the optimal terminal guidance law for gliding guidance bombs. J. Proj. Rocket. Missiles Guidance **30**(4), 51–54 (2012)
15. Ren, S., Chang, W.: Influence of geometric distortion on SAR image matching and its correction. J. Remote Sens. **16**(3), 467–473 (2012)
16. Wang, H., Cheng, Y.: A robust scene matching method for mountainous regions with illumination variation. Hangkong Xuebao/Acta Aeronautica Et Astronautica Sinica **38**(10), 321101 (2017)
17. Jin, Z., Wang, X.: Multi-region scene matching based localisation for autonomous vision navigation of UAVs. J. Navig. **69**(6), 1215–1233 (2016)
18. Chen, S., Liu, X.: Target location method based on homography and scene matching for micro-satellite images. In: International Conference on Optical & Photonics Engineering, vol. 10250, p. 102502U (2017)
19. Fu, Y., Cheng, G.: A fast scene matching method for navigation system based on the improved Hausdorff distance. In: Advanced Information Management, Communicates Electronic & Automation Control Conference, pp. 1825–1829 (2017)
20. Liu, H., Geng, B.: A coarse-to-precise matching strategy in navigation. In: Guidance Navigation & Control Conference, pp. 2170–2174 (2017)
21. Jiang, Y., Sun, C.: Orientation-guided geodesic weighting for PatchMatch-based stereo matching. Inf. Sci. Int. J. **334**, 293–306 (2016)
22. Pavic, M., Mandic, S.: A new type of flight simulator for manual command to line-of-sight guided missile. Int. J. Light Electron Opt. **125**(21), 6579–6585 (2014)
23. Hou, M., Liang, X.: Adaptive block dynamic surface control for integrated missile guidance and autopilot. Chin. J. Aeronaut. **26**(3), 741–750 (2013)
24. Sun, D., Wang, S.: A novel location method for an inconspicuous target based on affine invariability mapping. In: Intelligent Control & Automation, pp. 2247–2251 (2016)
25. Zhang, M.W., Peng, Z.K.: Location identification of nonlinearities in MDOF systems through order determination of state-space models. Nonlinear Dyn. **84**(3), 1–16 (2016)
26. Hu, L., Miao, D., Yang, X.: Modeling and simulation of geometric distortion in real-time image synthesis for scene matching. Missiles Guidance **26**(2), 743–745 (2006)
27. Gelman, N., Silavi, A.: A hybrid strategy for correcting geometric distortion in echo-planar images. Magn. Reson. Imaging **32**(5), 590–593 (2014)
28. Gao, X., Deng, C.: Geometric distortion insensitive image watermarking in affine covariant regions. IEEE Trans. Syst. Man Cybern. Part C: Appl. Rev. **40**(3), 278–286 (2010)
29. Xiao, L., Wu, H.: Modeling and simulation of real-time image synthesis under different wathers for scene matching. J. Syst. Simul. **17**(2), 378–383 (2005)
30. Singh, C., Ranade, S.K.: A high capacity image adaptive watermarking scheme with radial harmonic fourier moments. Digital Sig. Process. **23**(5), 1470–1482 (2013)

Research on Key Climatic Factors of Desert Based on Big Data

Xue Wang, Pingzeng Liu[(⊠)], and Xuefei Liu

Shandong Agricultural University, Tai'an 271000, China
lpz8565@126.com

Abstract. To analyse the correlations among the five factors of temperature, humidity, precipitation, sunshine and wind speed in the desert, the meteorological data of Hangjin Banner for a total of 52 years from 1959 to 2010 are used as the experimental data. Through correlation analysis and regression analysis, a regression equation is established between any factor as the dependent variable and the other four factors as independent variables. The test results show that each coefficient in the equation passes the 95% significance test. Among them, the regression equation has the best fitting degree when humidity and temperature are used as dependent variables, which are 0.520 and 0.514, respectively. Using the data from 2011–2016 of Hangjin Banner to test the regression equations of humidity and temperature, it is found that the model has better prediction ability. Therefore, it is feasible to apply the regression equation to the analysis and prediction of desert meteorological data.

Keywords: Meteorological data · Regression · Prediction

1 Introduction

Desert is potential wealth. Our country has accumulated a large amount of data in the collection of desert meteorology in the past decades. Moreover, the purpose of the meteorological data collection and processing is to obtain an understanding of the law of data changes during the process of collating, analysing, and excavating data, and to describe the regularity of the results in the form of a data model. Through data calculations, it can forecast and estimate the future state of the human living environment. In addition to performing microscopic weather and disaster prediction for a short period, it is also possible to carry out more long-term and macro environmental and ecological changes predictions. With the rapid development of the Internet of Things and big data technology, the use of big data analysis methods to guide desert transformation has become an effective method of desert management.

Regression analysis is one of the most traditional methods of big data analysis, and it is a common method to use it for data prediction [1–9]. In the papers gathered to predict weather data, a large part of the population used a stepwise regression approach to climate prediction [10]. Such as Huang [11], Chen [12] and so on through correlation analysis and stepwise regression achieved on rainfall forecast. Zhang [13], Jia [14], Whiteman [15] and others used multiple linear stepwise regression methods to analyse the impact of meteorological factors on PM2.5 comprehensively. Ceng et al. [16] used

© Springer Nature Switzerland AG 2018
X. Sun et al. (Eds.): ICCCS 2018, LNCS 11064, pp. 105–113, 2018.
https://doi.org/10.1007/978-3-030-00009-7_10

the winter temperature field in Guangdong Province as the forecast field. Through correlation analysis and stepwise regression, it was proved that the prediction error of the regression equation was slightly lower than the actual operational forecast error, which had certain reference significance for actual weather forecasting work. Others used different regression methods to make predictions. Jiang [17] applied the threshold autoregressive model to predict the atmospheric environment in Shanghai. Wang et al. [18] established a multivariate regression model based on the set pair analysis, which significantly improved the accuracy of weather forecasting. Some scholars have used the combination of regression and other methods to achieve the prediction [19, 20]. For example, Goyal et al. [21] used ARIMA and multiple regression to predict air quality in Delhi and Hong Kong. Yu et al. [22] combined the optimal subsets with the ridge trace analysis to obtain a better effect in the experiment of meteorological forecast statistical model of spring grain yield in Taihu plain. Shi et al. [23] studied the optimal climate prediction models based on all possible regressions. It can be seen that the types of regression analysis are diverse [24], but their core ideas are all seeking to establish a simple and stable statistical model. In practical problems, deserts are relatively less affected by human factors, and the correlation between meteorological factors is relatively large. There may be multicollinearity. To get a reliable regression model, it is necessary to select the factors that most influence the dependent variable from many factors. At present, the stepwise regression method has not yet carried out prediction analysis for this special region of the desert, but this method can handle more factors [25], and the prediction model is simple to build and easy to implement. Therefore, the multistep stepwise regression method is considered to be applied to desert meteorological prediction.

Since 2016, Elion Resources Group has cooperated with Shandong Agricultural University to build the "Elion Eco-desert Big Data Platform". To meet the needs of meteorological data analysis and prediction in the platform, starting from practical problems, the correlations between various meteorological factors were studied. Through regression analysis, it is shown whether the explanatory variables corresponding to the dependent variable are significant and whether the regression equation is worth relying on, and based on this, a correlation model is established for prediction. Finally, the test data set is used to verify the model. This experiment provides a theoretical basis and data support for the macro-control and management decision-making of the desert and is of great significance for subsequent deep-level data mining and analysis.

2   Experimental Materials and Methods

2.1   Research Area

Hangjin Banner is located in the northwest of Ordos, Inner Mongolia Autonomous Region. The terrain is high in the south and east, low in the north and west. The northern part is the alluvial plain on the south bank of the Yellow River. In the central and northern part is the Hobq Desert across the entire flag. It is 180 km long from east to west, 40–70 km wide from north to south, and has an area of 7668.50 km^2, accounting for 40.54% of the total land area of the entire flag. The southeast is the edge of Mu Us Desert. The climate characteristics of Hangjin Banner belong to the typical continental climate with a semi-arid plateau in middle temperate zone. There is strong solar radiation, abundant sunshine, and little rain. The precipitation of the entire flag decreases from east to west, and the evaporation is large. There are nine years of drought in every ten years and drought occurs every spring. Wind and sand are numerous, and the frost-free period is short. In early October, it is frozen, and in April of next year, it is thawed. It is hot and cold throughout the year, long and cold in winter, hot and short in summer an warmer in the spring. The falling temperature decreased significantly in autumn. As shown in Fig. 1, in the experimental area, the area near the Internet of Things site set up in Hobq Desert by the Key Laboratory of Smart Agriculture of Shandong Agricultural University was selected to facilitate the analysis of meteorological data in Hobq Desert and other places.

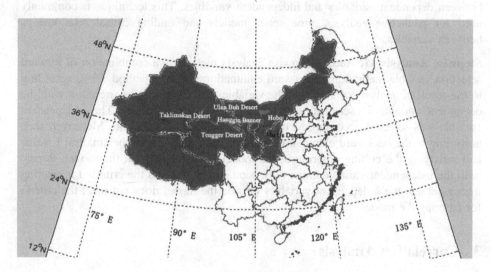

Fig. 1. Distribution of sites.

2.2 Data Screening

This study selected a total of 52 years of historical data from 1959-2010 in desert sand meteorological data from Inner Mongolia Autonomous Region. The data was sourced from the China Meteorological Data Network. Hangjin Banner (area code: 53533) was selected as the sampling point. The collected information included five meteorological data such as temperature, humidity, rainfall, wind speed, and sunshine hours. The data integrity and continuity were good.

SPSS was used for data processing and analysis. As shown in Table 1 for specific information and related treatment of each variable.

Table 1. Information of each variables.

Variable	Abbreviation	Dimension
Monthly average humidity	Humidity	1%
Monthly average temperature	Temperature	0.1 °C
Total annual rainfall	Rainfall	mm
Monthly average sunshine hours	Sunshine	h
Monthly average wind speed	Wind speed	0.1 m/s

2.3 Methods

Regression Analysis. Regression analysis is a statistical analysis method that determines the quantitative relationship between two or more variables. In big data analysis, regression analysis is a predictive modelling technique that studies the relationship between dependent variables and independent variables. This technique is commonly used for predictive analysis, time series models and finding causal relationships between variables.

Stepwise Analysis Method. Astepwise analysis method is a combination of forward selection variable method and backward elimination variable method. First, according to the result of analysis of variance, the variable with the highest correlation with the dependent variable is selected to enter the regression equation. The independent variable was selected according to the method of forward selection. Moreover, then according to the backward elimination method, the variable with the smallest F value and satisfying the culling criterion in the model is excluded from the model. Repeat until the independent variable in the regression equation meets the criteria for entering the model and the independent variables outside the model does not meet the criteria for entering the model.

3 Correlation Analysis

Table 2 shows the degree of interpretation of other variables when temperature, humidity, sunshine, rainfall and wind speed are used as dependent variables, respectively. Since the data used is panel data, the R-square value is relatively small. With the method of stepwise regression analysis, it can be seen that with 95% confidence, when rainfall is the dependent variable, rainfall, sunshine, and temperature have the most significant impact on it. The R-square value is 0.520, and the equation has the best fitting effect. The effect of temperature as a dependent variable is followed by the fitting of the equation. When the wind speed is used as the dependent variable, the effect of the equation is the worst, indicating that when the wind speed is used as the dependent variable, the influence of other factors on it is not significant enough. The following explains the result by selecting the humidity as the dependent variable.

As a dependent variable, humidity, rainfall, temperature, sunshine and wind speed are independent variables. The regression analysis is carried out in a stepwise approach. The first to enter the equation is rainfall, which shows that rainfall has the most significant effect on the humidity in predictors. The variable that entered the equation

Table 2. The results of regression analysis model.

Dependent variable	Independent variables	R	R^2	Standard estimate of the error	Durbin-Watson
Humidity	Constant, rain, sunshine, temperature	.721	.520	2.27257	1.655
Temperature	Constant, wind speed, rain, sunshine	.717	.514	6.10288	1.615
Sunshine	Constant, humidity, temperature	.683	.467	9.43189	1.044
Rainfall	Constant, humidity	.638	.407	62.63143	1.918
Wind speed	Constant, temperature	.568	.323	5.61755	.795

again is sunshine, indicating that the significance of sunshine is also greater, but it does not exclude the effect of rainfall on humidity. Finally, the predictive variable for entering the equation is the temperature, and the temperature does not exclude the effect of rainfall and sunshine on the humidity after entering the equation, indicating that in the case where the significance level is greater than 0.05, these three factors affect humidity. The impact of wind speed on humidity is small and therefore excluded. The model summary (humidity) is shown in Table 3.

Table 3. Model abstract (humidity).

Model	R	R^2	Adjusted R^2	The error of standard estimation	Durbin-Watson
1	.638[a]	.407	.395	2.47425	-
2	.677[b]	.458	.436	2.38907	-
3	.721[c]	.520	.490	2.27257	1.655

[a]Prediction variables: (constant), rainfall
[b]Predictive variables: (constant), rain, sunshine
[c]Predictive variables: (constant), rain, sunshine, temperature
[d]Dependent variable: humidity.

This table content is the F-test in the multiple linear regression tests, as shown in Table 4. The significance of the F-test is 0.000 less than 0.05, which means that the linear model established by temperature, rainfall, sunshine, and humidity is considered to have extremely significant statistical significance.

The regression analysis selects three factors with relatively large humidity-related coefficients: rainfall, sunshine, and temperature. Establish a linear regression relationship between the four factors, as shown in Table 5. The experimental results show that there is a positive linear correlation between humidity(y) and rainfall($x1$), and humidity(y) is negatively correlated with sunshine($x2$) and temperature($x3$). The linear equation is

$$y = 77.935 + 0.016x1 - 0.104x2 - 0.114x3. \tag{1}$$

Table 4. The result of F-test.

Model		Sum of square	Degree of freedom	Mean square	F	Significance
1	Regression	210.204	1	210.204	34.336	.000[b]
	Residual	306.096	50	6.122	-	-
	Total	516.300	51	-	-	-
2	Regression	236.625	2	118.312	20.729	.000[c]
	Residual	279.675	49	5.708	-	-
	Total	516.300	51	-	-	-
3	Regression	268.402	3	89.467	17.323	.000[d]
	Residual	247.899	48	5.165	-	-
	Total	516.300	51	-	-	-

[a]Dependent variable: humidity
[b]Prediction variables: (constant), total annual precipitation
[c]Prediction variables: (constant), annual total precipitation, monthly average sunshine
[d]Prediction variables: (constant), annual total precipitation, monthly average sunshine, monthly average temperature.

Table 5. Coefficient (humidity).

Model		Unstandardized coefficient		Standardized coefficient		Collinear statistics		
		B	Standard error	Beta	t	Significance	Tolerance	VIF
1	(Constant)	41.097	1.244	-	33.041	-	-	-
	Rainfall	.025	.004	.638	5.860	.000	1.000	1.000
2	(Constant)	58.054	7.973	-	7.282	.000	-	-
	Rainfall	.022	.004	.549	4.860	.000	.866	1.155
	Sunshine	−.061	.028	−.243	−2.152	.036	.866	1.155
3	(Constant)	77.935	11.034	-	7.063	.000	-	-
	Rainfall	.016	.005	.413	3.426	.001	.688	1.454
	Sunshine	−.104	.032	−.414	−3.242	.002	.614	1.628
	Temperature	−.114	.046	−.304	−2.480	.017	.668	1.497

4 Prediction

Since wind speed, rainfall, and sunshine are used as dependent variables, the fitting effect of the equation is not predicted. According to the regression equation, data for a total of six years are predicted for humidity and temperature in 2011–2016 as dependent variables respectively. Figure 2 shows the comparison between predicted and true values of humidity. Figure 3 shows the comparison between predicted and true values of temperature. The Mean Square Error values are 8.96 and 1.26, respectively. From the graph, it can be seen that the difference between the predicted value and the actual value is small, and the trend is more stable than the fluctuation of the real value. Therefore, it is feasible to use the method of regression analysis to predict desert meteorological data.

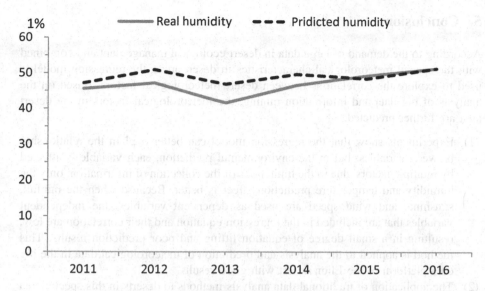

Fig. 2. Comparison of real and predicted values of humidity.

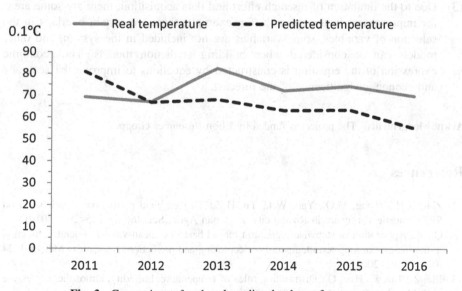

Fig. 3. Comparison of real and predicted values of temperature.

5 Conclusion

According to the demand of large data in desert ecological management and combined with the special meteorological characteristics in desert areas, the regression model is used to explore the correlations between desert meteorological factors. Based on the analysis of big data and information mining, the meteorological factors in the desert area are further predicted.

(1) Experiments show that the regression model can better explain the relationship between variables; but in the environmental prediction, each variable is affected by multiple factors, due to the limitations of the collection of information, only the humidity and temperature prediction effect is better. Because when the rainfall, sunshine, and wind speed are used as dependent variables, the independent variables that are included in the regression equation and their correlation are low, resulting in a small degree of equation fitting and poor prediction results. This method is applied to the analysis and prediction of meteorological data in the big data platform of the Elion desert with good results.

(2) The application of traditional data analysis methods to deserts in this special area of meteorological analysis and prediction can provide good theoretical support for the macro-planning and treatment of desert areas, making the purpose and pertinence of desert ecological governance more clear.

(3) Due to the limitation of research effort and data acquisition, there are some areas for improvement in the research. For example, there are certain overlaps in the selection of variables, some variables are not included in the system, and other models can be considered when building prediction models. The economic expression of the equation is constructed by equations to improve the accuracy and economic significance of the forecast.

Acknowledgements. The project is funded by Elion Resources Group.

References

1. Zhu, X.H., Zheng, M.Q., Yao, W.J., Yu, H.Z.: The tea yield prediction model based on SPSS statistical software in Rizhao city. J. Henan Agric. Sci. **26**(02), 295–297 (2010)
2. Qi, Z.: Application of stepwise regression model based on mean-valued generated function in the forecast of long-term temperature decreasing and prediction. J. Guangxi Meteorol. **24** (01), 15–17 (2003)
3. Ma, Z., Tan, F., Hou, Q.: Distribution rules of temperature, humidity, atmospheric pressure in Taklimakan Desert. J. Desert Res. **20**(3), 289–292 (2000)
4. Ruan, X., Xie, H., Wang, T.: A multivariate regression data estimation method based on correlation analysis. J. Shenyang Univ. Technol. **35**(02), 212–217 (2013)
5. Copas, J.B.: Regression, prediction, and shrinkage. J. Roy. Stat. Soc. **45**(3), 311–354 (1983)
6. Wu, C.H., Ho, J.M., Lee, D.T.: Travel-time prediction with support vector regression. IEEE Trans. Intell. Transp. Syst. **5**(4), 276–281 (2004)
7. Lehmann, A., Overton, J.M., Leathwick, J.R.: GRASP: generalised regression analysis and spatial prediction. Ecol. Model. **157**(2–3), 189–207 (2002)

8. Billings, S.A., Voon, W.S.F.: A prediction-error and stepwise-regression estimation algorithm for non-linear systems. Int. J. Control **44**(3), 803–822 (1985)
9. Cai, T.T., Hall, P.: Prediction in functional linear regression. Ann. Stat. **34**(5), 2159–2179 (2006)
10. Yin, J., Tan, J.: Statistical model of urban air quality forecast in Shanghai. Meteorol. Sci. Technol. **32**(06), 410–413 (2004)
11. Huang, L., Jian, Y.: Prediction of low temperature and rainy year in Guangdong. J. Sun Yat-sen Univ. (Nat. Sci.) **40**(06), 91–94 (2001)
12. Chen, D., Chen, C., Zhou, X., Sun, Q., Wei, J.: Study on the progressive regression prediction model of precipitation in flood season in Fujian. Meteorol. Mon. **39**(09), 1190–1196 (2013)
13. Zhang, S., Han, L., Zhou, W., et al.: Analysis of meteorological influence factors of PM2.5 in winter. Chin. J. Ecol. **36**(24), 7897–7907 (2016)
14. Jia, M., Zhao, T., Zhang, X., et al.: Seasonal changes of atmospheric pollutants in Nanjing and related meteorological analysis. China Environ. Sci. **36**(9), 2567–2577 (2016)
15. Whiteman, C.D., Hoch, S.W., Horel, J.D., et al.: Relationship between particulate air pollution and meteorological variables in Utah's Salt Lake Valley. Atmos. Environ. **94**, 742–753 (2014)
16. Zeng, C., Chen, C.M.: Application of stepwise regression of principal components in temperature prediction. Acta Scientiarum Naturalium Universitatis Sunyatseni **45**(04), 107–110 (2006)
17. Jiang, M., Zhang, Y.: Using threshold autoregressive model to predict ambient air quality. Shanghai Environ. Sci. (08), 375–377+405–406 (2001)
18. Wang, G., Zhao, K., Zheng, X.: Application of set pair analysis to fuzzy predictors of multiple regression weather forcast models. Bull. Sci. Technol. **20**(02), 151–155 (2004)
19. Mao, W., Liu, C., Chen, Y., Li, W.: Instability of climate prediction objects and impact factors and improvement of the statistical set prediction model. J. Arid Land Res. **34**(03), 564–574 (2017)
20. Harrell Jr., F., Lee, K.L., Califf, R.M., et al.: Regression modelling strategies for improved prognostic prediction. Stat. Med. **3**(2), 143 (1984)
21. Goyal, P., Chan, A.T., Jaiswal, N.: Statistical models for the prediction of respirable suspended particulate matter in urban cities. Atmos. Environ. **40**(11), 2068–2077 (2006)
22. Yu, S., Wang, W.: The method of combining the optimal subset with ridge trace analysis is used to determine the regression equation. Chin. J. Atmos. Sci. **12**(04), 382–388 (1988)
23. Shi, N., Cao, H.: Optimal climate prediction model based on all possible regressions. J. Nanjing Inst. Meteorol. (04), 459–466 (1992)
24. Qu, J., Ni, J.: Analysis and design implementation of the multivariate regression model. China Electr. Power Educ. (S1), 140–142 (2007)
25. Yu, S., Chen, X.: Some problems in the regression analysis of meteorological data and countermeasures. Acta Meteorol. Sinica (3), 73–78 (1988)

Research on Personalized Recommendation Case Base and Data Source Based on Case-Based Reasoning

Jieli Sun[1(✉)], Zhiqing Zhu[1], Yanpiao Zhang[1], Yanxia Zhao[1], and Yao Zhai[2]

[1] Hebei University of Business and Economics, Shijiazhuang 050061, HeBei, China
sunjieli@126.com
[2] The George Washington University, Washington, DC 20052, USA

Abstract. The research of the personalized recommendation system mostly concentrates on how to express, compute and update the interests of users. This article provides the research of personalizing recommendations based on personalized recommendation cases. The case base is the key to Case-Based Reasoning (CBR). To a large extent, the ability of case base to capture and reflect the interests of users determines the degree of personalization of recommendation results from a system. This paper puts forward a construction scheme for a case base of the personalized recommendation system based on CBR. The paper also analyzes the composition and design idea of the case base. It has built a personalized recommendation user case base, a similar user case base, a pattern case base and a knowledge base, which provides rich data for case-based reasoning. Results of the system's design show that the recommendation case base and data source construction have great significance in the quality of the personalization of the system's recommendation results.

Keywords: Case-based reasoning · Personalized recommendation
Data · Source

1 Intrduction

Case-based reasoning (CBR) is designed to use existing cases to solve new problems. The essence of CBR is to solve the current reasoning method of similar problems by analogy and association, using previous experience and methods of solving problems. Currently, CBR is an important area of research in the field of artificial intelligence [1–3]. Results of CBR techniques have been applied in many application fields. Some examples of CBR application results include emergency decision-making methods [4, 5], transfer of learning research [6], online customer consumption behavior research [7], grid application scheme [8], traffic path problem research [9], medical applications [10], etc. However, the application of CBR in books and archives management is still insufficient.

Personalized service is a service mode that provides different service strategy and service content according to the characteristics of different users, not only reflects the

© Springer Nature Switzerland AG 2018
X. Sun et al. (Eds.): ICCCS 2018, LNCS 11064, pp. 114–123, 2018.
https://doi.org/10.1007/978-3-030-00009-7_11

user's clear demand and latent demand, current demand and long-term demand, but also can effectively reveal the structure of user information requirement. Compared with the search engine, the recommendation system studies the user's interest preference, carries on the personalized computation, discovers the user's interest point by the system, thus guides the user to discover own information demand [11]. Its essence is a kind of service mode of information looking for people, which can reduce the time of searching information and improve browsing efficiency. At present, the research of personalized recommendation system mainly focuses on user model establishment and algorithm design, literature [12, 13] studies the design and implementation of user interest modeling of personalized recommendation system, and the application of case-based reasoning technology to personalized recommendation system design is very few.

In this paper, the personalized recommendation system based on case-based reasoning (C-PRS, case-based reasoning Personal recommender System) is personalized recommendation based on personalized recommendation. The multiple case base and knowledge base of personalized recommendation system is the main data source to produce personalized recommendation, and its ability to capture and reflect users ' interests determines the degree of personalization of system recommendation results to a great extent. The design and establishment of pattern case base and Knowledge Base is a basic data work of personalized recommendation system based on case-based reasoning.

2 Personalized Recommendation System Case Base

The data source means the source of the data, which provides the raw media the data needed for a personalized recommendation system. The main data sources of the personalized recommendation system based on case-based reasoning include case base and knowledge base.

2.1 Multiple Case Database

In the personalized recommendation system based on case-based reasoning, the case base serves the whole inference process and is the basis of the work of other modules.

The representation and acquisition of cases and the organization and construction of case base are the key of case reasoning. According to the expert experience and thinking mode, combined with the traditional case organization method, the personalized recommendation system based on case-based reasoning adopts multiple case base to organize personalized recommendation system cases. The personalized recommendation cases consist of user information, user interest type information, and recommended document item information. The increasing number of users has led to a large number of user interest types and recommended items, the number of different combinations of personalized recommendations produced by a very substantial, in order to control the personalized referral system case base scale, improve the efficiency of case retrieval, using multiple case base for personalized referral case organization.

According to the needs of personalized recommendation and the role in personalized recommendation system, the C-PRS system has three main parts: Personalized recommendation user case base, similar user case base and pattern case base.

2.2 Knowledge Base

Knowledge base is a collection of declarative and process-oriented knowledge that is reasonably organized in a particular field. The difference between a knowledge base and a traditional database is that the knowledge base contains not only a large number of simple facts, but also rules and process knowledge. Knowledge base system is based on knowledge base as the core, including human, software and hardware resources, and used to implement knowledge sharing, the knowledge base system study the general method and principle of knowledge representation, organization, reasoning and acquisition, it can be used for various purposes. The knowledge base of personalized recommendation system based on case-based reasoning the implication is that with the help of knowledge base system, the user data and document resource data of personalized recommendation system are classified accurately into the categories they should belong to, and replace human mental work completely or partially.

3 Multiple Case Base Construction of Personalized Recommendation System

The case base is composed of all user information behavior model case. Case Base is the most important part of the user information behavior model based on case-based reasoning, which contains the historical experience in the field of application, and the organization form of case Base and the representation of case are closely related. The establishment of the case base is a process of continuous improvement and updating, through the continuous learning (inference) process to maintain the purpose of the case base. The main purpose of the case base maintenance is to limit the size of the case base, and to maintain the performance of the system, the main task is to make the cases in the case base representative, increase the coverage of cases in the case base and reduce the degree of redundancy.

The system case design adopts adaptive dynamic strategy, which completes the acquisition, generation and update of personalized cases based on user's dynamic behavior data. Because of the complex and changeable characteristics of user interest, in order to provide the user with relatively accurate recommendation results, it is necessary to analyze the user's behavior data, so the recommender system needs to collect the user's behavior information continuously, and the data information of the personalized recommendation case database can be perfected gradually by feedback the user case data to the user case base, gradually improve the data information of the personalized recommendation case base.

Multi-case base of personalized recommendation system includes user case pase–basic data source, similar user case database–main data source, pattern case Base–abstract and generalization of personalized recommendation cases.

3.1 User Case Base Construction

The construction of user case base of personalized recommendation system includes the following aspects: (1) through the user case management module for personalized user information collection, a more comprehensive understanding of user needs, as a self-organizing dynamic user case input. (2) use the rules and process knowledge in the knowledge base to analyze and deal with the user's information and classify the basic data. (3) automatically and continuously track and record the status of the system registered users, for example, the user's download information, browsing information, feedback on the results of recommendations and use of system time, etc., and then analyze the behavior for the user, record down in the user behavior log and user staging database, provide case data preparation for the next step of personalized recommendation. Finally, the user case generation operation analyzes the data of the user staging database, and obtains the user's useful behavior data and generate the user case.

3.2 Similar User Case Base Construction

Personalized recommendation system needs to recommend the user to infer the recommended results, for the general case inference system retrieval process, to find the user case base of the corresponding cases can get the results, but the user case base stored is the document data items that has been browsing. This does not have much meaning to meet the needs of personalized recommendation service users. The personalized recommendation system based on case reasoning consider the recommendation result to refer to the data information of similar neighbors to be more practical and personalized recommendation value, which is also one of the characteristics of this system recommendation reasoning, similar user case base construction is based on this background [14–16].

The generation of similar user cases is the key to realize the recommendation function of personalized recommendation system, so it is necessary to design and create a similar user case base in order to get the data information of similar users.

Firstly, calculate case similarity for the user case base, generate case feature attribute vector. Secondly, the case similarity is judged with the content of knowledge base. When judging the similarity of cases, we can carry out similarity calculation by using the characteristic vectors (user interest feature word vector) of the case to be judged and the similarity case characteristic vector (similar case feature word vector) of similar user case base, so as to reduce the computational amount of case similarity judgment [17–20]. Finally the resulting data from similar user case libraries are updated continuously with similar user cases increase. In addition, the system will choose the case similarity calculation method (calculation formula) as the configuration parameter of the recommendation system, which can be selected by the recommendation system manager according to the recommendation, meanwhile increasing the flexibility and scalability of the recommendation system.

The key to the construction of similar user case database is how to judge the case similarity. The main content of similarity judgment based on similarity case feature vectors includes two aspects, first, calculating user case category. In the personalized recommendation system, the user's characteristic words are regarded as the embodiment of the user's dynamic interest. Because each feature word has a similarity to the category, so the user case category can be computed based on the characteristic words retrieved by the user. For each user, according to their search of the characteristic words in the word-category table, add the word category vector of these characteristic words, and get the user class vector. Each element of the category vector represents the similarity of the user to the category. Finally, find a class with the highest similarity as the representative category of the user case. Second, generate similar users.

Since there may be a lot of registered users, and the user's demand interest is classified, it is not necessary to compute the similarity between all the user cases. Only calculates the similarity between user cases that represent the same category. Firstly, according to the representative category of user cases, find and compute the similarity in the similar user case base, according to the similarity threshold of the recommended system, the cases exceeding this threshold are similar and recorded in the similar user case base [21, 22]. Because of the similar user case is a set of the user case meeting the similarity requirements, so the similar user cases can also be called the similar user group [23–25].

The steps of personalized recommendation system's case similarity determination are as follows: (1) Obtain the case category and the feature words according to the case feature vector to be determined. (2) Finding and locating similar user cases in a similar user case library. (3) Get eigenvectors for similar user cases and calculate similarity. (4) Comparison of similarity value and system similarity threshold. (5) If the user is similar to a similar user case, the similar case is positioned to update the similar user case and related attribute values. (6) If the user is not similar to a similar user case, the user's data is inserted into a similar user case library as a new similar user case. (7) Update the related attribute values of the similar user case library. (8) Update similar user case library.

3.3   Model Case Base Construction

Personalized recommendation system mode case Base has two sources of data: first, from the user staging database, select more than a certain number of query number of features (related weight parameters can be adjusted), fully considering the impact of user staging database. The second is by the field expert audit decision. Case data selection should be carefully selected under the audit of experts in the field.

The Pattern case Base has three attributes, pattern ID, pattern representation, and pattern recommendation document. Where the pattern ID is the category ID of the category table in the repository. In the personalized recommendation system, the pattern ID is relatively stable, and the pattern representative characteristic word and the pattern recommendation document change accordingly along with the recommendation system foundation recommendation data and personalized recommendation user Data change.

The construction of the pattern case base is mainly from two aspects: (1) analyzer design. In this method, we should select mode representative feature words and get the mode feature. In the feature word-category table, the contribution of the feature word to the category and the category of the greatest contribution are recorded. For each type of representative feature word selection, the maximum contribution for the category of the feature words retrieved should be displayed to the domain experts, let the field expert audit and determine whether it can be used as a representative of the pattern of the word, domain experts can set a value, and the contribution of less than a threshold of the feature words filtered out do not show.(2) the inference device design, select mode case recommended document that is recommended mode, and get the recommended records. From the document list, retrieve the documents with higher browsing and downloads in each category (field experts give a threshold, such as the first n or the number of clicks above a value m), which should be displayed to field experts, and allows field experts to select which documents can be used as recommended documentation for the model case. It is also possible for a field expert to add a document as a recommended document, mainly to recommend the latest literature, as well as high-quality literature that has not been browsed or downloaded by the user.

4 Knowledge Base Construction of Personalized Recommendation System

The knowledge base of personalized recommendation system includes system category information, characteristic word information, word segmentation dictionary information and system parameter information.

4.1 The Significance of the Knowledge Base Construction

The process of classifying personalized recommendation systems is divided into three steps: (1) scan the document data and user case data. (2) extract the corresponding data characteristics (document data characteristic word and user case to represent the user interest characteristic word, etc. (3) according to the corresponding data characteristic word, to assign a classification number for the classify the data to, it is necessary to use knowledge and inference mechanism of knowledge base in classification.

In the practical application of personalized recommendation system, the meaning of knowledge base lies in the first, auxiliary extraction of the characteristic words of literature resources. Because the characteristic word of a document is the enrichment and refinement of the content of the document, so it can be classified by the characteristic words of the document. Second, the guidance classification. Knowledge base is the wisdom crystallization of domain experts, these experts have domain knowledge, are familiar with the classification of recommendation system, and have certain experience, such as can extract the concept, deal with the problem of many subjects, etc., they play an important role in the process of document resource data and user case data classification. Third, supporting the personalized recommendation inference process based on case-based reasoning. In the personalized recommendation system based on case-based reasoning, the key is to collect, standardize and tidy up the knowledge and experience of field experts to form and perfect the knowledge base of personalized recommendation system. The relationship between the knowledge base and the multiple case libraries is shown in Fig. 1.

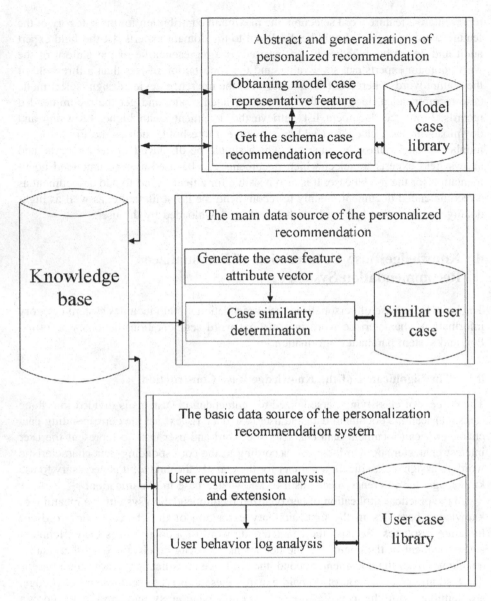

Fig. 1. Knowledge database and multiple case database diagram

4.2 Knowledge Base Composition

The requirements and functions of the personalized recommendation system based on case-based reasoning determine the composition and content of the knowledge base, and the knowledge base system data must be audited by a field expert with practical experience before it can be stored in the knowledge base of personalized recommendation system. The system Knowledge Base is composed of personalized recommendation system classified information, characteristic word information, word segmentation dictionary information and recommendation system parameter information, credibility, feedback times and so on.

Chinese library classification is a general classification system, now the system this paper is based on the classification of Chinese libraries in the case of users. Case-based reasoning based personalized recommendation system contains four kinds of parameters:

(1) recommended input parameters. Refers to the decision personalized recommendation system input production case data related parameters.
(2) recommended control parameters. Refers to the condition parameters produced by personalized recommendation system.
(3) recommended policy parameters. Refers to the selection of the recommended method parameters.
(4) recommended output parameters. Refers to the relevant parameters of recommended data produced by personalized recommendation inference.

The knowledge Base contains facts and rules, so you can use the Knowledge base to infer new facts. As the external world continues to evolve and evolve, knowledge in the knowledge base needs to be continuously increased and updated.

The key to update the Knowledge base data is the reliability and the number of feedback corresponding to the data information. The steps of the knowledge base of personalized recommendation system based on case-based reasoning are as follows: 1. obtain feedback from users on data information; 2, read the reliability and feedback times corresponding to the data information. 3, updating corresponding credibility, feedback times and feedback information according to the data information. The credibility of the data information in the knowledge base is not fixed, and it changes with the change of the user's feedback information, which is updated by reference to the feedback information of the users, so that the data information in the knowledge base is optimized continuously with the improvement of people's understanding level. This method improves the reliability of the data information in the knowledge base and makes it more accurate, thus effectively improves the accuracy of data access.

5 Conclusion

The realization of personalized recommendation system based on case-based reasoning is to classify user case data and document resource data so that the personalized recommendation system can organize relevant case data. The key technology of the personalized recommendation system based on case-based reasoning lies in the representation of cases, the acquisition of cases and the organization and application of cases, and the basic data work is to design and establish case base and knowledge base. The multiple case base (user case base, similar user case base, pattern case base) and knowledge base are the main data sources of personalized recommendation, which is of great significance to the quality of personalized degree of the system recommendation results.

Acknowledgements. This paper is supported by Education technology research Foundation of the Ministry of Education (No. 2017A01020) and the Science and technology plan project of Hebei Province (No. 16960314D).

References

1. Aamodt, A.: Case-based reasoning: foundational issues, methodological variations, and system approaches. AI Commun. **7**(1), 39–59 (1994)
2. Gilboa, I.: Case-based decision theory. Q. J. Econ. **110**(3), 605–639 (1995)
3. Xia, L., Yang, B., Tu, H.: Recognition of suspicious behavior using case-based reasoning. J. Central South Univ. **22**, 241–250 (2015)
4. Zhang, X.: Emergency decision method research based on case reasoning. Computer Science and Technology College, Tianjin University, Tianjin (2012)
5. Li, L.: Research on the intelligent decision support system of group events based on case reasoning. Economics and Management College, Xi'an Science and Technology University, Xi'an (2012)
6. Yang, H.: Study transfer research based on case reasoning. Journalism and Communication College, Yangzhou University, Yangzhou (2012)
7. Jia, H.: Research on online customer consumption behavior based on case reasoning. Information Management and Electronic Commerce College, Electronic Science and Technology University, Chengdu (2013)
8. Chen, S.: Grid application scheme generation system based on case reasoning. Huazhong Science and Technology University, Control Science and Engineering System, Wuhan (2012)
9. Wang, T.: Research on the uncertain information vehicle routing problem based on case reasoning. Economics and Management College, Nanjing University of Science and Technology, Nanjing (2013)
10. Bi, L.: Research on TCM clinical decision support system based on case reasoning. Computer and Information Technology College, Beijing Jiaotong University, Beijing (2012)
11. Wang, G.: Personalized recommendation system review. Comput. Eng. Appl. **48**(7), 66–76 (2012)
12. Hua, Q.: Research and realization of personalized recommendation system on the user interest modelling. Information and Communication Engineering College, Beijing Posts and Telecommunications University, Beijing (2013)
13. Li, N.: Design and implementation of personalized recommendation system based on user interest self adaptation. Software, Beijing College, Jiaotong University, Beijing (2012)
14. Juell, P.: Using reinforcement learning for similarity assessment in case-based systems. IEEE Intell. Syst. **18**(4), 60–67 (2003)
15. Pearce, M.: Case-based design support: a case study in architectural design. IEEE Expert **7** (5), 14–20 (1992)
16. Wei, C.: The application of an improved nearest neighbor case-based reasoning. J. Syst. Simul. **17**(5), 1045–1047 (2005)
17. Schafer, J.B.: Recommender systems in e-commerce. In: Proceedings of the 1st ACM conference on Electronic commerce. ACM (1999)
18. Liu, T.: Introduction to Information Search System. Mechanical Engineering Press, p. 150 (2008)
19. Xu, Z.: A discussion of similarity measures in case-based recommendation system. J. Xiamen Univ. (Nat. Sci.) **39**(4), 441–445 (2000)

20. Liao, T.: Similarity measures for retrieval in case-based reasoning systems. Appl. Artif. Intell. **12**(4), 267–288 (1998)
21. Shuguang, Z.: A model of case matching method in case-based reasoning. Pattern Recogn. Artif. Intell. **3** (2002)
22. Ying, J.: A case-based search model. Acta Scientiarum Naturalium Universitatis Sunyatseni **38**(2), 1–5 (1999)
23. Zhong, S.: A case-based hybrid search model. J. Softw. **10**(5), 521–526 (1999)
24. Melville, P.: Recommender systems. In: Sammut, C., Webb, G.I. (eds.) Encyclopedia of Machine Learning, pp. 829–838. Springer, Boston (2010). https://doi.org/10.1007/978-0-387-30164-8
25. Wu, D.: An electronic commerce recommendation algorithm joining case-based reasoning and collaborative filtering. In: Proceedings of 2015 International Industrial Informatics and Computer Engineering Conference (IIICEC 2015), pp. 1222–1225 (2015)

Research on Real-Time Monitoring of Human Body Temperature Based on Fiber Bragg Grating Sensing Technology

Bin Ma and Yecheng Sun$^{(\boxtimes)}$

School of Information Science,
Qilu University of Technology (Shandong Academy of Sciences), Jinan, China
qluxxsyc@163.com

Abstract. Aiming at the current needs of the medical industry for measuring human body temperature and the deficiencies of several traditional temperature measurement methods, a real-time monitoring method of human body temperature using fiber Bragg grating with light weight, small size, anti-electromagnetic interference, good biocompatibility, intrinsic safety, and other characteristics is proposed. In this paper, firstly the temperature sensing characteristics of the fiber grating are theoretically analyzed. Then four fiber grating temperature sensors are calibrated by thermostatic water bath and the corresponding curve fitting is performed. Finally, the experimental results of fiber grating sensors at room temperature and fiber grating sensors under thermostatic water bath heating environment were compared and analyzed, thus verifying the advantages of fiber grating sensors. The experimental results show that in the range of 25 °C–75 °C, the center wavelength of the fiber grating has a good linear relationship with the temperature change, and temperature measurement error is less than 0.1 °C, and the accuracy is effectively improved. It can be applied to real-time monitoring of human body temperature in medical treatment.

Keywords: Human body temperature measurement
Fiber Bragg grating temperature sensor · Curve fitting · Real-time monitoring

1 Introduction

In the medical process, real-time monitoring of the patient's body temperature is necessary in many cases to accurately track the patient's condition and ensure good treatment. Some treatments (such as tumor hyperthermia) require the accurate temperature monitoring of the patient in strong electromagnetic or ultrasonic environments. Commonly used thermal resistance or thermocouple type temperature sensors are susceptible to strong electromagnetic fields, unable to meet the measurement requirements in such environments, it is difficult to measure temperature accurately. The traditional mercury thermometer needs to manually reset when used, the operation inconvenience also can not meet the requirements of real-time monitoring, and is not suitable for medical measurement [1]. Most temperature sensors can measure temperature accurately, but there are not many temperature sensors that have both anti-electromagnetic interference and high precision. A wide variety of fiber gratings can measure many physical parameters with high resolution, compared with the traditional electrical and mechanical sensors, FBG sensors have the following advantages: the temperature detection system has a very low cost, strong ability of resisting electromagnetic interference, high corrosion resistance and high temperature resistance, small size and light weight, easy to manufacture and high precision, distributed measurement can be carried out [2]. Besides, FBG sensors not only have the characteristics of common sensors, but also have their own unique advantages. They are wavelength-modulated sensors immune to fluctuations in light sources power and loss of connections. They have high measurement resolution and are easy to implement quasi-distributed measurement [3]. Fiber Bragg grating temperature sensing system has broad application in harsh environments such as high temperature, strong magnetic field, etc., and can realize real-time on-line temperature measurement accurately. The practical research of fiber grating sensing system has been a hot research topic both at home and abroad [4]. At present, fiber gratings play an important role in biomedicine. Fiber grating sensors are small in size, biocompatible, chemically inert, immune to electromagnetic immunity, intrinsically safe and can be implanted into patients for continuous monitoring of some parameters [5]. Yu and Li et al. [6] established a theoretical model of temperature measurement of fiber Bragg gratings in smart clothing according to the heat transfer mechanism, and the temperature measurement value is corrected with the model. The human body wearing intelligent clothing experiment results show that the temperature measurement error is ± 0.2 °C, which can be used for high-precision monitoring of human body temperature. Yu and Chen et al. [7]. Developed a fiber grating temperature sensor for human body temperature measurement, the temperature calibration was performed on two FBG sensors operating at 1557 nm and 1547 nm with thermostatic water bath. The experimental results show that the standard deviation of temperature measurement of the sensor is less than 0.3 °C, which basically meets the needs of medical temperature measurement. Zhang and Wei et al. [8].used finite element analysis methods to design and implement a new fiber grating temperature monitoring system based on human body temperature characteristics. The experimental results show that the dynamic range of the system detection temperature is 28 °C–48 ° C, and the measurement accuracy is 0.1 °C.

At present, there are few temperature sensors with anti-electromagnetic interference and high measurement accuracy. The human body temperature measurement accuracy of the fiber Bragg grating temperature sensor used in literatures 6–8 still needs to be improved. In this paper, the measurement accuracy of fiber Bragg grating temperature sensor is further enhanced through theoretical and experimental analysis, which can be applied to medical real-time monitoring of human body temperature.

2 Theoretical Analysis of Fiber Bragg Grating Temperature Sensing

2.1 Fiber Bragg Grating Temperature Sensing Principle

After the broad-spectrum light source enters the fiber, the transmitted light passes through the coupler and reaches the sensing grating. At this point, the light satisfying the Bragg condition is reflected by the fiber grating and reach the fiber grating demodulator through the coupler, and the other light will pass through. When the temperature of the optical fiber in the environment changes, the grating period and core refractive index will change, leading to the change of the reflection spectrum. By measuring the change of the reflective center wavelength, the temperature variety can be obtained. Sensing schematic diagram is shown in Fig. 1.

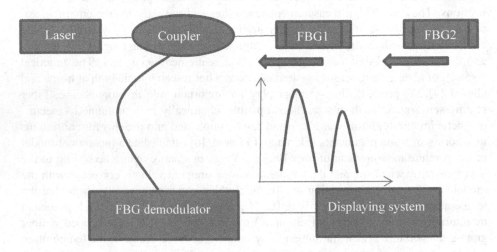

Fig. 1. Fiber Bragg grating sensing principle diagram

2.2 Fiber Bragg Grating Temperature Sensing Characteristics

After the incident light reaches the sensing grating, the light satisfying the Bragg condition is reflected by the fiber grating, and the reflection spectrum shows a peak at the Bragg wavelength. For the specific space refractive index modulation period (Λ) and the core effective refractive index (n_{eff}), the Bragg wavelength is:

$$\lambda_B = 2n_{eff}\Lambda \tag{1}$$

In the above equation, the changes of Λ and n_{eff} will cause the FBG reflected light center wavelength change. The change of temperature, stress or pressure will lead to the change of Λ and n_{eff}, so that the FBG can reach its sensitive purpose.

In terms of temperature sensing, the main factors that cause the wavelength shift of the FBG are the change of the grating period caused by the thermal expansion effect of the FBG and the change of the effective refractive index caused by the FBG thermal effect. Differentiate the two sides of the formula (1), and then take the derivative of the temperature to get the formula (2):

$$\frac{d\lambda_B}{dT} = 2(\frac{1}{n_{eff}}\frac{dn_{eff}}{dT} + \frac{1}{\Lambda}\frac{d\Lambda}{dT})$$ (2)

The formula (2) is divided by the formula (1), and the formula (3) can be obtained:

$$\Delta\lambda_B = \lambda_B(\alpha + \zeta)\Delta T = K_T\Delta T$$ (3)

In the formula: α is thermal expansion coefficient, $\alpha = \frac{1}{\Lambda}\frac{d\Lambda}{dT}$; ζ is thermal coefficient, $\zeta = \frac{1}{n_{eff}}\frac{dn_{eff}}{dT}$; K_T is temperature sensitivity coefficient.

From Eq. (3), we can see that the change of the FBG reflection center wavelength is linear with the change of temperature. Therefore, if the wavelength shift of the fiber grating is measured, the change of the temperature can be obtained. For pure silica fiber, its thermal coefficient is $6.45 \times 10^{-6}/°C$, its thermal expansion coefficient is $5.5 \times 10^{-7}/°C$, then the relative sensitivity coefficient of fiber grating is about $0.7 \times 10^{-5}/°C$, for a fiber grating sensor operating at a wavelength of 1550 nm, it is known that the wavelength shift caused by a change in the unit temperature is 10.8 pm/°C.

3 Experimental Analysis of Fiber Bragg Grating Sensing

3.1 Fiber Bragg Grating Temperature Sensing Experimental Device

Fiber grating temperature sensing experimental system consists of fiber grating temperature sensor, transmission cable, fiber grating signal demodulator and monitoring computer. Fiber grating sensor is the system temperature sensing device, installed directly at the temperature measurement point to measure the temperature. Its core component is a fiber grating, its role is to collect the temperature signal of the temperature measurement point and convert it into light wavelength signal; Transmission cable is the signal transmission channel, which has a strong anti-extrusion performance; Fiber grating signal demodulator's role is to demodulate the temperature signal, the core component is BaySpec FBGA demodulator module. The temperature-sensing grating in each fiber grating temperature sensor has a reflection effect only on light of a specific wavelength range so that the temperature of each sensor can be determined based on the wavelength signal. Therefore, FBG demodulator is the core of the whole temperature measurement system, which is crucial to the whole temperature measurement system. The stability of its work also directly determines the stability and reliability of the whole system. The device has a wavelength resolution of 1 pm, a wavelength scan range of 1525 to 1565 nm and a sampling frequency of 5 to 5 k Hz. The FBGA protocol interface is simple, using RS232 and USB parallel communication, the connection is simple and common, and has strong applicability [9]; The monitoring computer collects the temperature information from the fiber grating demodulator and displays the temperature data of each sensor in real time, thereby analyzing and processing the data through the full-featured software.

3.2   Calibration Experiment of Fiber Bragg Grating Temperature Sensor

In order to effectively adjust and maintain the temperature, it also ensures that the fiber grating can uniformly sense the temperature, as far as possible to reduce the error, a thermostatic water bath was adopted to calibrate the fiber grating sensor. Four optical fiber grating temperature sensors with center wavelengths of 1530.13 nm, 1553.13 nm, 1543.10 nm, 1548.11 nm (They were numbered 1001, 1002, 1003, 1004 respectively) respectively were placed in the temperature-adjustable thermostatic water bath. The temperature range of the water bath is room temperature ~ 100 °C, temperature control accuracy ≤ 0.5 °C. Experimental controlled temperature range was from 25 °C–75 °C, observed every 5 °C, and the wavelength value of FBG was recorded at 10 min after the temperature reached the set value. Since the thermostat water bath changes little after reaching the set temperature and the temperature in the bath environment is relatively uniform, the influence of uneven temperature distribution can be ignored. Wavelength values were read by the built-in software of the Sense 20/20 Revision 1.5.8.2 Wavelength Demodulator manufactured by BaySpec company, as shown in Fig. 2. Due to the limited space inside the thermostat water bath, four sensors were tested separately and four experiments were performed.

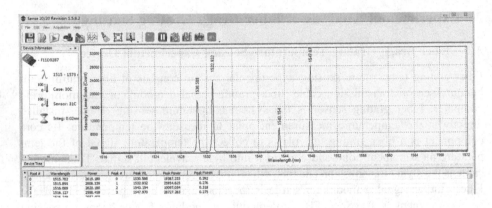

Fig. 2. Fiber Bragg grating wavelength display software

Using the measured four sets of data (that is, the center wavelength values measured by the four sensors at each temperature) and performing curve fitting respectively, the relationship between temperature and wavelength can be obtained. In this data processing system, the following relationship exists between temperature and wavelength:

$$y = ax^2 + bx + c \tag{4}$$

therefore, in the calibration experiment, this relationship is used as the calibration formula. Where: y represents temperature, x represents the center wavelength, a, b, c, are determined coefficients [10]. This experiment uses MATLAB for curve fitting, the coefficients a, b, c can be obtained. For sensor number 1001, the coefficients are:

$$a = -12.26$$
$$b = 37636.48$$
$$c = -28884422.84$$

Fitting curve is shown in Fig. 3.

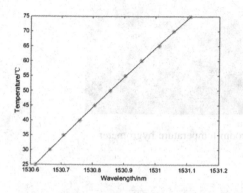 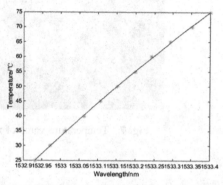

Fig. 3. Temperature fitting curve of sensor 1001

Fig. 4. Temperature fitting curve of sensor 1002

Similarly, Figs. 4, 5 and 6 show the temperature and wavelength fitting curves of the sensors 1002, 1003 and 1004, respectively.

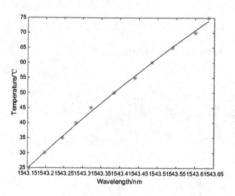 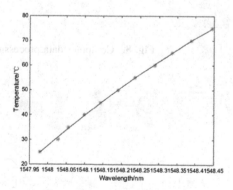

Fig. 5. Temperature fitting curve of sensor 1003

Fig. 6. Temperature fitting curve of sensor 1004

For different sensors, the values of parameters a, b, and c are different. The central wavelength values of each sensor recorded at each temperature are curve fitted to the temperature values, The values of the coefficients a, b, c for each sensor can be obtained and stored in the system for actual monitoring. When the room temperature meter is displayed as shown in Fig. 7, the computer data processing system interface displayed data is shown in Figs. 8 and 9.

Fig. 7. Temperature value of room temperature hygrometer

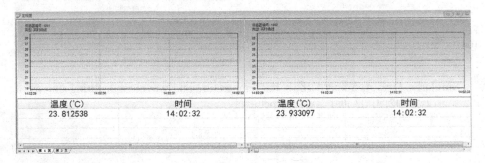

Fig. 8. Computer data processing system display interface (1)

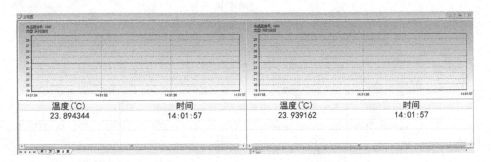

Fig. 9. Computer data processing system display interface (2)

3.3 Analysis of Experimental Results of Fiber Bragg Grating Temperature Sensing

It can be seen from Figs. 7 and 8 that the temperature measured by the fiber Bragg grating temperature sensor is very close to the actual ambient temperature, and the deviation is about 0.1 °C, further improving the accuracy of temperature measurement. There are two main reasons for the error: the inherent error in the working accuracy of the temperature measurement device and the fiber grating demodulator, and the measurement error caused by improper reading or timing when recording the data. When the experimental setup does not reach true thermal equilibrium, the recorded wavelength and temperature are not strictly corresponding.

For pure silica fiber used in this experiment, the thermal expansion coefficient of $\alpha = 5.5 \times 10^{-7}/°C$, thermal coefficient of $\zeta = 6.45 \times 10^{-6}/°C$, the center wavelength is 1530 nm, 1533 nm, 1543 nm, 1548 nm, respectively. Calculated by $K_T = \lambda_B(\alpha + \zeta)$, the temperature sensitivity theoretical values K_T of four fiber sensors are: 10.71 pm/°C, 10.73 pm/°C, 10.80 pm/°C, 10.83 pm/°C. By analyzing the results of the curve fitting in the experiment and combining Eq. (3), the temperature sensitivity coefficients of the four sensors can be obtained respectively: 9.88 pm/°C, 9.36 pm/°C, 9.60 pm/°C, 9.34 pm/°C, and the theoretical value is relatively close.

In summary, the temperature and wavelength fitting curves of FBG sensors show a good linear relationship. The temperature measurement error is less than 0.1 °C, which is able to meet the requirements of less than 0.3 °C in medical temperature measurement. It has practical application value.

4 Experimental Comparison

Since the temperature sensors in the thermostat water bath used in the calibration experiment are electromechanical sensors, these sensors are susceptible to electromagnetic interference and the measurement may be less than ideal. Therefore, it is very necessary to compare the wavelength measurement results of the FBG sensor under the heating condition of the thermostat water bath with the wavelength measurement result of the FBG sensor at room temperature. The temperature value at room temperature can be directly read out by the room temperature meter. In this paper, the number 1001 sensor is taken as the experimental object, the wavelength change is observed at the temperature range of 20 °C–30 °C at every 1 °C and is recorded after the temperature is stable. The comparison experiment was divided into two groups, which were conducted at room temperature and in a water bath heating environment.

The two sets of data measured by the fiber grating sensor under room temperature environment and water bath heating environment were respectively used to fit, and the obtained curves were shown in Figs. 10 and 11.

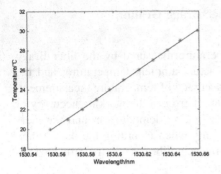

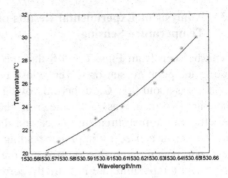

Fig. 10. At room temperature

Fig. 11. Under water bath heating condition

From Eq. (3) we can see that at room temperature, the sensitivity of FBG sensor is 10.3 pm/°C, while in a water bath environment, the sensitivity is 8.4 pm/°C. In addition, fiber grating temperature sensor curve fitting at real ambient temperature is more accurate. Under the environment of water bath heating, the measurement result of the FBG sensor is not higher than that measured directly at room temperature. This is because the electric temperature sensor in the thermostat water bath has been subjected to electromagnetic interference, which affects the measurement accuracy of the FBG sensor. Therefore, compared with the traditional electromechanical sensor, the fiber grating temperature sensor has obvious advantages.

5 Conclusion

A real-time monitoring of human body temperature based on FBG sensing technology was studied in this paper. Through the water bath experiment of the fiber grating temperature sensor, an accurate measurement of the temperature signal is achieved and the advantages of the fiber grating sensor are further verified. The results show that the center wavelength of FBG shows a good linear relationship with the temperature within the range of 25 °C–75 °C and has good accuracy. Temperature measurement error is less than 0.1 °C, which further improves the accuracy of temperature measurement. In addition, compared with the traditional electric sensors, the FBG temperature sensor has the advantages of good sensitivity, anti-electromagnetic interference and other prominent features, which can be used for the real-time monitoring of human body temperature. By using the characteristic of WDM sensing, the distributed sensing network can be constructed and the multi-channel temperature monitoring can be realized. The next step is to continue to improve the precision of the temperature sensor, the temperature sensitivity coefficient and the stability of the sensor work.

References

1. Song, D., Zhou, D., Li, G.: Study on the temperature sensing technology of medical fiber Bragg grating. Med. Equip. China **10**(4), 13–14 (2013)
2. Lixia, Yu., Qin, L.: Study on the improved fiber Bragg grating temperature detection system. Spectro. Spectral Anal. **36**(1), 283–286 (2016)
3. Zhang, S., Wang, J.: Application of fiber grating sensing technology in tunnel fire monitoring. Lasers Infrared **40**(2), 178–180 (2010)
4. Pang, D.: Research on novel fiber Bragg grating sensing technology. Shandong University, Shandong (2014)
5. Guoquan, X., Xiong, D.: Application of optical fiber sensing technology in engineering. China Opt. **6**(3), 306–314 (2013)
6. Yu, X., Li, H., Miao, C.: Research on human body temperature measurement models of intelligent clothing based on optical fiber Bragg grating. Opt. Tech. **37**(6), 704–708 (2011)
7. Yu, Q., Chen, H., Dong, Y.: Study on optical fiber Bragg grating temperature sensors for human body temperature monitoring. In: International Symposium on Photonics and Optoelectronics, Shanghai, China, pp. 460–468 (2012)
8. Zhang, Y., Wei, B., Huang, B.: Research on Bragg fiber optic body temperature detection system. Opt. Commun. Technol. **14**(1), 38–40 (2011)
9. Zhang, M.: Design of Software Platform for Bridge Security Optical Fiber Sensing Technology Monitoring System. Shandong University, Shandong (2015)
10. Li, X., Li, Y.: Research on fiber grating sensing system for measuring temperature distribution of seawater. J. North China Electric Power Univ. **38**(2), 80–83 (2011)

Revisiting Anonymous Two-Factor Authentication Schemes for Cloud Computing

Yaosheng Shen[1,3], Ding Wang[2,3], and Ping Wang[1,3,4(✉)]

[1] School of Electronic and Computer Engineering,
Peking University Shenzhen Graduate School, Shenzhen, China
[2] School of EECS, Peking University, Beijing 100871, China
[3] National Engineering Research Center for Software Engineering, Beijing, China
{ysshen,wangdingg,pwang}@pku.edu.cn
[4] School of Software and Microelectronics, Peking University, Beijing 100260, China

Abstract. Investigating the security pitfalls of cryptographic protocols is crucial to understanding how to improve security. At ICCCS'17, Wu and Xu proposed an efficient smart-card-based password authentication scheme to cope with the vulnerabilities in Jiang *et al.*'s scheme. However, in this paper, we reveal that Wu-Xu's scheme actually is subject to critical security defects, such as offline password guessing attack and replay attack. Besides security, user friendly is also another great concern. In 2017, Roy *et al.* found that in most previous two-factor schemes a user has to manage different credentials for different services, and further suggested a user-friendly scheme which is claimed to be suitable for multi-server architecture and robust against various attacks. In this work, we show that Roy et al.'s scheme cannot achieve truly two-factor security and is of poor scalability. Our results invalidate any use of the scrutinized schemes for cloud computing environments.

Keywords: Cloud computing · Two-factor authentication
Offline password guessing attack · User untraceability

1 Introduction

With the emerging paradigm of cloud computing, various services are provided over the cloud. As cloud-based services can be accessed anytime and anywhere just with a connection to the Internet, it is important to protect users and cloud servers from severe security threats, such as fraudulence, eavesdropping and falsification, posed either by external attackers or malicious internal entities. To guarantee that the resources and services can only be accessed by legitimate parties, user authentication plays an important part in securing electronic transactions by acquiring collaborative evidence. In 2011, Hao *et al.* [5] suggested the first two-factor authentication protocol which combines passwords and smart cards

© Springer Nature Switzerland AG 2018
X. Sun et al. (Eds.): ICCCS 2018, LNCS 11064, pp. 134–146, 2018.
https://doi.org/10.1007/978-3-030-00009-7_13

for the cloud computing environments. This initial work has brought about a number of enhanced proposals [9,16,24,25,27] with each different in terms of security, anonymity, usability and efficiency.

Without loss of generality, we consider the most common client-server architecture in which two participants (i.e. a server S and a user U) get involved in two-factor authentication. User U holds a memorable password and a smart card stored with some initial security parameters, and server S only needs to keep some secret key material of the system. Since there is no need to keep a table with password-related verification information on the server side, the server is free from the threat of password dataset leaks and ameliorated from the burden of maintaining a large password dataset. This feature that makes this type of schemes rather desirable, considering that there are incessant leakages of password databases from large websites [1]. The most important security goal of this kind of schemes is the so-called "two-factor security" [23]. This security concept essentially means that only the user who has the smart card as well as knows the right password can be verified by the server.

Most of existing two-factor schemes (e.g., [9,16,25]) for cloud computing are built on the basis of generic two-factor schemes like [24,29]. Nevertheless, past research [7,12,13,21] have, again and again, proved that designing a "password+smart-card" two-factor authentication scheme that can attain "two-factor security" is a tough task. In 2009, Xu et al. [28] developed such a two-factor authentication scheme relying on the intractability of computational Deffie-Hellman problem, and stated that their scheme is able to support "two-factor security" under the hypothesis that smart cards can be tampered. In addition, their scheme was "proved secure" in the random oracle model. Later on, Sood et al. [19] however illustrated that Xu et al.'s scheme cannot resist against user impersonation attack if the parameters kept in the smart cards can be extracted, invalidating Xu et al.'s claim of ensuring "two-factor security". In 2010, Song [18] independently found this severe flaw in Xu et al.'s scheme. Furthermore, Song presented an improvement to counter the problem emerged in Xu et al.'s scheme.

In 2012, Chen et al. [3] pointed out that various security drawbacks still existed in both Sood et al.'s [19] and Song's [18] schemes. More specifically, Sood et al.'s scheme is unable to withstand server impersonation attack and Song's scheme is vulnerable to offline password guessing attack, in case the attacker can obtain those sensitive information kept in the smart card. Chen et al. [3] also put forward an improvement and argued that their improvement is robust under the condition that the sensitive data in smart card has been revealed by the attacker. It should be noted that, recent rapid developments in side-channel attacks have proved that the sensitive information kept in general commercial smart cards could be extracted by power analysis or reverse engineering [11,15]. Based on a weak yet realistic assumption, Chen et al.'s scheme [3] appears very practical.

However, soon after Chen et al.'s scheme [3] was presented, Ma et al. [13] figured out that it is susceptible to exactly the same problem (i.e., prone to offline password guessing attack and no supply of forward secrecy) with the original scheme (i.e., Song's scheme [18]). Based on their past experience of protocol design and analysis, for the first time Ma *et al.* [13] suggested three generic principles for designing a secure and efficient two-factor protocol, namely, the public-key principle, the forward secrecy principle and the security-usability balance principle. Nevertheless, none of the two-factor authentication protocols mentioned above can satisfy all these three design principles and moreover, as we illustrate, all the schemes studied in this work fail to comply with at least one of these principles.

In 2017, Wu and Xu [26] also observed that previous schemes (e.g., [3,18]) are prone to various security loopholes (e.g., user impersonation attack and insider attack), and also developed an enhanced scheme. Wu-Xu argued that their new scheme not only eradicates the security pitfalls being overlooked in previous schemes but also maintains strengths of previous schemes. Notwithstanding their claims, we will show that this scheme still has serval serious defects be overlooked: (1) It cannot withstand offline password guessing attack once the parameters in smart card can be extracted out, which means that the primary goal of "truly two-factor security" cannot be satisfied with; (2) It is subject to replay attack; (3) It ensures no timely typo detection.

More recently, Roy *et al.* [17] found that, in Tsai-Lo's scheme [20], a user has to manage different credentials for different services, and further suggested a user-friendly scheme which is claimed to be suitable for multi-server architecture and robust against various attacks. Therefore, this protocol shows a good application potential in multi-server cloud computing environments. In this work, we show that Roy et al.'s scheme cannot provide truly two-factor security and user untraceability. We observe that the first failure of Roy *et al.*'s scheme is due in large part to the non-compliance with Ma et al.'s [13] security-usability tradeoff principle. Our attacks highlights the necessity of being aware of basic protocol design principles.

The remainder of the paper is organized as follows: We review Wu-Xu's scheme in Section 2, and describe its security loopholes in Sect. 3; Roy et al.'s scheme are presented in Section 4 and cryptanalyzed in Sect. 5; Finally, we conclude the paper in Sect. 6.

2   Cryptanalysis of Wu-Xu's Scheme

In this section, we briefly review the chaotic-map based authentication scheme for cloud computing proposed by Wu and Xu [26] in ICCCS 2017. Their scheme consists of four phases: initialization, registration, authentication and password change. For better presentation, we will follow the notations in Wu-Xu's scheme as closely as possible and list the notations in Table 1.

Table 1. Notations and abbreviations

Symbol	Description
U_i	i^{th} user
S	Remote server
$\mathcal{M}$	Malicious attacker
ID_i	Identity of user U_i
PW_i	Password of user U_i
x	The secret key of remote server S
$\oplus$	The bitwise XOR operation
$\parallel$	The string concatenation operation
$h(\cdot)$	Collision free one-way hash function
$A \rightarrow B : C$	Message C is transferred through an open channel from A to B
$A \Rightarrow B : C$	Message C is transferred through a secure channel from A to B

2.1 Registration Phase

At the beginning, the server S creates a random positive number $s \in Z_p^*$ and a symmetric key cryptosystem with $E_k(.)$ and $D_k(.)$, then chooses a secret key x, and two one-way hash functions $h(.)$ and $h_1(.)$.

Step R1. U_i chooses her identity ID_i, PW_i and b_i, then computes $HPW_i = h(PW_i \parallel b_i)$

Step R2. $U_i \Rightarrow S : \{ID_i, HPW_i\}$.

Step R3. S selects a random integer r_i, computes $IM_i = E_x((ID_i \oplus r_i) \parallel r_i)$ and $B_1 = h(ID_i \parallel HPW_i) \oplus HPW_i \oplus h(x \parallel IM_i)$, and stores IM_i, B_1, $h(.)$, $E_k(.)/D_k(.)$, s and p into the smart card.

Step R4. $S \Rightarrow U_i$: A smart card containing $IM_i, B_1, E_k(.)/D_k(.), h(.), s, p$.

Step R5. U_i computes $B_2 = h(ID_i \parallel PW_i) \oplus b_i$ and stores B_2 into the card.

2.2 Login and Mutual Authentication Phase

When wanting to login, U_i performs as follows:

Step 1. U_i inserts the smart card into card reader and inputs ID_i and PW_i.

Step 2. Smart card computes $b_i' = B_2 \oplus h(ID_i \parallel PW_i)$.

Step 3. Smart card generates two random integers $u \in [1, p + 1]$ and r_u and computes $HPW_i = h(PW_i \parallel b_i')$, $C_1 = T_u(s)$, $C_2 = B_1 \oplus h(ID_i \parallel HPW_i)$, $C_3 = h(ID_i \parallel C_1 \parallel C_2 \parallel r_u)$, $C_4 = C_2 \oplus C_3$, $C_5 = EC_3(ID_i \parallel C_1 \parallel r_u)$.

Step 4. Smart card$\rightarrow S : \{C_4, IM_i, C_5\}$.

Step 5. On receiving the message from U_i, S decrypts IM_i and gets ID_i' and r_i', then computes $C_2' = h(x \parallel IM_i)$, $C_3' = C_4 \oplus C_2'$.

Step 6. S decrypts C_5 to obtain ID_i'', C_1', and r_u', then checks if $ID_i' \overset{?}{=} ID_i''$ and $C_3' \overset{?}{=} h(ID_i' \parallel C_1' \parallel C_2' \parallel r_u')$. If both verifications are correct, S proceeds. Otherwise, the login request is interrupted.

Step 7. S prefers three random numbers $v \in [1, p+1]$, r_s and r_i^{new}, computes $IM_i' = E_x((ID_i' \oplus r_i^{new}) \parallel r_i^{new})$, $C_6 = T_v(s)$, $sk_s = T_v(C_1')$, $C_7 = h(x \parallel IM_i')$, $C_8 = h_1(ID_i' \parallel IM_i' \parallel C_1' \parallel C_2' \parallel C_6 \parallel C_7 \parallel sk_s \parallel r_s)$, $C_9 = C_2' \oplus C_8$, $C_{10} = E_{C_8}(IM_i' \parallel C_6 \parallel C_7 \parallel r_s)$, where sk_s is server-side session key.

Step 8. $S \rightarrow U_i : \{C_9, C_{10}\}$.

Step 9. Smart card calculates $C_8' = C_9 \oplus C_2$ and obtains IM_i'', C_6', C_7', r_s' by decrypting C_{10}. Smart card further computes $sk_u = T_u(C_6')$ and checks $C_8' \overset{?}{=} h_1(ID_i \parallel IM_i'' \parallel C_1 \parallel C_2 \parallel C_6' \parallel C_7' \parallel sk_u \parallel r_s')$. If they are unequal, U_i aborts the protocol. Otherwise, smart card computes $B_1' = C_2 \oplus C_7' \oplus B_1$ and replaces (B_1, IM_i) with (B_1', IM_i'').

3 Flaws in Wu-Xu's Scheme

In this section, the security loopholes of Wu-Xu's scheme [26] will be pointed out. More specifically, it cannot resist offline password guessing attack and suffers from replay attack, which make this scheme unpractical for real use. Before giving the detailed security analysis, we first define the various adversary models for smart-card-based password authentication.

3.1 Adversary Models

To analyze the security provisions of password-based authentication schemes with smart cards, generally three assumptions about the attacker's capabilities are made since the landmark work of Yang et al. [29], and we summarize them as follows:

Assumption 1. The malicious attacker $\mathcal{M}$ is able to eavesdrop, delete, insert, modify or block any transcripts communicated in the public channel. That is to say, the communication channel between the common users and the server can be completely manipulated by $\mathcal{M}$. This well complies with the standard adversary model that is widely accepted for distributed computing [4];

Assumption 2. The malicious attacker $\mathcal{M}$ can somehow got the victim user's smart card and use side-channel attack techniques to acquire sensitive security parameters from the card memory, which is realistic according to the recent research advancements in side-channel attacks [11,15];

Assumption 3. User's password space is very constrained and the malicious attacker $\mathcal{M}$ can offline enumerate it. To be user-friendly, most protocols (e.g., the ones in [10,24,29]) enable the users to select their own password at will in the initial process of registration or later process of password change. Because human beings are incapable of memorizing random strings, instead they are likely to choose passwords that relate to their personal lives or short strings for convenience. As a result, these human generated passwords often are very weak and belong to a small dictionary.

Obviously, if both *Assumptions* 2 and 3 hold simultaneously, then an attacker (without any other assumptions/abilities) can successfully impersonate a victim user and any scheme is trivially insecure. Therefore, it is widely regarded that attackers should not be granted to obtain a victim user's smart card as well as his password [8,24,29].

In [26], Wu and Xu reported that their scheme is secure under the above three assumptions. For example, they stated that their scheme can resist offline password guessing attacks even when the security parameters in smart card have been extracted. However, contrary to their claims, we will illustrate that this scheme is still prone to offline guessing as well as other pitfalls. Based on the above listed assumptions, we cryptanalyze the security provisions of Wu-Xu's scheme in the following, and assume that $\mathcal{M}$ can extract the secret data $\{B_1, B_2, h(\cdot), E_k(\cdot), D_k(\cdot)\}$ stored in U_i's smart card, and $\mathcal{M}$ can also eavesdrop the messages $\{C_4, IM_i, C_5\}$ exchanged between the parties.

3.2 Offline Password Guessing Attack

It is known that password-based authentication schemes are apt to be subject to two kinds of attacks regarding guessing [7,23], i.e., offline password guessing and online password guessing, due to the limited size of the password space. Among them, the online guessing can be relatively easily detected due to the abnormal number of login requests issued by the attacker against the victim account within a short duration, and thus it can be countered by rate-limiting [2]. In contrast, offline password guessing attack cannot be easily detected. In this attack, the attacker $\mathcal{M}$ first attempts to look for some pieces of information that can be exploited as the comparison target of his password guesses, and then locally determines the exactly correct password by repeatedly testing all the candidates. Since this attack is executed without online communication with the server, there is no means for the server to detect and thwart. Consequently, offline password guessing is considered to be a more serious threat.

Wu and Xu [26], claimed that an attacker is unable to, in an offline manner, determine a user's password even if the sensitive data B_1 has been revealed from user's smart card. However, the following attacking procedure illustrates that this claim is not tenable. Suppose that U_i's smart card is lost/stolen and the attacker $\mathcal{M}$ obtains it. Then $\mathcal{M}$ extracts the content $\{B_1, B_2, h(\cdot)\}$ by using the methods introduced in [15]. The following procedure describes our proposed offline password guessing attack:

Step 1. $\mathcal{M}$ choose a pair (ID_i^*, PW_i^*) from the identity space $\mathcal{D}_{ID}$ and password space $\mathcal{D}_{PW}$, respectively.

Step 2. $\mathcal{M}$ computes $b_i^* = B_2 \oplus h(ID_i^* \| PW_i^*)$, where B_2 is revealed from U_i's smart card.

Step 3. $\mathcal{M}$ computes $C_2^* = B_1 \oplus h(ID_i^*\|h(PW_i^*\|b_i^*)) \oplus h(PW_i^*\|b_i^*)$, where B_1 is extracted from U_i's smart card.

Step 4. $\mathcal{M}$ calculates $C_3^* = C_2^* \oplus C_4$, where C_4 is eavesdropped from the open channel.

Step 5. $\mathcal{M}$ decrypts C_5 by using C_3^* to obtain $ID_i' \oplus C_1' \oplus r_u'$, where C_5 is eavesdropped from the open channel.

Step 6. $\mathcal{M}$ calculates $C_3^* = h(ID_i^*\|C_1'\|C_2^*\|r_u')$;

Step 7. $\mathcal{M}$ examines the authenticity of (ID_i^*, PW_i^*) pair by verifying if $C_4 \overset{?}{=} C_2^* \oplus C_3^*$.

Step 8. $\mathcal{M}$ return to Step 1 of this procedure until the right pair of (ID_i, PW_i) is obtained or all pairs in $\mathcal{D}_{ID} \times \mathcal{D}_{PW}$ are exhausted.

It is obvious that the above procedure is with a time complexity of $\{\mathcal{O}(|\mathcal{D}_{ID}|* |\mathcal{D}_{PW}|)\} * (T_D + 4T_H + 7T_X)$, where T_E, T_H and T_X denote the execution time of modular exponentiation, hash and XOR operation, respectively. Based on the results reported in [6,23], the offline password guessing attack is able to be carried out in seconds on a common computer, for in practice the size of identity space $\mathcal{D}_{ID}$ and the size of dictionary space $\mathcal{D}_{PW}$ are rather limited and $\mathcal{M}$ could try all the possible passwords through an offline method [8,13]. All in all, the attacker $\mathcal{M}$ can guess (ID_i, PW_i) within polynomial time bound, it follows that our suggested attack is indeed effective.

3.3 Replay Attack

Resistance to replay attack is a very basic security goal of any cryptographic protocol [23,29]. However, Wu-Xu's scheme fails to achieve this goal. More specifically, Wu-Xu's scheme employs random numbers but not timestamps to achieve the freshness of messages. Yet, this scheme has only two protocol flows, making it inherently vulnerable to replay attack. As is well known that, any two-flow random number based scheme is unable to achieve explicit authentication while resisting replay attack, because $\mathcal{M}$ can simply replay the first message of a successful protocol run to impersonate the legitimate user, and the server can never know whether the replayed message is fresh or not unless the server maintains a table of all received messages. However, maintaining a table of all received messages is practically undesirable. In all, replay attack is quite realistic against Wu-Xu's scheme.

4   Review of Roy *et al.*'s Scheme

In this section, we first concisely review Roy *et al.*'s scheme [17] proposed in 2017. This scheme improves over Tsai-Lo's scheme [20] and aims to attain forward secrecy that is lacked in Tsai-Lo's scheme. Roy et al.'s protocol involves three participants, i.e., the mobile user (MU_i), the cloud server (CS_j) and registration center (RC). Five phases are involved in their scheme: registration, login, authentication and key establishment, password change, and revocation of mobile device. The notations and initial system parameters employed in Roy *et al.*'s scheme are same as employed in the scheme of Wu-Xu (see Table 1).

4.1   Mobile User Registration

Step 1. MU_i chooses her identity ID_i, password PW_i, biometrics B_i and two 128-bit random numbers b and k.

Step 2. MU_i produces $(\theta_i, \phi_i) = Gen(B_i)$ and computes the masked password $RPWB_i = H(ID_i \parallel H(PW_i \parallel \theta_i \parallel b))$.

Step 3. $MU_i \Rightarrow RC : \{ID_i, (RPWB_i \oplus k)\}$.

Step 4. RC selects an 1024-bit master secret key X_j for server CS_j. RC also selects an 1024-bit random number r_{ij} for each MU_i and CS_j pair.

Step 5. RC computes $A_{ij} = H(H(ID_i \oplus r_{ij}) \parallel X_j)$, $V_{ij} = A_{ij} \oplus RPWB_i$ and $RID_{S_j} = H(ID_{S_j} \parallel X_j)$ as the pseudo-identity of CS_j.

Step 6. RC selects a unique and random temporary identity TID_i for MU_i and saves n server key-plus-id combinations $\{TID_i, (ID_{S_j}, V_{ij}, RID_{S_j}) | 1 \leq j \leq n\}$ in mobile device of MU_i.

Step 7. $RC \Rightarrow MU_i$: A mobile device contains $\{TID_i, (IDS_j, V_{ij}, RID_{S_j}) | 1 \leq j \leq n\}$.

Step 8. MU_i computes $D_i^1 = H(PW_i \parallel \theta_i) \oplus b$, $D_i^2 = H(ID_i \parallel PW_i \parallel \theta_i \parallel b)$, $V'_{ij} = V_{ij} \oplus k = A_{ij} \oplus H(ID_i \parallel H(PW_i \parallel \theta_i \parallel b))$, $RID_{ij} = TID_i \oplus H(ID_i \parallel V'_{ij})$ and $RID'_{S_j} = RID_{S_j} \oplus H(\theta_i \parallel b)$ for $1 \leq j \leq n$.

Finally, MU_i stores ϕ_i, D_i^1, D_i^2, V'_{ij}s, RID_{ij}s and RID'_{S_j}s into her own mobile device, and deletes V_{ij}s, TID_i and RID_{S_j}s from the mobile device.

4.2   Cloud Server Registration

Step 1. CS_j chooses her identity ID_{S_j}.

Step 2. $CS_j \Rightarrow RC : \{ID_{S_j}\}$.

Step 3. RC provides the master secret key X_j to each CS_j.

Step 4. For all MU_is, the RC saves the credentials $\{TID_i, (ID_i, r_{ij})\}$ (for $1 \leq i \leq m$) in database of CS_j, and also stores $\{ID_{S_j}, X_j\}$ in the database of CS_j.

Finally, RC saves pair (ID_i, SN_i) in its own database, where SN_i is the serial number of MU_i's mobile device.

4.3   Login Phase

When wanting to login to CS_j, MU_i performs the following operations:

Step L1. MU_i inputs her identity ID_i, password PW_i and biometrics B'_i into her own mobile device. MU_i computes $\theta_i = Rep(B'_i, \phi_i)$ with ϕ_i through the fuzzy extractor reproduction procedure and generates $b' = D_i^1 \oplus H(PW_i \parallel \theta_i)$ with the stored parameter D_i^1, MU_i.

Step L2. MU_i computes $H(ID_i \parallel PW_i \parallel \theta_i \parallel b')$ and checks whether $D_i^2 = H(ID_i \parallel PW_i \parallel \theta_i \parallel b')$. An equality indicates that MU_i is legal.

Step L3. MU_i calculates $RPWB_i = H(ID_i \parallel H(PW_i \parallel \theta_i \parallel b'))$. MU_i also generates $A_{ij} = V'_{ij} \oplus RPBW_i$ using the device parameter V'_{ij}.

Step L4. MU_i selects an 128 bit random number RN_i, generates the current timestamp TS_i, and then computes $C_1 = A_{ij} \oplus RN_i \oplus TS_i \oplus H(IDS_j)$, $H_1 = H(ID_i \parallel C_1 \parallel RN_i \parallel TS_i)$, $TID_i = RID_{ij} \oplus H(ID_i \parallel V'_{ij})$, $RIDS_j = RID'_{S_j} \oplus H(\theta_i \parallel b')$, $TID_i^* = TID_i \oplus H(RIDS_j \parallel TS_i)$.

Step L5. $MU_i \rightarrow CS_j : \{TID_i^*, C_1, H_1, TS_i\}$.

4.4 Authentication Phase

In this phase, CS_j and MU_i mutually verify each other and agree on a session key. Since this phase is unrelated to our discussions, we omit it.

5 Flaws in Roy *et al.*'s Scheme

Recall that the three assumptions listed in Sect. 3 are also clearly made in Roy *et al.*'s scheme. However, we observe that this scheme still remains feasible for an attacker to offline guess a user's password and break forward secrecy. This means that the primary goal of "truly two-factor security" cannot be satisfied with. In addition, the scheme cannot provide forward secrecy and sound scalability.

5.1 Offline Password Guessing Attack

Note that Roy et al.'s scheme [17] is originally a three-factor one, here we are only interested in its two-factor version by assuming that the third factor (i.e., the biometric) has been known to $\mathcal{A}$. This is realistic as user biometrics are constant during their lives, and how to protect user biometric template is still an open issue [14]. We find that this scheme cannot achieve truly two-factor security: it is subject to two types of offline password guessing attack. This in turn indicates that it cannot achieve truly three-factor security.

Type-I Attack. Suppose U_i's biometric B_i and the secret parameters $\{D_i^1, D_i^2, \varphi_i, h(\cdot)\}$ stored in the smart card are somehow obtained by $\mathcal{A}$. At this point, $\mathcal{A}$ can find out U_i's identity and password as follows:

Step 1. Guesses U_i's identity ID_i^* and password PW_i^* from dictionary space $\mathcal{D}_{id}$ and $\mathcal{D}_{pw}$.

Step 2. Computes $\theta_i = Rep(B_i, \varphi_i)$, $b^* = H(PW_i \parallel \theta_i) \oplus D_i^1$, where D_i^1 is extracted from the smart card.

Step 3. Computes $D_i^{2*} = H(ID_i^* \parallel PW_i^* \parallel \theta_i \parallel b^*)$, where θ_i is extracted from the smart card.

Step 4. Checks the validity of (ID_i^*, PW_i^*) by comparing the calculated D_i^{2*} with the extracted D_i^2.

Step 5. Repeats Step 1–4 until find the correct pair of (ID_i^*, PW_i^*).

The time complexity of this attack is $\mathcal{O}(|\mathcal{D}_{id}| * |\mathcal{D}_{pw}| * 2T_H + T_B)$ [23,24]. Generally, it is only needed to calculate the bio-hashing function once, thus T_B can be ignored in practice. According to the running time in [23], $\mathcal{A}$ may complete the above attacking procedure within 17.6 days on a Laptop. This issue arises due to the inherent "usability-security tension": to achieve local password change (i.e., C-2 in [24]) and timely typo detection (i.e., C-9 in [24]), there is an explicit password verifier $D_i^2 = H(ID_i \parallel PW_i \parallel \theta_i \parallel b)$ stored in U_i's smart card, yet this verifier leads to a Type-I offline password attack.

To eliminate this security issue without loss of usability, a promising countermeasure is to adopt the "fuzzy-verifier" technique [13] and store $D_i^2 = h((H(ID_i \parallel PW_i \parallel \theta_i \parallel b)) \bmod n)$ in U_i's smart card, where n determines the capacity of (ID, PW) pair, $2^4 \leq n \leq 2^8$. In this way, even if $\mathcal{A}$ obtains D_i^2, she can not determine the correct (ID, PW) from the above attack, because there will be $\frac{|\mathcal{D}_{id}*\mathcal{D}_{pw}|}{n} \approx 2^{32}$ candidate (ID, PW) pairs that make $D_i^{2*} = D_i^2$ in Step 4. To further identify the exactly correct (ID, PW) pair, $\mathcal{A}$ needs to interact with the server, and we can adopt the "honeywords" technique [22,24] to confine $\mathcal{A}$'s advantage to a very limited value.

Type-II Attack. In the above attack, $\mathcal{A}$ does not need the protocol messages. In this attack, we presume that $\mathcal{A}$ can somehow obtain user's smart card and extract its secret parameters $\{D_i^1, D_i^2, V_{ij}', \varphi_i, h(\cdot)\}$, and also can eavesdrop the login messages $\{TID_i^*, C_1, H_1, TS_i\}$ from the open channel. Now, $\mathcal{A}$ can *offline* guess U_i's password and identity simultaneously as follows:

Step 1. Pick a pair of ID_i^*, PW_i^* from dictionary space $\mathcal{D}_{id}$ and $\mathcal{D}_{pw}$.
Step 2. Computes $\theta_i = Rep(B_i, \varphi_i)$, $b^* = H(PW_i \parallel \theta_i) \oplus D_i^1$, where D_i^1 is extracted from the smart card.
Step 3. Computes $A_{ij}^* = V_{ij}' \oplus H(ID_i^* \parallel H(PW_i^* \parallel \theta_i \parallel b^*))$.
Step 4. Computes $RN_i^* = C_1 \oplus A_{ij}^* \oplus TS_i \oplus H(ID_{S_j})$;
Step 5. Computes $H_1^* = H(ID_i^* \parallel C_1 \parallel RN_i^* \parallel TS_i)$;
Step 6. Checks the correctness of (ID_i^*, PW_i^*) by comparing if the calculated H_1^* equals the intercepted H_1.
Step 7. Repeats Step 1–6 of the above procedure until find the correct value of (ID_i^*, PW_i^*).

To conduct the above attack, the time complexity is $\mathcal{O}(|\mathcal{D}_{id}| * |\mathcal{D}_{pw}| * (5T_H + T_B))$, and $\mathcal{A}$ may complete the procedure within 44 days on a Laptop. In comparison, the Type-I attack is more practical.

5.2   No Forward Secrecy

A scheme that supports forward secrecy ensures that, even after the long-term private key(s) of one or more participants were leaked, previously agreed session keys remain secure [21]. This is important, especially when considering the serious situations of today's clouds like the compromise of cloud servers (e.g., [1]).

If an attacker $\mathcal{M}$ has obtained the server CS_j's long-term key X_j from the breached server S and intercepted the messages $\{TID_i^*, C_1, H_1, TS_i\}$ that are exchanged between U_i and S's authentication process from the public channel. $\mathcal{M}$ is able to figure out the session key using the following method:

Step 1. $\mathcal{M}$ computes $RID_{S_j} = H(ID_{S_j} \parallel X_j)$, extracts $TID_i = TID_i^* \oplus H(RID_{S_j} \parallel TS_i)$

Step 2. $\mathcal{M}$ computes $A_{ji} = H(H(ID_i \oplus r_{ij}) \parallel X_j)$, $RN_j = C_1 \oplus TS_i \oplus H(ID_{S_j}) \oplus A_{ji}$, $M_1 = C_1 \oplus TS_i \oplus H(ID_{S_j}) \oplus B_{ji}$;

Step 3. $\mathcal{M}$ gets the session key $sk = H(ID_i \parallel ID_{S_j} \parallel A_{ji} \parallel M_1 \parallel RN_j \parallel TS_i \parallel TS_j)$.

With the session key sk computed, the entire session will be no secret to $\mathcal{M}$.

5.3   Poor Scalability

In Roy *et al.*'s scheme, the user side stores all the cloud servers (i.e., $CS_j, 1 \leq j \leq n$) related information: $RID_{ij} = TID_i \oplus H(ID_i \parallel V'_{ij})$ and $RID'_{S_j} = RID_{S_j} \oplus H(\theta_i \parallel b)$ for $1 \leq j \leq n$. This means that, when a new server arrives, all the users have to re-register with the registration center RC. This show poor scalability. Similarly, the server side stores all the users (i.e., $U_i, 1 \leq i \leq m$) related information: the credentials $\{TID_i, (ID_i, r_{ij})\}$ (for $1 \leq i \leq m$) in database of CS_j. This means that, when a new user arrives, all the servers have to re-register with the registration center RC.

6   Conclusion

A large mount of efforts have been directed to the design of smart-card-based password authentication scheme, yet it is still an open challenge to devise an efficient, secure and privacy-preserving scheme based on the assumption that smart cards can be tampered. Very recently, Wu-Xu and Roy *et al.* made two another attempts. However, through careful analysis we show that all of them still have several serious drawbacks being overlooked. Taken our attacks in mind, we are considering to design an efficient scheme with provable security.

Acknowledgments. This research was supported by the National Natural Science Foundation of China under Grants No. 61472016, and by the National Key Research and Development Plan under Grants Nos. 2016YFB0800603 and 2017YFB1200700.

References

1. All Data Breach Sources, February 2018. https://breachalarm.com/all-sources
2. Alsaleh, M., Mannan, M., Van Oorschot, P.: Revisiting defenses against large-scale online password guessing attacks. IEEE Trans. Dependable Secur. Comput. **9**(1), 128–141 (2012)
3. Chen, B., Kuo, W.: Robust smart-card-based remote user password authentication scheme. Int. J. Commun. Syst. **27**(2), 377–389 (2014)
4. Dolev, D., Yao, A.: On the security of public key protocols. IEEE Trans. Inf. Theory **29**(2), 198–208 (1983)

5. Hao, Z., Zhong, S., Yu, N.: A time-bound ticket-based mutual authentication scheme for cloud computing. Int. J. Comput. Commun. Control **6**(2), 227–235 (2011)
6. He, D., Chen, J., Hu, J.: An ID-based client authentication with key agreement protocol for mobile client-server environment on ECC with provable security. Inf. Fusion **13**(3), 223–230 (2012)
7. Huang, X., Chen, X., Li, J., Xiang, Y., Xu, L.: Further observations on smart-card-based password-authenticated key agreement in distributed systems. IEEE Trans. Parallel Distrib. Syst. **25**(7), 1767–1775 (2014)
8. Islam, S.: Design and analysis of an improved smartcard-based remote user password authentication scheme. Int. J. Commun. Syst. **29**(11), 1708–1719 (2016)
9. Jiang, Q., Khan, M.K., Lu, X., Ma, J., He, D.: A privacy preserving three-factor authentication protocol for e-Health clouds. J. Supercomput. **72**(10), 3826–3849 (2016)
10. Jiang, Q., Ma, J., Li, G., Li, X.: Improvement of robust smart-card-based password authentication scheme. Int. J. Commun. Syst. **28**(2), 383–393 (2014)
11. Kocher, P., Jaffe, J., Jun, B.: Differential power analysis. In: Wiener, M. (ed.) CRYPTO 1999. LNCS, vol. 1666, pp. 388–397. Springer, Heidelberg (1999). https://doi.org/10.1007/3-540-48405-1_25
12. Li, X., Niu, J., Liao, J., Liang, W.: Cryptanalysis of a dynamic identity-based remote user authentication scheme with verifiable password update. Int. J. Commun. Syst. **28**(2), 374–382 (2015)
13. Ma, C.G., Wang, D., Zhao, S.D.: Security flaws in two improved remote user authentication schemes using smart cards. Int. J. Commun. Syst. **27**(10), 2215–2227 (2014)
14. Memon, N.: How biometric authentication poses new challenges to our security and privacy [in the spotlight]. IEEE Signal Process. Mag. **34**(4), 194–196 (2017)
15. Messerges, T.S., Dabbish, E.A., Sloan, R.H.: Examining smart-card security under the threat of power analysis attacks. IEEE Trans. Comput. **51**(5), 541–552 (2002)
16. Odelu, V., Das, A.K., Kumari, S., Huang, X., Wazid, M.: Provably secure authenticated key agreement scheme for distributed mobile cloud computing services. Future. Gener. Comput. Syst. **68**, 74–88 (2017)
17. Roy, S., Chatterjee, S., Das, A.K., Chattopadhyay, S., Kumar, N., Vasilakos, A.V.: On the design of provably secure lightweight remote user authentication scheme for mobile cloud computing services. IEEE Access **5**, 25808–25825 (2017)
18. Song, R.: Advanced smart card based password authentication protocol. Comput. Stand. Interfaces **32**(5), 321–325 (2010)
19. Sood, S.K., Sarje, A.K., Singh, K.: An improvement of Xu et al'.s authentication scheme using smart cards. In: Proceedings of ACM COMPUTE 2010, pp. 1–5. ACM (2010)
20. Tsai, J.L., Lo, N.W.: A privacy-aware authentication scheme for distributed mobile cloud computing services. IEEE Syst. J. **9**(3), 805–815 (2015)
21. Wang, C., Xu, G.: Cryptanalysis of three password-based remote user authentication schemes with non-tamper resistant smart card. Secur. Commun. Netw. (2017). https://doi.org/10.1002/sec.817
22. Wang, D., Cheng, H., Wang, P., Yan, J., Huang, X.: A security analysis of honeywords. In: Proceedings of NDSS 2018, pp. 1–16. ISOC (2018)
23. Wang, D., He, D., Wang, P., Chu, C.H.: Anonymous two-factor authentication in distributed systems: certain goals are beyond attainment. IEEE Trans. Dependable Secur. Comput. **12**(4), 428–442 (2015)

24. Wang, D., Wang, P.: Two birds with one stone: two-factor authentication with security beyond conventional bound. IEEE Trans. Dependable Secur. Comput. **15**(4), 708–722 (2018). https://doi.org/10.1109/TDSC.2016.2605087
25. Wei, F., Zhang, R., Ma, C.: A provably secure anonymous two-factor authenticated key exchange protocol for cloud computing. Fundam. Inform. **157**(1), 201–220 (2018)
26. Wu, F., Xu, L.: A chaotic map-based authentication and key agreement scheme with user anonymity for cloud computing. In: Sun, X., Chao, H.-C., You, X., Bertino, E. (eds.) ICCCS 2017. LNCS, vol. 10603, pp. 189–200. Springer, Cham (2017). https://doi.org/10.1007/978-3-319-68542-7_16
27. Xie, Q., Wong, D.S., Wang, G.: Provably secure dynamic ID-based anonymous two-factor authenticated key exchange protocol with extended security model. IEEE Trans. Inf. Forensics Secur. **12**(6), 1382–1392 (2017)
28. Xu, J., Zhu, W., Feng, D.: An improved smart card based password authentication scheme with provable security. Comput. Stand. Interfaces **31**(4), 723–728 (2009)
29. Yang, G.M., Wong, D.S., Wang, H.X., Deng, X.T.: Two-factor mutual authentication based on smart cards and passwords. J. Comput. Syst. Sci. **74**(7), 1160–1172 (2008)

Serialization of Lifecycles in ACBP Model as Regular Expressions

Junbao Zhang, Guohua Liu$^{(\boxtimes)}$, and Zhao Chen

School of Computer Science and Technology,
Donghua University, Shanghai 201600, China
junbaozb0451@163.com, {ghliu,chenzhao}@dhu.edu.cn

Abstract. Dictated by government regulations and user requirements, organizations are driven to change their business process continuously. The task of understanding current business process is one of the key stages in a business process improvement project. In Artifact-Centric Business Process (ACBP) modeling paradigm, figuring out the relationships between lifecycles is important to understanding the whole business process. To improve the efficiency of com-prehending the relationships, we serialize lifecycles of an ACBP model as regular expressions. By serializing the lifecycles, its presentation is transformed from graph to string, so that multiple lifecycles can be presented simultaneously. Combined with text searching and highlighting techniques, ad-hoc query and analysis can be implemented easily. From the experiment result, the efficiency of figuring out relationships between lifecycles is greatly improved in terms of time cost and accuracy.

Keywords: Artifact-Centric Business Process · Lifecycle · Regular expression Serialization

1 Introduction

Recently, service-oriented architecture (SOA) has become a predominant tool for facilitating businesses to meet the changing requirements of the market. SOA particularly enables the business collaboration across organizations by composing Web services to achieve a mutual business goal without comprising the autonomy of participating organizations. Business process environments are complex and changes of the collaboration are ubiquity. Organizations are undergoing rapid and significant process improvements under the pressure of government regulations, user requirements and growing global competition.

This research has been financially supported by grants from the National Key R&D Program of China (No. 2017YFB0309800), the National Natural Science Foundation of China (No. 61702094), the Young Scientists' Sailing Project of Science and Technology Commission of Shanghai Municipal (No. 17YF1427400) and the Fundamental Research Funds for the Central Universities (No. 17D111206).

X. Sun et al. (Eds.): ICCCS 2018, LNCS 11064, pp. 147–156, 2018.
https://doi.org/10.1007/978-3-030-00009-7_14

According to the Model-based and Integrated Process Improvement methodology for implementing process-based change and improvement, understand the business process is one key step of implementing a business process improve project [1]. Currently there is hardly any support in ACBP modeling tools to adequately support the task of figuring out relationships between lifecycles, which is important to understanding an ACBP model. In form of graphs, process manager need to examine these lifecycles file by file if they want to figure out the relationships between these lifecycles. And it is hard to present multiple graphs simultaneously so that scrutiny of multiple lifecycles at the same time is impossible.

In this paper, we serialize the lifecycles as regular expressions to overcome the aforementioned obstacles. Firstly, multiple lifecycles are presented at the same time for they are serialized as strings. Secondly, the keyword-based query helps process manager to find related lifecycles of concern. Thirdly, text highlighting techniques is used to make process manager interested information prominent. Although there exists other graph serialize methods, we choose to serialize lifecycles as regular expressions for the natural relationships between FSMs and regular expressions.

The rest of the paper is organized as follows: Sect. 2 overviews the related work. Section 3 introduces the ACBP modeling method and some basic definitions. Section 4 introduces the methods of serializing a lifecycle. Discussions and experiments are presented in Sect. 5. Finally, conclusions are given in Sect. 6.

2   Related Work

2.1   Artifact-Centric Business Process

In the past a few years, a new modeling approach has emerged, i.e., Artifact-Centric Business Process modeling. Compared with traditional activity-centric business process modeling paradigm, artifact-centric paradigm is proved to be more flexible in process modeling and execution for its adequate supports of automated tools for business process inter-operation and process schema reuse [2, 3]. Instead of control flows of a business process, business documents and their evolution through a business process become the main modeling objects. This approach depicts a business process in two dimensions, viz., business artifacts (business documents) and lifecycles of the artifacts. The lifecycle of an artifact is defined in terms of "business stages" and the possible evolution of the artifact. Up to present, artifact-centric approach has been applied to several industry domains such as healthcare (e.g., PHILharmonicFlows framework [4, 5]), insurance (e.g., in [6]), and finance (e.g., IBM global Financing [7]). ACBP modeling has been received much contributions in the area of foundations [8], design methodologies [9], model specification, construction, and verification [10–15], workflow realization/execution [16, 17] and monitoring supports [18].

2.2   Understanding Business Process

Although understanding business process is important in a business process improvement project, few works concentrated on this area. A conceptual framework was proposed in [19] to organize different view of business process to help under-standing the business process. Studies in the area of Business Process Model Abstraction (BPMA) [20], i.e., the business process model is abstracted as a more coarse-grained model and highlight the significant model components from the insignificant ones depending on user interests, provide different views of a business process model either. Syntax highlighting techniques is used in [21] to help users to understand the structural information of business process model. However, these researches all concentrate on the activity-centric workflow business process model.

Our work is different from the above research, because we focus on the text-based presentation of lifecycles of ACBP model and highlighting the user interested com-ponents of lifecycles and enumerating the correlated text-based lifecycles to make the relationships between lifecycles prominent.

3 Basic Definitions

In this section, we use a purchasing process as an example to illustrate the ACBP modeling paradigm and present the basic definitions.

In Fig. 1, the simplified purchasing process is presented in artifact-centric per-spective [12]. There are *Purchase Order, Picking List, Shipping Order, Quote, Pay-ment, Shipping List* and *Invoice* as artifacts. The lifecycles of the artifacts are depicted as Finite State Machines (FSMs). Each arrow represents a transition of the FSMs. The circled indexes above the arrows are the labels of *business rules*. These *business rules* encapsulate the services of the ACBP model and read/update some artifacts under some conditions. If a *business rule* appears in multiple FSMs, there are associations among the corresponding artifacts.

Definition 1 (Business Rule). A *business rule* r is triple (λ, β, v), where λ and β are the pre-condition and the post-condition, respectively. λ and β are propositions over arti-facts. v is a service that read/update one or more artifacts.

For example, the *business rule* of *buyer confirm* in Fig. 1 is listed as Table 1, where *po* is an artifact of *Purchase Order*, *q* is an artifact of *Quote*, and *instate* and *defined* are two predicates over the artifacts in the ACBP model.

Definition 2 (Lifecycle). A lifecycle is tuple $(Q, \Sigma, \delta, s_0, F)$, where Q is a finite set called the *states*, Σ is a finite set called the *alphabet*, $\delta : Q \times \Sigma \to Q$ is the transition function, $s_0 \in Q$ is the *start state* and $s_0 \notin F, F \subset Q$ is the set of *final states*.

With slight abuse, for all $\delta(q_x, l) = q_y$, we call (q_x, l, q_y) as a transition. Notice that any lifecycle satisfies following property: symbols in Σ present and only present once in the lifecycle, and there is no duplicate state in one lifecycle.

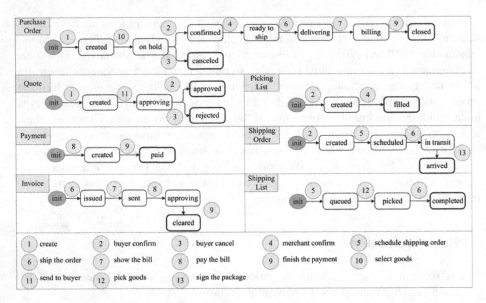

Fig. 1. Artifact-centric modeling of purchasing process

Table 1. An example of *business rule*

Pre-condition	instate(po, on_hold) ∧ instate(q, approving) ∧ defined(po, orderID)
Service	confirm(po, q)
Post-condition	instate(po, confirmed) ∧ instate(q, approved)

4 The Proposed Method: Serialization of a Lifecycle as a Regular Expression

In this section, we propose the serialization method in Subsect. 4.1, prove that the serialized regular expression is valid to maintain all the information of the lifecycle in Subsect. 4.2, present the deserialization method in Subsect. 4.3.

4.1 Serialization Method

In order to serialize a lifecycle without loss of information, firstly we construct a new FSM according to the lifecycle. Then we convert the FSM as a regular expression.

Given a lifecycle L, another FSM, $D = (Q', \Sigma', \delta', s_0', F')$, is constructed according to L, denoted as Cons(L): (1) $\Sigma' = \{f(x) | x \in L.Q \text{ or } x \in L.\Sigma\}$, where f is a function that encodes states of $L.Q$ and symbols of $L.\Sigma$ to strings and there exists a function f^d that decodes the strings to the original states or symbols. (2) $|Q'| = |L.Q| + |L.\Sigma| + 1$, and if $L.\delta(q_x, l) = q_y$, then there exists mappings $\delta'(q_a, f(q_x)) = q_b, \delta'(q_b, f(l)) = q_c$ and $\delta'(q_c, f(q_y)) = q_d$ in δ'. (3) s_0' is the state q_a, where $\delta'(q_a, f(q_x)) = q_y$ and q_x is the *start state* of L. (4) $F' = \{q_a | \delta'(q_b, f(q_x)) = q_a)\}$, where q_x is the *final state* of

L. Notice that a b c d and x y are variables of subscript of states in Cons(L) and L, respectively. In this paper, suppose the input of f is denoted by a. If $a \in L.\Sigma$, the output is "$<a>$"; if $a \in L.Q$, there are three cases: (i) a is a *start state*, the output is "$[\#a]$"; (ii) a is a *final state*, the output is "$[a\#]$"; (iii) a is not a *start state* or a *final state,* the output is "$[a]$". For example, the new FSM constructed according to lifecycle of *Quote* is presented as Fig. 2.

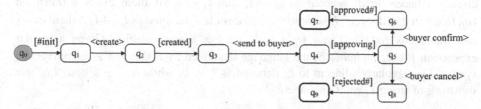

Fig. 2. The new FSM constructed according to lifecycle of *Quote*

The aforementioned step is added because the converted regular expression only maintains the information of the *alphabet* of an FSM. After the step, the information of an FSM can be maintained by a regular expression. For saving the space, the conversion process from an FSM to its equivalent regular expression is omitted. Details of the conversion process can be found in [22]. The steps of serialization of a lifecycle as a regular expression are summarized in Algorithm 1.

```
Algorithm 1. SERIALIZATION
Input: a lifecycle L
Output: a regular expression R
1. Construct another FSM D according to L.
2. Transform D to a GNFA G.
3. Convert G to regular expression R using algorithm
CONVERT.
4. Return R.
```

Using Algorithm 1, the FSM in Fig. 2 can be converted to a regular expression as "[#init] <create> [created] <send to buyer> [approving] (<buyer confirm> [approved#] ∪ <buyer cancel> [rejected#])".

To help figuring out the relationships between lifecycles, we collect these serialized lifecycles as a lifecycle repository. Moreover, we create an inverted index based on the repository. Thus, an ad-hoc keyword-based query can be made to retrieve the related lifecycles. To make the information of interest more predominant, the keywords and their regular adjacent symbols are highlighted in the result lifecycles. These symbols can be extracted by Function REG_POST proposed in Subsect. 4.3. We set up an experiment to validate the proposed method, which will be presented in Sect. 5.

4.2   Valid Proof

In this subsection, we prove that the serialized regular expression is valid to represent the original lifecycle, i.e., the regular expression maintains all the information of the lifecycle, although it is known that an FSM can be transformed to multiple regular expressions. Before starting the proof, we give a theorem that will be used in the proof.

Definition 3 (Adjacent). In a lifecycle, we say that q_i is directly adjacent to l_x and l_x directly adjacent to q_j denoted as $q_i \rightharpoonup l_x$ and $l_x \rightharpoonup q_j$, if there exists a transition (q_i, l_x, q_j) in the lifecycle; l_x is indirectly adjacent to l_y denoted as $l_x \rightleftharpoons l_y$ if there exists two transitions (q_i, l_x, q_j) and (q_j, l_y, q_k), i j k x y are variables. Given a regular expression R over *alphabet* Σ, the language described by R denoted as Language(R), symbol l_x is regularly adjacent to l_y, denoted as $l_x \Rightarrow l_y$, while $l_x, l_y \in \Sigma$ and "$l_x l_y$" are substring of string s, $s \in$ Language(R).

Theorem 1. Given a lifecycle L, suppose the regular expression corresponds to Cons (L) is R_L. Then $q_i \rightharpoonup l_x$ in L, iff $f(q_i) \Rightarrow f(l_x)$ in R_L, and $l_x \rightharpoonup q_i$ in L iff $f(l_x) \Rightarrow f(q_i)$ in R_L, $q_i \in L.Q$, $l_x \in L.\Sigma$.

Proof Sketch. Here we prove "$q_i \rightharpoonup l_x$ in L, iff $f(q_i) \Rightarrow f(l_x)$ in R_L", while "$l_x \rightharpoonup q_i$ in L iff $f(l_x) \Rightarrow f(q_i)$ in R_L" can be proved similarly. (1) Firstly, according to the construction method in 4.1, $q_i \rightharpoonup l_x$ iff $f(q_i) \rightleftharpoons f(l_x)$ in Cons(L). (2) Secondly, string s in Language(R_L) can be recognized by Cons(L) for R_L describes the same language that can be recognized by Cons(L). Thus, $f(q_i) \rightleftharpoons f(l_x)$ in Cons(L) iff $f(l_x) \Rightarrow f(q_i)$ in R_L. Combine (1) an (2), $q_i \rightharpoonup l_x$ in L, iff $f(q_i) \Rightarrow f(l_x)$ in R_L. ∎

Notice that there is no duplicate state in one lifecycle is considered in (1). And due to the property, there is no duplicate symbols in Cons(L). Thus, (2) is correct.

Valid Proof Sketch. In a lifecycle, the information contains five parts Q Σ δ s_0 and F. According to requirement of f, information of Q Σ s_0 and F can be found in the regular expression. And according to Theorem 1 and the language semantics of the regular expression, all the adjacent information of the lifecycle can be found in the regular expression so that information of δ can be found in the regular expression. ∎

4.3   Deserialization Method

In this subsection, we present the deserialization method, i.e., the method that extracts the lifecycle information from the serialized regular expression.

Information of Q Σ s_0 and F is easy to obtain if f^d is known. To acquire information of δ, we introduce two functions REG_PRE and REG_POST to find the set of symbols that regularly adjacent to symbol l and l regularly adjacent to, respectively. Information of δ can be obtained via f^d when all the regular adjacent information is got. Here we only present pseudo code of REG_POST, as REG_PRE can be coded similarly.

Suppose $R = (R_x)(R_y) * ((R_p) \cup (R_q))$. According to semantics of regular expression, $(R_x)(R_y) * ((R_p) \cup (R_q))$ and $(R_x)(R_y) * (R_p) \cup (R_x)(R_y) * (R_q)$ describe the same language. $\{(R_x)(R_y) * ((R_p) \cup (R_q))\}$ and $\{(R_x)(R_y) * (R_p), (R_x)(R_y) * (R_q)\}$ imply the same regular adjacent information, while $\{(R_x)(R_y) * (R_p)\}$ and

```
Function 1. REG_POST
Input: symbol l and regular expression R
Output: a set of symbols S
Initialize: S = null
1. Unfold R using following formula (1) as a set of regu-
lar expressions that implies the same regular adjacent
information as R recursively, until there does not exist
any operators and parentheses in the regular expression.
2. For each regular expression R' in the set, if there is
a symbol l' that l' right behind l in R', add l' to S.
3. Return S.
```

$\{((R_x)(R_p), (R_x)(R_y)(R_p), (R_x)(R_y)(R_y)(R_p)\}$ imply the same regular adjacent information. Therefore, Unfold(R), which is defined in Eq. (1), acquires a set of regular expressions that imply the same regular adjacent information as R.

$$\text{Unfold}(R) = \{(R_x)(R_p), (R_x)(R_y)(R_p), (R_x)(R_y)(R_y)(R_p), (R_x)(R_q), (R_x)(R_y)(R_q), \\ (R_x)(R_y)(R_y)(R_q)\} \tag{1}$$

Notice that all regular expressions can be presented in form of $(R_x)(R_y)*$ $((R_p) \cup (R_q))$. Some of $R_x R_y R_p R_q$ may be null. If there is no "*" and "$\cup$" operation in a regular expression, all the parentheses can be deleted.

5   Experiments

5.1   Experiment Setup

We set up an experiment to validate the effectiveness of our proposed regular expression based approach as compared to the traditional graph-based approach. In the experiment, there are some randomly generated lifecycles, with fifteen states in average and ten problems about relationships between lifecycles. An on-line instrument, running in the container of Apache Tomcat 8, is developed to conduct the self-administered experiment. We use lucene 7 as search engine. Screenshots of the instrument is shown in Fig. 3. Figure 3(a) is the screenshot of regular expression based approach, Fig. 3(b) is graph-based approach. One human participant in our test is assigned to only one kind of testing, either graph-based or text based. For each test, we record the time of answering all the ten problems and the number of correct answers. These records are the reference for evaluation of our experiments results of the serialization methods. The experiment result is the average of multiple tests.

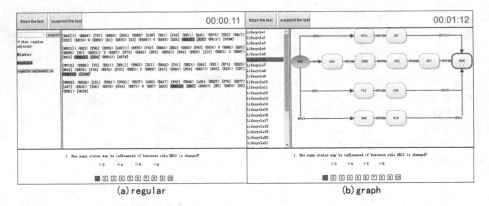

Fig. 3. Screenshots of the online instruments

5.2 Experiment Results and Discussions

In Fig. 4(a), we can see that in traditional graph-based approach, participants use more time to answer all ten questions while the number of lifecycles is increasing, and there is an obvious positive correlation between number of lifecycles and the cost time. Compared to traditional graph-based approach, participants use approximately the same time to answer these ten questions in our proposed regular expression approach. In Fig. 4(b) we can see that, in the traditional graph-based approach the accuracy of answering questions are lower than our proposed regular expression approach, which is 100%. There is also a decline of accuracy while the number of lifecycles is increasing. From these observations, we can conclude that in traditional graph-based approach, the time cost and the accuracy is closely related to the number of lifecycles, where the efficiency of these two performance indicators are declined while the number of life-cycles is increasing. Compared to traditional graph-based approach, our proposed approach is superior to the traditional graph-based approach both in time cost and accuracy. The time cost and the accuracy of our proposed approach are independent of the number of lifecycles.

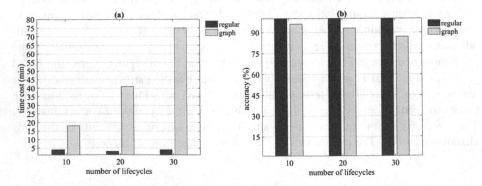

Fig. 4. Comparison of two paradigms (a) time cost (b) accuracy

Compare with traditional graph-based approach, we can see that our proposed regular expression representation of lifecycle combined with key words search and highlighting techniques of figuring out the relationships among ACBP model is effective in time cost and accuracy, especially ACBP model has large amount of lifecycles.

6 Conclusions

In this paper, we serialize the lifecycles of ACBP models as regular expressions. Based on the serialized lifecycle, keyword search techniques are used to help process modeler understanding relationships among the lifecycles. Compare with traditional graph-based approach, we proved that our proposed regular expression approach improves the efficiency of figuring out the relationships among the lifecycles in terms of accuracy and time cost.

References

1. Baines, T., Adesola, S.: Developing and evaluating a methodology for business process improvement. Bus. Process Manag. J. **11**(1), 37–46 (2005)
2. Hull, R., Su, J.: Report on NSF workshop on data-centric workflows (2012)
3. Hull, R., Su, J., Vaculin, R.: Data management perspective on business process management: tutorial overview. In: ACM SIGMOD International Conference on Management of Data. ACM (2013)
4. Künzle, V., Reichert, M.: PHILharmonicFlows: towards a framework for object-aware process management. J. Softw.: Evol. Process **23**(4), 205–244 (2011)
5. Chiao, C., Künzle, V., Reichert, M.: Object-aware process support in healthcare information systems: requirements, conceptual framework and examples. J. Adv. Life Sci. **5**(1 & 2), 11–26 (2013)
6. Kumaran, S., Liu, R., Wu, F.Y.: On the duality of information-centric and activity-centric models of business processes. In: Bellahsène, Z., Léonard, M. (eds.) CAiSE 2008. LNCS, vol. 5074, pp. 32–47. Springer, Heidelberg (2008). https://doi.org/10.1007/978-3-540-69534-9_3
7. Chao, T., et al.: Artifact-based transformation of IBM global financing. In: Dayal, U., Eder, J., Koehler, J., Reijers, Hajo A. (eds.) BPM 2009. LNCS, vol. 5701, pp. 261–277. Springer, Heidelberg (2009). https://doi.org/10.1007/978-3-642-03848-8_18
8. Bhattacharya, K., Caswell, N., Kumaran, S., et al.: Artifact-centered operational modeling: lessons from customer engagements. IBM Syst. J. **46**(4), 703–721 (2007)
9. Bhattacharya, K., Hull, R., Su, J.: A data-centric design methodology for business processes. In: Handbook of Research on Business Process Modeling, vol. 26, pp. 503–531 (2009)
10. Bhattacharya, K., Gerede, C., Hull, R., Liu, R., Su, J.: Towards formal analysis of artifact-centric business process models. In: Alonso, G., Dadam, P., Rosemann, M. (eds.) BPM 2007. LNCS, vol. 4714, pp. 288–304. Springer, Heidelberg (2007). https://doi.org/10.1007/978-3-540-75183-0_21
11. Estañol, M., Queralt, A., Sancho, M.R., Teniente, E.: Artifact-centric business process models in UML. In: La Rosa, M., Soffer, P. (eds.) BPM 2012. LNBIP, vol. 132, pp. 292–303. Springer, Heidelberg (2013). https://doi.org/10.1007/978-3-642-36285-9_34

12. Yongchareon, S., Liu, C., Yu, J., et al.: A view framework for modeling and change validation of artifact-centric inter-organizational business processes. Inf. Syst. **47**(C), 51–81 (2015)
13. Damaggio, E., Hull, R., Vaculín, R.: On the equivalence of incremental and fixpoint semantics for business artifacts with guard-stage-milestone lifecycles. In: Rinderle-Ma, S., Toumani, F., Wolf, K. (eds.) BPM 2011. LNCS, vol. 6896, pp. 396–412. Springer, Heidelberg (2011). https://doi.org/10.1007/978-3-642-23059-2_29
14. Nigam, A., Caswell, N.: Business artifacts: an approach to operational specification. IBM Syst. J. **42**(3), 428–445 (2003)
15. Fritz, C., Hull, R., Su, J.: Automatic construction of simple artifact-based business processes. In: International Conference on Database Theory Proceedings, DBLP, St. Petersburg, Russia, pp. 225–238 (2009)
16. Kan, N., Yongchareon, S., Liesaputra, V., et al.: An artifact-centric business process execution platform. In: Enterprise Distributed Object Computing Workshop, pp. 1–4. IEEE (2016)
17. Liu, G., Liu, X., Qin, H., Su, J., Yan, Z., Zhang, L.: Automated realization of business workflow specification. In: Dan, A., Gittler, F., Toumani, F. (eds.) ICSOC/ServiceWave-2009. LNCS, vol. 6275, pp. 96–108. Springer, Heidelberg (2010). https://doi.org/10.1007/978-3-642-16132-2_9
18. Liu, R., Vaculín, R., Shan, Z., Nigam, A., Wu, F.: Business artifact-centric modeling for real-time performance monitoring. In: Rinderle-Ma, S., Toumani, F., Wolf, K. (eds.) BPM 2011. LNCS, vol. 6896, pp. 265–280. Springer, Heidelberg (2011). https://doi.org/10.1007/978-3-642-23059-2_21
19. Melão, N., Pidd, M.: A conceptual framework for understanding business processes and business process modelling. Inf. Syst. **10**(2), 105–129 (2000)
20. Smirnov, S., Reijers, H., Weske, M., Nugteren, T.: Business process model abstraction: a definition, catalog, and survey. Distrib. Parallel Databases **30**(1), 63–99 (2012)
21. Reijers, H., Thomas, F., Jan, M., et al.: Syntax highlighting in business process models. Decis. Support Syst. **51**(3), 339–349 (2011)
22. Sipser, M.: Introduction to the Theory of Computation, 2nd edn. Addison-Wesley Longman Publishing Co., Inc., Reading (1997)

Social Networks Node Mining Algorithm
of Based on Greedy Subgraph

Hongbin Wang[1] ⓘ, Guisheng Yin[1] ⓘ, Lianke Zhou[1](✉) ⓘ, Yupeng Zhang[1] ⓘ,
and Zhen Cao[2] ⓘ

[1] College of Computer Science and Technology, Harbin Engineering University, Harbin, China
zhoulianke@hrbeu.edu.cn
[2] Beijing General Institute of Electronic Engineering, Beijing 100854, China

Abstract. The method of node mining in social networks is divided into heuristic method and greedy method, in which the former mainly measures the importance degree of each node in the networks according to its own attributes or networks topology. As a result, it is fast but with bad accuracy. In the latter algorithm, however, spread simulation has been conducted for each node by adopting diffusion model, and then the importance of each node is calculated through comparison of the spread size. Therefore, this kind of algorithm is inefficient and inappropriate to large-scale social networks. This paper, therefore, proposes a new node mining algorithm based on greedy subgraph, having taken into account the unsatisfactory node mining results in the heuristic method and the highly complexity in greedy algorithm. In this new algorithm, the heuristic method is used first and then the greedy method is also adopted. Then, the author compares the differences of heuristic algorithm, the greedy algorithm and the algorithm proposed in this paper on the effect of node selection, the effectiveness of algorithm, the spread range and so no. it concludes that the node mining algorithm based on greedy subgraph can guarantee good optimal solution on the basis of ensuring a better node selection effect and efficiency than the classical algorithm. Besides, the theoretical applicability and actual spread effect of the proposed algorithm has also been verified.

Keywords: Social networks · Influence node mining
Greedy subgraph algorithm · Linear threshold model

1 Introduction

Society is a network of various relationships and the concept of "social networks" has first been proposed and adopted by anthropologist Radcliffe Brown around 1930 [1] in his concern about the real-life structure. It can be defined as a community of social groups and their interrelated relationships [2].

There are many different branches of social networks research [3], with increasing concern in all the research. As a consequence, more and more attention on information exchange has been paid in daily life, with the flourish of many platforms that can facilitate communication between people, which has greatly promoted the exchange and contact between people without restrictions like geographical conditions. Nevertheless,

© Springer Nature Switzerland AG 2018
X. Sun et al. (Eds.): ICCCS 2018, LNCS 11064, pp. 157–168, 2018.
https://doi.org/10.1007/978-3-030-00009-7_15

those networks cannot be said of without problems and limitations, so it becomes a top priority for us to solve them. For example, the source of public opinion in the networks can be traced down so as to curb its malicious spread [4]; the terrorist leaders can be found out by digging important nodes in their relationship networks in order to carry out precise strikes [5]; top and high-yield authors in a field or major can be dug out in the collaborative research and paper writing networks so as to promote the scientific research development of the field; the highlight of information must be seized considering rules and patterns of information dissemination in the Twitter networks so that important target information can be delivered [6]. Based on above, it can be safely concluded that either the initiator of malicious opinion, the leader of the terrorist organization gang or the core research scholars and so on have something in common, that is, they are in the core position of their communities, i.e., the key nodes of the networks.

The node mining algorithms of social networks influence maximization can be mainly divided into the following categories:

Degree Centrality (DC). It is the most direct and primitive index in measuring Centrality [7, 8]. The degree of node importance drawn by this algorithm is dependent on degree of nodes: the larger the number of neighboring nodes in the networks is, the greater the degree, the greater the networks centrality of the node, the more critical of the node and its influence in the networks.

Closeness Centrality (CC). This index, also known as the centrality of compactness, has been proposed by Freeman [9], which reflects the distance between a node and the other nodes in the networks. The basic idea of the algorithm is that the smaller the sum of the total distances of the node between all the other nodes in the networks, the smaller the cost of the node's communication with all the remaining nodes in the networks, the more vital of the node's position in the social networks and the greater the influence.

Betweeness Centrality (BC). Betweeness is used to describe the capacity of a node to carry the shortest path number in a networks. It equals to the sum of the number of all critical paths that pass the node in any pair of nodes in the networks and the ratio of this node to the number of critical paths, which describes the influence and degree of centrality of the node in the networks.

Semi-local Centrality (SLC). The Degree Centrality algorithm is efficient but with low accuracy while the Closeness Centrality and betweenness Centrality algorithm are more precise but of greater complexity. Consequently, these algorithms are not very satisfactory in practical application. On this basis, Chen et al. [3] have proposed a centrality measurement based on semi-local information of nodes. This method weighs the low correlation centrality and other time-complex methods, which involves the neighboring node information of the node being evaluated. What is important is that it covers not only its direct neighbors, but also the nearest neighbor and its nearest neighbor, that is, the information of the neighbor's neighbor.

Hill Climbing Greedy Algorithm (HCGA). The four methods of calculating the importance of nodes are often called heuristic algorithms, which have long been regarded as important algorithms for their short function time and high efficiency in solving the problem of node influence maximization mining [10, 11]. The greedy algorithm can guarantee a higher accuracy of the solution, but each time when the algorithm chooses a node, it broadcasts to all the other nodes in the networks respectively (the next section will give a detailed description of the diffusion model). Therefore, it still cannot process massive data timely and effectively despite the repeated optimization, because its calculation complexity is too high and runs too long.

This paper proposes and presents a detailed description of the social networks node mining algorithm based on the greedy subgraph. The algorithm firstly achieves the mining effect of the node information in the layout of topology by calculating the influence potential of the nodes in the social networks and then improves the method of calculating the influence of nodes in the linear threshold model. Furthermore, the strategy of the greedy subgraph is introduced in this paper and the node of maximized social networks influence is chosen and the selection effect in the whole graph is proved.

2   An Estimation of Node Influence Potential

2.1   Formal Definition of the Estimation Formula

First, we calculate the effect of the node on node i in the neighbor subgraph, and introduce the aggregation coefficient $C(i)$ in the formula to measure the ring (i.e., triangle) of length 3 in the networks. To put it simply is that two friends of yours may also be friends themselves, which is easy to be found in a social networks map. When calculating the effect of a node, we consider some of the topological metric of the node itself and the neighbor subgraph, that is, the degree of the neighborhood subgraph node and the aggregation coefficient of the node. The estimation formula of node influence potential is defined as formula (1).

$$P_i = d_i + \sum_{j \in \Gamma(i)} d_j (1 - C(j)) \tag{1}$$

Where $\Gamma(i)$ is the set of adjacent nodes of node i, and $C(j)$ represents the aggregation coefficient of node j, that is, the influence of the node itself is reflected linearly by the neighboring nodes around the node.

2.2   The Calculation Process of Node Influence Potential

In the calculation of influence potential of any node in the networks, there is a need for pre-processing first, that is, to calculate aggregation coefficient of each node in the networks, for which a mature algorithm has been developed in today's social networks research. The pseudocode of the estimation algorithm of node impact potential is described as follows.

Algorithm :The basic process of the estimation algorithm of node influence potential:

Input: G (V, E) // enter the nodes and edges of the networks

Output: Pi // output the influence potential value of each node in the networks

1: for i = 1 to N // calculate each node's aggregation coefficient in the networks
   graph

2: // calculate the aggregation coefficient C (i) for each node

3: end for

4: for j in Γ(i) do // calculate the node's influence potential of each node in the
   networks graph

5: if (C(j) == 0) // the node is a local bridge node

6: P(i) is equal to the sum of the degree of a node and of the neighboring node

7: else if (C(j) == 1) // the topological structure of node layout is the full graph

8: P(i) is equal to the degree of the node itself, and the algorithm is the same with
   degree centrality

9: else

10: P(i) is equal to the node degree + neighbor node degree * (1- aggregation coef-
    ficient of the neighboring node)

11: end for

3 Improvement of Influence in Linear Threshold Model

In this paper, the calculation formula of the influence in the linear threshold model has
been improved, that is to say, the effect of the node's influence potential on the local
topology is taken into account, instead of simply adopting the traditional b_{ij} to estimate
the effect between the node i and the node j. It reflects the degree of closeness of the
nodes in the neighborhood subgraph (NSG), and the influence of the source node (node
i) to the audience node (node j) is mainly considered when considering the influence of
node i on node j (b_{ij}). When applied in the linear threshold model, the influence of node
i on node j is calculated by the formula (2).

$$b_{ij} = \frac{P_i}{P_i + P_j} * (1 - C(i)) \tag{2}$$

Where Pi represents the influence potential of node i and $C(i)$ is the aggregation
coefficient of node i. 10 the above formula, in calculating the influence of node i on node
j, does not simply consider the degree attribute of node j, but combines the topological
structure of its surrounding nodes.

The above formula, in calculating the influence of node i on node j, does not simply
consider the degree attribute of node j, but combines the topological structure of its
surrounding nodes. It is found in the research and analysis that interaction between two
nodes is mostly generated from the topology between the two nodes, while the other
nodes around have a relative weak influence on this, which is often related with their
local topology. For example, if the local networks has a larger density, then the

neighboring nodes have more even edges and the other nodes around play a greater role. Mining algorithm of social networks nodes based on greedy subgraph.

3.1 Algorithm Description

In this paper, a social networks node mining algorithm based on dynamic hill climbing greedy strategy, which improves the final influence spread and decreases time complexity at the same time, is proposed. The algorithm which simply adopts the node mining based on the node influence potential does not influence the dynamic process of the diffusion, so it is still a heuristic algorithm. This paper, having taken into account the advantages of the greedy algorithm in the influence spread, chooses the greedy strategy to ensure the final effect of the algorithm. A further analysis will show that there are "zombie nodes" in the social networks. Before giving the definition of the zombie node, it is necessary to offer the concept of the average threshold of the networks, whose definition is shown in formula (3).

$$<\theta> = \frac{1}{|V|} \sum_{i \in V} \theta_i \tag{3}$$

Where $|V|$ is the number of nodes in the networks and θ_i is the specific threshold of node i, whose value is given randomly according to the characteristics of the networks before the first diffusion of the networks. The value is [0, 1], and if $\Theta i == 0$, it denotes the minimum activation threshold of the node, that is, once its neighbor is activated, it is also activated, which rarely exists in the actual networks, however. If $\theta_i == 1$, it means that the node can not be activated, that is, it is the highest activation threshold. The node's specificity threshold is used to represent the ease of activation of each node in the social networks, which remains constant in subsequent transmissions.

3.2 The Algorithm Flow and Pseudo-Code Description

In the social networks node mining algorithm based on greedy subgraph, the selection of k seed nodes is divided into the following parts: the influence potential node part and the zombie node part. The former chooses the nodes with the largest Pi value successively while the latter selects the node with the highest specificity threshold in turn. At the same time, the potential factor α ($\alpha \in [0, 1]$) is introduced in the algorithm, and $\lceil \alpha k \rceil$ represents the proportion of the potential nodes in the k node set while $k - \lceil \alpha k \rceil$ represents the proportion of the zombie nodes.

The basic steps in the actual mining of influence maximized node are as follows:

(1) Obtain the influence potential of each node according to the influence potential algorithm for subgraph nodes, sort the nodes according to the influence potential progressive order, and add $\lceil \alpha k \rceil$ nodes with the greatest potential to the candidate set C1;

(2) Extract matching in the graph according to the definition of "zombie node", sort them according to their specificity threshold from high to low, and add the former $k - \lceil \alpha k \rceil$ nodes to the candidate set C2;

(3) For the set C3 composed of candidate nodes in C1 and C2, use the linear threshold model with improved influence, expressed as the hill climbing greedy algorithm, to attempt the diffusion activation. Initially, the node mining result set is $S = \varnothing$, then carry out diffusion simulation of each node in C3, add the node with the largest activation spread to set S, thus completing the selection of the first node. Mark each activated node at the same time, and set the default that those activated nodes will not be calculated next time. Remember to remove activated node from the graph after each calculation and extract the subgraph for the next broadcast.

(4) Through the diffusion of step 3, it is possible that the nodes in set C3 have been marked as activated nodes in the diffusion process. Remove these nodes then. As a result, the number of nodes in C3 is reduced, so repeat step 1 and step 2 node selection process, and select k nodes to fill set C3.

(5) Repeat step 3 to activate the diffusion process until the node mining result set S reaches the scale of k, and the algorithm ends.

The pseudo-code of the social networks node mining algorithm based on the greedy subgraph is described as follows:

Algorithm :The basic process of greedy subgraph algorithm

Input: G (V, E) // enter the nodes and edges in the networks

Output: S // output the set of initial mining nodes with maximized social networks influence

1: for i = 1 to N // calculate the influence potential of each node in the networks graph

2: // calculate the influence potential Pi of each node

3: end for

4: Sort (Pi) // sort the nodes' influence and make selection

5: Sort (zombie node) / / sort and select the zombie node

6: for i = 1 to k do // select the node with maximized influence through the greedy subgraph algorithm

7: for j = 1 to $\lceil \alpha k \rceil$ do // select $\lceil \alpha k \rceil$ influence potential nodes and add them to candidate set C1

8: C1 ← V (Pmax)

9: end for

10: for j = 1 to k-$\lceil \alpha k \rceil$ do // select k-$\lceil \alpha k \rceil$ zombie nodes and add them to candidate set C2

11: C2 ← V (zombie node)

12: end for

13: Greedy Algorithm // Perform the actual broadcast through the linear threshold model with improved influence, expressed as the greedy strategy

14: S ←the node with the largest incremental impact spread

15: if (| S | == k)

16: break

17: end for

3.3 Simulation Analysis of Node Mining Results

This section mainly compares the differences of several node mining algorithms, that is, degree centrality algorithm, closeness algorithm, betweeness algorithm, semi-local algorithm and the mining algorithm based on the greedy subgraph in their node influence mining results. Besides, an in-depth study and analysis of the node mining results of each algorithm has been offered in this part (Table 1).

Table 1. Experimental data set

Dataset feature	The dolphin social networks	Email communication networks	Wikipedia data set	Enron email data set
Number of nodes(N)	62	1133	7115	36692
Number of edges(E)	159	5451	103698	367662
Average degree(<k>)	5.129	5.129	——	——
Maximum degree(Kmax)	12	71	——	——
Average path length L(G)	3.357	3.606	——	——
Networks densityd(G)	0.084	0.009	——	——
Average aggregation coefficient C	0.303	0.254	0.1409	0.4970
Networks diameter D	——	——	7	11

Evaluation Criteria. In this paper, the classical social networks influence broadcast model, namely, SIR epidemic model, is used to simulate the influence transmission, and the real influence of the node is simulated. There are three states of nodes in the SIR model: the susceptible, infected and immune state. The infection probability ρ is the random value between [0, 1], and the immune probability λ of the infected node is <1/ K>, where <k> is the average degree of nodes in the networks. The transmission algorithm begins from the initial node and terminates until there is no infected nodes in the networks. In order to calculate the influence of a single node in a social networks, only one node is selected as a seed node for each infection, and the other nodes in the networks are used as susceptible nodes and then the transmission starts according to the classical SIR epidemic model. $F(t)$ in the model represents the sum of the number of infected nodes and immune nodes in the networks, which is used to evaluate the influence of the initially selected node after t-step diffusion. With the same condition and diffusion time, the node that infects more nodes has higher $F(t)$ value, that is, the influence centrality of the node is greater. According to the characteristics of the SIR model, the $F(t)$ value tends to stabilize over time.

Comparison of Node Mining Results. Rank nodes in the dolphin social networks data set according to DC, CC, BC, SLC and GSG node mining algorithm. TOP-K results (the top 15 nodes) of each algorithm in the networks is considered because people are more concerned about the important nodes in the networks. It is necessary to note that when the GSG algorithm selects the node, the optimal average is obtained by multiple tests. It is found that the node selection result is the most stable and the effect is better when the influence factor $\alpha = 0.7 \pm 0.1$. Therefore, in this paper, all the influence potential factors take the value $\alpha = 0.7$ whenever GSG algorithm is mentioned.

It can be seen from Fig. 1 that the social networks node mining algorithm based on greedy subgraph proposed in this paper is better than other comparison algorithms for node selection. In these five algorithms, the positional deviation distance of the GSG algorithm is the smallest in the five cases of the influence node TOP-K, followed by CC) algorithm. DC algorithm and BC algorithm are the largest in terms of the position offset distance, which indicates that the two algorithms have the worst effect on the node influence mining in the dolphin social networks. In a word, the following conclusions can be drawn: for the dolphin social networks, the effectiveness of the above several node mining algorithms can be ranked from high to low: GSG algorithm $\geq$ CC algorithm > LC algorithm > DC algorithm $\geq$ BC algorithm.

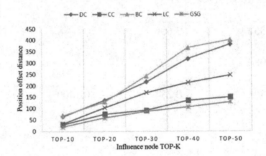

Fig. 1. Dolphin social networks node mining algorithm TOP - K position offset diagram

According to Fig. 2, we can see that in the email data set, GSG algorithm proposed in this paper is still promising. In the five algorithms, the DC algorithm and the BC algorithm are relatively inconstant and volatile in the choice of nodes of different sizes while the other three algorithms are more linear with the increase of linearity of the initial activation node set scale. From the effect point of view, it is difficult to tell which is better for GSG algorithm and CC algorithm, although both of them have more obvious advantages compared to the other three algorithms. The gap between LC algorithm, DC algorithm and BC algorithm is significantly widened as TOP-K set Scale increases, in which the LC algorithm performs the best. In summary, it can be concluded that in the email data set, the performance of these algorithms are sorted by: GSG algorithm $\approx$ CC algorithm > LC algorithm > DC algorithm > BC algorithm.

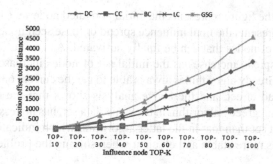

Fig. 2. Email dataset node mining algorithm TOP - K position offset graph

3.4 Analysis and Comparison of Greedy Sub-graph Strategy

In order to illustrate the validity and correctness of the social networks node mining algorithm based on the greedy, this chapter carries out the multi-angle comparison experiment by validating the public data set in the social networks analysis. The following section will explain this from the aspects of diffusion, algorithm execution time, and algorithmic stress testing.

Diffusion Spread. In this paper, the GSG algorithm defines the initial greedy nodes in the networks and selects specific nodes to spread from the candidate set at each time. What is more, the node candidate set is modified and the node activated by it is marked at each diffusion. The hill climbing greedy algorithm, however, following the traditional idea of greedy algorithm, always choose the node with the current largest influence scope as the optimal node for this step until the selected node size achieves the expected scale.

The experiment first examines the final influence spread of the two algorithms when their eigenvalues in the dataset are the same and their size of the seed nodes sets are different. The results are shown in Fig. 3, in which the hill climbing greedy algorithm is represented as Greedy while the node mining algorithm based on the greedy subgraph is GSG.

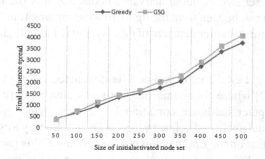

Fig. 3. The diffusion effect of GSG algorithm and Greedy algorithm on Wiki-Vote data set

The abscissa in the figure represents the initial activated node set (the seed set size), and the ordinate represents the final influence spread of these seed node set in the scale, that is, the number of nodes that can be finally activated. As can be seen from Fig. 3, the final influence spread increases as the initial set of nodes increases in both of the algorithms. As the Greedy algorithm is always able to get the current 63% of the approximate optimal spread effect, and the above analysis shows that the GSG algorithm, compared to climbing greedy algorithm in the same data set, has no less activated nodes by the selected seed set than that in the latter algorithm, which indicates that the effect of GSG algorithm is more stable and efficient when solving the problem of maximum node mining.

Algorithm Running Time Analysis. In the previous section, we have analyzed the influence spread of the two algorithms under the same scale of initial activated node set. The experiment in this section is a progressive experiment of the previous experiment, choosing 10 sets of seed nodes from the scale of 50,100,150,200 to 400,450,500 to simulate the spread, and the comparison results are shown in Fig. 4.

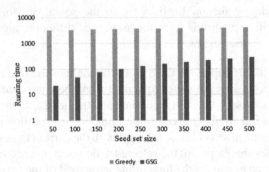

Fig. 4. Running time of GSG algorithm and Greedy algorithm in different seed node set scale

By analyzing the experimental data, it can be concluded that the GSG algorithm requires about k/n time of the Greedy algorithm with the same initial activated node set size, where k is the set size of initial activated nodes and n is the total node size of experimental data. It can be seen from the figure that the running time required for GSG algorithm spread is much shorter than that of Greedy algorithm with the same seed node set size.

Algorithm Pressure Test. This experiment is conducted only on the Enron email networks dataset [12] whose communication networks covers approximately 500,000 e-mail due to computer hardware conditional resources, which were originally is surveyed, analyzed and published online by the US Federal Energy Regulatory Commission. In the experiment on the Enron email networks dataset, this paper focuses on the time it takes for the GSG algorithm to select a particular size of initial activated node set, as results shown in Fig. 5. The abscissa in the figure represents the size of the selected initial set of activated nodes, and the ordinate represents the running time required to select the corresponding size of initial activated node.

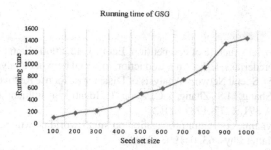

Fig. 5. Running time of the GSG algorithm on the Enron email networks dataset

It can be seen from Fig. 5 that the running time of GSG algorithm in the data set size of tens of thousands of nodes on the social networks to mine the initial activated node is still acceptable. For example, when 500 initial activated nodes are selected on the Enron email networks dataset, the time required for the GSG algorithm to be executed is 513 s $\approx$ 8.5 min. And when 1000 initial activation nodes are selected on the data set, it takes the GSG algorithm 1456 s $\approx$ 24 min to finish its calculation, and the size of the data set has reached a scale of 36k, which is a medium-sized large data set in the social networks analysis.

4   Conclusion

The research on the maximum social networks node influence mining algorithm has been related to many fields. And scholars have proposed many related algorithms according to the characteristics of the networks and the research method, in which the node mining algorithm can be summed up in two categories. One is the algorithm based on mining of the node's own topology information, and the other is by analyzing the nature of the overall social networks to identify a single node's influence. In this paper, we summarize the research results of scholars in recent years and put forward the social networks node mining algorithm based on greedy subgraph. Besides, detailed comparison experiments on the proposed algorithm have been conducted, further discussing the accuracy of the nodes mined, the stability of the spread results, the running time of the algorithm, the stress test of the algorithm, and so on. At the same time, the paper also validates the advantages of the proposed algorithm in the above aspects.

Acknowledgments. This work was funded by the National Natural Science Foundation of China under Grant (No. 61772152 and No. 61502037), the Basic Research Project (No. JCKY2016 206B001, JCKY2014206C002 and JCKY2017604C010), and the Technical Foundation Project (No. JSQB2017206C002).

References

1. Burt, R.S.: The social structure of competition. Econ. J. **42**, 7060–7066 (1992)
2. Durland, M.M., Fredericks, K.A.: An introduction to social network analysis. New Dir. Eval. **2005**, 5–13 (2005). Social Network Analysis of Disaster Response Recovery and Adaptation
3. Chen, D., Lü, L., Shang, M.S., Zhang, Y.C., Zhou, T.: Identifying influential nodes in complex networks. Phys. A **391**, 1777–1787 (2012)
4. Zanette, D.H.: Dynamics of rumor propagation on small-world networks. Phys. Rev. E Stat. Nonlinear Soft Matter Phys. **65**, 041908 (2002)
5. Xu, J., Chen, H.: Criminal network analysis and visualization. ACM (2005)
6. Wu, S., Hofman, J.M., Mason, W.A., Watts, D.J.: Who says what to whom on Twitter. In: International Conference on World Wide Web, WWW 2011, Hyderabad, India, 28 March–1 April, pp. 705–714 (2011)
7. Burt, R.S., Minor, M.J.: Applied network analysis: a methodological introduction. Can. J. Sociol. **63** (1983)
8. Bonacich, P.: Factoring and weighting approaches to status scores and clique identification. J. Math. Sociol. **2**, 113–120 (1972)
9. Aadithya, K.V., et al.: Centrality in social networks conceptual clarification. Soc. Netw. **1**, 215–239 (2010)
10. Chen, W., Yuan, Y., Zhang, L.: Scalable influence maximization in social networks under the linear threshold model. In: IEEE International Conference on Data Mining, pp. 88–97 (2010)
11. Vichaya, A., Joseph, K., Fredrickson, P.A., Lin, S.C., Castillo, P.R., Heckman, M.G.: IRIE: a scalable influence maximization algorithm for independent cascade model and its extensions. Rev. Crim. **56**, 1451–1455 (2011)
12. Leskovec, J., Lang, K.J., Dasgupta, A., Mahoney, M.W.: Community structure in large networks: natural cluster sizes and the absence of large well-defined clusters. Internet Math. **6**, 29–123 (2008)

Study on Cloud Logistics Distribution Model of Agricultural Products

Jianbiao Huang and Linli Tao[✉]

Xiangnan University, Chenzhou 42300, China
123472880@qq.com

Abstract. In the context of intensified market economic competition, logistics distribution still shows some lags in terms of efficiency, cost and effect speed. And the problems of agricultural products logistics are particularly acute. In order to further integrate and optimize the social logistics resources, improve the logistics efficiency of agricultural products, In this paper, an agricultural product logistics distribution model is proposed combined with the cloud computing technology, and the IDEF0 method is used to construct a model of cloud logistics' agricultural product distribution model. It analyzes its architecture from three levels: online system, online and offline link system and offline physical distribution system, which providing new thoughts for the development of agricultural products' logistics. The modernization of agricultural product logistics is the focus of China's agricultural modernization, and the improvement of the logistics efficiency of agricultural products involves many factors. This paper combines the characteristics of agricultural logistics and the cloud logistics service model to demonstrate the basic structure of the proposed model. However, in the actual situation, the logistics of agricultural products may be more complicated.

Keywords: Cloud computing · Cloud logistics
Logistics of agricultural products · Logistics distribution · IDEF0

1 Introduction

In the 21st century, the development of the Internet technology supports the large-scale, social and real-time social collaboration, which greatly improves the efficiency of collaboration among consumers, businesses and different entities and enables the personalized logistics needs to be met. Subsequently, the collaboration platform based on the Internet and big data is gradually becoming mature, forming a logistics distribution division and collaboration model centered on consumers. Based on this, the concept of cloud logistics is proposed. Cloud logistics is defined as an innovative logistics model using the cloud computing to change and renovate the traditional logistics industry. During the transformation and development of logistics giants such as China Post's "cloud warehouse", Suning's "cloud merchant" and Alibaba's "Cainiao", the logistics innovation development model is introduced and practiced, and studies and application of cloud logistics are becoming increasingly extensive and mature. China is a big agricultural country, in which the modernization of agricultural

X. Sun et al. (Eds.): ICCCS 2018, LNCS 11064, pp. 169–181, 2018.
https://doi.org/10.1007/978-3-030-00009-7_16

products is a key issue in the transition from traditional agriculture to modern agriculture. Based on the thought of efficiency integration of the logistics resources by cloud logistics, the thought of cloud computing is combined to analyze the agricultural product logistics distribution model by relevant technologies, and an agricultural product cloud logistics distribution model based on the IDEF0 model is proposed.

2 Preliminaries

Cloud computing was first proposed by Google CEO Eric Schmidt in 2006. Since then, with the development of information technology, cloud computing methods have been applied to different fields, and relevant theories and practices at home and abroad have also been gradually improved. Cloud computing typically involves the provision of dynamically scalable and often virtualized resources over the Internet. Foster [1] described cloud computing as providing abstract, virtual, dynamically scalable, and manageable computing capability services, storage services, and platform services to external users over the Internet.

In China, the concept of cloud logistics was first proposed by logistics companies in 2010. At present, relevant theories and technologies are still in the initial stage, and the research results are relatively limited. Liang [2] analyzed the mechanism of improving logistics efficiency by using big data and cloud computing, and put forward three innovative logistics models of logistics supermarkets, logistics supply chain integration and virtual anhydrous ports. Wang [3] conducted a more in-depth study of cloud logistics, conducted modeling and analysis of the "cloud storage" problem under big data, and designed a set of cloud logistics service quality evaluation system.

The cloud logistics is likened to a "reservoir". In this system, the pool integrates a large number of logistics resources and orders, and the water pipes are like various transportation methods. The faucets are all logistics enterprises. Integrating the resources of a "water reservoir" requires a huge computing integration capability, which is cloud computing. On the cloud platform, all logistics companies, express delivery companies, manufacturing companies, warehousing companies, sales companies, e-commerce companies, transportation companies, and logistics hubs are all focused on the organic integration of cloud platforms [4]. Each resource module is displayed and coordinated with each other to reduce costs and improve efficiency as shown in Fig. 1.

Cloud logistics introduces the concept of big data and cloud computing into the logistics field, as shown in Fig. 2. Using the powerful processing capabilities of cloud computing, a service platform based on big data was established to complete the resource integration and distribution activities for the logistics industry and departments.

First of all, it is necessary to integrate the supply and demand information of a large number of logistics and distribution services to form a huge pool of logistics resources in order to build a "cloud logistics" information platform. The information platform integrates a large number of user order information, information of distribution service providers such as logistics, express delivery, and carriers, etc. The demand side can

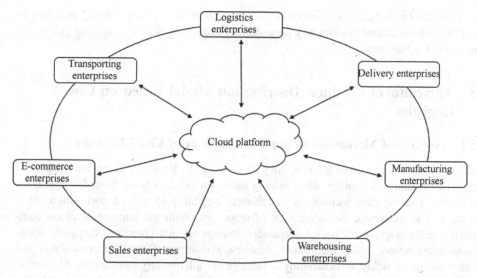

Fig. 1. Diagram of cloud logistics structure

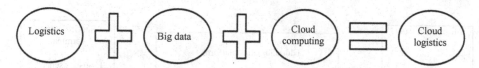

Fig. 2. Composition of cloud logistics

easily obtain the required information and services. On this basis, a unified standard is established to ensure the uniformity and scalability of the cloud platform.

China's agricultural product logistics has existed in the market for a long time in the form of simple and extensive, scattered distribution of agricultural products with low degree of resource integration and insufficient information sharing, which has caused agricultural product logistics to become a major obstacle to agricultural modernization. Therefore, some scholars have tried to use the concept of cloud logistics for agricultural logistics. Yu [5] proposed the logistics distribution model of agricultural products based on cloud logistics and constructed the framework of agricultural product logistics and distribution service system. They are: service requester, service provider, and resource integration manager. Lu [6] studied the model of agricultural and commercial integration under the cloud logistics and proposed the development ideas for the circulation mode of agricultural and commercial integration.

At present, the relevant research on cloud logistics can be summarized as follows: the discussion of cloud logistics service model; the application of cloud logistics in e-commerce; the application of cloud logistics in the express industry; the research of big data in cloud logistics Research on "cloud warehousing"; research on cloud logistics delivery service quality evaluation [7]; benefit and cost issues under cloud logistics model [8]. In general, the application of cloud logistics has a short research time. It is worthwhile to study the service model of cloud logistics for agricultural products to explore a low-cost, high-efficiency agricultural product logistics distribution model that meets the actual needs.

3 Agricultural Products Distribution Model Based on Cloud Logistics

3.1 Analysis of Mechanism to Improve Efficiency of Cloud Logistics

The improvement of logistics efficiency of cloud logistics depends on the support of cloud computing technology. Data mining based on big data is the basis for intelligent logistics. Use big data technology to enhance the ability to collect, sort, and analyze data, and to maximize the integration of resources. With the support of cloud computing technology, each logistics and distribution service company complete information collection, order integration, business convergence, intelligent analysis and other services quickly and efficiently to achieve complementary advantages. They unite and cooperate with each other, and a smart logistics ecosystem is formed [9]. The operating mode structure of cloud logistics is shown in Fig. 3.

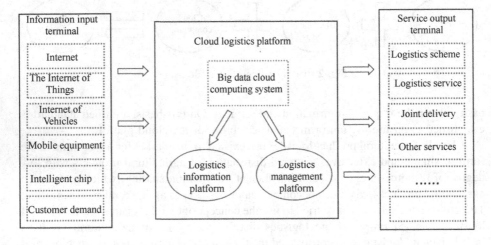

Fig. 3. Big data cloud logistics model

The specific implementation process is described as follows: The first step is to use big data technology to collect, sort, extract, and analyze logistics data. In the big data system, a large data warehouse is established by collecting users' social network information, exchange information, sensors, and other data to lay a data foundation for carrying out data mining and customizing personalized services. This creates the basic conditions for the construction of quick logistics, smart logistics, and ecological logistics.

The second step is the operation of the cloud logistics information platform. On the one hand, it provides the user with an interface for data. On the other hand, the platform collects a large amount of data of the user and the operating parameters of the platform.

The third step is to run a logistics management platform. As a comprehensive service platform for intelligent analysis and auxiliary decision-making in the operation of cloud logistics, it is a key step for improving logistics efficiency at the management level and strategic level. The platform can accurately process orders for enterprises, coordinate various types of logistics service resources, and provide a full range of logistics and distribution services.

3.2 Design of Agricultural Product Logistics Distribution Model Under Cloud Logistics Architecture

Combining the logistics business needs and characteristics, the cloud logistics distribution service platform can be divided into three modules: the cloud logistics request end, the cloud logistics provision end, and the cloud logistics distribution service integration end, as shown in Fig. 4 [10].

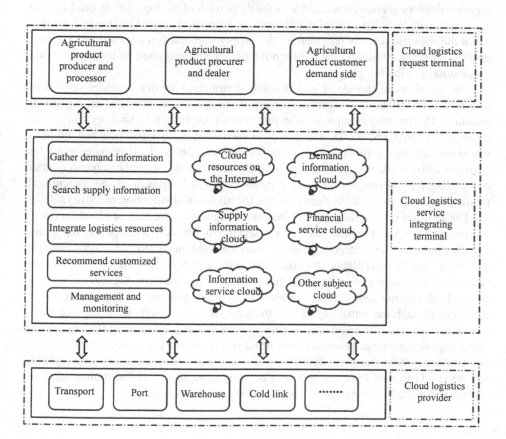

Fig. 4. Architecture of cloud platform

Based on the openness and coordination of the cloud service platform, both the supply and demand parties of logistics services can easily join the platform and complete the integration of resources [11]. The request side of the agricultural product cloud logistics constitutes the platform around the demand main body, and both the supply and demand sides of the logistics service can exchange and share information. The integration of distribution services is the core of cloud logistics. Its role is to complete the integration, classification, monitoring and optimization of resources.

Any node user on the agricultural product supply chain can request the product through the request of the agricultural product logistics and distribution service at any time. Taking the "agricultural super docking model" as an example, the agricultural product logistics process can be roughly described as: agricultural producer - agricultural - association - processing - cooperative supplier - wholesale r – supermarket - consumer. The stakeholders in the supply chain obtain the required services from the cloud platform; various types of logistics and distribution services in the supply chain can also cooperate with other logistics functional units through the platform, such as the storage and transportation of different logistics and distribution service units, and warehousing, cooperation with circulation processing, etc. For the realization of the logistics delivery service demand, due to the dispersion of the logistics demand in time and space, and the uniqueness of the demand, so response received by the demand side is not the response directly provided by the supply side, but is a personalized logistics distribution service solution that has been integrated and integrated by the logistics and distribution service integration.

The members of the cloud logistics and distribution service provider consist of logistics and distribution companies that fulfill the specific functions of all aspects of logistics. The member companies use the Internet of Things technology, their own databases, ERP, GPS, RFID, and bar code technologies to input rich and multidimensional logistics information into the "cloud" to form a cloud resource pool for logistics distribution services for agricultural products. As with the requester, after completing the information processing in the integrated segment of the agricultural product cloud logistics, it is released to the logistics and distribution company.

The logistics distribution service integration segment is the core of cloud logistics. It connects the service request side and the service supply side. It effectively integrates logistics resources and integrates logistics service solutions through resource consolidation, mining, and calculation. Its main functions are as follows: First, directly link the "cloud" of user information and logistics resources information; Second, accept the demand information sent by the requester at any time, and allocate logistics resource resources through the actual capacity of the massive service units to ensure that users can obtain the required resources on time and on demand; Thirdly, in the concept of cloud logistics, logistics resources are virtual in the cloud. Therefore, in actual operations, there is still a need for effective contacts between enterprises to achieve logistics operations. Therefore, the integration and delivery of logistics and distribution services should also have functions such as fee settlement and payment.

4 Design of Agricultural Product Logistics Distribution Model Based on IDEF0 Model

4.1 Distribution IDEF0 Model Based on Agricultural Product Cloud Logistics

The meaning of IDEF (Integrated Computer-Aided Manufacturing Definition) is to integrate calculator-aided manufacturing. The role of the first type of IDEF method is to exchange information between system integration personnel. IDEF0 is used to analyze the internal functional processes of the enterprise. The logical relationship between input, output, control and function of the entire system can be represented by the top-level relational model A-0 of the agricultural product distribution IDEF0 of cloud logistics, as shown in Fig. 5.

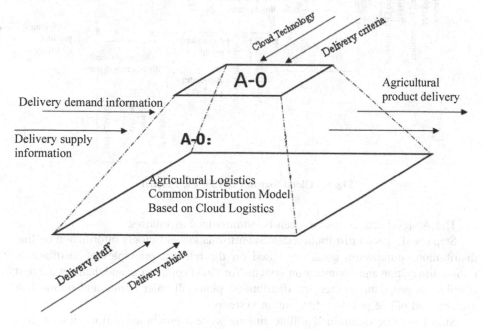

Fig. 5. IDEF0 model based on cloud logistics

The A-0 map reflects the system boundary of the agricultural product distribution of cloud logistics. The input of the system is the distribution requirements of agricultural products and the information and resources of distribution supply. The output is the user's needs are met. The control of the system is that the cloud server statistics and calculation of these information, and then according to the constraints of the distribution program to optimize, through distribution vehicles, distribution centers and other resource conditions for agricultural products delivery, complete the output.

The A0 map is further subdivided on the basis of the A-0 chart. The overall system of the model is divided into three subsystems: the online distribution optimization system, the offline online link system, and the offline physical distribution system, as shown in Fig. 6. In this way, the process and structure of the cloud logistics agricultural product distribution system model and the relationship between the various model sectors can be more clearly described.

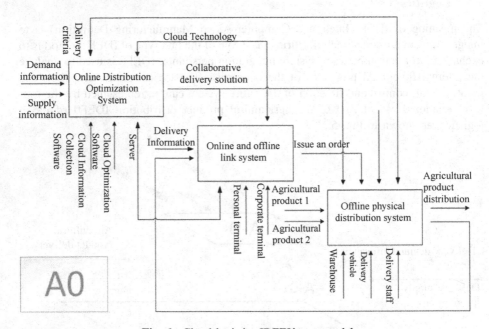

Fig. 6. Cloud logistics IDEF0's top model

The A0-level activity process can be summarized as follows:

Step one: Logistics distribution demand information and supply information on-line distribution optimization goals are based on the relevant principles of distribution, online distribution and optimization systems for cloud computing, and then get the best distribution program. Further, the distribution plan will enter online and offline link systems and offline physical distribution systems.

Step two: The online and offline linking system combines various information orders issued by individuals and enterprises to timely update the relevant information of agricultural product distribution in the cloud and convey relevant delivery instructions.

Step three: After the issuance of the delivery instruction, the physical delivery under the line is completed according to the related service standards of the delivery. Offline logistics resources work together to complete delivery operations. At the same time, the offline entity system collects all kinds of logistics information and feeds it back to the cloud. After the orders are settled online by the payment system in the online-linked system, the distribution plan is completed.

4.2 Online System's IDEF0 Model

The online system is the key point in the agricultural product distribution model based on cloud logistics, and it is also the core of resource integration. The cloud resource integration is reasonable to achieve a better distribution plan, so that the offline distribution can achieve economic efficiency and high efficiency. The online system model structure of agricultural product cloud logistics is shown in Fig. 7.

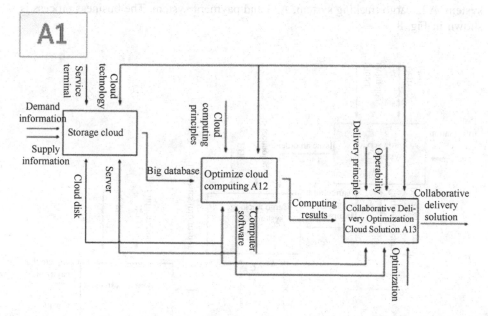

Fig. 7. Cloud logistics IDEF0 model's online framework

The online system A1 of the agricultural product distribution model can be divided into three parts: A11 storage cloud, A12 optimized computing cloud and A13 distribution optimization plan cloud. The specific operation flow is described as follows. The first step: the user uploads demand information through the service request port, and the enterprise also uploads the available service information to the cloud storage area A11. The storage cloud initially collates and analyzes various kinds of information to form a huge big database. The second step: the information of the large database enters into the optimization cloud computing system. Under the constraint conditions of the relevant calculation criteria, the preliminary distribution plan is calculated. The third step is to further enter the preliminary distribution plan into the optimization plan area of the distribution, and carry out optimization of the plan under the constraints of the distribution criteria and operability of the distribution to form the final distribution plan.

4.3   Online and Offline Link System's IDEF0 Model

The main function of the online and offline link system IDEF0 model is to connect online and offline of the agricultural product cloud logistics distribution platform. After the online system concludes that the best delivery plan has been completed, issue an order to the offline delivery entity. In this process, the link system acts as a bridge, processing settlement and payment services at the same time, and the system has the function of cargo tracking. Its structure consists of three parts: A21 online service system, A22 cargo tracking system, A23 and payment system. The business process is shown in Fig. 8.

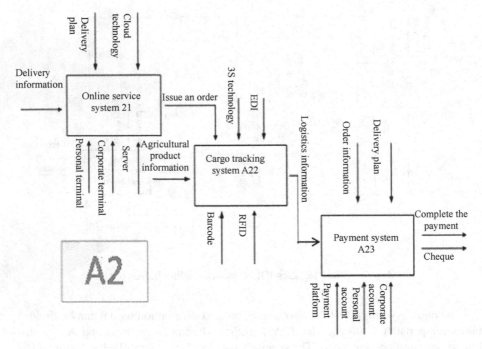

Fig. 8. Agricultural product cloud logistics IDEF0 model's online and offline link framework

The first step: After the distribution information enters the online cloud service system, the online service system gives the best distribution plan according to the distribution constraints. The offline company issues the delivery instruction and starts delivery. The second step: the delivery instruction is sent to the cargo tracking system and the goods are tracked using barcode, RFID, 3S technology, etc. to form the logistics information. The third step: The payment system receives the logistics information and autonomously judges the completion of the distribution. When the delivery is completed, the order directly enters the payment system, and according to the order information, the corresponding service fee is deducted, and then the proceeds are distributed according to the proportion of each participating enterprise that is involved in the integrated delivery plan, and the income is allocated to each distribution enterprise account. At the same time, the cloud platform issued the relevant electronic receipt certificate.

4.4 Offline Physical Distribution System's IDEF0 Model

The physical distribution system is the basic support for completing the logistics service and is the ultimate goal of the entire distribution system. The integrated solution for online distribution is only a virtual solution. To achieve distribution, the offline distribution system is indispensable. Based on the characteristics of offline distribution, the offline physical distribution model is summarized into three modules: A31 Distribution Center Management Information System, A32 Warehouse Management System, and A33 Distribution Management System. The business process is shown in Fig. 9.

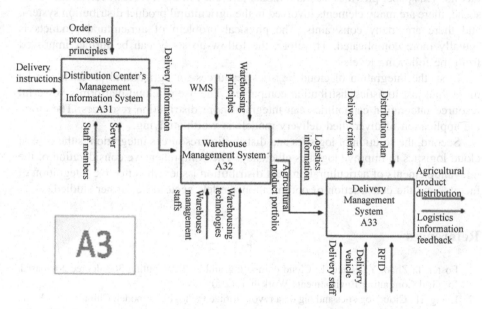

Fig. 9. Agricultural product cloud logistics IDEF0 model's offline architecture

Step one: the distribution management center receives the optimized delivery instructions from the online platform and passes the delivery information to the warehouse management system.

Step two: After the warehouse manager receives the delivery information, he will follow the principles of warehouse management and deliver it to the delivery area.

Step three: After the delivery personnel receives the delivery order and the goods to be delivered, it implements the delivery. During the delivery process, relevant technologies are used to collect information such as RFID, GPS, and bar code technology, and then the feedback information is transmitted to the cloud for tracking of the items until the delivery operation is completed.

5 Conclusion

The modernization of agricultural product logistics is the focus of China's agricultural modernization, and current IT technologies such as cloud computing and big data are widely used in all walks of life, and the results are significant [12]. Combining the characteristics of agricultural logistics and the service model of cloud logistics, this paper proposes a distribution logistics service model based on cloud logistics. Taking the distribution of agricultural products as an example, the model of agricultural logistics distribution based on cloud logistics was modeled using the method of IDEF0. The basic structure of the model was demonstrated in detail, trying to bring the logistics of agricultural products into the era of "cloud" and improving the logistics of agricultural products. The efficiency of reducing the logistics costs of agricultural products.

The improvement of the logistics efficiency of agricultural products involves many factors. This paper provides a certain model reference in theory. However, in the actual scene, there are many elements involved in the agricultural product distribution system, and there are many constraints. The physical problem of agricultural products is actually more complicated. Therefore, the follow-up study can be further improved from the following levels.

First, the integration of cloud logistics resources for agricultural products can be more than just logistics distribution companies. The use of cloud platform's powerful resource integration capabilities can integrate more distribution resources. Therefore, the application of diversified delivery models is worth studying.

Second, the solution of logistics and distribution resources integration is the core of cloud logistics to improve logistics efficiency. The comprehensive consideration of the relevant elements of agricultural product distribution issues, the effective integration of factors, and the construction of optimization models need to be further studied.

References

1. Foster, I., Zhao, Y., Raicu, I.: Cloud computing and grid computing 360-degree compared. In: Grid Computing Environments Workshop (2008)
2. Liang, H.: Cloud logistics and big data revolutionize the logistics model. China's Circ. Econ. (2014)
3. Wang, X.: Research on theory, method and application of smart cloud logistics based on big data. Zhejiang University of Technology (2015)
4. Jiang, Y., Fang, Z.: Virtual enterprise production logistics system modeling and simulation. J. Ningbo Univ. (Nat. Sci. Eng. Ed.) (2015)
5. Yu, Z.: Study on logistics distribution service model of agricultural products based on cloud logistics framework. In: Conference on Web Based Business Management (2012)
6. Lu, H., Zhang, J.: Innovation of logistics integration model integrating agriculture, logistics and business under cloud logistics. Bus. Times (2015)
7. Ramanathan, R.: The moderating roles of risk and efficiency on the relationship between logistics performance and customer loyalty in e-commerce. Transp. Res. **46**, 950–962 (2010)
8. Subramanian, N.P., Abdulrahman, M.D., Zhou, X.: Integration of logistics and cloud computing service providers: cost and green benefits in the Chinese context. Transp. Res. Part E: Logist. Transp. Rev. **70**, 86–98 (2014)

9. Lin, Y., Tian, S.: Logistics cloud service: innovation model of logistics service oriented to supply chain. Appl. Res. Comput. **29**, 224–228 (2012)

10. Fu, P.: Smart logistics model construction based on big data. Logist. Technol. (2018)

11. Nowicka, K.: Smart city logistics on cloud computing model. Procedia - Soc. Behav. Sci. **151**, 266–281 (2014)

12. Wang, X.: The logistics mode innovation of e-commerce enterprises in China and the development prospect discussion of "cloud logistics". J. Commer. Econ. (2017)

Teaching Video Recommendation Based on Student Evaluation

Jie Zhang[1], Yongsheng Zhang[1(✉)], Xiaolong Wu[1], and Guoyun Li[2]

[1] School of Information Science and Engineering, Shandong Normal University,
Jinan, China
elegantzhang@outlook.com, zhangys@sdnu.edu.cn,
sdnuwuxl@163.com
[2] Zhongtai Securities, Jinan, China
lgy9106@outlook.com

Abstract. At present, online education gradually changes the traditional education model, but the development of students is diverse. Because of the lack of interaction, teaching videos can hardly meet the individual needs of students. Nowadays, online teaching videos are mixed and it is very difficult for students and parents to choose suitable teaching videos for students. However, the uniform education does not accord with the characteristics of middle school students' physical and mental development at the present stage, and it is difficult to achieve the expected effect of teaching. This paper analyzes the characteristics of instructional videos from a professional point of view, combined with the physical and mental development characteristics of high school students to collect student evaluation of teaching video from a student point of view, to extract the students study preferences, use Collaborative filtering algorithm recommended teaching in line with students will be taught the way for students. This not only applies the convenience of online teaching, but also achieves personalized teaching services. At the same time, it also conforms to the characteristics of physical and mental development of middle school students, and greatly improves students' enthusiasms and efficiency in learning.

Keywords: Individuation · Video recommendation
Physical and mental development · Collaborative filtering

1 Introduction

With the entry of the Internet into the field of education, students' learning methods has also changed from traditional classroom learning to online learning supported by the Internet. Video teaching plays an important role in online teaching with its characteristics of "intuition", "visualization" and "authenticity".

However, for non-professional students and parents, it is very difficult to vast amounts of instructional video in a reasonable choice for students to learn video. Only by following the law of students' physical and mental development and choosing their preferred teaching mode can they improve the efficiency of listening and learning with pleasure and achieve twice the result with half the effort. In order to make the teaching of network recording and broadcasting more pertinence and inter-active, this paper puts

© Springer Nature Switzerland AG 2018
X. Sun et al. (Eds.): ICCCS 2018, LNCS 11064, pp. 182–190, 2018.
https://doi.org/10.1007/978-3-030-00009-7_17

forward the personalized recommendation of teaching video based on the idea of Collaborative filtering algorithm. Firstly, the feedback data are collected according to the evaluation criteria of video teaching, and then, according to the feedback of each student, a personalized map of students' listening tendency is formed. According to each student's preference for teaching characteristics, it is possible to recommend courses that are more suitable for students. In addition, the personalized recommendation result is changed with the change of the user's history information. In other words, when the user's behavior data changes, the results of personalized recommendation will change accordingly [1].

2 Related Work

We need to set up both a scientific and consistent evaluation system for middle school students understanding, so we first studied the characteristics of high school students, and secondly, they studied the domestic network of more mainstream course evaluation system. The final recommendation algorithm mainly uses Collaborative filtering technology, we also studied the basic idea of Collaborative filtering.

2.1 Study on Characteristics of Middle School Students

A. Middle school physical and mental development characteristics
The general rules of individual physical and mental development of sequential, stage, imbalance, complementarity and individual differences. Recognizing the laws and following the rules can better help learning and learning. To adapt to the theory of mastering students' physical and mental development, to familiarize themselves with the characteristics of physical and mental development of students of different ages, and to conduct education and teaching activities in accordance with the laws and characteristics of students' physical and mental development, so as to effectively promote the healthy development of students' physical and mental health.

The development of each student is unique. The student is a complete person, and each student has his own uniqueness. It is necessary to face up to the individual differences of the students and teach them according to their own circumstances. There is a huge difference between students and adults, students' observation, thinking, choice and experience are obviously different from adults. Therefore, we must consider the problem from the perspective of students.

B. Cognitive development on characteristics of middle school students
The consciousness and purpose of middle school students have been further improved, the accuracy and generality of intuitive things have been improved constantly, and the spatial intuition has more abstract, selective, understanding, integrity and constancy.

Learning and memory can basically be divided into image memory, logical memory, emotional memory, and motion memory. The memory of the intuitive material is better than the vocabulary. Intentional memory gradually dominates, understanding memory as the main means of memory.

The main feature of the development of thinking is that abstract logical thinking occupies a dominant position and can form complete abstract symbols in the mind and analyze and solve problems under the guidance of theory.

C. The Personalization Research of Middle School students

The greatest highlight of this topic is the study of student-centered personalization. Individual's personality and develop a process, and the pursuit of self-worth is a real process of individuation, is for the student's personality characteristics and to develop their potential and to take the appropriate methods and means, to encourage students in all aspects to get full, free, harmonious development process [2].

The individualized learning theory shifts the emphasis of education and teaching from teachers' teaching to students' learning, emphasizing on learning. While paying attention to the social value of learning, it pays more attention to the value of people [3].

2.2   Study on Education Evaluation System

Taylor R. W. Tyler, an American scholar, believes that educational evaluation is the process of measuring the degree to which educational goals are actually achieved. So we need to develop a scientific evaluation system to serve as the basis for our research. According to some foreign standards, several evaluation systems have been published and implemented in China, and we mainly refer to two domestic traditional evaluation systems.

A. Standard for Courseware Evaluation for Web-based Courses

This standard is only the lowest standard that can meet the requirements of network courseware. It can be divided into three types: required option, optional option and encouraging option. It summarizes teaching design, teaching content, usability, technology, etc. There are six first-level indicators of media characteristics and documents, and several sub-indicators are subdivided under each index, and there are one or two third-level indicators under second-level indicators.

B. CELTS-22.1: Specifications for Evaluating Web-Based Courses

In 2002, the Education Informatization Technology Standards Committee of the Ministry of Education issued the Education Informatization Technology Standard CELTS-22.1: Web-based course Evaluation Standard (specification for Evaluating Web-Based course). Through a set of specific indicators system to evaluate the quality attributes of network courses from multiple dimensions. They are: course content, teaching design, interface design, Technology. Each dimension contains specific evaluation indicators. There are 7 indicators in the curriculum content dimension, which are used to evaluate the quality and organizational structure of the curriculum content itself. There are 14 indicators in the instructional design dimension. The design of teaching goal, the design of teaching process strategy and the design of evaluation method are measured. There are 9 indexes in the interface design dimension, and the factors that affect the usability of the online course are evaluated. There are 6 indexes in the technical dimension. The reliability and suitability of the adopted technology are evaluated. The whole specification includes 36 evaluation indicators [4].

2.3   Collaborative Filtering

Collaborative filtering is one of the most common and successful technologies in the field of recommendation. Its core idea is to calculate a sort of directory according to their preferences by looking for the similar "neighbor" of the research object, and then recommend it to the research object.

According to the general model of personalized recommendation system given by Goldberg et al., the workflow of recommendation system can be summarized as follows:

(1) In order to obtain the interest preference of the user, it can be either active or passive, that is, it can be the preference description provided by the user actively, or the recommendation system can analyze the historical behavior data of the user. The interest preference of users is mined by correlation algorithms.

(2) The recommendation system builds the user model based on the interest preference of the users.

(3) According to the constructed user model, a corresponding recommendation algorithm is selected, the recommendation items are filtered, the recommendation list is generated, and the recommendation list is feedback to the user to be recommended [1].

3   Model Overview

First, we develop an evaluation system of educational video, then analyze the data according to the feedback data of users, construct a user preference vector, and then calculate the similarity between users according to the recommendation algorithm model. The recommendation model as shown in Fig. 1.

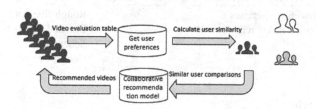

Fig. 1. The recommendation model graphic.

3.1   The Design of Educational Video Evaluation System

Because the system pays more attention to the teaching characteristic of the educational video content, but neglects the "technology" characteristic of the network video. Four of them are selected as the evaluation characteristics of the system, including: teaching design, teaching content, teaching implementation, teaching style. Each level of heading is subdivided into several secondary headings.

According to the needs of this research topic, because the target population is a middle school student, it has a certain ability to distinguish itself and has its own preferences. However, the formulation of this evaluation content should be made from the perspective of middle school students, not too professional. After all, the audience is after all a student, not a professional educator, we subdivide the options of each index again, so that students can understand and evaluate accurately.

A. Teaching Design

Teaching design includes three two-level indicators: knowledge introduction, motivation and interest, and practice design. The breakdown of options for each secondary indicator is shown in Table 1.

Table 1. Table of teaching design evaluation.

Knowledge representation mode	Attention guiding mode	Methods of solving questions
Introducing examples	Task driven	Multiple solutions
Experimental demonstration	Playing games	Classic solution
Interlocution	Scenario simulation	Targeted solutions
Analogy	Animation demonstration	Only results
	Challenging activities	

B. Teaching Content

The teaching content includes the consistency of two secondary indicators contents and the logical structure. The breakdown of options for each secondary indicator is shown in Table 2.

Table 2. Table of teaching content evaluation.

Conformity between teaching content and goal	Course structure
Providing exercises	Rough title list
Course meets requirements	Detailed title list
	Schematic
	Concept map

C. Teaching Style

Teaching style includes two secondary indicators: language style, professionalism. The breakdown of options for each secondary indicator is shown in Table 3.

Table 3. Table of teaching style evaluation.

Class atmosphere	Professionalism
Funny humor	Academic
Professional rigor	User-friendly

D. Teaching Implementation

Teaching implementation includes three secondary indicators: teaching process, teaching methods, and teaching tools. The breakdown of options for each secondary indicator is shown in Table 4.

Table 4. Table of teaching implementation evaluation.

Teaching process	Attention guiding mode	Teaching tools
Teaching and practice	Practical teaching	Picture
Experimental demonstration	Lecture-based teaching	Animation
		Text
		Audio

3.2 Video Evaluation Model

For video v, we use y_{uv} to represent the user's overall preference for video v. $\vec{x}_v = (x_{v1}, x_{v2} \cdots x_{vi} \cdots x_{vn})$ is the corresponding evaluation vector. n is the number of evaluation items. x_{vi} is the score of video v in item i. Its value is the average number of votes for all users on video v. The formula is as follows:

$$x_{vi} = \frac{t_1 + t_2 + \cdots t_j \cdots + t_m}{m} \tag{1}$$

$t_j \in \{0, 1\}$, $t_j = 1$ indicates that user j think video has the feature, $t_j = 1$ otherwise. After the calculation, we get the user's universal view of the video on feature i. represents score of video on feature j. The closer the x_{vi} is to 1, the more users think video v has the feature i.

3.3 User Preference Learning Model

The degree of user preference for the video and the video evaluation can be represented by linear regression model:

$$y_{uv} = \beta_{u0} + \beta_{u1}x_{v1} + \beta_{u2}x_{v2} \cdots + \beta_{ui}x_{vi} + \cdots + \beta_{un}x_{vn} + \varepsilon, \tag{2}$$

and β_{ui} make up the vector $\vec{\beta}_u$:

$$\vec{\beta}_u = (\beta_{u0}, \beta_{u1}, \cdots \beta_{ui}, \cdots \beta_{un}) \tag{3}$$

We expand the dimensions of $\vec{x}_v$ to $\vec{x}'_v$, which can be given by:

$$y_{uv} = \vec{x}'_v \vec{\beta}_u^T + \varepsilon \tag{4}$$

The parameter vector $\vec{\beta}_u$ is the user preference for u.

3.4 Video Recommendation Algorithm

This paper uses the idea of Collaborative filtering algorithm to perform video recommendation. The key is to calculate the distance between users after obtaining the user preference, and get the closest user. Commonly used similarity calculation methods for Collaborative filtering include Euclidean Distance, Pearson Correlation Coefficient, and Tanimoto Coefficient.

This paper uses the Euclidean Distance formula to calculate the distance between user preference. The calculation method is as follows, in this formula d_v^u is the distance between u and v.

$$d_v^u = dist\left(\vec{\beta}_u, \vec{\beta}_v\right) = \sqrt{\sum_{i=1}^{n}\left(\beta_i^u - \beta_i^v\right)^2} \qquad (5)$$

The distance between users can be calculated by the formula for the distance between vectors defined by $dist()$. Then using the following formula for a user and converts the similarity distance, where sim_v^u represents the degree of similarity, i.e. the distance is smaller, the similarity of the user about the big.

$$sim_v^u = \frac{1}{1 + d_v^u} \qquad (6)$$

The user v closest to the user u can be obtained through calculation. The video scored by the two users is represented by the sets E_u and E_v. And the video set recommended by the candidate to the user is represented by E. The calculation method is as follows:

$$E = E_v - (E_u \cap E_v) \qquad (7)$$

Set E represents videos that user v watched and user u didn't watched. After getting E, we select the video with the highest rating in this set as a recommendation for user u.

4   Experiments and Analysis

4.1 Datasets Description

We use one real dataset, MovieLens [6], to experimentally evaluate the proposed method. This dataset describes 5-star rating and free-text tagging activity from [MovieLens], a popular movie recommendation platform. It contains 20000263 ratings and 465564 tag applications across 27278 movies. These data were created by 138493 users between January 09, 1995 and March 31, 2015. We select a part of the dataset which is created from January 2011 to March 2015, in which there have 2142 users who had rated at least 20 movies exist during this period. Each pair of movie and tag is associated with a relevance score ranging from 0 to 1, using the Tag Genome approach [7].

4.2   Evaluation Metrics and Result Discussion

In our experiments, the evaluation metrics is to calculates the video which has highest rating by the most similar user and verify whether the target user like it. To evaluate our method, we partition the selected dataset into two parts according to time period: the training dataset D_1 covers ratings from January 2011 to January 2015, and the test dataset D_2 from January 2015 to March 2015.

For training dataset D_1, we calculate the Euclidean distance between target user u and other users. Then we select one user who has closet distance of u as the most similar user s. We recommend the video which has highest rating from the user s to user u. After the recommendation, we evaluate the method by dataset D_2. If user u having seen the recommended video in dataset D_2, we call it as one finished recommendation. If user u had not seen the recommended video in dataset D_2, that we can not be sure whether user u like it. So we only evaluate these finished recommendation in our experiments. In one finished recommendation if the rating of recommended video from user u being bigger than 3-star(), it indicates user u like it, we call it as hit recommendation.

Let U_{test} denote the set of target users, the accuracy of our method calculated by the follow formula:

$$acc = \frac{\sum_{u \in U_{test}} hit(u)}{\sum_{u \in U_{test}} finish(u)} \tag{8}$$

In this formula, the function $finish(u)$ is used to verify whether the recommendation to user u is a finished recommendation. $finish(u) = 1$ indicates that is a finished recommendation, $finish(u) = 0$ otherwise. Similarly, the index function $hit(u)$ is used to verify whether user u like recommended video. $hit(u) = 1$ indicates that user u like video v, $hit(u) = 0$ otherwise.

After the recommendation for 2142 users, we get 64 finished recommendation and 53 hit recommendation. The accuracy that we calculated is 82.8%. This result shows our model has the ability to explore user preferences and make recommendations. Thought we got a nice accuracy, we must admit that there are fewer finished recommendation. This is because our datasets are separated by time, resulting in two datasets being too independent. In the following work, we need to establish a suitable sampling model to redefine the training set and optimize the recommended model to obtain better experimental results.

5   Conclusions and Future Work

In this paper, according to the mainstream online course evaluation system, combined with the characteristics of middle school students' physical and mental development, an evaluation system of educational video course is developed, and based on the idea of Collaborative filtering algorithm, two models are proposed. The first one is the video evaluation model, the second is the user preference learning model. Finally, the Euclidean distance formula is used to calculate the user similarity and complete the final recommendation. We used the real data set to validate our model, and obtained 82.8% of the recommended accuracy by calculating the data of 2142 users. The above work demonstrates that our model can learn user preferences and recommend appropriate video. But in feature work, we need to establish a suitable sampling model to redefine the training set and optimize the recommended model to obtain better experimental results.

This paper provides the education video but the lack of relevant data set in the experimental process, we can only use of film rating data sets - MoveLens, education video and film have the characteristics of different obviously, this can lead to recommend model is the result of the deviation, so in the next step we will collect education video ratings data sets, remove the impact.

The development of computer network and artificial intelligence provides a way to scale and individualize education. Network distance education provides an open, equal, cooperative and active learning environment. To promote the realization and popularization of lifelong learning and learning society [5]. In the 10-year plan for the development of education informatization (2011–2020), it was pointed out that school education and teaching methods should be changed in terms of teachers' information-based teaching habits, ways of presenting knowledge, diversification of students, and individualized learning.

That is, "everything is for the development of every student" from the perspective of students and through data analysis, we can understand students' preference for attending classes. Then, we can specifically recommend appropriate teaching videos for students. To help the breakthrough reform of education and teaching. We hope our work can develop towards the above goal, help students to study better and more efficiently.

References

1. Gao, R.: An online video recommendation system based on deep neural network. Shenzhen University (2017)
2. Li, G.: The theoretical construction and characteristic analysis of personalized learning. J. Northeast Normal Univ. **37**(3), 152–156 (2005)
3. Chen, G.: The evaluation criterion of the implementation quality of college online courses. Tsinghua J. Educ. **23**(5), 97–102 (2003)
4. Gao, J.: Research on evaluation index system of micro-video teaching resources. Nantong University (2016)
5. Zhang, S.: Research on personalized learning support system based on learner feature analysis. Tianjin Normal University (2003)
6. Harper, M., Konstan, J.A.: The MovieLens datasets: history and context. ACM Trans. Interact. Intell. Syst. **5**(4), 19–20 (2015)
7. Vig, J., Sen, S., Riedl, J.: The tag genome: encoding community knowledge to support novel interaction. ACM Trans. Interact. Intell. Syst. **2**(3), 13–14 (2012)

A Temporal Collaborative Filtering Algorithm Based on Purchase Cycle

Yixuan Chai, Guohua Liu[✉], Zhao Chen, Feng Li, Yue Li,
and Esther Astaewwa Effah

School of Computer Science and Technology,
Donghua University, Shanghai 201620, China
{chaiyixuan, estereffah}@mail.dhu.edu.cn,
{ghliu, chenzhao, lifeng, frankyueli}@dhu.edu.cn

Abstract. Existing Temporal Collaborative Filtering (TCF) recommendation algorithms exploit the time context to capture the user-interest drift. They have been used in the movie and music recommendation domain successfully. In online wholesale domain, e.g. Alibaba B2B online trading platform, most of the customers are wholesalers. Unlike individual customers, the wholesaler's demand dominates their purchase intentions rather than their interest. Hence, detecting the user-interest drift is not appropriate in the online wholesale domain. In order to capture the user-demand drift, we make use of customer's historical purchased records to predict the next purchase cycle (from the last purchase date to the next purchase date). We assume that the user's demand for the target product will reach the peak in the next purchase date, so the product should have a highest probability to be recommended in this date. Our proposed algorithm uses a deep neural network to predict the next purchase cycle, then incorporating next purchase cycle to the TCF recommender by a time-demand function. We evaluate our method on an online wholesale dataset. The experimental results demonstrate that our approach significantly improves the recommendation accuracy and ensures an acceptable novelty effect on the recommendation result.

Keywords: Temporal collaborative filtering · Recommendation system
Purchase cycle

1 Introduction

Collaborative Filtering (CF) plays an important role in recommendation systems. However, classical CF algorithm ignores temporal context information (e.g. user interest drifts over time), so that the recommendation systems run the risk of

This research has been financially supported by grants from the National Key R&D Program of China (No. 2017YFB0309800), the National Natural Science Foundation of China (No. 61702094), the Young Scientists' Sailing Project of Science and Technology Commission of Shanghai Municipal (No. 17YF1427400) and the Fundamental Research Funds for the Central Universities (No. 17D111206).

X. Sun et al. (Eds.): ICCCS 2018, LNCS 11064, pp. 191–201, 2018.
https://doi.org/10.1007/978-3-030-00009-7_18

recommending the outdated items to users. As an improvement method of classical CF, temporal collaborative filtering (TCF) recommendation system has been developed. It exploits temporal context to capture the user-interest drift. Although existing TCF recommendation algorithms regard the time factor as an important role and have an accuracy improvement on movie and music recommendation domain, they only capture the user-interest drift. In the online wholesale domain, e.g. Alibaba B2B online trading platform, most customers are wholesalers. Unlike individual customers, the wholesaler's demand dominates their purchase intentions rather than their interest. Hence, the interest-detection based recommendation algorithms are not appropriate in the online wholesale application field. In order to capture the user-demand drift, we exploit the repeat purchase cycle sequence to predict the next purchase date. We assume that the user's demand for the target product will reach the peak in the next purchase date, so the product will have a high probability to be recommended near this date. Our proposed method uses a deep neural network to predict next purchase cycle (the time interval from the last purchase date to the next purchase date), then incorporating the next purchase cycle to the TCF recommender by a time-demand function. We evaluate our method on an UK's online wholesale dataset. The results demonstrate that our approach significantly improves the recommendation accuracy and ensures an acceptable novelty effect on the recommendation result.

The rest of this paper is arranged as follows. Section 2 outlines the related work. Section 3 describes our proposed recommendation method. Section 4 describes the experimental results and analysis. Finally, we draw conclusions of our paper and present future work in Sect. 5.

2 Related Work

Collaborative filtering recommender systems [1] are widely used in various application domains, such as movie [2–4], music [5] and online retail [6, 7]. The collaborative filtering algorithm attempts to recommend items to target user based on similar users (i.e. user-based collaborative filtering) or similar items (i.e. item-based collaborative filtering). Classical CF is based on an assumption: users' preferences will not change over time [8].

In order to capture the change of users' preferences, temporal collaborative filtering (TCF) has been proposed. Ding and Li [9] proposed an exponential time decay function which represents Ebbinghaus Forgetting Curve. The time decay function curve is shown in Fig. 1. They got a weight from this time function, then assigned the weight to the predicted rating. This method is based on the assumption that the more recent rating is better reflect the current user preference. Ren et al. [10] employed the weight not only in the phase of rating prediction but also on similarity computing. Zhang [11] employed the weight on similarity computing and incorporated a covering degree into the phase of rating prediction. Ma et al. [8] proposed a hierarchical temporal collaborative filtering method. They exploited a hierarchical structure between items to improve the accuracy of similarity computation, then utilized the time decay function to improve the prediction accuracy. Vaz et al. [12] used similar time decay function by different way to define the value of decay coefficient. These time decay functions are not appropriate in the online wholesaler application field, because the wholesalers usually buy the same product repeatedly rather than just buy once and forget it. Hence, we exploiting the repeat purchase cycle to capture the user-demand drift in our proposed method which will be described in Sect. 3. Beside these time decay functions, Blanco et al. [13, 14] took advantage of different kinds of time function curve in different categories of product. This method is more appropriate for online wholesaler domain, but the choice of time function is hand-crafted and depends on experience.

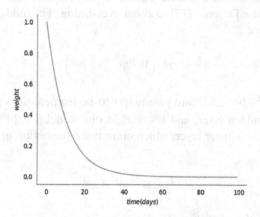

Fig. 1. The time decay function curve

3   Proposed Method

The main idea of our algorithm is to predict the user's next purchase date for the target item so that the item will contribute more probabilities to be recommended at the next purchase date. Intuitively, we speculate that the date when the user purchases the product is the user's peak demand for the product. Our proposed method has two phases: predict the next purchase cycle and incorporate the purchase cycle into collaborative filtering.

3.1   Next Purchase Cycle Prediction

We denote the repeat purchase behavior as a function $p : U \times I \rightarrow \mathcal{P}(T \times T)$, where $U = \{u_1, u_2, \ldots, u_m\}$ is the set of users, $I = \{i_1, i_2, \ldots, i_n\}$ is the set of items, T is the set of purchase timestamps and $\mathcal{P}(\cdot)$ is the notion of power set. For example, a repeat purchase behavior of a user $u \in U$ for the target item $i \in I$ is $p(u, i) = \{(t^1, t^2), (t^2, t^3), \ldots, (t^{t-1}, t^t)\}$. A purchase cycle (PC) of a repeat purchase behavior is the interval of time between purchases, denote as $p^l = t^l - t^{l-1}$. where t^l is the lth purchased date and $t^l - t^{l-1}$ is measured at the day level. A purchase cycle sequence is $P_{u,i} = (p^1, p^2, \ldots, p^t)$. Our objective is to predict p^{t+1}, given $P_{u,i}$.

We use a deep neural network model to predict the next purchase cycle. Figure 2 shows our proposed model, namely NN-PC model. It has five neural layers.

The first layer is an embedding layer. Inputs are the userID, the itemID, the purchase quantity and the purchase cycle. We first transform the userID and the itemID to distributed representations respectively, where each user is represented as a vector $u \in R^{|U|}$, and each item is represented as a vector $i \in R^{|I|}$. Both u and i are learned during the training process, which is similar as Wan [15] did. Then, we concatenate the two vectors with the purchase quantity and the purchase cycle as the final input $x \in R^{|U|+|I|+1+1}$.

The next three layers are nonlinear hidden layers. Here we use ReLU [16] as the active function, and use Dropout [17] to avoid over-fitting. The hidden representation h is obtained as follows:

$$h^{[l]} = relu\left(W^{[l]}h^{[l-1]} + b^{[l]}\right) \tag{1}$$

where $W^{[l]} \in R^{|l|*|l-1|}$, $b^{[l]} \in R^{l*1}$ are parameters to be learned, $|l|$ is the number of the hidden units in lth hidden layer, and $h^{[0]} = x$. In our model, $l \in \{1, 2, 3\}$.

The output layer is a linear layer, which outputs the prediction of the next purchase cycle p^{t+1}.

$$p^{t+1} = W^{[4]}h^{[3]} + b^{[4]} \tag{2}$$

where $W^{[4]} \in R^{1*|h^3|}$, $b^{[4]} \in R^{1*|h^3|}$. We use mean square loss as the loss function and Adam gradient decent [18] for optimization.

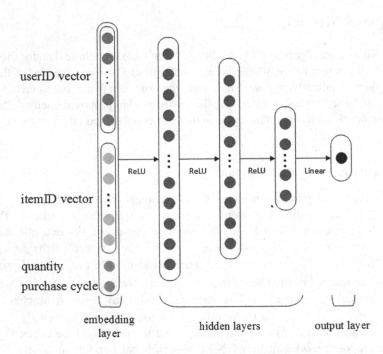

Fig. 2. Architecture of the NN-PC model

3.2   Incorporating Purchase Cycle into Collaborative Filtering

After we get the predicted next purchase cycle, we will incorporate it into the CF algorithm. There are two steps in the phase: Firstly, we predict the item ratings for the target user, just as the classical CF does. Secondly, we assign the demand weight to each rating. This weight is obtained from our proposed time-demand function f(dt).

Ratings Prediction
The input of CF method is user-item rating matrix $R = (r_{u,i}), u = 1, \ldots, M$ (total number of U), $i = 1, \ldots, N$ (total number of I), So R is a M × N matrix. The uth row and ith column cell is indicated as $r_{u,i}$. The value of $r_{u,i}$ is not rated by the user explicitly. In our task, it represents the user's purchase record (e.g. set 1 if the user has purchased the item otherwise is 0).

The CF computes the similarity between user u and user v by their historical purchase records. Several algorithms can be used to derive the similarity computation, but the *cosine similarity* is appropriate for our task. Because the value of ratings is the purchase records rather than rated by the users subjectively. The cosine similarity is defined as follows:

$$sim(u, v) = \frac{\sum_{i \in I_u \cap I_v} r_{u,i} \cdot r_{v,i}}{\sqrt{\sum_{i \in I_u \cap I_v} r_{u,i}^2 \cdot \sum_{i \in I_u \cap I_v} r_{v,i}^2}} \tag{3}$$

where $r_{u,i}$ and $r_{v,i}$ are user u and user v's ratings on item i, respectively. $i \in I_u \cap I_v$ denotes that the item i which is both rated by user u and v.

Then we predict the rating $r_{u,i}$ for the target user u:

$$r_{u,i} = \frac{\sum_{v \in N(u)} (r_{v,i}) \cdot sim(u, v)}{\sum_{v \in N(u)} |sim(u, v)|} \tag{4}$$

where $N(u)$ are the neighbors of user u. We can obtain the neighbors by getting the K most similar users after the computation of similarity. Then we select N items with the highest value of ratings, which is called Top-N recommendation.

Time-Demand Function
In order to capture the user-demand drift, we obtain a demand weight from a time-demand function, then assign the weight to each predicted rating. We define the time-demand function as follows:

$$f(dt) = e^{-\frac{(dt - p^{t+1})^2}{(\alpha p^{t+1})^2}} \tag{5}$$

Where $dt = |t^{rec} - t^{last}|$.that is to say, the dt is the time from recommended time t^{rec} to the last purchase time t^{last}, and dt is measured at the day level. The p^{t+1} is our predicted next purchase cycle, and α is a constant value.

Then we assign the demand weight to each rating. That is to say, in our proposed algorithm, the Eq. (5) is revised in Eq. (7) as follows:

$$r_{u,i} = \frac{\sum_{v \in N(u)} (r_{v,i}) \cdot sim(u,v) f(dt)}{\sum_{v \in N(u)} |sim(u,v)|} \tag{6}$$

where $sim(u,v)$ is the similarity computation function. $N(u)$ are the set of neighbors of the user u. After we compute the ratings, we can select N items to generate Top-N recommendation.

The time-demand function curve is shown in Fig. 3. We can see from Fig. 3 that there will be a longer time range of high demand if we select a big α. This function curve with different p^{t+1} is shown in Fig. 4. As we can see, the peak location and the time range of high demand are both associated with p^{t+1}.

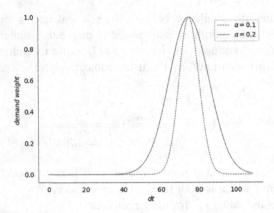

Fig. 3. The time-demand function curve with different α.

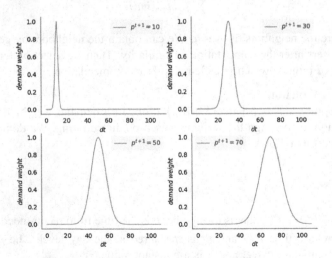

Fig. 4. The demand-time function curve with different next purchase cycle p^{t+1}.

4 Experiments

4.1 Dataset

We evaluate our algorithm on the UK Online Retail[1] public dataset [19]. Most customers of the dataset are wholesalers. This dataset contains the transactions occurring from 2010-01-12 to 2011-09-12. Table 1 shows a sample of the dataset. In addition, Table 2 shows the summary of the dataset. All source code and cleaned dataset used in our experiments can be found online[2].

Table 1. A sample of the UK online retail dataset.

CustomerID	StockCode	InvoiceDate	InvoiceNo	Description	Quantity	UnitPrice	Country
17850	85123	2010/12/1 8:26:00 AM	536365	WHITE...	6	2.55	United Kingdom
17850	71053	2010/12/1 8:26:00 AM	536365	WHITE...	6	3.39	United Kingdom
17850	84406	2010/12/1 8:26:00 AM	536365	CREAM...	8	2.75	United Kingdom

Table 2. A summary of the UK online retail dataset.

Users	Items	Purchase records
4372	3958	541909

4.2 Evaluation Metrics

In general, rating prediction metrics such as mean absolute error (MAE) and the root mean squared error (RMSE) are used to evaluate to rating prediction tasks, while ranking precision metrics are used to evaluate a Top-N recommendation task [20]. The ranking precision metrics such as *precision*, *recall*, and *F1-measure* are better suited for online shopping recommendation purpose which requires to present a limited number of the most appealing items for a user instead of rating predictions for individual items [21]. The precision is defined as follows:

$$\text{precision} = \frac{Number\ of\ hits}{Number\ of\ items\ in\ recommendation\ list} \tag{7}$$

---

[1] http://archive.ics.uci.edu/ml/datasets/Online+Retail

[2] https://github.com/chaiyixuan/NN-PC

The recall is defined as follows [7]:

$$recall = \frac{Number\ of\ hit}{Number\ of\ products\ in\ the\ testing\ set\ with\ which\ user\ u\ interacted} \tag{8}$$

The F1-measure is the harmonic mean of precision and recall:

$$F1 = \frac{2(precision)(recall)}{(precision + recall)} \tag{9}$$

Apart from accuracy metrics, more recently, the novelty has also become an important evaluation metrics especially in practical applications. The novelty [22] is defined as follows:

$$novelty = \frac{Number\ of\ items\ has\ been\ purchased\ in\ recommended\ list}{Number\ of\ items\ in\ recommendation\ list} \tag{10}$$

The lower the value of novelty, the better the performance in recommendation of novelty effect.

4.3   Evaluation Methodologies

Availability of timestamps causes the difference in the evaluation methodologies between the TCF and the classical CF. The major difference is how to perform the training-test set splitting (e.g. order by timestamp or random). In this paper, we follow Campos [20] proposed evaluation framework.

Base Set Condition
The base set condition states whether to split the training-test set from the whole dataset (named community-centered method) or on each of the user-based sub-datasets independently (named user-centered method). The community-centered method may cause some users have none or all of their ratings in the test set. Hence, we use user-centered method to ensure that all the user will have ratings in both training and test sets.

Rating Order Condition
The ratings order condition is to define the order of ratings used in the training-test set splitting. In our evaluation, we use time-dependent order to mimic real-world conditions. The time-dependent order is ordered according to the rating timestamps so that the ratings of test set are always later than the training set ratings.

Size Condition
Size condition decides how many ratings are included in the training and test sets. We select users who purchased more than 10 times to avoid that some users may have none

ratings in the test set. Next, we select last three records of each user as the test set. The final total number of users is 3780. The total number of items is 3676.

4.4 Experimental Results

Experiment 1: Tuning the Parameters

The objective of this experiment is to find an appropriate value of parameter α. We test all the values of α from 0.01 to 0.1 by 0.01 with 5 neighbors per user and Top-10 recommendations. From Table 3 we can see that the larger the value of α, the better the performance of precision, but the worse the novelty effect. In our task, we limit the novelty can't larger than 0.2 (i.e. The proportion of purchased items can't larger than 20%.). That is, when $\alpha = 0.08$ our algorithm shows the best performance.

Table 3. Parameter tuning results with different α.

α	0.01	0.02	0.03	0.04	0.05	0.06	0.07	0.08	0.09	0.10
Precision	0.0074	0.0075	0.0078	0.0080	0.0082	0.0084	0.0089	0.0093	0.0097	0.0099
Recall	0.0249	0.0253	0.0260	0.0267	0.0274	0.0282	0.0299	0.0313	0.0324	0.0332
F1-measure	0.0115	0.0116	0.0120	0.0123	0.0126	0.0130	0.0138	0.0144	0.0149	0.0153
Novelty	0.1484	0.1523	0.1562	0.1614	0.1673	0.1738	0.1814	0.1944	0.2054	0.2095

Experiment 2: Comparison with Other Algorithms

This experiment compares the performance between our method (NN-PC), the traditional user-based CF (UBCF) and the time decay TCF (TD-TCF) [9]. We can see from Table 4 that our NN-PC model achieves an average improvement of 60.3% on F1-measure as compared with the traditional UBCF, but the novelty effect is 37.7% worse than UBCF. In a way, our method sacrifices the novelty effect in an acceptable way for better accuracy.

However, as a feature of the time-demand function, the demand weight will decrease after the predicted purchase date. This means the novelty effect will get well over time. To confirm this theory, we add D days to the recommendation date t^{rec}, where D is from 0 to 100. As shown in Fig. 5, the NN-PC model's novelty effect will get well after 20 days. However, the novelty rises at the beginning which is different from what we expected. That because of the prediction error of the next purchase cycle. The mean error of next purchase cycle predictions is 19.25 (days).

Table 4. The accuracy and the novelty results comparison between NN-PC, UBCF and TD-TCF with different Top-N (bold indicates the best performance of each metric).

Metrics	Top-5			Top-10			Top-15		
	NN-PC	UBCF	TD- TCF	NN-PC	UBCF	TD- TCF	NN-PC	UBCF	TD- TCF
Precision	**0.0100**	0.0051	0.0044	**0.0093**	0.0061	0.0056	**0.0092**	0.0069	0.0061
Recall	**0.0167**	0.0085	0.0074	**0.0313**	0.0205	0.0188	**0.0463**	0.0349	0.0309
F1-measure	**0.0125**	0.0064	0.0055	**0.0144**	0.0094	0.0087	**0.0154**	0.0116	0.0103
Novelty	0.2030	0.1454	**0.1351**	0.1944	0.1324	**0.1364**	0.1920	0.1518	**0.1427**

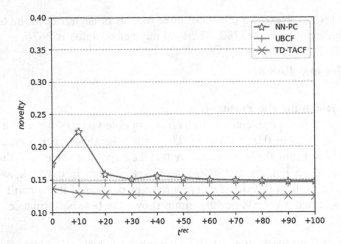

Fig. 5. The novelty in different recommended date t^{rec} (days).

5 Conclusions and Future Work

In this paper, we present a new temporal collaborative filtering algorithm based on the purchase cycle. Our method is designed for online wholesale recommendation domain. We use a DNN model to predict the next purchase cycle. When the date comes, the recommender will give a higher recommendation probability for the target item. Moreover, when the date is exceeded, the recommender will decay the recommendation probability.

Experimental results show that our method significantly improves the recommendation accuracy in the UK Online Retail dataset. However, the prediction error of the next purchase cycle will affect the performance of the novelty effect. In our further work, we will further improve the accuracy of the next purchase cycle prediction.

References

1. Resnick, P., Iacovou, N., Suchak, M., Bergstrom, P., Riedl, J.: GroupLens: an open architecture for collaborative filtering of netnews. In: Proceedings of the 1994 ACM Conference on Computer supported Cooperative Work, pp. 175–186 (1994)
2. Jeong, W.H., Kim, S.J., Park, D.S., Kwak, J.: Performance improvement of a movie recommendation system based on personal propensity and secure collaborative filtering. J. Inf. Process. Syst. **9**, 157–172 (2013)
3. Subramaniyaswamy, V., Logesh, R., Chandrashekhar, M., Challa, A., Vijayakumar, V.: A personalised movie recommendation system based on collaborative filtering. Int. J. High Perform. Comput. Netw. **10**, 54 (2017)
4. Chen, M.H., Teng, C.H., Chang, P.C.: Applying artificial immune systems to collaborative filtering for movie recommendation. Adv. Eng. Inform. **29**, 830–839 (2015)
5. Koenigstein, N., Dror, G., Koren, Y.: Yahoo! music recommendations. In: Fifth ACM Conference, pp. 165–172 (2011)

6. Linden, G., Smith, B., York, J.: Amazon.com Recommendations Item-to-Item Collaborative Filtering (2003)
7. Huang, Z., Zeng, D., Chen, H.: A comparison of collaborative filtering recommendation algorithms for e-commerce. IEEE Intell. Syst. **22**, 68–78 (2007)
8. Ma, T., Guo, L., Tang, M., Tian, Y., Al-rodhaan, M.: A collaborative filtering recommendation algorithm based on hierarchical structure and time awareness. IEICE Trans. Inf. Syst. **99**, 1512–1520 (2016)
9. Ding, Y., Li, X.: Time weight collaborative filtering. In: Proceedings of the ACM International Conference on Information and Knowledge Management, pp. 485–492 (2005)
10. Ren, L.: A Time-enhanced Collaborative Filtering Approach, pp. 7–10 (2016)
11. Zhang, Z.: Improvement of item-based collaborative filtering by adding time factor and covering degree (2016)
12. Vaz, P.C., Ribeiro, R., De Matos, D.M.: Understanding temporal dynamics of ratings in the book recommendation scenario (2013)
13. Blanco-Fernández, Y., López-Nores, M., Pazos-Arias, J.J., García-Duque, J.: An improvement for semantics-based recommender systems grounded on attaching temporal information to ontologies and user profile. Eng. Appl. Artif. Intell. **24**, 1385–1397 (2011)
14. Blanco-fernández, Y., et al.: Incentivized provision of metadata, semantic reasoning and time-driven filtering: making a puzzle of personalized e-commerce. Expert Syst. Appl. **37**, 61–69 (2010)
15. Wan, S., Lan, Y., Wang, P., Guo, J., Xu, J., Cheng, X.: Next basket recommendation with neural networks. In: CEUR Workshop Proceedings, vol. 1441, pp. 1–2 (2015)
16. Glorot, X., Bordes, A., Bengio, Y.: Deep sparse rectifier neural networks. In: Proceedings of the 14th International Conference on Artificial Intelligence and Statistics, AISTATS 2011, vol. 15, pp. 315–323 (2011)
17. Srivastava, N., Hinton, G., Krizhevsky, A., Sutskever, I., Salakhutdinov, R.: Dropout: a simple way to prevent neural networks from overfitting. J. Mach. Learn. Res. **15**, 1929–1958 (2014)
18. Kingma, D.P., Ba, J.: Adam: A Method for Stochastic Optimization, pp. 1–15 (2014)
19. Chen, D., Sain, S.L., Guo, K.: Data mining for the online retail industry: a case study of RFM model-based customer segmentation using data mining. J. Database Mark. Cust. Strateg. Manag. **19**, 197–208 (2012)
20. Campos, P.G., Díez, F., Cantador, I.: Time-aware recommender systems: a comprehensive survey and analysis of existing evaluation protocols. User Model. User-Adapt. Interact. **24**, 67–119 (2014)
21. Cosley, D., Lam, S.K., Albert, I., Konstan, J.A., Riedl, J.: Is seeing believing? How recommender interfaces affect users' opinions. In: Proceedings of the Conference on Human Factors in Computing Systems, CHI 2003, p. 585 (2003)
22. Hurley, N., Zhang, M.: Novelty and diversity in top-n recommendation – analysis and evaluation. ACM Trans. Internet Technol. **10**, 1–30 (2011)

Temporal Evolution Data Model for Heterogeneous Entities: Modeling with Temporal and Evolution Information

Dan Yang[1(✉)], Tiezheng Nie[2(✉)], and Jing Zhang[1]

[1] School of Software, University of Science and Technology LiaoNing,
Anshan 114051, China
asyangdan@163.com, aszhangjing9312@163.com
[2] College of Computer Science and Engineering, Northeastern University,
Shenyang 110004, China
nietiezheng@ise.neu.edu.cn

Abstract. Though many research efforts have been spent on data model of heterogeneous entities, temporal and evolution information have little been considered. In this paper we propose a graph-based temporal evolution multi-layered data model called TEM-Network which can capture temporal information and evolution features of heterogeneous entities and their associations. TEM-Network can not only capture associations among entities but also capture associations among entity groups. We present temporal multi-modality query models that TEM-Network can support in detail. Extensive experiments on two real data sets show the feasibility and effectiveness of proposed temporal evolution data model.

Keywords: Temporal evolution data model · Heterogeneous entities
Entity groups

1 Introduction

Entities and their associations usually have time information and revolve over time. Temporal and evolution information is very useful in many applications such as entity management, data lineage management, data integration. Entity-centric Data model has been studied extensively, but existing works pay less attention to entities' temporal and evolution features. It is necessary to provide a unified temporal evolution data model for the large number of heterogeneous entities with time information and evolved over time. Temporal information is useful for temporal data mining tasks such as prediction, pattern discovery, and trend analysis. However the most existing entity- centric data model lacks the description of the time information of entities and associations. How to enable the data model to properly capture temporal and evolution information is a non-trivial task. Many issues are aroused when extending entity data model with temporal and evolution information. (1) Different time types may be used when modeling the valid-time aspect, e.g., single time point, or time interval. (2) In addition to valid and transaction time, a temporal data model should support arbitrary time attributes, namely support user defined time, e.g., for employee entities, such as birth dates, hiring dates, etc. (3) Due to the time-varying features of entities and their associations, temporal evolution data model should describe their evolution information, i.e., to record their variation over time..

1.1   Contributions

The main contributions of this paper can be summarized as follows. (1) We propose a temporal evolution multi-layer data model TEM-Network taking into account of temporal and evolution features of entities, which explores not only associations among heterogeneous entities, but also inter-links among entity groups (i.e., aggregate entities). (2)We present temporal multi-modality query models based on characteristic of TEM-Network. (3) We have conducted extensive experiments on two real data sets to evaluate effectiveness and correctness of TEM-Networks.

1.2   Outline

The rest of the paper is organized as follows: Sect. 2 gives related work; Sect. 3 introduces our proposed temporal evolution data model TEM-Networks in detail. Section 4 introduces multi-modality query model in detail. Section 5 presents experimental results and analysis. Section 6 summarizes the main contributions of the paper.

2   Related Work

With respect to temporal data model, the related works are mainly on two fields: temporal ER data model [1] and temporal RDF data model [2, 4]. Related work [5] presents a formal framework for modeling, querying and managing concept evolution. Related work [6] introduces the theory of database dependencies as a tool for reasoning about RDFS schema evolution problems. There are at least two temporal dimensions considering when dealing with temporal databases: valid time and transaction time. Valid time is the time when data is valid in the modeled world; transaction time is the time when data is actually stored in database. The versioning approach captures transaction time, while labeling is mostly used when representing valid time. The approach we present in this paper supports both time dimensions.

Related works [7, 11] are all about temporal knowledge base building. YAGO2 [11] is an extension of the YAGO knowledge base with focus on temporal and spatial knowledge. Spatio-temporal information in YAGO2 can be explored either graphically or through a special time-and space-aware query language. Related work [8, 12] are about temporal scoping facts. Related work [12] focuses on extracting associations and their temporal extent. Related work [13] infers typical temporal order of relations which can be used to assign temporal scope to specific instances of relations.

Different from the above related work, our proposed temporal evolution data model for heterogeneous entities TEM-Network is entity-centric graph–based multi-layer data model which provides users with various logical views (i.e., abstract levels) on entities: higher-order overviews. Besides temporal information TEM-Network can keep track of evolution information. Moreover it can capture various associations among hetero-gonous entities, i.e. entity level, also associations among entity groups, i.e., aggregate level.

3 TEM-Network Overview

In this section, we first give the related definitions and problem statement, then present the temporal and evolution aspects of TEM-Network in detail, finally introduce the multi-granularity associations of TEM-Network.

3.1 Basic Definitions

Definition 1 (*entity type*) is the type which entity belongs to. E.g, entity type from the academic domain may contain the following entity types: *Person*, *Author*, *Paper*, and *Conference* etc. Type (e) denotes entity type of entity e.

Definition 2 (*temporal entity*) is instance of entity type which is denoted as a triple $e = <E_{type}, Attr, [@time point$ or *time interval*$]>$, where E_{type} is the entity type the entity belongs to; *Attr* is composed of a set of *Attr* = <attribute, value, [@*time point* or *time interval*]>, where the last temporal part is default; the value can be an atomic value (e.g., *string*, *char*, *int*, *bool*) or composite value. For example, a person entity: Tom = <Person, {<name, '*Tom*'>, <email, '*tom@yahoo.com*'>, <affiliation, '*Google*'>, <title, '*manager*'>},@2015>.

Definition 3 (**temporal association**) i.e., time-varying association is directional binary association with temporal information between two entities, is denoted as triple $ass = <e_{Source}, e_{Target}, temporal part>$, where the temporal part is composed of {*ass-Name*, @ [time point tp or time interval ti]}. We use $ti.start$ and $ti.end$ to refer the starting and ending time points of a time interval ti. E.g., Mary $\xrightarrow{SpouseOf@[2001,2013]}$ Tom indicates Mary and Tom were couples during 2001 and 2013. The temporal part is optional due to some associations are not time-varying such as $2 \xrightarrow{largerThan} 1$. Each entity attribute value can be history or current. The current and future value not known beforehand can be assigned UNTILL_CHANGED. E.g., the temporal information [2009, Until_Changed].

Definition 4 (*entity group*) is collection of semantically related entities of same entity type denoted as $Group = \{e_i|e_iE_i\}$. E.g., author groups, paper groups and venue groups, as dashed ellipse shown in Fig. 1.

Definition 5 (*temporal evolution Multi-layer network TEM-Network*) is multi-layer graph-based data model consists of n ($n \geq 1$) layers and each layer is represented by network $N_k = (V_k, E_k)$, where k is the entity type id, V_k and E_k are sets of vertices and edges. Specifically, $V_k = \{v_{k1}, v_{k2}, ..., v_{kz}\}$, where Z is the number of entities in V_k.

According to different entity types, entities and their associations are modeled as multi-layer entity network. Figure 1 shows an example of TEM-Network which is composed of three types of entities: authors, papers and venues.

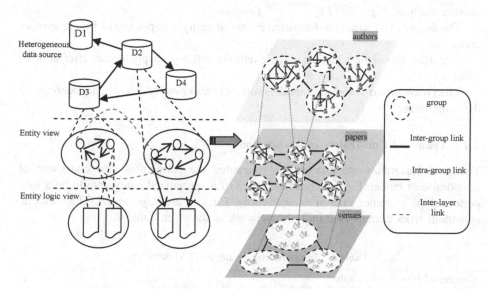

Fig. 1. An example of TEM-Network

3.2   TEM-Network: Introducing Time and Evolution Information into Data Model

To support the temporal dimension, we adopt the approach similar to Temporal RDF [9]. We not only add time semantics to entity associations (i.e., temporal associations), but also to entities (i.e., temporal entities). Capturing the temporal information of entities and associations can help us to better analyze the entities on the timeline, and then semantically search for entities with time context. E.g., temporal queries 'Halevy's papers, [2010, 2013]', 'Halevy's job title, 2016'.

3.3   Modeling Evolution with Evolution Associations

Entity evolution is about how the semantics of an entity change over time. TEM-Network introduces some special associations representing the entity evolution process or event to facilitate answering historical queries of the form 'How does entity e_i evolved over time interval ti'. To model various kinds of evolution events that may exist, currently TEM-Network introduces five evolution associations: *become, join, split, merge,* and *detach.* To model sequential relations, TEM-Network introduces two time sequence associations: *before, after* and *synchronous.*

The ***become*** association models that an entity e_i becomes another entity e_j. E.g., $AliPay \overset{become@2013}{\longrightarrow} ePay$

The **split** association models that an entity e_i becomes more than one another entity e_j. E.g., *Germany* $\overset{Split@1949}{\longrightarrow}$ *EastGermany*

The **merge** association models that at least a part of an entity e_i becomes part of another entity e_j. E.g., *IBM PC* $\overset{merge@2004}{\longrightarrow}$ *Lenovo*

The **before** association models some events or entity e_i happen/exist before another entity e_j.

The **after** association models some events or entity e_i happen/exist after another entity e_j.

The **synchronous** association models some events or entity e_i and e_j happen/exist at the same time.

3.4   Temporal Constraints of Associations

Temporal constraints are essential to guarantee the correctness and consistent of temporal data model. E.g., the existence time of a specialized entity should be a sub-period of the existence time of another entity. E.g., *isPartOf, parentOf*. The temporal constraint types current used in TEM-Network is shown in Table 1.

Table 1. Temporal constraints in TEM-Network

Constraint Type	Example
Attribute value range	In *citedBy* association, the publish date of the cited paper must be earlier than the citing paper
Temporal consistency	Two papers published in the same conference cannot form *citedBy* association
Temporal mutex	One person cannot be the reviewer of the paper and the author of the paper at the same time
Temporal parallel	The year of an author *publishedIn* and *submitIn* paper in a conference is temporal parallel

3.5   Multi-granularity Associations

Links (i.e., associations) in TEM-Network are divided into the following categories.

(1) **Intra-group link**: i.e., entity association, association among entities of the same group of the same layer, e.g., links between author$_1$ and author$_2$ as shown in Fig. 1.

(2) **Inter-group link**: association among different entity groups of the same layer or different layers, e.g., links between author group A and author group B, links between author group A and paper group A as shown in Fig. 1.

(3) **Inter-layer link**: represents entity association among entities or entity groups of different layers. E.g., links between author a_1 and paper p_1, links between author group A and paper group A.

The links on the same layer represent the associations among homogeneous entities, or associations among homogeneous entity groups. The links between different layers capture associations among heterogeneous entities, or associations among heterogeneous entity groups.

4 Temporal Multi-modality Query Models

TEM-Network can support the following four types of multi-modality query models for temporal semantic entity search as follows:

4.1 Temporal Entity Association Query

Temporal entity associated query Teaq is a form of temporal query as follows:

$$Teaq : \forall e : pq_1 \, ass_1 \, pq_2 \ldots ass_n \, pq_n \wedge ass_i = k_i[Q_t]$$

Where, k_i is query keyword; pq_i represents a predicate queries; ass_i is association between entities. Q_t is the query's temporal context which is optional. The format of Q_t can be time point tp or time interval ti. *Treq* returns a set of e_i related entities in the same layer. For example, user submits keyword query 'entity resolution, published in, SIGMOD, 2016' to find all papers about entity resolution published in SIGMOD 2016.

4.2 Temporal Related Entity Query

Temporal related entity query Treq is temporal query with the form of:

$$Treq : \forall e, k_i \rightarrow e_i \wedge e \, ass_i \, e_i \wedge ass_i \in \{\text{intra-group link, inter-group link}\}[Q_t]$$

Where, k_i is the query keyword mapped to an entity e_i; $ass_i \, e_i$ entity is involved in any associations, that by the entity e_i as intra-group or inter-group link vertices of the query results are related entities. *Treq* returns a set of e_i related entities in the same layer. E.g, the user submits the query 'Halevy' intend to find Halevy related entities such as Halevy's co-authors, his similar researchers.

4.3 Temporal Multi-modality Query

Temporal multi-modality query Tmmq is temporal query with the form of:

$$Tmmq : \forall e, k_i \rightarrow e_i \wedge e \, ass_i \, e_i \wedge ass_i \in \{\text{inter-layer link, inter-group link,}$$
$$\text{intra-group link}\} \wedge \text{Type}(e) \neq \text{Type}(e_i)[Q_t]$$

Where, k_i is query keyword mapped to a certain type of entity e_i; ass_i is any associations among layers among the participating entities e_i, i.e., the inter-layer entity as e_i link of vertices, intra-group link e entity type entity and entities belong to different outcomes e_i *Tnmq* returns all relevant entities located on a different layers. For example, user researching social network wants to do reviewer recommendation; he/she may find 'social network' in the *papers* or find 'social network' in the *topics*.

4.4   Temporal Association Query

Temporal association query Taq is temporal query with the form of:

$$Taq : \forall ass : k_i \rightarrow e_i, k_j \rightarrow e_j \wedge e_i \, ass_i \, e_j [Q_t]$$

Where, k_i and k_j are query keywords mapped to e_i, e_j respectively. ass_i is any associations between entities e_i, e_j. The *Taq* returns all associations between the two entities e_i, e_j.

5   Experiments

We perform a series of experiments using real world dataset to evaluate performance of proposed data model TEM-Network.

5.1   Experimental Setup

We conduct the experiments on a 3.5 GHz Pentium 4 machine with 8 GB RAM and 500 GB of hard disk.

Data set and query set: we use two real datasets DBLP and Cora which both include 4 entity types: Paper (*P*), Author (*A*), Venue (*V*) and Topic (*T*). Table 2 is the statistics of experimental data sets. The query set includes *Teaq*, *Treq*, *Tmmq* and *Taq* queries.

Table 2. Statistics of experimental data sets

Data set	Entity type	#entities	Timespan(Year)
DBLP	Paper	1041	[1990, 2012]
	Author	335	[1991, 2012]
	Venue	103	[1991, 2012]
	Topic	351	[1991, 2012]
Cora	Paper	768	[1974, 1998]
	Author	238	[1974, 1998]
	Venue	236	[1974, 1998]
	Topic	255	[1974, 1998]

5.2   Experimental Results and Analysis

Effectiveness of Query: Experimental evaluations of the average query precision (*P*), recall(*R*) and F-score are shown in Fig. 2. From Fig. 2 we observe that on both data sets *Tmmq* queries have the lowest average precision about 78%, followed by *Teaq* queries which are about 80%. The average precision of *Treq* and *Taq* queries are between 86% and 91%.

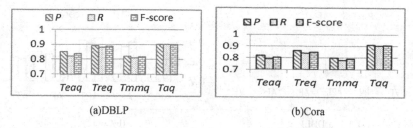

Fig. 2. Average precision, recall and F-score

Query Response Time: experimental results of the average query response time are shown in Fig. 3. It can be seen from Fig. 3 that on both data sets *Tmmq* queries have the longest average response time, followed by *Teaq* and *Treq* queries. And *Taq* queries have the least average response time.

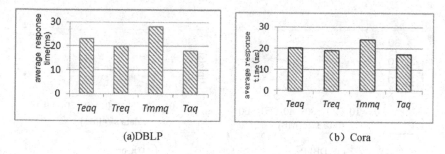

Fig. 3. Average query response time

Performance of TEM-Network: The performance of different number of layers of TEM-Networks on the temporal queries is compared on two datasets. The average precision (P), recall (R) and F-score are shown in Fig. 4.

- APVT:4-layers network including Author, Paper, Venue and Topic.
- APV:3-layers network including Author, Paper and Venue.
- APT:3-layers network including Author, Paper and Topic.
- AP:2- layers network including Author and Paper.
- AT:2-layers network including Author and Topic.
- VT: 2-layers network including Venue and Topic.

From Fig. 4 we can observe that the average precision of 3 layers are higher than those of 2 layers. The precision of 4 layers network APVT is lower than those of 3 layers. Because though APVT introduces more relevant information, it also brings unnecessary noise, therefore has a negative effect on the precision. In addition, it is noticed that the average precision of 3 layers network APT is higher than that of APV, which indicates that the topic information is more important than the conference information when searching for *authors*.

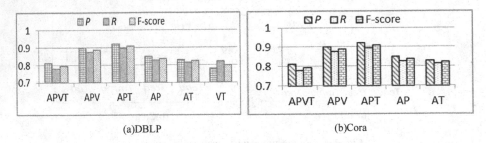

(a)DBLP   (b)Cora

Fig. 4. Comparison of different layers of TEM-Networks

Scalability TEM-Network: experimental comparison of the temporal evolution data model set up time under different data sizes (10 MB–50 MB), as shown in Fig. 5. We can see from Fig. 5 that on two datasets with the increasing of data sizes the overall execution times grow sub-linearly which show scalability of TEM-Network.

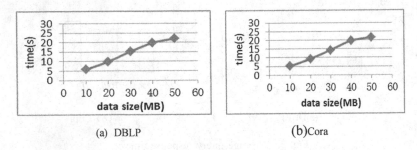

(a) DBLP   (b)Cora

Fig. 5. Scalability of TEM-Network

6   Conclusions

Aiming at temporal heterogeneous entities and their associations evolved over time, this paper proposes entity-centric multi-layer temporal evolution data model TEM-Network which can capture the temporal features and evolution features of entities and their associations. And TEM-Network can support four types of multi-modality temporal semantic entity search. The experimental results on two real datasets show the feasibility and effectiveness of TEM-Network.

Acknowledgments. This research was supported by the National Natural Science Foundation of China (Grant number 61672142); the Natural Science Foundation of Liaoning province (Grant number 20170540471).

References

1. Gregersen, H., Jensen, C.S.: Temporal entity-association ship models-a survey. IEEE Trans. Knowl. Data Eng. **11**(3), 464–497 (1999)
2. Gutierrez, C., Hurtado, C.A., Vaisman, A.A.: Introducing time into RDF. IEEE Trans. Knowl. Data Eng. **19**(2), 207–218 (2007)
3. Pugliese, A., Udrea, O., Subrahmanian, V.S.: Scaling RDF with time. In: Proceeding of WWW 2008, pp. 605–614 (2008)
4. Gutierrez, C., Hurtado, C., Vaisman, A.: Temporal RDF. In: Gómez-Pérez, A., Euzenat, J. (eds.) ESWC 2005. LNCS, vol. 3532, pp. 93–107. Springer, Heidelberg (2005). https://doi.org/10.1007/11431053_7
5. Chirkova, R., Fletcher,G.H.L.: Towards well-behaved schema evolution. In: WebDb (2009)
6. Rizzolo, F., Velegrakis, Y., Mylopoulos, J., Bykau, S.: Modeling concept evolution: a historical perspective. In: Laender, Alberto H.F., Castano, S., Dayal, U., Casati, F., de Oliveira, José Palazzo M. (eds.) ER 2009. LNCS, vol. 5829, pp. 331–345. Springer, Heidelberg (2009). https://doi.org/10.1007/978-3-642-04840-1_25
7. Wang, Y., Yang, B., Qu, L., et al.: Harvesting facts from textual web sources by constrained label propagation. In: CIKM (2011)
8. Talukdar, P.P., Wijaya, D., Mitchell, T.: Coupled temporal scoping of associational facts. In: WSDM (2012)
9. Wang, Y., Zhu, M., Qu, L., et al.: Timely YAGO: harvesting, querying, and visualizing temporal knowledge from Wikipedia. In: EDBT (2010)
10. Wang, Y., Yang, B., Zoupanos, S., et al.: Scalable spatio-temporal knowledge harvesting. In: WWW (2011)
11. Hoffart, J., Suchanek, F.M., Berberich, K., et al.: YAGO2: exploring and querying world knowledge in time, space, context, and many languages. In: WWW (2011)
12. Reinanda, R., Odijk, D., de Rijke,M.: Exploring entity associations over time.In: TAIA (2013)
13. Talukdar, P.P., Wijaya, D., Mitchell,T.: Acquiring temporal constraints between relations.In: CIKM (2012)

The Application of Distributed Database on Spectrum Big Data

Zhenjia Chen, Yonghui Zhang[(✉)], and Xia Guo

College of Information Science and Technology, Hainan University,
Haikou 570228, China
zhyhemail@163.com

Abstract. The management and utilization of spectrum resources has always been an important issue. The data of radio signals from the time domain, frequency domain, and space domain is tremendous. The current spectrum databases are mainly centralized and the disaster recovery capacity of centralized database is insufficient. In the future, cognitive radio network (CRN) will be the development trend of mobile communications. The access to the spectrum database by a large number of cognitive radio (CR) terminals and the uploading of spectrum detection data by the spectrum detection terminal in real time will exert tremendous pressure on CRN. This paper proposes use of distributed spectrum databases instead of centralized database architectures in the spectrum big data to improve the fault tolerance of spectrum databases. Multi-node collaborative electromagnetic detection method with source parameter is proposed to replace the traditional wide-band energy detection method. The traditional spectrum database stores spectrum data with energy values, and the redundancy of data is really high. We propose to store the instantaneous parameters of signal source with the structure of blockchain. The timestamp is used as the link ID of the block to connect each block end-to-end, and a distributed spectrum database is established. With the timestamp as a unique identifier, the nodes locally interact with real-time detection data. Secondary user (SU) achieve the complete electromagnetic spectrum data by access each node. SUs can analyze the electromagnetic spectrum environment, and formulate appropriate strategies for rapid dynamic spectrum access (DSA).

Keywords: Distributed database · Spectrum big data · Cooperative detection
Blockchain · Spectrum visualization

1 Introduction

With the continuous development and wide application of radio technology, the demand for radio spectrum in society is increasing day by day, resulting in an increasing gap between the supply and demand of the spectrum. A large number of licensed spectrum are not fully utilized in time and space, and there are a large number of spectrum holes, which results in a low utilization of spectrum resources. Continuous large-scale spectrum detection big data requires real-time processing. The maintenance and analysis of the spectrum database is a significant issue.

X. Sun et al. (Eds.): ICCCS 2018, LNCS 11064, pp. 212–222, 2018.
https://doi.org/10.1007/978-3-030-00009-7_20

DSA technology utilizes spectrum holes to achieve spectrum sharing for improving spectrum utilization and alleviating the shortage of spectrum resources. CR technology provides the foundation for the realization of DSA. The main idea of CR is that SUs perceive spectrum holes through spectrum monitoring and intelligently select the free spectrum without affecting primary users (PU), thereby improving spectrum utilization. [1] implemented wide band spectrum holes detection using software defined radio. Comparing the two algorithms of energy detection and cyclostationary detection, energy detection is used to achieve blind spectrum hole detection. However, the literature is only the detection of single cognitive users. In the actual electromagnetic environment, due to the influence of multi-path fading and shadows, cognitive users who are distributed in some geographical locations receive weak signal strength. In this case, the individual perceived users cannot detect the PU and spectrum hole well. [2] analyzed the effect of imperfect spectrum monitoring on the performance of CRN. The result indicated that spectrum monitoring error would misdirect SU and interfere with normal communication of PU. In order to more accurately perceive spectrum holes, the concept of cooperative spectrum sensing was proposed.

Cooperative spectrum sensing establishes multiple cognitive nodes to perform collaborative detection, reducing the errors caused by channel fading and shadow effects to user detection and the interference interference between cognitive users and PU. At present, cooperative spectrum sensing models are basically centralized, that is, the detection data of each cognitive user is aggregated into the spectrum database of the central node. All data are processed according to the set data fusion scheme for final decision. This kind of centralized collaborative awareness model requires that the central node has a strong calculation processing capability. Moreover, the central node contains data information of all cognitive users. Once the central node crashes, the data may be completely lost, and the entire system will be paralyzed. In the distributed collaborative awareness model without central node, each node establishes a local spectrum database, and exchanges information with each other to make a final decision. The distributed type distributes cumbersome data processing to various nodes, thereby improving the data processing efficiency.

With the rapid scanning speed of spectrum monitoring equipment, the widening of real-time bandwidth and the increasing deployment of CR terminal. The amount of data sensed by electromagnetic spectrum has increased exponentially, and there are various data from the three dimensions of time domain, frequency domain and spatial domain. The big data of the information society has the characteristic of "4 V" in [3]. That are, volume, velocity, variety and value. Assume that there are N detection nodes in the area of 10 km × 10 km. Each detection node takes 100 kHz as the sampling interval, and 1 s as the scanning interval. The frequency bin data is stored in 4 bytes and energy data is stored in 4 bytes. The node collects the spectrum data of the 30 MHz–1 GHz frequency band in real time and stores it in a local database. The amount of data is about $6 \times N$ GB/day. [4] proposed that the spectrum data presented strong character characteristics of big data, the electromagnetic spectrum data had ushered in big data era.

I/Q original RF data includes holographic information of electromagnetic signals. The multidimensional analysis of I/Q data in the time domain, frequency domain, and modulation domain can reflect more abundant signal characteristics, thus laying a solid foundation for signal identification. We can apply big data technology to spectrum data analysis. [5] designed the radio spectrum utilization evaluation system based on big data. The system applied the big data technology to spectrum data analysis, realizing the analysis of the spectrum focus band, detecting band occupancy rate and illegal use of spectrum. For the analysis of spectrum big data, the construction of the database is critical. Compared to traditional centralized databases, distributed databases can dynamically add cognitive nodes and distribute data across multiple cognitive nodes. [6] proposed the blockchain is a chained data structure in which data blocks are connected in a sequential manner in chronological order. It is a new application mode of distributed data storage and can be applied to the construction of distributed spectrum database. The spectrum sensing data is combined in a chronological order and stored in each node, which is jointly maintained by each node. Failure of one node does not cause the entire system to crash, which enhances system scalability and reliability.

This paper sets up a system model to illustrate the application of distributed database on spectrum big data. There is a spectrum database base on blockchain in each node in the CRN to implement distributed storage of spectrum data. The system applies the big data technology to realize the spectrum visualization analysis from three dimensions (time domain, frequency domain and spatial domain), and achieves the cooperative perception of multi-node. This architecture can provide a basis for DSA and improve spectrum utilization.

2 System Model

The development trend of future wireless communications must be a self-organizing network composed of CRs. At present, spectrum resources are allocated by the centralized Radio Surveillance Authority. However, the PU's utilization of allocated spectrum resources is low, which results in the waste of spectrum resources. On the other hand, today's CR devices that are being vigorously developed can achieve dynamic access to the spectrum, but SU often cause interference with the PU. In order to solve this problem, the release of real-time dynamic spectrum resource information has been noticed by many researchers [7–9]. The spectrum database began to be applied to many systems. However, most of the analysis of spectrum data is in a centralized processing mode. This puts tremendous pressure on CRN and processing centers. Moreover, this centralized system has poor disaster tolerance and system flexibility.

This paper proposes that multi-node are used to traverse the direction of the signal source as the transaction content. The collaborative energy detection modified signal source energy distribution parameter algorithm is a consensus algorithm [10]. The co-estimation results of the signal sources within a region are stored in blocks in the form of distributed database. All CR devices can provide collaborative detection data in a distributed spectrum database, and contribute their own arithmetic force of spectrum detection, so they are allowed to perform DSA within the region as a corresponding reward. The distributed spectrum database obtained through multi-node cooperative detection is stored in every node. CR devices can analyze spectrum holes based on the local spectrum database, and calculate the frequency bands, bandwidth, and transmit power parameters of the blank spectrum. The priority of accessing the blank spectrum depends on the contribution value of CR devices.

2.1 Block Data Format of Broadcast in Distributed Spectrum Database

Each node can obtain the I/Q original RF data of the target frequency band through the form of frequency sweep, and from which the amplitude and phase information of the signal source can be parsed out. Then, the direction finding (DF) angle of the signal source relative to the north can be obtained through the principle of phase difference measurement. Each node broadcasts block data to the network. The block data storage the detection time and the local coordinates in block header, and storage the DF angle and source detection energy of signals in block data (see Fig. 1).

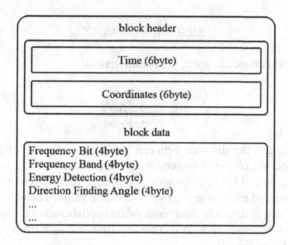

Fig. 1. Block data format of broadcast in distributed spectrum database. The data in the block contains the signal source information detected by each node. The data is mainly used for multi-node collaborative detection.

The node direction measurement will have a certain error, so it is necessary to eliminate DF error through cooperative detection and improve the accuracy of signal source positioning.

2.2 Signal Location Algorithm Base on Cooperative Detection

The coordinates of the two nodes are known as $A(x_A, y_A)$ and $B(x_B, y_B)$. The coordinates of the signal is known as $S(x_S, y_S)$. The DF angles of nodes to the same source are known as α, β. According to the trigonometric function formula, the coordinates of the signal source can be calculated by the following formula.

$$\begin{cases} x_S = \frac{x_B \tan\alpha - x_A \tan\beta + (y_A - y_B)\tan\alpha\tan\beta}{\tan\alpha - \tan\beta} \\ y_S = \frac{x_A - x_B - y_A \tan\alpha + y_B \tan\beta}{\tan\alpha - \tan\beta} \end{cases} \tag{1}$$

At the same time, the number of submissions within the network is n. According to the formula of the permutation and combination, $G = \frac{n!}{2!(n-2)!}$ kind of signal source coordinates can be obtained. At this point, a convention is needed to pick the best solution. In free space, [11] proposed electromagnetic wave propagation damage characteristics be described with the RSSI characteristics as (2). It contains the antenna parameters of the receiver and the transmitter, as well as the channel attenuation. Therefore, as long as we get the detection value of the node and the distance between the node and the signal source, we can obtain the parameter a and the parameter c in the formula.

$$\text{RSSI} = a \log d + c \tag{2}$$

Simultaneous equations can solve (2) parameters as

$$\begin{cases} a = \frac{r_A - r_B}{\log d_{SA} - \log d_{SB}} \\ c = \frac{r_A \log d_{SB} - r_B \log d_{SA}}{\log d_{SB} - \log d_{SA}} \end{cases} \tag{3}$$

where d_{SA} and d_{SB} are the distance between nodes and signal. (2) can be used to describe the distribution of signal sources in the target area.

Due to the existence of DF error in node, we need to use a mechanism to determine which detection result of each node is closer to the true value. Then all nodes select the detection value of that node as the final result of this collaborative detection. We define that the DF error of detection node as θ. The deviation distance from the signal source is described as Δd (see Fig. 2).

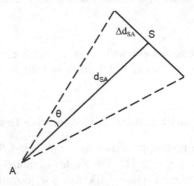

Fig. 2. The deviation distance from the signal source. The farther the detection node is from the signal source, the greater the deviation distance. The closer the detection node is to the signal source, the more accurate DF value.

So Δd can be expressed by the trigonometric function formula as

$$\Delta d_{SA} = d_{SA}\tan\theta \tag{4}$$

Then a predicted value offset distance is $\Delta d = \Delta d_{SA} + \Delta d_{SB}$. Therefore, we determine that when *min(Δd)*, the prediction values of the corresponding two detection nodes are the optimal values. After each node calculates the optimal prediction value of all frequency points, the optimal values are linked to the previous block with the detection time as a timestamp, and a reward is added to all the nodes participating in the cooperative detection. The detection node defaults to the unit of the minimum detection time in whole seconds in the distributed system. That is, the millisecond unit is ignored. The minimum unit of timestamp is one second. The distributed spectrum database structure (see Fig. 3).

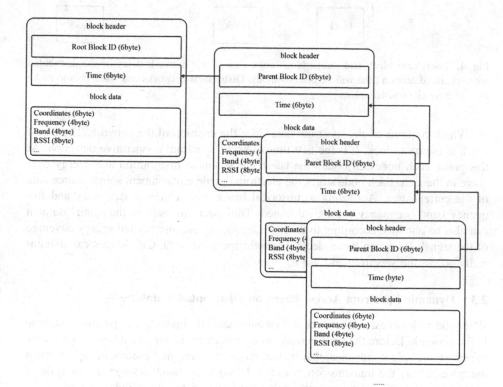

Fig. 3. The structure of distributed spectrum database. Data blocks are linked in the order of time stamps in the form of linked lists. Block data stores signal data at each moment. The parent block ID stores the ID of the last timestamp block.

The node broadcasts its own blockchain to the CRN at regular intervals. Receiving blockchain of the network, nodes update their own local database. With the timestamp as an index, the block content source data can be updated, and the spectrum data of different networks can be merged. Different timestamp blocks can be inserted directly into the local database (see Fig. 4). The traditional centralized network must rely on the Internet, 2G/3G/4G and other networks to aggregate the data of each detection node to the server. The detection range of the node is generally limited. Distributed networks can autonomously integrate local data of different networks through spectrum data sharing between different networks. After multiple iterations of merge, each node will have integrated spectrum data of the CRN.

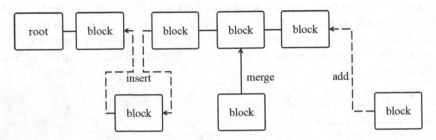

Fig. 4. Insert new block and merge block data. Due to the network delay of the distributed network, the detection time will be discontinuous. Distributed networks can share data to make the database close to complete.

Which contains all the spectrum data since the creation of the network. The oldest block is the root block. It is the first timestamp of spectrum cooperative detection. At this point, each node can obtain the latest signal source distribution and energy coverage in the area. Each node stores the electromagnetic environment signal source data of the current area. According to historical block data, channel occupancy and frequency band occupancy can be calculated. The spectrum map on the spatial domain can also be obtained according to the radio frequency parameters and energy coverage of the signal. Based on these electromagnetic spectrum data, CR devices can dynamically access the spectrum and use it.

2.3   Dynamic Spectrum Access Based on Distributed Database

When the node access the network, it first automatically updates the spectrum database in the network. Before the node is ready to use spectrum resources, it needs to perceive the spectrum hole in advance, that is, the frequency band that are not occupied. Then the node selects the transmission power and frequency band through the analysis of cooperative detection data currently being broadcasted by other nodes. Based on the spectrum database and broadcast data packets, the terminal can analyze the distribution of wireless devices in the current area. The terminal can indirectly obtain the signal coverage of each detection frequency band and visualize the radio frequency spectrum data (see Fig. 5). According to the spectrum access requirements, such as the communication frequency band, communication bandwidth, and coverage (transmission power), the terminal judges whether it will affect the normal operation of the nearby nodes or the signal source. The terminal can access the blank spectrum to communicate automatically by ensuring that other detection nodes and signal source location are not within the signal range of the node.

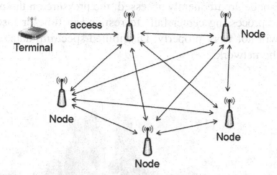

Fig. 5. CR equipment access to distributed spectrum database and dynamic spectrum access. The terminal can access the complete spectrum database through any node in the distributed network.

When the frequency band requested by the node is the same as that of other detection nodes, the contribution value of the node in cooperative detection needs to be verified. The nodes with higher contribution values use spectrum resources preferentially. SU can accumulate their own contribution value by participating in collaborative detection activities. So, the number of nodes in the distributed network is variable, and the dynamic access and exit make the data volume of the network always fluctuate. Node movement can also cause changes in the spectrum environment. Once the terminal starts to access the spectrum, it needs to participate in cooperative spectrum detection. As long as the primary user starts to use the frequency band, the SU will automatically exit the frequency band to prevent the spectrum collision from occurring.

3 Spectrum Data Processing and Analysis

3.1 Channel Occupancy Calculation

The nodes access the network and update the local distributed database. The spectrum information of the current area is extracted from each block. In order to better understand the spectrum utilization of the current channel, we often calculate the channel occupancy [12, 13], that is the probability that this frequency point is used in history. We define the number of current blocks as b, and the number of times that a certain frequency signal appears in the block is t. The channel occupancy rate can be expressed by

$$R_C = \frac{t}{b} \times 100\% \tag{5}$$

Then we can get the spectrum occupancy in the target frequency band (see Fig. 6). Channel occupancy will be an important parameter for measuring spectrum utilization. In a centralized spectrum database network, each node needs to query the processing center. When multi-node are frequently accessed, the pressure on the processing center will increase. If the processing center fails to respond in time or loses physical connection, the node will not work properly. Distributed spectrum databases increase the fault tolerance of the network.

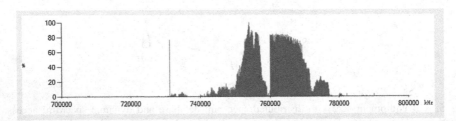

Fig. 6. The channel occupancy rate. According to the channel occupancy rate, the utilization of spectrum resources can be analyzed from the time-frequency joint domain.

3.2   Spectrum Map and Spectrum Visualization

The spectrum is an invisible radio resource. Spectral visualization integrates multi-dimensional electromagnetic spectrum monitoring information such as time domain, frequency domain and space domain. It can present intangible spectrum resources in a

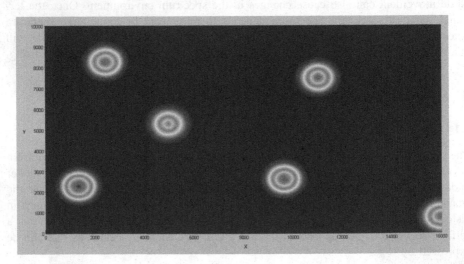

Fig. 7. Spectrum Map and Spectrum Visualization. The distribution of electromagnetic signals can be described more fully by recording the location of the signal source and the propagation loss characteristic parameters in free space. The point where the color is reddish in the figure is the position of the signal source. The darker color indicates that the higher the transmit power of the signal source, the greater the coverage. (Color figure online)

more simple and easy-to-understand manner, enabling users to easily identify valid information of spectrum data. According to the distributed spectrum database, the spectrum occupancy is calculated in real time, and the spectrum map is mapped in the form of a map for visualization. By detecting the signal source parameters, we detect the distribution of radio signals in the target area more directly by distributed spectrum database (see Fig. 7).

4 Conclusion

In the centralized spectrum database, the energy values of each frequency point of each node will be stored, including too much noise data, and the amount of redundant data is huge. When calculating the channel occupancy, the distributed block-chained spectrum database replaces the centralized database mode by storing the signal source parameters, which greatly reduces the data retrieval time. In this paper, a distributed spectrum database is constructed by using the blockchain method to improve the performance of multi-node cooperative spectrum detection under the scenario of spectrum big data. In the distributed network, nodes frequently join or leave the network with minimal impact on the spectrum database. Spectral data is permanently stored in the network in the form of blockchain and is maintained by all nodes. According to the contribution of each node to the spectrum detection work, the priority of dynamic spectrum access is defined. Under the trend of spectrum big data, distributed spectrum database will be more applied in wireless communication networks.

Acknowledgment. In this paper, the research was sponsored by the National Natural Science Foundation of China (61561018).

References

1. Frasch, I., Kwasinski, A.: Wideband spectrum holes detection implementation for cognitive radios. In: IEEE Global Conference on Signal and Information Processing, pp. 278–282 (2017)
2. Thakur, P., Kumar, A., Pandit, S.: Effect of imperfect spectrum monitoring on cognitive radio network performance. In: The Fourth International Conference on Image Information Processing, pp. 1–5 (2017)
3. Xueqi, C., Xiaolong, J., Yuanzhuo, W.: A review of big data systems and analytical techniques. J. Softw. **25**(9), 1889–1908 (2014)
4. Zheng, L.: Electromagnetic Spectrum Sensing Data Management and Mining Based on Big Data. Information and Communications, pp. 137–138 (2016)
5. Qian, Z., Fei, W., Xie, L.: Design and implementation of radio spectrum utilization evaluation system based on big data. In: IEEE 9th International Conference on Communication Software and Networks, pp. 362–366 (2016)
6. Bracamonte, V., Okada, H.: The issue of user trust in decentralized applications running on blockchain platforms. In: IEEE International Symposium on Technology and Society, pp. 1–4 (2017)

7. Hu, Y., Hu, J., Song, T.: Joint energy and spectrum detection in cooperative cognitive radio under noise uncertainty. In: 9th International Conference on Wireless Communications and Signal Processing, pp. 1–5 (2017)
8. Jing, Y., Ma, L., Li, P.: A novel spectrum sensing algorithm for small-scale primary users detection. In: IEEE International Conference of IEEE Region, vol. 10, pp. 1–4 (2013)
9. Liu, C., Qi, A., Zhang, P.: Wideband spectrum detection based on compressed sensing in cooperative cognitive radio networks. In: 8th International Conference on Communications and Networking in China, pp. 638–642 (2013)
10. Kwok, P., Li, H., Teh, K.C.: Dynamic cooperative Sensing-Access policy for energy-harvesting cognitive radiosystems. IEEE Trans. Veh. Technol. 65(12), 10137–10141 (2016)
11. Beaudeau, J.P., Bugallo, M.F., Djurić, P.M.: RSSI-based multi-target tracking by cooperative agents using fusion of cross-target information. IEEE Trans. Signal Process. 63(19), 5033–5044 (2015)
12. Lehtomäki, J.J., Vuohtoniemi, R., Umebayashi, K.: On the measurement of duty cycle and channel occupancy rate. J. Select. Areas Commun. 31(11), 2555–2565 (2013)
13. Lehtomäki, J.J., Löpez-Benłtez, M., Umebayashi, K.: Improved channel occupancy rate estimation. IEEE Trans. Commun. 63(3), 643–654 (2015)

The Benchmark Performance Testing Method for Cluster Heterogeneous Network Based on STC Platform

Junhua Xi[✉] and Kouquan Zheng

National University of Defense Technology, Xian 710106, Shannxi, China
10110091123@163.com

Abstract. For BDC (Big Data Center) cluster heterogeneous network lack of accurate, systematic and standardized performance evaluation and optimization problems, a BDC cluster heterogeneity network benchmark performance test index system was set up, a BDC cluster heterogeneous network benchmark performance test model based on STC (Spirent Testing) platform was established, and a cluster heterogeneous network benchmark performance test method and index optimization scheme were proposed. Through experimental verification, the model in this paper can analysis base on BDC topology, quickly locate network performance bottlenecks, and achieve intelligent iterative optimization of evaluation indicators, significantly reducing system response time under the premise of improving network performance.

Keywords: Spirent testing · Benchmark performance
Cluster heterogeneous network

1 Introduction

With the rapid development of information and communication technology, the continuous improvement of network equipment performance, the highly integrated network service platform, and the continuous deepening application of cloud computing and heterogeneous cluster networks, modern network services have entered the era of big data [1, 2]. In the situation of large-scale data operations with quantified, complex, complicated and discrete, the important issues that need to be addressed in the development of data services are how to optimize deployment of network resources, reduce system response time, improve network service quality, and build a network service system with stability, scalability, and flexibility [3]. BDC (Big Data Center) is an operational management technology framework that has been generated and continuously improved in the context of highly concentrated services such as data calculation, network transmission, and backup storage. It has realized the integration and centralized management of IT (Information Technology) resources and reduced Business cost, shortened the business development cycle, and provided open, flexible, and uniform interfaces to external and internal users, to meet the diversified data service needs of users, and has attracted the attention of the academic community and the application fields of the information and communication industries [4]. However,

© Springer Nature Switzerland AG 2018
X. Sun et al. (Eds.): ICCCS 2018, LNCS 11064, pp. 223–231, 2018.
https://doi.org/10.1007/978-3-030-00009-7_21

with the explosive growth of network service requests, the scale of network data has expanded geometrically, and the collaborative operation of cluster heterogeneous networks has become normal. BDC's position in the entire network is also increasingly important. The network topology becomes extremely complex, and the bottleneck of network performance is becoming increasingly prominent. This makes it urgent to extract and analyze the indicators of the heterogeneous network of the BDC cluster, optimize the network configuration, and improve and enhance the BDC network service quality. However, the traditional data center network operation system lacks a standardized performance test program, and it is difficult to understand, master, and adjust the network behavior through the verification of new technologies and the evaluation of network key performance to ensure the high-performance and stable operation of the BDC network system [5]. Therefore, the BDC cluster heterogeneous network benchmark performance is tested by scientific and effective method, and the operation state of BDC network is revealed in a quantitative way, so as to realize the management, predictability and adjustable target of system network resources. It has become a key issue in the field of information communication network service.

STC (Spirent Testing) is the industry's first overall data center test platform launched by Spirent Communications. It covers all aspects of the data center from basic network architecture evaluation to upper application verification. It can simulate the real-time and effective BDC network operation status, monitor the client in real time, achieve comprehensive testing of the network benchmark performance, and quickly locate the performance bottleneck of the system under test based on the analysis of the data center topology, and provide a complete network performance index optimization solution [6]. Because it can automatically provide data center standardized test suites, support single-device or data center effective cluster heterogeneous network test extensions, providing the industry's highest test accuracy and the best compensation algorithm, Because it can automatically provide data center standardized test suites, support single-device or data center effective cluster heterogeneous network test extensions, providing the industry's highest test accuracy and the best compensation algorithm, the STC platform is widely used in network product development, verification and performance optimization of network equipment manufacturers, in network performance evaluation and system operation and maintenance of network operators, in technological innovation of scientific research institutes and network service organizations, and other related fields [7–9]. In view of this, this article cuts through the network performance test under the condition of BDC operation, builds the heterogeneous network benchmark performance test model of BDC cluster based on STC platform, realizing intelligent monitor for information users and application customization network service quality, providing effective ideas and methods for BDC network comprehensive performance monitoring and optimization.

2 BDC Cluster Heterogeneous Network Benchmark Performance Test Model

2.1 BDC Cluster Heterogeneous Network Benchmark Performance Test Index System

Network (device) benchmark performance is closely related to system applications, but not entirely dependent on the application network (device) performance characteristics. The BDC network benchmark performance test is to measure, analyze, and evaluate the benchmark performance characteristics of the BDC network (device) hardware, software, and system operation modules, which can solve the problems that the network service quality is not high, network operation is difficult to locate and system performance cannot be optimized occurring during the BDC operation, providing assistance for targeted high-performance security and stable operation of BDC and meeting the needs of users. In addition, modern mass data services and large-scale cloud computing tasks often require the cooperation of multiple clustered heterogeneous networks, which leads to BDC's dependence on network performance is growing. Therefore, we must research and establish a scientific and reasonable cluster heterogeneity network benchmark performance test index system to provide support for BDC network evaluation optimization.

The STC platform provides a standard and systematic automated test suite for data center network benchmark performance test. It also provides optimized compensation algorithms while providing network benchmark performance test, as well as convenient and quick test wizards to quickly complete complex BDC networks testing system configuration. Therefore, this paper focuses on the Spirent Data Center network benchmark performance optimization solution to build a BDC cluster heterogeneous network benchmark performance test index system. According to the test indicators, the impact of the heterogeneous network operation on the BDC cluster is sorted, as shown in Fig. 1.

2.2 BDC Cluster Heterogeneous Network Benchmark Performance Test Model

The STC platform complies with industry-wide standards for network (device) benchmark performance, defines the overall network performance test suite for Data Center. Therefore, in order to effectively evaluate the overall performance of the heterogeneous network of BDC clusters, analyze the operation status of the data center system and the utilization of network resources, quickly locate the bottleneck of cluster heterogeneous networks, facilitate network assessment and optimization, and realize real-time intelligent monitoring of heterogeneous network performance in BDC clusters. This paper sets up a BDC cluster heterogeneity network benchmark performance test model to provide overall monitoring of network performance for the efficient operation of BDC systems and realizes intelligent monitoring of service quality across the entire network.

As shown in Fig. 2, the BDC cluster heterogeneous network benchmark performance test model consists of five subsystems: management control, data collection,

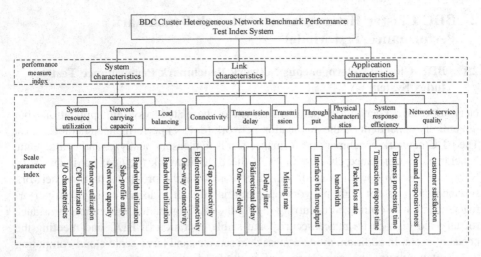

Fig. 1. BDC cluster heterogeneous network benchmark performance test index system

performance testing, evaluation optimization, and data support. The management control subsystem is responsible for network test parameter setting, script definition, node design, task management, and interaction configuration with the network test main system and data support subsystem. The data collection subsystem is responsible for the collection of BDC system equipment, network, and performance parameters. The performance testing subsystem is responsible for testing benchmark performance parameters such as BDC communication contact, resource equipment and network coordination. The evaluation optimization subsystem is responsible for network test data display, data analysis, performance evaluation, index optimization, and evaluation of intelligent feedback. The data support subsystem is a backend database support for the test model, including a configuration database, a record database, a test database, and an analysis database. The configuration database is mainly used for storing various configuration management information required for test evaluation, such as test interval time, test node, test tasks and detailed path information, the record database is mainly used to store various types of parameter information collected by the system, the test database is mainly used to store test data, and the analysis database is mainly used to store the statistical information after the evaluation and analysis. Each database uses Orcal database standard, using a text file format, which supports data migration integration between heterogeneous databases.

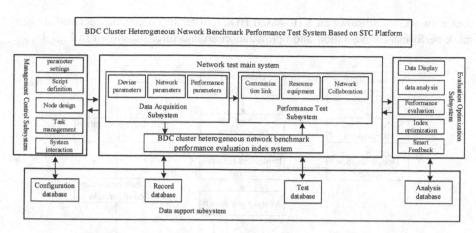

Fig. 2. BDC cluster heterogeneous network benchmark performance test model

3 Design and Implementation of BDC Cluster Heterogeneous Network Benchmark Performance Test System

3.1 BDC Cluster Heterogeneous Network Evaluation Optimization Process

BDC cluster heterogeneous networks are generally used to carry network computing, data disaster recovery, and system optimization that require large-capacity network resources. They require high system network bandwidth, and each cluster is deployed across regions, and the link latency is relatively high, which results in a need for optimizing the full-time system evaluation for BDC network bearer service features. The specific test process is shown in Fig. 3.

In the BDC cluster heterogeneous network evaluation and optimization, the optimal number of iterations needs to be selected according to user requirements and evaluation costs, and each round of testing is required to statistically analyze BDC network benchmark performance evaluation indexes and generate evaluation reports. Then according to the requirements of data analysis, to find the system network performance bottlenecks, and combined with the test results to give an optimized program for real-time feedback-type performance optimization.

3.2 BDC Cluster Heterogeneous Network Benchmark Performance Test Scene Design

The BDC cluster heterogeneous network benchmark performance test is a comprehensive system test. It is required to test and analyze the capabilities of the system, discover system operation problems, and locate system performance bottlenecks. Therefore, in order to eliminate the effects of network bandwidth and system delay on the test results, it is possible to discover system performance bottlenecks with minimal test iterations and reduce network transmission uncertainties, the STC platform and the BDC cluster heterogeneous network service application model are deployed in the local area network, establishing an STC-based BDC cluster heterogeneous network benchmark performance evaluation and optimization architecture. As shown in Fig. 4.

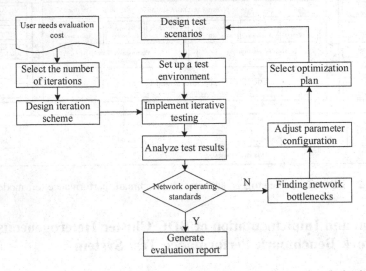

Fig. 3. BDC cluster heterogeneous network performance evaluation and optimization process

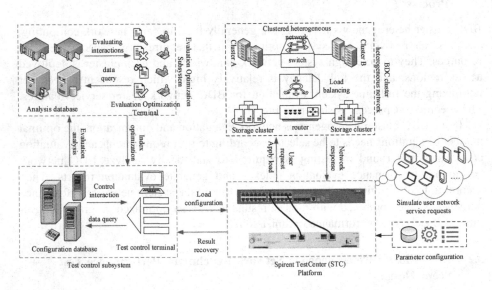

Fig. 4. BDC cluster heterogeneous network benchmark performance test environment architecture

The management control subsystem implements the test scenario configuration and test process monitoring. Build BDC cluster heterogeneous network business application system, simulate massive users through STC platform and send random network service requests, monitor system response status in real time, analyze various performance indicators online in real time, and generate test reports. The evaluation and optimization subsystem combines the BDC cluster heterogeneous network benchmark performance index system, analyzes the BDC network operating status, locates the network bottleneck, and solves the problem when found, ensuring the successful deployment of BDC network applications.

3.3   BDC Cluster Heterogeneous Network Benchmark Performance Test Method

BDC cluster heterogeneous network benchmark performance test is based on the STC platform to impose load on the network system, obtain system response, use the connection between the input load and output results, analyze the performance characteristics of heterogeneous BDC cluster network performance, locate system performance bottlenecks, and optimize network system configuration, this will improve BDC network service quality. The key part of the test is the STC platform load generator creates load pressures which meet the requirements of virtual users and generates. To impose a load on the virtual user, the core step is how to configure the platform parameters to complete the analysis of the test target and test log to find the system performance bottlenecks, and through parameter adjustment, intelligent iteration is performed to optimize the network indicators.

Therefore, in order to make the design of the test model conform to the operation of the heterogeneous network of BDC clusters as much as possible, this paper has improved and innovated in the testing method. The specific test steps can be described as:

(a) Initialization of BDC cluster heterogeneous network system and STC platform configuration.
(b) The STC test platform simulates a multi-domain multi-user to issue a large-scale concurrent random network service request to the BDC, and applies the process load in a pre-warming, pressurizing, maintaining, and descending manner according to an exponentially progressive ratio.
(c) Based on the BDC network response, the STC platform generates test logs in collaboration with the data acquisition subsystem and the performance evaluation subsystem.
(d) The evaluation and optimization subsystem analyzes the performance indicators according to the test logs. If the best performance is achieved, the evaluation report is generated. Otherwise, the performance bottleneck of the positioning system is analyzed, the configuration of the system platform parameters is adjusted, and the number of iterations is determined according to the system requirements and the test costs. Cycle test optimization until the optimization evaluation has been achieved.
(e) Generate a BDC cluster heterogeneous network benchmark performance evaluation report.

4   Analysis of Benchmark Performance Test of Heterogeneous Network in BDC Cluster

In order to verify the performance of the algorithm, this paper simulates the large-scale concurrent random network service requests based on the STC platform and tests the cluster heterogeneous network benchmark performance, it runs on the real-time sampling of indicators such as disk utilization, average CPU performance, system usage, and network load operation of BDC cluster network servers, the BDC's benchmark performance such as network load capacity, resource utilization, and system response efficiency is analyzed. From the test results, it was found that the average CPU usage within the 45 min of normal operation of each cluster server is below 23%, and the peak value only reached 50%. The BDC network system runs smoothly, the parameter configuration is reasonable, and the overall resource utilization rate is high. In particular, after iterative optimization, the maximum write/read speed of the network server disk is 200 Mbit/s and 500 Mbit/s respectively, far from the disk application performance bottleneck. Although the network load fluctuates greatly during the initial period of pressurization, the system can quickly analyze the positioning performance bottleneck and perform load balancing iterative optimization.

By adjusting cluster network servers, load balancing servers, system management, and security systems to different network card outlets respectively, network bandwidth usage can be reduced to less than 4 Mbit/s to avoid network congestion. After 3 h of exponential progressive pressurization and reverse decompression testing, the overall use of the BDC network is in good condition, and the utilization rate of network resources is maintained at a high level for a long time. Through system evaluation and intelligent iterative optimization, the network operating status can be monitored in real time and the entire network computing resources can be flexibly scheduled.

It can be seen that optimizing and benchmarking the performance of the heterogeneous network of the BDC cluster based on the STC platform can effectively improve the bearing capacity, resource utilization, and service processing efficiency of the cluster heterogeneous network, simplify the operation and maintenance of the system, reduce energy consumption, and avoid network congestion. At the same time, the stability and scalability of BDC operations have been improved, and the timeliness of network services has been enhanced. This makes the BDC resource configuration more reasonable and the network runs more smoothly.

5   Conclusion

In view of the deficiencies of BDC cluster heterogeneous network testing methods, this paper introduces the STC platform into the BDC cluster heterogeneous network benchmark performance evaluation optimization process. The BDC cluster heterogeneity network benchmark performance test index system is designed, and the BDC cluster heterogeneity network benchmark performance evaluation optimization model is built. The BDC cluster heterogeneous network benchmark performance evaluation and optimization method based on STC platform is proposed. Through simulation experiments, this method can effectively enhance the flexibility, stability and scalability of BDC cluster heterogeneous network performance evaluation optimization, real-time monitoring of system operation status, accurate positioning of network bottlenecks, and intelligent optimization evaluation indicators. In essence, BDC network service quality will be improved, providing effective support for BDC business expansion.

References

1. Yi, W.: Analysis of satellite network performance testing technology. Ship Electron. Eng. (3), 153–155 (2014)
2. Wang, E.-S., Li, R., Tang, Y.: Research and analysis of GNSS performance test methods. J. Navig. Position. (2), 21–25 (2016)
3. Zhan, J.-F., Gao, W.-L., Wang, L.: BigDataBench: open source large data system evaluation benchmarks. J. Comput. Sci. (1), 196–211 (2016)
4. Jiang, D.-Y., Chen, H.-X.: Discussion of inter cluster network performance optimization in cloud data center. Telecommun. Sci. (5), 138–142 (2015)
5. Wan, Y., Yu, Y.-H.: Performance analysis of NPB based on heterogeneous network cluster environment. J. Nat. Sci. Harbin Norm. Univ. (2), 75–78 (2016)
6. Li, T.: Research and design of performance evaluation system based on spirent for high-performance fault-tolerant computer. Harbin Institute of Technology, Harbin (2010)
7. Zhou, P., Zhou, H.-Y., Zuo, D.-C., Li, T.: Spirent-based web application performance evaluation. Comput. Eng. (24), 57–61 (2012)
8. Zhang, C., Xiong, Y., Fang, W.-D.: Research on ZigBee network performance testing system. Foreign Electron. Meas. Technol. **34**(8), 74–81 (2015)
9. Song-Wei, Shen, J.-X., Sun, Y.: Method for performance testing of large-scale mail server and its practice. Comput. Appl. Softw. (12), 130–131 (2010)
10. Zheng, K.-Q., Hui, J.-H., Zhang, Q.-H.: The benchmark performance testing of ISC based on STC platform. J. Xi'an Commun. Inst. (4), 35–38 (2016)

The Classification of Traditional Chinese Painting Based on CNN

Qingyu Meng[1,2,3], Huanhuan Zhang[1,2,3], Mingquan Zhou[1,2,3(✉)],
Shifeng Zhao[1,2,3], and Pengbo Zhou[1,2,3]

[1] College of Information Science and Technology, Beijing Normal University,
Beijing 100875, People's Republic of China
qy@mail.bnu.edu.cn, mqzhou@bnu.edu.cn
[2] Engineering Research Center of Virtual Reality and Applications,
Ministry of Education (MOE), Beijing 100875, People's Republic of China
[3] Beijing Key Laboratory of Digital Preservation and Virtual Reality for Cultural
Heritage, Beijing 100875, People's Republic of China

Abstract. Traditional Chinese painting has an extremely long and uninterrupted history, which makes it valuable for people to study and analyze it. Meanwhile, the convolutional neural network has achieved a great success in the field of image processing. However, there are relatively less research in applying the convolutional neural network to traditional Chinese painting images. Based on the content of the painting, traditional Chinese paintings are categorized into three types—figure painting, flower-and-bird painting and landscape painting. In this article, we use serval classical convolutional neural network to classify traditional Chinese painting images according to the content of the painting. Although some networks achieve an ideal classification accuracy, they still cost a large amount of time and memory. To address this problem, we modify the architecture of VGG-16 network—deleting a convolutional layer and adding dropout to the network. Finally, the VGG-15 (with dropout) achieves a classification accuracy with 93.8%, while still maintaining a relatively low time and memory consumption.

Keywords: Content of painting · CNN · Tradition chinese painting
VGG

1 Introduction

As one of the oldest and uninterrupted forms of traditional art in the world, traditional Chinese painting has extremely high artistic and cultural values. The research of traditional Chinese painting has never stopped. With the rapid development of computer technology, using computer has been a prevalent way to do the research and the analysis to the traditional Chinese painting. However, some main problems still hampering the research work. For instance, even though different painters are trying to paint the same one thing, there would be huge differences between their paintings. What's more, when painters drawing, they do not simply map the objects they see to canvas, but reflect through their own processing, conciseness, and sublimation [1]. In

© Springer Nature Switzerland AG 2018
X. Sun et al. (Eds.): ICCCS 2018, LNCS 11064, pp. 232–241, 2018.
https://doi.org/10.1007/978-3-030-00009-7_22

summarize, traditional Chinese painting's style and expression form are highly abstract and subjective. These characteristics have brought great difficulties for the use of computer to research and analyze the traditional Chinese painting.

Although the style of each painting is different, we can still categorize them into serval different type according to different standard. For example, according to the way of expression, traditional Chinese painting could be categorized into gongbi painting (which means meticulous, usually uses highly detailed brushstrokes and highly colored) and xieyi painting (which also known as literati painting or freehand style). Another standard is according to the content of painting. By using this standard, traditional Chinese paintings can be categorized into three main type: figure painting, landscape painting and flower-and-bird painting. These three main type are showed in the following figure (Figs. 1, 2 and 3):

Fig. 1. Figure painting.

In recent years, with the rapid improvement of computer computing capabilities, deep learning has achieved remarkable results in various fields. Meanwhile, convolutional neural networks have also been applied in many aspects such as image classification and edge detection. Considering that with the deepening of the convolutional neural network, the nonlinear expression ability of the entire network gets stronger. With that ability, the convolutional neural network can handle the abstract features relatively easy. However, relatively few researches have been done to apply convolutional neural networks to traditional Chinese painting.

Taking into account the above characteristics of deep neural networks, this article tries to use deep neural networks to classify traditional Chinese painting according to the content of painting. What's more, these work would facilitate the future research to the painting, like detecting if there are boys, girls, old people or young people in the painting.

2 Related Work

Research on the classification of images using computers has achieved relatively remarkable results. However, most of the research results are mainly achieved in the classification of natural images, or images containing realistic scenery. For the classification of abstract images such as traditional Chinese painting, development is relatively backward, but recent progress has also been made.

Fig. 2. Flower-and-bird painting.

Fig. 3. Landscape painting.

For the natural image classification, Corridoni [2, 3] et al. used color feature as the classification standard. Stricker [4] et al. proposed color-moment based on color feature which partly solved the problems of low color quantification and feature dimension. Lowe [5] et al. proposed Scale Invariant Feature Transform (SIFT) algorithm, which extremely simplify the expression form of image by using the SIFT features. Herbert [6] et al. proposed Speeded-Up Robust Features (SURF) algorithm, which improves the speed of feature extraction by a factor of 3 to 5. Yang [7] and Gao [8] did some research on sparse coding image classification algorithm.

For the research of image with relatively abstract style, like traditional Chinese painting, Li [9] et al. used wavelet transformation to extract features and designed a mixed 2d multi-resolution Markov model. However, the classification effect was not ideal. Jiang [10] et al. proposed an algorithm which firstly extract color and texture which are relatively low-level feature information. Then they use support vector machines (SVM) to classify. This algorithm finally achieved 90% classification accuracy which were relatively ideal. Gao [11] et al. proposed an algorithm with key area detection and cascade classification strategy. Guan [12] et al. used color histogram and Gabor feature fusion to classify traditional Chinese painting according to content. Du [13] et al. proposed using color and shape features to construct painting features and used support vector machine (SVM) to perform semantic classification. Although they achieved some better accuracy, still under 86% in 500 examples. In 2010, Hong [14] et al. proposed image semantically significant region extraction and multi-task joint sparse method based on BOF to classify the content of painting, which cost less time.

With the rapid improvement of computer computing capability, convolutional neural network has achieved more and more achievement in image appliance. In 2012, Krizhevsky [15] et al. trained a large, deep convolutional neural network to classify the 1.2 million high-resolution images into the 1000 different classed and used it to classify the test data set which finally achieved top-1 and top-5 error rates of 37.5% and 17.0%. In 2015, Simonyan [16] et al. proposed VGG network which performs better than AlexNet. In the same year, Szegedy [17] proposed a deep convolutional neural network architecture codenamed Inception which can enlarge the depth and width of the network and finally improved the performance by a factor of 2 to 3. In 2016, He [18] et al. proposed a network which contained residual block. It is easy for residual block to learn the identity function which guarantee the deeper neural network would perform not worse than the shallower neural network.

In this article, we trained serval classical deep neural networks. After that, we randomly chose a traditional Chinese painting as the input of the network. Then the network output the probability of the image belonging to figure painting, landscape painting, and flower-and-bird painting. We also modified the classical VGG-16 network which finally achieved 93.8% classification accuracy.

3   The Implementation of Different CNN to Traditional Chinese Painting

Using the same experimental platform and the same data set, we trained the serval classical convolutional neural network and compared the classification accuracy. There are 4% gap between the best and the worst. However, even though the ResNet achieved the best classification accuracy. It also consumed the most memory and time.

With regard to VGG network, we delete a convolutional layer and add dropout to the fully connected layer. The VGG-15(with dropout) finally achieved the best classification accuracy, Meanwhile, the memory consumption and the training time are still ideal.

3.1   The Modified VGG Network

Dropout
With the deepening of the deep neural network, the capability of expressing the non-linearity gets stronger and stronger, which also means the network can be very expressive model which can study complicated relationships between input and output. However, during the training stage, some noises in the training data set would also be learned by the network, which is not really exists in test data set. This kind of problem is called overfitting which finally makes the network behaves badly.

With regard to the overfitting problem, some methods have been proposed to address it. For instance, early stopping, weight penalty and drop out et al. [19].

The term dropout means that drop out units in the network. During the training stage, we temporarily delete a unit along with the incoming connections and the outgoing connections with a fixed probability p. This operation makes that, for each mini-batch during the training stage, we try to train a thinned network. By doing like that, for a deep neural network with n units, we could generate 2^n thinned networks. However, each thinned-network shares the same weights, which makes dropout would not slow down the training speed. The following figure show the difference between the networks with or without dropout (Fig. 4):

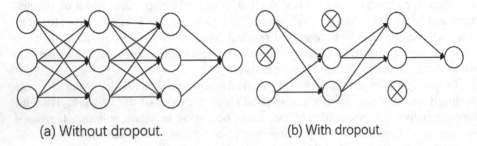

(a) Without dropout.   (b) With dropout.

Fig. 4. The differences between the networks with or without dropout.

During the testing stage, all units in the network are retained and kept alive. The weights learned before are multiplied by p. Like the following figure shows (Fig. 5):

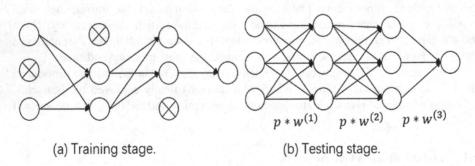

$$p * w^{(1)} \quad p * w^{(2)} \quad p * w^{(3)}$$

(a) Training stage.   (b) Testing stage.

Fig. 5. The differences between the training and testing stage.

The VGG-15

We firstly used an unmodified classical VGG-16 network. However, the outcome was not good enough. So we deleted a convolutional layer and add dropout in fully connected layer. By utilizing these, the modified VGG network achieved the highest classification accuracy with least time consumption and least memory cost compared with Alexnet, ResNet and GoogLeNet.

At the training stage, the traditional Chinese painting image was scaled into a resolution with 256*256. After that, we have implanted the gamma correction algorithm which can effectively enhanced the contrast of images. Meanwhile, the gamma correction algorithm also enlarges the data set which helps to address the overfitting problem.

After that, the preprocessed image is sent to the VGG-15 network as the input; The batch size is set to 25; After each convolutional operation and fully connected layer, we utilize the ReLU activation function. Compared with the original VGG-16 network, we add the dropout after a pooling layer and the first two fully connected layer.

The detailed architecture is depicted in the following figure (Fig. 6):

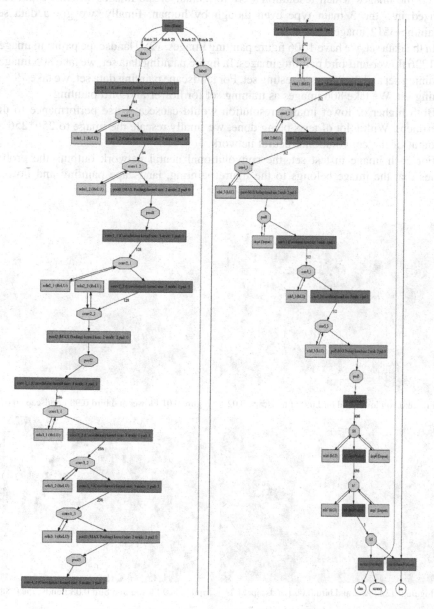

Fig. 6. The architecture of VGG-15 (with dropout).

4 Experiment

During the implementation stage, we used Intel Xeon CPU 2.4 GHz, 32 GB Memory and a GPU with 8 GB memory.

As for the data set, because there were not enough off-the-shelf traditional Chinese paintings images, we used the web crawler to download the images from the China Central Museum of Art. After that, we manually screened the downloaded images and deleted the images which resolution were too small or the images which cannot categorized into the 3 main type even though by human. Finally, we got a data set containing 3512 images.

In the data set, we have 1006 figure painting images, 1280 landscape painting images and 1226 flower-and-bird painting images. In figure painting data set, we take 805 images as training set and the others as testing set. For landscape painting data set, we take 797 as training set. We take 806 images as training set for flower-and-bird painting.

Both higher or lower images resolution would cause a worse performance to the experiment. With a lot of tests being done, we finally rescale the image to 256*256 as the input of the convolutional neural network.

For each image in test set, the convolutional neural network outputs the probabilities that the image belongs to the figure painting, landscape painting and flower-

Figure:0.96 Flower and bird:0.02 Landscape:0.02   Figure:0.01 Flower and bird:0.98 Landscape:0.01

Figure:0.12 Flower and bird:0.06 Landscape:0.82   Figure:0.09 Flower and bird:0.03 Landscape:0.88

Fig. 7. The output examples of three main type painting.

and-bird painting. For the three main type of traditional Chinese painting, we give some example in the following figure (Fig. 7):

In this article, we conducted the experiments in two main ways: Firstly, we used the original AlexNet, VGG-16, GoogLeNet and ResNet to see which achieved the best outcome using the same data set and experimental platform. Secondly, we used the modified VGG network (VGG-15 with dropout added) which finally achieved the state-of-the-art accuracy.

4.1 The Comparison Between Original CNN

The Correlation Between Loss, Accuracy and Iteration

During the experiment, to improve training speed, we used batch gradient descent. We choose the training batch = 25, testing batch = 25. To see the correlation between loss, accuracy and iteration, we draw the following figure (Fig. 8):

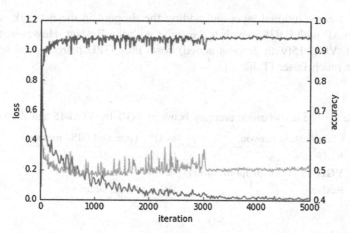

Fig. 8. The correlation between loss, accuracy and iteration. (Color figure online)

In the figure above, the red line stands for the change of test accuracy. The yellow line stands for the change of test loss. And the green line stands for the change of training loss. The learning rate started with 0.001 and after each 5000 iterations, the learning rate reduced by a factor of 10. The figure above only shows the experiment result before 5000 times iteration.

The Accuracy of AlexNet, VGG-16, GoogLeNet and ResidualNet

In this section, we used the same data set and the same experimental platform to train the classical convolutional neural network (all introduced fine-tuned). Then we compared the accuracy which showed in the following table (Table 1):

Table 1. The classification accuracy.

Classification network	mAP
AlexNet	0.90
VGG-16	0.912
GoogLeNet	0.92
ResNet	0.938

By analyzing the chart above, we can easily find out that the ResNet achieved the best classification accuracy. However, with the best accuracy achieved, ResNet also cost too much GPU memory and time compared with the rest three neural network. In such a case, we tried to modify the VGG-16 architecture and add dropout to the network. The outcome shows in the next section.

4.2   The VGG-15(with Dropout Added)

By deleting a convolutional layer and adding the dropout in the network, we finally achieved a mAP with 0.938, which is the same with the ResNet. However, compared with ResNet, VGG-15(with dropout added) costs little GPU memory and reaches the convergence much faster (Table 2).

Table 2. The classification accuracy between VGG-16, VGG-15 and ResNet.

Classification network	mAP	Time and GPU memory
VGG-16	0.912	–
VGG-15 (With dropout added)	**0.938**	–
ResNet	0.938	Much larger

5   Conclusions

In this article, we train serval classical convolutional neural network and use it to predict that if a traditional Chinese painting belongs to figure painting, flower-and-bird painting or landscape painting. Although some networks achieve relatively ideal classification accuracy, they still consume large memory and a lot of time to train. To address this problem, we delete a convolutional layer and add dropout to the VGG-16 network. Finally, the VGG-15(with dropout) achieves a classification accuracy with 93.8%, while maintaining an ideal memory and time consumption.

For future work, firstly, we would try to enlarge out data set. We believe that would improve the classification accuracy for a big step. Secondly, we will try to classify traditional Chinese paintings according to other standard, like painting style or expression style.

References

1. Zheng, W., Meijun, S., Yahong, H., et al.: Supervised heterogeneous sparse feature selection for Chinese paintings classification. J. Comput.-Aided Des. Comput. Graph. **25**(12), 1848–1855 (2013)
2. Corridoni, J.M., Del Bimbo, A., De Magistris, S., et al: A visual language for color-based painting retrieval. In: Proceedings of the 1996 IEEE Symposium on Visual Languages, pp. 68–75. IEEE (1996)
3. Chang, P., Krumm, J.: Object recognition with color cooccurrence histograms. In: 1999 IEEE Computer Society Conference on Computer Vision and Pattern Recognition, vol. 2, pp. 498–504. IEEE (1999)
4. Stricker, M.A., Orengo, M.: Similarity of color images. In: Storage and Retrieval for Image and Video Databases III 1995, vol. 2420, pp. 381–393. International Society for Optics and Photonics (1995)
5. Lowe, D.G.: Object recognition from local scale-invariant features. In: The Proceedings of the Seventh IEEE International Conference on Computer Vision 1999, vol. 2, pp. 1150–1157. IEEE (1999)
6. Bay, H., Tuytelaars, T., Van Gool, L.: SURF: speeded up robust features. In: Leonardis, A., Bischof, H., Pinz, A. (eds.) ECCV 2006. LNCS, vol. 3951, pp. 404–417. Springer, Heidelberg (2006). https://doi.org/10.1007/11744023_32
7. Yang, J., Yu, K., Gong, Y., Huang, T.: Linear spatial pyramid matching using sparse coding for image classification. In: IEEE Conference on Computer Vision and Pattern Recognition 2009. CVPR 2009, pp. 1794–1801. IEEE (2009)
8. Gao, S., Chia, L.-T., Tsang, I.W.-H.: Multi-layer group sparse coding—For concurrent image classification and annotation. In: 2011 IEEE Conference on Computer Vision and Pattern Recognition (CVPR), pp. 2809–2816. IEEE (2011)
9. Li, J., Wang, J.Z.: Studying digital imagery of ancient paintings by mixtures of stochastic models. IEEE Trans. Image Process. **13**(3), 340–353 (2004)
10. Jiang, S., Huang, Q., Ye, Q., et al.: An effective method to detect and categorize digitized traditional Chinese paintings. Pattern Recognit. Lett. **27**(7), 734–746 (2006)
11. Feng, G., Jie, N., Lei, H., et al.: Traditional Chinese painting classification based on painting techniques. Chin. J. Comput. **40**(12), 2871–2882 (2017)
12. Guan X.: Research on Computer-aided Classification, Authentication and System of Chinese Traditional Painting. Zhejiang University (2005). Chinese
13. DU Yajun, F.: The Study of Feature Extraction and Classification Algorithm in Traditional Chinese Paintings. Chinese: Taiyuan University of Technology (2008)
14. Bao, H., Liang, Y., Liu, H.-Z., et al.: A novel algorithm for extraction of the scripts part in traditional Chinese painting images. In: 2010 2nd International Conference on Software Technology and Engineering (ICSTE), vol. 2, pp. V2–26. IEEE (2010)
15. Krizhevsky, A., Sutskever, I., Hinton, G.E.: Imagenet classification with deep convolutional neural networks. In: Advances in Neural Information Processing Systems, pp. 1097–1105 (2012)
16. Simonyan, K., Zisserman, A.: Very deep convolutional networks for large-scale image recognition. arXiv preprint arXiv:1409.1556 (2014)
17. Szegedy, C., Liu, W., Jia, Y., et al.: Going deeper with convolutions. In: CVPR (2015)
18. He, K., Zhang, X., Ren, S., et al.: Deep residual learning for image recognition. In: Proceedings of the IEEE Conference on Computer Vision and Pattern Recognition 2016, pp. 770–778 (2016)
19. Srivastava, N., Hinton, G., Krizhevsky, A., et al.: Dropout: a simple way to prevent neural networks from overfitting. J. Mach. Learn. Res. **15**(1), 1929–1958 (2014)

The Design and Implementation of a Backup and Disaster Recovery System for vSphere Data Center Based on Swift Cloud Storage

Yanchao Guo[1]([✉]), Linfeng Wei[2], and Jianzhu Lu[2]

[1] Information Network Center, Guangzhou Light Industry Technician College,
Guangzhou 510220, China
457900493@qq.com
[2] College of Information Science and Technology/College of Cyber Security,
Jinan University, Guangzhou 510632, China
{twei,tljz}@jnu.edu.cn

Abstract. In a college or university, data is an important resource for guiding instruction and improving student learning. A backup and recovery strategy is necessary to protect the critical data against data loss incidents. Based on Swift cloud storage, this thesis explores how to design and implement a backup and disaster recovery system for vSphere data center being deployed in College where the author works. The Swift, which is suitable for storing large unstructured data, provides a flexible, scalable and highly available distributed object storage service. By integrating Swift cloud storage with VMware vSphere, this thesis presents an efficient solution to design a backup and disaster recovery system.

Keywords: vSphere · Swift cloud storage · Backup and disaster recovery
Data deduplication · Storage policy

1 Introduction

As informatization has been widely accepted in schools and a concept of "smart campus" has been proposed, the school data center carries multiple application systems and growing business data of various departments. Provided that key data in data centers is lost, it will cause disruption of critical businesses and services, or even lead to severe economic losses. therefore it is particularly important to configure a powerful disaster recovery system within data centers against such risks.

In addition, the relationship between data recovery time and costs is also required to take into consideration. The small and medium-sized enterprises and institutions urgently need to adopt a low-cost disaster recovery solution with short recovery time.

Virtualization technology provides data centers with a new direction for backup and disaster recovery technology. Cloud storage technology provides a new storage environment for disaster recovery.

© Springer Nature Switzerland AG 2018
X. Sun et al. (Eds.): ICCCS 2018, LNCS 11064, pp. 242–253, 2018.
https://doi.org/10.1007/978-3-030-00009-7_23

2 Related Works

Disaster recovery methods are increasingly rich for data centers. For data centers that currently employ virtualization technology, disaster recovery generally takes the form of remote replication. The VDP (vSphere Data Protection) solution is a powerful and easy-to-deploy disk disaster recovery solution for vSphere virtualized data centers [1].

Disaster recovery costs are getting higher and higher for data centers. At present, the active-active data center disaster recovery is used more as solutions [2]. The data is synchronized in real time through storage technology. Once a malfunction occurs in the local data center, it can be switched to a data center platform on an off-site network to achieve continuous operation of applications and data.

Cloud storage brings new directions for data center disaster recovery. At present, the research on mainstream OpenStack Swift cloud storage in China and abroad mainly emphasizes how to deploy [3, 4], how to study the experimental performance of Swift cloud storage [5], how to optimize the storage performance of small files uploaded to Swift cloud storage by using the Flash cache and how to write the metadata information that is frequently read and written to the SSD media [6] and so on.

Researches on Swift cloud storage also focus on the load balancing algorithms in cloud environments [7], including the inclusion of multi-factor weights, virtual node access rankings, etc., in Swift load balancing based on I/O, so that the client has access to use the optimal storage node in load balancing read policy to provide services [8–10].

Swift cloud storage has been researched and applied in the implementation of educational resource sharing platform [11], private cloud disk for users, mail service platform, multimedia image and video website platform. It is stored as an object and has a great advantage in the storage of unstructured data. With the development and application of big data, Swift, as an object storage component of OpenStack, is one of the most prevailing cloud storage solutions in recent years [12, 13].

In the era of cloud computing and big data, the application of cloud storage in the data centers disaster recovery backup will be an important form of future disaster recovery backup and development.

3 Requirements Analysis of Data Center Disaster Recovery System

3.1 Analysis of Status Quo of Disaster Recovery System in a School

The school where the author works uses the VMware vSphere 6.0 architecture in its data center. The virtualized data center runs on 10 physical servers and 80 virtual machines. The virtual machines in the data center run on the server array hard disk of each ESXi architecture, failure of which will give rise to the virtual machine running on it to fail.

Currently, the data center stores 97.68 TB of data, uses LAN-based VCB for data backup, adopts IP SAN for backup storage and mounts a 30 TB Hitachi memory. The

ESXi hosting in vSphere runs the VCB backup program, reads data from its array hard disk, and sends the data over the LAN network to IP SAN backup storage for backup.

3.2   Existing Problems of Disaster Recovery System

Due to the importance of key data in the data center, construction of disaster recovery backup is intensely urgent. The disaster recovery of the virtual data center established by the author's school has the following problems:

Due to the increasing use of the vSphere virtualized data center and increasing data volume in the data center, the total volume of data in the vSphere data center reaches 97.68 TB, and the backup data volume reach 1465.2 TB in total–a number that has far surpassed the current space for backup storage devices, which cannot meet the demand.

At present, data center disaster recovery mainly uses the form of local replication of virtual machines to back up the virtual machine data of the data center to local storage devices. This kind of backup method is prone to a single point of failure and the malfunction of a single backup storage medium will result in the loss of the entire backup data, which cannot meet the requirements, either.

The current backup method does not have the characteristic of off-site disaster recovery. Once a force majeure situation leading to disaster recovery data loss occurs in the computer room, it will result in serious outcomes.

At present, the data center virtual machine runs on the application server array hard disk. If the server fails, it takes a long time to recover data from the backup storage, while along with a low efficiency of disaster tolerance.

In order to improve disaster recovery efficiency, disaster recovery construction requires the purchase of a large number of high-end storage arrays, redundant application servers, and redundancy devices. Meanwhile, a large amount of funds is also required for the project. Nonetheless now that quite a few organizations cannot implement them due to financial problems, there is an urgent need for a cost-effective, high-reliability disaster recovery backup solution.

3.3   Analysis of Existing Problems of Backup Files

The backup files obtained from the VCB backup of the vSphere data center are VMDK files and VMX files, respectively, the key file of which is the VMDK (Virtual Machine Disk) file-a file format of the VMware virtual machine to store a virtual disk image. The virtual machine disk file represents the virtual machine's storage volume [14], on which hexadecimal data analysis can be performed by using the WinHex software. We found the following problems as the difference bytes of backup data are more concentrated; the repeatability of backup data is high; there is a continuous repetition of the backup data; and there are some duplicate data in the backup files of the identical operating system.

3.4   Overall Architecture Design Requirements of Virtual Data Center Disaster Recovery System

The application-level disaster recovery is introduced based on the need of disaster recovery system of the virtual data center using cloud storage. Deduplication and backup data compression are required for disaster recovery data. Cloud storage applications are introduced to cope with the single-point failure problem of disaster recovery data, to address remote disaster recovery and disaster recovery costs as well as other issues. The system mainly includes backup users, system administrators and other roles and its overall architecture mainly includes functional modules such as system interface management, data center fault management, and deduplication management.

4   Data Center Disaster Recovery System Design

Based on the current status, problem analysis and design requirements of the disaster recovery system for cloud storage virtual data centers, the relevant technologies of vSphere data centers and Swift cloud storage technologies are studied. This paper presents a new data center disaster recovery backup system design scheme. By linking the vSphere data center to Swift cloud storage, the distributed, scalable, and highly available features of Swift Cloud Storage provide strong support for vSphere data center disaster recovery backup.

4.1   System Design and Planning

The Swift cloud storage-based vSphere data center disaster recovery system is designed as a local production environment data center, a local disaster recovery center, and an off-site disaster recovery center. The specific system overall design is as shown in Fig. 1.

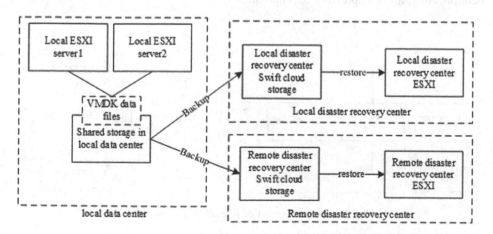

Fig. 1. Overall design of backup and disaster recovery system

In this 'two-site three-center' design, the local production environment data center establishes multiple application-layer servers ESXi. Through virtualization technology, virtual machine VMDK files originally stored on the server ESXi local array hard disk are stored in a shared storage, and the ESXi application server is connected to the shared storage through the fiber optic switch. In this way, the separation of the computing layer and storage layer of the local production environment data center is thus formed, and high-availability cluster design and local application level disaster recovery are achieved.

In the local disaster recovery center, a disaster recovery data storage environment based on OpenStack Swift cloud storage is designed. The VM data is backed up to the local disaster recovery center cloud storage environment from the shared storage of the local production environment data center through a backup program, and subsequently the disaster recovery application server ESXi is established in the local disaster recovery center. Provided that the local center has a malfunction in the storage, data and applications are restored to the server ESXi through a data recovery program.

In the remote center, a cloud storage disaster recovery environment based on OpenStack Swift is also designed. The virtual machine data in the local production environment data center is remotely backed up to a remote cloud storage environment through a backup program. When a sectional fault occurs in the local production data center or the local disaster recovery center, the remote disaster recovery center initiates the data recovery process and restores the applications and data to the remote disaster recovery server ESXi.

4.2   Overall System Functions Module Design

The overall system module in Fig. 2 includes the functional design of a Swift cloud storage interface module, a system data backup module, a disaster recovery data storage module, and a post-disaster data recovery module. The system is at the bottom of the ESXi server in the local data center, improving VCB backups, partitioning, deduplicating, and compressing backup data.

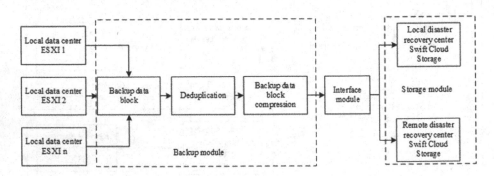

Fig. 2. Design diagram of overall system module

Swift's cloud storage interface module stores backup data in the Swift cloud storage environment of local and remote disaster recovery centers through API interfaces. When a disaster occurs, backup data is restored to the local and remote disaster recovery servers through the post-disaster data recovery module server ESXi, fulfilling the overall design of disaster recovery for the data center.

In the system data backup module, as the backup data is often duplicated, an improved multiple hash algorithm is applied to dice, deduplicate, and compress the backup data, saving the storage resources and increasing the backup speed at the most extent.

In the disaster recovery data storage module, a storage strategy is adopted to optimize the cloud storage and a single copy storage method of a traditional backup is transformed by using a data block multi-copy storage method to form a set of multiple copies, distributed, highly available, extensible and cost-effective cloud storage disaster recovery system.

In the local and remote disaster recovery modules, the system obtains disaster recovery data blocks in the cloud storage environment of the disaster recovery data center. Through the Swift cloud storage interface module, the data blocks are reassembled and restored to the server ESXi in the disaster recovery data center. The standby data center server ESXi continues to assume business application services, as shown in Fig. 3.

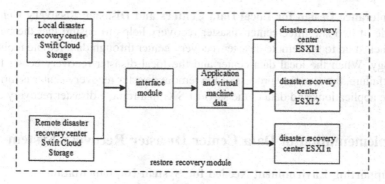

Fig. 3. Design diagram of overall system module

4.3   System Disaster Recovery Design

The system disaster tolerance design is based on the combination of local application-level disaster recovery and off-site asynchronous data disaster recovery. It mainly embraces application-level disaster recovery for local server failures, disaster recovery for shared storage faults in the local data center, a storage node failure in the local disaster recovery center and malfunctions in the local data center and disaster recovery center.

Application Level Disaster Recovery for Local Server Failure. Virtualization technology is used to place business system virtualization into shared storage and applications and data are hierarchically designed. When a local server ESXi fails, VM virtual machines running on ESXi are automatically migrated to other running ESXi servers through Distributed Resource Scheduler (DRS) of the vSphere. This kind of application-level disaster recovery switching recovery time indicator RTO (Recovery Time Object) is overwhelmingly small, which meets the application-level disaster recovery requirements.

Shared Data Storage Disaster Recovery Design in the Local Data Center. When the shared data in the local data center fails, the recovery process of the local disaster recovery center is enabled, and the disaster recovery data in the cloud storage is restored to the ESXi server in the disaster recovery center, application services continuing to be provided. As there are many backup data in the shared storage, multiple ESXi servers are designed to run the recovery program at the same time to obtain disaster recovery data in the cloud storage, and thereafter recover the business system after reorganization.

Design of a Disaster-Tolerant Design for a Storage Node in a Local Disaster Recovery Center. The use of the distributed multi-copy design of Swift cloud storage will not affect the disaster recovery data in the entire cloud storage when a node in the Swift cloud storage fails. The disaster recovery data will select copy information from other storage nodes in the process of business data recovery to reorganize business data.

Fault Tolerance Design for Local Data Centers and Disaster Recovery Centers. The mode of two-site three-center disaster recovery helps to ensure that the business data is backed up to the remote disaster recovery center through data remote replication technology. When the local data center and the local disaster recovery center have a regional failure, the recovery process of the remote disaster recovery center is turned on to restore applications and data to the server ESXi in a remote disaster recovery center.

5 Implementation of Data Center Disaster Recovery System

5.1 Supporting Environment Needed for System Implementation

As the Linux is an environment for the development and implementation of virtual data center disaster recovery backup system based on cloud storage, the ubuntu 14.04.5 LTS version is used to install a python 2.7.13 compiler and the IDE tool pycharm professional 2016 to develop. As for the version of cloud storage and data center, the Mitaka of OpenStack Swift and VMware vSphere 6.0.0 are options. The NOSQL database SSDB 1.9.3 is an alternative for the database.

5.2 Implementation of System Data Backup Module

The core of the design of backup module in the vSphere data center is to delete a miraculous number of duplicate data in backup data [15, 16]. The main process of deduplication is as follows: slice the flat. VMDK, the main backup file [17]; and afterward calculate the hash function of each file's slicing block to obtain a 32-bit or

64-bit hash string output; the hash value is used to determine whether the data is duplicated. As the collision rate of the hash function required by the data block file repetitiveness detection is low and several gigabytes of data require faster hash functions, we have integrated the characteristics of the two kinds of hash functions and bettered the two algorithms, designing a multiple hash function algorithm. The mixed formula followed is used to improve the hash function algorithm:

$$R = Murmurhash3(xxhash(S) + Key) \tag{1}$$

S is the input data block, xxhash and Murmurhash3 are two different hash functions, and Key is the Key value that is introduced into the hash function. The first byte data of the data block, the $(n + 1)/2$nd-byte data and the nth byte data are taken as the Key value, in which n = data block length. Consequently, the random Key value composed of the three bytes $K_1 K_{\frac{n+1}{2}} K_n$ has Key $= K_1 K_{\frac{n+1}{2}} K_n$ which is finally converted to a hexadecimal form appended to the end of the xxhash function by the hex function. After these steps, it is hashed twice with the Murmurhash3 function. The collision rate of the hash function value thus obtained will be lower and meet the expected requirements.

5.3 Implementation of Disaster Recovery Data Storage Module

The data Block obtained in the backup module will be used as the starting point of the process. The vSphere data center connects to the OpenStack Swift through the API interface and uses different storage strategies according to different requirements.

In the storage module, in order to meet the storage requirements of disaster recovery data, off-site multiple replica storage of disaster recovery data can further improve the capability of data center against disaster. The author's school's data center not only applies a storage strategy for local backup but also uses a remote disaster recovery backup storage strategy. The storage data block adopts a multiple-copy and distributed disaster recovery scheme.

5.4 Implementation of System Disaster Recovery

Implementation of Local Application-Level Disaster Recovery. Local application-level disaster recovery technology is the key to improving the disaster recovery speed of the overall system. The VMs originally running on the ESXi server are decentralized into the shared storage and the computing layer and the storage layer are separated. When the application server ESXi fails, the heartbeat network between the ESXi servers of the HA cluster responds in a very short period of time, using DRS technology and vMotion technology to migrate the virtual machines in the failed ESXi server to other ESXi servers for continuous running. The RTO time reaches minute level.

Implementation of Data-Level Disaster Recovery of Disaster Recovery Center. The disaster recovery center's data-level disaster recovery is mainly implemented in the event of a disaster, when the Restore.py program of the ESXi server in the Center is operated, through post-disaster recovery, to reorganize the data block copy that is stored in the disaster recovery center cloud storage so that the business data is thus obtained, continuing to provide services. Due to the distributed nature of cloud storage, failure of a storage node on the cloud platform does not affect data recovery. This kind of disaster recovery method takes longer than the application-level disaster recovery, but the cost is intensively low and the recovery time is within the user's tolerance range.

6   Overall System Performance Testing and Analysis

6.1   Introduction to Testing Platform

The test platform is deployed across two campuses in the south and north of the school where the authors work. The vSphere 6.0 data center is deployed in the local data center of the South Campus, while the South Campus Disaster Recovery Data Center deploys a disaster recovery ESXi server and two object cloud storage servers. The North Campus as an offsite disaster recovery data center deploys two ESXi servers, two Proxy Server servers, one control server, one load balancing server, two object cloud storage servers and an SSDB database server as tests.

6.2   Deduplication Rate, Compression Ratio, Backup Speed Test of Backup Data

Deduplication Rate Test of Backup Data. The rate of data deduplication for the first backup in the test is more than 50%, and that for the second and subsequent backups is more than 95%. The first backup removes the redundant part of the VMDK file, and the 2nd and subsequent backups deduplicate data already existing in the cloud storage environment and incremental data redundancy.

For the backup of the same operating system, since there is already some of the same operating system data in the cloud storage, the first backup test has a higher deduplication rate. As an example, the test system's first backup deduplication rate reaches 80% and the first backup deduplication rate in the internship management system reaches 95%. As shown in Fig. 4, the system will effectively delete redundant data in the identical operating system, greatly setting aside the disk space.

Compression Ratio Test of Backup Data. The lz4 algorithm is used to compress the data blocks stored in the Swift cloud storage and to analyze the compression ratio of the data blocks. As shown in Fig. 4, the data block compression rate of the windows operating system is relatively large, while that of the Linux operating system is smaller. The compression rate of the data block after the first compression is relatively large, while that after the second time is reduced.

6.3   System Disaster Recovery Test

Local application level disaster recovery test. In the test, failure of the local ESXi server is simulated in the South Campus data center. As shown in Fig. 5, the average system failure recovery time is within 25 s.

Local disaster recovery center data disaster recovery test. As the test data Block is stored in the sdb hard disk of the object1 storage node, the sdc hard disk, and the sdc hard disk of the object2 storage node, the local data center can enable other storage nodes and use the recovery program to recover the test data Block normally when a shared memory of the local data center and a storage node of the local disaster recovery center fail. As shown in Fig. 5, the average system failure recovery time is 740 s.

As the test data Block is not only stored in object1 and object2 but also stored in object3 and object4 in the remote disaster recovery center, when the local data center and local disaster recovery center have a regional failure, the recovery program is run on the ESXi server in the remote disaster recovery center. The system can use the Block copy in Swift-object3 and Swift-object4 for a successful recovery. As shown in Fig. 5, the average system failure recovery time is 699 s.

6.4   Test Results and Analysis

The backup and disaster recovery system for vSphere data center based on Swift cloud storage has a good performance in deduplicating the redundancy of VMDK data, with the average compression ratio of the system in the test data up to 34% and the backup speed particularly after the second time having been greatly improved. Due to the use of vSphere HA cluster technology, vMotion technology and Swift distributed cloud storage design, system failures disaster recovery capabilities have been greatly bettered.

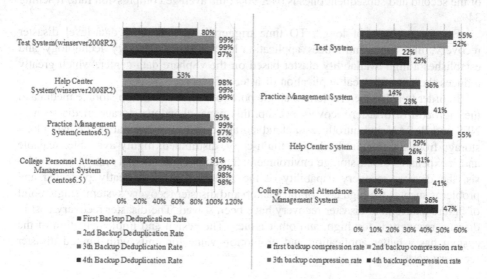

Fig. 4. Deduplication rate and compression ratio test of disaster recovery system for virtual data center based on cloud storage

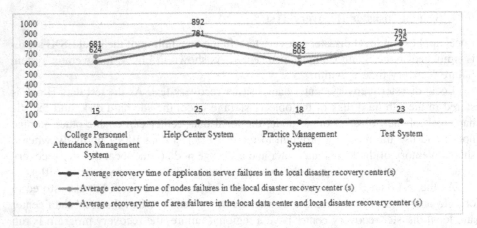

Fig. 5. Average failure recovery time of disaster recovery system for virtual data center based on cloud storage

7 Conclusions

Aiming at the problem of the increasing volume of backup data in vSphere virtualized data centers, this paper studies the characteristics and structure of duplicate data of the backup target files, performs segmentation and data hash calculations on backup files and removes duplicate data at the source side. Each data block that needs to be backed up is compressed efficiently, setting aside maximum storage space. According to the experimental test and analysis, a virtual data center disaster recovery system based on Swift cloud storage is used. The removal rate of the first backup is over 50%, and that of the second and subsequent ones is over 90%, the average compression ratio reaching 34%.

For the problem of long RTO time triggered by traditional data-level disaster recovery, this paper introduces application-level disaster recovery technology and establishes a high-availability cluster based on the vSphere data center, which greatly reduces the time for local application disaster recovery.

In order to solve the problem of single point of failure of backup storage media and the high cost of disaster recovery backup, this paper abandons storage media such as NFS and IP SAN and introduces a cloud storage architecture to change the data block storage from single-point backup to multi-copy, distributed, highly available, scalable and inexpensive cloud storage environment. Through experimental testing and analysis, the disaster recovery capability of the system has been greatly perfected and problems such as the high cost of the backup and disaster recovery system, single point of failure and remote disaster recovery have been solved. The disaster recovery cost in disaster recovery is too high, and other issues. The design and implementation of the system has a better application and promotion value for units with limited disaster recovery costs.

References

1. Yang, X., Peng, Y.M., Xing, C.J., Li, R.M.: The backup system of VMware vSphere 5 virtual machine. J. East China Normal Univ. (Nat. Sci. Ed.) **61**(S1), 252–256 (2015)
2. Wu, L.L.: Design and application of cloud computing data center based on double living capacity storage technology. Electron. Des. Eng. **22**(06), 190–192 (2015)
3. Xia, Z.X.: Research and implementation of OpenStack cloud storage technology. Master's thesis, Institutes of Technology of South China (2016)
4. Li, Z.J., Li, H.J., Wang, X.C., Li, K.Q.: A generic cloud platform for engineering optimization based on OpenStack. Adv. Eng. Soft. **75**(6), 42–57 (2014)
5. Zheng, C., Zhao, J.J., Li, C.J., Lou, T., Tang, X.: Experiment and research of object storage performance based on OpenStack. Microcomput. Appl. **33**(18), 13–16 (2014)
6. Zhou, Y.P.: Cloud storage product optimization based on swift and cloud virtual machine scheduling algorithm research. Master thesis, East China University of Science and Technology (2014)
7. Zhen, H., Wang, H.P., Chen, Y., Fu, D.L., Liu, Y.M.: Workload balancing and adaptive resource management for the swift storage system on cloud. Future Gener. Comput. Syst. **51**(1), 120–131 (2015)
8. Bian, N.Z., Yuan, H.: The load balancing algorithm based on I/O in the swift cloud storage environment. Comput. Eng. Appl. **52**(2), 70–80 (2016)
9. Jiang, Y., Sun, X.T., Yang, C.: Swift cloud storage environment base on I/O load balanced reading strategies. Comput. Eng. Des. **34**(9), 3024–3027, 3032 (2013)
10. Shan, X.Y.: Research on resource load balancing strategy based on swift. Master thesis, Harbin Institute of Technology (2015)
11. Fu, S.P.: Design and implementation of education resource sharing platform based on swift. Master's thesis, Xi 'an University of Electronic Science and Technology (2014)
12. Huo, J.Y., Qu, H., Wu, L.: Design and implementation of private cloud storage platform based on OpenStack. In: IEEE International Conference, pp. 1098–1101. SmartCity (2015)
13. Corradi, A., Fanelli, M., Foschini, L.: VM consolidation: a real case based on OpenStack cloud. Future Gener. Comput. Syst. **32**(1), 118–127 (2014)
14. Lai, Z.Q.: Design and implementation of a VMDK application virtualization system. Jiangxi Normal University of Science and Technology (2012)
15. Cai, S.X.: A backup system design and implementation based on repetitive data deletion. Beijing University of Posts and Telecommunications (2010)
16. Huang, C.B., Hu, X.Q., Ma, X.X., Wang, J.: Design and implementation of winnowing based deduplication data backup and recovery system. J. SiChuan Univ. (Nat. Sci. Ed.) **57**(03), 535–542 (2012)
17. Shi, J.J.: The design and implementation of a de-duplication file system based on cloud storage. HuaZhong University of Science and Technology (2013)

The Handoff Mechanism Based on Mobile Location Prediction

Yu-xiang Wang[1,2(✉)], Qi Wang[1,2], and Zhi-feng Zhou[1]

[1] Jiangsu Engineering Center of Network Monitoring, Nanjing University of Information Science and Technology, Nanjing 210044, China
wangyx@nuist.edu.cn
[2] School of Computer and Software, Nanjing University of Information and Science, Nanjing 210044, China

Abstract. The handoff mechanism is a key technology to support the user seamless mobile application services in wireless communication system, which has a great impact on users' services experiences and application. This paper presents the handoff mechanism based on mobile location prediction, using the modified Dempster-Shafer (D-S) theory together with a variety of context information is adopted to predict the location of mobile users. The method proposed in this paper can effectively avoid the "ping-pong" handoff, shorten the handoff delay, and reserve the resources in advance. It can provide fast, accurate and reliable basis for decisions, thus significantly improve the QoS of network. Theoretical analysis and simulation results show that location prediction is closer to the real trajectory of the user. Also, the RMSE of position is smaller, which indicates the success rate of handoff has been greatly improved.

Keywords: Handoff mechanism · Context · Dempster-Shafer (D-S) theory
GIS (Geographic Information System) · Hausdorff distance

1 Introduction

At present, there are a lot of researches on the handoff mechanism, for example, Mao and Liu [1, 2], et al., judge the terminal switching between different base stations by predicting terminal signal strength. They take the signal strength as the only criterion of judgment for the handover, which tends to cause "ping-pong" handoff when under the high building shadow. Pei [3] conducted the dynamic switching by considering several factors of terminals such as the current location, direction and velocity vector, and a fairly good efficiency is achieved. Yang [4] utilized the Sequential Monte Carlo Filter to predict the terminal location and assist terminal to switch. He designed the state transition and the particle weight adjustment equation. This method has better handover accuracy when each location prediction interval is very short, but if the sampling interval is longer or terminal trajectory is uncertain, location prediction failure may occur. Marmasse [5] established markov model and bayesian model for path learning and prediction, the use of fuzzy reasoning method [6] and multiple neural network method [7] for mobile location prediction. These models and methods are not suitable for switching real-time applications since a large number of users' history prior data is

© Springer Nature Switzerland AG 2018
X. Sun et al. (Eds.): ICCCS 2018, LNCS 11064, pp. 254–264, 2018.
https://doi.org/10.1007/978-3-030-00009-7_24

required and a much longer time is needed to train fitting the real moving track users. Khan [8] and so on only used the road topology information for mobile station switching, the mobile station signal strength and user context information are not involved Sanabani [9] et al., divided the base station coverage area into sub-areas. When the mobile station enters the edge area of the base station, the base station coverage area is switched. However, they did not consider the mobile station movement state factor. In fact, the user context information is an important clue to characterize the user behavior, and can assist location prediction effectively. In [11–13], context is used to make semantic search. However, this stored context information is not used to predict some mobile location information.

2 Architecture Based on Mobile Location Prediction Switching

In this paper, we propose a handoff mechanism based on mobile location prediction. The architecture based on mobile location prediction switching is shown in Fig. 1.

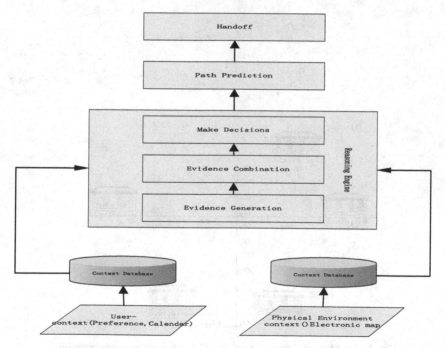

Fig. 1. Switching architecture based on mobile location prediction

3   Concrete Steps Based on Mobile Location Prediction Switching

3.1   Context Information Acquisition and Formalized Expression

In order to predict the user's location information accurately, we have collected and edited the information from Google Maps (Fig. 2a) in the area of Gulou in Nanjing, using the Geographic Information Systems GIS [14] method to formalize the electronic map information.

(a)

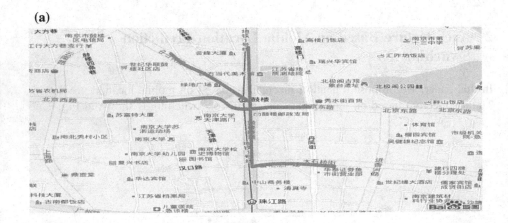

(b)

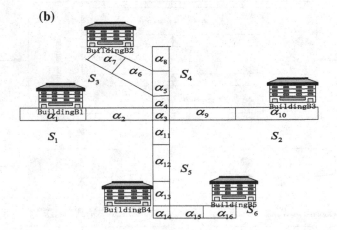

Fig. 2. (a) Map of Gulou district. (b) GIS information representation

In GIS, we first select all possible locations for the users. These locations are mainly some landmark buildings such as the Carrefour supermarkets, the libraries, etc., which can be represented as: $B_{GIS} = \{B_1, B_2, \ldots, B_n\}$, in which, $B_i(i = 1, 2, \ldots, n)$ denotes the location of the user, that is the building near the user. Then we select the streets through which the user can reach the predicted location, such as Beijing West Road, Zhongshan North Road, etc., These streets can be expressed as: $S_{GIS} = \{S_1, S_2, \ldots, S_m\}$ in which, $S_i(i = 1, 2, \ldots, m)$ represents a street through which the user has reached the predicted location. Finally each street $S_i(i = 1, 2, \ldots, m)$ can be subdivided into connected path segments $S_i = \{\alpha_1^i, \alpha_2^i, \ldots, \alpha_k^i\}$, in which, the rule of subdivision for $\alpha_j^i(j = 1, 2, \ldots, k)$ is:

(1) The buildings adjacent to S_i are divided into separate sections α_j^i.
(2) The cross between S_i is divided into a section α_j^i.
(3) Base station boundaries are divided into sections α_j^i, that one sections α_j^i cannot have two different *cell_id*.

The GIS information of Nanjing Gulou area is shown in Fig. 2(b).

The independent variable function is first defined with Mark buildings $F(B_i)$, The range is a collection of mark building attributes, for example, if the mark building B_i is a shopping mall, then $F(B_i) = \{a_1^i, a_2^i, \ldots, a_l^i\}$, in which, $a_1^i = $ Mall, $a_2^i = $ France, $a_3^i = $ Low cost; if B_i is a library, then $F(B_i) = \{a_1^i, a_2^i, \ldots, a_l^i\}$, in which, $a_1^i = $ Library, $a_2^i = $ China, $a_3^i = $ Cost free; furthermore, for high-rise building B_i, it can be subdivided as B_{ih}, in which h represents floor, each floor has different attributes as $F(B_{ih}) = \{a_{1h}^i, a_{2h}^i, \ldots, a_{lh}^i\}$, Therefore, the introduction of landmark buildings floor parameters, converts the spatial geographic information into a three dimensional space.

In order to predict the user path sequence based on the path information, the path segments α_i is introduced, α_j as the matrix R, shown in Fig. 3. The matrix R represents formalized GIS information, the element r_{ij} in R can be expressed as:

$$r_{ij} = \begin{cases} \text{The direction of the adjacent } \alpha_i \text{ to } \alpha_j & i \neq j \\ \text{Attribute information of building } B_i \text{ adjacent to } \alpha_i & i = j \end{cases}$$

In which, when $i \neq j$, represents the direction of the adjacent path segments α_i to α_j, the value range is from $0°$ to $360°$. For simplicity, we use the east (E) south (S) west (W) north (N) direction value. Because the landmark building floor parameters are introduced, thus we add (U), under(D) two direction value, which constitutes the GIS three-dimensional spatial information model; when $i = j$, it indicates the attribute information of adjacent landmark building B_i with path segments α_i as $F(B_i) = \{a_1, a_2, \ldots, a_l\}$. For multi-storey buildings B_{ih}, the attribute information is $F(B_{ih}) = \{a_{1h}^i, a_{2h}^i, \ldots, a_{lh}^i\}$, at this point the matrix R is the nested matrix R^*. Moreover, since y represents the adjacency, direction, and sign attribute of the adjacent path segment, the non-adjacent path segments are empty. Therefore, R^* is an sparse matrix.

3.2 Inference Engine

The Dempster-Shafer theory was proposed by Dempster in 1968, and was developed by his student Shafer [15] in 1971. The D-S theory divides the research questions into mutually exclusive and exhaustive identification frameworks as Θ, for any subset A belonging to the identification frame Θ, if $m(\Phi) = 0$ and $\sum_{A \subseteq \Theta} m(A) = 1$, it is called m

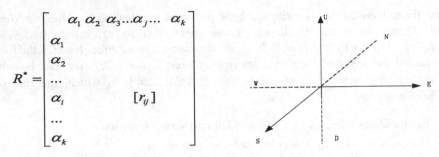

Fig. 3. GIS information matrix

is BPA (Basic Probability Assignment) function on Θ, also known as mass function. In order to express the degree of trust in the proposition, the D-S theory introduces the concept of the credibility function Bel and the likelihood function Pls, its relationship with BPA satisfies $Bel(A) = \sum\limits_{B \subseteq A} m(B)$, $Pls(A) = \sum\limits_{A \cap B \neq \Phi} m(B)$, in which, B is a subset of the identification frame Θ, Bel and Pls are the credibility and likelihood functions of hypothesis A, respectively. The interval $[Bel, Pls]$ represents the degree of confidence in the hypothesis.

In order to synthesis of different sources of evidence, D - S theory of Dempster synthesis rules are put forward. Set Bel_1 and Bel_2 are two credibility functions in the same identification frame Θ, m_1 and m_2 are respectively corresponding to the basic probability assignment, A_i and B_j is focal element, then the two credibility functions of the synthesis law is:

$$m(A) = m_1 \oplus m_2 = \frac{\sum\limits_{A_i \cap B_j = A} m_1(A_i)m_2(B_j)}{1 - \sum\limits_{A_i \cap B_j = \Phi} m_1(A_i)m_2(B_j)} \tag{1}$$

$m(A)$ reflects the degree of joint support of proposition A with the two evidences corresponding to m_1 and m_2, $k = \sum\limits_{A_i \cap B_j = \Phi} m_1(A_i)m_2(B_j)$ is conflict factor, reflecting the degree of conflict between evidence. When $k = 0$, it is called no conflict, when $0 < k < 1$, it is called non-complete conflict, when $k = 1$, it is called complete conflict.

Evidence Generation

First we construct the identification frame Θ to represent all future possible locations for the user. that is, all the possible landmark buildings the users are in. $\Theta = \{B_{ih} : B_{ih} \in B_{GIS}\}$, B_{GIS} represents the target location of the user in the GIS, 2^{Θ} is a subset of Θ represents the different hypotheses of the user's possible location, each hypothesis can use the mass function to assign basic credibility values, and use different cloud computing information for generating evidence to predict the user's future target location.

(1) Cloud computing evidence based on user preference

We generate a set of evidence based on user preferences, current location and calendar information matching with the attributes of possible locations $F(B_{ih}) = \{a^i_{1h}, a^i_{2h}, \ldots, a^i_{lh}\}$. Assume that any user preference has n properties, the evidence H for n hypotheses is E_p. For any one hypothesis $H_i(i = 1, 2, \ldots, n)$ represents a set of user possible locations as $B_{ih} \in \Theta$, attributes of B_{ih} has a certain degree of matching with the user preferences P of the property. Therefore, $H_i = \{B_{jh} : B_{jh} \in \Theta | a^i_{jh} \in F(B_{jh})\}$, set:

$$m(H_i) = \frac{1}{n} \tag{2}$$

In which, $m(H_i)$ represents the basic probability assignment function of hypothesis H_i.

(2) Cloud computing evidence based on user schedules

Cloud computing information based on user schedule is another powerful evidence to predict the user mobile location. Assuming B_{yh} represents the location of the user who will arrive setting in the schedule, t_y is the rest time that user does not reach the set location. Therefore, n hypothetical evidence E_y is generated. Each hypothesis H_i represents a set of possible locations B_{jh}, then $H_i = \{B_{jh} : B_{jh} \in \Theta | (t(B_{xh}, B_{jh}) + t(B_{jh}, B_{yh})) \leq i \times \frac{t_y}{n}\}$, in which, B_{xh} is the user current location, $t(B_{ih}, B_{jh})$ is the user moving from the current location B_{ih} to the target location B_{jh}, set

$$m(H_i) = \frac{1}{n} \tag{3}$$

Evidence Synthesis

All of the evidence participated in the synthesis has the same importance in the classic evidence combination formula (1), evidence synthesis needs weighted correction for the basic credibility of evidence [16] to reflect the importance and credibility of evidence, the corrected credibility formula as formula (4):

$$m^\beta(A_i) = \begin{cases} (1 - \beta)m(A_i) & C \neq \Theta \\ \beta + (1 - \beta)m(\Theta) & 其他 \end{cases} \tag{4}$$

In which, the value of evidence importance factor β is [0, 1].

Therefore, the paper proposes to use the modified evidence theory, that is, weighted evidence combination rule formula (5) to the fusion of different sources of evidence as follows:

$$m(A) = m_1 \oplus m_2(A) = \frac{\sum\limits_{A_i \cap B_j = A} w_1 m^\beta_1(A_i) w_2 m^\beta_2(B_j)}{1 - \sum\limits_{A_i \cap B_j = \phi} w_1 m^\beta_1(A_i) w_2 m^\beta_2(B_j)} \tag{5}$$

In which, $w_i = \dfrac{\sum\limits_{j=1, j \neq i}^{n} (1-d(m_i, m_j))}{\sum\limits_{i=1}^{n} \sum\limits_{j=1, j \neq i}^{n} (1-d(m_i, m_j))}$, $d(m_i, m_j)$ is the distance between m_i and m_j.

For the evidence obtained from the different sources of formula (2) and formula (3), we use the corrected evidence synthesis formula (5) to synthesize.

Decision Making

After synthesizing the evidence of different evidence sources, the candidate set of all possible active locations of the user is formed, then the user's active location of the maximum credibility value is selected as the target location of the predicted according to the credibility value.

3.3 Path Prediction

Each element in path sequence can be represented by a binary as (α_i, D_i), in which, D_i represents the direction value. For example, in the Fig. 2(b), if the current location is α_7, the target location by predicted is α_{10}, then the predicted path sequence is (α_7, ES), (α_6, ES), (α_5, S), (α_4, S), (α_3, E), (α_9, E), (α_{10}, B_3), B_3 is the predicted target location.

If there are multiple paths to choose from α_7 to α_{10}, we can predict the path based on other relevant cloud computing information, such as path distance and traffic congestion and so on.

3.4 Handoff Mechanism Based on Cloud Computing and Mobile Location Prediction

The base station *cell_id* where the path is located, therefore, the path element can be represented as $(\alpha_i, D_i, cell\_id)$, shown in Fig. 4.

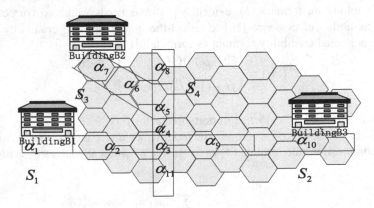

Fig. 4. Handoff mechanism based on context-aware and mobile location prediction

4 Simulation

4.1 Experimental Environment

The experimental simulation environment is shown in Fig. 2(a), shown in Fig. 5.

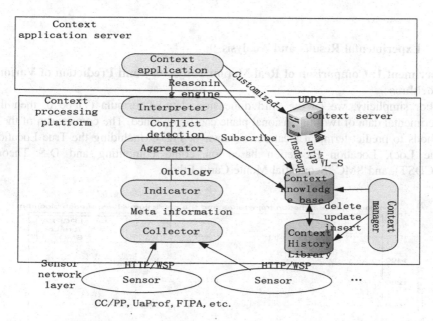

Fig. 5. Cloud computing information processing system

4.2 Experimental Method

In this paper, the classical Hausdorff (HD) distance algorithm [17] is improved to construct a new three-dimensional distance function.

If the sampling points on the real trajectories HD_λ and the predicted trajectories HD_ω is expressed respectively as $\{\lambda_1, \lambda_2, \ldots, \lambda_n\}$ and $\{\omega_1, \omega_2, \ldots, \omega_m\}$, we can calculate the error between the point ω_j and the real motion trajectory HD_λ as $\delta(\omega_j, HD_\lambda)$, shown in formula (6):

$$\delta(\omega_j, HD_\lambda) = \| \lambda_i - \omega_j \|_{\min_{\lambda_i} |t(\lambda_i - \omega_j)|} \tag{6}$$

In which, $\| \cdot \|$ is euclidean norm, to $\forall \ \lambda_i \in HD_\lambda$ 和 $\omega_j \in HD_\omega$, the euclidean norm can be obtained by formula (7):

$$\| \lambda_i - \omega_j \| = \sqrt{(\lambda_i^x - \omega_j^x)^2 + (\lambda_i^y - \omega_j^y)^2 + (\lambda_i^z - \omega_j^z)^2} \tag{7}$$

Therefore, the error between the predicted trajectories HD_ω and the real trajectories HD_λ is:

$$\delta_m(HD_\lambda, HD_\omega) = \sum_{\omega_j \in HD_\omega} \delta(\omega_j, HD_\lambda) \bigg/ m \tag{8}$$

4.3   Experimental Results and Analysis

Experiment 1: Comparison of Real Motion Trajectory and Prediction of Various Algorithms

For simplicity, we let the third dimension data of formula (7) be 0, then the experimental data of two-dimensional plane can be obtained. The comparison of these methods to predict terminal location is shown in Fig. 6, including the True Location (True Loc), Location Prediction based on could computing and D-S Theory (LPCDST), and SMC (Sequential Monte Carlo Filter).

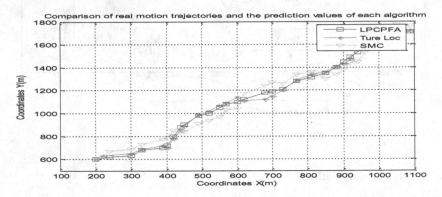

Fig. 6. Comparison of real motion trajectories and LPCDST, SMC predictions

It can be seen from the figure that the accuracy of the user mobile location prediction based on the cloud computing and D-S theory is relatively high.

Experiment 2: The Comparison of User Movement Location HD Error Value Comparison

Using the formula (5) can get the terminal HD location error value of LPCDST and SMC method, as shown in Fig. 7.

It can be seen from the figure that the user mobile location prediction LPCDST based on the cloud computing and D-S theory, the user HD location error is smaller than the other method SMC location prediction, thus effectively improves the handover success rate.

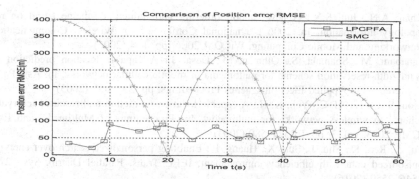

Fig. 7. Comparison of HD position errors

5 Conclusions

The paper proposes a handoff mechanism based on cloud computing and mobile location prediction, the method does not require users to have a lot of historical activities information as a priori knowledge, it is only based on user cloud computing (user preferences, schedules, etc.) and the user physical environment cloud computing (GIS, base stations, etc.) to accurately predict the user activities of the location and path sequence in the future. The simulation results show that the method has high accuracy to predict the mobile location of the user, which can provide reliable decision basis for the handover decision.

Acknowledgement. This work was supported by Natural Science Foundation of Jiangsu Province under Grant BK20160955, the Priority Academic Program Development of Jiangsu Higher Education Institutions (PAPD) and Jiangsu Collaborative Innovation Center on Atmospheric Environment and Equipment Technology funds (CICAEET).

References

1. Mao, W., He, Z., Liu, N., Yang, M., Liu, D.: Study on the soft handoff simulation based on received signal strength in CDMA. In: 2009 International Conference on Artificial Intelligence and Computational Intelligence, AICI, vol. 2, pp. 145–149 (2009)
2. Liu, X., Jiang, L., He, C.: A novel vertical handoff algorithm based on fuzzy logic in aid of pre-decision method. Acta Electronica Sinica **35**(10), 1989–1993 (2007)
3. Pei, T., Guo, D., Wang, Y.: Dynamic rate handoff algorithm based on LBS information. Comput. Eng. Appl. **44**(15), 110–112, 130 (2008)
4. Yang, Z., Wang, X.: Joint mobility tracking and handoff in cellular networks via sequential monte carlo filtering. IEEE Trans. Sig. Process. **51**(1), 269–281 (2003)
5. Marmasse, N., Schmandt, C.: A user-centered location model. Pers. Ubiquit. Comput. **6**(5–6), 318–321 (2002)
6. Shen, X., Mark, J.W., Ye, J.: User mobility profile prediction: an adaptive fuzzy inference approach. Wirel. Netw. **6**, 363–374 (2000)
7. Kumar, V., Venkataram, P.: A prediction based location management using multi-layer neural networks. J. Indian Inst. Sci. **82**(1), 7–21 (2002)

8. Khan, A.N., Jun, S.X.: A new handoff ordering and reduction scheme based on road topology information. In: 2006 International Conference on Wireless Communications, Networking and Mobile Computing, WiCOM 2006, pp. 1–4 (2006)
9. Sanabani, M., Shamala, S., Othman, M., Desa, J.: A capable location prediction and bandwidth reservation scheme for multimedia in mobile cellular networks. In: Asia-Pacific Conference On Applied Electromagnetics Proceedings, pp. 351–355 (2005)
10. Liou, S.-C., Lu, H.-C., Yeh, K.-H.: A capable location prediction and resource reservation scheme in wireless networks for multimedia. In: Proceedings of Multimedia and Expo, ICME 2003, vol. 3, pp. III-577–580 (2003)
11. Fu, Z., Ren, K., Shu, J., Sun, X., Huang, F.: Enabling personalized search over encrypted outsourced data with efficiency improvement. IEEE Trans. Parallel Distrib. Syst. 27(9), 2546–2559 (2016)
12. Xia, Z., Wang, X., Sun, X., Wang, Q.: A secure and dynamic multi-keyword ranked search scheme over encrypted cloud data. IEEE Trans. Parallel Distrib. Syst. 27(2), 340–352 (2015)
13. Fu, Z., Sun, X., Liu, Q., Zhou, L., Shu, J.: Achieving efficient cloud search services: multi-keyword ranked search over encrypted cloud data supporting parallel computing. IEICE Trans. Commun. E98-B(1), 190–200 (2015)
14. Yuan, L.W., Yu, Z.Y., Luo, W., et al.: A 3D GIS spatial data model based on conformal geometric algebra. Sci. China Earth Sci. 54, 101–112 (2011)
15. Shafer, G.: A Mathematical Theory of Evidence. Princeton University Press, Princeton (1976)
16. Miao, Y.Z., Zhang, H.X., Zhang, J.W., et al.: Improvement of the combination rules of the D-S evidence theory based on dealing with the evidence conflict. In: 2008 IEEE International Conference on Information and Automation, Shanghai, pp. 331–336, June 2008
17. Peterfreund, N.: Robust tracking of position and velocity with Kalman snakes. IEEE Trans. Pattern Anal. Mach. Intell. 22(6), 564–569 (2000)

The New Progress in the Research of Binary Vulnerability Analysis

Tiantian Tan[✉], Baosheng Wang[✉], Zhou Xu[✉], and Yong Tang[✉]

National University of Defense and Technology, Changsha 410073, CS, China
happinesschild@126.com, wangbaosheng@126.com, {zhouxu,ytang}@nudt.edu.cn

Abstract. Although vulnerability analysis based on source code has achieved a significant progress, large numbers of software exist in binary code, research of binary vulnerability analysis is more important. This paper presented an overview of the field of binary vulnerability analysis framework, classified typical vulnerability analysis technologies into intermediate language, taint analysis, symbolic execution, and fuzzing, classified current framework based on typical analysis technologies, summarized limitations of current framework and design a next generation automatic binary vulnerability analysis framework, and then we summarized the core principles, process, and limitations of each analysis technology in next generation frameworks, and discussed possible optimizations that could improved vulnerability analysis. This survey on binary vulnerability analysis can provide theoretical guidance for the development of the future binary analysis.

Keywords: Vulnerability analysis · Intermediate language
Taint analysis · Symbolic execution · Fuzzing

1 Introduction

With the rapid development of cloud computation, software has increasingly wide in utilization, privacy leaking has been becoming the major limitation of cloud computation application. Focus on privacy protection, lots of privacy protection scheme has been proposed, such as the improved content based image retrieval (CBIR) in cloud computation which protects privacy by local sensitive hash (LSH) search algorithm [1,2], multimonitor joint detection with lower communication overhead proposed by Cai et al. [3], the distributed Ternary Content Addressable Memory (TCAM) coprocessor architecture proposed by Cai et al. for Longest Prefix Matching (LPM), Policy Filtering (PF), and Content Filtering (CF) [4]; the detection approach of DDoS attacks based on Conditional Random Fields model etc. [5]. However, no matter how secure a scheme is, the vulnerabilities in execution files can always cause the risks and privacy leaking, such

Supported by National University of Defense and Technology and National Natural Science Foundation No. 61402492.

X. Sun et al. (Eds.): ICCCS 2018, LNCS 11064, pp. 265–276, 2018.
https://doi.org/10.1007/978-3-030-00009-7_25

as the vulnerability of the "OpenSSL" heart bleeding which caused worldwide damage with a high encryption strength. In addition, various vulnerabilities have been found in Shellshock, LibTIFF, Libpng, OpenJPEG, FFm-peg, Libav. 75% of the attacks relies on the security vulnerabilities of software [6]. Because of vulnerability exploits, attackers can obtain root privilege by running malicious code or implanting the back doors. The vulnerability has become the hotspot in information security field.

There are a variety of the classification methods for binary vulnerability analysis [6]. According to different classification criteria, we consider different methods which can together cover all categories in all classification criteria as typical techniques, including fuzzing, symbolic execution and taint analysis, these can represent every scope of binary vulnerability analysis technology. According to the theory of vulnerability exploits, taint analysis is effective in principle [7]. Symbolic analysis is focus on control flow while taint analysis is focus on data flow, these two technologies can complement each other [8]. Fuzzing has the most widely utilization for no dependence on source code and high efficiency.

The organization framework of this paper is shown as Fig. 1. The current framework will be introduced in Sect. 2, the research status and future optimizations of the specific techniques in each type of framework will be discussed in Sects. 3–6, conclusion will be summarized in Sect. 7.

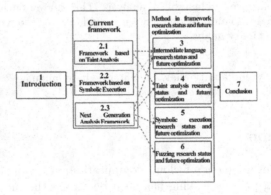

Fig. 1. The framework of the paper.

2 Binary Vulnerability Analysis Framework

Focus on vulnerability analysis, researchers had proposed several analysis frameworks, include framework based on taint analysis (such as BitBlaze, proposed by SONG, etc. [9,10]), and framework based on symbolic execution (such as Anger proposed by Shoshitaishvili, etc. [11]), but most of them only suit for vulnerabilities in some specific types, or improve current methods, and these binary vulnerability analysis frameworks have some limitations:

- Firstly, lots of work can not be reuse, and can not further extended on current work, only can re-implement on current framework which only has one function, it wastes more efforts and time;
- Secondly, each current method has its limitations. How to combine two or more methods to complement each other will be the future research.

A better solution is to construct a more comprehensive binary analysis framework, and integrate major analysis techniques, and subsequent researchers can do some optimizations or extensions on the basis of current work.

2.1 Next Generation Binary Vulnerability Analysis Framework

In future work, a comprehensive binary vulnerability analysis platform will be constructed by integrating all typical technologies to form a more comprehensive binary vulnerability analysis framework. Detailed construction includes:

- Add binary model and establish the security policy library based on formal description.
- Optimize the intermediate language conversion, solve the problems of information loss and low efficiency, further supplement and improve conversion process to obtain more accurate information (including data flow and control flow).
- Integrate and optimize symbolic execution technology to achieve automatic analysis.
- Integrate taint analysis technology to limit the range of symbolic execution for alleviating the path explosion. In addition, the taint analysis can also be combined with the security strategy library established above.
- Integrate fuzzing technology to generate the test cases according to path constraint solver, and then detect the vulnerabilities. The next generation binary vulnerability analysis framework is shown in Fig. 2.

Limitations and optimizations of specific technologies integrated in next generation will be discussed respectively in Sects. 3, 4, 5 and 6.

3 Research on Intermediate Language

It is difficult to analyze binary program directly because of the complexity of binary program. There are two major reasons for this:

- The number of underly instructions is more, such as the x86 instruction set which is hundreds in number and more complex;
- Separate the code from the data, meaning that the binary code lacks the corresponding semantics and type information.

Intermediate language [10] was proposed to translate the binary code into intermediate code with semantic information in order to facilitate analysis. The

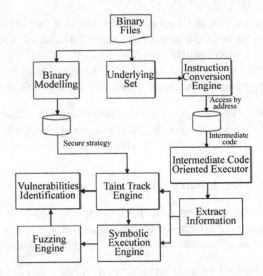

Fig. 2. The future framework of binary vulnerability analysis

conversion to intermediate language is one of the most important step in analyzing binary vulnerability, the conversion need analyze the semantic information of intermediate language to generate the CFG figure, and further obtain control flow and data flow. However, there are some limitations in current methods based on intermediate language.

– Firstly, there will be some information missing in the translation process, such as the Valgrinds VEX does not save the EFLAGS register [12];
– Secondly, translating an instruction into two or more intermediate instructions may decrease the efficiency, such as the VEX used by Valgrind, and VINEIL used by BitBlaze.

Due to intermediate language is the basis of vulnerability analysis, how to increase efficiency and accuracy is an urgent problem. The future research of intermediate language major includes:

– Firstly, using each instruction to achieve one function is main target of conversion process, and reduce redundant information as far as possible;
– Secondly, it is necessary to ensure complete semantic information during reducing redundant process.

Therefore, Information missing needs to be further solved. It can be solved by comparing intermediate language with the corresponding assembly language, and check the integrity of important semantic information in order to improve the problem of semantic information missing, provide complete data flow and control flow as much as possible.

4   Research on Taint Analysis

Taint analysis technology, first proposed by Denning in 1976 [13], is a technique to track and analyze taint propagation at run time. The main principle of taint analysis is to mark input data as taint data, the new data generated by a series of arithmetic and logical operations based on "taint data" will inherit the property of "taint data" [6]. Analyze these properties to obtain features of the program. Taint analysis technology can be classified into dynamic taint analysis and static taint analysis [14] from the perspective of execution. Dynamic taint analysis can be classified into Fine-grained dynamic taint analysis technology and Coarse-grained dynamic taint analysis technology [15]. Shi et al. [15] proposed a method of dynamic taint analysis by combining Coarse-grained with Fine-grained.

In recent years, scholars focus on taint analysis has carried on the thorough research, Yin et al. [14] proposed a TEMU extension based on QEMU virtual machine platform, it can analyze the kernel activity and interact with multiple processes from all system perspective, and analyze in-depth by fine-grained taint analysis. Kang et al. [16] proposed a dynamic taint transmission scheme DTA++, it can find the paths of incomplete taint control flow to solve the path constraints by symbolic execution and the method based on path predicates. In symbolic execution, paths can be expressed as a series of constraints of branch conditions. Ma et al. [17] proposed a taint analysis method based on execution trace offline index which can track program execution by dynamic instrument tool, record execution status information, then analyze off-line records, and establish the index file, It is only focus on operations related to taint data, skip the instructions which have nothing to do with the taint data for high efficiency.

4.1   Existing Problems

There are several problems in current dynamic taint analysis.

Implicit Flow Problem. In the process of pollution transmission analysis, according to the different dependence, it can be classified into explicit flow analysis and implicit flow analysis. The explicit flow analysis is to analyze the taint propagation according to data dependence among program variables, while the implicit flow analysis is to do analysis according to control dependence among program variables. The implicit flow taint propagation is important in taint analysis technique [18]. There are two main situations: under-taint and over-taint. Under-taint pollution is that some tags missing due to improper handling of the implicit flow taint data. The problem of over-taint pollution is that the number of tags is too large to cause a lot of contamination. Current solution for implicit flow problem is to reduce under-taint and over-taint.

– The first problem of dynamic implicit flow is how to identify the range of statements that need to be marked. Offline static auxiliary analysis is an effect solution.

- The second problem is the leakage of some taint information. The current solution is to combine the offline static analysis with dynamic analysis.
- The third problem is how to choose the right taint branch to propagate the taint data. Propagating all the branches that contain the taint tags will lead to contamination, so the taint data need to be filtered for limiting pollution. The DTA++ tool proposed by Kang et al. [19] can find branches which propagate taint data using the symbolic execution based on offline execution trace.

Taint Removal Problem. In taint analysis, if taint data is illegal increased and propagates continuously, the existence of taint data which should be eliminated can lead to false positives [21]. Analysis results with higher accuracy need reduce the number of taint data, improve the efficiency of the taint analysis, and avoid the inaccurate analysis results caused by the propagation of the additional taint data. Therefore, in some special cases, such as encrypting sensitive data or constant functions, removing the taint marks can be considered.

Expensive Cost. Some of taint analysis tools use instrument or dynamic code rewriting technology which can bring huge consumption [18], such as Dytan [20]. One solution is selective taint propagation analysis in system instructions. For example, the fast path optimization proposed by Qin et al. [21] can identify vulnerabilities before input and output of a taint data analysis module, only propagate taint data for lower consumption. Peng et al. [22] limited taint propagation range by establishing a suspicious taint data set, and identified taint source using taint tracking back technology (a propagation of taint reverse analysis) for reducing the consumption. Lin et al. [23] proposed the effective taint propagation method based on semantic rules, further improved efficiency of taint propagation reverse analysis by tracking records. All the methods have a negative effect on accuracy, further study need to reduce cost and increase accuracy.

Higher Leakage Rate. Different test cases lead to different execution. Therefore, the dynamic taint analysis may only cover the partial path with high leakage rate. Dynamic taint analysis need to analyze entire codes and functions, and construct appropriate test cases to cover more path. Zhu et al. [24] proposed a dynamic symbolic taint analysis method, the method uses symbols to represent taint information and the risk rules, if it finds a violation of the certain risks rules, it will detect the unsafe behavior. Cui et al. [30] proposed an offline taint analysis method including two modules (dynamic record module and static replay module), and reduced the leakage rate of dynamic analysis by combining with the static analysis.

Lack of High-Level Semantic Information. Because binary code lacks the necessary semantics and type information, it limits the application of binary oriented dynamic taint analysis technique. Jianwei et al. [7] proposed a dynamic taint analysis based on type perception and type variable oriented symbols execution technology, effective resolve the problem that current binary oriented dynamic taint analysis can not provide high-level semantic. By propagating and deducting input data type information, combining with type information of taint source, it improved dynamic taint analysis in variable-grained. It can better support vulnerability analysis and semantic feature extraction better.

Low Path Cover. The advantage of dynamic taint analysis is to obtain accurate runtime information by execution, but run once can only perform one path, path unaccessible always exists after re-execution, and vulnerabilities in these path have to be ignored. Combining with symbolic execution technology can improve the path coverage. Current dynamic taint analysis research focus on the design of communication logic, the efficiency optimization and implicit flow analysis. To solve the problem that current taint analysis tool can not make the balance between speed and accuracy, some researchers proposed a corse-fined grained dynamic taint analysis method, it used on-line coarse-grained model to increase the efficiency of information collection of taint analysis, improved the accuracy of the taint analysis and limited time consumption into a reasonable range by off-line fine-grained mode. In the future, information flow obtained by intermediate language will be used to analyze taint dynamically, security policies and concolic execution will be used to detect vulnerabilities.

5   Concolic Symbolic Execution

To obtain running information, researchers proposed the concept of concolic execution, and implemented a series of tools, such as CUTE [27], DART [28]. CUTE combined random test with symbolic execution to reduce the consumption. It tends to test randomly and use symbolic execution for generating the test cases when random test can not find new path. The open source tools KLEE was developed for C language program analysis in Linux by Cadar et al. [29]. It generates the test cases by symbolic execution, analyzes the range of symbol value at key position using symbolic execution and constraint solving, and checks whether the symbol value satisfy the range or not, vulnerabilities is considered exist, if corresponding symbol value can not meet the range. In test cases construction, KLEE considers not only path conditions, but also the conditions which can triggering the vulnerabilities.

Source code is always unable to obtain, therefore, relevant researchers proposed concolic execution in binary level, and developed corresponding tools, such as SAGE [26], BitBlaze [10], SmartFuzz [25], etc. Using legitimate input, SAGE tests program dynamically tracks and records instruction execution by binary platform iDNA, and collects path constraint conditions in instruction replaying, solves the path constraint conditions one by one to generate a new test set for driving the program execution. SmartFuzz [25] is on the basis of Valgrind (binary instrument platform), converts binary code to VEX intermediate language by online symbolic execution and constraint solving, and dynamically generates test cases to detect vulnerabilities in Linux system.

5.1   Existing Problems

At present, Path explosion and performance problems are two main problems which limit the development of symbolic execution technology.

Path Explosion. Path explosion is a major problem of symbolic execution technology. Because that every branch condition can increase a new path. The path grows exponentially. There are several methods to solve the problem of path explosion:

- Similar to limit symbolic execution, Limit the number of paths in each process.
- Improve performance of symbolic execution analysis by improving the path scheduling algorithm. for example, according to the methods and characteristics of program execution, Boonstoppel et al. [30] proposed the idea of cutting paths on the basis of the EXE tool, cut some unnecessary path, alleviated symbolic execution path explosion problem effectively.
- Adopt parallel symbolic execution strategy [29] to improve efficiency of constraint solver according to current parallel computing technology.

Performance Problems. Symbolic execution technology uses constraint solver to solve the path condition expression, and it needs to break in instrument during the procedure analysis. According to statistics, the 2000 lines C code can increase to 40,000 lines [30] after instrument, which increases the number of code lines and the number of constraint solver calls, the efficiency of symbolic execution is up to the performance of solver. The current solution is to decrease the number of solver calls, there are mainly two methods, one is caching the common constraint expression or part of middle expressions produced during solving process by cache technology, thus reducing unnecessary repetition [26, 29]. The other is improving speed through further optimization constraints, such as elimination constraints, rewrite the expression and simplify the constraint set.

5.2   Future Optimization

Unlike traditional static symbolic execution, concolic execution technology makes full use of runtime information, improves the accuracy of symbolic execution, and promotes the development of symbolic execution. In addition, with the rapid growing of analysis demand, concolic execution for binaries becomes more and more important. The major optimizations in the future include:

- Further combined with other technologies to complement each other for solving the problems of each method.
- Further alleviate path explosion in symbolic execution. Design abstract methods to handle and abstract path information into a higher level set which has less path, thus alleviate the path explosion problem by greatly reducing the number of paths.

6   Fuzzing

6.1   Principles and Classification of Fuzzing

Fuzzing, first proposed by Miller et al. [31] in 1989, and the core principle of Fuzzing is to generate special structure or random data as input, monitor the process of program execution, record input that result in crash, and then locate the vulnerability position [3] in target program by artificial analysis. From the scope of test case generation strategy, Fuzzing can be classified into the Fuzzing based on generation and the Fuzzing based on mutation [6]. From the scope of source code dependence, Fuzzing can be classified into Black-box Fuzzing, White-box Fuzzing and Grey-box Fuzzing.

Some scholars have developed some tools for applying fuzzing to detect vulnerabilities. For passing input check and other protect mechanism, in 2010, Wang et al. [32] proposed a method by the combination of concolic execution and fine-grained dynamic taint propagation, and developed a corresponding tool TaintScope, achieved vulnerabilities detection in deep logic. Since 2011, genetic algorithms and heuristic algorithms, etc. have been used by many researchers to assist in generating test cases, it improved the efficiency of test cases generation.

6.2   Existing Problems

Compared to other vulnerabilities detection method, one important disadvantages of fuzzing is not to guarantee high path coverage rate and high automatic level. Therefore, optimizing test case generation strategy is the major research direction for improving fuzzing efficiency.

Test Case Generation Strategies. Test case generation is the most critical part of the fuzzing, and its efficiency determines the efficiency of fuzzing. The early fuzzing was a Black-box test, the test results were not ideal, and cannot be used in the program with input check. How to optimize the test case generation strategy is the problem that needs to be studied.

Currently, researchers have introduced some similar concepts into test case generation strategies to optimize the test result. For example, concepts of selection, cross and mutation. Using genetic algorithms to generate specific test cases has been proven to greatly improve the test case generation efficiency with higher automatic level [33].

Combined with other binary vulnerability analysis is taken to consideration by fuzzing researchers. For example, dynamic taint analysis can extract the dynamic data flow or control flow, and integration into the binary vulnerability analysis process, guide the generation of input data, it greatly improved the efficiency of traditional fuzzing.

Automatic Level. Manual testing relies on prior knowledge, it also takes more time, and results in low practical value. Common fuzzing frameworks often require manual participation in determining input data constraints and generating test cases. Therefore, the current research focuses on automation and intelligence. One solution is to apply genetic algorithms to improve automatic level.

Multi-point Triggered Vulnerability. Traditionally, fuzzing can only detect vulnerabilities caused by one condition, and there is no way to find vulnerabilities that require multiple conditions [34]. Recently some researchers have tried to use fuzzing for detecting vulnerabilities which can be triggered by multi-point and proposed the concept of multi-dimensional fuzzing [35]. However, the multi-dimensional fuzzing currently has a combinatorial path explosion problem which limits its development.

6.3 Future Optimization

Compared with other methods, fuzzing has a great advantage for unnecessary to understand the internal structure of the program, so it costs less overhead. However, large blindness, low efficiency and no guarantee of code coverage rate limit fuzzing development. It is possible to combine fuzzing with other binary vulnerability analysis techniques for making up disadvantages, such as the combination with dynamic taint analysis or symbolic execution. In future work, the fuzzing will tend to be integrated into the binary analysis framework, which is combined with the symbolic execution. To obtain a high path coverage rate, constraints solving of symbolic execution can used to obtain a path constraint set, and then design test cases based on the path constraint set for fuzzing.

The combination of fuzzing and symbolic execution to generate test cases can greatly improve the efficiency of fuzzing, and efficiency will be improved obviously. In addition, improving genetic algorithm to generate test cases is also a good way. In future, fuzzing can also be further combined with other subjects for new breakthroughs.

7   Conclusion

Vulnerability analysis is a relatively difficult subject, it became an emerging international study in recent 20 years, and the related work in China has just started in recent years. The future development direction will be mainly combined with several vulnerability analysis technology, such as intermediate language, taint analysis, symbolic execution, and fuzzing to complement each other, optimize limitations in these current vulnerability analysis technologies. In addition, in order to obtain higher efficiency and extend scope of application, vulnerability analysis in parallel and scale is also an important research point.

In this paper, we make full study of binary code oriented vulnerability analysis technology, classify the current binary vulnerability analysis framework, summarize the limitations and optimizations of each types of framework, propose a more powerful integrated binary vulnerability analysis framework on the basis of current typical binary vulnerability analysis framework for large-scale, automatic efficient analysis. We also introduce the research status of key technologies in each framework in detail, summarize limitations of each key technology, propose further optimizations of each key technology.

References

1. Xia, Z., Zhu, Y., Sun, X., et al.: Towards privacy-preserving content-based image retrieval in cloud computing. IEEE Trans. Cloud Comput. 2015 **99**, 1 (2016)
2. Xia, Z., Xiong, N.N., Vasilakos, A.V., et al.: EPCBIR: an efficient and privacy-preserving content-based image retrieval scheme in cloud computing. Inf. Sci. **387**, 195–204 (2016)
3. Cai, Z.P., Chen, M., Chen, S., et al.: Searching for widespread events in large networked systems by cooperative monitoring. In: IEEE International Conference on Network Protocols, San Francisco, pp. 123–133 (2015). https://doi.org/10.1109/icnp.2015.46
4. Cai, Z., Wang, Z., Zheng, K., et al.: A distributed TCAM coprocessor architecture for integrated longest prefix matching, policy filtering, and content filtering. IEEE Trans. Comput. **62**(3), 417–427 (2013). https://doi.org/10.1109/tc.2011.255
5. Liu, Y., Cai, Z.P., Zhong, P., et al.: Detection approach of DDoS attacks based on conditional random fields. J. Softw. **22**(8), 1897–1910 (2011)
6. Wu, S., Guo, T., Dong, G., et al.: Software vulnerability analysis: a road map. J. Tsinghua Univ. (Sci. Technol.) **10**, 1309–1319 (2012)
7. Jianwei, Z., Chen, L., Fan, T., et al.: Type-based dynamic taint analysis technology. J. Tsinghua Univ. **52**(10), 1320–1328 (2012)
8. Bai, H., Chang-Zhen, H.U., Zhang, G., et al.: Binary oriented vulnerability analyzer based on hidden Markov model. IEICE Trans. Inf. Syst. **93**(12), 3410–3413 (2010)
9. Li, X., Zheng, D., Ma, R., Liang, A., Guan, H.: MTCrossBit: a dynamic binary translation system using multithreaded optimization framework. In: Hua, A., Chang, S.-L. (eds.) ICA3PP 2009. LNCS, vol. 5574, pp. 502–512. Springer, Heidelberg (2009). https://doi.org/10.1007/978-3-642-03095-6_48
10. Song, D., et al.: BitBlaze: a new approach to computer security via binary analysis. In: Sekar, R., Pujari, A.K. (eds.) ICISS 2008. LNCS, vol. 5352, pp. 1–25. Springer, Heidelberg (2008). https://doi.org/10.1007/978-3-540-89862-7_1
11. Yan, S., Kruegel, C., Vigna, G., et al.: SOK: (state of) the art of war: offensive techniques in binary analysis. In: IEEE Security and Privacy, pp. 138–157 (2016). https://doi.org/10.1109/sp.2016.17
12. Nethercote, N., Seward, J.: Valgrind: a framework for heavyweight dynamic binary instrumentation. ACM SIGPLAN Not. **42**(6), 89–100 (2007)
13. Denning, D.E.: A lattice model of secure information flow. Commun. ACM **19**(5), 236–243 (1976)
14. Qiang, H., Zeng, Q.K.: Taint propagation analysis and dynamic verification with information flow policy. J. Softw. **22**, 2036–2048 (2011)
15. Shi, D.W., Yuan, T.W.: A dynamic taint analysis method combined with coarse-grained and fine-grained. Comput. Eng. **40**(3), 12–17 (2014)
16. Dai, W., Liu, Z., Liu, Y.H.: Binary code-based dynamic taint analysis. Appl. Res. Comput. (2014)
17. Ma, J.-X., Li, Z.-J., Zhang, T., et al.: Taint analysis method based on offline indices of instruction trace. J. Softw. (2017)

18. Wang, L., Li, F., Li, L., et al.: Principle and practice of taint analysis. J. Softw. (2017)
19. Newsome, J., Song, D.: Dynamic taint analysis for automatic detection, analysis, and signature generation of exploits on commodity software. Chin. J. Eng. Math. **29**(5), 720–724 (2005)
20. Clause, J., Li, W., Orso, A.: Dytan: a generic dynamic taint analysis framework. In: Proceedings of the 2007 International Symposium on Software Testing and Analysis, pp. 196–206. ACM (2007). https://doi.org/10.1145/1273463.1273490
21. Qin, F., Wang, C., Li, Z., et al.: LIFT: a low-overhead practical information flow tracking system for detecting security attacks. In: IEEE/ACM International Symposium on Microarchitecture, pp. 135–148. IEEE (2006).https://doi.org/10.1109/micro.2006.29
22. Ouyang, Y., Wang, Q., Peng, J., et al.: An advanced automatic construction method of ROP. Wuhan Univ. J. Nat. Sci. **20**(2), 119–128 (2015)
23. Lin, W., Cai, R., Zhu, Y., et al.: Optimization method of taint propagation analysis based on semantic rules. J. Comput. Appl. (2014)
24. Zhu, Z.X., Zeng, F.P., Huang, X.Y.: Dynamic symbolic taint analysis of binary programs. Comput. Sci. (2016)
25. Molnar, D., Li, X.C., Wagner, D.A.: Dynamic test generation to find integer bugs in x86 binary linux programs. In: Conference on Usenix Security Symposium, pp. 67–82. USENIX Association (2009)
26. Molnar, D.A.: Automated whitebox fuzz testing. In: Network and Distributed System Security Symposium. NDSS, California (2008). DBLP, USA (2011)
27. Sen, K., Marinov, D., Agha, G.: CUTE: a concolic unit testing engine for C. In: European Software Engineering Conference Held Jointly with, ACM SIGSOFT International Symposium on Foundations of Software Engineering, pp. 263–272. ACM (2005). https://doi.org/10.21236/ada482657
28. Sen, K.: DART: directed automated random testing. In: Namjoshi, K., Zeller, A., Ziv, A. (eds.) HVC 2009. LNCS, vol. 6405, pp. 213–223. Springer, Heidelberg (2011). https://doi.org/10.1007/978-3-642-19237-1_4
29. Cadar, C., Dunbar, D., Engler, D.: KLEE: unassisted and automatic generation of high-coverage tests for complex systems programs. In: USENIX Conference on Operating Systems Design and Implementation, pp. 209–224. USENIX Association (2009)
30. Boonstoppel, P., Cadar, C., Engler, D.: RWset: attacking path explosion in constraint-based test generation. In: Ramakrishnan, C.R., Rehof, J. (eds.) TACAS 2008. LNCS, vol. 4963, pp. 351–366. Springer, Heidelberg (2008). https://doi.org/10.1007/978-3-540-78800-3_27
31. Miller, B.P., Fredriksen, L., So, B.: An empirical study of the reliability of UNIX utilities. Commun. ACM **33**(12), 32–44 (1990)
32. Wang, T., Wei, T., Gu, G., et al.: TaintScope: a checksum-aware directed fuzzing tool for automatic software vulnerability detection. In: IEEE Symposium on Security and Privacy, pp. 497–512. IEEE Computer Society (2010). https://doi.org/10.1109/sp.2010.37
33. Zhu, X.Y., Wu, Z.Y.: A new fuzzing technique using niche genetic algorithm. Adv. Mater. Res. **756–759**, 4050–4058 (2013)
34. Wu, Z.Y., Wang, H.C., Sun, L.C., et al.: Survey on fuzzing. Appl. Res. Comput. **27**(3), 829–832 (2010)
35. Heelan, S., Gianni, A.: Augmenting vulnerability analysis of binary code. In: Computer Security Applications Conference, pp. 199–208. ACM (2012). https://doi.org/10.1145/2420950.2420981

The New Progress in the Research of Binary Vulnerability Exploits

Tiantian Tan$^{(\boxtimes)}$, Baosheng Wang$^{(\boxtimes)}$, Zhou Xu$^{(\boxtimes)}$, and Yong Tang$^{(\boxtimes)}$

National University of Defense and Technology, Changsha 410073, China
wangbaosheng@126.com

Abstract. The vulnerabilities exploitable validation is the core of vulnerability analysis technology. To solve the limitations of manual reappearance and exploits of vulnerabilities, current vulnerability automatic exploit technology has achieved preliminary progress. This paper presented an overview of the field of automatic vulnerability exploits, and classified current automatic vulnerability exploits method into 3 categories: patch comparison scheme, control flow oriented scheme and data flow oriented scheme, introduced the core principle, process, research status of each category, summarized the advantages and limitations of each category, and proposed the direction of future research. This survey on software vulnerability automatic exploits can provide a theoretical guidance for the future research work.

Keywords: Patch comparison · Control flow oriented
Data flow oriented · Exploits generation

1 Introduction

The storage and sharing of vast amounts of data has increase the widespread utilization of cloud computation. In the cloud computation environment, more users are participating in the storage, acquisition and exchange of data, this results in higher risk of privacy leaking, privacy has been a research hotspot in the field of cloud computation security problems, domestic and foreign researchers have proposed lots of solutions, such as improved content-based image retrieval scheme proposed by Xia et al. [1,2], it increased the efficiency by the secure k-nearest neighbor (KNN) algorithm to encrypt images without revealing the sensitive information, a solution for multi-monitor joint detection with lower communication overhead designed by Cai et al. [3]; a distributed Ternary Content Addressable Memory (TCAM) coprocessor architecture proposed by Cai et al. for Longest Prefix Matching (LPM), Policy Filtering (PF), and Content Filtering (CF) [4]; a more robust detection approach of DDoS attacks based on Conditional Random Fields model proposed by Cai et al. [5].

Supported by National University of Defense and Technology and National Natural Science Foundation No.61402492.

X. Sun et al. (Eds.): ICCCS 2018, LNCS 11064, pp. 277–286, 2018.
https://doi.org/10.1007/978-3-030-00009-7_26

However, no mater how strength an encryption algorithm has, the vulnerabilities of the encryption algorithm can always led to privacy leaking, the attackers can detect cloud computing vulnerabilities to intercept and steal personal information, such as "Amazon EC2 crash", "GoogleApps service interruption", "Azure stop operation" etc. Therefore, vulnerability relevant technologies are the core solution and the hotspot of the implement of cloud computation security in recent years.

In the fields of vulnerability technologies, detection and exploitation of software vulnerability are current hot issues. Although fuzzing can solve the problem of automatic vulnerabilities detection, and parallel fuzzing platform can efficiently find a lot of vulnerabilities, both the defender and attacker are more concerned about whether these vulnerabilities can be reappearanced and exploited. How to quickly analyze and assess the exploits of vulnerability is one of the key problems in current vulnerability exploit and analysis technology [6,7].

Using the data structure in manual way, not only underlying knowledge of a relative comprehensive system (including file format, the assembly code, internal mechanism of the operating system and processor architecture, etc.), but also the method for analysis the mechanism of the vulnerabilities indepth, traditional software vulnerabilities can be successfully exploited. Recently, complex functions of software and the diversity of vulnerabilities tend to increase rapidly, traditional vulnerability exploitation methods have been unable to meet the challenges.

At present, with the continuous development of program analysis technologies, especially these technologies, such as taint analysis [8–11], symbolic execution [12–15], successfully applied in the software and software vulnerability dynamic analysis [16–19] etc., the researchers tried to use these techniques to automatic construct software vulnerability exploits efficiently. Figure 1 shows the existing work and detailed description will be discussed in Sects. 2, 3, 4.

2   Automatic Vulnerability Exploits Based on Binary Patch Comparison

In IEEES&P conference 2008, Rumley et al. first proposed the automatic generation method of exploits on the basis of binary patch comparison [20,21]. The core principle is the assumption that the patch increases the filter condition which can triggers the crash of the original program. Therefore, a candidate exploits can be generated by constructing illegal input different from data structure of the filter conditions after finding the position of filter condition in a patch. According to the detailed content, the work mainly includes three steps:

- Find the position of the patch (Patch Testing Point) by binary comparison tools (such as BinDiff and EBDS, etc.);
- Find the input data not meet the patch test point as a candidate of exploits of the original program;

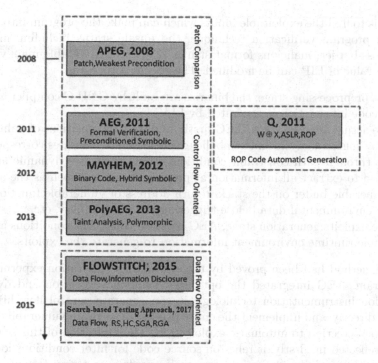

Fig. 1. The categories of vulnerability exploits

Identify the effective exploits that can trigger overflow or the control flow hijacking of the original program by taint propagation or other monitoring methods. According to the experimental results of several patches released by Microsoft, this method has strong reliability and practicability. APEG is the first attempt to automatic generate vulnerability exploits, although the core idea is relative simple, strong operability makes it has been obtained the general recognition of researchers. However, the limitations of APEG mainly include two aspects:

- The method cannot deal with the patch which has no filter conditions, for example, the patch increasing the length of buffer in order to repair the buffer overflow;
- From the actual exploit effect, the exploitations can mainly trigger denial of service which can only cause the crash rather than control flow hijacking.

3 Control Flow Oriented Automatic Vulnerability Exploits

3.1 Automatic Vulnerability Exploits Based on Source Code

In order to overcome dependence on patch and unable to construct control flow, T.A vgerinos firstly proposed an effective automatic method AEG [22] for vulnerability detection and exploit in NDSS conference, 2011. The core idea of the method is to find the exploitable inputs which can make the program into unsafe state by program verification technique, the unsafe status including memory write cross-border, malicious format strings [23], etc. Exploitable mainly refers that the value of EIP can be modified. The specific process is:

- In the preprocessing stage, the binaries are built by GNU C compiler and the byte code information is generated by LLVM;
- In the actual analysis stage, AEG firstly finds out the positions of vulnerabilities by source analysis and symbolic execution, and generates corresponding input through path constraint conditions. AEG then uses dynamic analysis method to extract all information at program run time, such as the address of vulnerable buffer on the stack, return address of vulnerable function, and other environmental data before triggering the vulnerability, etc.
- In the exploits generation stage, AEG uses the constraint conditions and the dynamic runtime environment information to generate the exploits.

This method had been proved by the automatic exploitation experiment of 14 program. AEG integrated the optimized symbolic execution and dynamic instruction instrumentation technology, it can generate control flow hijacking exploits directly, and implement the entire process of software vulnerability from automatic detection to automatic exploitation. The limitation of this scheme is mainly reflected in: firstly, it relies on source code for filter conditions location; Secondly, the exploits are mainly for stack overflow or string format vulnerabilities, and the exploits is limited by the compiler and dynamic operating environment.

3.2   Binary Oriented Automatic Vulnerability Exploits

In order to get rid of the dependence on the source and guarantee the universality scene, Ha et al. proposed binary oriented automatic vulnerability exploits method Mayhem [24] in IEEE, the S&P 2012. Mayhem construct memory model based on index to achieve a more practical vulnerability detection and exploits generation by combining on-line symbolic execution with off-line symbolic execution for high speed and low memory consumption. The specific process includes:

- Firstly, construct two parallel subsystems: symbolic execution subsystem and execution subsystem;
- Secondly, for a specific execution subsystem, using taint analysis to all the input which can control the JMP or call instructions at run time, and send these input as a vulnerability candidate items to symbolic execution subsystem;
- Finally, the symbol execution system converts all received instructions into the intermediate instructions, and construct path accessible constraint conditions and exploitable constraint conditions by constraint solver.

In actual symbolic execution process, in order to ensure efficiency, Mayhem system uses a memory model based on index to optimize the symbolic memory load problem, which makes it become a vulnerability exploit automatic generation with high usability. At present, the limitations of Mayhem mainly focus on:

- Firstly, the system can only model part of systems or library functions, so it cannot efficiently handle large programs;
- Secondly, the system cannot handle interaction issues among multi-thread, such as shared-memory and message transformation;
- Finally, due to the use of the taint propagation, there are also typical problems such as data missing and miss propagation.

3.3   Diverse Vulnerability Exploits Automatic Generation

Due to exploits with high quality and the diversity is great importance for vulnerability risk assessment, therefore in SecureComm conference 2013, Wang proposed a diverse vulnerability exploits automatic generation method PolyAEG [25]. The core principle of PolyAEG is to find out all control flow hijacking through dynamic taint analysis, and construct the diverse exploits by constructing different control flow transfer modes. The specific process is:

- Firstly, implement dynamic execution monitoring and extract the runtime information through the expanded hardware virtualization platform QEMU;
- Secondly, build instruction level taint propagation flow graph iTPG and global taint state record GTSR on the basis of the dynamic information collection, and then obtain all possible control flow hijacking in the program, available springboard instructions and taint memory areas which can deposit attack code, etc.;
- Finally, use solver to solve path constraint conditions for generating a set of diverse exploits through the construction of different jump instruction chain and attack code in different taint memory areas.

According to the experimental results on 8 programs, the scheme has generated a maximum of 4724 exploits for one control flow hijacking. PolyAEG has implemented a complete diverse vulnerability exploits automatic generation for control flow hijacking, and has provided effective support for the vulnerability assessment. However, the limitations of the scheme include mainly two aspects:

- There are certain limitations in the implementation of the protection mechanism of data execution;
- In the construction process, the scheme only considers the existing instructions in itself or other libraries, and does not consider the use of dynamic code generation.

3.4   ROP Code Automatic Generation

In order to solve the data protection and address randomization which prevent control flow hijacking, in USENIX Security 2011, Schwartz et al. implemented a set of high reliability vulnerability exploit oriented ROP code automatic generation Q [26]. The core principle is to collect the gadgets in the target program and automatic build ROP code through the Gadget - oriented programming language. The specific process is as follows:

- Firstly, use Q to find the Gadget collection with specific functions in program without randomization or other binary library provided to Q;
- Secondly, realize the target code that satisfies the specific semantic function, and compile the target code into Gadget oriented instruction sequences by QooL (a programming language provided by Q);
- Subsequently, the final ROP code is formed by using obtained Gadget collection to fill in the obtained instruction sequence.

The experiment on nine real software vulnerabilities had shown that Q can ensure vulnerability exploits execute normally whether it exists data execution protection and address randomizing function or not. Q had proved in system containing only a small amount code with randomization, ROP code can still be automatic generated effectively, thus it strengthen the effect of control flow hijacking oriented vulnerability exploits in real environment. The limitations of Q scheme mainly include:

- Firstly, Q scheme does not consider the ROP code automatic construction without ret instruction;
- Secondly, Q scheme only starts from the actual effect and does not consider to satisfy the Turing completeness.

4   Data Flow Oriented Automatic Vulnerability Exploits

The methods used by most attackers has been changed from control flow hijacking exploit to data flow oriented exploits under the condition of data protection, address randomization and control flow integrity protection.

4.1   Data Flow Exploits Automatic Construction by Tampering Key Variables

Hu et al. first time proposed a data flow exploits automatic construction method FlowStitch in USENIX Security conference 2015 [27]. The core principle of the method is to use the known memory error directly or indirectly tamper with variables in the key position in the original program data flow for exploits automatic generation without changing the program control flow. The specific process includes the following steps:

- Firstly, define the programs which contain memory error, input which can trigger a memory error and special normal input as the preconditions of the automatic vulnerability exploitation system, special normal input refers that execution path must be the same as path which can trigger a memory error before triggering the error;

- Secondly, obtain the corresponding error execution record and normal execution record by normal input and wrong input, and on this basis further extract the affect range of respective memory errors and the sensitive data in normal data flow;
- Finally, find the sensitive data may be involved in affect range of respective memory errors by comparing error execution records and normal execution records, eventually select all sensitive variables which may be tampered with sensitive data and construct the data flow oriented automatic exploit.

The results of experimental on eight programs can be seen that 19 exploits automatically generated by FlowStitch cannot only bypass data execution protection and control flow integrity measures, such as fine-grained control flow integrity, and 10 samples of exploits can also execute in address randomization environment successfully. FlowStich is the first data flow oriented vulnerability automatic exploitation scheme, although it cannot run any malicious code directly, the leakage of sensitive data on the target host make it a strong practical value. The limitations of the scheme mainly include:

- Firstly, data flow oriented is dependent on the known memory errors in the program.
- Secondly, in the process of construction and exploitation, not only the corresponding error execution record is required, but also the corresponding normal input and normal execution path need to be constructed.

4.2 Search-Based Testing Approach

Jan et al. proposed an search-based testing approach. The core principle of the method is to automatically generate malicious inputs to web services by testing 2 fitness function in Random Search (RS), Hill Climbing (HC), Standard Genetic Algorithms (SGA) and Real-coded Genetic Algorithms (RGA) [28]. The specific process includes the following steps:

Encode Scheme. Encode the input for algorithm, one candidate test case for the SUT with n input parameters is a strings tuple $T = <S1, S2, ..., Sn>$. A generic string in T is an array of k characters, i.e., $Si = <c1, c2, ..., ck>$. The array length k is fixed based on the expected maximum length of the corresponding input parameter. Use a special symbol to denote the empty character to allow input strings with different length, the lengths of input strings can vary during the search no matter if the length of the array (i.e., k) in the encoding schema is fixed. Fill the array $Si = <c1, c2, ..., ck>$ with the empty character to represent shorter strings.

Fitness Function. Use two fitness function to compute the distance d(TO, SUT(T)) between the target TO and the XML message that the SUT produces upon the execution of T, i.e., SUT(T). The first fitness function use the Levenshtein distance to compute string edit distance and the second function use the real-coded edit distance which modified the Levenshtein distance to focus the search on sub-regions of the large ASCII neighborhood of the target TO.

Solver. Investigate random search(RS) for functions with plateaus, hill climbing (HC) for unimodal functions (i.e., with only one optimum), the standard genetic algorithm (SGA) for multimodal functions (i.e., with multiple local optima), and the real-coded genetic algorithm(RGA) for problems whose solution encoding contains numbers (real-coded).

Validation. Use 4 algorithm and 2 fitness function to run experiments on 5 application, and obtain the success rate and execution time by computing the average value of the records of each algorithm and fitness function.The Realcoded Genetic Algorithm(RGA), using a fitness function minimizing a real-coded edit distance between TOs and generated XML messages, is proved to be the best option.

The proposed search-based testing approach is not only limited to XML injection detection, but can be generalized to detection of other types of vulnerabilities. For instance, to apply it to Cross-site scripting or SQL injection vulnerabilities, one would only need to modify the TOs according to the corresponding types of attacks for that vulnerability. The limitations of the scheme mainly include:

- The target program must has the corresponding function implemented by XML file, such as web application.

5   Summary and Prospect

Around how to rapid analyze and determine the reappearance the exploits of software vulnerabilities generated by fuzzy testing technology, researchers have proposed a series of efficient vulnerability exploit automatic generation, including patch comparison, control flow oriented scheme and data flow oriented scheme, etc. The implementation of these solutions can not only efficiently identify high risk vulnerabilities from a large number of vulnerabilities, as well as to a certain extent, it can prevent the high risk vulnerabilities from be exploited. Although the software automatic exploit technology has achieved preliminary progress, the increase of the complexity of the software, control flow integrity detection and the diversity of software vulnerability types, bring vulnerabilities exploits assessment more challenges. Therefore, we need to further explore and study the software vulnerabilities and propose more efficient and reliable automation solutions. This survey on software vulnerability automatic exploits can provide a theoretical guidance for the combination of muti-scheme software vulnerability automatic exploits with higher efficiency and reliability.

References

1. Xia, Z., Xiong, N.N., Vasilakos, A.V., et al.: EPCBIR: an efficient and privacy-preserving content-based image retrieval scheme in cloud computing. Inf. Sci. **387**, 195–204 (2016)
2. Xia, Z., Zhu, Y., Sun, X.: Towards privacy-preserving content-based image retrieval in cloud computing. IEEE Trans. Cloud Comput. **2015**(99), 1–1 (2016). https://doi.org/10.1109/srds.2015.27
3. Cai, Z.P., Chen, M., Chen, S., et al.: Searching for widespread events in large networked systems by cooperative monitoring. In: IEEE International Conference on Network Protocols, pp. 123–133, San Francisco (2015). https://doi.org/10.1109/icnp.2015.46
4. Cai, Z., Wang, Z., Zheng, K.: A distributed TCAM coprocessor architecture for integrated longest prefix matching, policy filtering, and content filtering. IEEE Trans. Comput. **62**(3), 417–427 (2013). https://doi.org/10.1109/tc.2011.255
5. Liu, Y., Cai, Z.P., Zhong, P.: Detection approach of DDoS attacks based on conditional random fields. J. Softw. **22**(8), 1897–1910 (2011)
6. Miller, C., Caballero, J., Berkeley, U.: Crash analysis with BitBlaze. Revista Mexicana De Sociologa **44**(1), 81–117 (2010)
7. Heelan, S., Kroening, D.: Automatic generation of control flow hijacking exploits for software vulnerabilities. M.Sc. Computer Science Dissertation (2009)
8. Tang, H., Huang, S., Li, Y., et al.: Dynamic taint analysis for vulnerability exploits detection. In: International Conference on Computer Engineering and Technology, vol. 2, pp. 215–218 (2010). https://doi.org/10.1109/iccet.2010.5485224
9. Ma, J.X., Li, Z.J., Zhang, T., Shen, D., Zhang, Z.K.: Taint analysis method based on offline indices of instruction trace. J. Softw. **28**, 2388–2401 (2017)
10. Sheth, M.: System and method for facilitating static analysis of software applications, US 20160179486 (2016)
11. Schutte, J., Brost, G.S.: A data usage control system using dynamic taint tracking. In: International Conference on Advanced Information Networking and Applications, pp. 909–916, IEEE Computer Society (2016). https://doi.org/10.1109/aina.2016.127
12. King, J.C.: Symbolic execution and program testing. Commun. ACM **19**(7), 385–394 (1976)
13. Berdine, J., Calcagno, C., OHearn, P.W.: Symbolic execution with separation logic. In: Yi, K. (ed.) APLAS 2005. LNCS, vol. 3780, pp. 52–68. Springer, Heidelberg (2005). https://doi.org/10.1007/11575467_5
14. Khurshid, S., PǍsǍreanu, C.S., Visser, W.: Generalized symbolic execution for model checking and testing. In: Garavel, H., Hatcliff, J. (eds.) TACAS 2003. LNCS, vol. 2619, pp. 553–568. Springer, Heidelberg (2003). https://doi.org/10.1007/3-540-36577-X_40
15. Boyer, R.S., Elspas, B., Levitt, K.N.: SELECT-a formal system for testing and debugging programs by symbolic execution. In: International Conference on Reliable Software, vol. 10, pp. 234–245 (1975). https://doi.org/10.1145/800027.808445
16. Basu, J.P.: Vulnerability analysis. In: Basu, J.P. (ed.) Climate Change Adaptation and Forest Dependent Communities, pp. 57–58. Springer, Cham (2017). https://doi.org/10.1007/978-3-319-52325-5_4
17. Ghaffarian, S.M., Shahriari, H.R.: Software vulnerability analysis and discovery using machine-learning and data-mining techniques: a survey. ACM Comput. Surv. **50**(4), 1–36 (2017)

18. Albab, K.D., Issa, R., Lapets, A., et al.: Scalable secure multi-party network vul-
    nerability analysis via symbolic optimization. In: IEEE Security and Privacy Work-
    shops, pp. 211–216. IEEE Computer Society (2017). https://doi.org/10.1109/spw.
    2017.21
19. Sheth, M.: System and method for facilitating static analysis of software applica-
    tions. US 20160179486 (2016)
20. Brumley, D., Poosankam, P., Song, D., et al.: Automatic patch-based exploit gen-
    eration is possible: techniques and implications. In: IEEE Symposium on Security
    and Privacy, pp. 143–157 (2008). https://doi.org/10.1109/sp.2008.17
21. Allodi, L., Massacci, F.: Comparing vulnerability severity and exploits using case-
    control studies. ACM Trans. Inf. Syst. Secur. 17(1), 1–20 (2014)
22. Avgerinos, T., Sang, K.C., Hao, B.L.T., et al.: AEG: automatic exploit generation.
    In: Network and Distributed System Security Symposium. NDSS. DBLP, USA
    (2011)
23. Tsai, T., Singh, N.: Libsafe 2.0: detection of format string vulnerability exploits.
    White Paper (2001)
24. Avgerinos, T., Rebert, A., Brumley, D., et al.: Unleashing mayhem on binary code.
    vol. 19, pp. 380–394 (2012)
25. Wang, M., Su, P., Li, Q., Ying, L., Yang, Y., Feng, D.: Automatic polymorphic
    exploit generation for software vulnerabilities. In: Zia, T., Zomaya, A., Varad-
    harajan, V., Mao, M. (eds.) SecureComm 2013. LNICST, vol. 127, pp. 216–233.
    Springer, Cham (2013). https://doi.org/10.1007/978-3-319-04283-1_14
26. Schwartz, E.J., Avgerinos, T., Brumley, D.: Q: exploit hardening made easy. In:
    Usenix Conference on Security, pp. 25–25. USENIX Association (2011)
27. Hu, H., Zheng, L.C., Adrian, S., et al.: Automatic generation of data-oriented
    exploits (2015)
28. Jan, S., Panichella, A., Arcuri, A., et al.: Automatic generation of tests to exploit
    XML injection vulnerabilities in web applications. 99, 1–1 (2017)

The Quasi-circular Mapping Visualization Based on Extending and Reordering Dimensions for Visual Clustering Analysis

Shan Huang[2], Ming Li[1], and Hao Chen[1(✉)]

[1] National Key Laboratory of Image Processing and Pattern Recognition in Jiangxi, Nanchang Hangkong University, Nanchang 330063, Jiangxi, China
chenhaoshl@nchu.edu.cn
[2] School of Information Engineering, Nanchang Hangkong University, Nanchang 330063, Jiangxi, China

Abstract. Radial coordinate visualization (RadViz) and Star Coordinates (SC) can effectively map high dimensional data to low dimensional space, owing to which can place an arbitrary number of Dimension Anchors (DAs). Nevertheless, the problem owner is faced with ordering DAs, which is a NP-complete problem and visual results of crowding which hamper clustering analysis. We introduce a new radial layout visualization, called the Quasi-circular mapping visualization (QCMV), to address those problems in this paper. Firstly, QCMV extend the original dimension of datasets by the probability distribution histogram of the dimension and affinity propagation (AP) algorithm. In additional, distributing them on the unit circle by their correlation according to the correlation of the extended dimensions. Then, mapping the dimensions extended and reordered data to integrate a polygon in the Quasi-circular space and visualizing them by the geometric center and area of the polygon in the three dimension. Finally strengthening their visual clustering effect with t-SNE. We also compare the visual clustering results of RadViz, SC and QCMV with two indexes, correct rate and Dunn index on visually analyzing the three datasets. It shows better effect of visual clustering with QCMV.

Keywords: Quasi-circular mapping visualization · Visual clustering
Multi-dimensional data

1 Introduction

As the computer and sensor equipment develop rapidly, multi-dimensional and even high-dimensional data have been widely used in numerous fields, such as economics, medical, military and industrial, etc. For example, high dimensional functional magnetic resonance imaging data [1], the spectrometry data in air quality research [2], multi-dimension architecture of three-layers defense [3] and so on. Their increasing dimensions and sizes bring new opportunities and challenges to analysis. Visualization technology is an important tool of data analysis, which refers to express the internal structure, information and knowledge of data with computer graphics, image

X. Sun et al. (Eds.): ICCCS 2018, LNCS 11064, pp. 287–299, 2018.
https://doi.org/10.1007/978-3-030-00009-7_27

processing, signal processing and other methods. It can help users qualitatively analyze data and conduct pattern recognition, outlier detection and other research.

However, the limitations of display devices and our visual systems are the impediments to direct display and quickly analyze the structures of more than three-dimensional data. Many excellent visualization analysis methods for high dimensional data are studied with the deep research. One class of them is dimension-reduction methods (DR), which maps data from high dimensional target space to low dimensional space and display the dimensionality reduction data with the scattered points or other symbols. It mainly includes principal component analysis (PCA) [4], self-organizing map (SOM) [5], Neuroscale [6], generative topographical mapping (GTM) [7] and so on. PCA is one of the most common linear dimensionality reduction methods. Xie et al. [8] combined Terahertz time-domain spectroscopy with PCA to perform visual classification on the materials, thus facilitating substance identification. SOM is an important type of neural network based on unsupervised learning method. Sarlin et al. [9] gained the factors and conditions that contribute to the emergence of currency crises in various parts of the world by SOM. Although DR try to preserve the original characteristics and clustering relations of high-dimensional space in low dimensional space, it may cause the loss of potentially important information and cannot express the relationship between dimensions.

Another class of method result in a visualization without using dimensionality reduction technique, such as scatterplot matrix [10], parallel coordinate plots (PCP) [11], the radial layout visualization [12–14] and heatmap [15] and so on. PCP is a typical multidimensional visualization technique based on a coordinate axis, which represented by a series of parallel coordinate axes for each variable of high dimensional data. Li et al. [16] applied PCP to compare the quality of solution sets, analyze the shape and distribution of a solution set and the relation between objectives in evolutionary many objective optimization. Heatmap is a graphical representation the value as colors. David et al. [17] improved the readability of the traditional heatmap by ordering the rows and columns together according to their correlation. Comparing with DR, scatterplot matrix, PCP and heatmap can produces a visual result from which all of the original data can be recovered. Furthermore, they can express the relationship between dimensions well. However, with the increase of data dimension and scale, a large number of curves or patches may be intertwined due to the limitation of screen.

The radial layout visualization, represented by Radial coordinate visualization (RadViz) and Star Coordinates (SC), can effectively map high dimensional data to low dimensional space, owing to which can place an arbitrary number of Dimension Anchors (DAs) on the circumference of the circle flexibility. However, one obstacle in the radial layout visualization is that the optimal order of DAs is a NP complete problem [18]. Although many methods have been put forward to solve the problem of visual dimension ordering in radial layout visualization, most of them are exhaustive or greedy local searches [19]. Another way is to enhance the flexibility of the DAS layout by extending the number of dimensions. Sharko [20], Zhou [21] et al. extended the dimension by segment the probability distribution histogram of dimensions. In Sharko' study, the probability distribution histogram in the dimension shows obvious pulse characteristics only at discrete values. Therefore, it can be directly divided according to the impulse location, but his dimension partitioning strategy may not only suitable for the continuous multidimensional data. Zhou segments the probability distribution histogram by mean shift, but it causes local optimal dimension division results. Another problem is that the mapping space is not fully utilized in the visualization of radial coordinates, that is to say, the inter class distance is too small and the intra class distance is too large, hampering visual clustering analysis.

In this paper, we first propose the Quasi-circular mapping visualization (QCMV) based on extending and reordering dimensions for visual clustering analysis. QCMV extend the original dimension of datasets by the probability distribution histogram of the dimension and affinity propagation (AP) algorithm [22]. In additional, distributing them on the unit circle by their correlation according to the correlation of the extended dimensions. Moreover, mapping the dimensions extended and reordered data to integrate a polygon in the Quasi-circular space and visualizing them by the geometric center and area of the polygon in the three dimension. We also compare the visual clustering results of RadViz, SC and QCMV with two indexes, correct rate and Dunn index. Finally, we strengthen their visual clustering effect with t-SNE [23].

The remainder of this paper is structured as follows. In Sect. 2, we present some related work with the radial layout visualization and t-SNE. Section 3 introduces the proposed method. Section 4 is devoted to describe experimental comparison of three methods. Conclusions and future work are drawn in Sect. 5.

2   Related Work

2.1   The Radial Layout Visualization

RadViz is a nonlinear mapping, which based on the model of a physical spring system where the data dimension constitute anchor points. Many researches have put forward some ideas to enhance the visual result of RadViz [20, 24]. SC instead generates linear mappings by calculating linear combinations of a set of low-dimensional vectors that represent radial axes. Like RadViz, SC allows modifying the direction and length of the axis to change the projection. Lehmann et al. [25] preserve the structure of the original dataset in the projection by the concept of orthogonal constraint. Zanabria et al. [26] design a clustering mechanism, which can be performed automatically as well as interactively to mitigate visual clutter.

Although the two methods have different motivations and principles, they are equivalent in some conditions [27]. They can effectively save visual space and achieve the visual clustering effect of multidimensional data in two-dimensional space by observing the clustering structure of the data points projected into the circle intuitively.

2.2   t-SNE

The t-SNE algorithm [23] is proposed by Maaten et al. It models the distribution of the nearest neighbor of each data point, in which the nearest neighbor is a set of data points that are close to each other. It models the high dimensional space and the two-dimensional output space as the Gauss distribution and T distribution separately.

The goal of the process is to find the transformation of a high dimensional space into a two-dimensional space to minimize the difference between all points in the two distribution.

The main advantage of t-SNE is to maintain a local structure, which means that the projection of a point with close distance in a high dimensional data space is still close to a low dimension.

3 Method

Our method of visual clustering analysis is based on QCMV. Firstly, extending the original dimension of dataset by the probability distribution histogram of the dimension and affinity propagation (AP) algorithm. Then, analyzing the correlation of the extended dimensions and distributing them on the unit circle by their correlation. Finally, mapping the extended data to integrate a polygon in the Quasi-circular space and visualizing them by the geometric center and area of the polygon in the three dimension.

3.1 Dimension Expansion

Throughout this paper, we are concerned with visual clustering the data set F includes K records with N dimension. Firstly, normalization for each dimension so that the normalized data set F^* values for each dimension, ranging from zero to one.

$$F^*_{kn} = \frac{F_{kn} - \min(F_n)}{\max(F_n) - \min(F_n)} \tag{1}$$

Where $\max(F_n)$ and $\min(F_n)$ are the maximum value and minimum value of F in n dimension respectively. Then dividing 0 to 1 into r parts, and the probability of data F^* in r sections can be calculated. Finally, the histogram for each dimension are ready.

However, one impediment to extend a dimension to multiple new dimensions is now appropriately segmenting the probability distribution histogram. In this paper, we use AP [22] to segment the probability distribution histogram. AP is a clustering algorithm based on the communication of near neighbor information. The aim is to find the best class to find the sum of the similarity of the representative points and it can be guaranteed to converge to the global optimal. In practice, the AP algorithm can obtain more stable results. At present, this algorithm has been successfully applied to face recognition [28], gene discovery [29], image segmentation [30], etc.

AP algorithm partition dataset according to each data point and the affiliation between data points and the clustering center, which searched through the message transfer mechanism in the network. In fact, the partition of the histogram of probability distribution can be seen to classify a two-dimensional data by AP. One dimension is the value of probability and the other is the value of X-axis of the histogram. After that, each dimension can been extended to a number of new dimensions where one dimension has the original value and the remaining have value zero. And which new dimension have the original value dependent on which partition the value of F^* belongs to in this dimension. So, dimension extended data set $F^\otimes$ can be represented as Eq. (2)

$$F^\otimes = \left(f_1^\otimes(x), f_2^\otimes(x), \ldots, f_N^\otimes(x), \ldots, f_M^\otimes(x)\right) \tag{2}$$

Obviously, $F^\otimes$ have K records with M dimension and $M > N$.

3.2 Dimension Reorder

We rearrange the dimension of $F^\otimes$ based on the similarity between dimensions in this section. The similarity can be measured in various ways, and we choose the Fiedler vector [31] metric.

We begin to denote the M ranks for each record of $F^\otimes$ by their the value, which called rank matrix T

$$T = \left(t_{ij}\right)_{K \times M} \tag{3}$$

Where $t_{ij} = 1, 2, 3, \ldots, M$, $i = 1, 2, \ldots, K$, $j = 1, 2, \ldots, M$. So analyzing of the similarity of the dimension of $F^\otimes$ is equivalent to the similarity of matrix T. Moreover, building up a similarity matrix A to describe the similarity between t_j and t_m based on the squared difference.

$$A = \left(a_{jm}\right)_{M \times M} \tag{4}$$

Where $a_{jm} = 1 - \frac{1}{K(K-1)^2} \sum_{k=1}^{K} \left(t_{kj} - t_{km}\right)^2, j, m = 1, 2, \ldots, M$. Clearly, the greater the rank difference between j dimension and m dimension, the greater the value of a_{jm} is. That is to say, the more similar the two dimensions are, the greater the value of a_{jm} is. And since $\sum_{k=1}^{K} \left(t_{kj} - t_{km}\right)^2 \leq K(K-1)^2$, $0 \leq a_{jm} \leq 1$.

Then, According to formula Eq. (5), the Laplace matrix [32] L is obtained by the similar matrix. And Laplace matrix's the eigenvector corresponding to the maximum eigenvalue is the Fiedler vector. We find the Fiedler vector based on the similar matrix now. Finally, the dimensions are arranged such that the dimensions with the kth smallest value in the Fiedler vector occupies the kth position in the permutation.

$$L = \left(l_{ij}\right)_{M \times M} = D - S \tag{5}$$

Where $D = \left(d_{ij}\right)_{M \times M}$, $d_{ii} = \sum_{j} s_{ij}$. We define the data set of dimension-reordered data set to be F^Δ for convenience.

$$F^\Delta = \left(f_1^\Delta(x), f_2^\Delta(x), \ldots, f_N^\Delta(x), \ldots, f_M^\Delta(x)\right) \tag{6}$$

3.3   The Quasi-circular Mapping

The Quasi-circular Mapping Visualization (QCMV) maps the reordered data F^Δ obtained by Sects. 3.1 and 3.2 to integrate a polygon in the Quasi-circular space and visualizing them by the geometric center and area of the polygon in the three dimension.

The similar circular space C_O is defined as the inner space of a unit circle in a two dimensional Cartesian coordinate system. The ordered dimensions are sequentially distributed on the arc, which called DAs V_i, as shown in Fig. 1(a).

$$V_i = (\cos(\theta_i), \sin(\theta_i)) \tag{7}$$

Where $\theta_1 = 0$, $\theta_i = \dfrac{\sum\limits_{j=1}^{i-1}(s_{\lambda(j)\lambda(j+1)})}{\sum\limits_{j=1}^{M-1}(s_{\lambda(j)\lambda(j+1)})}, i = 2, 3, \ldots, M$, $\lambda(j)$ represents the original

dimension position before the dimension rearrangement of jth dimension for F^Δ.

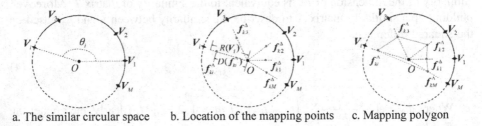

a. The similar circular space   b. Location of the mapping points   c. Mapping polygon

Fig. 1. The schematic diagram of the Quasi-circular mapping

QCMV maps the kth record of F^Δ into M projection points f_{ki}^Δ, $k = 1, 2, \ldots, K$, $i = 1, 2, \ldots, M$, in The Similar Circular space C_O. Figure 1(b) presents that the projection point f_{ki}^Δ, the center O of C_O and dimension anchor V_i are collinear and the distance between f_{ki}^Δ and O is determined by the value of data f_{ki}^Δ and the radius of the kth dimension anchor point.

$$D(f_{ki}^\Delta) = f_{ki}^\Delta * R(V_i) \tag{8}$$

Where $R(V_i) = \dfrac{\sum\limits_{k=1}^{K} f_{ki}^\Delta}{\max\limits_{i=1,\ldots,M} \sum\limits_{k=1}^{K} f_{ki}^\Delta}$. Then, we can construct a polygon $f_{k1}^\Delta f_{k2}^\Delta \cdots f_{kM}^\Delta$ by join

the projection point f_{ki}^Δ with straight lines in turn, which determined by the global information of the dataset. It is easy to get the geometric center of a polygon P_k

$$P_k = (p_{k1}, p_{k2}) = \frac{1}{M} \sum_{i=1}^{M} D(f_{ki}^{\Delta}) V_i \qquad (9)$$

Where $\qquad p_{k1} = \frac{1}{M} \sum_{i=1}^{M} D(f_{ki}^{\Delta}) \cos(\theta_i), \qquad p_{k2} = \frac{1}{M} \sum_{i=1}^{M} D(f_{ki}^{\Delta}) \sin(\theta_i),$

$\theta_i = \dfrac{\sum_{j=1}^{i-1} (s_{\lambda(j)\lambda(j+1)})}{\sum_{j=1}^{M-1} (s_{\lambda(j)\lambda(j+1)})}$ $(i = 2, 3, \ldots, M)$, $\theta_1 = 0$. We further divide the polygon $f_{k1}^{\Delta} f_{k2}^{\Delta} \cdots f_{kM}^{\Delta}$

into the triangle $f_{k1}^{\Delta} O f_{k(i+1)}^{\Delta}$, $i = 1, 2, \ldots, M-1$, so the area S_{Fk} of the polygon is equal to the sum of M triangles area.

$$S_{Fk} = \sum_{i=1}^{M} S_i \qquad (10)$$

Where S_i represents the area of the triangle $f_{k1}^{\Delta} O f_{k(i+1)}^{\Delta}$. So we can build a three-dimensional visualization space containing the geometry center location information P_k and area information S_{Fk} of the polygon, which mapping point coordinates is Q

$$Q = (p_{k1}, p_{k2}, S_{Fk}) \qquad (11)$$

4 Experiments

4.1 Datasets and Metrics

In the experiments, we assess the performance of QCMV based on extending and reordering dimensions when compared traditional RadViz and Star Coordinates by three datasets in Table 1.

Table 1. Datasets description

Name	Instances	Attributes	Class
Iris	150	4	3
Seeds	210	7	3
Ecoli	336	7	8

In addition, we rely on two different metrics to assess the quality of the methods mentioned above. One metric is the correct rate (CR) to evaluate the accuracy of clustering results based on true classification. The other is Dunn Index (DI) [33] which assess the clustering effect by a non-linear combination of intraclass and interclass distances. DI is defined as follows:

$$D = \min_{i=1,\ldots,nc}\left\{ \min_{j=i+1,\ldots,nc}\left\{ \frac{\min\limits_{x\in C_i, y\in C_j} d(x,y)}{\min\limits_{k=1,\ldots,nc}\{\max\limits_{x,y\in C_k} d(x,y)\}} \right\} \right\}$$ (12)

Where nc is the number of clusters, $d(x,y)$ is the Euler distance of point x and point y, $\min\limits_{x\in C_i, y\in C_j} d(x,y)$ is the distance between clusters C_i and clusters C_j, $\max\limits_{x,y\in C_k} d(x,y)$ is the diameter of the cluster C_k. It is obvious that the more compact within the cluster and the more separation between the clusters, the smaller the maximum distance in the cluster is and the larger the minimum distance between the clusters is. So large values of D suggest well-separated clusters.

4.2   Results and Analysis

In the first experiment, we use the iris data to describe the process of our method in detail again. Figure 2 depicts the probability distribution histogram of iris's four dimensions. We divide 0 to 1 into 20 parts, i.e. $r = 20$. Furthermore, Fig. 3 shows the segmentation results of four dimensions in the iris data by AP. For example, the first dimension, sepal length in the iris data are divided into 3 parts, including the number of probability 6, 7, 7, respectively. That is to say, the first dimension of the iris data is expanded into three new dimensions. In additional, the histogram is divided where the probability is 0.3 and 0.65. If the values of 3 records in the original first dimension of the iris data are 0.2, 0.5, 0.8, their values in the new extended dimensions are [0.2, 0, 0], [0, 0.5, 0], [0, 0, 0.8] respectively.

We only extend the fourth dimension of the iris data and rearrange the extended dimension according to their correlation in the Fig. 4(c) and (d). Figure 4(d) is a three-dimensional visualization of the information of the geometric center and area. However, Fig. 4(c) only express the information of the geometric center. The other two figure in Fig. 4 are RadViz and SC. Figure 4 represent the three-class iris by red, green, and blue data points. Figure 4 show that RadViz and SC are overlapped on some red and blue points, which means only one class of iris can be easily distinguished. Moreover, we can clearly see that one blue point clustering is mistaken in the SC method. Nevertheless, the points of three colors are ideally separate separated into 3 classes by QCMV in Fig. 4(c) and (d) and the number of erroneous classification points is only 6.

Figures 5 and 6 show the other two groups of data, the seeds data and the Ecoli data, visualizations. In Fig. 5(a) and (b), the points of the three clusters are mapped to a similar position, that is, RadViz and SC cannot distinguish the three class of seeds. But achieving the better visual effect by QCMV in Fig. 5(c) and (d). Especially in Fig. 5(d), however the blue and green points can still not be separated; most of the red points have been separated from those. Nevertheless, comparing with the RadViz and SC, although QCMV also cannot classify the data, its clustering visualization is improved.

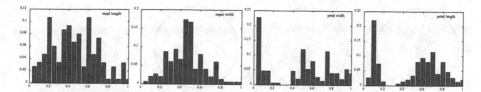

Fig. 2. Probability distribution histograms of four dimensions in the iris data

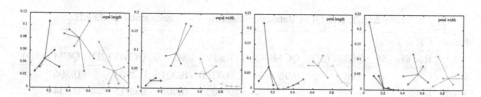

Fig. 3. The segmentation results of four dimensions in the iris data by AP

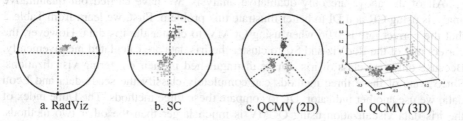

a. RadViz   b. SC   c. QCMV (2D)   d. QCMV (3D)

Fig. 4. The visualization methods in the iris data

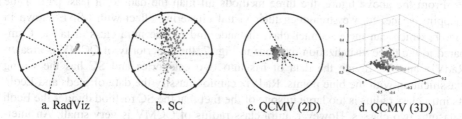

a. RadViz   b. SC   c. QCMV (2D)   d. QCMV (3D)

Fig. 5. The visualization methods in the seeds data

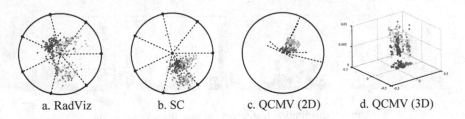

a. RadViz   b. SC   c. QCMV (2D)   d. QCMV (3D)

Fig. 6. The visualization methods in the Ecoli data

Table 2. CR and DI of datasets clustering ('-' means not calculated)

Name	CR				DI			
	RadViz	SC	QCMV(2D)	QCMV(2D)	RadViz	SC	QCMV(2D)	QCMV(3D)
Iris	–	–	0.96	0.96	0.0250	0.0016	0.2903	0.3061
Seeds	–	–	–	–	0.0055	0.0054	0.0015	0.0344
Ecoli	–	–	–	–	0.0022	0.0016	0.0043	0.0049

All of the above are only qualitative analysis, we have carried out quantitative analysis using CR and DI to better illustrate this problem. First, we learn from Table 2 that the correct rate is 0.96 when using QCMV to cluster the iris data. However, the correct rate of the RadViz and SC to cluster the iris data are calculated inconveniently. Because only one class of iris can be distinguished in their clustering visualizations. Since none of these three methods can completely classify the seeds data and Ecoli data, we use another indicator, DI, to compare these three methods. The Dune index of the iris data visualization using QCMV is much larger than the other two methods. Combined with the previous CR, it advise that QCMV improve the cluster analysis effect. Most of the cases that the Dune index of QCMV is the largest, followed by the RadViz, and the minimum of SC. Only when visualizing the seeds data, QCMV's Dunn indicator is smaller than the other two methods in two dimension.

From the above figure, the three methods all map the data to at least part of the mapping space. So we strengthen their visual clustering effect with t-SNE shown in Fig. 7, which can increase inter class distance and reduce intra class distance. Compared to the three visualization methods in Fig. 7, the superiority of QCMV is greater. RadViz and SC divide the data of iris into two categories and SC has the wrong classification with the blue points. RadViz cannot classify the data of seeds and Ecoli. Its intra class radius is too large in spite of the fact that the SC method divides the Ecoli data into two classes. However, intra class radius of QCMV is very small. An interesting phenomenon is that the QCMV separates the classes of the seed represented by the most of the blue points and the most of the red points in two dimension and three dimension separately.

Name	RadViz	SC	QCMV(2D)	QCMV(3D)
Iris				
Seeds				
Ecoli				

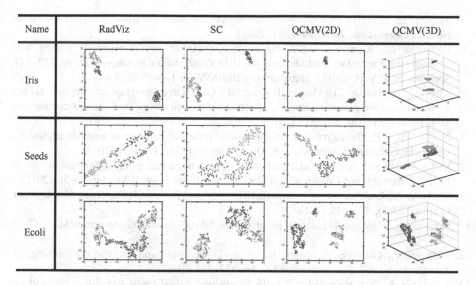

Fig. 7. Strengthening visual effect with t-SNE

5   Conclusions and Future Work

In this, we recommend QCMV to solve the problem of DAs sorting and cluster crowding. QCMV solves the first issue by extending and sorting dimension and use the characteristics of t-SNE algorithm to address the second problem. It shows better effect of visual clustering and better value of metrics with QCMV, when comparing to RadViz, SC.

As a future work, we will focus on finding out which dimensions and their combination extensions will optimize the visual clustering results. Therefore, we will call for more intelligent and efficient criteria for judging.

For another work, we want to improve ability of our method to solve the problem dimensional disasters. Because QCMV which utilizes the method of dimension extension lead to the dimension of the high dimension data to rise again.

References

1. Wang, Y., Li, Z., Wang, Y., et al.: A novel approach for stable selection of informative redundant features from high dimensional fMRI data. Comput. Sci. **146**, 191–208 (2016)
2. Engel, D., Hummel, M., Hoepel, F., et al.: Towards high-dimensional data analysis in air quality research. In: Eurographics Conference on Visualization. The Eurographs Association & John Wiley & Sons, Ltd., pp. 101–110 (2013)
3. Zhang, X., Lai, S.Q., Liu, N.W.: Research on cloud computing data security model based on multi-dimension. In: International Symposium on Information Technology in Medicine and Education, IEEE, pp. 897–900 (2012)
4. Wold, S., Esbensen, K., Geladi, P.: Principal component analysis. Chemometr. Intell. Lab. Syst. **2**(1), 37–52 (1987)

5. Mohebi, E., Bagirov, A.: Constrained self organizing maps for data clusters visualization. Neural Process. Lett. **43**(3), 849–869 (2016)
6. Dzemyda, G., Kurasova, O., Žilinskas, J.: Combining multidimensional scaling with artificial neural networks. Multidimensional Data Visualization. SOIA, vol. 75, pp. 113–177. Springer, New York (2013). https://doi.org/10.1007/978-1-4419-0236-8_4
7. Kireeva, N., Baskin, I.I., Gaspar, H.A., et al.: Generative topographic mapping (GTM): universal tool for data visualization, structure-activity modeling and dataset comparison. Mol. Inform. **31**(3–4), 301–312 (2012)
8. Xie, Y., Sun, P.: Terahertz data combined with principal component analysis applied for visual classification of materials. Opt. Quant. Electron. **50**(1), 46–57 (2018)
9. Sarlin, P., Marghescu, D.: Visual predictions of currency crises using self-organizing maps. In: IEEE International Conference on Data Mining Workshops. IEEE, pp. 15–38 (2011)
10. Sarikaya, A., Gleicher, M.: Scatterplots: tasks, data and designs. IEEE Trans. Vis. Comput. Graphics **24**(1), 402–412 (2018)
11. Heinrich, J., Weiskopf, D.: State of the art of parallel coordinates. Eurographics **34**(1), 17–25 (2012)
12. Hoffman, P., Grinstein, G., Marx, K., et al.: DNA visual and analytic data mining. In: Visualization 1997, Proceedings. IEEE, pp. 437–441 (1997)
13. Kandogan, E.: Star coordinates: a multi-dimensional visualization technique with uniform treatment of dimensions. In: Proceedings of the IEEE Information Visualization Symposium Late Breaking Hot Topics, pp. 9–12 (2000)
14. Kandogan, E.: Visualizing multi-dimensional clusters, trends, and outliers using star coordinates. In: ACM SIGKDD International Conference on Knowledge Discovery and Data Mining, DBLP, pp. 107–116 (2001)
15. Cerdas, F., Kaluza, A., Erkisi-Arici, S., et al.: Improved visualization in LCA through the application of cluster heat maps. Procedia CIRP **61**, 732–737 (2017)
16. Li, M., Zhen, L., Yao, X.: How to read many-objective solution sets in parallel coordinates [educational forum]. IEEE Comput. Intell. Mag. **12**(4), 88–100 (2017)
17. Walker, D.J., Everson, R., Fieldsend, J.E.: Visualizing mutually nondominating solution sets in many-objective optimization. IEEE Trans. Evol. Comput. **17**(2), 165–184 (2013)
18. Ankerst, M., Berchtold, S., Keim, D.A.: Similarity clustering of dimensions for an enhanced visualization of multidimensional data. In: IEEE Symposium on Information Visualization, 1998. Proceedings. IEEE, vol. 153, pp. 52–60 (1998)
19. Di Caro, L., Frias-Martinez, V., Frias-Martinez, E.: Analyzing the role of dimension arrangement for data visualization in RadViz. In: Zaki, M.J., Yu, J.X., Ravindran, B., Pudi, V. (eds.) PAKDD 2010. LNCS (LNAI), vol. 6119, pp. 125–132. Springer, Heidelberg (2010). https://doi.org/10.1007/978-3-642-13672-6_13
20. Sharko, J., Grinstein, G., Marx, K.A.: Vectorized RadViz and its application to multiple cluster datasets. IEEE Trans. Vis. Comput. Graph. **14**(6), 1427–1444 (2008)
21. Zhou, F., Huang, W., Li, J., et al.: Extending dimensions in RadViz based on mean shift. In: Visualization Symposium. IEEE, pp. 111–115 (2015)
22. Dueck, D., Frey, B.J.: Non-metric affinity propagation for unsupervised image categorization. IEEE International Conference on Computer Vision. IEEE, pp. 1–8 (2007)
23. Maaten, L.V.D., Hinton, G.: Visualizing data using t-SNE. J. Mach. Learn. Res. **9**(2605), 2579–2605 (2008)
24. Russell, A., Daniels, K., Grinstein, G.: Voronoi diagram based dimensional anchor assessment for radial visualizations. In: International Conference on Information Visualisation, pp. 229–233. IEEE (2012)
25. Lehmann, D.J., Theisel, H.: Orthographic star coordinates. IEEE Trans. Vis. Comput. Graph. **19**(12), 2615–2624 (2013)

26. Zanabria, G.G., Nonato, L.G., Gomez-Nieto, E.: iStar (i*): an interactive star coordinates approach for high-dimensional data exploration. Comput Graph. **60**, 107 118 (2016)
27. Rubiosanchez, M., Raya, L., Diaz, F., et al.: A comparative study between RadViz and star coordinates. IEEE Trans. Vis. Comput. Graph. **22**(1), 619–628 (2015)
28. Gan, H., Sang, N., Huang, R.: Self-training-based face recognition using semi-supervised linear discriminant analysis and affinity propagation. J. Opt. Soc. Am. A **31**(1), 1–6 (2014)
29. Sharma, S., Agrawal, A., Patel, D.: Class aware exemplar discovery from microarray gene expression data. In: Kumar, N., Bhatnagar, V. (eds.) BDA 2015. LNCS, vol. 9498, pp. 244–257. Springer, Cham (2015). https://doi.org/10.1007/978-3-319-27057-9_17
30. Xie, Q., Remil, O., Guo, Y., et al.: Object detection and tracking under occlusion for object-level RGB-D video segmentation. IEEE Trans. Multimed. **20**(3), 580–592 (2018)
31. Kaveh, A., Rahimi Bondarabady, H.A.: Finite element mesh decomposition using complementary Laplacian matrix. Commun. Numer. Methods Eng. **16**(6), 379–389 (2000)
32. Fiedler, M.: Algebraic connectivity of graphs. Czechoslovak Math. J. **23**(23), 298–305 (1973)
33. Wunsch, D., Xu, R.: Clustering (IEEE Press Series on Computational Intelligence). IEEE Computer Society Press, Washington DC (2008)

The Research on Security Audit for Information System Classified Protection

Hui Lu[1]([✉]), Xiang Cui[1], Le Wang[1], Yu Jiang[1], and Meng Cui[2]

[1] Cyberspace Institute of Advanced Technology, Guangzhou University,
Guangzhou 510006, China
luhui@gzhu.edu.cn
[2] Research Center of Computer Network and Information Security Technology,
Harbin Institute of Technology, Harbin, Heilongjiang Province, China

Abstract. In the first part of this article, we'll introduce the security problem and the shortage of the now-widely-used security tools to expatiate on why we need Security Audit System. In the second part what is Security Audit System will be introduced. After this part we'll also introduce the techniques related to Security Audit. And in the forth part some methods to implement Security Audit System will be analysed. Some essential points when implementing a Security Audit System will be talk about in the last part.

Keywords: Security audit · User authentication
Techniques of security events correlation

1 The Meaning of Security Audit System

In recent years, network technology has developed rapidly. Internet has deeply into our lives. With the rapid development of Internet, network security and information security issues are also increasingly serious. Faced with these problems have been proposed a variety of security methods, which are used widely as firewall technology and intrusion detection technologies (IDS). But the two technologies mentioned above are not perfect, there are many problems and limitations. And the details will be introduced below.

1.1 The Now-Used Security System's Shortage

(1) The Shortage of Firewall

Firewall was earlier applicated than most of other security systems. Firewall technology is a security technology can be divided into packet filtering firewall and proxy gateway firewall. But both of the two categories's main idea is to be established isolation between the external network and the internal net work, control external access to protect the internal network, which by controlling the flow of data through a firewall to shield sensitive information from the internal network from external threats as well as block [3].

X. Sun et al. (Eds.): ICCCS 2018, LNCS 11064, pp. 300–308, 2018.
https://doi.org/10.1007/978-3-030-00009-7_28

Although the development of this technology is a long time, relatively mature, but its shortcomings are obvious. First, the internal firewall can only prevent external attacks, not prevent attacks from within. Second, in most cases firewalls are implemented on coarse-grained access control, inspection and control of communications content rarely [4, 7, 9]. Another point is firewall always to be very complex configuration management. Network administrators have to own a higher professional quality, making the technology difficult to use

(2) The Shortage of Intrusion Detection System

Intrusion Detection System (IDS) can detect many kinds of intrusion attacks, and its greatest feature is real time. It can generate warning at the first time when attacked to the network administrator. But it is this characteristic is the speed of the performance of intrusion detection is critical, therefore decided to use the data analysis of their algorithm can not be too complicated, it is impossible to use for a long time or window of historical data combined with real-time data analysis. So now most of the intrusion detection system is, only a single data packet or packets within a short time, a simple analysis to make judgments, which will inevitably result in higher false positive rate and false negative rate. Generally only 20% of the attacks intrusion detection system that is not surprising. And while technology continues to evolve with the hackers, more and more attacks then turned to the attacks on intrusion detection systems, intrusion detection system because there are defects, so a growing number of hacker attacks to bypass intrusion detection systems.

1.2 The Current Network Security Situation

Existing network security situation has the following characteristics: a. Network systems have more unsafe factors: the communication lines are weak links in network security, line interference, eavesdropping interception and other attacks penetrate security capabilities of the system put forward new requirements; b. Network security is more breadth and depth: on the one hand, the hidden network security threats and potential increased the difficulty of security and resistance. Extensive and difficult to prevent objects clearly; the other hand, the system faces against the various means and strong attacks, and the trend of increasing complexity; C. Network security is more relative: There is no absolute security of computer systems, any system of security is relative, and computer networks need to consider more comprehensive sets of factors, the greater the relative safety; d. Network Security has a more important role and significance: Once the network security system has been compromised, often lead to very serious consequences and even result in paralysis of the entire network.

The existing security system, the biggest problem is that the invasion from within and attack detection and prevention is weak, not only highly vulnerable to destruction from within, and often resulted in huge losses, and later held responsibility there are many difficult issues. Violations within the staff generally has two forms: one is the internal staff operate out of the result is the impact of system security; the other is a purpose to steal resources.

In summary, the current system provides many security audit is only part of the network range (such as a host or part of the network segment) within the recorded security-related events and do a preliminary audit analysis, is neither comprehensive nor profound. Especially for large, distributed network system even more so. And network security is a whole concept in itself, need to develop a global system of safety audits to ensure that range across the network to provide effective security auditing services. Security for the current form, we need a system to compensate for the deficiencies of existing security systems, while integrating various security devices from the safety record of the corresponding analysis and processing, and timely reports to the invasion, and subsequent provide the basis for accountability, which is made to the system security audit.

2 Introduction to Security Audit

2.1 The Concept of Security Audit

Information security audit system mainly refers to the activities of security-related information such as identification, recording, storage and analysis. Information security audit log to check what security-related activities happened on the network, who is responsible for this activity. Normally the Security Audit System's structure as shown below (Fig. 1).

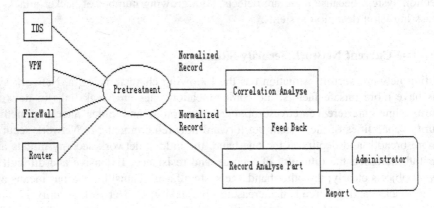

Fig. 1. Security audit system structure chart

2.2 The Requirements of the Security Audit System

In 1999, the International Standards Organization and International Electrotechnical Commission published "Information Technology- Security Techniques - Evaluation Criteria for IT Security - Part 2: Security Functional Requirements First Edition", referred as the CC quasi-side. CC criteria with the use of information technology security evaluation criteria, in which the definition of network security audit a complete set of features, such as automatic response to security event, security audit event generation, security audit analysis, security audit browsing, security audit events storage and a series of functions.

In the TCSEC (Trusted Computer System Evaluation Criteria) guidelines, but also on the safety audit system for the basic requirements, including: Audit information must be selectively retained and protection, and security-related activities can be traced to the responsible party, the audit system can be effectively analyzed.

From the above criteria which points out several important requirements for the security audit system, it is not difficult to see that the security audit system is not just a simple log system. Especially as network attacks and destruction become more and more serious, security audit system was put forward higher requirements. We should be guided by these international standards, according to our own system conditions, security needs and problems faced by the specific needs to develop our safety audit system.

3 Technologies Related to Security Audit System

Security audit system is an integrated system, its functions are extremely complex, it must not only be able to handle security log from different data systems or safety equipment, in a timely manner and make the appropriate response, but also need to be able to analyze the safety record of relationship between intrinsic. In order to achieve these functions, we need a range of technologies to support, the following were the two major technologies: authentication technologies and associated technical analysis techniques will be introduced respectively [1, 2].

3.1 Authentication Technology

To nensure the safety record's identify characteristic abd non-repudiation characteristic, we need to use authentication technology. The following is a brief introduction for authentication technologies.

(1) The concept of identity authentication technology

Authentication technology is the process that operator's identity is recognized by the computer. In the secure network communication, the parties involved in the communication must be through some form of authentication mechanism to prove their identity. Must firstly verify the identity of the user are consistent with the claims, and then to achieve access control for different users and records [5, 6].

(2) Several popular authentication technologies
(a) Based on DCE/Kerberos authentication mechanism
Based on DCE/Kerberos the user authentication to log on through a secure server. Obtain proof of identity. Of course, the user must log on before has been registered. At the same time the client must be running DCE client software.

DCE/Kerberos is a proven approach for the very secure authentication technology. DCE/Kerberos authentication stressed client authentication on the server or other products, only to solve the authentication server to the client.

(b) Public key-based authentication mechanism
Internet is also used the public key-based authentication security policy. In particular, the use of consistent x.509 identity. Using this method proved to be a third-party authorization center of the company issued identification. Client and server to obtain their certificate from a certificate authority center, and trust the certification authority center. And communications in the session when the first exchange of identification, which include their public key guitar that will give the other side, then use the other's public key to verify the digital signature of each other and exchange encryption keys and other communications in determining whether to accept each other's identity certification, the need to check on the server to confirm that the certificate is valid, the specific process as shown below (Fig. 2).

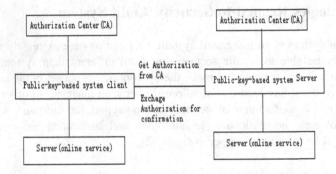

Fig. 2. Public key based authentication system flow chart

(C) Based on challenge/response authentication mechanism
Based on challenge and response (Challenge/Response) authentication mechanism is the mode of authentication, authentication server each time gave the client sends a different challenge string, the client program after receiving the challenge string, to make the appropriate response. Radius authentication mechanism is known in this way. Its design idea is to use UDP between client and server interact to make light of; using challenge/response authentication to avoid password transmitted over the network; certification carried out from time to time, and each certified message different, and prevent others to "replay" attacks, but also to ensure that users will not be damaged by other fraudulent use of the address (Fig. 3).

3.2 Correlation Analysis Technology

To many of the current security system, on one hand due to the limitations of the individual tools, there are many fake warning because they can not identify normal behavior; the other hand, a single attack may caused multiple repeated warnings, to create difficulties for the administrator to make the right judgments; more importantly, network attacks become more complex, the distribution of an offensive attack by a number of steps in the process of composition, multiple steps and completely may be implemented in different places, so relying on a single event log, is too trivial, not

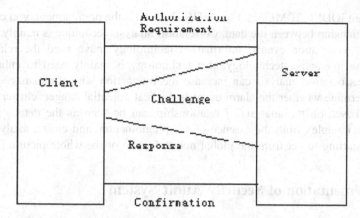

Fig. 3. Challenge/response mechanism for the certification process

reflect complete picture of the aggressive behavior and, therefore, can not capture those who planned, complex attack steps. [11–13] Therefore, we need correlation analysis technology to security audit system for all security incidents to support the overall management.

(1) The concept of association analysis

To the security audit system, the correlation analysis is on distributed nodes (IDS, FireWall and Anomaly Detectors) provide a comprehensive analysis of security incidents in order to facilitate management of a comprehensive monitoring network security technology. Correlation analysis to solve the problem such as analysis may be a single alarm event by contacting the different security scene, in order to avoid false alarms; deal with the same, similar alarm event to avoid duplication of alarms; improve the analysis of real-time, in order to facilitate timely response; mining deep-seated, complex attacks, to identify the planned attack, thereby increasing the attack detection rate. Association analysis in general can be regarded as subordinate event generator presented the findings of the comprehensive analysis, in a sense, association analysis engine itself into a monitor [15–17]. It may like rule-based IDS with the same working principle, but it's "rules" more complex.

(2) The key technologies Correlation Analysis associated with

Correlation analysis can usually be divided into three phases: pretreatment, analysis, and present the results for the response. During the pretreatment, pretreatment technology used mainly for integration of the safety record for future work, we must first get rid of duplicate reports, while the grading of events for more targeted after the treatment. Association analysis is to rely on the node under the jurisdiction of the IDS, VPN gateway, firewall, routers, security devices, these security features to provide information to the global situation of network security to make judgments. Therefore, another task for pretreatment is carried out on normalized event record, the record of events from different security devices, formats often vary widely, in order to facilitate the work needed after the record format of these. The description of standards for reference are IODEF, IDMEF and so on [18–20]. After the pretreatment, you can study on the relationship between the data. Correlation analysis technique is mainly used for analysis of association events, information technology, have used the relationship between the interactive technology, this technology is mainly used to enhance the relevance association analysis can increase the interaction with the managed system link to determine whether the alarm event is the real potential danger; cluster analysis technique based on the analysis of relationship can be seen as the details begin to analyze the complex from the essence of the phenomenon, and cluster analysis technology is starting to get from the global network state of the whole picture [21].

4 Implementation of Security Audit System

There are many types of security audit system implementation, the following implementation of the more popular ways to make a brief introduction.

4.1 Rule-Based Database Security Audit System

Rule-based security audit database of known attack method is to conduct feature extraction, these features of scripting languages and other methods used to describe the rule base after the release, when the security audit, network data will be collected with these rules a comparison and matching operations (keywords, regular expressions, fuzzy approximation degree, etc.), to discover possible network attacks. This method is characterized by simple matching networks to filter out a lot of data, hacker tools for the use of a particular network attacks are particularly effective. Because of its simple structure makes the system scalability is very good. However, this approach is that the attack must first know the type or specific software. But the attacks used by hackers on the slightest change to the possible omission. This variant of the current hacker attacks do nothing more than the status quo.

4.2 Based on Statistics of the Security Audit System

Mathematical statistics is the first to create a statistics object description, such as a network traffic, on average, variance, etc., the statistics of these characteristics under normal circumstances, the amount of value, then the actual network packets used to compare the situation, When they find out the actual value from the normal value, can be considered a potential attack. However, the biggest problem of mathematical statistics is how to set the statistics of the "threshold", which is the normal value and abnormal cutoff point values, which often depends on the administrator's experience, inevitably prone to false positives and false negative.

4.3 Based on Data Mining Security Audit System

To address the detection of unknown attacks, people are increasingly concerned about the learning ability of safety systems. With learning ability using data mining methods, to achieve a general framework for network security audit system prototype. The main idea of the system is "normal" network traffic data found in the "normal" network traffic patterns. And a number of attacks and conventional rules of library association analysis, to achieve the purpose of detecting network intrusions [3].

5   Security Audit System Design POINTS

Our security audit system in the design of the main aspects to be concerned about are:
Data sources, source of data in security audit system, mainly through the intrusion detection system, fire walls, embedded module available; audit system's analysis mechanism is the core of the audit system. A system without the ability to analysis and judge the abnormal is not required to play the role of the audit system. The audit system includes real-time analysis mechanisms and after analysis. Real-time analysis gives the network administrator the report as an exception at the first time [7]. Achieved through hindsight can enhance event processing and record to audit records to perform a better destination for emergency treatment and exercises as well as realize the organic integration of technology and management; the relationship between the original system, in the important areas of information systems, we need to implement multi-angle multi-level security audit, the audit system and the relationship between the original system also needs further attention. System of relations, including: fully transparent type, the original system does not know the existence of security audit system, the original operation of the system without regard to security audit system; loosely coupled type, in order to achieve security audit system for only a small amount of the original system change; closely bound, legacy systems need to make a major change in security audit system; integrated design, the time in the system design, security auditing system to consider with an excuse, so that all modules of the original system contains audit system interface [8, 9]. We consider the original system and the relationship between security audit system in the design criteria is that we should be but at the same time the audit system to ensure the normal operation of the existing system and make changes to the original system and impact to a minimum.

Acknowledgment. This paper is supported by the National Natural Science Foundation of China under Grant No. 61572153 and the National Key research and Development Plan (Grant No. 2018YFB0803504).

References

1. Habra, N., Le Charlier, B., Mounji, A., Mathieu, I.: Preliminary Report on Advanced Security Audit Trail Analysis on Unix (ASAX also called SAT-X)
2. CCITT Recommendation X.740 Information Technology – Open System Interconnection - System Management: Security Audit Trail Function
3. Lee, W., Stolfo, S.J.: Data Mining Approaches for Intrusion Detection. Computer Science Department, Columbia University (1998)
4. Safford, D.R., Schales, D.L., Hess, D.K.: The TAMU Security Package: An Ongoing Response to Internet Intruders in an Academic Environment. Supercomputer Center, Texas A&M University (1993)

5. Vigna, G.: Inspect: A Lightweight Distributed Approach to Automated Audit Trail Analysis
6. Bishop, M., Wee, C., Frank, J.: Goal Oriented Auditing and Logging. Department of Computer Science, University of California at Davis (1996)
7. U.S. National Computer Security Center. A Guide to Understanding Audit in Trusted System (1988)
8. Moeller, R.R.: Computer Audit. Control and Security. Wiley, New York (1989)
9. U.S. National Computer Security Center Trusted Network Interpretation of the Trusted Computer System Evaluation Criteria
10. Haines, J.: Ryder, DK: Validation of sensor alert correlators. IEEE Secur. Priv. 1(1), 46–56 (2003)
11. Kliger, S., Yemini, S.: A coding approach to event correlation. In: Proceedings of 4th International Symposium on Integrated Network Management (IFIP/IEEE), Santa Barbara, CA (1995)
12. Gruschke, B.: Integrated Event Management Event Correlation Using Dependency Graphs (1998)
13. Hasan, M., Sugla, B., Viswanathan, R.: A conceptual framework for network management event correlation and filtering systems. In: Proceedings of the Sixth IFIP/IEEE International Symposium on Integrated Management (1999)
14. Liu, G., Mok, A.K., Yang, E.J.: Composite events for network event correlation. In: Proceedings of the Sixth IFIP/IEEE International Symposium on Integrated Network Management, Distributed Management for the Networked Millennium, pp. 247–260. IEEE (1999)
15. Ohsie, D., Mayer, A., Kliger, S.: Event modeling with the MODEL language: a tutorial introduction (2004)
16. Cuppens, F., Miege, A.: Alert correlation in a cooperative intrusion detection framework. In: Proceedings of 2002 IEEE Symposium on Security and privacy, pp. 202–215. IEEE (2002)
17. Gula, R.: Correlating IDS alerts with vulnerability information (2004)
18. Debar, H., Wespi, A.: Aggregation and correlation of intrusion-detection alerts. In: Lee, W., Mé, L., Wespi, A. (eds.) RAID 2001. LNCS, vol. 2212, pp. 85–103. Springer, Heidelberg (2001). https://doi.org/10.1007/3-540-45474-8_6
19. Lee, W., Stolfo, S.J.: A framework for constructing features and models for intrusion detection systems. ACM Trans. Inf. Syst. Secur. 3(4), 227–261 (2000)
20. Stolfo, S.J., Lee, W.: Data mining-based intrusion detectors: an overview of the Columbia IDS project. SIGMOD Rec. 30(4), 5–14 (2001)
21. Lee, W., Stolfo, S.J.: Real time data mining-based intrusion detection. In: Proceedings of DISCEX II (2001)
22. Locasto, M.E., Parekh, J.J., Stolfo, S., Keromytis, A.D., Malkin, T.G., Misra, V.: Collaborative distributed intrusion detection (2004)

Topk Service Composition Algorithm Based on Optimal QoS

Gen Li[1,2], Kejie Wen[1,2(✉)], Yaxuan Wu[1,2], and Baili Zhang[1,2]

[1] School of Computer Science and Engineering,
Southeast University, Nanjing 211189, China
913106903@qq.com
[2] Research Center for Judicial Big Data,
Supreme Count of China, Nanjing 211189, China

Abstract. The existing QoS-based Topk service composition algorithm can not guarantee the accuracy and time performance of the service composition. This paper proposes a QoS optimal Topk service composition algorithm based on service dependency graph. The algorithm aims to construct the relationship between services by applying the service dependency graph model and to reduce the traversal space through effective filtering strategies. On the basis of a combined path traversal sequence, the generated service composition is represented directly to avoid retrospective searching. Meanwhile, the process removes the redundant service from the service composition with the idea of dynamic programming. Experiments show that the algorithm has better time performance and higher service composition accuracy for large data sets.

Keywords: Service composition · Graph model · Path traversal sequence
Optimal QoS

1 Introduction

In recent years, with the emergence of service-oriented computing frameworks such as SOA, cloud computing and microservices, web services have played an increasingly important role as the most basic logical computing unit of these frameworks. However, the functionality provided by single web service is limited. How to combine existing web services to user's complex needs has become a research hot spot [1]. The current research of most Web service composition algorithms focuses on finding a QoS-optimal service composition scheme [2–10]. However, a single service composition does not meet user's preference requirements well. Meanwhile, service failure caused by the change of the network environment, reduces the availability of a single service composition greatly. Therefore, it becomes urgent to provide users with QoS-based Topk service composition solutions.

Topk service composition solutions can not only provide users with more choices but also avoid the occurrence of "service overheating" caused by frequent selection of a single service composition, making it possible to provide better load balancing for service composition system. Many researchers have proposed their own solutions to the problem of Topk service composition based on optimal QoS [11–15]. However, most

© Springer Nature Switzerland AG 2018
X. Sun et al. (Eds.): ICCCS 2018, LNCS 11064, pp. 309–321, 2018.
https://doi.org/10.1007/978-3-030-00009-7_29

of their algorithms have problems such as poor accuracy and poor algorithm performances. Therefore, this paper proposes a Topk service composition algorithm QWSC-K based on service dependency graph. According to a combined path traversal sequence, the generated service composition is represented directly to avoid retrospective searching. Meanwhile, the process removes the redundant service from the service composition with the idea of dynamic programming.

2 Related Knowledge and the Definition of Problems Connected

2.1 Service Dependency Graph Model

This paper uses the service dependency graph $G = (V, E)$ to model the Web service set.

In G, the node set V represents a set of Web services. Each Web service Wi in the Web service set is represented as a node in G. The directed edge set E represents a set of service matches. The set satisfies: $\forall e_k \in E, e_k = (v_n, v_m, tag_k)$. Among them, v_n and v_m respectively represent the service nodes corresponding to the start and the end of the edge, and tag_k satisfies the following relationship: $tag_k \in v_n . O$; $tag_k \in v_m . I$.

When there is a service request R, the entrance service node *Start* and the exit service node *End* are dynamically generated in the figure, and the two service nodes satisfy the following relationship: $Start.I = \emptyset$; $Start . O = R . I$; $End . I = R . O$; $End . O = \emptyset$.

If the service set is the described service in Table 1, the service request is $R = <I, O>$. The request input parameter $I = \{A, B, C\}$ and the request output parameter $O = \{D\}$. The service dependency graph constructed is shown in Fig. 1.

Table 1. Service node

Service name	Input parameters	Output parameters	QoS value
v_1	A ,B, C	D	900
v_2	A, B	E, F	100
v_3	C, E	H	200
v_4	C, F	G	500
v_5	L, J	D	600
v_6	K	H	500
v_7	H	D	200
v_8	G	H	500

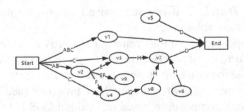

Fig. 1. Service dependency graph

2.2   The Definition of Problems Concerned

Definition 1 (QoS-based Topk Service Composition). Given a service request R and a service dependency graph $G = (V, E)$, a sub-atlas SG is found from G. SG is the QoS-optimized top k service composition. Each sub graph SG_i represents a service composition that satisfies R and satisfies the following conditions:

(1) $SG_i . I = R . I$; $SG_i . O = R . O$
(2) $|SG| = k$
(3) $\forall SG_i \in SG, \neg(\exists SG_i' \in (SG_{all} - SG) \wedge SG_i' . QoS \succ SG_i . QoS)$

Where $\succ$ denotes $SG_i' . QoS$. QoS is better than $SG_i . QoS$. QoS (e.g. the response time of the service composition is less), and SG_{all} represents all subgraphs satisfying R in the service dependency graph G.

2.3   Global QoS Calculation Rules

In the service dependency graph, the global QoS (GQoS) calculation rule is mainly determined by the combination mode and QoS type of the graph.

QoS type is generally divided into two types. One type is negative, that is, the greater the QoS value, the worse the service QoS, such as response time and price. The other is the affirmative type, that is, the greater the QoS value, the better the service QoS. In order to perform unified metrics on multiple QoS, QoS can be divided into the four categories according to different measurement methods: (1) Accumulation type (2) the minimum type (3) Product type. (4) Maximum type.

In the combination mode of the graph, since the sub-graphs obtained by the service composition mostly appear as a directed acyclic graph (DAG), they mainly contain three kinds of combination modes: Sequence, Joint, and Split.

According to different combinations of graphs, the response time is taken as an example. The global calculation rules for QoS as a service are shown in Table 2.

Table 2. GQoS calculation rules

Mode	Calculation rules
Sequence	$w . GQ = w . Q + \sum_{i=1}^{n} w_i . Q$
Joint	$w . GQ = w . Q + \max\{w_i . GQ\}|_{i=1}^{n}$
Split	$w_k . GQ = w . GQ + w_k . Q (1 \leq k \leq n)$

3   Combination Algorithm Description

The overall structure of the QWSC-K algorithm and its related processes mainly include three modules: layered filtering module, a combined sequence module and combination path conversion module. The main framework is shown in Fig. 2.

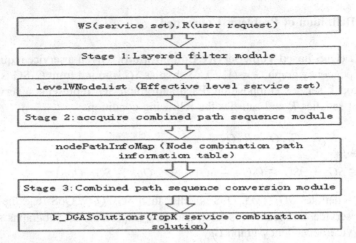

Fig. 2. Combination algorithm flow

3.1   Layered Filter Module

For user's service request, the number of services ultimately, which is associated in the service composition, is often very small, compared with the entire service set. Therefore, these unrelated services can be eliminated before the service composition is generated. Thereby they will reduce the search space in the service composition process.

To meet this end, an effective hierarchical filtering algorithm is proposed (*Hierarchical filtering algorithm, HF_Alg*). The algorithm is divided into two stages. In the first stage, a parameter set is initialized by using the service request input parameter I_R, and then the entire service set is traversed. The service which is triggered by the parameter set is added to the hierarchical service list in each round of exam. Meanwhile, the output parameters of this service are added to the parameter set. Until no service can be triggered by the parameter set. The positive filtering ends (*HF_Alg* Algorithm, lines 4–10). This phase can filter out services that are not related to service request and service input parameters. In the second stage, the hierarchical service list, which is saved in the first stage, is traversed from the highest level to the lowest level. Similar to the first stage, a temporary parameter set is initialized by using the output parameters of the service request. This is to determine whether the traversed service can be triggered. If the service cannot be triggered, it will be deleted from the hierarchical service list. The service, which filtered out at this stage, has nothing to do with the service request output parameters (*HF_Alg* Algorithm, lines 11–17). Therefore, when the entire algorithm ends, if the services still exist in the hierarchical service list, they are valid services and are associated with the requested service. The specific algorithm pseudocode is shown in Algorithm 1.

Algorithm 1 : *HF_Alg*

Input: *W*(Service set), *R*(Request for service)

OutPut: *levelWNodeList* (Effective level service list)

1. Initial **Start** node and **End** node by *R*
2. *layer* = 0; *levelWNodeList[layer]← Start;*
3. *allActivePars← Start.O*; *tempLevelPars←end.I;*
4. **while** *allActivePars* is extensible or not contain *end.I* **do**
5.   **for every** *service* **in** *W* **do**
6.   **if** *service* can be triggered by the elements in *allActivePars* **do**
7.   *levelWNodeList[layer]← service;*
8.   *allActivePars← service.O;*
9.   *layer++;*
10. **end while**
11. **for** *i* **from** *layer* **to** 0 **do**
12.   **for every** *s* **in** *layerList* **do**
13.   **If** *S.O∪tempLevelPars ≠ ∅* **do**
14.   *tempLevelPars←s.I;*
15.   **else** *layerList* remove *s*;
16.   **end for**
17. **return** *levelWNodeList*

Taking the service and service request described in Table 1 as an example: $R = <I, O>$, $I = \{A, B, C\}$, $O = \{D\}$, after passing the *HF_Alg* algorithm, the original service set v5, v6, and v9 services are irrelevant services, which are determined by request R, thus are removed. The service dependency graph built at this time is shown in Fig. 3.

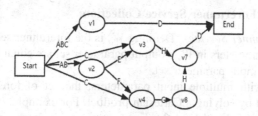

Fig. 3. Service dependency graph after reducing service

3.2   A Combined Sequence Module

This paper proposes an algorithm (combination path sequence traversal algorithm, *CPST_Alg*), which is based on the traversal sequence of the combined path in the traversal search process. During the traversal searching, the algorithm records the top k GQoS optimal combination path traversal sequences, which is associated with each service node. We only need to convert the combined path traversal sequence at the egress service node to the final service composition at the end of the search traversal. The solution can avoid the process of retrospective combination.

The breadth-first search traversal is performed according to the service hierarchy relationship. While traversing each service node, it needs to save its associated top k GQoS optimal combined path information sequence. For each service node, it is required to obtain its associated top k GQoS optimal set of predecessor service nodes, and then merge the sequence traversal sequence of service nodes in the set of predecessor service nodes. The specific algorithm pseudo code is shown as follows.

Algorithm 2: *CPST_Alg*

Input: *levelWNodeList* (Effective service set),*k*

OutPut: *nodePathInfoMap*(Combined path information table)

---

1. create *WSDG* by *levelWNodeList*
2. *nodePathInfoMap*←∅;
3. *OutParsInvertedMap*←*levelWNodeList*;
4. **for each** *snode* by level **in** *WSDG* **do**
5.   *k_preMergeNodes*←getKPreNodeSet(*snode*,*k*, *OutParsInvertedMap*); //get the Forerunner service collection
6.   *k_mergePathInfo*←getKMergePathInfo(*snode*,   *k_preMergeNodes*, *nodePathInfoMap*); //combining path traversal sequence
7.   *nodePathInfoMap*.put(*snode*, *k_mergePathInfo*);
8. **end for**
9. **return** *nodePathInfoMap*;

The whole process of CPST_Alg algorithm mainly involves the calculation of the current service node's forerunner service set and the merging of the combined path traversal sequence. Two important processes are discussed separately as follows.

Calculation of the Forerunner Service Collection

Definition 2 (Forerunner Service). Defining W_a is the forerunner service of W_b, if and only if part of the parameters in W_a's output parameter set are equal to part of the input parameters of W_b's input parameter set.

For a service with multiple input parameters, the set of forerunner services is generally performed by solving a Cartesian product. For example, the input parameter set for a service is *{a, b, c}*, and the input parameter a is associated with for the forerunner service node *{W₁}*, the forerunner service node associated with the input parameter *b* is *{W₁, W₂}*, and the forerunner service associated with the input parameter *c* is *{W₁, W₃}*. After the Cartesian product is obtained, four forerunner service sets are obtained: *{W₁}, {W₁, W₂}, {W₁, W₃}, {W₁, W₂, W₃}*. It can be concluded that when there are too many input parameters of the service node, the set of forerunner services obtained by doing Cartesian product calculation is very large. If each one is considered, the performance of the algorithm will drastically decrease.

Therefore, we adopt the dynamic programming approach to solve the current k-optimal pre-service service set with the first GQoS. First, we consider whether each Forerunner service can trigger the service node, and add the Forerunner service which can trigger into the Forerunner service set queue (in accordance with the Forerunner service in gathering priority queues of GQoS ordering, the size of the queue is k). The forerunner service that can not trigger the service node is added to the queue and will be investigated. In addition to verifying whether it can directly trigger the current service node, each preemption service also needs to merge with each service set that waits to be examined, and then verify whether the current service node can be triggered. This method can reduce the number of forerunner service compositions, and avoid the existence of redundant services in the preemption service set.

The Merging of Combination Path Traversal Sequence. A combined path traversal sequence is a sequence of all traversed service nodes in a process of traversing from a *Start* node to a previous service node. Each element in the sequence is associated with a traversed service node, consisting of service nodes and related forerunner service nodes. The services of the forerunner service node are also currently traversed. Such a two-tuple is generally used to represent the elements in the combined path traversal sequence, such as $RP_a = <W_a.name, WS_a>$, where $W_a.name$ represents the ID or name of the service node and WS_a represents the set of Forerunner services of W_a. The service is also represented by its ID or name of the service. It's note-worthy that for the start node *Start*, $RP_{start} = <start, null>$, because it does not have a set of forerunner services.

For a service node, its associated combined path traversal sequence is generally merged from the combined path traversal sequence, which is associated with its forerunner service node. The sequence after the merging is added to the sequence element, which is associated with the current service node. The traversal sequence of the combined path associated with the current service node is obtained.

Then taking the *v3* service node in Fig. 3 as an example, its forerunner service node set is *{start, v2}*. The combined service path information sequence, which is associated with the *Start* service node, is *<start, null>*. The combined path information sequence which is associated with the *v2* service node is <start, null> <v2, {start}>. Then, the combined path information sequence of *v3* needs to combine the sequence information of *Start* and *v2*. The sequence elements which are associated with the *Start* service node have duplicates and need to be de-duplicated. Then the sequence elements associated with *v3* itself should be added, and then the combined path information sequence of *v3* as *<start, null> <v2, {start}> <v3, {start, v2}>* is achieved. Finally, the CPST_Alg algorithm is run for the combined path information sequence associated with each service node in Fig. 3 as shown in Fig. 4:

service node	Node hierarchy	Combined path traversal sequence	GQoS
Start	0	⟨start, null⟩	0
v1	1	⟨start, null⟩⟨v1, {start}⟩	900
v2	1	⟨start, null⟩⟨v2, {start}⟩	100
v3	2	⟨start, null⟩⟨v2, {start}⟩⟨v3, {start, v2}⟩	300
v4	2	⟨start, null⟩⟨v2, {start}⟩⟨v4, {start, v2}⟩	600
v8	3	⟨start, null⟩⟨v2, {start}⟩⟨v4, {start, v2}⟩⟨v8, {v4}⟩	1100
v7	3	⟨start, null⟩⟨v2, {start}⟩⟨v3, {start, v2}⟩⟨v7, {v3}⟩	400
		⟨start, null⟩⟨v2, {start}⟩⟨v4, {start, v2}⟩⟨v8, {v4}⟩⟨v7, {v8}⟩	1300
End	4	⟨start, null⟩⟨v2, {start}⟩⟨v3, {start, v2}⟩⟨v7, {v3}⟩⟨end, {v7}⟩	400
		⟨start, null⟩⟨v1, {start}⟩⟨end, {v1}⟩	900

Fig. 4. Combination path sequence information of service node

3.3   Combination Path Conversion Module

The *CPST_Alg* algorithm finally obtains its associated top k QoS-optimal combined path traversal sequence at the egress service node *End*. The path traversal sequence has a corresponding relationship with the final service composition solution (represented as a DAG subgraph). In the traversal sequence, all the service nodes (DAG node sets) required to constitute the service composition are recorded. At the same time, each service node's forerunner service set corresponds to the call relationship between services (the edge set of the DAG). It is easy to construct a composite path traversal sequence into a service composition solution in the form of a DAG subgraph. Therefore, in this section, a composite path traversal sequence conversion algorithm (*CPTSC_Alg*) is proposed to transform the combined path traversal sequence into a solution of the DAG form. The algorithm is shown below.

Algorithm 3: *CPTSC_Alg*

Input: *nodePathInfoMap* ,*End*

OutPut: *k_DAGSolution*(DAG service composition solution)

---

1.   initial *k_DAGSolution*;   initial *SingelDAGSolution*;
2.   *k_mergePathInfo* ← nodePathInfoMap.get(*End*);
3.   **for every** *mergePathInfo* in *k_mergePathInfo* **do**
4.   **for each** RP in *mergePathInfo* **do**
5.   *SingelDAGSolution*.addNode(*RP.W*);
6.   *SingelDAGSolution*.addEdge(*RP.W,RP.WS*);
7.   **end for**
8.   *k_DAGSolution*.add(*SingelDAGSolution*);
9.   **end for**
10. **return** *k_DAGSolution;*

Taking the combined path traversal sequence associated with the *End* node in Fig. 5 as an example, the two combined path traversal sequences are converted into a DAG service composition solution, as shown in Fig. 5 below.

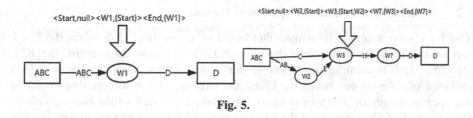

Fig. 5.

3.4 Algorithm Performance Analysis

The algorithm mainly consists of three stages. First, in the worst situation, the hierarchical filtering algorithm requires the entire service set that is accessed both in the forward filtering and the reverse filtering. Therefore, the time complexity of the algorithm is $O(2n)$, where n is the number of services in the service set. In the $CPST\_Alg$ algorithm, when obtaining a set of Forerunner services for each service node, if the number of forerunner services for each service is c, the time complexity of the process is $O(c^2)$. When merging the combined path traversal sequence, if the average length of the combined path is p and the average number of preemption service sets per service is m, the time complexity of the merge process is $O(kp * \log m)$. Therefore, the time complexity of the entire $CPST\_Alg$ algorithm is: $O(n'(c^2 + kp * \log m))$, where n' is the number of valid services and n is the worst case. The $CPTSC\_Alg$ algorithm only needs to traverse k combination path traversal sequences. So its time complexity is $O(kp)$. For the whole algorithm, the time complexity is: $O(n + kp + n(kp * \log m + c^2))$.

4 Experiment

4.1 Experiment Procedure

All of the algorithms in this paper are based on the Java language. Except for the use of SAX-related software packages in the xml file parsing module, no other third-party software packages are used.

The experimental test set applies the WSBen [18] tool to generate a data set containing five test sets with different service sizes (200–5000). Each test set contains three types of files: The WSDL file describes the input and output parameters of the service; the WSLA file describes the QoS of the service; the request file describes the user's request. Each experiment selects a data set as the input of the system. The input file is parsed by the xml parsing module into the data formats of the standard service node and the service request node. These nodes are then processed by the combined algorithm module. At the end, the Topk service compositions with the best QoS are obtained. In addition, the test hardware environment is Intel Core PC.

4.2   Accuracy Evaluation of Experiment Results

The Topk service composition algorithm based on the optimal QoS solves the first k service compositions that satisfy the optimal QoS condition. In contrast, the KPL algorithm in [14] identifies the Topk service compositions in accordance with QoS rankings of different combinations. Using the experimental procedure described, the accuracy of the returned service composition results is verified for the two algorithms. Here *ratio*, the GQoS average of the k results returned from the two algorithms is taken as a measure of accuracy for the two algorithms.

$$ratio = \frac{\frac{\sum_{i=1}^{i=k} top\ i\ DAG\ GQoS\ value\ by\ KPL}{k}}{\frac{\sum_{i=1}^{i=k} top\ i\ DAG\ GQoS\ value\ by\ QWSCK}{k}}$$

Experiment 1. Algorithm accuracy comparison based on different service sets.

Figure 6 shows a comparison of the accuracy of the KPL algorithm and the QWSC-K algorithm under different service set sizes. From Fig. 6, it can be concluded that the Topk service composition algorithm based on the optimal QoS is superior to the KPL algorithm in accuracy of the result.

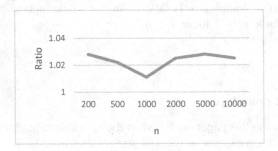

Fig. 6. Algorithm accuracy comparison

4.3   Experimental Effect of Hierarchical Filtering Algorithm

To verify the filtering effect of the hierarchical filtering algorithm, we run the filtering algorithm on the six data sets and obtain the number of valid service levels. Since the filtering algorithm is related to the input and output of the requesting service, eight randomly generated request services are run for each service set. The final result is the average of eight results. Experimental results are shown in Fig. 7.

It's easy to find that the hierarchical filtering algorithm can generally reduce the initial service set size by about 90%, which can greatly reduce the search space in the *CPST_Alg* algorithm and improve the operating efficiency of the entire algorithm.

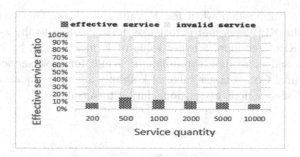

Fig. 7. Hierarchical filtering algorithm effect

4.4 Algorithm Performance Comparison

The comparison experiment is mainly the time performance comparison between the above-mentioned KPL algorithm and the optimal QoS-based topk service composition algorithm proposed in this paper. The comparison is divided into two aspects. One is to verify different k values to impact of the time performance for the two algorithms under the same data set. The other is, under the same K value, to verify the impact of different service set size upon time performance.

Experiment 2. Effects of different service set sizes on the algorithm.

Figure 8 shows the time consumption of the two algorithms when the k value is 10 based on different service sets. By analyzing the graph, the time consumption of the two algorithms as a whole shows an upward trend as the scale of the service set increases. This paper directly uses an effective filtering policy to filter the service set size. It avoids access to invalid services during traversal, which makes the algorithm in the overall time consumption slightly better than the KPL algorithm.

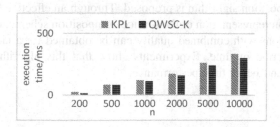

Fig. 8. Relationship between algorithm time performance and service set size

Experiment 3. The effect of different k-values on the algorithm.

It can be seen from Fig. 9 that the KPL algorithm and the algorithm of this paper both increase with the increase of the K value, and the running time of the algorithm also increases. The main reason is that both algorithms need more time to solve the increased service composition when the K value increases. The advantage of this algorithm over the KPL algorithm is that it is less sensitive to the k-value. This is because for the KPL algorithm, a larger value of K means more backtracking combination process and more time consumption. While for topk service composition algorithm of optimal QoS, a larger value of k simply affects a sequence of combined paths which find service node associations during traversal.

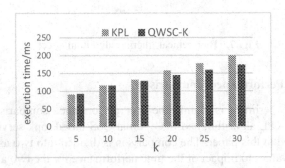

Fig. 9. Relationship between algorithm time performance and k

5   Conclusion

With an acceleration of the growth rate of Web services and the expansion of service composition applications, the academic and industrial communities are increasingly demanding higher requirements for automatic service composition technologies. In addition to satisfying functional requirements, service quality must also be considered. Topk service composition solutions can provide users with more service options, meet diversified application requirements, and eliminate the "overheating" of services brought by the centralized selection of optimal solutions. In this paper, a QoS-based Topk service composition algorithm is proposed. Through an effective filtering strategy and the serialization representation of the service composition scheme, the top k service composition solutions with combined quality can be obtained for a large data set in a relatively short period of time. Experiments show that this algorithm can promise reliable accuracy and better time performance.

References

1. Yin, R.: Study of composing web service based on SOA. In: Yang, Y., Ma, M. (eds.) Proceedings of the 2nd International Conference on Green Communications and Networks 2012 (GCN 2012): Volume 2. LNEE, vol. 224, pp. 209–214. Springer, Heidelberg (2013). https://doi.org/10.1007/978-3-642-35567-7_26
2. Oh, S.C., Lee, D., Kumara, S.R.T.: Web service planner (WSPR): an effective and scalable web service composition algorithm. Int. J. Web Serv. Res. (IJWSR) **4**(1), 1–22 (2007)

3. Wagner, F., Ishikawa, F., Honiden, S.: QoS-aware automatic service composition by applying functional clustering. In: 2011 IEEE International Conference on Web Services (ICWS), pp. 89–96. IEEE (2011)
4. Alrifai, M., Risse, T., Nejdl, W.: A hybrid approach for efficient web service composition with end-to-end QoS constraints. ACM Trans. Web (TWEB) 6(2), 7 (2012)
5. Zeng, L., Benatallah, B., Ngu, A.H.H., et al.: QoS-aware middleware for web services composition. IEEE Trans. Softw. Eng. 30(5), 311–327 (2004)
6. Huang, Z., Jiang, W., Hu, S., et al.: Effective pruning algorithm for QoS-aware service composition. In: 2009 IEEE Conference on Commerce and Enterprise Computing, CEC 2009, pp. 519–522. IEEE (2009)
7. Yan, Y., Xu, B., Gu, Z., et al.: A QoS-driven approach for semantic service composition. In: 2009 IEEE Conference on Commerce and Enterprise Computing, CEC 2009, pp. 523–526. IEEE (2009)
8. Jiang, W., Zhang, C., Huang, Z., et al.: Qsynth: a tool for QoS-aware automatic service composition. In: 2010 IEEE International Conference on Web Services (ICWS), pp. 42–49. IEEE, (2010)
9. Wagner, F., Klein, A., Klöpper, B., et al. Multi-objective service composition with time-and input-dependent QoS//Web Services (ICWS), 2012 IEEE 19th International Conference on. IEEE, 234–241 (2012)
10. Jaeger, M.C., Rojec-Goldmann, G., Muhl, G.: QoS aggregation for web service composition using workflow patterns. In: 2004 Eighth IEEE International Enterprise Distributed Object Computing Conference, EDOC 2004, Proceedings, pp. 149–159. IEEE (2004)
11. Benouaret, K., Benslimane, D., Hadjali, A., et al.: Top-k web service compositions using fuzzy dominance relationship. In: 2011 IEEE International Conference on Services Computing (SCC), pp. 144–151. IEEE (2011)
12. Almulla, M., Almatori, K., Yahyaoui, H.: A QoS-based fuzzy model for ranking real world web services. In: 2011 IEEE International Conference on Web Services (ICWS), pp. 203–210. IEEE (2011)
13. Wang, X.L., Huang, S., Zhou, A.Y.: QoS-aware composite services retrieval. J. Comput. Sci. Technol. 21(4), 547–558 (2006)
14. Jiang, W., Hu, S., Liu, Z.: Top k query for QoS-aware automatic service composition. IEEE Trans. Serv. Comput. 7(4), 681–695 (2014)
15. Deng, S., Huang, L., Tan, W., et al.: Top-k automatic service composition: a parallel method for large-scale service sets. IEEE Trans. Autom. Sci. Eng. 11(3), 891–905 (2014)
16. Menasce, D.A.: Composing web services: a QoS view. IEEE Internet Comput. 8(6), 88–90 (2004)
17. Jaeger, M.C., Rojec-Goldmann, G., Muhl, G.: QoS aggregation for web service composition using workflow patterns. In: 2004 Eighth IEEE International Enterprise Distributed Object Computing Conference, EDOC 2004, Proceedings, pp. 149–159. IEEE (2004)
18. Oh, S.C., Kil, H., Lee, D., et al.: WSBen: a web services discovery and composition benchmark. In: 2006 International Conference on Web Services, ICWS 2006, pp. 239–248. IEEE (2006)
19. JianMin, B., Jie, L.: An integrated algorithm for QoS-aware logistics service composition. In: Proceedings of 2017 IEEE 2nd Advanced Information Technology, Electronic and Automation Control Conference (IAEAC 2017), p. 5 (2017)
20. Huo, L., Wang, Z.: Service composition instantiation based on cross-modified artificial bee colony algorithm. China Commun. 13(10), 233–244 (2016)

Towards Multi-task Fair Sharing for Multi-resource Allocation in Cloud Computing

Lihua Zhao[1]([✉]) [iD], Minghui Du[1], Weibao Lei[1], Lin Chen[2], and Lei Yang[1]

[1] School of Electronic and Information Engineering,
South China University of Technology, Guangzhou 510641, China
`zhao.lihua@mail.scut.edu.cn`, `ecmhdu@scut.edu.cn`
[2] Lab. Recherche Informatique (LRI-CNRS UMR 8623) Univ. Paris-Sud,
91405 Orsay, France
`chen@lri.fr`

Abstract. This paper addresses multi-resource fair allocation: a fundamental research topic in cloud computing. To improve resource utilization under well-studied fairness constraints, we propose a new allocation mechanism called *Multi-task Share Fairness for Efficiency-Aware Allocation (MTSFEAA)*, which generalizes Bottleneck-aware Allocation (BAA) to the settings of users with multiple heterogeneous tasks to run. We classify users into different groups by their dominant resources. The goals are to ensure that users in the same group receive allocations in proportion to their fair shares while users in different groups receive allocations that maximize resource utilization subject to the well-studied fairness properties such as those in DRF. Under MTSFEAA, no user (1) is worse off sharing resources than dividing resources equally among all users; (2) prefers the allocation of another user; (3) can improve their own allocation without reducing other users' allocations. Experiments demonstrate that the proposed allocation policy performs better in terms of total number of tasks than does DRF.

Keywords: Multi-resource fairness allocation · Cloud computing Resource utilization

1 Introduction

Cloud computing has become increasingly popular and attractive as a modern application-specific clusters in the current era of big data. Multi-resource fair allocation is a fundamental problem in any shared cloud system, with which users

Supported by the Oversea Study Program of the Guangzhou Elite Project (GEP), Also supported by the National Natural Science Foundation of China under Grant 61701181 and the Guangdong Natural Science Foundation under Grant 2017A030325430.

© Springer Nature Switzerland AG 2018
X. Sun et al. (Eds.): ICCCS 2018, LNCS 11064, pp. 322–333, 2018.
https://doi.org/10.1007/978-3-030-00009-7_30

are guaranteed to receive fair shares of cloud resources, without considering the behavior of others. Unlike traditional clusters and grids, modern cloud computing systems are not only diversity in their hardware components, but also present highly heterogeneous in resource demand profiles between the sharing clouds users.

For the diversity of hardware components, for example, as observed from Google compute clusters, there is approximately 50% of jobs that users run have specific requirements on the server (or machine) they can execute [7]. For the unprecedented heterogeneity of the clouds users, different jobs can have widely different resource demands for CPU, memory, and I/O resources. For instance, database operations are usually memory-heavy tasks, while video transcoding tasks are typically CPU-intensive. The heterogeneity of both hardware and resource demands increases significant challenges to solve the multi-resource fair allocation problem.

To address the fair problem of multi-resource allocation, one of the state-of-art resource allocation schemes is namely *Dominant resource fairness (DRF)* [4], which is a generation of *max-min fairness* for multi-resource environment. DRF provides several highly desirable fairness properties, called Sharing Incentive (SI), Envy-freeness (EF), Pareto Efficiency (PE) and Strategy-proofness (SP). Therefore, recent work, notably [1,3,6], have extended DRF in different dimensions in the literature. While DRF and its variants investigate the demand heterogeneity of multi-resource, based on a *single job* abstraction, they ignore the heterogeneity of the tasks that users run, limiting the discussions on a hypothetical scenario *where all jobs of users are considered have the same task to run multiple times*. If users may have *multi-task* to run, and each task has different utility for the user, this case is common in practice. So, achieving fair allocation of multi-resource with users have multi-task to execute, however, exists non-trivial technical challenges, due to the presence of hardware heterogeneity and different multi-resource demands.

In this paper, we present the study of the fair resource allocation problem in shared computing systems with multi-task, all of the tasks need to be finished before a job is considered complete. We consider a fundamental question of resource allocation, that is, how would fair sharing be defined and achieved for jobs with multi-task and multi-resource demands? The contributions of this paper are summarized as follows:

- We propose a new allocation policy, namely Multi-task Share Fairness for Efficiency-Aware Allocation (MTSFEAA), which equalizes the multi-task share of users as much as possible. *Multi-task share* is defined for each user as the ratio between the gross number of tasks allocated and the maximum number of tasks the user monopolizes the entire resource pool.

- We prove that MTSFEAA still inherits the three highly attractive properties of DRF, that is, they meet Sharing Incentive (SI), Envy-freeness (EF), Pareto Efficiency (PE). To our knowledge, MTSFEAA is the first extended multi-resource allocation policy of Bottleneck-aware allocation (BAA) [8] on dealing with multi-task scheduler, while meeting optimal fairness guarantees as does DRF.

- Our experimental results show that MTSFEAA significantly outperforms the current state-of-the-art in terms of reducing the waste of resources while improving resource efficiency.

The remainder of this paper is organized as follows. In Sect. 2, we introduce the system model and formalize the multi-task multi-resource fair allocation problem. In Sect. 2.3, we describes three well-recognized fairness properties nice to have for multi-resource allocation in the literature, then we propose a new allocation policy, called Multi-task share fairness for efficiency-aware allocation. Formal proofs are presented in Sect. 4. We evaluate the performance of our proposed algorithm in Sect. 5. Finally, we conclude the paper in Sect. 6.

2   System Model and Allocation Properties

2.1   System Model

We define some terminology for multi-resource fair allocation. We consider a system with m types resources, *e.g.*, CPU, memory, disk, etc. Let $R = \{1, \ldots, m\}$ be the set of m resources and C_r be the total amount of resources r available in the system. Each resource is divisible, meaning that it can be divided into arbitrarily small pieces. Let $U = \{1, \ldots, n\}$ be the set of users sharing the system. We consider a setting in which the job of some users have multi-task to run, where multi-task means different tasks have different demands. For example, the job of user l has two tasks (task1 and task2) to run, and its resource demands are (1 CPU, 1 GB) and (2 CPU, 4 GB) separately. Let M_i represents the set of tasks that user i ($i \in U$) wants to execute in the system. Each task j ($j \in M_i$) requires a set of resources in the resource pool provided by the system. For any user i ($i \in U$), let *demand set* D_i be a m-dimensional matrix, where $D_i = \{D_i^1, \ldots, D_i^{M_i}\}$, and D_i^j is the demand vector of the j-th task in M_i of user i. The preference of the j-th task is characterized by a *demand vector*, that is, $D_i^j = \{D_{i,j1}, \ldots, D_{i,jm}\}$, where each element in D_i^j is a m-dimensional vector that specifies the amount of each of the m resource required by the j-th task.

For simplicity, in this paper we assume positive demands for all users, *i.e.*, $D_{i,jr} > 0, \forall j \in M_i, r \in R$. We define

$$d_{i,jr} = \frac{D_{i,jr}}{C_r}$$

as the *fraction demand* of each resource r that the j-th task of user i.

For now, we assume users have an infinite number of tasks to be scheduled, and all tasks are divisible [2,4,6].

2.2   Problem Formulation

The multi-task fair allocation problem is formally defined as follows.

Problem 1 (Multi-task fair allocation problem). Given a system with m types resources, n users sharing the system. For any user i ($i \in U$), M_i represents its set of tasks. Given each task's resource demand is characterized by $D_i{}^j = \{D_{i,j1}, \ldots, D_{i,jm}\}$. The multi-task fair allocation problem is to devise a fair allocation mechanism satisfies the well-recognized fairness properties and tries to capture a trade-off between multi-resource fairness and resource efficiency.

Table 1. Main terminologies

Symbols	Descriptions
R	Set of resource types in the cloud's resource pool
C_r	Capacity of resource $\tilde{r}$
U	Set of users share the cloud's resource pool
M_i	Set of tasks of user i
D_i	Resource demands of user i
$D_i{}^j$	Resource demand vector of the j-th task of user i
$d_{i,jr}$	Fraction demand of resource r that the j-th task of user i
S_{r^*}	Set of tasks bottlenecked on resource r^*
N_{fij}	Minimum number of tasks allocated to the j-th task of user i
N_{ij}	The number of tasks allocated to the j-th task of user i
ρ_{r^*}	Amplification factor that tasks bottlenecked in the queue S_{r^*}
N_i	Total number of tasks allocated to user i
X_{ij}	Allocation of the j-th task of user i
X_i	Allocation of user i

Table 1 summaries the main terminologies used in the paper. To streamline the paper, in what follows, we will present the well-recognized fairness properties and then design the multi-task fair allocation mechanism to meet the fair requirements.

2.3   Allocation Properties

We are interested in mechanisms that meet the well-recognized fairness properties proposed by Ghodsi et al. in [4], specially, they are sharing incentive, envy-freeness and Pareto efficiency. These desirable properties are very important to guide the devise of a multi-resource fair allocation.

We present below the three well-studied notions of fairness from economic theory:

Sharing Incentive (SI): An allocation mechanism is SI if each task of any user runs no fewer tasks than the task would have run in the setting of getting a fraction of $\frac{1}{n}$ of each of the resources among all the tasks of the shared users. *i.e.*, for every j-th task in M_i of user i, $N_{ij}(X_{ij}) \geq N_{ij}(\frac{1}{n}, \ldots, \frac{1}{n})$, where X_{ij} specifies the amount of the resource allocated to j-th task.

Envy-Freeness (EF): An allocation mechanism is EF if each user just prefers her own allocation. *i.e.*, for every pair of users $i, v \in U(i \neq v)$, $N_i(X_i) \geq N_v(X_v)$, where X_i and X_v are the amount of resources allocated to user i and user v separately.

Pareto Efficiency (PE): An allocation mechanism is PE is no users can increase their gains without decreasing the gains of other users. If an allocation is not PE, it exists other allocation could improve system performance.

3   Multi-task Share Fairness with Efficiency-Aware Allocation

In this section, we propose Multi-task Share Fairness with Efficiency-Aware Allocation (MSFEAA), a new multi-resource allocation policy that provides all the fairness properties described in Sect. 2.3. We start with core fair policy of the MSFEAA and the related notations used in MSFEAA. Finally, we present the scheduling algorithm of MSFEAA.

3.1   Multi-task Share Fairness with Efficiency-Aware Allocation

We say resource r^* is the *dominant resource* of the j-th task if its fraction demand d_{i,jr^*} is the largest one in all $d_{i,jr}$.

Remark 1. Note that, different task has different dominant resource, so, tasks maybe are divided into different groups.

For every user i and its every task j, let $X_{ij} = (X_{i,j1}, \ldots, X_{i,jm})$ be the *resource allocation vector*, where $X_{i,jr}$ is the amount of resource r allocated to the j-th task in M_i of user i. Let $X_i = (X_i^1, \ldots, X_i^{M_i})$ be the *allocation set* of user i, and $X = (X_1, \ldots, X_n)$ the overall allocation for all users.

For each user i, let N_{ij} be the number of tasks allocated to the j-th task that corresponding to the allocation X_{ij} in M_i. We have

$$X_{ij} = N_{ij} D_i^j, \forall r \in R.$$

Inspired by the SI fairness property in which each user should receive at least $\frac{1}{n}$ of each of resource, where n is the number of users sharing the system. So, we define the N_{fij} be the *minimum number of tasks* j-th task receives, where minimum number of tasks corresponding to dividing each kind of resources equally among all of tasks in the system.

Because the users sharing the system with multiple tasks is the context that we concern, in order to state clearly, we only focus on the task to be implemented.

Therefore, in the rest of this paper, N_{fij} can be simplified as N_{fj}, similarly, we use N_j replace N_{ij}. Since a user prefers an allocation that allows it to schedule more tasks, note that, N_{fj} is the minimum number of tasks of the j-th task receives, thus, we have

$$N_j/N_{fj} \geq 1, \forall j \in M_i.$$

where M_i is the *demand set* defined in Sect. 2.1 for every user i.

Furthermore, each task is characterized by the demand vector, so, we capture each task's preference by judging its dominant resource. Let $\rho_{r*} = N_j/N_{fj}$ be the *amplification factor* of the j-th task, and its dominant resource is resource r^*.

If all tasks bottleneck on the same resource (i.e., having the same dominant resource), then the resulting allocation should be reduced to a max-min fair allocation for that resource [3]. It implies the notion of *bottleneck fairness*, motivated by this, we introduce the idea of dividing the tasks of users into different groups, which is determined by each task's dominant resource. Specially, like Bottleneck-aware allocation [8], we define the bottleneck group for the different tasks, then we give the two rules as our fair policy to guide and devise allocation mechanism to meet the proposed fair properties. The specific steps are presented below.

Definition 1. *For* $\forall j \in M_i$, *we define* S_{r*} *as the* bottleneck queue *of the tasks that are bottlenecked on the same dominant resource* r^*.

For any pair of tasks j and j', $j \neq j'$, if they bottleneck on the same dominant resource, according to the definition of bottleneck queue, task j and task j' are in the same queue.

We use the rules below to measure the fairness between any pair of tasks j and j'.

1. If task j and task j' are in the same bottleneck queue S_{r*}, let $\frac{N_j}{N_{j'}} = \frac{N_{fj}}{N_{fj'}}$.

Note that, $\rho_{r*} = N_j/N_{fj}$, hence task j and task j' have the same *amplification factor*.

2. If task j and task j' are in the different queue, $\forall j \in S_{r*}, j' \in S_{r*'}$. Suppose that the dominant resources of task j and task j' are r^* and $r^{*'}$, respectively. Then, for $\forall r^* \neq r^{*'}$, $\min_{j \in S_{r*}} N_j D_{jr*} > \max_{j' \in S_{r*'}} N_{j'} D_{j'r*'}$.

Remark 2. Rule (1) states that when two tasks have the same dominant resource, the number of tasks between the two tasks are in proportion to *the minimum number of tasks* defined above. So, actually $\rho_{r*} \geq 1$ is implied in Rule (1).

Rule 2 is an enforced constraint that ensures the envy-free property is satisfied between any pair of tasks of different bottleneck queues. Note that, for Rule (2), there is a special case: if a task has more than two dominant resources, i.e., $d_{i,jr_1} = d_{i,jr_2}$, we divide the task into bottleneck queue S_{r_1} or S_{r_2} randomly.

A resource allocation mechanism takes user requirements as input and outputs the quantity of each resource allocated to each user. In this paper, our objective is to design an allocation mechanism that guarantees the well-recognized properties defined in Sect. 2.3, which are widely deemed as the most important fairness and efficiency measures in both cloud computing systems [3,5].

All computed allocations must be feasible in the sense that they must satisfy the capacity constraints:

$$\sum\nolimits_{i \in U} X_{i,jr} \leq C_r, \forall j \in M_i, r \in R. \tag{1}$$

Different tasks may have different dominant resources. For example, the dominant resource of a task with CPU-intensive jobs is CPU, while the dominant resource of another task with I/O-intensive jobs is bandwidth.

To balance the fairness between different users with multi-task, we define *multi-task share* to equalize the allocation of users received as much as possible. The formal definition of the *multi-task share* is shown as follows.

Definition 2. *For each user i, we define* multi-task share MS_i *as the ratio between the gross number of tasks allocated and the maximum number of tasks the user monopolizes the entire resource pool.*

Its muti-task share is denoted as $MS_i = \frac{N_i}{H_i}$.

Remark 3. For $\forall i \in U$, the gross number of tasks allocated to user i is computed as

$$N_i = \sum_{j \in M_i} N_{ij} \tag{2}$$

where N_{ij} is the number of tasks of the j-th task in M_i for user i.

N_{ij} be the number of tasks scheduled of each task, can be received by solving the linear program (LP) optimization; Its objective function is maximizing users' total number of tasks, and the constraints are formula expressed in Rule (2) and the formula (1). H_i represents the maximum number of tasks user i can run when it monopolizes the entire resource pool, it is computed as the sum of maximum number of tasks allocated to each task (considered user i with multi-task to run), each maximum number of tasks can be computed in a hypothetical scenario where it monopolizes the resource pool.

MSFEAA applies local bottleneck fairness with respect to the users multi-task share to capture a tradeoff between fairness and efficiency for multi-task allocation. Moreover, MSFEAA meets all the attractive properties such as SI, EF, PE.

3.2 Scheduling Algorithm of Multi-task Share Fairness with Efficiency-Aware Allocation

Instead of considering a single task like the existing works did [1,4], these approaches fall short when it comes to support users with heterogeneous multi-task to run. In this paper, MSFEAA solves the multi-task fair allocation problem for multi-resource in cloud computing environment, the core idea of MSFEAA is focusing on generalizing BAA approach [8] to model the multi-task allocation problem. The detail of the decision procedure is shown in Algorithm 1.

Algorithm 1. Algorithm 1 Implementation of Multi-task Share Fairness with Efficiency-Aware Allocation

---

Require: Resource types $R = \{1, \ldots, m\}, \forall r \in R$; User set $U = \{1, \ldots, n\}$; $C = \{C_1, \ldots, C_m\}, \forall C_r \in C$; User may have multi-task to run, each task is characterized by a demand vector $D_i{}^j$ for the j-th task of user i;

Ensure: Gross number of tasks allocated to user i N_i and corresponding allocation X_i;

  1: Capturing each task's dominant resource then sort the task into the corresponding bottlenecked queue S_{r*}.

  2: Define the minimum number of tasks allocated to the each task according to the notion of the SI fairness property;

  3: Use the computed results denoted by ρ_{r*} for the dominant resource as weights for the allocations of the tasks;

  4: Solve the LP Problem of N_{ij} with unknowns ρ_{r*}, Constraint (1) and condition of Rule (2);

  5: Obtain N_i and X_i;

  6: if $\sum X_i \leq C_r$ **then**

  7: $MS_i = \frac{N_i}{H_i}$

  8: else

  9:   **return** the cloud cluster is full.

  10: end if

MSFEAA first calculates the dominant resource of the each current task in the cluster according to the definition of the *dominant resource*. Then, it divides different tasks into different groups based on the calculation results of the above step. Next, the number of tasks scheduled of each task can be received by solving the linear program (LP) optimization. Finally, multi-task share is calculated by the definition for every user sharing the cloud system. Algorithm 1 maintains and updates the system status periodically.

4   Analysis of Fairness Properties

In this section, we start to analyze and prove the three well-recognized fairness properties (i.e., SI, EF, PE) presented in Sect. 2.3.

Lemma 1. *For any two tasks l and k of two different users($k \neq l$), we have*

$$h_l \geq \rho_{kl} h_k$$

where $\rho_{kl} = min_{r:D_{lr}>0} \frac{D_{kr}}{D_{lr}}$

Proof. For task k, when it is in a hypothetical scenario, it monopolizes the resource pool. Let h_k be the maximum number of tasks allocated to task k in the hypothetical scenario. Thus, the amount of resource r allocated to task k is computed $h_k D_{kr}$. Now allocate the resources that have been allocated to task k in the hypothetical scenario, with which task l can run n_i number of tasks, we have

$$n_l = min_{r:D_{lr}>0} \frac{h_k D_{kr}}{D_{lr}} = h_k \rho_{kl}$$

where $\rho_{kl} = min_{r:D_{lr}>0} \frac{D_{kr}}{D_{lr}}$

On the other hand, by the definition of h_l, we have

$$h_l \geq n_l$$

Thus, that is, $h_l \geq \rho_{kl} h_k$.

Having established Lemma 1, we next prove envy-freeness of MSFEAA.

Theorem 1. *MSFEAA satisfies envy-freeness (EF) property.*

Proof. To prove MSFEAA satisfies envy-freeness (EF) is equivalent to prove $N_l(X_k) \leq N_l(X_l)$. Let X_{lr} be the amount of resource r allocated to the task l, we have $X_{lr} = N_l(X_{lr}) D_{lr}$, where $N_l(X_{lr})$ is the number of tasks of the task l can run given allocation X_{lr}.

To see $N_l(X_k) \leq N_l(X_l)$, we first show that the task l does not envy the task k as follows:

Since $N_l(X_k) = min_{r:D_{lr}>0} \frac{X_{kr}}{D_{lr}} = min_{r:D_{lr}>0} \frac{h_k D_{kr}}{D_{lr}} = h_k \rho_{kl}$ where $\rho_{kl} = min_{r:D_{lr}>0} \frac{D_{kr}}{D_{lr}}$

Because $N_l(X_l) = min_{r:D_{lr}>0} \frac{X_{lr}}{D_{lr}} = min_{r:D_{lr}>0} \frac{h_l D_{lr}}{D_{lr}}$, therefore, we have

$$\frac{N_l(A_k)}{N_l(X_l)} \leq min_{r:D_{lr}>0} \frac{h_k D_{kr}}{h_l D_{lr}} = \rho_{kl} \frac{h_k}{h_l}$$

Since $h_l \geq h_k \rho_{kl}$, it follows from Lemma 1, so,

$$\frac{N_l(X_k)}{N_l(X_l)} \leq 1$$

This completes the proof.

Theorem 2. *MSFEAA satisfies Pareto efficiency (PE).*

Proof. By construction, MSFEAA satisfies Pareto efficiency.

Theorem 3. *MSFEAA satisfies the sharing incentive (SI) property.*

Proof. We prove the theorem using the following lemmas.

Lemma 2. *By Lemma 2 in [8], all tasks in the same bottleneck group receive equal allocations on the dominant resource. Specifically, all tasks in the same group receive $\rho_{r^*} C_{r^*}/n_t$ from its dominant resource r^*, where n_t is the number of total tasks running in the system.*

Lemma 3. *By Lemmas 4, 5 and 6 from [8], we have the amplification factor* $\rho_{r^*} > 1$.

Since it follows from Lemmas 2 and 3, we have amplification factor $\rho_{r^*} > 1$.

Therefore, each task of any user runs no fewer tasks than the task would have dividing each of the resource equally among all total running tasks. Furthermore, no user is worse off sharing the resource pool than by dividing each resource equally among all the users. That is, MSFEAA meets sharing incentive property.

5   Performance Evaluation and Analysis

In order to evaluate MSFEAA at a larger scale users, we conduct an experiment with 100 users and we use a cloud simulation software CloudSim3.0.0 to evaluate MSFEAA with DRF. We assume that there are two types of resources: CPU and memory, provided by the resource pool. Firstly, we present the multi-task share proposed by MSFEAA, then we compare the resource utilization for the two types of resources. Finally, the total number of tasks of all users are compared for both schedulers DRF and MSFEAA.

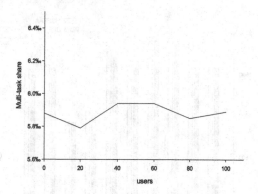

Fig. 1. Multi-task share for 100 users in resource pool.

As shown in Fig. 1, for the multi-task share of 100 shared users, we observe that each task share's value is between 5.7‰ and 6.0‰. So, the experimental results show that MSFEAA tries to balance the multi-task share for the shared users, in order to achieve better fair sharing for multi-resource.

In Fig. 2(a) and (b), we evaluate the resource utilization of CPU and memory under the two schedulers, DRF and MSFEAA. Specially, we compare the average resource utilization using the data of 10 randomly extracted, which are the calculation results of scheduling algorithms by taking 10 times every 100 times in the 1000 times experiments. For each experiment, we compute resource utilization of the two types of resources, then we get the average utilization of 10 times experiments. As shown in Fig. 2(a), for CPU, there is a slight gap

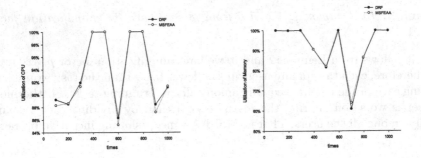

(a) Utilization of CPU with DRF and (b) Utilization of memory with DRF and MSFEAA.   MSFEAA.

Fig. 2. Resource utilization comparison under DRF and MSFEAA.

exists between the two schedulers DRF and MSFEAA. Apparently, however, for memory, as shown in Fig. 2(b), MSFEAA has higher resource utilization than DRF.

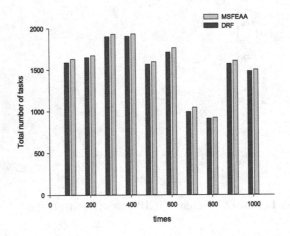

Fig. 3. Total number of tasks with DRF and MSFEAA.

Figure 3 shows the total number of tasks under DRF and MSFEAA. We compare total number of tasks using the data of 10 randomly extracted; these data are the calculation results of scheduling algorithms, by taking one times every 100 times, then, taking 10 times in the 1000 times experiments. As can be seen from Fig. 3, we make the following observation that the MSFEAA achieves better performance on the total number of tasks compared to the DRF. Hence, MSFEAA captures a tradeoff between fairness and resource efficiency.

6   Conclusions

We initiated the study of multi-resource fair allocation in the presence of users with multi-task. Specifically, our goal is to devise a new multi-resource sharing policy subject to the well-recognized fairness properties. We have introduced a new allocation mechanism called *Multi-task Share Fairness with Efficiency-Aware Allocation* (MSFEAA). MSFEAA uses *multi-task share* to balance the allocation received by each user, and it is shown that MSFEAA satisfies the highly desirable fairness properties, *i.e.,* Sharing Incentive (SI), Envy-freeness (EF) and Pareto Efficiency (PE). With MSFEAA, no user is worse off when sharing resources than if resources are divided equally across all users; no user would prefers to receive another users allocation; no user can improve their own allocation without decreasing the allocation of others; Our experimental simulation studies further showed that MSFEAA getting greater total number of tasks than Dominant Resource Fairness (DRF).

References

1. Chowdhury, M., Liu, Z., Ghodsi, A., Stoica, I.: HUG: multi-resource fairness for correlated and elastic demands. In: 13th USENIX Symposium on Networked Systems Design and Implementation (NSDI 2016), pp. 407–424 (2016)
2. Dolev, D., Feitelson, D.G., Halpern, J.Y., Kupferman, R., Linial, N.: No justified complaints: on fair sharing of multiple resources. In: Proceedings of the 3rd Innovations in Theoretical Computer Science Conference (2012)
3. Ghodsi, A., Sekar, V., Zaharia, M., Stoica, I.: Multi-resource fair queueing for packet processing. ACM SIGCOMM Comput. Commun. Rev. **42**(4), 1–12 (2012)
4. Ghodsi, A., Zaharia, M., Hindman, B., Konwinski, A., Shenker, S., Stoica, I.: Dominant resource fairness: fair allocation of multiple resource types. NSDI **11**, 24–24 (2011)
5. Joe-Wong, C., Sen, S., Lan, T., Chiang, M.: Multiresource allocation: fairness-efficiency tradeoffs in a unifying framework. IEEE/ACM Trans. Netw. **21**(6), 1785–1798 (2013)
6. Parkes, D.C., Procaccia, A.D., Shah, N.: Beyond dominant resource fairness: extensions, limitations, and indivisibilities. ACM Trans. Econ. Comput. **3**(1), 3 (2015)
7. Sharma, B., Chudnovsky, V., Hellerstein, J.L., Rifaat, R., Das, C.R.: Modeling and synthesizing task placement constraints in Google compute clusters. In: ACM Symposium on Cloud Computing, p. 3 (2011)
8. Wang, H., Varman, P.J.: Balancing fairness and efficiency in tiered storage systems with bottleneck-aware allocation. In: FAST, pp. 229–242 (2014)

Towards the Cloud Computing from Services to Securities and Challenges

Shuyan Yu[✉]

College of Management and Information,
Zhejiang Post and Telecommunication College, Shaoxing 312000, China
shuyanyu1231@qq.com

Abstract. Cloud computing is ideal for running data intensive and computational intensive applications whether it is business applications or scientific applications. It raises the requirement of reducing the running costs and maximizing the revenues while maintaining or even improving the service quality. It is predicted that cloud computing is the mainstream technology and development in the future 100 years in IT industry. But cloud computing is also facing a lot of questions such as complex industrial environment and technical problems. This paper provides the readers with a basic understanding of services, securities, and challenges in cloud computing, it also enables the application developers and security researchers to acquire the current development status about the cloud computing.

Keywords: Cloud computing · Services · Securities

1 Introduction

Cloud Computing is a growing field in the area of computing, which aims to maximize the utilization and computing capabilities without spending much into purchasing new infrastructures, and cloud computing services are having various features such as liability, versatility, dependability, adaptability, profitability, and element property [1]. Cloud computing is a distributed network computing technology [2] in that it conveys infrastructure, programming and application as administrations to the client through the internet. According to the recent survey [3], cloud computing acquires 12% of software market in the last 5 years and the value will reach up to 95 billion USD.

Cloud computing can be defined as the aggregation of computing as a utility and software as a service [4] where the applications are delivered as services over the Internet and the hardware and systems software in data centers provide those services [5]. Also called *on demand computing, utility computing* or *pay as you go computing*, the concept behind cloud computing is to offload computation to remote resource providers [6].

Cloud computing has derived from grid computing and utility computing [7]. According to [7], the major difference between cloud computing and grid

© Springer Nature Switzerland AG 2018
X. Sun et al. (Eds.): ICCCS 2018, LNCS 11064, pp. 334–343, 2018.
https://doi.org/10.1007/978-3-030-00009-7_31

computing is its wide use of virtualization, cloud computing also has the *pay as you go* model like the utility computing, the service oriented architecture and Web 2.0 technologies also have significant contributions in the wide spreading of the cloud based technologies, and Fig. 1 shows the relationship between these technologies [7].

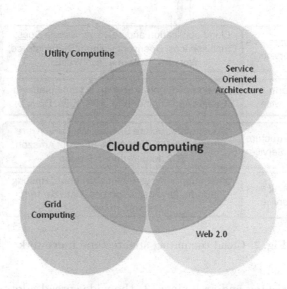

Fig. 1. Cloud computing and related technologies

To understand the basic concept and framework of cloud computing, the basic cloud computing architectural framework is presented in Fig. 2 [8]. In addition, cloud computing has many applications [9], among this applications, using the cloud technology in the eHealth domain [10] has improved quality of services due to the cloud characteristics such as economical, scalable, expedient, ubiquitous, and on demand access to shared resources [11,12]. Cloud computing improves efficiency health care not only by the use of different medical resources but also with achieving a strong information technology resources and optimizing patient flow [13].

Cloud provides four deployment models [7]: (1) public cloud which is sold to the public by big organizations or companies who have mega scale infrastructure; (2) private cloud that is owned or leased by big organizations or companies; (3) hybrid cloud is the composition of two or more cloud; (4) community cloud is shared infrastructure for specific community.

According to [7], there are three main factors contributing to the surge and interests in cloud computing: (1) rapid decrease in hardware cost and increase in computing power and storage capacity, and the advent of multi-core architecture and modern supercomputers consisting of hundreds of thousands of cores; (2) the exponentially growing data size in scientific instrumentation or simulation

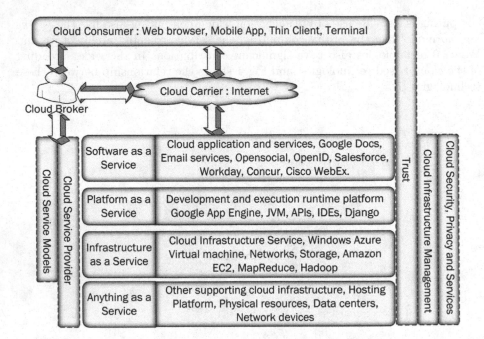

Fig. 2. Cloud computing architectural framework

and Internet publishing and archiving; (3) the wide-spread adoption of services computing and Web 2.0 applications [15].

In spite of all the advantages of the cloud, cloud security is a major area of concern that is restricting its use for certain applications, security concerns are preventing some organizations from adopting cloud computing at all, others are considering using a combination of a secure internal private cloud, along with public clouds [7].

This paper provides the readers with a basic understanding of services, securities, and challenges in cloud computing, it also enables the application developers and security researchers to acquire the current development status about the cloud computing. The organization of the article is as follows: an introduction is presented in Sect. 1; services provided by cloud computing are shown in Sect. 2; security issues and challenges are discussed in Sects. 3 and 4; conclusion is drawn in Sect. 5.

2   Services Provided

Three major service models are provided by cloud computing as is shown in Fig. 3 [7], i.e., Software as a Service, Platform as a Service, and Infrastructure as a Service.

The SaaS provides least flexibility as the end users have to use the application as provided and cannot make any changes to the application [7]. Saas replaces

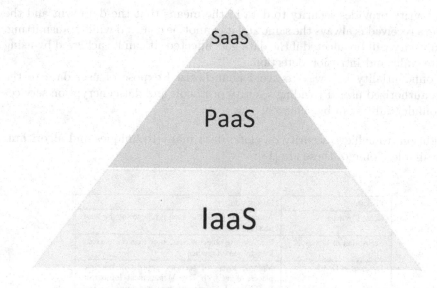

Fig. 3. Cloud computing service models

the applications running on PC onto the cloud computing environment, covers a wide range of simple to complex services, and provides GUI interaction to the user for service [15].

In case of PaaS, the end users have the flexibility to deploy their own applications in the platform [7]. PaaS abstracts the infrastructures, supports a set of application program interface to clod applications, and is responsible to provide the risk free and robust environment for software product development [15].

IaaS provides the most flexibility so that end users can make use of the infrastructure provided in any way they want [7]. Iaas deals with the delivery of computing resources such as servers, storage, network, and other computing resources in the form of virtualized systems, which can be accessed through the internet, offers the infrastructure as-a-service, to execute appropriate applications, and can be combined or layered to derive customized environment with various building blocks [15].

3   Security Issues

Despite of increased hacking of data in public cloud, data security in public cloud can be achieved with the use of high quality cloud security [16]. The three issues need to be addressed to provide security in cloud computing are: Availability, Confidentiality and Integrity [17] described as follows.

(1) Availability is a mechanism by which data will be available to the user in a manner irrespective of location of the user. It can be achieved by providing authentication and network security.

(2) Integrity provides security to data in the means that the data sent and the data received is always the same and it cannot be changed while transmitting. Integrity will be affected if the data gets affected. It can be achieved by using fire walls and intrusion detection.

(3) Confidentiality is a way to avoid unauthorized expose of user data to the unauthorized user. Providing security protocols and data encryption services confidentiality can be achieved.

In addition, to achieve security on cloud data many techniques and algorithms are available. Some of these are [18]:

Principle	Description
Least Privilege	An entity is given the least privilege for the least acceptable time
Separation of Duties	For Sensitive object access, more than one persons have to come together
Defense in Depth	Multiple layers of security, applied in multiple places, along with Key Management Infrastructure/Public Key Infrastructure and Intrusion Detection systems.
Fail Safe	On failure, system goes to a state with least access privileges and recovers to a secure state
Economy of Mechanism	Simple, comprehensible design and implementation of protection mechanisms.
Complete Mediation	Every subject to object request undergoes authorization procedure
Open Design	More secure when reviewed by a number of experts
Least Common Mechanism	Multiple users should share least common security mechanism
Psychological Acceptability	Ease and intuitiveness of the interfaces with which the users interact
Weakest Link	The whole security of the system is only that much of the weakest security mechanism in place
Leveraging Existing Components	Existing components partitioned into a sub units so that compromising one unit does not affect the whole system.

Fig. 4. Cloud security principles

(1) Authorization practice provides authorization to clients, who can access data stored on cloud system.

(2) Authentication process creates a user name and password to access the data.

(3) Encryption uses complex algorithm to hide the original information with the help of encryption key.

[19] provides insight into securing the cloud through its chapters. The security of the system is enhanced by keeping the security in mind when the software itself is developed. Secure cloud software requires secure development practices

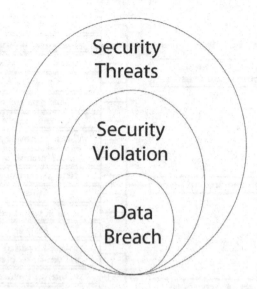

Fig. 5. Cloud security and data breach

and secure testing practices. The security requirements have to be identified in the requirement phase itself and the security principles and the security services are to be kept in mind while designing and developing the system. Figure 4 gives some of the relevant cloud security design principles in [19] that needs to be followed while developing a software [7].

According to [1], data breach is the key security issue in cloud computing environment. The sensitive data of user or organization are stolen and they are become victims of financial fraud and identity theft. There are different sorts of data breaches, for example, [20,21] representative manhandle, Human oversights, system bugs, malicious assaults, intrusions with no robbery of information and intrusions with burglary of information. A data breach takes place when there is an impact related to the data such as the data being lost or illegitimately accessed, and effects have repercussions not only on the system security but also on the protection of personal data of the individual affected. Figure 5 shows the relationship between security threats, security violation and data breaches [1].

Security testing also plays a major role in securing the software, Source code analysis, property based testing, source code fault injection, dynamic code analysis, binary code analysis, byte code analysis, black box debugging, vulnerability scanning and penetration testing are the common security testing techniques applied [7].

In addition, [8] provides a through summarization for cloud computing securities as is shown in Fig. 6, which creates a building block in the reader's mind that is helping to understand the current security issues.

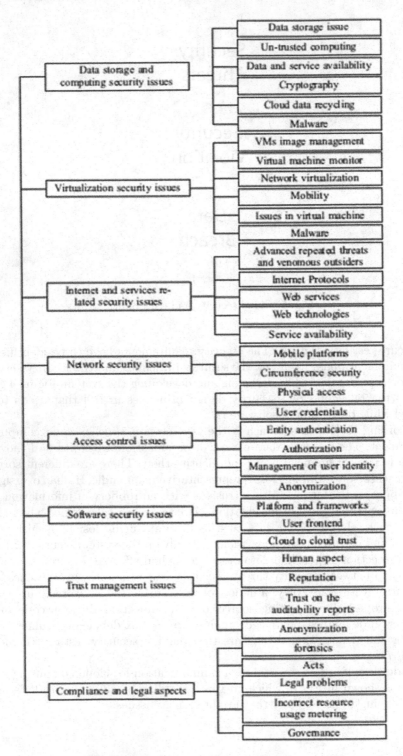

Fig. 6. Cloud security principles

4   Challenges

There are numerous security challenges associated with cloud computing and some of them are as follows [1]:

(1) Privileged user access. If any of the confidential information of the client is accessed by an unauthorized user then the client should acquire a new membership to verify the unauthorized access, or else the leakage of information will be increased. The owner of the data is having full privilege rights over the data stored, and other users are owning only certain set of privileges or access rights.
(2) Regulatory compliance. Cloud provider performs internal audit to the cloud systems and processes, but never permits any external auditing processes, and installing new security certificates to the network is also dropped by the cloud provider.
(3) Data location. In cloud computing conditions, the client is ignorant of the storage areas of the information.
(4) Investigative support. An exact request concerning the unlawful access to the customer information in cloud computing is troublesome. The unapproved access is finished by either inside or remotely.
(5) Data segregation. In cloud computing, the data from one client can be made available to other clients through sharing process, so more than one client can access the data in parallel with each other.
(6) Recovery. If the server or the data farm utilized by the cloud provider for putting away the customer information is flopped because of characteristic catastrophes or framework disappointments, then it's the obligation of the cloud provider to suggest the status of the customer information to the customer.

High availability of usersdata is also a great challenge to service providers, so data security and privacy have become users concerns, and diversified and personalized access technology in clouds are key points related to widespread usage of clouds [22].

5   Conclusion

The future of cloud computing is invaluable. It is even predicted that cloud computing is the mainstream technology and development in the future 100 years in IT industry. But cloud computing is also facing a lot of questions such as complex industrial environment and technical problems. In addition, relevant laws and regulations needed to be improved. This paper provides the readers with a basic understanding of services, securities, and challenges in cloud computing, it also enables the application developers and security researchers to acquire the current development status about the cloud computing.

References

1. Barona, R.: Survey on data breach challenges in cloud computing security: issues and threats. In: 2017 International Conference on Circuits Power and Computing Technologies, pp. 1–8. College of Pune, India (2017)
2. Jitender, G., Shikha, M., Mohit, S.: Cloud computing and its security issues-a review. In: IEEE 5th ICCCNT, Hefei, China, pp. 208–213 (2014)
3. Kanickam, S.: A survey on layer wise issues and challenges in cloud security. In: 2017 World Congress on Computing and Communication Technologies, New York, USA, pp. 168–171 (2017)
4. Vogels, W.: A head in the clouds the power of infrastructure as a service. In: Proceedings of the 1st Workshop on Cloud Computing and Applications, Barcelona, Spain, pp. 132–140 (2013)
5. Armbrust, M., et al.: Above the clouds: a Berkeley view of cloud computing. EECS Department, University of California, Berkeley, vol. 53, no. 4, pp. 50–58 (2009)
6. Kulkarni, P., Khanai, R.: Addressing mobile cloud computing security issues: a survey. In: IEEE ICCSP 2015 Conference, Tamilnadu, India, pp. 1463–1467 (2015)
7. Anupa, J., Sekaran, K.: Cloud workflow and security: a survey. In: 2014 International Conference on Advances in Computing, Communications and Informatics, Calcutta, India, pp. 1598–1607 (2014)
8. Singh, A., Chatterjee, K.: Cloud security issues and challenges: a survey. J. Netw. Comput. Appl. **79**, 88–115 (2017)
9. Gourav, K.: Mobile cloud computing architecture, application model and challenging issues. In: 2014 Sixth International Conference on Computational Intelligence and Communication Networks, Ghaziabad, India, pp. 613–617 (2014)
10. Ida, I., Jemai, A., Loukil, A.: A survey on security of IoT in the context of eHealth and clouds. In: Design & Test Symposium 2017, pp. 25–30 (2017)
11. Duan, Q., Yan, Y., Vasilakos, A.: A survey on service-oriented network virtualization toward convergence of networking and cloud computing. IEEE Trans. Netw. Serv. Manag. **9**(4), 373–392 (2012)
12. Abbas, A., et al.: A cloud based health insurance plan recommendation system: a user centered approach. Future Gener. Comput. Syst. **43–44**, 99–109 (2015)
13. Bai, Y., et al.: Access control for cloud-based eHealth social networking: design and evaluation. Secur. Commun. Netw. **7**(3), 574–587 (2014)
14. Foster, I., Zhao, Y., Raicu, I., Lu, S.: Cloud computing and grid computing 360-degree compared. In: 2008 Grid Computing Environments Workshop, West Lafayette, USA, pp. 1–10 (2008)
15. Raja, K., Hanifa, S.: Bigdata driven cloud security: a survey. Mater. Sci. Eng. **225**(1), 12–18 (2017)
16. Geetha, V.: Survey on security mechanisms for public cloud data. In: International Conference on Emerging Trends in Engineering, India, pp. 1–8 (2016)
17. Agarwal, A., Agarwal, A.: The security risks associated with cloud computing. Int. J. Comput. Appl. Eng. Sci. **1**, 108–116 (2011)
18. Selvamani, K., Jayanthi, S.: A review on cloud data security and its mitigation techniques. In: International Conference on Intelligent Computing, Communication and Convergence, pp. 347–352 (2015). Procedia Comput. Sci
19. Krutz, R., Vines, R.: Cloud Security: A Comprehensive Guide to Secure Cloud Computing. Wiley, New Delhi (2010)
20. Algarni, A., Malaiya, Y.: A consolidated approach for estimation of data security breach costs. In: International Conference on Information Management, India, pp. 26–39 (2016)

21. www.cyberriskhub.com/breach. Accessed 4 Oct 2017
22. Ma, W., Zhang, J.: The survey and research on application of cloud computing. In: 7th International Conference on Computer Science & Education, Melbourne, Australia, pp. 203–206 (2012)

Traffic Accident Time Series Analysis

Chao Zhang[1], Junmei Wang[1(✉)], Pingzeng Liu[1], Wanming Ren[2],
Weijie Chen[1], and Yanyan Wang[1,2]

[1] College of Information Science and Engineering,
Shandong Agricultural University, Tai'an 271000, China
jmwang@sdau.edu.cn
[2] Shandong Provincial Department of Agriculture Information Center,
Jinan 250013, China

Abstract. Traffic accident hidden behind a lot of factors, although the rapid development of China's transportation infrastructure, traffic management level is increasing, but the development of social economy and daily living travel traffic caused by the supply and demand contradiction is prominent. The traffic safety management situation is still grim, needs to be based on existing management, through the analysis of massive traffic the management of data mining, finding the underlying changes in the law, for the transportation departments to effectively carry out the administration of road traffic safety, more in-depth mining the potential causes of traffic accidents. In this paper, we first use the Baidu map API interface to transform the street information to the specific latitude and longitude. Then we divide the morning and evening peak and non peak hours, working days and non working days, and analyze the time characteristics of the accidents based on the MATLAB 3D data imaging principle. Secondly, the stability analysis is carried out after the data collection, and the occurrence trend and periodic law of the accident are obtained by using the Holt - Winters filter prediction and test and STL decomposition. Finally, in view of the above analysis, the reasonable countermeasures are given in order to reduce the incidence of traffic accidents and build a harmonious travel environment.

Keywords: Traffic · Data mining · MATLAB 3D modeling
Time series analysis

1 Introduction

1.1 Research Background

Guiyang Geographical Location and Geomorphic Features. Guiyang is located in the middle of Guizhou Province, the east of Yunnan Guizhou Plateau, the watershed of the Yangtze River Basin and the Pearl River Basin. High altitude, low latitude, located in the east longitude 103 36′ to 109° 31′, north latitude 24 37′ to 29° 13′. The highest elevation of the city is 1762 m, the lowest is 506 m, and the average elevation of the main city is 1070 m. Guiyang City area of 176 thousand and 100 km^2, the specific administrative divisions as shown in Fig. 1 [1].

© Springer Nature Switzerland AG 2018
X. Sun et al. (Eds.): ICCCS 2018, LNCS 11064, pp. 344–356, 2018.
https://doi.org/10.1007/978-3-030-00009-7_32

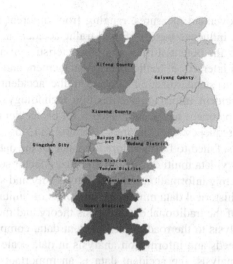

Fig. 1. The administrative division of Guiyang

The Guiyang landform belongs to the Hilly Basin area, which is mainly mountainous and hilly. The mountainous area of 4218 km², hilly area of 2842 km²; the dam is less, only 912 km². In addition, there are about 1.2% gorge landform. The layered landform is obvious, mainly in Guiyang - in our Cao synclinal basin and Baiyun Huaxi constitute multi platform and Qingyan karst depression landforms. Flat Bazi Huaxi, Meng Guan, Wudang, Jinhua, Zhu Chang, etc. The Nanming river runs from the southwest to the northeast, which accounts for about 70% [2] of the total area of the urban area.

In Guiyang, there were 273486 kinds of traffic accidents in 2015, 803 people died and 3494 were injured, the total amount increased by 2.42%.

1.2 The Purpose and Significance of the Study

In recent years, China's social and economic development has maintained a relatively high speed, and the road traffic infrastructure has been gradually improved. The number of drivers, vehicle ownership and road traffic volume continue to grow. As an indispensable part of life, road traffic plays a more and more important role in supporting and guiding the social and economic development. However, all kinds of traffic accidents also seriously affect the safety of people's life and property, and restrict the quality and benefit of social and economic development.

Road traffic accident is a process that people or things are damaged at the same time due to the coupling of dynamic and static factors such as people, vehicles, roads and environment. The historical data of road traffic accidents can directly reflect the relationship between people, vehicles, roads and environment. Because the road traffic accident has many factors, contingency and fuzzy characteristics, analysis of road traffic accidents in general historical data for the study of the related theories and methods to study the accident also historical data and the specific research contents include accident inquiry, statistics, forecast, cause analysis and evaluation of traffic safety and safety improvement measures, ranging from different aspects from macroscopic to microcosmic, influence factors of road traffic accident analysis to multi angle and multi-level, reveals the potential rules and characteristics of all kinds of accidents between historical data interaction, traffic safety management and accident prevention.

With the continuous standardization of road traffic accident management information system and accident information collection technology, China's road traffic safety management department has accumulated a lot of accident data. These data in practice for "accident frequency" and "injured", "death" and "loss" of four indicators of the descriptive statistics, failed to fully explore the value of the data; on the other hand, discrete, accident history data multi dimension and fuzzy factor set and characteristics. In the process of collecting information integrity, objectivity and standardization of the cause of the accident, historical data mining has all kinds of limitations, which directly affect the application of the traditional data analysis theory and method. In addition, in the choice of data analysis to the road traffic accident data, complex characteristics to adapt to the various needs and information analysis in data scale [3].

From the above analysis, the accident data is an important basis for correlative research of road traffic safety, data for rational and efficient application is an effective way to fully reflect the value of the accident data. For a large number of road traffic accident historical data, it is very necessary to find latent characteristics, rules and other useful information behind data, which has important theoretical research significance and application prospect.

1.3 The Purpose and Significance of the Study

Due to road traffic accidents data is discrete, multi dimension, fuzzy factor set characteristics, coupled with China's traffic accident information collection started late, there are many defects in application of historical data in a series of accidents, including integrity, objectivity and non standardization, the problems that reduced the application quality of road traffic accident data then, a direct impact on the application of traditional data analysis theory and method [4].

Data mining is a process of extracting hidden information from a large number of incomplete, noisy, fuzzy and random practical application data, which people don't know before, but potentially useful information and knowledge. The process is user oriented, knowledge discovery oriented data analysis process [5]. Through the data mining research of a large number of road traffic accident historical data, we can analyze the influencing factors of road traffic accidents from multiple angles, multi-level and more comprehensively, and reveal the potential rules and characteristics of the interrelated effects between different kinds of accident data [6].

This paper uses MATLAB three-dimensional modeling, classification analysis, simple linear regression, cluster analysis, association rules mining data mining theories and methods, focusing on spatial and temporal characteristics of the accident, for traffic accident causes, and puts forward the improvement measures, in order to create a better and safer travel environment.

2 Data Preprocessing

2.1 Data Overview

Analyze the competition provided by Guiyang traffic accident data, and data driver violation records, weather records and other data of Guiyang traffic data race series data used in this paper sources jointly organized by the Guiyang Municipal Traffic Management Bureau and Data Castle the causes of traffic accidents, and all the data has been desensitization.

The Guiyang Administration provided accident data, illegal data and meteorological data. Among them, the accident data is divided into 21 fields, a total of 56651 accident record; illegal data is divided into 6 fields, including 65535 illegal records, the jszh field and accident data in the driver license table matching fields; meteorological data is divided into 4 fields, recorded the weather throughout the year in Guiyang city.

We use Excel PivotTables, preliminary to false: such as "mass" and "mass card", "Volkswagen brand" duplicates unified into "public"; relates to the driver's age, driving age can not modify the input error directly to delete.

2.2 Address Resolution

Open platform Baidu map Geocoding API interface, including address resolution and reverse address resolution functions: address resolution is to address the streets are structured with Baidu latitude and longitude information, reverse address resolution from Baidu latitude and longitude information structured address information. It is used to provide transformation service from address to latitude and longitude coordinate or from latitude and longitude coordinate to address. Users can send requests and receive data from JSON and XML by using C#, C++, Java and other development languages. Geocoding API has fully supported two forms of request [3], which are as follows (Fig. 2):

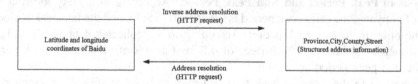

Fig. 2. Geocoding API service schematic

This time mainly uses its geographical analysis function, the street information contained in the accidentaddr field of the accident data is converted to the latitude and longitude information. After the merger, the address record is still more, so it is divided into batch processing to improve the efficiency. For the two analysis of the records that failed to be parsed correctly, the information comparison was carried out, and the data that were obviously beyond the scope of Guiyang were removed to ensure the accuracy of the information.

The longitude and latitude data obtained by the final analysis are limited to the six bits in the decimal point, and the corresponding accuracy is meter.

2.3   Taxonomy

The following fields are mainly divided into the following fields: month, date, peak and non peak, working day and non working day. Combined with the latitude and longitude of subtotals, in addition the total number of each longitude accident and the total number of all kinds of accident type statistics.

The data treated above, as shown in the following figure, are shown in the following figure (Fig. 3):

Fig. 3. Post processing data partial screenshot

3   Time Series Analysis of Accident Time

3.1   Accident Time Analysis

Analysis of Peak Period and Non Peak Period. According to the city location and habit of Guiyang, the early peak period is set at 6:30 to 8:30, and the late peak period is that the other is the non peak period. According to the collected data and MATLAB three-dimensional imaging, the images of different angles of view in the peak period and the non peak period are drawn.

According to the morning peak time 3D map and profile (Fig. 4), evening peak three-dimensional map and profile (Fig. 5), non peak period of three-dimensional map and profile (Fig. 6) the four picture shows that the total number of image features and the characteristics of accidents during peak periods are basically the same, the image non peak time it showed different characteristics.

But the characteristics of the morning peak image is more obvious. The area where the municipal government is located is particularly prominent, which indicates that traffic accidents are more likely to happen at the rush hour, which can be seen more clearly from the front view.

The high incidence places in the late peak period are more concentrated, and the phenomenon of serial is appeared. This indicates that the traffic volume of the peak

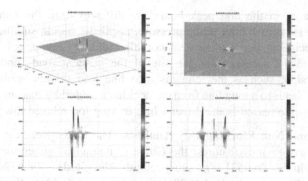

Fig. 4. The three dimensional map and the profile of the early peak period

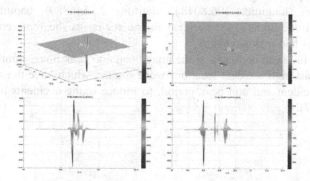

Fig. 5. Three dimensional map and section map in the late peak period

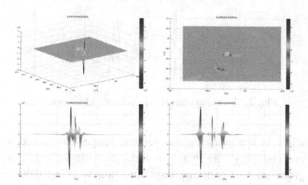

Fig. 6. The non peak period of three dimensional map and profile

hours is large, the driver's mood is impatient, and the unclear vision at night makes the accident happen more likely, which leads to a large number of traffic accidents.

By comparing the peak time with the off peak time, we found that the difference between the two images is quite large, and the location of the accident has changed a lot, and the images in the non peak hours are different from the total number of accidents. There is no rush hour traffic pressure, accidents should significantly reduce the number of accidents, but in some areas not fall, indicating non peak hours the main factors leading to the accident was the site of the incident road conditions or the unreasonable design, such as the long distance line lead drivers because of visual fatigue, speeding leads to a long line from car accidents caused by inaccurate judgment; secondly the possible reason is the driver while driving too relaxed this time [7].

Working Day and Non Working Day Analysis. The image from the working day can see it has two obvious features: the Guiyang municipal government (longitude 106.643358, latitude 26.653148), show South (longitude 106.672405, latitude 106.672405), orchard (longitude 106.701707, latitude 26.57595), Nanming Airport Road (longitude 106.760438, latitude 26.564122) as the representative of the accident area with the approaching location had a significant jump; and in Nanming Long-dongbao Airport (longitude 106.804843, latitude 26.546889), bapima (longitude 106.606437, latitude 26.847448) accident image region as the representative of the neighboring sites had a slow change.

At the same time can be found on the image and non peak image similarity is high, the image contrast high accident locations were similar, which have the same place in its work day accident and non peak period, to reduce traffic accidents have a certain reference (Fig. 7).

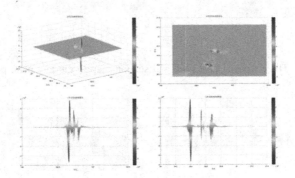

Fig. 7. Working day 3D drawings and sections

The image below is non working day related image. Compared with the image, there is no obvious change in the image. It indicates that the traffic pressure is very large in both regions on both working days and non working days. Therefore, reasonable arrangements can be made in these sections properly (Fig. 8).

Figure 9 shows the frequency of the accident from Monday to Sunday. From Monday to Friday, the frequency of accidents increased first and then increased, and the frequency of accidents on Friday was larger than that of weekly. At the end of the week, the frequency of accidents dropped sharply and decreased to the lowest level on Sunday.

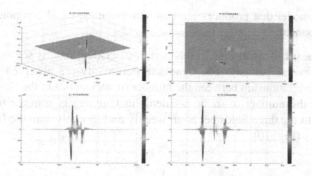

Fig. 8. Non working day 3D drawings and sections

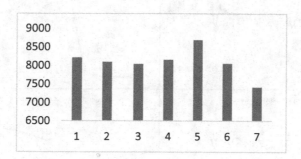

Fig. 9. The frequency of accidents from Monday to Sunday

3.2   Accident Timing Analysis

STL Decomposition. A time series may be composed of some or all of the three components of a trend, a season, a cycle and a random component. If these components can be broken down, the problem can be simplified. Of course, not all the sequences can be disassembled. The simplest form of a decomposed sequence is an additive model [8]:

$$X_t = m_t + g_t + e_t \tag{1}$$

In the form of m_t, the trend component is expressed as the g_t seasonal component, while e_t is the remaining disturbance component or error component. If the model is generally correct, the disturbing component is considered to be random. Sometimes other components, such as random or irregular cyclic or fluctuating components, are also considered. However, they are often not placed in the model [9]. The influence is considered to be added to the disturbance components. Therefore, to be more precise, the disturbance component should be called the residual component.

The STL decomposition method [10] is based on the loess smoothing method, which is based on the local polynomial regression method. Specifically, the STL is based on the formula (1), so the STL is the simplest non-parametric seasonal-trend decomposition model that produces seasonal components, trend components, and the rest Error component.

Process and Result of Analysis. In this part, the accident data is set up according to the number of events per day. The trend and periodicity are observed through STL analysis, and the relationship between the number of accidents and the time is analyzed.

First of all, the number of traffic accidents in Guiyang is summarized daily, and then according to the three fields per hour, weekly and monthly, and the folding map is made as follows (Fig. 10).

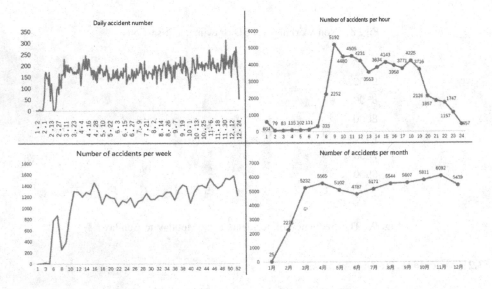

Fig. 10. A summary of the number of accidents

A corresponding scatter plot is made according to the date and the total number of accidents. The left is a scatter diagram based on the number of accidents per day and the date. The time axis is in days. The longitudinal axis is the number of accidents X, and the right is its ACF diagram, that is, sequence autocorrelation function diagram (Fig. 11).

For this data, the Holt - Winters filter [11] can be used for exponential smoothing or decomposition into three components of level, trend and season. The trend and level of this combination is roughly corresponding to the trend of subsequent STL. The residual error of original data minus the fitting value is roughly equivalent to the residual error component of STL method [12]. Using Holt - Winters filtering for daily accident data, Fig. 12 can be obtained. From top to bottom, the map is followed by the fitting sequence, the horizontal component, the trend component and the seasonal component [13]. From the graph, when the truncation lag parameter is 4, the trend of using filtered sequence is not obvious, basically a horizontal line, and the horizontal component is very close to the data itself.

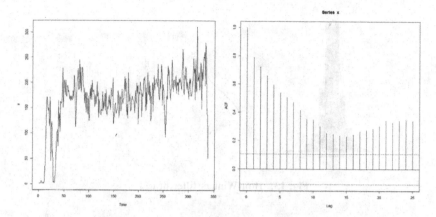

Fig. 11. Ordinary scatter plot and ACF diagram

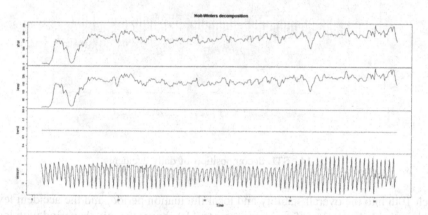

Fig. 12. Holt - Winters filter for daily accident number

Following a series of tests, from left to right, the residuals density histogram, the normal QQ map and the residual sequence [14] fitted by the Holt - Winters filter are in turn. From the figure, the overall fitting effect is better (Fig. 13).

Due to the use of filtering to eliminate the original trend of the data, STL decomposition was performed again. In Fig. 14, from top to bottom, there are sequence diagrams, seasonal effect diagrams, trend graphs, and random fluctuation items. The figure shows that the seasonal influence is minimal (according to the scale) and can be completely ignored; it is mainly the influence of the trend.

According to the above image shows, the overall incidence of accidents in January is the lowest, the number of accidents after the climb quickly, to the middle of February reached the first peak, then the Spring Festival is approaching, the overall level showed a decreasing trend, and realize the lowest accident rate during the Spring Festival holiday, the specific date of February 21st, only 2 accidents; vacation after people started to work, traffic gradually increased, increasing the number of accidents, since

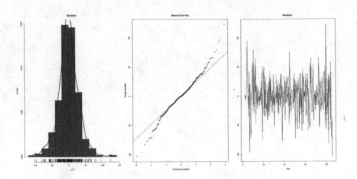

Fig. 13. Holt-Winters filter fit test

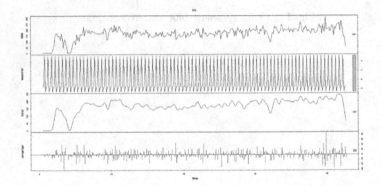

Fig. 14. STL decomposition of daily accidents

March 10th into the overall stability and local fluctuation period, and the accident level is higher, the daily number of accidents is up to 110 above; the middle period with local fluctuations for holidays, people travel demand is day decline, the number of accidents will decrease slightly. The number of accidents decreased obviously the National Day holiday, to achieve second obvious trough in October 3rd, there were 93 accidents; then continue to rise back to the previously stable level, continued until December 25th again near the new year, a larger decline in accident rate.

As a result, holidays have a certain regulating effect on the incidence of traffic accidents. During the holidays, there are regional and time traffic jams. But at this stage, people have strong sense of their own, and the number of outbound travelers is more, which eases the traffic pressure in the center of the city, and the accident rate decreases slightly, and minor accidents account for a large proportion, and major accidents are less. Rather than during holidays, whether traffic is going to work or going out, traffic flow is increasing rapidly, and traffic participants are in urgent need, resulting in high and high accidents [15].

4   Countermeasures

In view of the above analysis, the causes of traffic accidents in Guiyang are summarized, and suggestions for improving the traffic accidents are given.

(1) The traffic management department can manage accurately according to the time series analysis of the accident period, and use the human resources efficiently and reasonably.

According to the different accidents in different periods, the police command traffic is targeted, and traffic information is released ahead of schedule according to the accident situation, through WeChat, SMS and other platforms [16], to guide the driver's choice of driving path.

The government encourages local enterprises to carry out flexible work system [17] to reduce traffic pressure at peak hours. During weekends and holidays, multiple solutions are launched for tour drivers to stagger the peak of travel.

(2) The individual reasonably arranges the travel time and chooses the appropriate means of transportation.

According to the specific situation of our own, we should take a reasonable way to deal with the problem of rush hour congestion in the morning and evening. Go out ahead of time, or take public transport. Do not violate traffic rules in order to squeeze time and cause safety hazards.

Holiday travel, whether to go out or take a vacation, should keep in mind, strengthen the sense of safety, and do not drive.

References

1. National data. http://data.stats.gov.cn/easyquery.htm?cn=C01
2. A brief introduction of Guiyang City. https://zh.wikipedia.org/wiki/%E8%B4%B5%E9%98%B3%E5%B8%82#.E5.9C.B0.E7.90.86
3. Baidu API introduction. http://lbsyun.baidu.com/index.php?title=webapi/guide/webservice—geocoding
4. Wu, X., Liu, M.: Application of Time Series Analysis: R Software Accompanying. Machinery Industry Press, Beijing (2014)
5. PPG Corporate Communications, Automotive Color Trends 2015, America (2015)
6. Han, J., Kamber, M., Pei, J.: Data Mining: Concepts and Techniques. Morgan Kaufmann, Burlington (2011)
7. Yongqiang, X.H.Y.B., Jiang, H.L.: Research on data analysis and mining of road traffic accidents. J. Chin. People's Public Secur. Univ. (Nat. Sci. Ed.) (04), 69–73 (2008)
8. Tan, C.: Research on Data Mining and Application of Road Traffic Accidents. Harbin University of Technology, Heilongjiang
9. Dong, L., Liu, G., Yuan, S.: Application of data mining technology in traffic accident analysis. J. Jilin Univ. (Sci. Ed.) 44(06), 951–955 (2006)
10. Sun, X.: Analysis and simulation of vehicle-bicycle traffic accidents. Harbin Institute of Technology, Heilongjiang (2015)

11. Kabacoff, R.I.: R in Action: Data Analysis and Graphics with R, 2nd edn. Manning Publications, Shelter Island (2015)
12. Savolainen, P.T., Mannering, F.L.: The statistical analysis of highway crash—injury severities: a review and assessment of methodological alternatives. Accid. Anal. Prev. **43** (05), 1666–1676 (2011)
13. Al-Ghamdi, A.S.: Using logistic regression to estimate the influence of accident factors on accident severity. Accid. Anal. Prev. **34**(06), 729–741 (2002)
14. Yau, K.: Risk factors affecting the severity of single vehicle traffic accidents in Hong Kong. Accid. Anal. Prev. **36**(03), 333–340 (2004)
15. Li, S., Sun, M., Guan, H.: Prediction model of traffic accident severity based on cumulative Logistic model. Traffic Stand. (03), 168–171 (2009)
16. Zhao, Z.: The application of hidden Markov model in the field of intelligent transportation. Transp. Technol. Econ. **14**(01), 120–122 (2012)
17. Xia, M.: Analysis on the impact of meteorological conditions on road traffic accidents. Nanjing University of Information Engineering, Jiangsu (2014)

VAT: A Velocity-Aware Trajectory Privacy Preservation Scheme for IoT Searching

Yuhang Wang[1], Hongli Zhang[1], and Shen Su[2(✉)]

[1] Research Center of Computer Network and Information Security Technology,
Harbin Institute of Technology, Harbin 150001, China
[2] Cyberspace Institute of Advanced Technology, Guangzhou University,
Guangzhou 510006, China
sushen@gzhu.edu.cn

Abstract. As the rapid development of the IoT infrastructure and searching technologies, the potential of to-be-located of IoT user has caused the privacy concerns. Although the privacy issue of trajectory privacy has gain much attention in the mobile Internet and the IoT researches, these efforts are also in some degree omitted some high level features of the trajectory information. In this paper, we introduce a type of trajectory privacy attack named "Velocity Inference Attack", and we shows that the preservation schemes which left out to protect the velocity information will fail to resist this attack. Then, a velocity-aware trajectory privacy preservation scheme named VAT was propose. Experimental result shows the effectiveness of VAT while against the velocity inference attack.

Keywords: Location privacy · Trajectory privacy
Internet of Things · IoT searching · Privacy attack

1 Introduction

The Internet of Thing enables the pervasive searching of the location and the trajectory of every smart device and the mobile user. In spite of the next generation search engine of IoT greatly expand the spatial-temporal range of search, it also brings the unprecedented privacy concerns. Among those privacy-concerning information, The trajectory of the user is one of the most crucial part, it contains rich dimension of other privacy, such as lifestyle, social relationship and others.

Much efforts have been put into the trajectory privacy preservation, among these proposed schemes, trajectory k-anonymity method, mixzone and the dummy-based method are the most popular approaches. Beside the mixzone-based approaches which rely on the cloaking method, the basic idea of k-anonymity and the dummy method are focusing on adding the noise trajectory into the real trajectory, and then make further efforts to improve the authenticity of the noise trajectories. However, most of these efforts will to a certain

© Springer Nature Switzerland AG 2018
X. Sun et al. (Eds.): ICCCS 2018, LNCS 11064, pp. 357–365, 2018.
https://doi.org/10.1007/978-3-030-00009-7_33

extent lose the effectiveness when they fontal defense the inference attacks which rely on those advanced human activity recognition technologies. We argue that this defect is caused by the lack of consideration on the high level trajectory features, such as the velocity information. High convincing noise trajectory should be used to confuse the inference attack.

In this paper, we take the velocity feature of the trajectory into consideration, and proposed a dummy trajectory-based approach. We first introduces a trajectory inference attack based on the abnormal behavior detection technology, and we will shows the effect of this attack on those approaches which do not take the high level movement features into consideration. Then, we proposed our trajectory privacy preserving scheme named VAT. The experimental result and the comparison shows the effectiveness of our approach against the inference attack.

The contributions of this paper are as follows:

1. We introduce a trajectory inference attack based on the abnormal behavior detection, and shows its threat effect on recognising the raw noise trajectories.
2. We proposed a noise trajectory generation scheme which take the velocity information into consideration, and higher similarity to the real trajectory a ensured by our scheme.
3. We make a comprehensive evaluation of both the effectiveness and the comparison, the result shows the effectiveness of our work.

The rest of this paper is organized as follows. Section 2 illustrate the fundamental of trajectory privacy in IoT searching. Section 3 introduce the trajectory privacy attack and the VAT scheme. We provide the experimental result of VAT against the inference attack as well as the comparison with other works in Sect. 4. Finally, Sect. 5 concludes the paper.

2   Background Knowledge

The trajectory are being considered as a moving path or trace reported by a moving object in the geographical space [1]. Formally, in most of the researches, if we use the 2 dimension Euclidian coordinates $l(x, y)$ to represent the location, a trajectory T can be defined as:

$$T : \{identity, [l_1, t_1], [l_2, t_2], \cdots , [l_n, t_n]\}$$

where $identity$ is the identifier of user, and t_i is the time stamp of l_i.

Much efforts had been given on improving the fidelity of Tr, and these approaches are surveyed comprehensively in [1]. In general, the anonymity-based approach and the dummy-based approach tend to add (or, for anonymity method, to induce the attack from leaning) the dummy trajectories and mix them with the real trajectory. [2] tried to mix the real trajectory with the noise and minimal the whole cover area of all the trajectories, [3] proposed a randomization-based dummy trajectory generating method, and ensured a certain extent of similarity by imitating the "swerve" feature of the real trajectory. In general, the information in Tr was used to generate dummies.

T basically outline the fact of trajectory, however, it is lack of the high level features of the object movement. Specially, the velocity information of the object contains abundant information of the moving pattern and the human active information. Although it could be get from T by the indirect calculation, but the result is tend to the average velocity of each interval, and the instantaneous velocity was lost. In this paper, we take the (instantaneous) velocity of the object in each time stamp into consideration, extend the definition of Tr as:

$$Tr : \{identity, [l_1, t_1, v_1], [l_2, t_2, v_2], \cdots, [l_n, t_n, v_n]\}$$

We take Tr as the fundamental of the inference attack and the VAT scheme, which will be showed in the next section.

3 VAT Scheme

As the low similarity noise trajectories are generated by some imitation methods which works on T, as the result, from the perspective of the behavior detection, these trajectories tend to be considered as the abnormal data. On the basis of this concept, we introduce our privacy attack.

3.1 Trajectory Inference Attack

The threat model of our approach is concise and practical, we consider the search engine of the IoT is an honest-but-curious service provider, and it possesses large scale of historical data of trajectories of the underlying user and devices, these data could be used as the basis of the inference attack.

From the perspective of the attacker, he first train his balance matrix upon the historical real trajectories data. With the help of the matrix along with the feature vectors, he will perform the curve comparison to recognize the abnormal trajectories. In our work, we define the detail process of this attack as follow: First, the trajectory clipping are carried out on the historical trajectories for the PCA process. Second, the normal principal component analysis process will be performed on, and get the balance matrix and the feature vectors $D^m = \{y_1^m, y_2^m, \cdots, y_n^m\}$, note that the velocity of each location will be considered as one of the dimension of the input data. Then, with the feature vector of the to be detected trajectory $t = \{x_1, x_2, \cdots, x_n\}$, calculate the projection distance between t and D^m follow:

$$d_t = (\sum_{i=1}^{n} \|x_i - y_i^m\|^2)^{\frac{1}{2}}$$

The threshold δ of d_t controls the discovery of the suspicious trajectory, when $d_t > \delta$, the attacker assert a dummy trajectory was found. Through this process, the attacker will narrow the guess range of the trajectories in the candidate set which generated by the privacy preserving scheme. The following experiment will show the effect of this inference attack against the raw dummy trajectories.

3.2 Velocity-Aware Preservation Scheme

In this paper, we propose a enhanced dummy trajectory generating method which take Tr in to consideration. We further use the reverse engineering method to refine the dummy location in order to achieve higher privacy.

In our scheme, we further divide the velocity v_i in Tr as the magnitude and the direction, denote as $v_i = \{m_i, d_i\}, d_i \in [0, 2\pi]$. For each location l_i in Tr in sequence, we first choose a random coordinate as the origin of the dummy trajectory, together with the approximate random magnitude. Then, for each next location in the real trajectory, the direction of the dummy location is generated in two phrase. In the first phrase, a random increment value between $(d_{i+1} - d_i)$ will be added to the previous location, then, in the second phrase, we calculate the projection distance d_t of the dummy trajectory, if $d_t > \delta$, repeat the first phrase and check the distance again.

As VAT continuously adjust the projection distance of the dummy trajectory, the time complexity will be determined by the possible number of randomization. This number can be controlled by adjusting the interval of randomization, obviously, the time of re-random will decline as the interval narrows, when the interval is 0 (deterministic direction dummy), only one randomization is needed and the dummy trajectory will have the same "swerve" feature as the real trajectory does.

We design the Self-generating R-tree (SGR) algorithm to enable each device to create its own Noise Library. Algorithm 1 shows the details of SGR based on the standard R-tree operation introduced in [40]. The SGR involves three operations:

1. Snippet merging, in which we do not insert any vertex in T but merge some information (not geolocation information) into the existing snippet vertex in some leaf node.
2. Insertion, in which we perform a insertion on T.
3. Splitting, in which we split T when a node overflows; here, we follow the quadratic split heuristic.

The threshold γ represents the maximum number of vertexes a snippet can have; this value controls whether SGR performs a merge or an insert operation. Although SGR enables the device to conduct privacy preservation by itself, it may reduce the scale and diversity compared to the global situation. However, this tradeoff is worthwhile, and will be analyzed and evaluated in the following two sections. In practice, the outcome when using SGR is sufficiently robust.

Algorithm 1. SGR algorithm

Require:
    APs in proximity $\{AP\}$;
    current geolocation L;
    R-tree T;
Ensure:
    R-tree T;
1: $SNIPPETS$ = searchTree(L);
2: **if** $SNIPPETS \cap AP \neq \emptyset$ **then**
3:    **if** vetex number of $snippet + |AP| \leq \gamma$ **then**
4:      merge AP into $snippet$;
5:    **else**
6:      insert AP into T;
7:    **end if**
8: **else**
9:    insert AP into T;
10: **end if**
11: **if** leaf node exceed the maximum record number **then**
12:    split leaf node and adjust T;
13: **end if**

---

4   Experimental Results

In our experiment, the historical trajectory data comes from the open public trajectory data collected from the Borlange, Sweden, containing totally 4503 of available trajectories, 4403 of them are used as the training data of the attacker, and 100 of them are used as the input real trajectories. For simulating the privacy inference attack, we use the training and the trajectory matching method proposed in [4–42] to perform the inference. We run our simulation experiment on the DELL laptop with Intel i7 CPU and 16 GB DDR4 RAM. For the purpose of comparison, we simulate the method proposed in [2,3], we omit the anonymity part of [2] because the anonymity process is irrelevant to our scope of discussion.

For each real trajectory, we generate several dummy trajectories with three trajectory generating scheme independently. Then, we perform the inference attack on these trajectories. Figure 1 shows the comparison of these approaches, the hit ratio of the inference attack is with a constantly high level for the other two schemes and declines slightly with the k rises from 5 to 20, here k denotes the number of dummy trajectories we added for one real trajectory. As a contrast, the k of VAT remains at a much lower level (0.14 to 0.035 in our experiment), k of VAT in our experiment is closed to the probability of the blind random selection, which is the minimum expectation of the evaluation. This result verify the effectiveness of our proposed scheme.

We further investigate the effect of the threshold δ on the hit ratio and the CPU time of VAT. Figure 2 shows this result. As the threshold tighten from 0.5 to 0.2, the hit ratio declines from 0.194 to 0.114, however, the CPU time will increase due to the multi-time of randomization. But in general, the 100 ms level of time cost is acceptable for the IoT searching scenario.

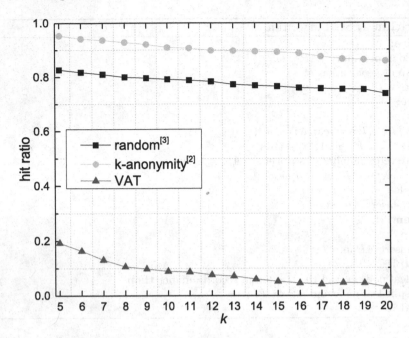

Fig. 1. Hit ratio of inference attack against three approaches as k increases from 5 to 20 using a fixed δ of 0.2.

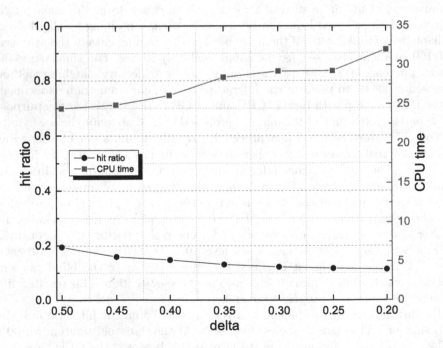

Fig. 2. Hit ratio and CPU time of VAT as δ tightened from 0.5 to 0.2 using a fixed k of 15.

5   Conclusion

In this paper, we proposed a trajectory privacy preserving scheme named VAT for the IoT searching scenario. Based on the dummy trajectory method, people and the device of IoT could publish their trajectory information with a privacy preserved way, and more realistic feature of the trajectory was considered into our method. By introduce the privacy inference attack based on the abnormal behavior detection, we perform VAT against this attack in our experiment as well as some approaches which do not take the high level feature of trajectory into consideration. The result verifies the effectiveness of VAT, and future work may concentrate on the universality of our work.

Acknowledgement. This work was supported by National Natural Science Foundation of China (Grant No. 61572153, 61723022, 61601146), and the National Key research and Development Plan (Grant No. 2018YFB0803504, 2017YFB0803300).

References

1. Chow, C.Y., Mokbel, M.F.: Trajectory privacy in location-based services and data publication. ACM SIGKDD Explor. Newsl. **13**(1), 19–29 (2011)
2. Bamba, B., Liu, L., Pesti, P., et al.: Supporting anonymous location queries in mobile environments with privacygrid. In: Proceedings of the 17th International Conference on World Wide Web, pp. 237–246. ACM (2008)
3. Kido, H., Yanagisawa, Y., Satoh, T.: An anonymous communication technique using dummies for location-based services. In: 2005 Proceedings International Conference on Pervasive Services. ICPS 2005, pp. 88–97. IEEE (2005)
4. Li, Z., Katsaggelos, A.K., Gandhi, B.: Fast video shot retrieval based on trace geometry matching. IEE Proc. Vis. Image Signal Process. **152**(3), 367–373 (2005)
5. Bhatia, N.: Survey of nearest neighbor techniques. arXiv preprint arXiv:1007.0085 (2010)
6. Sun, G., Chen, J., Guo, W.: Signal processing techniques in network-aided positioning: a survey of state-of-the-art positioning designs. IEEE Signal Process. Mag. **22**(4), 12–23 (2005)
7. Ni, W.W., Chen, X.: User privacy preference support in location privacy-preserving nearest neighbor query. J. Softw. **27**(7), 1805–1821 (2016)
8. Yiu, M.L., Jensen, C.S., Huang, X., et al.: SpaceTwist: managing the trade-offs among location privacy, query performance, and query accuracy in mobile services. In: 2008 IEEE 24th International Conference on Data Engineering. ICDE 2008, pp. 366–375. IEEE (2008)
9. Schlegel, R., Chow, C.Y., Huang, Q.: User-defined privacy grid system for continuous location-based services. IEEE Trans. Mobile Comput. **14**(10), 2158–2172 (2015)
10. Xu, H., Guo, S., Chen, K.: Building confidential and efficient query services in the cloud with RASP data perturbation. IEEE Trans. Knowl. Data Eng. **26**(2), 322–335 (2014)
11. Gedik, B., Liu, L.: Protecting location privacy with personalized k-anonymity: architecture and algorithms. IEEE Trans. Mob. Comput. **7**(1), 1–18 (2008)

12. Chow, C.Y., Mokbel, M.F., Aref, W.G.: Casper*: query processing for location services without compromising privacy. ACM Trans. Database Syst. **34**(4), 1–45 (2009)
13. Khoshgozaran, A., Shahabi, C.: Blind evaluation of nearest neighbor queries using space transformation to preserve location privacy. In: Papadias, D., Zhang, D., Kollios, G. (eds.) SSTD 2007. LNCS, vol. 4605, pp. 239–257. Springer, Heidelberg (2007). https://doi.org/10.1007/978-3-540-73540-3_14
14. Damiani, M.L., Cuijpers, C.: Privacy challenges in third-party location services. In: 14th IEEE International Conference on Mobile Data Management, pp. 63–66. IEEE Press, Milan (2013)
15. Jiang, F., Fu, Y., Gupta, B.B., et al.: Deep learning based multi-channel intelligent attack detection for data security. IEEE Trans. Sustain. Comput. (2018)
16. Tippenhauer, N.O., Rasmussen, K.B., Pöpper, C.: Attacks on public WLAN-based positioning systems. In: 7th Proceedings of the International Conference on Mobile systems, pp, 29–40. ACM, Wroclaw (2009)
17. Li, H., Lim, S., Hao, Z.: Achieving privacy preservation in WiFi fingerprint-based localization. In: IEEE INFOCOM Proceedings, pp. 2337–2345. IEEE, Toronto (2014)
18. Wang, X., Liu, Y., Shi, Z., et al.: A privacy-preserving fuzzy localization scheme with CSI fingerprint. In: 2015 IEEE Global Communications Conference (GLOBECOM), pp. 1–6 (2015)
19. Bomze, I.M., Budinich, M., Pardalos, P.M., Pelillo, M.: The maximum clique problem. In: Du, D.Z., Pardalos, P.M. (eds.) Handbook of Combinatorial Optimization. Springer, Boston (1999). https://doi.org/10.1007/978-1-4757-3023-4_1
20. Christin, D.: Privacy in mobile participatory sensing: current trends and future challenges. J. Syst. Softw. **116**, 57–68 (2016)
21. Theodorakopoulos, G., Shokri, R., Troncoso, C., et al.: Prolonging the hide-and-seek game: optimal trajectory privacy for location-based services. In: Proceedings of the 13th Workshop on Privacy in the Electronic Society, pp. 73–82. ACM (2014)
22. He, D., Chan, S., Guizani, M.: User privacy and data trustworthiness in mobile crowd sensing. IEEE Wirel. Commun. **22**(1), 28–34 (2015)
23. Giannetsos, T., Gisdakis, S., Papadimitratos, P.: Trustworthy people-centric sensing: privacy, security and user incentives road-map. In: 2014 13th Annual Mediterranean Ad Hoc Networking Workshop (MED-HOC-NET), pp. 39–46. IEEE (2014)
24. Zhang, B., Liu, C.H., Lu, J.: Privacy-preserving QoI-aware participant coordination for mobile crowdsourcing. Comput. Netw. **101**, 29–41 (2016)
25. Gisdakis, S., Giannetsos, T., Papadimitratos, P.: Security, privacy, and incentive provision for mobile crowd sensing systems. IEEE Internet Things J. **3**(5), 839–853 (2016)
26. Niu, B., Gao, S., Li, F., et al.: Protection of location privacy in continuous LBSs against adversaries with background information. In: 2016 International Conference on Computing, Networking and Communications (ICNC), pp. 1–6. IEEE (2016)
27. Boutsis, I., Kalogeraki, V.: Location privacy for crowdsourcing applications. In: Proceedings of the 2016 ACM International Joint Conference on Pervasive and Ubiquitous Computing, pp. 694–705. ACM (2016)
28. Shokri, R., Theodorakopoulos, G., Troncoso, C.: Privacy games along location traces: a game-theoretic framework for optimizing location privacy. ACM Trans. Priv. Secur. (TOPS) **19**(4), 11 (2017)
29. Peng, T., Liu, Q., Meng, D.: Collaborative trajectory privacy preserving scheme in location-based services. Inf. Sci. **387**, 165–179 (2017)

30. Liu, B., Zhou, W., Zhu, T.: Invisible hand: a privacy preserving mobile crowd sensing framework based on economic models. IEEE Trans. Veh. Technol. **66**(5), 4410–4423 (2017)
31. Tang, D., Ren, J.: A novel delay-aware and privacy-preserving data-forwarding scheme for urban sensing network. IEEE Trans. Veh. Technol. **65**(4), 2578–2588 (2016)
32. Zhang, S., Wang, G., Liu, Q., et al.: A trajectory privacy-preserving scheme based on query exchange in mobile social networks. Soft Comput. 1–13 (2017)
33. Liu, H., Darabi, H., Banerjee, P.: Survey of wireless indoor positioning techniques and systems. IEEE Trans. Syst. Man. Cybern. Part C (Appl. Rev.) **37**(6), 1067–1080 (2007)
34. Ahmadi, H., Bouallegue, R.: Exploiting machine learning strategies and RSSI for localization in wireless sensor networks: a survey. In: 2017 13th International Wireless Communications and Mobile Computing Conference (IWCMC), pp. 1150–1154. IEEE (2017)
35. Chow, C.Y., Mokbel, M.F.: Trajectory privacy in location-based services and data publication. SIGKDD **13**, 19–29 (2011). ACM
36. Krumm, J.: A survey of computational location privacy. Pers. Ubiquit. Comput. **13**, 391–399 (2009)
37. Wernke, M.: A classification of location privacy attacks and approaches. Pers. Ubiquit. Comput. **18**, 163–175 (2014)
38. Yu, W., Hong, Z., Xiang, Y.: Research on location privacy on mobile internet. Communication **36**, 230–243 (2015)
39. Zhang, D., Guo, L., Nie, L.: Targeted advertising in public transportation systems with quantitative evaluation. ACM Trans. Inf. Syst. (TOIS) **35**(3), 20 (2017)
40. Zhang, S., Liu, Q., Wang, G.: Enhancing location privacy through user-defined grid in location-based services. In: 2016 IEEE Trustcom/BigDataSE/ISPA, pp. 730–736. IEEE (2016)
41. Ziegeldorf, J.H., Henze, M., Bavendiek, J., et al.: TraceMixer: privacy-preserving crowd-sensing sans trusted third party. In: 2017 13th Annual Conference on Wireless On-demand Network Systems and Services (WONS), pp. 17–24. IEEE (2017)
42. Liu, H., Li, X., Li, H., et al.: Spatiotemporal correlation-aware dummy-based privacy protection scheme for location-based services. In: IEEE INFOCOM 2017-IEEE Conference on Computer Communications, pp. 1–9. IEEE (2017)

Video Quality Assessment Algorithm Based on Persistence-of-Vision Effect

Pai Liu[✉], Fenlin Liu, and Daofu Gong

State Key Laboratory of Mathematical Engineering and Advance Computing,
Zhengzhou, China
liupai_0701@163.com

Abstract. In order to assess video quality more accurately, this paper proposes an improved video quality assessment algorithm based on persistence-of-vision effect. This algorithm firstly adopts region partitioning, Just Noticeable Difference (JND) model, etc. to assess the quality of a video single frame; then conducts perceptual weighting on the several affected frames based on persistence-of-vision effect when the video scene changes; and finally assesses the video quality by using linear correlation coefficient and Peirman correlation coefficient and compares with the performance of the traditional algorithm through experiments. The experimental results show that the proposed algorithm in this paper can objectively describe the video quality and perform well in the materials with more radical scene changes.

Keywords: Video quality · Human vision characteristics
Perceptual weighting

1 Introduction

In today's society, video services have become a significant component of the Internet business [1]. Nevertheless, due to some objective restrictions like network costs, video compression often needs to be performed in the process of video transmission, which, to a large extent, may reduce the quality of the video, affect users' viewing experience as well as decrease the quality of service. How to save network bandwidth as much as possible while satisfying different users' viewing needs is an issue that network video service providers must pay attention to. Consequently, an effective video quality objective assessment method is required to guide the setting of video compression rate and other parameters during network transmission.

At present, numerous research institutions and scholars both at home and abroad have carried out in-depth research on the objective video quality assessment issue and yielded certain results, including pixel-based assessment algorithms such as mean squared error (MSE) and peak signal-to-noise ratio (PSNR) [2]. Donoho et al. hold that in an image, the marginal region gets the most attention from human eyes, and thus its quality has a great impact on the quality of the image [3]. Wang et al. believe that combining the structural information in different scales can effectively reflect image distortion and proposed multiscale structural similarity (MS-SSIM) [4]. Prison et al. proposed a video quality model (VQM) [5] to assess videos by using the correlation

© Springer Nature Switzerland AG 2018
X. Sun et al. (Eds.): ICCCS 2018, LNCS 11064, pp. 366–376, 2018.
https://doi.org/10.1007/978-3-030-00009-7_34

among the changing features such as image color, luminance and time-space domain. Li et al. proposed a video quality assessment algorithm for distinguishing detail distortions in combination of motion and space-time characteristics [6]. By considering factors such as video region division and structural similarity, Zhu Hong et al. proposed a video quality assessment method based on HVS [7], and Chou et al. proposed that the Just Noticeable Difference (JND) model can be used to simulate the invisible distortion and so on caused by human eye masking effects [8]. Appina et al. adopt the gradient structural similarity algorithm to calculate the sub-block average luminance, sub-block gradient contrast and sub-block gradient correlation coefficient of the original video disparity map and the distorted video disparity map by extracting the luminance contrast distortion assessment index, the structural similarity assessment index and the resolution distortion assessment index of the left and right view videos combined with luminance weights, obtain the depth fidelity assessment index of the entire stereoscopic video by averaging the depth fidelity of all the disparity map sub-blocks in the stereo video, and acquire the mathematical morphology and weight of each stereoscopic video quality assessment index via multiple non-linear regression analysis so as to construct a FR stereoscopic video quality assessment model SVQ [9].

Through the study on HVS, persistence of vision (i.e., the phenomenon that after light produces an effect on the retina, the effect still remains for a period of time when the effect stops) is used to interfere with the identified image content when dramatic changes occur in the video scene. That is, when the scene image changes, human eyes still retain the image vision of the previous scene within a certain period of time, which leads to certain fault tolerance when human eyes process and identify the content of a new scene. As a result, from the perspective of video quality assessment, while scene switching, observers, for a certain period of time, are not sensitive to the distortion in the scene after switching. According to this sort of influence, by using the scene division technology, this paper conducts perceptual weighting on the frames affected by persistence of vision after the scene changes to stimulate the influence of human eye persistence-of-vision effect on changing-scene perception, and proposes a video quality assessment method based on persistence of vision.

2 Algorithm Description

The basic principles of the algorithm is that: the morphological technique is used to perform region division on a video; the JND model is used to judge whether the frame distortion is visible to human eyes; perceptual weighting is carried out on different regions according to region division results and the judgment results of the JND model in order to give assessment on the single frame quality of the distorted video; then video frame sequences are perceptually weighted by using persistence of vision; and finally the overall quality of the video is obtained. The specific algorithm architecture is shown as Fig. 1.

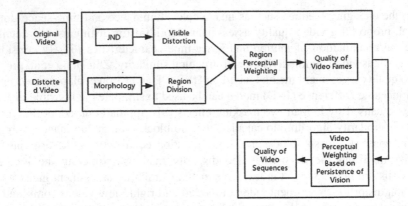

Fig. 1. Framework of the proposed algorithm in this paper

2.1   The Specific Steps in This Algorithm

STEP 1 Division of Textured and Smooth Regions [10]

STEP 1.1 Use the Laplacian Operator $\left\{ \begin{array}{ccc} 0 & -1 & 0 \\ -1 & 4 & -1 \\ 0 & -1 & 0 \end{array} \right\}$ to extract the edge of I_k,

the kth frame in video frames, then:

$$E = Edge(I_k) = \{(i,j) : L(i,j) > mean(L(I_k)) + std(L(I_k))\} \tag{1}$$

Where $L(\bullet)$ represents the convolution between image and the Laplacian Operator, and mean($\bullet$) and std($\bullet$) represent calculating the mean and standard deviation of the matrix elements respectively; after the results are binarized, the morphological closing operation is performed on the binary image, and then opening operation is performed on the results. The morphological closing operation refers to dilation operation first and then erosion operation. The morphological opening operation refers to erosion operation first and then dilation operation.

The dilation operation refers to using a structuring element B to act on each pixel in the image A, and the pixel value at the center position of B is changed to the maximum pixel value of A in $A \cap B$. The erosion operation refers to using the structuring element B to superimpose the image A, and the pixel value at the center position is changed to the minimum pixel value of the B coverage region. The overall operation in the calculation process is expressed as:

$$M = \{(A \bullet B) \circ B\} \tag{2}$$

Where $\bullet$ and $\circ$ represent the closing operation and opening operation; A is the binary image after the edge extracting; and B is the structural unit.

Suppose $M(i,j)$ are the results after morphological operation, then:

$$M(i,j) = \begin{cases} 1, & I_k(i,j) \in S \\ 0, & I_k(i,j) \in T \end{cases} \tag{3}$$

Where S represents the smooth region; T represents the textured region; and $I_k(i,j)$ represents the point at the kth frame (i,j).

STEP 2 Visible Distortion Judgment [11]
STEP 2.1 Calculate the luminance difference between the original frame and the corresponding distorted frame:

$$D_d(i,j) = |D_1(i,j) - D_2(i,j)| \tag{4}$$

Where $D_1(i,j)$ and $D_2(i,j)$ represent the luminance values of the single frame in the original video frame and the corresponding single frame in the distorted video at (i,j) respectively.

STEP 2.2 Calculate the JND threshold by using the calculation method in reference [12]:

$$Y(x) = \begin{cases} 22.98e^{-0.057}, & 0 \leq x \leq 64 \\ 1.683 - 0.0083x + 3.376 \times 10^{-5}x^2, & 64 < x \leq 255 \end{cases} \tag{5}$$

Where x is the background luminance, and $Y(x)$ is the JND threshold.

STEP 2.3 Calculate the background luminance $D_b(i,j)$ at the frame (i,j): using the 5×5 region at (i,j) and the convolution kernel shown in Fig. 2 as the convolution.

1	1	1	1	1
1	2	2	2	1
1	2	0	2	1
1	2	2	2	1
1	1	1	1	1

Fig. 2. Convolution kernel used for calculating background luminance

STEP 2.3 Compare the luminance difference $D_d(i,j)$ shown in formula (4) with the JND threshold to judge whether this point is visible distortion. The judgment function is as follows:

$$f(i,j) = \begin{cases} 1, & if\ D_d(i,j) > Y(x) \\ 0, & ELSE \end{cases} \tag{6}$$

Where 1 indicates that the point is visible distortion, and 0 indicates that the point is invisible distortion.

STEP 3 Region Perceptual Weighting

STEP 3.1 Calculate the peak signal-to-noise ratio at (i,j). For the point (i,j) in different regions, the peak signal-to-noise ratios thereof are:

$$p = \begin{cases} \alpha_1 p(i,j), \text{if } f(i,j)=1 \text{且} p(i,j) \in S \\ \alpha_2 p(i,j), \text{if } f(i,j)=1 \text{且} p(i,j) \in T \end{cases} \tag{7}$$

Where α_1 and α_2 are the weighting coefficient of the smooth region and the textured region, and $p(i,j)$ is the peak signal-to-noise ratio at (i,j).

STEP 3.2 Calculate the quality of the kth frame in the video:

$$p_{f_{lk}} = \frac{1}{N_1}\sum_{t=1}^{N_1} p_{t1} + \frac{1}{N_2}\sum_{t=1}^{N_2} p_{t2} \tag{8}$$

where p_{t1} and p_{t2} are the peak signal-to-noise ratios of each points in the smooth region and the textured region, and N_1 and N_2 are the numbers of points in the smooth region and the textured region.

STEP 4 Vedio Sequence Weighting Based on Persistence of Vision

STEP 4.1 Calculate the frame luminance difference between the kth frame and the $k+1$ th frame as follows:

$$S_d(k,k+1) = \frac{1}{EF}\sum_{t=1}^{E}\sum_{t=1}^{F} |I_{tk}(i,j) - I_{tk+1}(i,j)| \tag{9}$$

Where E is the number of pixels in the vertical direction of the frame; F is the number of pixels in the horizontal direction of the frame; and $I_{k-1}(i,j)$ and $I_k(i,j)$ are the luminance values of the kth frame and the $k+1$ th frame at the pixel (i,j). The threshold G is set, and whether a scene change occurs in the kth frame is judged according to the following formula:

$$g(k,k+1) = \begin{cases} 1, & \text{if } S_d > G \\ 0, & \text{else} \end{cases} \tag{10}$$

Where the result being 1 indicates that there is a scene change in the kth frame, and a result being 0 indicates that there is no scene change in the kth frame.

STEP 4.2 Suppose δ_1, δ_2, ... and δ_z are the weighting coefficient of these frames affected by persistence of vision. The rectified frame quality p_f' of the affected z frame is calculated according to the following formula:

$$p_f' = \begin{cases} \delta i \cdot p_{f_{k+i}}, & if \quad g(k)=1 \; \text{且} \; i=1,2,...,z \\ p_f, & else \end{cases} \tag{11}$$

STEP 4.3 Video sequence quality is:

$$Q = \frac{1}{H} \sum_{t=1}^{H} p_{fi}' \tag{12}$$

Where H is the number of frames in the video sequence.

3 Experiment and Result Analysis

According to the objective assessment algorithm and subjective assessment algorithm consistency test methods adopted by the video quality experts group (VQEG), this experiment assesses the validity of the proposed algorithm in this paper by using the linear correlation coefficient (LCC) and Spearman rank order correlation coefficient (SROCC) [13, 14].

3.1 Experimental Material and Algorithm Parameter Selection

The video data used in the experiment are taken from the LIVE VIDEO QUALITY DATABASE [15, 16] established by the Image and Video Engineering Laboratory at the University of Texas, Austin. The contents of the video sequences include ten categories of natural scene sequences with different characteristics, which are described in the following Tables 1 and 2:

Table 1. Description of experimental video scene contents

Scene name	Scene content
Pedestrian area	Walking pedestrians in the street scene
River bed	Flowing water and pebbles in the still river bed
Rush hour	Passing car clips in the movie
Tractor	The camera follows a moving tractor
Station	The camera gradually pulls to shoot slowly driving trains and surrounding pedestrians
Sunflower	The camera shoots bees and sunflowers via close-ups
Blue sky	Camera lens are vertically upward to shoot woods and sky
Shields	The Camera panning-shoots a person walking through displays
Park run	The Camera panning-shoots a person running in the square
Mobile&Calendar	The Camera panning-shoots a train model, whose traveling direction is perpendicular to the camera panning direction

Table 2. Setting of experimental parameters

Parameter name	Parameter value
Weighting coefficient in the smooth region α_1	0.9
Weighting coefficient in the textured region α_2	0.5
The number of the selected frames for persistence-of-video effect z	6
Weighting coefficient of the affected first frame δ_1	0.01
Weighting coefficient of the affected second frame δ_2	0.03
Weighting coefficient of the affected third frame δ_3	0.07
Weighting coefficient of the affected fourth frame δ_4	0.15
Weighting coefficient of the affected fifth frame δ_5	0.30
Weighting coefficient of the affected sixth frame δ_6	0.63

3.2   Experimental Results

Taking the LIVE database as the experimental sample, the 100 video sequences used for the test are objectively assessed according to the method in the previous section; the results are fitted by a multi-parameter nonlinear equation [17]; and the objective assessment results DMOSobj after the conversion are compared with the subjective assessment results DMOS given by the materials. According to reference [17], the Pearson LCC and SROCC are used to assess the accuracy and monotonicity of algorithms.

The proposed model in this paper is compared with the above-mentioned traditional methods, which include the PSNR [2], SSIM, MS-SSIM [4], VQM [5] and reference [9]. The performance in each scene content in the experimental materials is shown in following tables:

Tables 3, 4, 5, 6, 7, 8, 9, 10, 11 and 12 have listed different types of experimental materials in the LIVE database, as well as the LCC and SROCC correlation coefficient of each algorithm. It can be seen from the experimental results that the proposed algorithm in this paper shows relatively good performance in both consistency and monotonicity. Among the different experimental materials, the proposed algorithm works well in materials such as Rush hour, Station, whereas produces unsatisfactory results in materials such as Ricer bed, Tractor, Sunflower, Blue sky, Park run, which is related to the principles of this algorithm. Based on the influence of human eye persistence of vision on image perception when the scene is switched, the proposed algorithm conducts perceptual weighting on the affected part, thereby improving traditional algorithms. In materials like Rush hour, because there is normal scene switching, the proposed algorithm can work normally. Nonetheless, in materials like Ricer bed, Tractor, Sunflower, Blue sky and Park run, because such materials usually capture the shots with single image content, fixed angles, and fewer scene changes and accidental events, it is impossible to judge the key frames in the part of judging scene changes or to carry out perceptual weighting on the frame quality, and in this case,

Table 3. Performance of the proposed algorithm in this paper and other algorithms in the scene of Pedestrian area

Experimental material	Related algorithm	LCC	SROCC
Pedestrian area	PSNR	0.475	0.421
	SSIM	0.692	0.646
	MS-SSIM	0.773	0.746
	VQM	0.768	0.765
	Reference [9]	0.774	0.749
	Proposed algorithm	0.748	0.713

Table 4. Performance of the proposed algorithm in this paper and other algorithms in the scene of River bed

Experimental material	Related algorithm	LCC	SROCC
River bed	PSNR	0.425	0.420
	SSIM	0.690	0.631
	MS-SSIM	0.772	0.744
	VQM	0.768	0.752
	Reference [9]	0.784	0.787
	Proposed algorithm	0.718	0.701

Table 5. Performance of the proposed algorithm in this paper and other algorithms in the scene of Rush hour

Experimental material	Related algorithm	LCC	SROCC
Rush hour	PSNR	0.468	0.427
	SSIM	0.715	0.694
	MS-SSIM	0.771	0.773
	VQM	0.776	0.721
	Reference [9]	0.778	0.780
	Proposed algorithm	0.785	0.783

Table 6. Performance of the proposed algorithm in this paper and other algorithms in the scene of Tractor

Experimental material	Related algorithm	LCC	SROCC
Tractor	PSNR	0.443	0.456
	SSIM	0.672	0.641
	MS-SSIM	0.786	0.750
	VQM	0.779	0.737
	Reference [9]	0.781	0.775
	Proposed algorithm	0.727	0.758

Table 7. Performance of the proposed algorithm in this paper and other algorithms in the scene of Station

Experimental material	Related algorithm	LCC	SROCC
Station	PSNR	0.426	0.437
	SSIM	0.707	0.685
	MS-SSIM	0.761	0.745
	VQM	0.770	0.754
	Reference [9]	0.781	0.766
	Proposed algorithm	0.784	0.780

Table 8. Performance of the proposed algorithm in this paper and other algorithms in the scene of Sunflower

Experimental material	Related algorithm	LCC	SROCC
Sunflower	PSNR	0.435	0.419
	SSIM	0.710	0.699
	MS-SSIM	0.775	0.750
	VQM	0.770	0.749
	Reference [9]	0.777	0.779
	Proposed algorithm	0.729	0.715

Table 9. Performance of the proposed algorithm in this paper and other algorithms in the scene of Blue sky

Experimental material	Related algorithm	LCC	SROCC
Blue sky	PSNR	0.441	0.434
	SSIM	0.712	0.711
	MS-SSIM	0.758	0.741
	VQM	0.769	0.758
	Reference [9]	0.772	0.764
	Proposed algorithm	0.704	0.710

Table 10. Performance of the proposed algorithm in this paper and other algorithms in the scene of Shields

Experimental material	Related algorithm	LCC	SROCC
Shields	PSNR	0.441	0.437
	SSIM	0.721	0.713
	MS-SSIM	0.767	0.751
	VQM	0.772	0.726
	Reference [9]	0.770	0.745
	Proposed algorithm	0.773	0.758

Table 11. Performance of the proposed algorithm in this paper and other algorithms in the scene of Park run

Experimental material	Related algorithm	LCC	SROCC
Park run	PSNR	0.431	0.427
	SSIM	0.688	0.654
	MS-SSIM	0.785	0.758
	VQM	0.776	0.741
	Reference [9]	0.780	0.772
	Proposed algorithm	0.722	0.749

Table 12. Performance of the proposed algorithm in this paper and other algorithms in the scene of Mobile&Calendar

Experimental material	Related algorithm	LCC	SROCC
Mobile&Calendar	PSNR	0.456	0.431
	SSIM	0.710	0.691
	MS-SSIM	0.768	0.764
	VQM	0.772	0.724
	Reference [9]	0.776	0.772
	Proposed algorithm	0.782	0.779

utilizing the assessment model based on persistence-of-vision effect is hard to play a prominent role.

4 Conclusion

By combining the persistence-of-vision effect of human eyes, a video quality assessment algorithm based on human vision characteristics is proposed in this paper. According to the experiments of the LIVE video database, the proposed algorithm in this paper performs well in terms of consistency and monotonicity, and it has some advantages in the materials with frequent scene changes and more content accidental events. Furthermore, there is still plenty of room for improvement in parameter selection as well as the model mining of persistence of vision from more scenes, which will also be the main direction of further work.

References

1. Tong, Y., Hu, W., Yang, D.: A review on the video quality assessment methods. J. Comput.-Aided Des. Comput. Graph. **18**(5), 735–741 (2006)

2. Rohaly, A.M., Corriveau, P.J., Libert, J.M., et al.: Video quality experts group: current results and future directions. In: Proceedings of SPIE, pp. 742–753. Society of Photo-Optical Instrumentation Engineers, Bellingham (2000)
3. Donoho, D.L., et al.: Can recent innovations in harmonic analysis explain key findings in natural image statistics. J. Netw. Comput. Neural Syst. 12(23), 371–393 (2001)
4. Wang, Z., Simoncelli, E.P., Bovik, A.C.: Multiscale structural similarity for image quality asessment. In: Conference on Signals, Systems & Computers, vol. 2, no. 2, pp. 1398–1402 (2014)
5. Pinson, M.H., Wolf, S.: A new standardized method for objectively measuring video quality. IEEE Trans. Broadcast. 50(3), 312–322 (2004)
6. Li, S.N., Ma, L., Ngan, K.N.: Full-reference video quality assessment by decoupling detail losses and additive impairments. IEEE Trans. Circuits Syst. Video Technol. 22(7), 1100–1112 (2012)
7. Yuan, F., Huang, L.F., Yao, Y.: A video quality assessment algorithm based on human visual characteristics. J. Comput.-Aided Des. Comput. Graph. (2014)
8. Chou, C.H., Li, Y.C.: A perceptually tuned subband image coder based on the measure of just-noticeable-distortion profile. IEEE Trans. Circuits Syst. Video Technol. 5(6), 467–476 (1995). IEEE Press
9. Appina, B., Manasa, K., Channappayya, S.S.: IEEE International Conference on Acoustics. ISSN 2379-190X:2012-2016 (2017)
10. Zhou, Y.F., et al.: Double local Wiener filter image denoising algorithm based on mathematical morphology and direction window in wavelet domain. Syst. Eng. Electron. Technol. 29(8), 1238–1241 (2017)
11. Chen, Y., Zhan, D.: Combined JND model image stitching elimination method. J. Electron. Inf. 39(10), 2404–2412 (2017)
12. Wang, Z.F., Liu, Y.H., Wang, Y., et al.: Human visual contrast resolution limit measurement based on digital image processing. J. Biomed. Eng. 25(5), 998–1002 (2008)
13. Brunnstrom, K., Hands, D., Speranza, F., et al.: VQEG validation and ITU standardization of objective perceptual video quality metrics. IEEE Signal Process. Mag. 26(3), 96–101 (2009)
14. Seshadrinathan, K., Soundararajan, R., Bovik, A.C., et al.: Study of subjective and objective quality assessment of video. IEEE Trans. Image Process. 19(6), 1427–1441 (2010)
15. LIVE video quality data base. http://live.ece.utexas.edu/research/quality/live_video.html. Accessed 08 Apr 2013
16. Sheikh, H.R., Sabir, M.F., Bovik, A.C.: A statistical evaluation of recent full reference image quality assessment algorithms. IEEE Trans. Image Process. 15(11), 3440–3451 (2006)
17. Seshadrinathan, K., Soundararajan, R., Bovik, A.C., et al.: A subjective study to evaluate video quality assessment algorithms. In: Human Vision and Electronic Imaging (2010)

Workflow Task Scheduling Algorithm Based on IFCM and IACO

Qin Liu[1], Tinghuai Ma[1,2(✉)], Jian Li[1], and Wenhai Shen[3]

[1] School of Computer Software,
Nanjing University of Information Science Technology,
Nanjing 210-044, Jiangsu, China
thma@nuist.edu.cn
[2] CICAEET, Jiangsu Engineering Centre of Network Monitoring,
Nanjing University of Information Science Technology,
Nanjing 210-044, Jiangsu, China
[3] National Meteorological Information Center, Beijing 100-080, China

Abstract. To solve the scheduling problem of workflow tasks in cloud computing, this paper combined the improved fuzzy c-means clustering algorithm (IFCM) and the improved ant colony optimization algorithm (IACO) and proposed a new workflow task scheduling algorithm. Firstly, the proposed algorithm used the IFCM to classify resources. Then, tasks will be sorted by their priority. Based on the results of resource clustering and the distance between resources and expect of tasks, tasks will be assigned to the appropriate resources and the scheduling will be initialized. After that, the workflow tasks will be encoded based on the initial scheduling. At last, ant colony optimization algorithm will be improved by the cross and mutation operation in genetic algorithm and used to search optimal schedules. The experiments showed that the proposed algorithm could quickly and efficiently find appropriate scheduling scheme, effectively reduce the time span of workflow tasks and increase the utilization of resources.

Keywords: Cloud computing · Workflow task scheduling
Fuzzy clustering algorithm · Ant colony optimization algorithm

1 Introduction

In order to facilitate people to use resources, such as storage, software, services, etc., and to improve the convenience and availability of network access, cloud computing [14] gradually steps into people's lives. The cloud computing research includes storage, virtualization, computing, security and other aspects. Scheduling algorithm is one of the important research directions. The goal of cloud computing task scheduling is to realize the optimal scheduling for the tasks submitted by users based on certain principles and to maximize resource utilization [10].

© Springer Nature Switzerland AG 2018
X. Sun et al. (Eds.): ICCCS 2018, LNCS 11064, pp. 377–388, 2018.
https://doi.org/10.1007/978-3-030-00009-7_35

In the research of cloud computing task scheduling, tasks can be divided into independent tasks and workflow tasks. Among them, the workflow tasks [5] in the implementation of the pre-order relationship, that is, the implementation of a task depends on the implementation of its pre-order tasks. The cloud computing task scheduling problem is considered NP (Non-deterministic Polynomial)-Complete problem. Aiming at the task of workflow in cloud computing environment, considering the resources characteristic, the paper uses the IFCM to classify resources and proposes a workflow task scheduling algorithm based on the improved ant colony optimization algorithm (IACO). The main contributions of this paper are listed as follows:

1 The improved fuzzy c-means clustering algorithm (IFCM) is used for resource clustering cloud computing resources.
2 Combining with clustering resources and improved ant colony optimization algorithm (IACO), the workflow task scheduling is proposed.

The rest of the paper is as follows: Sect. 2 introduces the related work of task scheduling. In Sect. 3, the models of task and resource are described. The workflow task scheduling algorithm proposed in this paper is elaborated in Sect. 4. In Sect. 5, experiments verify the validity of the algorithm. Finally, conclusion and prospect are got in Sect. 6.

2   Related Work

2.1   Clustering Resource

Currently, the existing handwriting recognition solutions usually adopt (depth) cameras, motion controllers, Wi-Fi signals for data acquisition. Many researchers have stressed the impact of resource characteristics on task scheduling performance, so they classify resources [13] and then assign tasks. Considering the user's quality of service (QoS) requirements and the elasticity and heterogeneity of the computing resources, Rodrigue and Buyya [12] proposed an algorithm based resource provisioning and scheduling. For scientific workflows on Infrastructure as a Service (IaaS) clouds, particle swarm optimization is used to minimize the overall workflow execution cost to meet deadline constraints.

2.2   Ant Colony Algorithm

Ant colony algorithm is a heuristic bionics algorithm proposed by Dorigo in 1992 [3,7–9], which searches for the optimal solution or approximate optimal solution by imitating ant foraging process. For the conflict of service requirements in the cloud computing environment, Huang et al. [4] used the ant colony algorithm to find the optimal scheduling solution by analyzing service platform features and global service targets. Sinha et al. [11] used ant colony algorithm to find the optimal solution, and then initialize the workflow task scheduling scheme, and make use of the completion time limit to optimize the scheduling scheme, thus minimizing the workflow task execution cost.

3   Model Introduction

3.1   Problem Definition and Description

The model of workflow task scheduling can be expressed in triples $\langle WF, R, E \rangle$ (Fig. 1). Among them,

$WF = \{WF_1, WF_2, \ldots, WF_n\}$ represents a set of n workflows;

$R = \{R_1, R_2, \ldots, R_m\}$ represents a set of m virtual machines;

$E = \{\langle WF_i, R_j \rangle \,|\, WF_i \in WF, R_j \in R, 0 \le i < n, 0 \le j < m\}$ represents assignment relationship between workflow and resource.

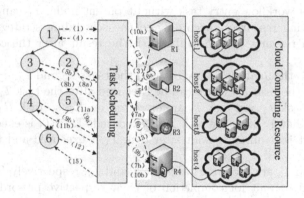

Fig. 1. The flow diagram of workflow task scheduling

3.2   Workflow Task Model

The workflow WF_i is a set of tasks with a pre-order relationship, which is usually described by two-tuples$\langle T, C \rangle$, where:

$T = \{T_1, T_2, \ldots, T_p\}$ represents tasks of forming workflow, the i-th task can be expressed as $T = \{T_{iid}, T_{ipri}, T_{iexp}, T_{ilocal}, T_{iin}, T_{iout}, T_{istatus}\}$, T_{iid} denotes the task number; T_{ipri} denotes the task priority; $T_{iexp} = \{T_{iexp\_comp}, T_{iexp\_stor}\}$ that the task of CPU and memory requirements;T_{ilocal} represents the data locality requirement of the task; T_{iin} represents the input position of the task; T_{iout} represents the output position of the task; $T_{istatus}$ indicates the task execution status, including waiting, running, finished and error.

$C = \{\langle T_a, T_b \rangle \,|\, T_a \in T, T_b \in T, 0 \le a, b < p, a \ne b\}$ represents the order between the task and the size of the traffic.

3.3   Resource Model

In the preceding text, the resource R_j represents a virtual machine in a cloud computing system, which can be expressed by tetrad $R_j = \{R_{jid}, R_{jhost}, R_{jcomp}, R_{jstor}\}$ where R_{jid} denotes the resource number, R_{jhost}

represents the host node to which the virtual machine belongs,$R_{j_{comp}}$ represents the CPU performance of the virtual machine, $R_{j_{stor}}$ represents the memory performance of the virtual machine.

3.4 Workflow Task Scheduling

The workflow in Fig. 1 consists of six tasks: T_1, T_2, T_3, T_4, T_5 and T_6. The data center consists of R_1, R_2, R_3, R_4. The data center virtualizes four resources R_1, R_2, R_3, R_4 to perform these tasks according to the task demand. As shown in the Fig. 2, workflow tasks include the implementation of the following points:

1 Task T_1 is a workflow entry task without parent node, T_1 can be executed after allocating resources. According to the scheduling strategy, task T_1 is executed on resource R_2. R_2 will return the result after the completion of task T_1.
2 According to the analysis of DAG graph, the tasks T_2 and T_3 are the sequential tasks of the task T_1, which can be executed after the task T_1 is executed. Since both task T_2 and task T_1 are executed on R_2, so task R_2 can be executed immediately after the task T_1 is executed. Task T_3 is executed on R_4. Therefore, it is required to wait after task T_1 is executed and transfer data to R_4.
3 Tasks T_2 and T_3 are pre-order tasks of T_4 and T_5, respectively. Therefore, T_4 and T_5 need to wait for completion of their respective pre-order tasks and transfer the execution results to resources to execute.
4 Task T_6 has two pre-order tasks T_4 and T_5, it must wait until T_4 and T_5 are completed and data is transferred, then can be executed.

4 Proposed Algorithm

4.1 Improved Fuzzy C-Means Clustering Algorithm

Improvement of FCM. FCM clustering algorithm is more sensitive to noise, so Mulier et al. [1] proposed an improved FCM clustering algorithm. The objective function of IFCM clustering algorithm is described as formula (1) in FCM clustering algorithm, but it relaxes the constraint on membership. In IFCM, the constraints subject to the following formulas (2) (3) (4):

$$MinJ_{fcm}(U, V) = \sum_{i=1}^{c} \sum_{j=1}^{n} u_{ij}^{m} d_{ij}^{2} \tag{1}$$

Subject to:

$$\sum_{i=1}^{n} u_{ij} > 0, 1 \leq i \leq c \tag{2}$$

$$u_{ij} \leq 0, 1 \leq i \leq c, 1 \leq j \leq n \tag{3}$$

$$\sum_{i=1}^{c}\sum_{j=1}^{n} u_{ij} = n \tag{4}$$

Similar to the FCM clustering algorithm, the IFCM clustering algorithm about the iteration equation about the centroid and membership can be calculated. The iteration equation of the centroid is the same as that of (5), while the iterative formula of membership is as formula(6):

$$v_i = \frac{\sum_{j=1}^{n} u_{ij}^m x_j}{\sum_{j=1}^{n} u_{ij}^m}, i = 1, 2, \ldots, c \tag{5}$$

$$u_{ij} = n \cdot \left[\sum_{k=1}^{c}\sum_{l=1}^{n} \left(\frac{d_{ij}}{d_{lk}}\right)^{\frac{2}{m-1}}\right]^{-1}, 1 \le i \le c, 1 \le j \le n \tag{6}$$

It can be seen that the formula (6) is a necessary condition for formula (3), that is, the IFCM clustering algorithm is a FCM clustering algorithm relaxing the constraint of membership essentially.

Resource Clustering. In this section, the IFCM clustering algorithm is used to cluster the virtual machines based on the performance of the virtual machines. Based on the description of virtual machine performance in Hadoop, the performance of the virtual machine CPU and the memory are mainly considered. Therefore, in each data center, the virtual machine resources are divided into two types. One type processes CPU with high speed, another type has larger memory. Before the clustering operation, fuzzy clustering and Max-Min method is used to preprocess the data. The process of resource clustering is performed according to the steps of IFCM. The flow diagram is shown in Algorithm 1:

Algorithm 1. Resource clustering based on IFCM

Input: vectors of resources
Output: centers and clusters of resource clustering
    Description:
        Step1: set parameters;
        Step2: calculate cluster centers according to the formula (5);
        Step3: calculate membership matrix according to the formula (6);
        Step4: repeat Step2 and Step3 until satisfying the termination conditions;
        Step5: output centers and clusters.

Expect of Task Resource. In our algorithm, the total amount of each available resource in the current data center is firstly obtained, such as computation or storage. Then, the expectations of the tasks for every resource are achieved through the task model vector. The ratio of task resource expectation and the current available expectation exp_i $(i = 1, \ldots, n)$ can be calculated, where exp_i is the ratio of the resource expect of the task $cloudlet_i$ and available resources. The formula is as follows:

$$exp_{i cata} = \frac{cloudlet_{i cata}}{VM_{cata}}, cata \in [stor, compute, bandwidth] \qquad (7)$$

$$VM_{cata} = vm_{1 cata} + \ldots + vm_{k cata} \qquad (8)$$

In formula (7), VM_{cata} refers to the total amount of available virtual machine resources in the current category, which can be calculated according to formula (8); k is the total number of virtual machines in the current category, and $vm_{k cata}$ represents the available of virtual machine.

According to ratio exp_i of three expected resources of the task $cloudlet_i$ selecting the corresponding resource category with maximum one, the task $cloudlet_i$ is put into the queue of it. Through the calculation of task resource expect and the initial classification of resources, some inefficient allocation results in the scheduling process can be reduced. And due to the reduction of the candidate virtual machines, time of searching for suitable resources will also be shortened, which can reduce the task waiting time. Later, we will adopt a modified FIFO algorithm to assign tasks.

4.2 Based Workflow Task Scheduling

Ant Colony Algorithm Based Workflow Task Scheduling. The workflow task scheduling problem can be solved on the basis of the idea of ant colony algorithm in cloud computing system.

In view of the characteristics of workflow scheduling problem, researchers usually use discrete encoding. Ants coding can effectively indicate the distribution sequence of workflow tasks, and can be easily scheduled according to the sequence. As shown in Fig. 1, each node in the workflow corresponds to a task, and each task corresponds to a bit in the encoded sequence. The number of bits in the encoding sequence is the number of tasks. As shown in Fig. 2, the number of workflow tasks is 6, and the coding sequence of each ant is 6 bits. The value of each bit indicates the ID of the virtual machine that executes the task, that is, the task corresponding to the bit is allocated to the corresponding virtual machine for execution. Taking a workflow task in Fig. 1 as an example, an ant encoding sequence is constructed as (1 3 3 2 4 2). This sequence has a total of 6 bits. The first one represents Task 1 in Fig. 2, which is the entry task. The virtual machine number 1 indicates that task 1 is executed on the virtual machine 1. The 6th bit is on behalf of task 6, for the export task, which is executed in the 6th virtual machine. Because of this, the assignment of tasks to the virtual machines is shown in Table 1. In the process of searching for the optimal solution by the ant colony algorithm, the values of all bits in the encoding sequence will be changed. After the path is selected, the ant's encoding will be reconstructed.

Table 1 reflects the allocation scheme of virtual machines, but execution order of the task in the virtual machine cannot be reflected. When considering virtual

Table 1. Task allocation in the virtual machine

Task	1	2	3	4	5	6
Virtual machine	1	3	3	2	4	2

machine allocation schemes, the order of execution of the tasks also needs to be taken into account. If we do not take the order of task into consideration, task 2 and task 3 in Table 1 are all assigned to the 3th virtual machine, while the virtual machine can only run one task at the same time. The pre-order task of task 2 and task 3 is task 1. While task 1 is finished, the 3th virtual machine will not know which task to execute firstly, if the task execution sequence is not provided. Therefore, it is necessary that the coding incorporate the order of execution of the tasks.

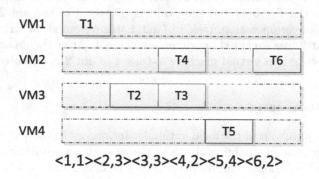

<1,1><2,3><3,3><4,2><5,4><6,2>

Fig. 2. Ant encoding with the order

In order to add the order of task execution into coding, ordered pair is used to present the ants in ant colony algorithm. The first number in the order pair represents the number of the task, the second number represents the number of the virtual machine where the task is located. As shown in Fig. 2, VM_j represents the virtual machine, T_i represents the task.

Improved Ant Colony Algorithm Based Workflow Task Scheduling. The convergence of ant colony algorithm is slow, and the solution is easier to fall into the local optimal rather than global optimal. Therefore, in this paper, ant colony optimization algorithm is improved by the cross and mutation operation in genetic algorithm to speed up the ant colony algorithm convergence, and avoid the local optimum.

(1) Crossover operation

As shown in Fig. 3(a), crossover operation actually indicates that the values of the selected positions are exchanged in the encoding sequence according to a

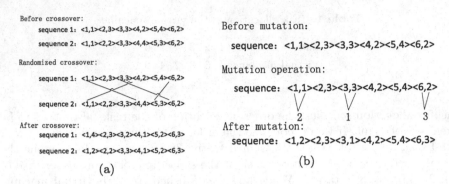

Fig. 3. (a) Crossover operation, (b) Mutation operation

certain crossover probability. For example, the position of task 1 in ant 1 (i.e., sequence 1) in the Fig. 3(a) and the position of task 4 of the ant 2 is crossed. Before the crossover operation, task 1 of ant 1 was executed on virtual machine 1, task 4 of ant 2 was executed on virtual machine 4. After the crossover, task 1 of ant 1 is executed on virtual machine 4, task 4 of ant 2 is executed on virtual machine 1.

(2) Mutation operation

In order to jump out of the local optimal solution, we introduce the mutation operation in genetic algorithm to introduce new solution sequence and increase the diversity of solutions. Mutation operation is shown in Fig. 3(b). Combined with modulo operation of random number, the sequence of coding is operated mutation. The main process of the Ant colony algorithm in this paper is shown in Algorithm 2.

Algorithm 2. the Ant colony algorithm in this paper

Input: initialized scheduling scheme
Output: the optimal solution
    Description:
        Step1: initialize scheduling scheme;
        Step2: combined crossover and mutation operations, select the next resource node according to the status transition probability;
        Step3: modify taboo table and update pheromone;
        Step4: operate iteratively until finding the optimal solution or t=reaching the iteration times;
        Step5: output the optimal solution.

---

5   Experiments

5.1   Experimental Methods

CloudSim is used to create a workflow generator, and according to the related configuration, workflow tasks is generated and written to a local disk. Upload files from local disk to Hadoop via Eclipse, perform tasks with Hadoop, and output the results.

The scheduler is one of the core components of Hadoop and is a plug-in service component of the ResourceManager. It is responsible for the management and distribution of the entire cluster resources. The Fair scheduler and Capacity scheduler which belong to an extended YARN scheduler can support multiple queues and multiple users [15]. Therefore, these schedulers are used as a comparison.

The Capacity scheduler [2] is developed by Yahoo!, which designs several queues for storing jobs. The principle of Capacity scheduler is shown in Fig. 4(a). The Fair Scheduler [6] designed by Facebook can be used to handle different types of jobs. The idea is to equally distribute system resources to tasks submitted by users. The principle of Fair scheduler is shown in Fig. 4(b).

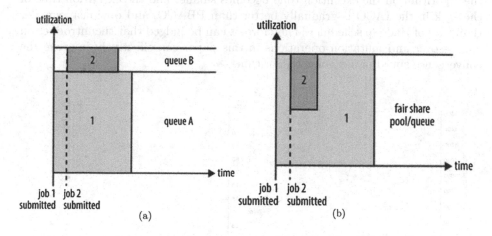

Fig. 4. (a) The principle of Capacity scheduler, (b) The principle of Fair scheduler

Apart from Hadoop own scheduler, another algorithm PBACO [16] is also compared to show the superiority of IACO. The primary targets of this scheduling method are performance and budget cost; because it is based on the ant colony optimization algorithm, it is named PBACO, which is a multi-objective optimization method for task-scheduling problems in cloud computing. First, with an aim toward the biodiversity of resources and tasks in cloud computing, we propose a resource cost model that defines the demand of tasks on resources with more details. This model reflects the relationship between the user's resource costs and the budget costs. A multi-objective optimization scheduling method has been proposed based on this resource cost model. This method considers the makespan and the user's budget costs as constraints of the optimization problem, achieving multi-objective optimization of both performance and cost. Two constraint functions were used to evaluate and provide feedback regarding the performance and budget cost. These two constraint functions made the algorithm adjust the quality of the solution in a timely manner based on feedback in order to achieve the optimal solution.

5.2   Experimental Results and Analysis

In this paper, we compare IACO algorithm with the algorithm PBACO and Hadoop own schedulers Capacity and Fair. The result is as follows:

As can be seen from Fig. 5(a), comparing with IACO algorithm and PBACO algorithm, IFCM can be used to cluster resources, which can effectively utilize the characteristics of resources and reduce the execution time of tasks. At the same time, the task execution time of the ant colony algorithm and its improved algorithm are slightly higher than that of Hadoop own scheduler. However, with the increase of the number of tasks, the influence of the convergence speed of the algorithm on the execution time becomes smaller and the execution time of the task in the IACO is gradually better than PBACO, and obviously smaller than that of Hadoop scheduler. Therefore, it can be judged that the introduction of crossover and mutation operations in this paper can effectively improve the convergence speed of ant colony algorithm.

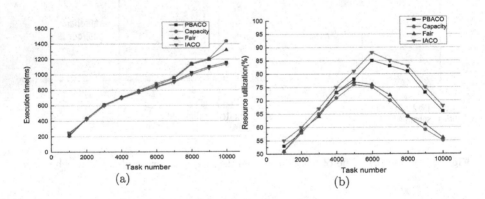

Fig. 5. Comparison of (a)task execution time, (b) resource utilization

As can be seen from Fig. 5(b), through the comparison of resource utilization between IACO and PBACO, it can be found that by using IFCM algorithm to cluster resources, the utilization of resources is more reasonable and the utilization rate is improved. The resource utilization of the improved algorithm is obviously higher than Hadoop own scheduler. When the number of tasks reaches a certain amount, the resource utilization rate reaches its peak. Further increasing the task, resource utilization rate becomes lower, but resource utilization of IACO algorithm is always higher than other algorithms. When the number of tasks exceeds the number, the average load of the virtual machines becomes larger. Due to the pre-order relationship between workflow tasks, some tasks may wait, resulting in a decrease in resource utilization.

6   Conclusion

In this paper, aiming at the workflow tasks in cloud computing system, IFCM clustering algorithm is used to reduce the sensitivity of clustering, which the resources in cloud computing system. Tasks are sorted by priority. Then the task scheduling solutions are initialized by computing the distance between expect of task resource and resources, and the task of workflow is coded. Combining with the crossover and mutation operation in genetic algorithm, the improved ant colony algorithm accelerates the convergence speed of ant colony algorithm and jumps out of the local optimal solution. The improved ant colony algorithm searches for the optimal scheduling scheme, which can effectively reduce the execution time of workflow tasks and improve the system resource utilization.

At present, only the fuzzy clustering algorithm is applied to the resource clustering, but the task has not been clustered. Clustering tasks, combined with resource clustering, should be able to improve the efficiency of task scheduling more effectively. This is our further work.

Acknowledgement. This work was supported in part by National Science Foundation of China (No. 61572259, No. U1736105) and Special Public Sector Research Program of China (No. GYHY201506080) and was also supported by PAPD.

References

1. Calheiros, R.N., Ranjan, R., Beloglazov, A., Rose, C.A.F.D., Buyya, R.: CloudSim: a toolkit for modeling and simulation of cloud computing environments and evaluation of resource provisioning algorithms. Softw. Pract. Exp. **41**(1), 23–50 (2010)
2. Chauhan, J.: Simulation and performance evaluation of hadoop capacity scheduler. MapReduce, MRPERF, Capacity Scheduler (2013)
3. Dorigo, M., Maniezzo, V., Colorni, A.: Ant system: optimization by a colony of cooperating agents. IEEE Trans. Syst. Man Cybern. Part B Cybern. **26**(1), 29 (1996). A Publication of the IEEE Systems Man and Cybernetics Society
4. Huang, X., Du, B., Sun, L., Chen, F., Dai, W.: Service requirement conflict resolution based on ant colony optimization in group-enterprises-oriented cloud manufacturing. Int. J. Adv. Manuf. Technol. **84**(1–4), 183–196 (2016)
5. Kaur, P., Mehta, S.: Resource provisioning and work flow scheduling in clouds using augmented shuffled frog leaping algorithm. J. Parallel Distrib. Comput. **101**(2017), 41–50 (2017). Academic Press, Inc.
6. Lo, S.C., Cheng, Y.W.: Improving the performance of fair scheduler in hadoop. Adv. Sci. Technol. Eng. Syst. J. **2**(3), 1050–1058 (2017)

7. Lv, Y.: An efficient and scalable density-based clustering algorithm for datasets with complex structures. Neurocomputing **171**(C), 9–22 (2016)
8. Ma, T., et al.: LED: a fast overlapping communities detection algorithm based on structural clustering. Neurocomputing **207**, 488–500 (2016)
9. Ma, T., Ying, C., Ying, C., Tian, Y., Al-Dhelaan, A., Al-Rodhaan, M.: Detect structural-connected communities based on BSCHEF in C-DBLP. Concurr. Comput. Pract. Exp. **28**(2), 311–330 (2016)
10. Ma, T., et al.: KDVEM : a k-degree anonymity with vertex and edge modification algorithm. Computing **97**(12), 1165–1184 (2015)
11. Sinha, N., Srivastav, V., Ahmad, W.: Deadline constrained workflow scheduling optimization by initial seeding with ant colony optimization. Int. J. Comput. Appl. **155**(14), 24–29 (2016)
12. Rodriguez, M.A., Buyya, R.: Deadline based resource provisioningand scheduling algorithm for scientific workflows on clouds. IEEE Trans. Cloud Comput. **2**(2), 222–235 (2014)
13. Rong, H., Ma, T., Tang, M., Cao, J.: A novel subgraph k^+ -isomorphism method in social network based on graph similarity detection. Soft Comput. **7**, 1–19 (2017)
14. Yu, J., Xiao, X., Zhang, Y.: From concept to implementation: the development of the emerging cloud computing industry in china. Telecommun. Policy **40**(2–3), 130–146 (2016)
15. Zhang, X., Hu, B., Jiang, J.: An optimized algorithm for reduce task scheduling. J. Comput. **9**(4), 965–970 (2014)
16. Zuo, L., Shu, L., Dong, S., Zhu, C., Hara, T.: A multi-objective optimization scheduling method based on the ant colony algorithm in cloud computing. IEEE Access **3**, 2687–2699 (2015)

Research on Intuitionistic Fuzzy Multiple Output Least Squares Support Vector Regression

Dingcheng Wang[✉], Yiyi Lu, Beijing Chen, and Liming Chen

Nanjing University of Information Science and Technology, Nanjing 210044,
Jiangsu, China
dcwang2005@126.com

Abstract. Support vector regression (SVR) is an important machine learning algorithm, although some successful applications have been achieved. The algorithm for complex system is still worth studying. Multiple output intuitionistic fuzzy least squares support vector regression (IFLS-SVR) is improved by using the intuitionistic fuzzy to solve the problem of the uncertain multiple output complex system. Compared with the traditional fuzzy support vector regression, the model with the fuzzy membership and non-fuzzy membership is more close to the practical system. Multiple output IFLS-SVR transforms the actual data into fuzzy data and transforms the quadratic programming optimization problem into a series of linear equations. Compared with the current fuzzy support vector regression, multiple output IFLS-SVR in this paper adopted the intuitionistic fuzzy method to calculate membership functions, improving the training efficiency of the algorithm and reducing the training time by using the least square method. Through the simulation model, multiple output IFLS-SVR has achieved good results compared with other methods. The application of multiple output IFLS-SVR to the prediction of complex wind weather has also achieved good results.

Keywords: Least squares support vector regression · Intuitionistic fuzzy
Multiple output · Wind weather prediction

1 Introduction

Support vector machine (SVM) is a machine learning method. It is a data based learning method based on statistical learning theory, VC, and structural risk minimization. It has been applied in pattern recognition field successfully. Support vector machine regression (SVMR) is the form of support vector machine in continuous function domain, and there have been many successful applications [1–5]. Compared with the traditional regression method, the support vector machine regression is based on structural risk minimization principle, which transforms complex nonlinear problems into linear problems, and successfully solves the problems of high-dimensional operation and so on. However, the two programming optimization method has the problem of training speed, and there is a problem of noise interference from sample data. Fuzzy support vector machine (FSVM) [6–8] combines the fuzzy set theory with

X. Sun et al. (Eds.): ICCCS 2018, LNCS 11064, pp. 389–398, 2018.
https://doi.org/10.1007/978-3-030-00009-7_36

the support vector machine model, and can effectively solve the noise interference problem. In FSVM, it is a key problem to select effective fuzzy membership function. [9–11] has studied the method of determining membership value function, and taken different weights according to different samples. In order to eliminate the effect of noise and outliers on the results, the weight of the noise points is smaller when the target function is constructed. A new membership function design method is studied in literature [12]. It not only considers the distance between sample and class center, but also considers the size of samples, and improves the classification performance. Based on distance samples, the class center method is often used to calculate membership degree. When the distance between sample and sample center is smaller, the membership degree of the sample is bigger. Conversely, the larger the distance is, the smaller the membership degree is. Because noise and outliers are far from the sample center, membership degree is very small, which can effectively solve the noise problem, but it has a negative impact on outliers.

Bulgarian scholar Atanassov extends the uncertainty of fuzzy set theory, membership degree, non-membership degree and intuitionistic fuzzy set. Compared with the traditional fuzzy set, the intuitionistic fuzzy set has a non-fuzzy membership, and reflect the actual things more accurately [13]. Literature [12] applies intuitionistic fuzzy to support vector machine (SVM) for C-means clustering, which is more efficient than K-means and fuzzy C-means. In [14], using intuitionistic fuzzy algorithm, least squares support vector regression and Sammon mapping, improved the traditional fuzzy C-regression algorithm to solve the clustering problem, and achieved good results.

In this paper, the intuitionistic fuzzy least squares support vector regression is studied, and intuitionistic fuzzy is applied to the support vector regression model to solve the problem of continuous function domain [15]. Because the actual system not only has noise and uncertainty, but also is a multi-output system, there is coupling between outputs. Therefore, this study is based on multi output least squares support vector regression.

2   Least Squares Support Vector Regression

Assuming that $D = \{(x_1, y_1), (x_2, y_2), \ldots, (x_l, y_l)\}, x_i \in R^n, y_i \in R, x_i$ and y_i are input vectors and output vectors respectively. LS-SVR maps the samples to high dimensional feature spaces. Based on the principle of structural risk minimization, LS-SVR needs to solve a planning problem:

$$\min \frac{1}{2}\|w\|^2 + \frac{\varsigma}{2}\sum_{i=1}^{l} e_i^2$$
$$\text{s.t. } y_i = W \cdot \varphi(x_i) + b + e_i \qquad (1)$$

e_i is an error variable; W is the weight; $\varphi(x_i)$ is a nonlinear mapping function, and b is a deviation. The Lagrange multiplier is introduced and we get the Eq. (2).

$$L(W, b, e; \alpha) = \frac{1}{2}\|W\|^2 + \frac{C}{2}\sum_{i=1}^{l} e_i^2 - \sum_{i=1}^{n} \alpha_i[W \cdot \varphi(x_i) + b + e_i - y_i] \qquad (2)$$

The Eq. (3) is obtained for solving the constrained optimization problem according to the KKT condition.

$$
\begin{cases}
\frac{\partial L}{\partial W} = 0 \rightarrow W = \sum_{i=1}^{n} \alpha_i \cdot \varphi(x_i) \\
\frac{\partial L}{\partial b} = 0 \rightarrow 0 = \sum_{i=1}^{n} \alpha_i \\
\frac{\partial L}{\partial e_i} = 0 \rightarrow \alpha_i = Ce_i \\
\frac{\partial L}{\partial \alpha} = 0 \rightarrow 0 = W \cdot \varphi(x_i) + b + e_i - y_i
\end{cases}
\tag{3}
$$

The LS-SVR solution is obtained by solving the two programming.

3 Intuitionistic Fuzzy Multiple Output Least Squares Support Vector Regression

The traditional fuzzy algorithm transforms the actual accurate data into fuzzy sets by membership function, and the membership function is commonly based on the distance from the sample to the center of the class.

(1) Calculate the center of class of two types of samples:

$$
(\overline{x_1}, \overline{y_1}) = \frac{1}{n_1} \sum_{i=1}^{n_1} (x_{1i}, y_{1i})
\tag{4}
$$

$$
(\overline{x_2}, \overline{y_2}) = \frac{1}{n_2} \sum_{i=1}^{n_2} (x_{2i}, y_{2i})
\tag{5}
$$

(2) Calculate the radius of the two types of samples:

$$
r_1 = \sqrt{(maxx_{1i} - \overline{x_1})^2 + (maxy_{1i} - \overline{y_1})^2}
\tag{6}
$$
$$
i = 1, 2, \ldots, n_1
$$

$$
r_2 = \sqrt{(maxx_{2i} - \overline{x_2})^2 + (maxy_{2i} - \overline{y_2})^2}
\tag{7}
$$
$$
i = 1, 2, \ldots, n_2
$$

(3) Calculate the membership of each sample:

$$
\mu_{1i} = 1 - \frac{\sqrt{(x_{1i} - \overline{x_1})^2 + (y_{1i} - \overline{y_1})^2}}{r_1} + \varepsilon
\tag{8}
$$
$$
i = 1, 2, \ldots, n_1
$$

$$
\mu_{2i} = 1 - \frac{\sqrt{(x_{2i} - \overline{x_2})^2 + (y_{2i} - \overline{y_2})^2}}{r_2} + \varepsilon
\tag{9}
$$
$$
i = 1, 2, \ldots, n_2
$$

In equations above, x_{1i} and x_{2i} are of two kinds of samples the input vector, n_1 and n_2 are the numbers of two class samples, $\overline{x_1}$ and $\overline{x_2}$ are the centers of class, r_1 and r_2 are the radius, μ_{1i} and μ_{2i} are memberships of two kinds of samples, ε is a very small positive number which is in order to avoid that the membership is zero.

However, the actual system is not a complete fuzzy set. Atanassov has put forward the intuitionistic fuzzy set, which adds a non-membership degree to the traditional fuzzy algorithm, which is a more practical algorithm.

Then the intuitionistic fuzzy set on λ is defined as:

$$A = \{ <x, \mu_A(x), v_A(x) > | x \in \chi \} \tag{10}$$

Among them, $\mu_A(x)$ and $v_A(x)$ are the subordinate function and the non-subordinate function respectively.

$$\mu_A(x) : \chi \to [0,1], x \in \chi \to \mu_A(x) \in [0,1] \tag{11}$$

$$v_A(x) : \chi \to [0,1], x \in \chi \to v_A(x) \in [0,1] \tag{12}$$

$\mu_A(x)$ and $v_A(x)$ satisfy that $0 \le \mu_A(x) + v_A(x) \le 1$.

$\pi_A = 1 - (\mu_A(x) + v_A(x))$ is the degree of hesitation or uncertainty, that is, the index of intuition. The training sample is modified according to the definition of intuitionistic fuzzy. The intuition index reflects the uncertainty of the sample.

$$\left. \begin{array}{c} \min \frac{1}{2} \sum_{j=1}^{k} \| W_j \|^2 + \frac{C}{2} \sum_{i=1}^{l} \sum_{j=1}^{k} (\mu_{i,j} - t \cdot \pi_{i,j}) e_{i,j}^2 + C_0 \sum_{i=1}^{l} \eta_i \\ \text{s.t. } y_{i,j} = W_j \cdot \varphi(x_i) + b_j + e_{i,j} \\ \eta_i = \sum_{j=1}^{k} |e_{i,j}| \\ i = 1, 2, \ldots, l; \ 0 \le \mu_{i,j} - t \cdot \pi_{i,j} \le 1 \end{array} \right\} \tag{13}$$

The parameter t needs to be satisfied $0 \le \mu_{i,j} - t \cdot \pi_{i,j} \le 1$.

The Lagrange multiplier is used, and the formula (14) is obtained.

$$L(w, b, e; \alpha) = \min \frac{1}{2} \sum_{j=1}^{k} \| W_j \|^2 + \frac{C}{2} \sum_{i=1}^{l} \sum_{j=1}^{k} (\mu_{i,j} - t \cdot \pi_{i,j}) e_{i,j}^2 + C_0 \sum_{i=1}^{l} \eta_i +$$
$$\sum_{i=1}^{l} \sum_{j=1}^{k} \alpha_{i,j} [W_j \cdot \varphi(x_i) + b_j + e_{i,j} - y_{i,j}]$$

$$\tag{14}$$

According to the KKT condition,

$$\begin{cases} \frac{\partial L}{\partial W_j} = 0 \to W_j = \alpha_{i,j} y_{i,j} \varphi(x_i) \\ \frac{\partial L}{\partial b_j} = 0 \to \sum_{i=1}^{l} \alpha_{i,j} y_{i,j} = 0 \\ \frac{\partial L}{\partial e_{i,j}} = 0 \to C(\mu_{i,j} - t \cdot \pi_{i,j}) e_{i,j} - \alpha_{i,j} = 0 \\ \frac{\partial L}{\partial \alpha_{i,j}} = 0 \to y_{i,j} \left[W_j^T \varphi(x_i) + b_j \right] - 1 + e_{i,j} = 0 \end{cases} \tag{15}$$

The variable W is eliminated by the transformation of the same solution.

$$\begin{bmatrix} 0 & \mathbf{1}^T \\ \mathbf{1} & K(x_i, x_j) + (\mu_{i,j} - t \cdot \pi_{i,j})C^{-1}I \end{bmatrix} \begin{bmatrix} b_j \\ \alpha_j \end{bmatrix} = \begin{bmatrix} 0 \\ Y_j^* \end{bmatrix} \tag{16}$$

The result of the corresponding multiple output IFLS-SVR can be obtained.

$$f^{(j)}(X) = \sum_{i=1}^{l} \alpha_{i,j} K(X, X_i) + b_j \\ j = 1, 2, \ldots, k; \tag{17}$$

4 Simulation

In general, the selection of the kernel function includes the selection of the type of kernel function and the selection of the related parameters after the kernel function. The radial basis function is chosen as the kernel function. The different parameters have influence on the experimental results, and the control variable method is adopted to select the parameters.

The data from −3 to 3 to 0.01 is the sampling interval, with a total of 300 input samples. The first 200 sample data are training samples, and the latter 100 are test samples.

Finally, we choose $\sigma = 0.5$, $C = 10$, $d = 0.6$, $k = 0.5$. The multiple output IFLS-SVR algorithm is compared with the multiple output LS-SVR algorithm and multiple single output SVR algorithms. The performance of the algorithm is analyzed by calculating the iterative time and comparing the root mean square error (RMSE). The results of the experiment are shown in Fig. 1, Tables 1 and 2. The root mean square error (RMSE) of the multiple output IFLS-SVM is shown in Table 1.

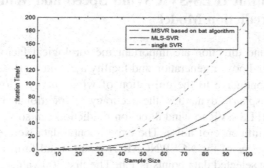

Fig. 1. Iterative time comparison of three methods

According to the root mean square error of Table 1, it can be seen that the generalization performance of the algorithm is better. The experimental results show that the multi output IFLS-SVM algorithm has a better effect compared with the multiple output LS-SVR algorithm.

Table 1. Experimental results of different methods

	Algorithm	Training sample	Test sample	RMSE
$\gamma = 0.5$	MIFLS-SVR	200	100	0.185
$\varepsilon = 0.1$	MLS-SVR	200	100	0.193
$\gamma = 0.5$	MIFLS-SVR	200	100	1.132
$\varepsilon = 1$	MLS-SVR	200	100	1.226
$\gamma = 0.1$	MIFLS-SVR	200	100	0.531
$\varepsilon = 1$	MLS-SVR	200	100	0.647
$\gamma = 0.1$	MIFLS-SVR	200	100	3.225
$\varepsilon = 3$	MLS-SVR	200	100	3.501

Table 2. Comparison of three methods of iterative time and iterative speed

Algorithms	Iteration time/s	Iteration speed/s^{-1}
Multiple output IFLS-SVR	87.55	2.28
MLS-SVR	99.07	2.02
Single SVR	165.34	1.21

Figure 1 shows the iteration time of the three algorithms, and it can be seen that the iterative time of the multiple output IFLS-SVR algorithm is the shortest.

In Table 2, the iteration time of the multiple output IFLS-SVR algorithm is the least of the three methods. Therefore, the multi-output IFLS-SVR algorithm proposed in this paper is more reasonable.

5 Multiple Output IFLS-SVR Wind Speed and Wind Direction Prediction Model

Wind speed and wind direction are important meteorological factors, which play an important role in wind power generation and facility agriculture. Reasonable prediction of wind speed is conducive to the utilization of wind energy. However, due to the complexity of atmospheric dynamics, the accuracy of traditional methods is limited. The application of IFLS-SVR to wind direction prediction can solve the uncertainty of the system and the influence of noise. The experimental data were extracted from the actual wind speed series of the NCEP/NCAR Xinjiang wind farm in April 2001. The interval between the selected data points is 1 h. The first 300 values are selected as the training samples of the model, and the last 50 values are used as the prediction samples.

In Fig. 2, the wind speed changes in the range of [4 14], the daytime wind speed is basically stable around [5 7], and the value of the wind velocity fluctuates at night. The temperature difference between day and night in Xinjiang in April is relatively large, but the fluctuation of wind speed values are generally greater than the end of the month. To the north of 0° clockwise direction as positive. Although the fluctuation of wind direction is very large, it fluctuates at 200°.

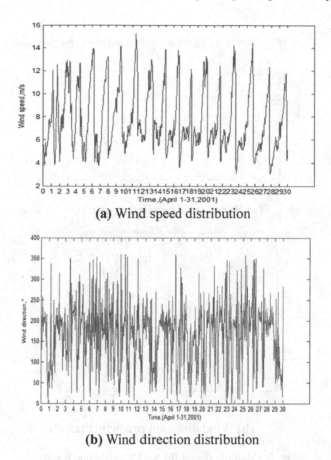

(a) Wind speed distribution

(b) Wind direction distribution

Fig. 2. The velocity and direction of the wind in the experimental sample

As shown in Fig. 3, the prediction results of wind speed and wind direction based on the multi-output IFLS-SVR can be shown that the difference between the predicted value and the actual value is small.

Figure 4 uses three different methods to predict wind speed and wind direction by using the multiple output IFLS-SVR, the multiple output LS-SVR, and the single output SVR.

The prediction result of multiple output IFLS-SVR is the closest to the actual value. Compared with the multiple output IFLS-SVR, the result of MLS-SVR has a certain deviation, and the prediction error of single output SVR is the largest. The experimental results prove the superiority of the multi output IFLS-SVR algorithm.

It is very important to choose a reasonable method of error analysis. We chose the root mean square error (RMSE) and the mean absolute percentage error (MAPE) to evaluate the experimental results.

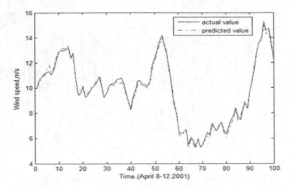

(a) Wind speed prediction results

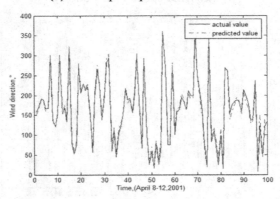

(b) Wind direction prediction results

Fig. 3. Multiple output IFLS-SVR prediction results

$$\text{MAPE} = \frac{1}{M} \left[\sum_{i=1}^{M} \frac{|y_i - f(x_i)|}{y_i} \right] \times 100\% \tag{19}$$

$$\text{RMSE} = \sqrt{\frac{1}{M} \sum_{i=1}^{M} [y_i - f(x_i)]^2} \tag{20}$$

From Table 3, we can see that the error of the multiple output fuzzy least squares support vector regression is the smallest, and the wind speed and the wind direction error are close to 15% and 17%, respectively. The errors of MLS-SVR and single output SVR are all 20%. Therefore, the multiple output IFLS-SVR algorithm with error of 15.09% and 17.51% performs well. The other two methods are chosen to predict the speed and direction of the wind to compare with the multiple output IFLS-SVR. These three methods are the machine learning algorithms. Compared with MLS-SVR, multiple output IFLS-SVR helps to overcome the influence of traditional SVR on noise and isolation. Compared with the single output SVR, the multiple output IFLS-SVR has a

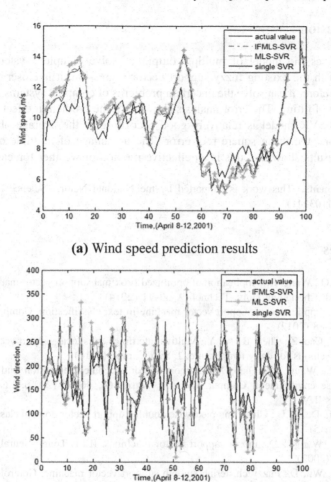

(a) Wind speed prediction results

(b) Wind direction prediction results

Fig. 4. Wind speed and wind direction prediction results of three methods

stronger generalization. The experimental results confirm the feasibility of the intuitionistic fuzzy multiple output regression model.

Table 3. Prediction error of three methods

Algorithms	MAPE (%)		RMSE(m/s, °)	
	Speed	Direction	Speed	Direction
IFMLS-SVR	15.09	17.51	0.3393	9.712
MLS-SVR	21.93	25.67	0.7375	17.2493
Single SVR	35.39	31.13	1.6799	39.7379

6 Conclusion

IFLS-SVR uses the model of multiple output to solve complex system problems. Compared with the existing fuzzy support vector regression, it is closer to the actual system. Therefore, it can solve the uncertain problems of complex systems and improve the accuracy of fitting. The error analysis shows that the prediction effect of the multi output IFLS-SVR model is relatively good according to the average absolute error percentage and the mean square root error. The advantage of multiple output IFLS-SVR. The results show that this is an effective method of weather forecasting.

Acknowledgments. This work is supported by the National Natural Science Foundation of China (No. 61103141).

References

1. Wang, H.Q., Wang, B.: Application of optimized proximal support vector machine in image retrieval. J. Chongqing Univ. Technol. **9**, 66–71 (2014)
2. Duan, Y.: Application of support vector machine in text classification. Comput. Digit. Eng. **40**(7), 87–88 (2012)
3. Wang, D., Cao, Z., Chen, B., Ni, Y.: Multivariate time series local support vector regression forecast methods for daily temperature. J. Syst. Simul. (2016)
4. Wang, D., Wang, M., Qiao, X.: Support vector machines regression and modeling of greenhouse environment. Comput. Electron. Agric. **66**, 46–52 (2009). Elsevier Science Publishers B.V.
5. Liang, J.J., De, W.U.: Clustering piecewise double support vector domain classifier. Control Decis. (2015)
6. Lin, C.F., Wang, S.D.: Fuzzy support vector machines. IEEE Trans. Neural Netw. **13**(2), 464–471 (2002)
7. Liu, S.Y., Wu, D.: Fuzzy clustering smooth support vector machine. Control Decis. **32**(3), 547–551 (2017)
8. Shang, Z.G., Yan, H.S.: Product design time prediction based on fuzzy support vector machine. **27**(4), 531–534 (2012)
9. Ding, S.F., Sun, J.G.: Fuzzy dual support vector machine based on mixed fuzzy membership degree. **30**(2), 432–435 (2013)
10. Ha, M., Wang, C., Chen, J.: The support vector machine based on intuitionistic fuzzy number and kernel function. Soft. Comput. **17**(4), 635–641 (2013)
11. Zhang, X., Xiao, X.L., Xu, G.Y.: Fuzzy support vector machine based on affinity among samples. J. Softw. **17**(5), 951–958 (2006)
12. Lin, K.P.: A novel evolutionary kernel intuitionistic fuzzy C-means clustering algorithm. IEEE Trans. Fuzzy Syst. **22**(5), 1074–1087 (2014)
13. Atanassov, K.T.: Intuitionistic fuzzy sets. Fuzzy Sets Syst. **35**(1), 1–137 (1986)
14. Lin, K.P., Chang, H.F., Chen, T.L.: Intuitionistic fuzzy C-regression by using least squares support vector regression. Expert Syst. Appl. Int. J. **64**(C), 296–304 (2016)
15. Hung, K.C., Lin, K.P.: Long-term business cycle forecasting through a potential intuitionistic fuzzy least-squares support vector regression approach. Inf. Sci. **224**(2), 37–48 (2013)

Cloud Security

A Blind Signature Scheme with Disclaimer Contract in the Standard Model

Liming Zuo[1,2(✉)], Mengli Zhang[1,2], Tingting Zhang[1,2], and Kaiyu Hu[1,2]

[1] College of Science, East China Jiaotong University, Nanchang 330013, China
limingzuo@126.com
[2] Institute of Systems Engineering and Cryptograph,
East China Jiaotong University, Nanchang 330013, China

Abstract. It is difficult to construct a blind signature scheme in the standard model that conforms to the formalized blindness. The difficulty lies in eliminating the blindness when the scheme is constructed. Focused on the blind nature and using the bilinear pairing, a signature scheme with disclaimer contract is proposed on the basis of the Waters signature scheme, which has provable security and blind features. Besides, the security proof of the scheme is given in the standard model. In general, the scheme has the characteristics of self-eliminating blindness and higher efficiency. It is easy to be realized in the standard model.

Keywords: Blindness · Standard model · Bilinear pairing · Disclaimer contract
Digital signature

1 Introduction

Blind signature that was firstly introduced by Chaum [1] is a kind of extremely important digital signature type in practical application, and has two prominent features: (1) Blindness, that is, the signer does not know the specific content of the signature message; (2) Non-degeneracy, that is, the signer only knows that the message has been signed, but there's no way to know when to sign this signature and whom it is signed to. These two properties can effectively protect the message from being tampered with, and can not track the correspondence between the signature and the message. Because blind signatures are widely used in practical projects and have been studied by many scholars deeply [2–7]. However, most blind signature schemes are provable secure under the random oracle model [8]. The random oracle model is an idealized model in which the random oracle does not exist in the real world. The random oracle is instantiated as the Hash function in the proof of the scheme. However, because the output of the Hash function is not random, many blind signature schemes under the random oracle model have some security loophole. In 2005, Waters [9] proposed provable encryption scheme in the standard model, and proposed a signature scheme in the standard model (Waters scheme). After that, more signature schemes were proposed in the standard model [10–15]. In 2011, Gu et al. [14] proposed a new efficient signature scheme that could reduce security protocols to CDH issues based on

© Springer Nature Switzerland AG 2018
X. Sun et al. (Eds.): ICCCS 2018, LNCS 11064, pp. 401–412, 2018.
https://doi.org/10.1007/978-3-030-00009-7_37

the Waters scheme. Subsequently, Yu et al. [15] pointed out that there are potential security risks in the scheme of Gu's scheme, and gave two types of attacks, but the efficiency is not high. In 2015, Chen [16] proposed an identity-based proxy blind signature under the standard model, and proved that this scheme has provable security under the standard model. In this paper, we propose a new blind signature scheme with the disclaimer contract by using bilinear pairing [17]. The scheme uses the disclaimer contract, and if it is determined that the message to be signed is harmful to the signer, the blind signature can be determined to be invalid according to the disclaimer contract, which protects the signer's interests from infringement. The scheme has the characteristics of self-eliminating blindness, so the message holder does not need to eliminate the blindness of the signature again.

2 Preliminaries

Before presenting our scheme, we review essential knowledge required in this paper, namely bilinear pairing, CDH problem and the definition of partially blind signature scheme.

2.1 Bilinear Pairing

Let g be a generator of G_1. Let G_1 and G_2 be multiplicative groups of the same order q. Let $e : G_1 \times G_1 \to G_2$ be a bilinear map which satisfies the following properties:

- Bilinearity: $e(P^a, Q^b) = e(P, Q)^{ab}$ for all $a, b \in Z_q$ and $P, Q \in G_1$.
- Non-degeneracy: $e(g, g) \neq 1$.
- Computability: There is an efficient algorithm to compute $e(P, Q)$ for all $P, Q \in G_1$.

2.2 CDH Problem

Given $g \in G_1$, the unknown $a, b \in Z_q^*$, given a tuple of values $(g, g^a, g^b) \in G_1 \times G_1 \times G_1$, the problem of solving g^{ab} is hard.

2.3 Definition of Partially Blind Signature Scheme

In the scenario of issuing a partially blind signature [18], the signer and the user are assumed to agree on a piece of common information, denoted as info. In some applications, info may be decided by the signer, while in other applications it may just be sent from the user to the signer. Anyway, this negotiation is done outside of the signature scheme, and we want the signature scheme to be secure regardless of the process of agreement.

A Partially blind signature scheme is made up of four (interactive) algorithms (machines) (G, S, U, V).

- G is a probabilistic polynomial-time algorithm that takes security parameter n and outputs a public and secret key pair (pk, sk).

- S and U are a pair of probabilistic interactive Turing machines each of which has a public input tape, a private input tape, a private random tape, a private work tape, a private output tape, a public output tape, and input and output communication tapes. The random tape and the input tapes are read-only, and the output tapes are write-only. The private work tape is read-write. The public input tape of U contains pk generated by $G(i^n)$ and info. The public input tape of S contains info. The private input tape of S contains sk, and that for U contains message m. S and U engage in the signature issuing protocol and stop in polynomial-time in n. When they stop, the public output tape of S contains either completed or not-completed. Similarly, the private output tape of U contains either $\perp$ or (m, σ).
- V is a (probabilistic) polynomial-time algorithm that takes (pk, info, m, σ) and outputs either accept or reject.

3 Blind Signature Scheme in the Standard Model

3.1 Disclaimer Contract

The definition of the disclaimer contract C is a binding statement. According to the disclaimer contract, the signature may be deemed invalid, if afterwards the arbitration finds that the message to be signed is harmful to the signer. Due to blind signature of the signer on file, the specific content can not be informed of the file, it can not guarantee that the signature results will be detrimental to their own interests, so before the blind signature is made, a binding statement is defined in advance to effectively ensure that the legitimate rights of the signer are not infringed.

3.2 Blind Signature Scheme

Key Generation: Running algorithm $\Re(1^k)$, it returns system parameters $params = (G, G_T, q, g, e)$. Pick a random number a from Z_q, and compute $g_1 = g^a$. Randomly choose $b, t_0, t_1, \cdots, t_k$ from Z_q, then compute $g_2 = g^b$ and $u_0 = g^{t_0}, u_1 = g^{t_1}, \cdots, u_k = g^{t_k}$. The public key is the tuple of values $(params, g_1, g_2, u_0, u_1, \cdots, u_k)$, and the private key is g_2^a. Define collision attack function $H_1 : \{0, 1\}^* \rightarrow \{0, 1\}^k$. Let

$$H(h) = u_0 \prod_{i=1}^{k} u_i^{h_i} (h = h_1 \cdots h_k \in \{0, 1\}^k) \tag{1}$$

Signature Generation: We sign through the following interactive methods, where Alice is the signer. Bob is the user.

- Alice picks a random number $r \in Z_q$ and disclaimer contract C, and then sends (g^r, C) to Bob.
- Bob selects a blinding factor randomly w from Z_q, and computes

$$h = H_1(m\|C) \tag{2}$$

$$U = g^{-w}H(h) \tag{3}$$

$$W = g^{rw} \tag{4}$$

Then Bob sends (U, W) to Alice.

- Alice computes

$$(\sigma_1, \sigma_2, C) = (g_2^a U^r W, g^r, C) \tag{5}$$

Signature Verification: To verify a signature (σ_1, σ_2, C) of a message m, check whether there is (2) to satisfy

$$e(g, \sigma_1) = e(\sigma_2, H(h)) \cdot e(g_1, g_2) \tag{6}$$

4 Analysis of the Proposed Blind Scheme

4.1 Completeness

For the blind signature $(g_2^a U^r W, g^r, C)$, we have

$$
\begin{aligned}
e(g, \sigma_1) &= e(g, g_2^a U^r W) \\
&= e(g, g_2^a g^{-rw} H(h)^r g^{rw}) \\
&= e(g, g_2^a H(h)^r) \\
&= e(g, g_2^a) e(g, H(h)^r) \\
&= e(g^a, g_2) e(g^r, H(h)) \\
&= e(g_1, g_2) e(\sigma_2, H(h))
\end{aligned}
$$

4.2 Blindness of Message

This scheme has message blindness. In this article, the message holder, Bob, does the following blind processing for m: (2) and (3), and the blinding factor w from Z_q selected by Bob randomly. It is required that w should face discrete logarithm problems, and satisfy blindness and unforgeability. So, it is believed that the proposed scheme has message blindness.

4.3 Analysis of Security

Theorem. If the CDH problem is hard, the above scheme is unforgeable under an adaptive chosen-message attack.

Proof. Given an adversary A for an attack signature scheme, making at most q_s signing queries, and having success probability ε (the ε is not negligible), we construct an adversary B solving the CDH problem with probability polynomially related to ε. Algorithm B is given $params = (G, G_T, q, g, e)$, and $g_1 = g^a$, $g_2 = g^b$. Let $l = 2q_s$, we assume $kl < q$, which holds for k large enough. Choose $x_0 \in \{-kl, \cdots, 0\}$, $x_1, \cdots, x_k \in \{0, \cdots, 1\}$ and $y_0, \cdots, y_k \in Z_q$. Compute $h = H_1(m\|C)$ that $h = h_1 \cdots h_k \in \{0, \cdots, 1\}$.

For $i = 0, \cdots, k$, set

$$u_i = g_2^{x_i} g^{y_i} \tag{7}$$

Define the functions

$$F(h) = x_0 + \sum_{i=1}^{k} h_i x_i \tag{8}$$

$$G(h) = y_0 + \sum_{i=1}^{k} h_i y_i \tag{9}$$

Run the algorithm A on the public key $(params, g_1, g_2, u_0, u_1, \cdots, u_k)$. When A requests a signature on a message m, do:

- If $F = F(h) = 0 (\mathrm{mod}\, q)$, then the algorithm B abort;
- If $F = F(h) \neq 0 (\mathrm{mod}\, q)$, set $\theta = F^{-1} \mathrm{mod}\, q$ and $G = G(h)$. Choose $r \in Z_q$ arbitrarily, return the signature $(g_2^{Fr} g^{Gr} g_1^{-G\theta}, g^r g_1^{-\theta}, C)$.

If A outputs a valid forgery $(m, (\sigma_1, \sigma_2, C))$, do:

If $F(h) \neq 0 (\mathrm{mod}\, q)$, then abort; Otherwise, output $\sigma_1 / \sigma_2^{G(h)}$.

As long as B does not abort, corresponding certificate shall be made of the following:

Let $a = \log_g g_1$ and $b = \log_g g_2$. Recall that a real signature on the message m would be computed as $(g_2^a U^{\bar{r}} W, g^{\bar{r}}, C)$ for a random $\bar{r}$. Setting $F = F(h)$, $G = G(h)$, $\theta = F^{-1} \mathrm{mod}\, q$ and $\bar{r} = r - a\theta$, and knowing that

$$H(h) = g_2^{F(h)} g^{G(h)} \tag{10}$$

we have:

$$
\begin{aligned}
g_2^a U^{\bar{r}} W &= g_2^a g^{-\bar{r}w} H(h)^{\bar{r}} g^{\bar{r}w} \\
&= g_2^a H(h)^{\bar{r}} = g_2^a H(h)^{r-a\theta} = g_2^a \cdot (g_2^F g^G)^{r-a\theta} \\
&= g_2^a g_2^{Fr-a} g^{Gr-Ga\theta} = g_2^{Fr} g^{Gr} g_1^{-G\theta}
\end{aligned}
$$

and

$$g^{\bar{r}} = g^{r-a\theta} = g^r g^{-a\theta} = g^r g_1^{-\theta} \tag{11}$$

exactly as returned by B.

A outputs a valid signature (σ_1, σ_2, C) on a message m for which $F(h) = 0 \bmod q$. By definition of the verification algorithm, we have:

$$e(g,g)^{ab} = e(g_1, g_2) = \frac{e(g, \sigma_1)}{e(\sigma_2, H(h))} = \frac{e(g, \sigma_1)}{e(\sigma_2, g_2^0 g^{G(h)})} \tag{12}$$

So we conclude that

$$\sigma_1 / \sigma_2^{G(h)} = g^{ab} \tag{13}$$

B outputs the solution of CDH instance.

Let E be the event in the following equation:

$$F(h_1) \neq 0 \bmod q \wedge \cdots \wedge F(h_{q_s}) \neq 0 \bmod q \wedge F(h) = 0 \bmod q \tag{14}$$

Fix arbitrary h and $h_i (h_i = H_1(m_i \| C))$, here $i \in (1, \cdots, q_s)$, we then have

$$\Pr(\bar{E}) \leq \Pr[F(h) \neq 0] + \sum_{i=1}^{q_s} [F(h) = 0 \wedge F(h_i) = 0] \tag{15}$$

For any $x_1, \cdots, x_k$, there is exactly one choice of x_0 for which $F(h) = 0$; thus,

$$\Pr[F(h) \neq 0] = kl/(kl+1) \tag{16}$$

Next consider any $i \in \{1, \cdots, q_s\}$, and let $\Gamma = h_i$. Since $h \neq \Gamma$, there must be some index j where they differ. Without loss of generality, say the jth bit of h is 1 and the jth bit of Γ is 0. Fixing some choice of $x_1, \cdots, x_{j-1}, x_{j+1}, \cdots, x_k$, we see that $F(h) = 0$ and $F(\Gamma) = 0$ only if

$$x_0 + x_j = -\sum_{i \neq j} h_i x_i \tag{17}$$

$$x_0 = -\sum_{i \neq j} \Gamma_i x_i \tag{18}$$

Therefore

$$\Pr[F(h) = 0 \wedge F(h_i) = 0] \leq \frac{1}{kl+1} \cdot \frac{1}{l+1} \tag{19}$$

Putting everything together, we have:

$$\Pr[\bar{E}] \leq \frac{kl}{kl+1} + \frac{q_s}{(kl+1)(l+1)} \tag{20}$$

and so:

$$\Pr[E] \geq \frac{1}{kl+1} \cdot (1 - \frac{q_s}{l+1}) \geq \frac{1}{4kq_s+2} \tag{21}$$

From this we conclude that B succeeds with probability at least $\frac{\varepsilon}{4kq_s+2}$ to solve CDH problem, the new scheme is unforgeable if the CDH problem is hard relative to $\Re$.

5 Key Technology Implementation and Efficiency

The basis of this algorithm's implementation is the PBC library, which is a kind of open source algorithm library implemented in the C language environment by using the bilinear pairings on elliptic curve. The PBC library has the characteristics of high speed and portability. We migrated the PBC library to the Windows 7 operation platform, improved and optimized the bilinear pairing operation library. And in the Visual Studio 2012 version, the specific implementation of the proposed scheme is given by using the PBC library.

5.1 Definition of Parameter and Function

Firstly, introduce the definitions of key functions and parameters. The definition of G_1 is a cyclic addition group of generating elements to q, and G_T is a multiplicative cycle group. Functions $element\_init\_G1()$, $element\_init\_Zr()$ and $element\_init\_GT()$ represent initialization functions of G, Z_q and G_T, $element\_random()$ represents a random function on a group, $element\_pow\_zn()$ is a modular exponent function on group G, $element\_from\_hash()$ is a hash function, $element\_mul()$ is the multiplication function on group G, $element\_invert()$ is a inverse function on group G, $element\_pairing()$ represents a bilinear pairing operation function under the discrete logarithm problem and $element\_cmp()$ is a comparison function on group G.

5.2 Signature Generation

This signature process mainly consists of three interactive phases. The implementation code of signature generation is as follows:

```
//signature generation
//1 compute gr=g^r
element_init_Zr(r, pairing);
element_random(r);//r is the element of Zr
element_init_G1(gr,pairing);
element_pow_zn(gr,g,r);//gr=g^r
//2 compute h=H1(m||c)、H(h)=u0*(u1^h1*u2*h2*···ui*hi)、
U=g^(-w)*H(h) and W=g^(rw)
element_init_G1(H, pairing);
element_init_G1(temp1, pairing);
element_init_G1(h, pairing);
unsigned char h_hash_array[256];//byte array message by
hashed
char m[128] = "message";//message
char C[128] = "message_c";//disclaimer contract
char mc[256];//m||C
int k = 0;//yhe length of bytearray
strcpy(mc, m);//mc||m
strcat(mc, C);//mc||C
element_from_hash(h, mc, strlen(mc));//m||C   hash
element_to_bytes(h_hash_array, h);//convert the hash
value to a byte array
k = element_length_in_bytes(h);//length of byte array
int int_ex = 0;
element_pow_zn(H, g, ti);//H(h)=u0    //   Initial H(h)
for (int i = 0; i < k; i++)//loop byte array
{
  for (int j = 0; j < 8; j++)//loop 8 bit of a byte
  {
    int_ex = pow((double)2, (int)j);//(2^j)
    //when h_hash_array[i]  is 1, ui participates in
    the operation- (h_hash_array[i]&(2^j))
    //when h_hash_array[i]  is 0, ui does not partici-
    pate it.
    if ((h_hash_array[i] & int_ex)>0)
    {
      element_mul(H, H, ui);//
    }
  }
}
//compute U=g^(-w)*H(h) and W=g^(rw)
```

```
element_init_G1(temp1, pairing);
element_init_G1(ivetemp1, pairing);
element_init_G1(U, pairing);//U is the element of G
element_init_G1(W, pairing);//W is the element of G
element_init_Zr(temp2, pairing);
element_init_Zr(w, pairing);//w is the element of Zr
element_random(w);
//compute U=g^(-w)*H(h)
element_pow_zn(temp1, g, w);//temp1=g^w
element_invert(ivetemp1, temp1);//compute the inverse
of g^w
element_mul(U, ivetemp1, H);//U=g^(-w)*H(h)
//compute W=g^(rw)
element_pow_zn(W, gr, w);//W=g^(rw)
//3 compute s1=g2^a*(U^r)*W and s2=g^r
element_init_G1(s1, pairing);
element_init_G1(s2, pairing);
element_init_G1(temp11, pairing);
element_init_G1(temp12, pairing);
element_init_G1(temp13, pairing);
///////////compute  s1=g2^a*U^r*W////////////
element_pow_zn(temp11, g2, a);//temp11=g2^a
element_pow_zn(temp12, U, r);//temp12=U^r
element_mul(temp13, temp11, temp12);//deta13=g2^a*U^r
element_mul(s1, temp13, W);//s1=g2^a*U^r*W
//compute s2 =g^r
element_pow_zn(s2, g, r);
```

5.3 Signature Verification

We now give the code of the specific implementation of signature generation as follows.

As shown in the code, initialize the parameters *left*, *right* and intermediate variables $r1, r2$ in the signature verification algorithm and perform bilinear pairing operations according to the *element_pairing*() function. The left side of the verification equation is *left* = *element_pairing* = $e(g, s1)$. Use the intermediate variables $r1, r2$ and *element_pairing*() function to compute $r1 = element\_pairing(s2, H(h))$ and $r2 = element\_pairing(g1, g2)$, so the right side of the verification equation is *right* = *element_mul*($r1, r2$) = $e(g_1, g_2)e(g_2, H(h))$. Finally, compare the verification equation based on the *element_cmp*() function and output the verification result.

```
//signature verification
element_init_GT(left, pairing);// left of equational
element_init_GT(right, pairing);//right of equational
element_init_GT(r1, pairing);
element_init_GT(r2, pairinsg);
//compute left=e(g,s1)
element_pairing(left, g, s1);
//compute  right=e(s2,H(h))*e(g1,g2)
element_pairing(r1, s2, H);//  r1= e(s2,H(h))
element_pairing(r2, g1, g2);//r2=e(g1,g2)
element_mul(right, r1, r2);//right=e(s2,H(h))*e(g1,g2)
//1. output verification results
if (!element_cmp(right, left)) {
  printf("verify Success! \n");
}
element_printf("left = %B\n", left);
element_printf("right = %B\n", right);
```

5.4 Efficiency of Scheme

We compare the computation costs of the schemes [19–22] and our scheme. Before that, let we introduce some notation firstly.Pr denotes the pairing operation, *Sm* denotes elliptic scalar multiplication,*Exp* denotes modular exponentiation and *H* denotes hash operation. From Table 1, we can see that our scheme uses three *Sm* and one *H* in the process of signature and uses two Pr and one *H* in the process of verification. Okamoto T's scheme [19] uses three *Sm* in the process of signature and uses two Pr and three *Sm* in the process of verification. Zhang F's scheme [20] uses five *Sm* and two *H* in the process of signature and uses two Pr, one *Sm* and one *H* in the process of verification. Ghadafi E's scheme [21] uses four *Sm* and one *H* in the process of signature and uses two Pr and four *Sm* in the process of verification. Verma G K's [22] scheme uses one Pr, three *Sm* and one *H* in the process of signature and uses one Pr and one *Exp* in the process of verification. Compared with those schemes, it can see that our scheme is more efficient.

Table 1. Efficiency comparison of schemes

Scheme	Sign	Verify
Our scheme	3Sm + 1H	2Pr + 1H
Okamoto T [19]	3Sm	2Pr + 3Sm
Zhang F [20]	5Sm + 2H	2Pr + 1H + 1Sm
Ghadafi E [21]	4Sm + 1H	2Pr + 4Sm
Verma G K [22]	1Pr + 3Sm + 1H	1Pr + 1Exp

6 Conclusions

The difficulty of building blind signature scheme in the standard model lies in increasing the blindness of the message to be signed and eliminating the blindness of the signature, because it's hard to introduce the blinding factor by using conventional methods when we normally treat each bit of the message as the index in the computation process. Focused on the essence of the blind signature, this paper proposed a blind signature scheme with disclaimer contract based on the Waters signature scheme by using the bilinear map, instead of taking common approaches. In this new scheme, if the signature is harmful to the signer, it will be invalidated according to the disclaimer contract. With the characteristics of self elimination, the message holder does not need to eliminate the blindness of the signature again. Thus the efficiency of blind signature in the standard model is improved. And we give the key technology implementation. Further, we will study the proxy blind signature and multi-signature scheme in the standard model.

Acknowledgements. This work is partially supported by the National Natural Science Foundation of China (11361024), the Natural Science Foundation Projects of Jiangxi Province (20171BAB201009), the Science and Technology Project of Jiangxi Province Office of Education (GJJ170386), the Innovation Fund Designated for Graduate Students of Jiangxi Province (YC2017-S257).

References

1. Chaum, D.: Blind signatures for untraceable payments. In: Chaum, D., Rivest, R.L., Sherman, A.T. (eds.) Advances in Cryptology, pp. 199–203. Springer, Boston, MA (1983). https://doi.org/10.1007/978-1-4757-0602-4_18
2. Choon, J.C., Hee Cheon, J.: An identity-based signature from gap Diffie-Hellman groups. In: Desmedt, Y.G. (ed.) PKC 2003. LNCS, vol. 2567, pp. 18–30. Springer, Heidelberg (2003). https://doi.org/10.1007/3-540-36288-6_2
3. Xun, Y.: An identity-based signature scheme from the Weil pairing. IEEE Commun. Lett. **7**(2), 76–78 (2003)
4. Zhang, B., Xu, Q.: Certificateless proxy blind signature scheme from bilinear pairings. In: The 2nd International Workshop on Knowledge Discovery and Data Mining, IWKDD 2009, Washington, vol. 47, pp. 573–576. IEEE Computer Society (2009)
5. Han, S., Chang, E.: A pairing-based blind signature scheme with message recovery. Int. J. Inf. Technol. **2**(4), 187–192 (2005)
6. Zhang, Y.H., Chen, M.: Extended identity-based partially blind signature scheme in the standard model. Comput. Eng. Appl. **46**(1), 95–101 (2014)
7. Deng, Y.Q., Du, M.H., Yao, Z.L.: A blind proxy re-signatures scheme based on standard model. J. Electron. Inf. Technol. **32**(5), 1219–1223 (2010)
8. Bellare, M.: Random oracles are practical: a paradigm for designing efficient protocols. In: Proceedings of the 1st Conference on Computer and Communications Security, vol. 27, pp. 62–73. ACM Press (1993)
9. Waters, B.: Efficient identity-based encryption without random oracles. In: Cramer, R. (ed.) EUROCRYPT 2005. LNCS, vol. 3494, pp. 114–127. Springer, Heidelberg (2005). https://doi.org/10.1007/11426639_7

10. Hwang, Y.H., Liu, J.K., Chow, S.S.: Certificateless public key encryption secure against malicious KGC attacks in the standard model. J. Univers. Comput. Sci. **14**(3), 463–480 (2008)
11. Boneh, D., Boyen, X.: Efficient selective identity-based encryption without random oracles. J. Cryptol. **24**(4), 659–693 (2011)
12. Boneh, D., Boyen, X.: Short signatures without random oracles. In: Cachin, C., Camenisch, J.L. (eds.) EUROCRYPT 2004. LNCS, vol. 3027, pp. 56–73. Springer, Heidelberg (2004). https://doi.org/10.1007/978-3-540-24676-3_4
13. Boneh, D., Shacham, H., Lynn, B.: Short signatures from the Weil pairing. J. Cryptol. **17**(4), 297–319 (2004)
14. Gu, K., Jia, W.J., Wang, S.C.: Proxy signature in the standard model: constructing security model and proving security. J. Softw. **23**(9), 2416–2429 (2012)
15. Yu, Y., Ni, J.B., Xu, C.X.: Cryptanalysis of a secure and efficient identity-based signature scheme. J. Softw. **25**(5), 1125–1131 (2014)
16. Chen, M.: Identity-based proxy blind signature scheme in standard model. J. Sichuan Univ. (Eng. Sci. Ed.) **51**(19), 103–109 (2015)
17. Boneh, D., Franklin, M.: Identity-based encryption from the Weil pairing. In: Kilian, J. (ed.) CRYPTO 2001. LNCS, vol. 2139, pp. 213–229. Springer, Heidelberg (2001). https://doi.org/10.1007/3-540-44647-8_13
18. Abe, M., Okamoto, T.: Provably secure partially blind signatures. In: Bellare, M. (ed.) CRYPTO 2000. LNCS, vol. 1880, pp. 271–286. Springer, Heidelberg (2000). https://doi.org/10.1007/3-540-44598-6_17
19. Okamoto, T.: Efficient blind and partially blind signatures without random oracles. In: Halevi, S., Rabin, T. (eds.) TCC 2006. LNCS, vol. 3876, pp. 80–99. Springer, Heidelberg (2006). https://doi.org/10.1007/11681878_5
20. Zhang, F., Kim, K.: Efficient ID-based blind signature and proxy signature from bilinear pairings. In: Safavi-Naini, R., Seberry, J. (eds.) ACISP 2003. LNCS, vol. 2727, pp. 312–323. Springer, Heidelberg (2003). https://doi.org/10.1007/3-540-45067-X_27
21. Ghadafi, E.: Efficient round-optimal blind signatures in the standard model. In: Kiayias, A. (ed.) FC 2017. LNCS, vol. 10322, pp. 455–473. Springer, Cham (2017). https://doi.org/10.1007/978-3-319-70972-7_26
22. Verma, G.K., Singh, B.B.: Efficient identity-based blind message recovery signature scheme from pairings. IET Inf. Secur. **12**(2), 150–156 (2018)

A CP-ABE Access Control Scheme Based on Proxy Re-encryption in Cloud Storage

Haiyong Wang$^{(\boxtimes)}$ and Yao Peng

College of Internet of Things,
Nanjing University of Posts and Telecommunications, Nanjing 210003, China
why@njupt.edu.cn

Abstract. With the popular application of cloud storage and the diversification of terminal devices, especially the widespread popularization of smart terminals. Users have more and more requirements for how to access information in the cloud safely and efficiently. Ciphertext policy attribute-based encryption (CP-ABE) is an effective method to achieve fine-grained access control of cloud data. However, the large decryption overhead is a potential problem of attribute-based encryption. In this paper, a CP-ABE access control scheme based on proxy re-encryption is proposed, it helps markedly reduce the user's decryption overhead. Meanwhile, attribute revocation is provided for key update while ensuring fine-grained access control, and an improved decryption key generation method is proposed, which solves the data leakage problem caused by illegal stealing private key in the traditional CP-ABE scheme. A comparison with other CP-ABE schemes shows that our scheme has better decryption performance for mobile devices accessing cloud data.

Keywords: Cloud storage · Attribute-based encryption · CP-ABE
Proxy re-encryption

1 Introduction

With the rapid development of information technology and the explosive growth of user data, it is becoming more and more convenient to share cloud data over the Internet [1]. Cloud computing is one of the most important technologies for cloud data sharing [2], it is a new computing paradigm that provides users with on-demand deployment, dynamic optimization and recovery, on-demand billing, and massive amounts of storage and computing resources available over the Internet at all times and places [3]. Shared data is remote storage, it is a threat to the privacy of the data owner, and the security of the shared data itself [4]. Therefore, enforcing the protection of personal, confidential and sensitive data stored in the cloud is extremely crucial. The simultaneous participation of a large number of users requires fine-grained access control for data sharing [5]. Attribute-based encryption (ABE) [6] provides a flexible access control scheme, it can implement one-to-many communication mechanism in cloud storage environment, which means that a single key can decrypt different ciphertexts or different keys can decrypt the same ciphertext [7]. ABE is divided into two categories: key policy attribute-based encryption (KP-ABE) and ciphertext policy

X. Sun et al. (Eds.): ICCCS 2018, LNCS 11064, pp. 413–425, 2018.
https://doi.org/10.1007/978-3-030-00009-7_38

attribute-based encryption (CP-ABE) [8]. For KP-ABE, the attribute set is associated with the ciphertext, and the access policy is associated with the decryption private key. For CP-ABE, the access policy is embedded into the ciphertext, and the attribute set is embedded into the private key. CP-ABE allows data owner can define their own access policy with an attribute set. Due to this property, CP-ABE is quite suitable for the construction of secure, fine-grained access control for cloud data sharing [1].

In 2005, Sahai and Waters [9] proposed a fuzzy identity-based encryption (FIBE) based on classic identity-based encryption. Since FIBE indicated some many key features of ABE, it laid a theoretical foundation of subsequent research into ABE. In 2006, Goyal *et al.* proposed a formal definition of ABE. With the rapid popularization of mobile intelligent terminals, a growing number of mobile devices participate in cloud data sharing, such as smartphones, wearable devices. Green et al. [10] indicated that ciphertext size and decryption cost are major drawbacks of practical ABE applications. At the same time, there are more and more illegal attacks on mobile terminals at present, and the user's private key is also likely to be stolen by illegal users. A mechanism for deferred re-encryption and proxy re-encryption based on HDFS was proposed in [11]. In this scheme, a large number of encryption and decryption computations are performed by the cloud server and reduces the computational overhead of data owner when the right is revoked. An absolute outsourcing decryption scheme for mobile devices was proposed in [12] to achieve the stability of network traffic of mobile devices. In [13], an attribute-based data sharing system is proposed. By introducing secure two-party computation (2PC) between the key generation center and the data storage center, a new solution to the key escrow problem in a single authorization system is provided.

In this paper, a CP-ABE scheme based on proxy re-encryption (CP-CPE-BPRE) is proposed aiming to solve key escrow problem and decrease decryption overhead. In CP-ABE-BPRE, the private key consists of two parts, the proxy server uses one of the keys to decrypt ciphertext to obtain the semi-decrypted message and sends it to terminal devices, and the devices decrypt the semi-decrypted message by the other key. The scheme can effectively reduce the decryption overhead of user, while guaranteeing flexible and fine-grained access control, but also reduces the data leakage problem caused by the private key exposure.

2   Preliminaries

In this section, we first give some basic definition. Then, we provide formal definitions for access structures and relevant background on Linear Secret Sharing Schemes (LSSS), as taken from [14]. Finally, we will briefly review the cryptographic background about the bilinear map and its security assumption.

Definition 1: The set of users is $U = \{u_1, u_2, \cdots, u_l\}$, where l represents the total number of users.

Definition 2: The set of attributes that have been authorized is $A = \{att_1, att_2, \ldots\ldots att_p\}$, where p represents the total number of attributes.

Definition 3: Let G_t denotes users with the same attribute att_t, and $G_t \subseteq U$. The collection of attribute group is represented as $\mathcal{G} = \{G_t \mid \forall att_t \in A\}$.

Definition 4: Let K_t denote the attribute group key associated with G_t. The collection of attribute group key is represented as $\mathcal{K} = \{K_t \mid \forall att_t \in A\}$.

Definition 5 (Access Structure): Let $P = \{P_1, P_2, \cdots, P_n\}$ be a set of parties. A collection $\mathbb{A} \subseteq 2^P$ is monotone if for arbitrary B and C we have that $B \in \mathbb{A}$ and $B \subseteq C$, and $C \in \mathbb{A}$ holds. An access structure (monotone access structure) is a collection (monotone collection) $\mathbb{A} \subseteq 2^P \mid \{\Phi\}$. We call sets in $\mathbb{A}$ authorized sets, and sets not in $\mathbb{A}$ unauthorized sets.

Definition 6 (Linear Secret Sharing Schemes, LSSS): Let P be a set of participants and M be a matrix with m rows and d columns. The map $\rho : \{1, 2, \cdots, m\} \to P$ associates each row with one participant for labeling. A secret sharing scheme Π over P for access structure $\mathbb{A}$ is a linear secret sharing scheme in Z_p^* represented by (M, ρ) if it consists of two polynomial-time algorithms:

Share (M, ρ): The share algorithm takes $s \in Z_p^*$ as an input secret to be shared. Share randomly chooses a group of elements $r_1, r_2, \cdots, r_n \in Z_p^*$ and generates a column vector $\vec{v} = (s, r_1, r_2, \cdots, r_n)^T$. Then, it outputs $M \cdot \vec{v}$ as a vector that l participants share such that they each possess an element. We define M_i as the ith row in M so that $\lambda_{\rho(i)} = M_i \cdot \vec{v}$ is the element belonging to participant $\rho(i)$.

Recovery (S): The recovery algorithm takes a set S of participants as input. We define a set $I = \{i : \rho(i) \in S\} \subset \{1, 2, \cdots, m\}$. If $S \in \mathbb{A}$, there exists a group of constants $\left\{\omega_i \in Z_p^*\right\}_{i \in I}$, it can recovery the shared secret by $\sum \omega_i \cdot \rho_{(i)} = s(i \in I)$.

Definition 7 (Bilinear pairings): Let $\mathbb{G}_0$ and $\mathbb{G}_T$ be two multiplicative cyclic groups of prime order p. Let g be a generator of $\mathbb{G}_0$ and $e : \mathbb{G}_0 \times \mathbb{G}_0 \to \mathbb{G}_T$ be a bilinear map with the properties:

- Bilinearity: For all $u, v \in \mathbb{G}_0$ and $a, b \in Z_p$, we have $e(u^a, v^b) = e(u, v)^{ab}$.
- Non-degeneracy: There exists a generator g of $\mathbb{G}_0$ such that $e(g, g) \neq 1$ holds.
- Computability: For all $u, v \in \mathbb{G}_0$, there exists an effective calculation $e(u, v)$.

Assumption 1 (Discrete Logarithm Assumption): Given two $X, Y \in \mathbb{G}_0$, no probabilistic polynomial-time algorithm can find an integer $k \in Z_p^*$ with a non-negligible advantage for which $Y = X^k$ holds.

Assumption 2 (Decisional Bilinear Diffie-Hellman Assumption): For an arbitrary group of exponents $a, b, c \in Z_p^*$, given a tuple $\left(g, g^a, g^b, g^c, e(g, g)^{abc}\right)$, no probabilistic polynomial-time algorithm can find an integer $z \in Z_p^*$ with a non-negligible advantage for which $e(g, g)^z = e(g, g)^{abc}$ holds.

3   CP-ABE Access Control Scheme Based on Proxy Re-encryption

The above introduced the existing scheme deficiencies and the basic concepts. This section details how to improve the scheme and reduce the decryption overhead.

3.1   Model Construction

The scheme proposed in this paper is shown in Fig. 1, which is mainly composed of 5 parts. The 5 components communicate through the Internet.

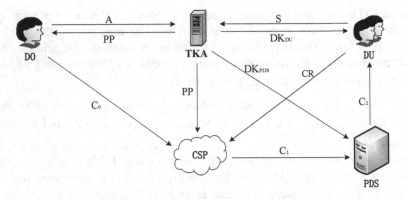

Fig. 1. CP-CPE-BPRE scheme model

- Trusted Key Authority (TKA): The TKA is a vital component in the system. The KA is responsible for most computing tasks, including key generation, key update, etc. The TKA is considered credible in our system.
- Data Owner (DO): DO is an authorized user who possesses data to be uploaded. DOs define their own explicit access policies. Only users whose attributes meet the access policy can obtain plaintext.
- Cloud Service Provider (CSP): CSP is responsible for data storage, management and ciphertext re-encryption. We assume that the CSP is semi-trusted in our system, meaning it is curious about the value of plaintext but has no intention of tampering with it.
- Proxy Decryption Server (PDS): PDS undertakes most of the decryption calculations in our model, it is also considered to be semi-trusted.
- Data User (DU): DO is an authorized user who accesses ciphertext. With the rapid development of cloud services, mobile devices have become the main devices for accessing cloud data. Therefore, we think there is a possibility that the private key of the terminal may be stolen.

We assume that all entities involved in data sharing does not collude with each other to access data illegally, otherwise the system model does not make any sense. The attributes submitted by users are authenticated by TKA. The user's attribute set is a set that uniquely identifies the user. Each authorized attribute is represented by a random number in public parameters (PP). When DO wants to upload data, it encrypts the data with its access policy and public parameters to obtain C_0. Then, C_0 is uploaded to the cloud server, which is re-encrypted to C_1 by the cloud server. When DU submits an attribute to TKA, TKA generates a private key composed of two parts, which are respectively distributed to DU and PDS. After the DU sends a ciphertext request (CR) to the CPS, the CPS sends C_1 to PDS. PDS decrypts C_1 using the key from TKA to obtain C_2, which can be decrypted by DU.

3.2 Scheme Construction

1. Setup

$\mathbb{G}_1$ and $\mathbb{G}_2$ are two multiplicative cyclic groups with prime order p. Let k be a security parameter and g be a generator of $\mathbb{G}_1$. The hash functions are defined as follows:

$$H : \{0,1\}^* \to \mathbb{G}_1$$

$$H_1 : \mathbb{G}_2 \to Z_P^*$$

TKA completes the initialization operation and returns a group of public parameters and master key of system.

***Algorithm 1**: Setup$\left(1^k, A\right)$*

Input: security parameter k and authorized attribute set A

Output: PP (public parameters) and MK (master key)

Step1: TKA selects a group of random elements $h_1, h_2, \cdots, h_m \in_R \mathbb{G}_1$ and $\alpha, \beta \in Z_p^*$, where the element h_t corresponds with an authorized attribute att_t $(t \in [1, m])$.

Step2: outputs the following public parameters and master key:

$$PP = \left\{ g, g^\beta, h_1, h_2, \ldots\ldots, h_m, e\left(g, g\right)^\alpha, H, H_1 \right\}$$

$$MK = \left\{ \beta, g^\alpha \right\}$$

2. Key Generation

This algorithm is run by the TKA, takes as input PP, MK and the attribute collection submitted by the DU. The private key is composed of DK_{PDS} and DK_{DU}, which are respectively saved by the PDS and the DU, the PDS cannot decrypt ciphertext alone.

Algorithm 2: $KeyGen(PP, MK, S)$

Input: PP, MK and S (the attribute collection submitted by the DU)

Output: DK_{PDS} and DK_{DU}

Step1: chooses a random exponent $\tau \in_R Z_p^*$. Then, computing the initial key $K_3 = g^{(\alpha+\beta\tau)r/\pi}$.

Step2: computes $K_2 = g^{\alpha+\beta\tau}$ using the random number α, β that generated the public parameters and τ in Step1.

Step3: chooses random exponents $r, \pi, \in_R Z_p^*$. Then, computing $K_3 = g^{(\alpha+\beta\tau)r/\pi}$.

Step4: uses the random number in Step3 to calculate $D = g^{\tau r/\pi}, \forall x \in S : D_x = h_x^{\tau r/\pi}$.

Step5: outputs private key as follows:

$$DK_{DU} = \pi/r$$

$$DK_{PDS} = \left\{ K_3 = g^{(\alpha+\beta\tau)r/\pi}, D = g^{\tau r/\pi}, \forall x \in S : D_x = h_x^{\tau r/\pi} \right\}$$

3. Encryption

The encryption algorithm, which is run by DO, takes as input the public parameter PP, an access structure $\mathbb{A}$ and plaintext $\mathcal{M}$ and guarantees the confidentiality and integrity of the data.

Algorithm 3: $Encrypt(PP, \mathcal{M}, \mathbb{A})$

Input: PP, $\mathbb{A}$ and $\mathcal{M}$

Output: initial ciphertext C_0

Step1: generates vector $\vec{v} = (s, y_2, y_3, \ldots\ldots, y_d)$ and linear secret sharing scheme (M, ρ).

Step2: computes $\lambda_i = \vec{v} \cdot M_i$ for each user $u_i \in U$.

Step3: the ciphertext is published as:

$$C_0 = \left((M, \rho), C = \mathcal{M} \cdot e(g, g)^{\alpha s}, C' = g^s, \forall att_t \in \mathbb{A} : C_t = g^{\beta\lambda_t} h_{\rho(t)}^{-s} \right)$$

4. Re-encryption

The re-encryption algorithm, which is run by CSP, takes as input the public parameter PP, initial ciphertext C_0, and the collection of attribute groups $\mathcal{G}$. When CSP receives C_0 and $\mathcal{G}$, the re-encryption algorithm selects two random numbers $\mu, \gamma \in_R Z_p^*$ to construct attribute group key set $\mathcal{K}$, and defines a unique identifier $ID_k \in \{0, 1\}^*$ for user $u_k \in \mathcal{G}$, which will not change with user attributes. We adopt the attribute group-based algorithm of [13] to re-encrypt the initial ciphertext.

Algorithm 4: $\text{Re}\,Encrypt\left(PP,C_0,\mathcal{G}\right)$

Input: PP, C_0 and $\mathcal{G}$

Output: ultimate ciphertext C_1

Step1: defines a unique identifier $ID_k \in \{0,1\}^*$ for user $u_k \in \mathcal{G}$.

Step2: selects two random numbers $\mu,\gamma \in_R Z_p^*$. Then, computing the session key of $SK_{DU_k} = H\left(ID_k\right)^\gamma$ and $SK_{CSP} = g^\gamma$ respectively for the DU and the CSP and the corresponding element $x_k = H_1\left(e\left(Q_k^\mu, SK\right)\right)$ for each DU.

Step3: constructs a polynomial $f_t\left(x\right) = \prod_{i=1}^{v}\left(x - x_i\right) = \sum_{i=0}^{v} a_i x^i \pmod{p}$ for each $G_t \in \mathcal{G}$, where v represents the number of DU in G_t.

Step4: defines $\left\{P_0, P_1, \cdots, P_v\right\} = \left\{g^{a_0}, g^{a_1}, \cdots, g^{a_v}\right\}$, and choosing random number $R \in_R Z_p^*$ to computing $Head_t = \left(K_t \cdot P_0^R, P_1^R, \cdots, P_v^R\right)$.

Step5: builds a header message $Head = \left(g^\mu, \gamma, \forall G_t \in \mathcal{G}: Head_t\right)$.

Step6: the ultimate ciphertext is published as:

$$C_0' = \left(\left(M, \rho\right), C = \mathcal{M} \cdot e\left(g,g\right)^{\alpha s}, C' = g^s, \forall att_t \in \mathbf{A}: \; C_t = \left(g^{\beta \lambda_t} h_{\rho(t)}^{-s}\right)^{K_t}\right)$$

$$C_1 = \left(Head, C_0'\right)$$

5. Decryption

The decryption algorithm takes as input DU's attribute set S, the ultimate ciphertext C_1, and all private key components DK_{PDS} and DK_{DU}. On receiving a ciphertext request from a DU u_k, the CSP and TKA send the ultimate ciphertext C_1 and the private key DK_{PDS} to the PDS immediately. The PDS decrypts C_1 outputs the partially decrypted ciphertext C_2. The PDS sends C_2 to u_k, and u_k decrypts it with its own private key DK_{DU}.

Algorithm 5: *Decrypt* $\left(S, C_1, DK_{PDS}, DK_{DU}\right)$

    Input: S, C_1, DK_{PDS} and DK_{DU}

    Output: plaintext $\mathcal{M}$

    Step1: the PDS constructs the attribute group key $\left\{K_t \mid \forall \theta_t \in S\right\}$ as follows:

$$H_1\left(e\left(SK_{DU_k}{}^{\mu}, SK_{CSP}\right)\right) = x_k$$

$$K_t \cdot P_0^R \prod_{i=1}^{v} P_i^{R \cdot x_k^i} = K_t$$

    Step2: the PDS extracts an elements C_2 as follows:

$$\prod_{\rho(t) \in S}\left(e\left(C_t^{1/K_t}, D\right) \cdot e\left(C', D_{\rho(t)}\right)\right)^{\omega_t}$$

$$= \prod_{\rho(t) \in S}\left(e\left(\left(g^{\beta\lambda_t} h_{\rho(t)}^{-s}\right)^{K_t \cdot 1/K_t}, g^{\tau r/\pi}\right) \cdot e\left(g^s, h_{\rho(t)}^{\tau r/\pi}\right)\right)^{\omega_t}$$

$$= \prod_{\rho(t) \in S}\left(e(g,g)^{\beta\lambda_t \tau r/\pi}\right)^{\omega_t}$$

$$= e(g,g)^{\beta s \tau r/\pi}$$

$$= C_1'$$

$$e\left(C', DK_{PDS}\right)/C_1'$$

$$= e\left(g^s, g^{(\alpha+\beta\tau)r/\pi}\right)/e(g,g)^{\beta s \tau r/\pi}$$

$$= e(g,g)^{\alpha s r/\pi}$$

$$= C_2$$

    Step3: on receiving C_2 from the PDS, the u_k extracts plaintext as follows:

$$C/C_2^{DK_{DU}}$$

$$= \mathcal{M} \cdot e(g,g)^{\alpha s} / \left(e(g,g)^{\alpha s r/\pi}\right)^{\pi/r}$$

$$= \mathcal{M}$$

4   Comprehensive Analysis

This section mainly analyses the proposed scheme CP-ABE-BPRE in this paper from attribute revocation, security requirements and efficiency. In our analysis, we use notation shown in Table 1.

4.1   Revocation

When a user comes to hold or drop an attribute, the private key should be updated to prevent the user from accessing the previous or subsequent encrypted data for backward or forward secrecy. On receiving a join or leave request for some attribute groups from a user (e.g., a user comes to hold or drop an attribute att_q at some time instance), the proposed CP-ABE-BPRE will execute the revoking operation immediately. At the beginning of revocation, the KA updates the attribute group from $\mathcal{G}$ to $\mathcal{G}'$ and the attribute group key of G_q and sends the updated membership list of the attribute group to CSP. The CSP runs the re-encryption algorithm upon receiving C_0 and $\mathcal{G}'$. The updated attribute group key set is:

$$\mathcal{K}' = \left\{ K'_q, \forall att_t \in A \backslash \left\{ att_q \right\} : K_t \right\}$$

The CSP constructs a new polynomial for G_q, where v' represents the number of DU in G_q:

$$f_q(x) = \prod_{i=1}^{v'} (x - x_i) = \sum_{i=0}^{v'} a'_i x^i (\bmod p)$$

Then, the re-encryption algorithm selects a new random number $R' \in_R Z^*_p$ to build a new header message as follow:

$$\{P_0, P_1, \cdots, P_{v'}\} = \left\{ g^{a'_0}, g^{a'_1}, \cdots, g^{a'_v} \right\}$$

$$Head'_q = \left(K'_q \cdot P_0^{R'}, P_1^{R'}, \cdots, P_{v'}^{R'} \right)$$

$$Head' = \left(g^{\mu}, Head'_q, \forall G_t \in \mathcal{G} \backslash \{G_q\} : Head_t \right)$$

Subsequently, the CSP re-encrypts the ciphertext as:

$$C'_0 = \left\{ C = \mathcal{M} \cdot e(g,g)^{\alpha s}, C' = g^s, C_q = \left(g^{\beta \lambda_q} h_{\rho(q)}^{-s} \right)^{K_q} \right.$$

$$(M, \rho), \forall att_t \in A \backslash \left\{ att_q \right\} : \left. C_t = \left(g^{\beta \lambda_t} h_{\rho(t)}^{-s} \right)^{K_t} \right\}$$

$$C''_1 = \left(Head', C''_0 \right)$$

Finally, the key generation algorithm is implemented to update the privacy key:

$$DK'_{DU} = \pi' / r'$$

$$DK'_{CSP} = \left\{ K'_3 = g^{(\alpha + \beta \tau) r' / \pi'}, D = g^{\tau r' / \pi'}, \forall x \in S : D_x = h_x^{\tau r' / \pi'} \right\}$$

Table 1. Notations relevant to efficiency comparision.

Symbol	Definition
$|A|$	Sum of attributes in an access structure
$|S|$	Sum of attributes held by a DU
S_T	Sum of threshold value of all "AND" gates in an access structure
S_G	Sum of gates in an access tree
v	Sum of DUs in a group attribute
t_h	A calculation of hash function
t_p	A calculation of pairing
t_e	A calculation of exponentiation
t_m	A calculation of multiplication
t_d	A calculation of division

4.2 Security Requirements

For the CP-ABE-BPRE scheme, we assume that TKA is trusted, the CSP and PDS are honest but curious about plaintext, and parties do not collude to access data illegally. In this scheme, the CSP re-encrypts the initial ciphertext. Like the trusted third party in [8, 10], the TKA generates and distributes the private key by the submitted attributes of user. However, the difference lies in that the private key of the user in the CP-ABE-BPRE scheme is composed of two parts, respectively stored in the PDS and the DU, and the PDS cannot decrypt the ciphertext only by the key kept in itself. In the process of PDS decrypting C_1 to C_2, since C_2 is encrypted by ElGamal algorithm, the PDS cannot obtain the plaintext. C_1' and C_2 cannot be accessed for user whose attributes do not satisfy the access policy.

In terms of backward and forward secrecy, we adopt an attribute group mechanism inspired [13] to guarantee backward and forward secrecy. Once a DU lose an attribute, the TKA will update the attribute group list immediately. Then, the CSP updates the set of attribute group keys for re-encrypting ciphertext by rebuilding the head message at once. Later, the TKA distributes updated private key components. For ciphertext accessible only to those who hold this attribute, those who no longer possess this attribute can by no means extract any information from the ciphertext. If a DU obtains a new attribute, the CSP updates the attribute group key. Then, it embeds the newly rebuilt head message into the ciphertext. Finally, all DUs in the new attribute group obtain new private key components. Even if this DU possesses ciphertext encrypted before acquiring this attribute, it cannot be correctly decrypted by this DU. Thus, backward and forward secrecy can be guaranteed.

For key exposure, the private key is directly stored in the mobile terminal [8]. When the private key is obtained by the unauthorized user, the illegal user can directly decrypt the ciphertext. In [10], the proxy decryption server is also introduced to reduce the user's decryption cost. However, the private key of the proxy decryption server is generated and distributed by the client. Therefore, the risk of private key exposure remains. The problem that the terminal private key may be stolen is solved by introducing secure two-party computation in [13], but there is a problem that the terminal has a larger decryption overhead. Mobile devices, such as smartphones, are far inferior to cloud storage servers in privacy protection, which may lead to the exposure of users' private keys stored in these devices. In the CP-ABE-BPRE scheme, the private key is composed of two parts, which are respectively stored at the PDS and DU. When the terminal's key is stolen illegally, unauthorized users can not directly decrypt the ciphertext stored in the PDS, thus effectively preventing the user from disclosing the key exposure problem.

4.3 Efficiency

In terms of efficiency, we assume that the time delay in this scheme is acceptable to the user and compare the CP-ABE-BPRE scheme with the [8, 10, 13]. Each scheme is compared in terms of total decryption overhead and client decryption overhead, the comparison results are presented in Tables 2 and 3. In CP-ABE, the calculation of bilinear pairs takes up most of the computational overhead. The introduction of attribute group encryption mechanism in CP-ABE-BPRE scheme adds an amount of computational overhead. However, most of the decryption computations are performed by PDS through proxy decryption, which obviously reduces user's decryption overhead. As shown in Table 2, compared with other schemes, the total decryption overhead in the CP-ABE-BPRE does not have obvious advantages. However, when the user decryption overhead is significantly reduced, server-side decryption overhead is appropriately increased, which is acceptable. As can be seen from Table 3, the CP-ABE-BPRE is similar to the scheme in [10], the mobile terminal only needs to perform an exponentiation and division operation to complete the decryption. However, the private key generation and distribution of the proxy decryption server in [10] adds the extra computation overhead of client. In the schemes [8, 13], the user has to bear all the computational decryption overhead in the system, which is not conducive to the safe and efficient access of the mobile terminal to the cloud storage data.

Table 2. Comparison of total decryption overhead

Scheme	Decryption overhead
[8]	$(2|A|+1)t_p + S_T \cdot t_e + (S_T - S_G)t_m + 2t_d$
[10]	$(|S|+2)t_p + (2|S|+1)t_e + (2|S|-1)t_m + 2t_d$
[13]	$1 \cdot t_h + (2|S|+2)t_p + (S_T + v)t_e + (S_T - S_G + v)t_m + 2t_d$
CP-ABE-BPRE	$1 \cdot t_h + (2|S|+2)t_p + (2|S|+v+1)t_e + (2|S|+v-1)t_m + 2t_d$

Table 3. Comparison of client decryption overhead

Scheme	Decryption overhead
[8]	$(2|A|+1)t_p + S_T \cdot t_e + (S_T - S_G)t_m + 2t_d$
[10]	$1 \cdot t_e + 1 \cdot t_d$
[13]	$1 \cdot t_h + (2|S|+2)t_p + (S_T + v)t_e + (S_T - S_G + v)t_m + 2t_d$
CP-ABE-BPRE	$1 \cdot t_e + 1 \cdot t_d$

In summary, our scheme has better decryption performance for mobile terminals accessing cloud data compared with the schemes of [8, 10, 13].

5   Conclusion and Future Work

Ciphertext policy attribute-based encryption achieves fine-grained access control in cloud storage. A CP-ABE scheme based on proxy re-encryption is proposed in this paper, which introduces the concept of attribute groups in [13] to implement ciphertext re-encryption. The proposed scheme perfectly optimizes clients' user experience since only a small amount of responsibility is taken by them for decryption. Meanwhile it addresses a worse problem called key exposure. Thus, the proposed scheme performs better in cloud data sharing system serving massive performance-restrained mobile devices with respect to either security or efficiency.

The user's encryption overhead and the size of the ciphertext are also the areas of great attention in the attribute encryption technology. We expect to improve the scheme by reducing the encryption overhead, total decryption overhead and ciphertext size of the system in our future work.

Acknowledgments. This research is supported by Education Information Research funded topic in Jiangsu Province (20172105), Nanjing University of Posts and Telecommunications Teaching Reform Project (JG06717JX66) and the special topic of Modern Educational Technology Research in Jiangsu province (2017-R-59518). The authors thank the sponsors for their support and the reviewers for helpful comments.

References

1. Sukhodolskiy, I.A., Zapechnikov, S.V.: An access control model for cloud storage using attribute-based encryption. In: Young Researchers in Electrical and Electronic Engineering, pp. 578–581. IEEE (2017)
2. Wang, S., Zhou, J., Liu, J.K., et al.: An efficient file hierarchy attribute-based encryption scheme in cloud computing. IEEE Trans. Inf. Forensics Secur. **11**(6), 1265–1277 (2016)
3. De, S.J., Ruj, S.: Efficient decentralized attribute based access control for mobile clouds. IEEE Trans. Cloud Comput. **PP**(99), 1 (2017)
4. Sun, G., Dong, Y., Li, Y.: CP-ABE based data access control for cloud storage. J. Commun. **32**(7), 146–152 (2011)
5. Yang, G., Wang, D.-Y., Zhang, T., et al.: Attribute-based access control with multi-authority structure in cloud computing. J. Nanjing Univ. Posts Telecommun. (Nat. Sci.) **34**(2), 1–9 (2014)
6. Goyal, V., Pandey, O., Sahai, A., et al.: Attribute-based encryption for fine-grained access control of encrypted data. In: ACM Conference on Computer and Communications Security, pp. 89–98. ACM (2006)
7. Yan, X., Meng, H.: Ciphertext policy attribute-based encryption scheme supporting direct revocation. J. Commun. **37**(5), 44–50 (2016)
8. Bethencourt, J., Sahai, A., Waters, B.: Ciphertext-policy attribute-based encryption. In: IEEE Symposium on Security and Privacy, pp. 321–334. IEEE Computer Society (2007)

9. Sahai, A., Waters, B.: Fuzzy identity-based encryption. In: Cramer, R. (ed.) EUROCRYPT 2005. LNCS, vol. 3494, pp. 457–473. Springer, Heidelberg (2005). https://doi.org/10.1007/11426639_27

10. Green, M., Hohenberger, S., Waters, B.: Outsourcing the decryption of ABE ciphertexts. In: Usenix Conference on Security, p. 34. USENIX Association (2011)

11. Zhang, R., Chen, P.S.: A dynamic cryptographic access control scheme in cloud storage services. J. Inf. Process. Manag. 4(1), 50–55 (2012)

12. Ohigashi, T., Nishimura, K., Aibara, R., et al.: Implementation and evaluation of secure outsourcing scheme for secret sharing scheme on cloud storage services. In: Computer Software and Applications Conference Workshops, pp. 78–83. IEEE (2014)

13. Hur, J.: Improving security and efficiency in attribute-based data sharing. IEEE Trans. Knowl. Data Eng. 25(10), 2271–2282 (2013)

14. Waters, B.: Ciphertext-policy attribute-based encryption: an expressive, efficient, and provably secure realization. In: Catalano, D., Fazio, N., Gennaro, R., Nicolosi, A. (eds.) PKC 2011. LNCS, vol. 6571, pp. 53–70. Springer, Heidelberg (2011). https://doi.org/10.1007/978-3-642-19379-8_4

A Delay Step Based Geolocation Data Verification Method

Zhang Xiaoming[1], Wang Zhanfeng[2(✉)], Wei Xianglin[3], Zhuo Zihan[1], and Hu Chao[4]

[1] National Computer Network Emergency Response Technical Team/Coordination Center of China, Beijing 100000, China
[2] School of Computer Science and Engineering, Southeast University, Nanjing 211189, China
hehengw@hotmail.com
[3] Nanjing Telecommunication Technology Research Institute, Nanjing 210007, China
[4] Command and Control Engineering College, Army Engineering University of PLA, Nanjing 210007, China

Abstract. IP Geolocation technology is widely used in network security, especially in attack tracing, cyberspace security situation analysis and display, which has attracked attentions both in academic research and commercial applications. At present, there are many commercial or open source IP geolocation databases on the Internet. These databases have different geolocation accuracy, can not provide consistent positioning results, and seriously affect the user's confidence in these databases. To create an accurate geolocation database, a delay step based geolocation data verification method was proposed to find suspicious data in the geolocation database, and then an adaptive localization algorithm is introduced to verify the questionable data and improve the accuracy of geolocation database. Experiments show that by this method nearly half of the geolocation data can be verified, and results on the test data show the proposed method can efficiently improve the geolocation database.

Keywords: Attack tracing · Network measurement · IP geolocation Landmark

1 Introduction

IP geolocation technology aims to locate the geographical position of the devices by IP address. In recent years, IP geolocation service has become a hot issue and widely used in various fields, such as content positioning, targeted advertisements, identity authentication, network security, network performance optimization and others [1–5]. Because of its wide range of applications and important value, it has been a great concern in academia and industry. At present, there are many open source and commercial IP geolocation databases, such as IP2Location, MaxMind, GeoBytes, NetAcuity, Akamai, Quova, IPIP.net, pure, Sina, Taobao, Baidu and so on.

© Springer Nature Switzerland AG 2018
X. Sun et al. (Eds.): ICCCS 2018, LNCS 11064, pp. 426–438, 2018.
https://doi.org/10.1007/978-3-030-00009-7_39

These data are derived from Who is data, or Internet service provider (ISP), or web data, thus the positioning accuracy of the geolocation data can not be guaranteed and greatly affecting the usage of IP geolocation data. The initial IP geolocation algorithms inference the geographic location of the IP device by querying the DNS server or mining the information implied in the host name [8, 17, 18]. Then, some positioning algorithms estimate the location of the hosts by linear relationship between the time delay and the geographical distance, and reduce the positioning errors [13–15] by topological information. In order to further improve the accuracy of IP geolocation, some nonlinear time delay geographical distance models are proposed [11]. Based on these algorithms, some comprehensive positioning algorithms are proposed using the end-to-end delay, network topology and reference nodes as parameters. The highest accuracy can reach the block level, such as Octant [1], TTG and other [1, 15].

Although many IP geolocation algorithms have been proposed, but in a large range high precision IP geolocation data is still a challenge, the main reasons are as follows: 1. the shortage of a large number of landmark nodes. IP geolocation algorithm is often based on delay or topological distance by estimating the destination nodes and land-mark nodes to infer the location, and therefore more landmark nodes will result in more precision. But a large number of landmark nodes is difficult to obtain. 2. As the IP addresses are allocated dynamically, even if the ISP can accurately tell the exact position of each IP. 3. As the performance of the network delay jitter, the effect of the delay jitter will incur wrong result the of geolocation algorithm. 4. Many destination nodes cannot be geolocated by active measurement based algorithm because they are connected with the Internet by NAT gateway or do not response to active measurement at all. 5. There are 4 billion of IP4 addresses, and a complete geolocation of all IP will result in a large measurement overhead.

An effective way to establish an available IP geolocation database is merging the existing IP geolocation database to one, and then detecting and verifying the error data in the database. Thus, there are two problems needed to be solved: how to effectively detect the wrong or doubtful data and verify or geolocate the wrong or doubtful record in the IP geolocation database. Base on this idea, a delay step based geolocation data verification method (DSGVM) is proposed. The basic idea of this algorithm is checking all the geolocation records by the delay step effect to find doubtful geolocation records, and then locating the doubtful records by a adaptive method.

Our contributions are as follows: 1. delay step is used to find the doubtful data without a larger number of landmarks; 2. an adaptive geolocation method is proposed, which adjust the measurement times according to the geolocation results, can effec-tively reduce the measurement overheads; 3. an effective way to construct an accurate IP geolocation database is outlined by merging and verifying existing databases.

This paper is organized as follows, firstly the IP geolocation technologies of IP are reviewed, then there is a formal statement of the IP geolocation and the delay step characteristic are revealed. Base on this observation, the delay step based Geolocation data verification method, and finally we verify it by experiments.

2 Related Work

The basic method of IP geolocation is to employ the name of IP device, registration information or delay information to estimate its geographical location. The basic designing principle of geolocation algorithm is to minimize the measurement cost while ensuring the geolocation accuracy, and it also has good scalability, and can protect the privacy of IP users. This paper groups the geolocation algorithms into two classes: client dependent geolocation algorithm and client independent geolocation algorithm.

The client dependent geolocation algorithm usually has higher accuracy compared to the client independent geolocation algorithm. But these algorithms often need the assistant of GPS, cellular base station, WiFi access point and other infrastructure. Recently, with the popularity of social networks, many applications have released the user's geographical location on the websites, which has provided a useful way to geolocate IP, and on the other hand, there is a risk of privacy leakage. The user position information is usually stored in the user information database by popular Internet application, such as Facebook, Yahoo, Tencent, Ali, and so on. However, it's difficult to access for most researchers.

The client independent geolocation algorithm can be divided into 3 categories according to the geolocation principle: reasoning based geolocation algorithm, the time delay based geolocation algorithm and the comprehensive geolocation algorithm. The reasoning based geolocation algorithm inferred the IP address of the street or through the IP address of the IP device to estimate the location position by querying the Whois database, the typical algorithms are IP2LL, NetGeo, GeoTrack, Quova, MaxMind, VisualRoute, GTrace, Neotrace, Software77, IPligence etc. This kind of algorithms can also be divided into 3 categories, the first one is directly querying the Whois database to get the location, the second one is to infer IP locations by the host names and address information, and the third one is to infer the host location through the network structure and the other information. The delay based geolocation by measuring the target host to the landmarks to estimate the position of the host, in order to improve the positioning accuracy, often combined with network topology information for localization, such as Geoping [13], Shortest Ping [3], Constraint-based Geolocation [14] (CBG), Topology-based Geolocation (TBG) [3], NBIGA [11], Posit, Spotter etc. Compared with the geolocation algorithm based on reasoning, this kind of geolocation algorithms has a relatively solid mathematical basis. The delay based algorithms are also divided into two categories, the geolocation algorithm based on the space embedding theory and probability model. None of the above methods can accurately locate the hosts or IP independently, so some researchers have proposed a comprehensive geolocation method, such as Octant [1], TTG [15]. These geolocation algorithms use the above two or three algorithms to locate the IPs, and then interactively verify the IP's location.

3 The Formulation of IP Geolocation

In this section, we firstly give a formal description of IP geolocation. Let the IP address set is noted as $IP = \{ip_1, ip_2, ..., ip_N\}$, and all of IP locations are represented as $Loc = \{loc_1, loc_2, ..., loc_M\}$, a geolocation record in the geolocation database is represented as a key value pair (ip_i, loc_j). Thus, the IP geolocation is converted into determine whether the mapping relation is established. The Mapping function Position (.) denotes a geolocation algorithm as shown Fig. 1, which can either be based on database query, or can be based on delay or topology, any algorithm listed above.

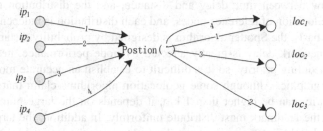

Fig. 1. The mapping between IP and geolocation

Next, a mathematical model of IP geolocation based on benchmark nodes is given. Let the landmark nodes denoted as $L = \{l_1, l_2, ..., l_W\}$, the distance between the ip_i and the landmark node is denoted as $distance(ip_i, l_k)$. The distance is substituted into the geolocation function and the formula is rewritten as follow.

$$loc_j = \text{Position}(.(ip_i)) = \text{Position}(distance(ip_i, l_k)) \tag{1}$$

Axiom 1: In a N-dimensional space, if the distance from a point to a $N + 1$ point is known, the location of this point can uniquely be determined.

In the network space, geographical distance can not be measured, and can only be replaced by delay or route hops.

$$loc_j = Position(ip_i) = Position(distance(ip_i, l_k))$$
$$\approx Position(delay(ip_i, l_k)) \text{ or } \approx Position(hop(ip_i, l_k)) \tag{2}$$

Intuitively, there is a linear relationship between delay and geodistance, as shown in Formula (3). In this formula, $delay(ip_i, l_k)$ denotes the delay between ip_i and landmark l_k, $G(ip_i, l_k)$ denotes the geodistance between two nodes, g denotes geodistance ratio, Δ is a random part of the delay.

$$delay(ip_i, l_k) = g \cdot G(ip_i, l_k) + \Delta \tag{3}$$

As the $delay(ip_i, l_k)$ can be retrieved by network measurement, the geodistance $G(ip_i, l_k)$ can be computed as Formula (4).

$$G(ip_i, l_k) = (delay(ip_i, l_k) - \Delta)/g \qquad (4)$$

For the coordinate of landmark l_k is already known, the coordinate of destination IP ip_i is on the cycle center with coordinate of landmark l_k and radius with $G(ip_i, l_k)$. In a 2-dimension plane, when the number of landmarks is over 3, the coordinate of ip_i can be located in a small area or a point.

The well-known geolocation algorithm CBG bases on this hypothesis. In fact, there is no an apparent linear relation between geodistance and network delay, so as route hop. In other words, the distance between two points in the geographical distance is not necessarily close in the delay space. Thus, Laki et al. [18] found that there is a uniform distribution law between time delay and distance, and the distribution rule is independent of the location of reference nodes, and each distribution is independent of each other. On this basis, the Spotter algorithm is designed by probability distance function.

Actually, network delay is greatly affected by node performance, network traffic and queue scheduling priority, so it is difficult to establish an accurate model between delay and geographic. Although some geolocation algorithms claim that their geolocation granularity can be higher than 1 km, it depends on the large number of landmarks and all the landmark must distribute uniformly. In addition, the target IPs must not be behind the NAT gateway, because the node access the Internet by NAT can not response to the measurement. Thus, it's impossible to provide high geolocation accuracy for every IP.

Though the high accurate geolocation for each IP cannot be reached, but it does not mean that the geolocation database is useless. For most of the network applications, the geolocation granularity at the city or county level is enough. In fact, even though the granularity at city or country level cannot be reached by these IP geolocation databases. To verify this, we took Chinese IPs as an example by comparing geolocation results between Maxmind database and the ones of the other three databases at different granularities of the country, province and city, as shown in Table 1. At the city level, the highest consistency rate between Maxmind and the other three data is less than 80%. This indicates that there is a big difference for different databases.

Table 1. The difference between Maxmind and Chunzhen, IP138 and IPIP.net

Database	IP number	Record count	Country	Province	City
Chunzhen	380,150K	350,509	98.3%	88.9%	46.4%
IP138	388,550K	91,216	97.6%	90.8%	76.7%
IPIP.Net	389,130K	128,298	98.1%	86.5%	78.1%

4   Step Effect Base IP Geolocation Data Verification Algorithm

4.1   Step Effect of Delay

Network delay is composed of 4 parts, such as transmission delay, propagation delay, processing delay and queuing delay. In the process of network measurement, due to the dynamic of network load and the scheduling scheme, the delay fluctuation often occurs, and it is very common that the delay of the previous hop is greater than the latter one. So, the delay usually (refers to round trip time, RTT) does not meet monotonicity constraints. However, it's known the RTTs from the same source to two adjacent IPs is similar. In other words, delay jitter happens when the geodistance are similar, but when geodistance are quite different, the delays will be not similar. As shown in Formula 3, if we ignore the random part of the delay, we repair the RTTs of a route into a monotonically increasing squences. Thus, a forward repair algorithm is proposed, as shown in Fig. 2.

Input: $Route(IP_{des})$
Output: $Route'(IP_{des})$

Begin
1: *Initialize;*
2: *Foreach* $i=0$ *to* $|Route(IP_{des})|-1$
3:    *if(* $rtt_i < rtt_{i+1}$ *){*
4:       *Foreach* $j=i-1$ *to* 0
5:          *if(* $rtt_j < rtt_{i+1}$ *){*
6:             $s=j;$
7:             *Foreach* $k= s+1$ *to* i *{*
8:                $rtt_s = rtt_{i+1}$
9:             }
10:          }
11:    }
12: }
13: $Route'(IP_{des}) = Route(IP_{des})$
17:
End

Fig. 2. The pseudocode of the forward repair algorithm.

Let IP_{des} denote the IP to be geolocated, $Route(IP_{des})$ denotes the set of IPs of each hop and RTT.

$$Route(IP_{des}) = <hop_1, hop_2, \ldots, hop_n>$$
$$= <(IP_1, rtt_1), (IP_2, rtt_2), \ldots, (IP_n, rtt_n)> \tag{5}$$

If the *RTT* of the i-th hop rtt_i is smaller than the *RTT* of the latter hop rtt_{i+1}, then scann forward until find a index h, while $rtt_h < rtt_{i+1}$ and $h < i$, then the *RTTs* of the $(h + 1)$-th to i equal with rtt_{i+1}. rtt_i is set as rtt_{i+1}. The repaired route is denoted as $Route'(IP_{des})$

$$Route'(IP_{des}) = \text{ForwardRepair}(DRoute) \tag{6}$$

To illustrate the step effect of delay, we take a route from Nanjing to Raleigh in North Carolina of United States as example. Figure 3(a) and (b) show the original data and repaired data respectively. It can be seen that there are two apparent steps in the two routes.

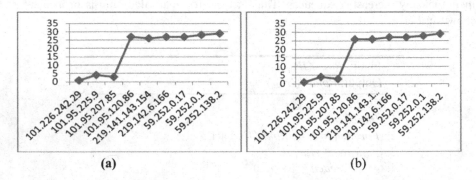

(a)   (b)

Fig. 3. The original delay curve and its corresponding repaired curve

Further observation shows that the step effect on the network path does not occur only once, but multiple times. The magnitudes of different steps have a strong relationship with the geodistance. A detail discussion about the way to detect the delay step is presented in the Sect. 5.

4.2   Detecting the Questionable Data

Base on this observation, we propose a delay step based geolocation data verification method (DSGVM). Let the whole IP set to be verified is denoted as C, then according to the geolocation granularity, we can get a partition of the set C, denoted as $C = \{C_1, C_2, ..., C_K\}$. Then each IP of the any subset C_i is measured to verify whether it belongs to the city. If it is locate in the city recorded in the geolocation database, then it is added to a set C_i', else it is added to another set C_i'', thus $C_i = C_i' \cup C_i''$. After verifying each subset, the questionable set $C'' = \{C_1'', C_2'', ..., C_K''\}$ is build. In the following, the IP in C'' is re-geolocated. Firstly, we illustrate how to filter the questionable IP geolocation record.

Theorem 1. Let $<J_1, J_2, J_M>$ is a partition of $Route(IP_{des})$, for any $ip_i, ip_j \in J_n$, while $0 \leq n < M$, Geolocate(ip_i) = Geolocate(ip_j)

Theorem 1 reveals a method for detecting inconsistent data in a database, that is dividing the route into a set by delay step and verifying if the locations of the IPs belong to the same Step is same. A threshold based method is proposed to divide the route to steps. From the first hop, if the RTT of i-th hop is smaller than the RTT of then next hop overcome a threshold δ, then the all of the IPs belong to step J_1. Next, repeat this procedure until all IPs are divided into different Steps, as Formula (7).

$$J = <J_1, J_2, J_m>$$
$$= < <(IP_1, d'_1), (IP_2, d'_2)> , \ldots, <(IP_{i+1}, d'_{i+1}), (IP_{i+2}, d'_{i+2}), \ldots, (IP_{i+m}, d'_{i+m})> >$$

$$(7)$$

So, the selection of the threshold is very important, and too big or too small will result in errors. Usually δ is 5 ms at the geolocation granularity of city. When the threshold can divide the route into steps, threshold is set One-third of the RTT difference of the first hop and the last hop, as formula (8).

$$\delta = 0.5 * (d_n - d_1) \tag{8}$$

By this way, the questionable record can be found in the geolocation database. In the next section, an adaptive geolocation algorithm is introduced to validate the real location of the questionable IPs.

4.3 An Adaptive Geolocation Algorithm

A large number of inconsistent data of the geolocation database can be obtained by the step based filtering algorithm in the previous section. In this section, an adaptive geolocation algorithm is introduced to assure the real location of each questionable IP. It's known that only the IPs which response the active measurement can be geolocated. The IP location itself is very complex, depending on the degree of response, and for the IP without any response, it is impossible to determine its geographical location.

The adaptive algorithm considers the hops and RTTs together. A possible location set loc_1 can be assured by a hop and a delay. If there is more than one location, another landmark is selected to get a new possible location set loc_2, and repeat this procedure until there is only one location in their intersection of location set.

The possible location set for a hop can be retrieved by a statistic way. We first select some measurement data and mapping each hop into a location and computer the frequency the location. Only the frequency of location overcome a percent can be treated as possible location. As the degree of node is not big, so the location possible set is not big either. The possible location set for a delay can be get by a similar way.

According to Axiom 1, in a two dimensional plane, it need at three landmark to position a point, so in the adaptive geolocation algorithm it initializes with 3 landmarks. The adaptive geolocation algorithm consist of six steps, as follows:

1. let the landmarks set denoted as L, and randomly select 3 landmarks measure the RTTs and host to the destination IP;
2. repair the measurement data as Sect. 4.1;
3. compute the possible location set $loc = \{loc_1, loc_2, loc_3\}$, according to RTTs to three landmarks;
4. filter the possible location set according to the hops to the three landmarks, and get the possible location set $loc = \{loc'_1, loc'_2, loc'_3\}$;
5. computer the intersection of the three possible location set, $City_{result} = loc' \cap loc'_2 \cap loc'_3$;

6. if the $City_{result}$ is empty or not only, selected one more landmark until there is only one location in $City_{result}$.

5 Experiments and Validation

In order to verify our proposed algorithm, we purchased and downloaded 6 IP geolocation databases, then merged the 6 databases into a comprehensive IP geolocation database named CyerBase. We hired 5 cloud computing servers to verify a subset of the IPv4, which is extracted from CyerBase and contains all the IPs assigned to the China. The subset is composed of 380 million IPs (including IPs assigned to Hongkong, Macao and Taiwan). Next, we the proposed algorithm DSGVM is used to find questionable IPs and geolocate them by the adaptive geolocation algorithm, and compare the result with the algorithm shortestping. The experiment results show our algorithms can efficiently improve the geolocation database.

5.1 Experiments Setup

In order to get the most accurate information IP positioning database, we collected 6 IP positioning databases from the Internet, including Maxmind, IPIP.net, Taobao, Baidu, Sina, DB-IP and so on. Firstly, the IP geolocation database files are parsed and standardized, then sorted with all the geolocation records, and the following rules are used to merge the geolocation records: (1) when the locations of a IP of different databases is inconsistent, the result is accepted by the voting; (2) if the location at upper granularity are same, the one will small gradulrity will be accepted; (3) if there is no record for a IP in the other databases, the record will be accepted.

We hired five cloud servers from Ali, Huawei and Tencent, and each server has 4 cores, 8 G memories, 100 G hard disk, and connected with Internet with 4 M bit/s bandwidth, which locates at Beijing, Shanghai, Nanjing, Guangzhou and Hongkong seperately.

It is should noted that this algorithm is fit for active IP, which is responsive to the measurement. In order to reduce the overhead of network measurement and improve the speed of measurement, we first divided all of 380 million IPs into 1,523,009 of/24 subnets. Through the measurements, 643,771 active subnet ware found covering IP range of 160 million IPs, accounting for about 42.3% of the total IP. The unresponding IPs may not be enabled, or the probings are filtered by firewall interception. At present, the all of IPv4 addresses has been assigned, according to Philipp Ritcher research, the routabled IPs is about 1.2 billion, about 42.8% of all assigned IP. At the macro scale, our measurement results are consistent with the conclusions of this study, which shows the validity of the data. This result also demonstrates that 42% of the assingen IPs can be geolocated by active measurement. So, if our proposed method was effective, it can be applied in a wide range and improve the geolocation database appearently.

5.2   Experiments on Step Effect

The step effect is base of our proposed algorithm, in this section the fact that the step effect is very common is illustrated by experiments. Therefore, a metric R_{PT} is introduced to show popularity of steps in the routes.

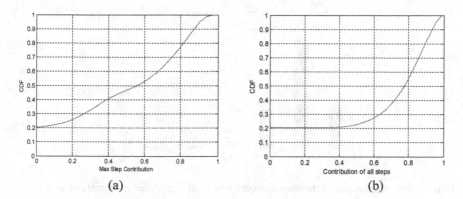

Fig. 4. The cumulative distribution function of the step effect.

Definition 2: Let RTT$_{Step}$ denote the RTT difference of the two adjacent Step,
RTT$_{Step}$ = {Step$_1$, Step$_2$, ..., Step$_n$}, R_{PT} = Step$_{max}$/d$_n$.
From the definition, the bigger R_{PT} is, the more apparent the step effect is. In the measurement data, we had extracted 19,233 routes which is has a complete response and compute the cumulative function of R_{PT} and the sum of all steps separately as Fig. 4. As shown in Fig. 4(a), there are nearly 70% paths, and the maximum delay step contributes more than 30% of delay in the path. Figure 4(b) is the contribution of all the delay steps in the network path to the whole path delay. From the graph, it can be found that all the paths with time delay step have more than 50% of their contribution, and there are nearly 50% paths whose delay step ratio is close to 80%. Thus, it is found that the delay step constitutes the main proportion of the network path.

In oneword, the delay step is very common in the network path, and it is the main component of the network path delay. This provides a theoretical basis for the use of step delay for location verification.

The above methods are easy to implement, however, in the discovery of step, DBSCAN Spatial Clustering of Applications with Noise (Density-Based) is used to divide the delay step in the path. There are two key parameter scanning radius (EPS) and minimum inclusion point (minPts) in DBSCAN algorithm, in which the scanning radius mainly refers to the radius of the cluster, and the minimum inclusion point is the threshold of the number of clusters. In this experiment, we set the clustering radius 10 ms, minPts designated as 2.

Next, we illustrate the selection of an important parameter step threshold. It's well known RTT have s a relation with the geodistance, thus different thresholds apply for different granularities. Figure 5 shows the result of the step thresholds of 10 ms. It can be found that 20% of the paths have no obvious step, 52.3% have only one step, 18.9% have two steps, 5.6% have 3 steps, the others are less than 3%, which means that 79.4% of network paths have more than one step. If the threshold of the delay step is set to 5 ms, 90% of the network paths have the above delay step. Thus, 5 ms is selected as the step detecting threshold.

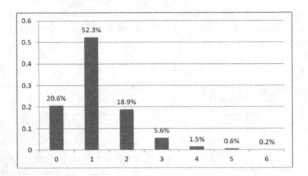

Fig. 5. The percentages of the step numbers when set step detecting threshold as 10 ms.

5.3   Validation of the Algorithm

On the above, the analysis of a large number of measurement data shows that the delay step is indeed exist. Thus, based on Axiom 1 and Theorem 1, the questionable data in the geolocation database can detected by the step effect to improve the quality of the database. In this section, the proposed algorithm is verified from two aspects: 1. how many questionable records found in the geolocation database; 2. the correctness of the inference results.

Large scale IP localization and verification is one of the important contributions of this paper. However, the effectiveness of the algorithm needs the support of ground-truth data. At present, most of the high-precision positioning algorithms can not be applied on large scale because of the lack of enough landmarks. In order to verify the effect of the algorithm, we use the Shortestping positioning method to test the results. The idea of Shortest Ping algorithm is to measure the delay of the landmark to the destination node, and to use the landmark's position as the location of destination node, whose delay to the destination node is shortest. Its geolocation accuracy is no less than the other algorithm, but need a lot of landmarks [3]. So we collect 88 nodes as landmarks, which support the measurement service, located in different city and have more stable performance. In the comparison, in order to ensure the correctness of the Shortestping algorithm, we only select the IPs in the city where the benchmarks are located. When the step based adaptive algorithm finds that the location of the error record is consistent with that of the Shortestping algorithm, it is considered correct, otherwise, the result of the step based adaptive algorithm is wrong.

Table 2 lists the result of step effect based detecting algorithm and adaptive geolocation algorithm. In the merged database CyberData, there are 263,071 records of IPs which are assigned to China. In the experiment, there are 183,129 questionable records which are detected by the step effect based algorithm, and these records are contained by 1,234 subnets. Among them there are 8,097 records are verified and the result verified by shortestping is 7,653. The results showed our proposed algorithm can efficiently detected and geolocated the locations of IPs.

Table 2. The verification of the algorithm

Total records	Questionable IPs	Verified IPs	Correct results
263,071	183,129	8,097	7,653

6 Conclusion

IP geolocation technology is widely used in user behavior analysis, network attack traceability, network performance optimization, network space situation analysis and other different fields. Although there are dozens of IP geolocation algorithm, it is still a hard to construct a geolocation database without errors even at granularity of city for the whole IPV4 space. In this paper, we find there is a step effect in the RTTs and verified it by a large number of measurements. Base on this observation, a delay step based geolocation data verification method is proposed to detect the error data of the IP geolocation data and repair the data. The advantage of this method is that it does not need to deploy a lot of network landmark nodes, but it can effectively improve the positioning accuracy of the IP geolocation database, so that it is possible to make large-scale positioning in the network space. In the future, we will further optimize the algorithm and improve its verification and geolocation effect.

Acknowledgment. This work was supported by the State Key Development Program for Basic Research of China Grant No. 2012CB315806, the National Natural Science Foundation of China under Grant No. 61379149 and No. 61402521, and Jiangsu Province Natural Science Foundation of China under Grant No. BK20140068 and No. BK2010133.

References

1. Wong, B., Stoyanov, I., Sirer, E.G.: Octant: a comprehensive framework for the geolocalization of internet hosts. In: Proceedings of NSDI 2007 Symposium, Cambridge, Massachusetts (2007)
2. Katz-Bassett, E., John, J., Krishnamurthy, A., Wetherall, D., Anderson, T., Chawathe, Y.: Towards IP geolocation using delay and topology measurements. In: Proceedings of ACM IMC 2006, Brazil, pp. 71–84 (2006)
3. Gill, P., Ganjali, Y., Wong, B.: Where's that IP? Circumventing measurement-based IP geolocation. In: Proceedings of Usenix Security Symposium (2010)
4. Gueye, B., Uhlig, S., Fdida, S.: Investigating the imprecision of IP block-based geolocation. In: Uhlig, S., Papagiannaki, K., Bonaventure, O. (eds.) PAM 2007. LNCS, vol. 4427, pp. 237–240. Springer, Heidelberg (2007). https://doi.org/10.1007/978-3-540-71617-4_26
5. Laki, S., Mátray, P., Hága, P., Csabai, I., Vattay, G.: A model based approach for improving router geolocation. Comput. Netw. **54**(9), 1490–1501 (2010)

6. Anderson, M., Bansal, A., Doctor, B., Hadjiyiannis, G., et al.: Method and apparatus for estimating a geographic location of a networked entity. United States Patent 6,684,250. Assigned to Quova, Inc. Filed 3 April 2001. Issued 27 January 2004
7. Eriksson, B., Barford, P., Sommers, J., Nowak, R.: A learning-based approach for IP geolocation. In: Krishnamurthy, A., Plattner, B. (eds.) PAM 2010. LNCS, vol. 6032, pp. 171–180. Springer, Heidelberg (2010). https://doi.org/10.1007/978-3-642-12334-4_18
8. Hu, Z., Heidemann, J., Pradkin, Y.: Towards geolocation of millions of IP addresses. In: IMC 2012 (2012)
9. Padmanabhan, V.N., Subramanian, L.: An investigation of geographic mapping techniques for Internet hosts. In: Proceedings of the ACM SIGCOMM Conference, August 2001, San Diego, California, USA, pp. 173–185. ACM (2001)
10. Gueye, B., Ziviani, A., Crovella, M., Fdida, S.: Constraint-based geolocation of Internet hosts. ACM/IEEE Trans. Netw. 14(6), 1219–1232 (2006)
11. Wang, Y., Burgener, D., Flores, M., et al.: Towards street-level client-independent IP geolocation. In: Proceedings of the 8th USENIX Conference on Networked Systems Design and Implementation, Berkeley, CA, USA. USENIX Association (2011)
12. Youn, I., Mark, B.L., Richards, D.: Statistical geolocation of Internet hosts. In: Proceedings of International Conference on Computer Communications and Networks (ICCCN) (2009)
13. Ziviani, A., Fdida, S., Rezende, J.F., Duarte, O.C.M.B.: Similarity models for Internet host location. In: Proceedings of ICON (2003)
14. Muir, J., Oorschot, P.C.: Internet geolocation: evasion and counterevasion. ACM Comput. Surv. 42, 4 (2009)
15. Arif, M.J., Karunasekera, S., Kulkarni, S., Gunatilaka, A., Ristic, B.: Internet host geolocation using maximum likelihood estimation technique. In: Proceedings of IEEE International Conference on Advanced Information Networking and Applications (AINA) (2010)
16. Shavitt, Y., Zilberman, N.: A study of geolocation databases. arXiv cs.NI/.5674v3 (2010)
17. Guo, C., Liu, Y., Shen, W., Wang, H.J., Yu, Q., Zhang, Y.: Mining the web and the internet for accurate IP address geolocations. In: Proceedings of INFOCOM (2009)
18. Laki, S., Mátray, P., Hága, P., Sebők, T., Csabai, I., Vattay, G.: Spotter: a model based active geolocation service. In: Proceedings of INFOCOM 2011 (2011)

A Distributed Security Feature Selection Algorithm Based on K-means in Power Grid System

Junquan Yang[1], Song Liu[1], Wenwei Tao[1], and Chao Hu[2(✉)]

[1] CSG Power Dispatching Control Center, Guangzhou 510670, China
{yangjq, liusong, taoww}@csg.cn
[2] NARI Information & Communication Technology Co., Ltd.,
Nanjing 210033, China
huchao@sgepri.sgcc.com.cn

Abstract. With the rapid development of power grid, the operational and operational characteristics of large scale power grid have become increasingly variable and complex, which greatly increases the operational risks of power grid. In this paper, an novel distributed security feature selection algorithm based on K-means clustering is proposed, which aims to offer effective information for power system security and stability. First, all the security features are collected and then clustered into several groups using K-means algorithm, which are distributed to different nodes. Then, the key features is selected and used to establish a fine operational rule, and helps operator to grasp the critical power security features and analysis the weak spots in power system. The numerical tests on power system show that the proposed algorithm can effectively select out the crucial status features with high accuracy.

Keywords: Power grid system · Information security
Security feature selection algorithm · K-means clustering

1 Introduction

With the rapid development of power grid, the operating modes of power grid are increasingly changing, which pose a great challenge to the safe operation of the power grid. How to ensuring its safety and stability in the context of energy internet is a problem that needs to be solved urgently [1]. In recent years, the value of power grid data has received increasing attention from the academic community. Many measurement devices in the power system, such as the wide area measuring system (WAMS) and advanced metering infrastructure (AMI), have produced huge amounts of data. These data have four typical characteristics: (1) Volume, the amount of data exceeds the traditional data processing; (2) Variety, data sources of big data are numerous, and it has a high degree of variety in content and structure; (3) Velocity, data processing should be relatively completed at a fast speed; (4) Value, power grid data has huge application values. Fully analyzing and digging power grid data can bring great benefits to power users, power retailers, and power generation companies [2–4].

© Springer Nature Switzerland AG 2018
X. Sun et al. (Eds.): ICCCS 2018, LNCS 11064, pp. 439–449, 2018.
https://doi.org/10.1007/978-3-030-00009-7_40

Based on the historical operating state data of the power system and the corresponding simulation data, a power security feature database is established, and can be used to guide the actual power grid operation [5–9]. In this paper, we propose a distributed security feature selection algorithm based on K-means algorithm (Km-DSFS), where the power system operational data is established according to the actual state of the power system and the simulation state, and further establish the feature set for each state. The K-means clustering and information gain index are used for feature clustering and distributed selection of key features in order to establish the power security knowledge base. Finally, the fine operational rules for the power system are established based on the key features and total transmission capacity (TTC). The example analysis shows the proposed the key feature selection algorithm can effectively establish the distributed security power system knowledge base and generate effective fine operational rules.

The rest of this paper is organized as follows, the framework of the Km-DSFS algorithm is described in Sect. 2, the key procedures of our algorithm are introduced in Sect. 3, the analysis of our algorithm example are discussed in Sect. 4, and the conclusion is summarized in Sect. 5.

2 Km-DSFS Framework

The K-means clustering-based power system key feature selection and framework of security fine operational rule generation algorithm are shown in Fig. 1. First, according to the characteristics of the feature selection task in this paper, the feature selection algorithm on a single computing node is designed. Second, due to the decoupling of active and reactive power flows in the power grid, hierarchical scheduling and other scheduling are used during power system operation and scheduling.

(1) Collect the current operating status of the power grid from the energy management system (EMS), and use the automatic key section discovery algorithm to find out the key sections in the current power grid. According to the current power grid operating status, using the Monte Carlo simulation to ensure the output and voltage of the unit are changed within the range, so that a large amount of neighborhood state data are obtained. Finally, the limit transmission capacity of the key sections under the current state and the simulation state is calculated according to the continuous power flow algorithm [10].

(2) A set of features of the grid operating state is established. Due to the large size of the actual power system, and the large number of features and redundant information, using the feature selection algorithms can reduce the dimension and improve the selection efficiency [11]. Firstly, all features are clustered according to the number of computing nodes using K-means clustering algorithm. Then, each feature is assigned to different nodes for feature selection. Finally, the features filtered by each node are merged. The algorithm is used to selected key features from a large number of power system operating features (i.e., tidal flows), which is related to the key transmission capacity of key sections. The key features not only

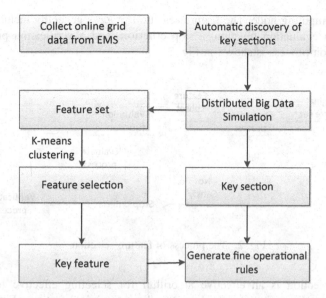

Fig. 1. Framework of distributed security feature selection algorithm.

represent the massive feature sets, but also are the essential factors of the key transmission capacity of key sections in power system operation, and have great practical significance.

(3) Using key features and limit transmission capacity to establish fine operational rules for online security power operations. The key features and the maximum transmission capacity under each simulation state are linearly fitted to obtain a local linearized fast calculation algorithm of the limit transmission capacity, thus it provides an auxiliary decision for the actual operation [12]. The linear expression of this key transmission capacity is a fine operational rule. This rule not only provides a fast calculation method and control scheme for the limit transmission capacity, but also reveals the influence of each key feature on the limit transmission capacity.

3 Key Procedures of Km-DSFS Algorithm

3.1 Features of Power Data

For the actual operation state and simulation state of a certain time section, the feature description set F is established by using the power flow feature quantity of the power system:

$$F = \{f_1, f_2, \cdots, f_n\} \tag{1}$$

where n is the number of features and $f_i (1 \leq i \leq n)$ is the i-th feature of the sample. After feature clustering is completed, distributed feature selection is performed on $F_{sub\,i}$

on a single computing node. The feature selection process generally includes a subset generation, an evaluation function, a stop criterion, and a verification process. The feature selection process is shown in Fig. 2.

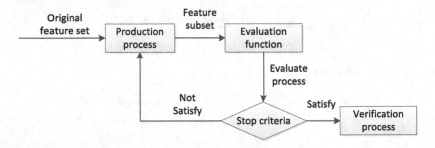

Fig. 2. The process of feature selection

Feature selection is an effective algorithm for selecting effective features and reducing feature dimensions from a large number of original features. First, a feature subset is generated from the feature full set, and then the feature subset is evaluated by an evaluation function, and then compare the evaluation result with stop criterion. If the evaluation result satisfies the criterion, the process stops, otherwise, it continues to generate the next set of feature subsets and performs feature selection.

3.2 Feature Clustering Based on K-means

K-means clustering algorithm is a typical distance-based clustering algorithm, which uses distance as the evaluation index of similarity (i.e., the closer the two objects are, the greater they are similar) [13]. In this paper, the euclidean distance is chosen as an indicator to measure the similarity between two features:

$$d_{ij} = \left\| f_i - f_j \right\|_2 \tag{2}$$

where d_{ij} represents the euclidean distance between two features. The class is composed of closely spaced objects and the final training target is to obtain a compact and independent class.

In the clustering process, we need to manually specify the number of clustering categories and use the average of all the objects in each class as the clustering center of the cluster:

$$C_k = \frac{1}{n_k} \sum_{i=1}^{n_k} f_i \tag{3}$$

where C_k is the cluster center of the k-th class, n_k is the number of clustering objects in the k-th class, and f_i is the i-th object in the k-th class.

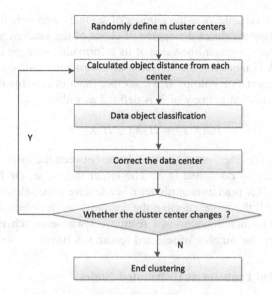

Fig. 3. The process of K-means clustering.

The clustering process with a clustering number of m is shown in Fig. 2. First, any m objects are randomly selected as the initial clustering center, and thereafter in each iteration, each of the remaining objects in the data set is reassigned to the nearest class according to its distance from each class center. When all data have been examined, an iterative calculation is completed and a new cluster center is calculated. If the results of clustering no longer change after an iteration, the algorithm has converged.

In order to select the distributed feature, the clustering algorithm selects an integer multiple of the number of computing nodes of the system as the number of clusters, so as to improve the overall calculation efficiency. After clustering, the original feature set F is divided into m subclasses:

$$F = \{F_{sub1}, F_{sub2}, \cdots, F_{subm}\} \tag{4}$$

where m is the number of clusters and $F_{subi}(1 \leq i \leq m)$ is the i-th subclass generated after the clustering process.

3.3 Evaluation Function

The core content of feature selection is the formulation of the evaluation function. This article focuses on this discussion and uses the Information gain evaluation algorithm to evaluate whether the candidate feature should be selected. First, for discrete random variables $X = \{x_1, x_2, \cdots, x_N\}$, we define the information entropy [14] $H(X)$ as:

$$H(X) = -\sum_{i=1}^{N} p_i \log_2 p_i \tag{5}$$

where X is a random variable, N is the number of samples, and p_i is the probability of x_i. Information entropy measures the degree of chaos of the random variable X. If the distribution of X is more regular, the value of its information entropy is smaller, else if the distribution of X is more mixed, the value of information entropy is larger.

Based on the information entropy $H(X)$, another random variable is known $Y = y_i$, the conditional information entropy of X is defined as follow:

$$IG(X|Y) = H(X) - H(X|Y) \tag{6}$$

where $IG(X|Y)$ indicates the degree of coincidence between the information contained in Y and the information contained in X. The larger the value, the higher the information coincidence. If X is a target attribute, Y is a feature to be selected, and the larger the value of $IG(X|Y)$, the more effective the feature Y to be selected. Therefore, the feature selection evaluation function is a feature set whose search maximizes information entropy when the number of selected features is fixed.

3.4 Merge Selected Features at Distributed Nodes

First, the original feature set F is divided into m subclasses after clustering. Secondly, the distributed feature selection is completed for m subclasses. Finally, the selected features of each node are combined to obtain the final key features:

$$F_{Key} = \{F_{KeySub1}, F_{KeySub2}, \cdots, F_{KeySub\,m}\} \tag{7}$$

where F_{Key} is the key feature set, and $F_{KeySub\,i}$ is the selected feature set of the i-th node.

3.5 Some Restrictions of Online Operational Distributed Security

In general, the power system operating status will not change greatly in a short time. Therefore, the neighborhood linearization algorithm can be used to approximate and concisely describe the operating status of the power grid, that is, to establish the regression relationship between the key transmission capacity and the key features. To generate online security fine operational rules and use this rule to guide grid operations, the specific relationship is as follows:

$$P_{TTC} = P_{TTCO} + b_1 \Delta_{f_1} + b_2 \Delta_{f2} + \cdots + b_l \Delta_{fi} \tag{8}$$

In the formula, P_{TTC} is the predicted value of the key transmission capacity of the key section, P_{TTCO} is the base value, $\Delta_{f_i}(1 \leq i \leq l)$ is the increment of the i-th key feature, and b_i is the regression coefficient. In the case of a short period of time or when the scope of the operating state of the grid is not large, this fine operational rule can be used to guide the actual grid operation.

4 Analysis of DSFS Algorithm

This article analyzes the example of the IEEE 9-node system. The continuous flow algorithm was used to calculate the limit transmission capacity of the section. $N-1$ static safety check and N-transient safety check [15] were all taken into account in calculating the power flow at each step. The modified IEEE 9-node system is shown in Fig. 4.

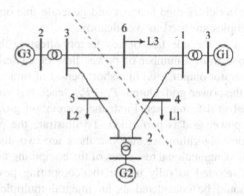

Fig. 4. IEEE 9-bus power system (Color figure online)

Figure 4 shows the number of nodes, generators, and loads in the system. This example illustrates the principle of the distributed feature selection algorithm based on the relevance grouping of grid feature quantities, and compares it with the randomized enumeration grouping algorithm and the centralized algorithm. The initial operating mode of this system is shown in Tables 1 and 2. The data used in the example are the standard value, in which the power base value is 100 MW, and it is assumed that the thermal stability limit value of all transmission lines in the power grid is 100 MW.

Table 1. Active power and terminal voltage of generators in IEEE 9-bus system

Generator number	Active output	Generator voltage
1	0.87	1.027
2	1.27	1.027
3	1.04	1.033

In this mode of operation, the transmission line cut by the red dotted line in Fig. 4 is a heavy-duty transmission channel. The load rate of the channel is high and the security margin is small. It reflects the weak link in the power grid and is needed to be focused on key sections.

The Monte Carlo method is used to generate large-scale simulation samples, which control 85% to 115% of the active power output of each generator and 95% to 105% of the machine terminal voltage to form 2000 simulation samples. 80% of simulation

Table 2. Active and reactive power of loads in IEEE 9-bus system

Load number	Active power	Reactive power
1	1.25	0.50
2	1.00	0.35
3	0.90	0.30

samples are used to select distributed features and generate fine operational rules, and 20% of simulation samples are used for verification.

This article focuses on the selection of key factors affecting the key transmission capacity of key sections from a number of power flow characteristics (for example, generator voltage, generator output, etc.) in a short period of time with little change in the operating state of the power grid. Output P_{G1}–P_{G3}, each bus voltage U_{G1}–U_{G3} and U_{L1}–U_{L3} are the initial grid feature set. First, the correlation grouping based on the characteristics of the power grid is performed. To illustrate the principle of the distributed feature selection algorithm, we suppose there are two distributed computing nodes, according to the computational resources of the computing node, the appropriate number of groups is selected to fully utilize the computing power. Generally, the number of groups should be considered as an integral multiple of the number of computing nodes. The abscissa in Fig. 5 represents the features of each grid, and the ordinate represents the degree of correlation between the clusters (the subsets of the grid features), and the correlation between the clusters uses the minimum correlation. In the process of grouping the number of packets from the maximum number of packets to one group, the group with the highest correlation degree is first merged, whereas the last combination is the same, and the threshold condition $\xi_{min} = 0.20$, it is divided into two groups as shown by the dashed line in Fig. 5.

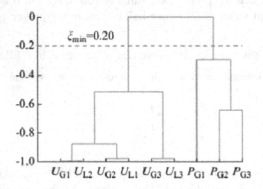

Fig. 5. Feature groups when correlation between feature subsets are defined as the minimum correlation

Similarly, the degree of correlation between the groups in Fig. 6 uses the maximum correlation, considering $\xi_{max} = 0.30$, they are divided into two groups as shown by the dashed line in Fig. 6.

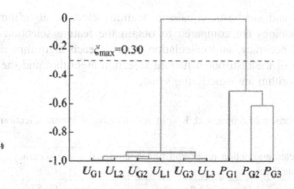

Fig. 6. Feature groups when correlation between feature subsets are defined as the maximum correlation.

Thus, it can be seen from both Figs. 5 and 6 that:

Firstly, due to the decoupling features of active and reactive power, the correlation between the node voltage and the active power output of the generator is not high;

Secondly, the correlation between the voltage of the entire network is large, In particular, the voltage between the generator node and the load node is more closely related, so the correlation between the two is relatively high, and the voltage between the generator nodes is relatively independent;

Thirdly, compared with the correlation between the voltage of the whole network The correlation between the active power output of each generator is relatively low, because the active power output is relatively independent. Comparing with Figs. 3 and 4, we can see that the grouping of attributes is the same under the definition of two types of correlation. It can be seen that the definition of the correlation between the features subsets of the grid is not sensitive. Therefore, after grouping, the network feature subsets I_{NP1} are formed as $U_{G1}-U_{G3}$, $U_{L1}-U_{L3}$, and the power grid feature of subset I_{NP2} is $P_{G1}-P_{G3}$.

Then the distributed feature selection is performed. The network feature subsets I_{NP1} and I_{NP2} are distributed to the computing nodes for grouping feature selection to obtain feature attribute subsets S_1 as U_{G1} and U_{G2}, and feature attribute subsets S_2 as P_{G1} and P_{G2}. For example, for the physical attribute subset S_1, the physical interpretation is that the active power flow of the key section in Fig. 3 flows from the lower left power generation zone to the upper right load zone. The voltage energy in the power generation zone and the load zone determines the transient stability of the system to a large extent. Improving the voltage of the power generation area U_{L2} and the voltage of the load area U_{G1} helps to improve the transient stability of the example system, and thus increase the key transmission capacity of the key sections. Therefore, the node voltages U_{G1} and U_{G2} have a greater influence on the key section transmission capacity P_{TTC}. Then, the feature attribute subset S_i is merged into S_F, and feature selection is performed on the coordination node. The final result of the distributed feature selection is P_{G1}, P_{G2}, and U_{L2}. In the end, the fine linearity-increasing rule is formed in the small neighborhood of the online power grid operating state, and the testing data set is used to test its accuracy. The distributed feature selection algorithm, centralized feature selection algorithm and stochastic-equalized feature selection algorithm based on related attribute groupings are compared to obtain the feature selection results and detailed rule forms, accuracy, and calculation time of each algorithm as shown in Table 3. The results of the distributed feature selection algorithm and the centralized feature selection algorithm are exactly the same.

Table 3. Result comparison of centralized, K-split and distributed feature selection algorithm in IEEE 9-bus system

Algorithm type	Feature selection result and fine operational rule form	Accuracy (%)	Time (s)
Centralized	$P_{TTC} = 2.15 - 0.76\Delta P_{G1} - 0.37\Delta P_{G2} + 0.30\Delta U_{1.2}$	99.57	487.0
Randomly divided	$P_{TTC} = 2.15 - 0.38\Delta P_{G1} - 0.37\Delta P_{G3} + 0.30\Delta U_{1.2}$	99.62	148.2
Distributed	$P_{TTC} = 2.15 - 0.76\Delta P_{G1} - 0.37\Delta P_{G2} + 0.30\Delta U_{1.2}$	99.71	173.2

The features extracted by the algorithm of average feature selection of the aircraft are slightly inconsistent with the centralized algorithm, and the accuracy is slightly lower.

5   Conclusion

With the development of smart grid, power system data mining and processing is a research direction. Based on the decoupling features of the power system, this paper proposes an online distributed security feature selection algorithm based on the relevance grouping of grid feature quantities and adapting to the grid operation big data. Compared with the centralized algorithm and the stochastic equalization algorithm, this algorithm has the advantages of high accuracy, less time-consuming and good stability. This algorithm of distributed feature selection can alleviate the dimension disaster problem in power system operation big data to a certain extent, dig out weak points of power grid operation quickly and accurately, help power grid operators to grasp grid security operating features and avoid the occurrence of grid operation accidents.

References

1. Tang, Y., Wang, Y.T., Tian, F., et al.: Research and development of stability analysis, early-warning and control system for huge power grid. Power Syst. Technol. **36**(7), 1–11 (2012)
2. Cheng, X.Q., Jin, X.L., Wang, Y.Z., et al.: Survey on big data system and analytic technology. J. Softw. **25**(9), 1889–1908 (2014)
3. Zhang, D.X., Miao, X., Liu, L.P., et al.: Research on development strategy for smart grid big data. Proc. CSEE **35**(1), 2–12 (2015)

4. Poudel, S., Ni, Z., Malla, N.: Real-time cyber physical system testbed for power system security and control. Int. J. Electr. Power Energy Syst. **90**, 124–133 (2017)
5. Zhang, B.M.: Concept extension and prospects for modern energy control centers. Autom. Electr. Power Syst. **27**(15), 1–6 (2003)
6. Sun, H.B., Xie, K., Jiang, W.Y., et al.: Automatic operator for power systems: principle and prototype. Autom. Electr. Power Syst. **31**(16), 1–6 (2007)
7. Huang, T.E., Sun, H.B., Guo, Q.L., et al.: Knowledge management and security early warning based on big simulation data in power grid operation. Power Syst. Technol. **39**(11), 3080–3087 (2015)
8. Sun, H.B., Huang, T.E., Guo, Q.L., et al.: Power grid intelligent security early warning technology based on big simulation data. South. Power Syst. Technol. **10**(3), 42–46 (2016)
9. Huang, T.E., Sun, H.B., Guo, Q.L., et al.: Distributed security feature selection online based on big data in power system operation. Autom. Electr. Power Syst. **40**(4), 32–40 (2016)
10. Zhao, F., Sun, H.B., Zhang, B.M.: Zone division based automatic discovery of flowgate. Autom. Electr. Power Syst. **35**(5), 42–46 (2011)
11. Jiang, W.Y., Sun, H.B., Zhang, B.M., et al.: Fine operational rule of power system. Proc. CSEE **29**(4), 1–7 (2009)
12. Sun, H.B., Zhao, F., Jiang, W.H., et al.: Framework and functions of fine operational rules online automatic discovery system for power grid. Autom. Electr. Power Syst. **35**(18), 81–86 (2011)
13. Han, J., Pei, J., Kamber, M.: Data Mining: Concepts and Techniques. Elsevier, Amsterdam (2011)
14. Kullback, S.: Information Theory and Statistics. Courier Corporation, Chelmsford (1997)
15. Jiang, W.Y., Zhang, B.M., Wu, W.C., et al.: A total transfer capability calculation method for power system operation and decision. Autom. Electr. Power Syst. **32**(10), 12–17 (2008)

A Network Illegal Access Detection Method Based on PSO-SVM Algorithm in Power Monitoring System

Yang Su[1], Wenzhe Zhang[1], Wenwen Tao[1], and Zhizhong Qiao[2(✉)]

[1] CSG Power Dispatching Control Center, Guangzhou 510670, China
{suyang, zhangwenzhe, taoww}@csg.cn
[2] NARI Information & Communication Technology Co., Ltd.,
Nanjing 210033, China
qiaozhizhong@sgepri.sgcc.com.cn

Abstract. In this paper, a network illegal access detection method based on PSO-SVM algorithm in the power monitoring system is proposed, where the particle swarm optimization (PSO) algorithm is used to optimize the parameters of support vector machine (SVM). And the proposed method is used to classify normal data flow and abnormal data flow in the network to detect whether there is illegal access behavior in the power monitoring system. Compared with the original SVM-based method and LS-SVM-based method, the proposed method not only improves the convergence speed of the network training, but also improves the accuracy rate. The proposed method can fleetly discovery and locate the illegal access behavior in the power monitoring system, which is a meaningful study in improving the security of the power monitoring system.

Keywords: Network illegal access detection · SVM · PSO
Power monitoring system

1 Introduction

With the popularity of Internet technology in scientific research, economy, military, education and people's daily lives, people are more and more inseparable from the Internet. And at the same time, the security problems of network are increasingly prominent, particularly in the power monitoring system. The power monitoring system belongs to the industrial control system, deployed in the enterprise intranet, and physically isolated from the outside public network or the Internet. Thus the power monitoring system requires very high security level, however with the development of network technology, it is becoming easy for some criminals or the internal staff to access the power monitoring system in the enterprise intranet without being authorized, the security and stability of the system is in tremendous risk. Therefore, it is very necessary to monitor and prevent the illegal access in the power monitoring system [1].

The commonly used illegal access behavior detection methods are: (1) Using TTL field of IP packet to detect illegal access device. (2) Using ID identification of IP packet to further confirm illegal access behavior and number of equipment stations confirming

© Springer Nature Switzerland AG 2018
X. Sun et al. (Eds.): ICCCS 2018, LNCS 11064, pp. 450–459, 2018.
https://doi.org/10.1007/978-3-030-00009-7_41

illegal access behavior. (3) Using User-Agent in HTTP protocol field to detect illegally accessed mobile devices. But these methods are inefficient and not suitable. Therefore the network illegal access detection is proposed.

The original network illegal access detection technology is a pattern matching detection method. This method is simple and easy to implement, but the flexibility and adaptability are poor, the accuracy of detection is low, the error detection and leakage rate are very high, and the new illegal access behavior cannot be identified. Later, many scholars have introduced statistical technology into network illegal access detection. Such as the K means clustering [2] and fuzzy C-mean clustering [3] algorithms. Compared with the traditional pattern matching detection algorithm, these algorithms have good detection performance, and the network illegal access detection misinformation rate is reduced. But there are still many shortcomings in these detection technology, such as complex detection process and unstable detection results. In recent years, artificial intelligence technology has been developed rapidly, which has attracted many scholars' attention, and was applied to network illegal access detection. There are network illegal access algorithms based on genetic algorithm [4] and artificial neural network [5]. These methods have strong nonlinear processing ability and can identify a new type of illegal access in network. The illegal access detection algorithms of the network has improved the network security.

The data flow of network is an important parameter to study the network performance and network operation. By analyzing and forecasting the data flow, we can find the problems in the network, such as illegal access behavior. Support vector machine (SVM) method in statistical theory and the particle swarm optimization (PSO) algorithm are introduced in this paper. The data flow in the enterprise network is monitored by the modified PSO-SVM, and the data flow acquired in real time is analyzed and predicted whether the data flow belongs to illegal access. The PSO-SVM method is suitable for the classifier design and anomaly detection in the high dimensional heterogeneous unbalanced data set in the field of illegal access detection, and has good generalization ability.

2 Review of SVM and PSO

2.1 Brief Review of SVM

SVM is a Machine Learning method based on Statistical Theory [6, 7]. It developed from finding the optimal classification surface under the condition of linear separability, and the linear separable set $(x_i, y_i), i = 1, 2, \cdots, n, x_i \in \{-1, +1\}$ meet the conditions,

$$y_i[((w \cdot x_i) + b) - 1] \geq 0 \tag{1}$$

The optimal classification surface means making the classification interval $2/\|w\|$ the largest. And then with the help of the Lagrange optimization method, the optimal classification surface problem can be transformed into the duality problem [8], that is, in the constraint condition,

$$\begin{cases} \sum_{i=1}^{n} y_i \alpha_i = 0 \\ 0 \le \alpha_i, i = 1, 2, \cdots, n \end{cases} \tag{2}$$

Calculated the maximum value of the following functions for α_i,

$$Q(a) = \sum_{i=1}^{n} \alpha_i - \frac{1}{2} \sum_{i,j=1}^{n} \alpha_i \alpha_j y_i y_j (x_i, x_j) \tag{3}$$

Where α_i is the Lagrange multiplier for each sample, it is a problem of quadratic function optimization under inequality constraints, which exists a unique solution. There will be only one part of the solution α_i are not 0. And the corresponding vector is the support vector, the optimal classification function obtained by solving the above problem is,

$$f(x) = \text{sgn}[(w \cdot x) + b] = \text{sgn}\left[\sum a_i^* y_i (x_i \cdot x) + b^*\right] \tag{4}$$

Where b^* is a classification threshold, it can be obtained by any support vector. Because the coefficient of a non-support vector is 0, the sum in the expression is actually only for the support vector. In the case of linear inseparability, a relaxation term $\xi_j, \xi_j \ge 0$ can be added to (1),

$$y_i[(w \cdot x) + b] - 1 + \xi_j \ge 0 \quad i = 1, \cdots, n \tag{5}$$

And at the same time make $\Phi(w, \xi) = \frac{1}{2} \|w\|^2 + C\left[\sum_{i=1}^{n} \xi_j\right]$ the minimum, where C is a penalty factor. Considering the minimum error sample and the maximum classification interval, the generalized classification surface is obtained. Where $C > 0$ is a regular number, which controls the punishment of the wrong sample. The dual problem of the generalized optimal classification plane is similar to the linear separable case, and (2) change to,

$$0 \le a_i \le C, i = 1, \cdots, n \tag{6}$$

The nonlinear problem can be transformed into a linear problem in a high dimensional space by nonlinear transformation, and the optimal classification surface can be obtained in the transformation space. If the kernel function is adopted in the optimal classification surface, the linear classification after a nonlinear transformation can be realized without increasing the computational complexity. The corresponding classification function is as follows,

$$f(x) = \text{sgn}\left[\sum a_i^* y_i K(x_i \cdot x) + b^*\right] \tag{7}$$

Different inner product kernel functions in SVM generates different forms of support vector machines, which corresponds to different optimal classification hyperplanes in the feature space. There are four kinds of kernel functions,
Linear kernel function,

$$K(x,y) = x \cdot y \tag{8}$$

Polynomial kernel function,

$$K(x,y) = [(\lambda \cdot x \cdot y) + \alpha]^d \tag{9}$$

Radial basis kernel function (RBF),

$$K(x,y) = \exp\left(\frac{\|x - y\|^2}{\sigma^2}\right) \tag{10}$$

Sigmoid kernel function,

$$K(x,y) = \tanh(v(x,y) + c) \tag{11}$$

The performance of SVM is greatly affected by kernel function. The selection of kernels and the determination of parameters in kernel functions are different in different problem areas. And it is usually selected according to the experience, which needs further study.

2.2 Brief Review of PSO

PSO algorithm [9] is a swarm intelligence algorithm derived from the study of bird predation behavior [10]. The PSO algorithm is first initialized into a set of random particles, which can be seen as a random initial solution, and the initial population is uniformly distributed in the solution space. If there are N particles in the D-dimensional target search space, the position and velocity of the i particle can be represented as $X_i = (x_{i_1}, x_{i_2}, \cdots, x_{i_p})$ and $V_i = (v_{i_1}, v_{i_2}, \cdots, v_{i_p}) i = 1, 2, \cdots, n$. Then the algorithm finds the optimal solution by iterative search. At each iteration, the particle updates its velocity and position by tracking the two optimal solutions [11, 12]. One of the best solutions is known as the best position of the individual, recorded as $P_{best_1} = (P_{best_1}, P_{best_3}, \cdots, P_{best_p})$. Another optimal solution is the best value the population has searched so far, which is called the global optimal location. Recorded as $G_{best_1} = (G_{best_1}, G_{best_3}, \cdots, G_{best_p})$. And particle update its speed and position according to formulas (12) and (13),

$$V_i^{k+1} = \omega \cdot V_i^k + c_1 \cdot rand() \cdot (P_{best} - X_i^k) + c_2 \cdot rand() \cdot (G_{best} - X_i^k) \tag{12}$$

$$X_i^{k+1} = X_i^k + V_i^{k+1} \tag{13}$$

3 Network Illegal Access Detection Method Based on PSO-SVM Algorithm in Power Monitoring System

3.1 SVM Parameter Optimization Using PSO

Through the above mentioned prediction principle of the SVM, the prediction performance is mainly determined by the disciplinary factor C and the corresponding kernel function parameters. There is no unified standard on how to choose the SVM parameters reasonably. In most cases, the gradient descent or grid algorithm is used, but these traditional methods are very slow. And also easy to obtain the local optimum value, which seriously limits the application of SVM. In the process of optimization, PSO is easy to be realized, and only a few parameters need to be adjusted. In general, it can quickly converge to the optimal solution and obtain the result of high quality optimization. Therefore, we using the PSO algorithm to optimizes the SVM parameters [13]. The specific process of optimizing SVM parameters is given as follows.

Step1: Parameter initialization. Set $t = 0$. Initialize the position of each particle z_j^0 and v_j^0, setting related parameters. Particle population n.

Step2: The average relative error predicted by support vector machine is taken as fitness function, as shown in formula 6, and the fitness of each particle is calculated. Confirm that p_j^t and np_j^t,

$$fitness = \frac{1}{m} \sum_{i=1}^{m} \left| \frac{x_i - x_i^*}{x_i} \right| \tag{14}$$

where x_i denotes the i observation of network data flow, and x_i^* denotes the i support vector machine prediction.

Step3: Update the particle velocity $vC_j^{t+1} v\varepsilon_j^{t+1} v\gamma_j^{t+1}$, besides the speed does not exceed the limit value.

Step4: Update the particle position $C_j^{t+1} \varepsilon_j^{t+1} \gamma_j^{t+1}$.

Step5: Calculate the fitness of the updated particle and update the p_j^t and np_j^t.

Step6: If the program termination condition is satisfied, the algorithm terminates, outputs the optimal solution, otherwise goes to step 3.

3.2 Procedures of Network Illegal Access Detection Method Based on PSO-SVM

For the illegal network access detection, firstly, some relevant data are extracted from a large number of network data flow for statistics, and then establish the feature profile, which is a statistical summary of normal data flow in the network. While the difference between network behavior and the currently established feature profile exceeds a threshold. Then the problem of illegal access detection in the power monitoring system is transformed into a problem of pattern recognition, and the more mature theory in the field of pattern recognition can be used to solve the problem in the network illegal access detection field. The data collected by the power monitoring system can be regarded as data points in n-dimensional space, and each dimension represents an attribute (feature) of the data. The function of kernel function is to insinuate these data from n-dimensional space to a higher dimensional space through inner product operation. This kind of mapping is very useful because the purpose of illegal access detection is to find a hyperplane to classify the data. Although this hyperplane cannot be found in n-dimensional space, it may exist in high-dimensional or infinite dimensional space. Therefore, the basic idea is to apply support vector machine (SVM) to train data from low-dimensional spatial shadow by kernel function. In high dimensional space, the data can be linearly separable in the high dimensional space. And with the help of the PSO algorithm, the parameters of SVM is optimized, which will improve the accuracy and the detection rate of the proposed method.

The detailed procedures of network illegal access detection method based on PSO-SVM are shown as bellows (also shown in Fig. 1).

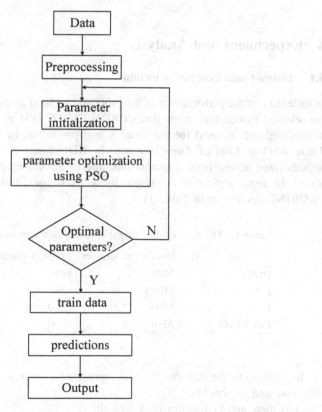

Fig. 1. Procedures of network illegal access detection method based on PSO-SVM

Step1: Collects raw data which is needed for the training and prediction of the PSO-SVM algorithm.

Step2: In order to reduce the training time of network data, speed up convergence and improve the accuracy of data, it is very necessary to normalize the collected raw data, which is aimed at normalizing the special large or very small sample vectors. The normalized data can greatly improve the performance of network illegal access detection method.

Step3: Then takes the normalized network illegal access detection data as the learning sample of PSO-SVM and optimizes the parameters of POS-SVM through PSO to obtain the optimal parameters of SVM.

Step4: The obtained optimal parameters is used to train the training samples of the network illegal access detection method. Then, a new set of network training samples is constructed by combining these two methods. Finally, create an optimal network illegal access detection method for the power monitoring system.

Step5: The established network illegal access detection method is used to monitor the Test sample.

Step6: Finally, the test results of the method is obtained.

4   Experiment and Analysis

4.1   Dataset and Feature Selection

In order to test the performance of the proposed method in the power detection system, we selected partial data in the dataset KDD CUP99 [14] as the needed raw data. The normalized data is used for the training and prediction of the PSO-SVM algorithm. There are four kind of illegal accesses in KDD data set, denial of service (DOS), unauthorized access from a remote machine to a local machine (R2L), unauthorized access to local superuser privileges by a local user and surveillance (U2R) and PROBING (as shown in Table 1).

Table 1. The four kind of illegal accesses in the power detection system

Illegal access type	Number of samples	Training samples	Test samples
DOS	2400	1850	550
R2L	11390	8395	1995
U2R	5500	3300	2200
PROBING	3380	2400	980

In addition to the fact that Normal represents a normal event, the rest of the signs are expressed as abnormal.

And there are 41 features [15], including:

(1) Basic attribute sets, such as continuous duration, protocols, services, Number of sending bytes, receiving bytes, etc.

(2) Content attribute set, such as the number of failed landings in the connection, whether the Landing, etc.

(3) Traffic attribute sets, such as in the past 2s with the current connection having In the connection of the same target host, statistics about protocol behavior, Statistical information, etc.;

(4) Host traffic attribute sets, such as the previous 100 connections with the current Connect the number of connections with the same destination host and have a phase with the current connection Percentage of connections to services, etc.

4.2   Data Preprocessing

Because the input space of the traditional SVM algorithm is induced in the inner product space, the inner product cannot usually be defined on the KDD data set. Therefore, the SVM method cannot be used to train the data set directly. In this paper, the distance metric function is used to preprocess the data set, and it is processed into $0 \sim 1$ real numbers.

4.3   Analysis of Experiment Results

SVM is used to train pre-selected training data, and training data is obtained by data preprocessing. After training, a group of SVM vectors will be obtained. Then the trained SVM vector is used to detect the network connection records that need to be monitored. The results of the detection are 1 normal, the −1 is abnormal, and the illegal access is taken. In this process, the PSO is used to optimize the SVM parameters.

In order to verify the effectiveness of the PSO-SVM parameter optimization proposed in this paper, the proposed model is compared with the classical SVM and the LS-SVM using the same data set. To ensure the accuracy of the experiment, the test results select the average of multiple experiments, the detection accuracy, false alarm rate and false alarm rate are defined as follows:

$$\text{Accuracy rate} = \frac{\text{accurate number of samples}}{\text{total number of samples}} \tag{15}$$

$$\text{Error rate} = \frac{\text{total number of normal samples}}{\text{total number of normal samples misreported as intrusions}} \tag{16}$$

$$\text{Omission rate} = \frac{\text{the total number of normal samples misreported as intrusions}}{\text{the total number of intrusion samples}} \tag{17}$$

The proposed PSO-SVM, the SVM and the LS-SVM experimental results are as follows (shown in Table 2).

From the simulation results of Table 1, we can see that the correctness of the network intrusion detection algorithm using PSO optimization SVM parameters proposed in this paper is higher than that of the traditional SVM and LS-SVM, while the false alarm rate and the missing report rate are reduced correspondingly. The result shows that the number of SVM parameters obtained through the PSO algorithm is the global optimal.

Table 2. Comparison of simulation results of SVM, PSO-SVM and LS-SVM

Model	Performance index	DOS result	R2L result	U2R result	PROBING result
SVM	Accuracy rate	80.32	84.51	79.53	78.31
	Error rate	9.50	7.42	9.21	10.82
	Omission rate	5.13	3.12	6.31	6.02
LS-SVM	Accuracy rate	83.16	87.56	82.15	79.74
	Error rate	7.42	5.23	7.44	9.10
	Omission rate	4.53	2.32	5.52	6.11
PSO-SVM	Accuracy rate	90.14	94.30	88.10	85.30
	Error rate	3.12	2.04	6.14	7.10
	Omission rate	3.74	1.66	3.76	5.60

5   Conclusion

In the power detection system, the security and stability is the top priority thing, however the illegal access behaviors destroy the independence of the system, the security and stability is threatened. Thus the security problems in the power monitoring system becomes a core problem which cannot be ignored in real life. In this paper, a network illegal access detection method based on PSO-SVM algorithm is proposed to protect the power monitoring system. By introducing the PSO algorithm into the optimization of SVM parameters, the method has a strong self-learning and adaptive capability for network illegal access detection. Experimental results compared with the classical SVM and LS-SVM algorithms, the network illegal access method based on PSO-SVM algorithm not only accelerates the learning speed, but also improves the correct rate of network detection, and reduces the false rate. Thus, the proposed method is more suitable for the network illegal access detection in the power monitoring system.

References

1. Luo, B., Xia, J.: A novel intrusion detection system based on feature generation with visualization strategy. Expert Syst. Appl. **41**(9), 4139–4147 (2014)
2. Liu, C., Hsaio, W., Chang, T.: Locality sensitive K-means clustering. J. Inf. Sci. Eng. **34**(1), 289–305 (2018)
3. Selvakumar, J., Lakshmi, A., Arivoli, T.: Brain tumor segmentation and its area calculation in brain MR images using K-mean clustering and Fuzzy C-mean algorithm. In: International Conference on Advances in Engineering, Science and Management, pp. 186–190 (2012)
4. Goldberg, D.E.: Genetic algorithms in search. Optim. Mach. Learn. **13**(7), 2104–2116 (1989). Addion wesley
5. Guyon, I., Elisseeff, A.: An introduction to variable and feature selection. In: Joint International Conference on Artificial Neural Networks and Neural Information Processing, pp. 737–744. Springer-Verlag (2003)
6. Zhang, X.H., Lin, B.G.: Research on internet of things security based on support vector machines with balanced binary decision tree. Netinfo Secur. **8**, 20–25 (2015)

7. Wang, J., Zhu, W., Zhang, W., et al.: A trend fixed on firstly and seasonal adjustment model combined with the SVR for short-term forecasting of electricity demand. Energy Policy **37** (11), 4901–4909 (2009)

8. Fukunaga, K.: Introduction to statistical pattern recognition. **60**(12–1), 2133–2143 (1972). (2nd edn.)

9. Wang, Y.Y., Xue, J.H.: Particle swarm optimization algorithm. J. Nantong Text. Vocat. Technol. Coll. **306**(3), 1369–1372 (2009)

10. Zhong, Y.H., Zhang, P.X.: Generalized trapezoidal decision-theoretic rough sets. Math. Pract. Theor. **6**, 9 (2015)

11. Faria, P., Soares, J., Vale, Z., et al.: Modified particle swarm optimization applied to integrated demand response and DG resources scheduling. Trans. Smart Grid **4**(1), 606–616 (2013)

12. Esmin, A.A.A., Coelho, R.A., Matwin, S.: A review on particle swarm optimization algorithm and its variants to clustering high-dimensional data. Artif. Intell. Rev. **44**(1), 23–45 (2015)

13. Yang, J.: Particle swarm optimization algorithm based on chaos searching. Comput. Eng. Appl. **16**, 69–71 (2013)

14. Xu, Z., Yager, R.R.: Some geometric aggregation operators based on intuitionistic fuzzy sets. Int. J. Gen Syst **35**(4), 417–433 (2006)

15. Lee, W., Stolfo, S.J.: Data mining approaches for intrusion detection. In: Conference on Usenix Security Symposium, pp. 79–93. USENIX Association (1998)

A New Steganographic Distortion Function with Explicit Considerations of Modification Interactions

Hongrun Zhang, Bin Li[✉], and Shunquan Tan

Guangdong Key Laboratory of Intelligent Information Processing and Shenzhen Key Laboratory of Media Security, Shenzhen University, Shenzhen, China
zhang_hr_szu@163.com, {libin,tansq}@szu.edu.cn

Abstract. Conventional steganographic schemes are based on optimizing an additive distortion function, which is defined by summing up the cost of modified pixels. Using such schemes, pixels with lower costs will be selected for modification. However, the interactions of embedding changes are not explicitly considered in the distortion function. In this paper, we propose a new framework for steganography that incorporates a term considering interactions of embedding changes in the distortion function. An algorithm is designed to minimize the distortion with an approximal but efficient solution using auxiliary costs. The proposed framework can eliminate the ambiguity in the definition of additive distortion caused by updated costs. Experimental results show the proposed framework is more resilient to steganalysis compared with the schemes with a conventional additive distortion function, and it works as best as the embedding schemes with synchronized modifications.

Keywords: Steganography · Embedding iteration
Distortion minimization

1 Introduction

Image steganography aims to embed data in a *cover image* to convey information [12,16]. The image carrying secret bits is referred to as *stego image*. A better steganographic scheme produces stego images with a lower risk of being detected by steganalysis algorithms. It is often achieved by making a stego image resemble to the corresponding cover image in terms of statistics.

Most steganographic algorithms are based on minimizing an additive distortion function [7,18]. Such an additive function sums up the individual costs of the modified pixels. Generally, pixels with lower costs are usually those in textured or the edge regions. Many works have been devoted to developing cost

---

This work is supported in part by NSFC (Grant 61572329, 61772349, and U1636202) and in part by the Shenzhen R&D Program (Grant JCYJ20160328144421330).

X. Sun et al. (Eds.): ICCCS 2018, LNCS 11064, pp. 460–471, 2018.
https://doi.org/10.1007/978-3-030-00009-7_42

assignment schemes, such as HUGO [19], WOW [11], UNIWARD [3,8,10], HILL [14], MG [9], and MiPod [20] etc.

Aside from modification costs, the interaction between neighboring embedding changes is another aspect related to embedding distortion. It is well accepted that synchronizing embedding changes can introduce less distortion in the corresponding stego images [2,15], due to the fact that correlations among pixels can be preserved to some extent. In fact, from the perspective of steganalysis, the steganalytic features are usually extracted by convolving an image with high-pass filters [6,17,22–24] in the beginning. When the pixels in a patch are embedded with synchronized values, the output of a high-pass filter from a stego image will be more similar to that from the pristine one. In this way, the stego patch provides less deviated features for a steganalyzer to distinguish. Since the costs are updated in an ad-hoc fashion in the steganographic schemes [2,15], the employed additive distortion function does not explicitly consider the cost of embedding interactions. It may cause a confusion in understanding the meaning of the optimization function.

Distinct from the prior framework, in this paper we propose a new framework which considers both the distortion caused by modifying individual pixels and a new kind distortion due to interaction of embedding changes of neighboring pixels. In other words, it combines two kinds of distortion in an unified optimization function. Minimizing the distortion function will simultaneously reduce these two types of distortion. It is worthy to notice that within our proposed distortion function, it is straightforward to incorporate other types of distortion. Therefore our proposed distortion function can be regarded as a generalized one.

The structure of this paper is as follows. In Sect. 2, we formulate the problem and present the proposed framework. In Sect. 3, we propose an embedding scheme with sub-images and updating auxiliary costs to solve the defined optimization problem. Experimental results to demonstrate the effectiveness of our framework are given in Sect. 4. Finally we make the conclusion in Sect. 5.

2 Proposed Framework

2.1 Notations

In this paper, matrix and vector are denoted by bold upper-case and lower case letters, respectively. We use $a_{i,j}$ to denote the (i,j) element of the matrix $\boldsymbol{A}$. Let $\boldsymbol{X} = \{x_{i,j}\}^{M \times N}$ denotes an greyscale image with $x_{i,j} \in \{0,1,...,255\}$, $1 \leqslant i \leqslant M, 1 \leqslant j \leqslant N$, and $\boldsymbol{Y} = \{y_{i,j}\}^{M \times N}$ is the stego version of $\boldsymbol{X}$. The stego image is embedded with a message $\boldsymbol{m}$. The $\Delta \boldsymbol{Y}$ is the difference image between $\boldsymbol{Y}$ and $\boldsymbol{X}$, i.e., $\Delta \boldsymbol{Y} = \{\Delta y_{i,j}\}^{M \times N} = \boldsymbol{Y} - \boldsymbol{X}$. We consider ternary embedding where $\Delta y_{i,j} \in \{-1,0,1\}$.

2.2 Problem Statement

Modern steganography aims to generate a stego image $\boldsymbol{Y}$ to carry embedding message $\boldsymbol{m}$ while minimize a distortion function. Lower distortion may reduce the probability of Y being recognized as stego by a steganalyzer. The process can be formulated by the following optimization problem:

$$\underset{\Delta Y}{\arg\min} \; \mathcal{D}(\Delta Y), \quad s.t. \; \text{Ext}(Y) = m, \tag{1}$$

where $\text{Ext}(\cdot)$ is the data extraction operation. The STC (syndrome trellis coding) scheme [5] can be used to address the coding problem.

In conventional approaches, it is assumed that the pixels in X chosen for modification contribute independently to the overall distortion, therefore, it is natural to construct the distortion in an additive form [7] as

$$\mathcal{D}(\Delta Y) = \sum_i \sum_j c_{i,j} |\Delta y_{i,j}|, \tag{2}$$

where $c_{i,j}$ is the cost of changing the pixel $x_{i,j}$. We can rewrite Eq. (2) in a matrix form as

$$\mathcal{D}(\Delta Y) = [C_X \odot |\Delta Y|_a]_s, \tag{3}$$

where $C_X = \{c_{i,j}\}^{M \times N}$ is the cost matrix, and $\odot$ is the element-wise multiplication. $[A]_s$ computes the sum of all elements in matrix A, and $|A|_a$ denotes a matrix with each element taking the absolute value of the corresponding element in A. Generation of an efficient cost matrix has been well established by many researches. For example, the cost matrix of the state-of-the-art scheme HILL [14] is proposed as

$$C_X = Rec\left([X \otimes \mathbf{H}]_a \otimes \mathbf{P}_1\right) \otimes \mathbf{P}_2, \tag{4}$$

where $\mathbf{H}$ is a high pass filter, $\mathbf{P}_1$ and $\mathbf{P}_2$ are two low pass filters, $\otimes$ represents the mirror-padded convolution operation, and $Rec(\cdot)$ computes the reciprocal values of matrix elements.

We can see that the distortion function in Eq. (2) is defined in an additive form, *i.e.*, a summation of costs of those pixels chosen to be modified. By minimizing $\mathcal{D}(\Delta Y)$, the embedding changes tend to reside in pixels with lower cost $c_{i,j}$. However, $\mathcal{D}(\Delta Y)$ does not explicitly consider the interactions of embedding changes within neighboring pixels. It is the main objective of this paper to redefine the distortion function so that it can take the interactions of neighboring embedding changes into account.

2.3   The Proposed Distortion Function

We redefine the distortion function $\mathcal{D}(\Delta Y)$ in Eq. (1) by adding a term called *modification correlation level* (MCL), which is denoted by $\mathcal{H}(\Delta Y)$. The new distortion function is reformulated as

$$\mathcal{S}(\Delta Y) := \mathcal{D}(\Delta Y) - \lambda \mathcal{H}(\Delta Y), \tag{5}$$

where λ is the weighted factor with a positive value. We use the new term $\mathcal{H}(\Delta Y)$ to model the interactions of embedding modifications. More specifically, when

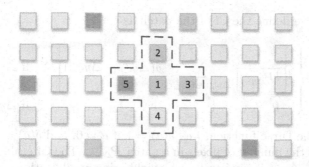

Fig. 1. An example to compute the clustering index. The blue, yellow and green squares represent the modification with 0, -1, and 1, respectively. (Color figure online)

the modifications to pixels have a high level of correlation in neighborhoods, $\mathcal{H}(\Delta Y)$ will have a large value. The optimization problem in Eq. (1) with the incorporated term is reformulated as

$$\underset{\Delta Y}{\arg\min}\ \ \mathcal{S}\left(\Delta Y\right),\quad s.t.\ \ \mathrm{Ext}(Y) = m. \tag{6}$$

Optimizing the above problem requires to simultaneously minimize $\mathcal{D}(\Delta Y)$ and maximize $\mathcal{H}(\Delta Y)$. In this way, reducing the distortion can explicitly encourage the increasement of the modification correlations.

2.4   Modification Correlation Level

The pixels within neighboring regions present high correlations. When the image is modified because of data embedding, such correlations will be deviated to some extent. The correlations have been exploited by many steganalysis algorithms to distinguish between covers and stegos. A good solution to steganography is to preserve the local correlations by using embedding modifications with the same values within local regions. It is evident that the more the same modification values being clustered in a local region, the more correlations in the original cover image can be preserved.

Motivated by the above analysis, we define $\mathcal{H}(\Delta Y)$ in a way with patches. Denote $P_{\Delta y_{i,j}}$ as a patch of modification centered at the (i,j)-th position, and denote $h\left(P_{\Delta y_{i,j}}\right)$ as the *clustering index* (CI) of a patch. The MCL can be defined as the summation of CIs of all patches as follows.

$$\mathcal{H}(\Delta Y) = \sum_i \sum_j h\left(P_{\Delta y_{i,j}}\right). \tag{7}$$

Therefore, with the conventional additive distortion as Eq. (2), the integrated distortion is derived as

$$\mathcal{S}\left(\Delta Y\right) = \sum_i \sum_j \left(c_{i,j}\left|\Delta y_{i,j}\right| - \lambda h\left(P_{\Delta y_{i,j}}\right)\right). \tag{8}$$

In this paper, we define the CI of the patch as

$$
h\left(\boldsymbol{P}_{\Delta y_{i,j}}\right) = \begin{cases} \left[\dfrac{1}{\left|\boldsymbol{P}_{\Delta y_{i,j}}\right|} \displaystyle\sum_{\Delta y_{u,v} \in \boldsymbol{P}_{\Delta y_{i,j}}} \delta(\Delta y_{i,j} - \Delta y_{u,v})\right]^2, & \text{if } \Delta y_{i,j} \neq 0, \\[4mm] 0, & \text{if } \Delta y_{i,j} = 0, \end{cases} \tag{9}
$$

where $\delta(\cdot)$ is the Dirac function, $i.e.$, $\delta(a) = 1$ if $a = 0$, and $\delta(a) = 0$ otherwise. The $\left|\boldsymbol{P}_{\Delta y_{i,j}}\right|$ is the number of pixels in a patch $\boldsymbol{P}_{\Delta y_{i,j}}$. The CI evaluates whether a modification $\Delta y_{i,j}$ is similar to its neighboring modifications in the patch $\boldsymbol{P}_{\Delta y_{i,j}}$. When the modifications in a patch are similar, it leads to a large value of CI, and thus increasing the MCL and reducing the distortion.

Let $\boldsymbol{P}_{\Delta y_{i,j}}$ be formed by $\Delta y_{i,j}$ and its 4-neighborhood elements, $i.e.$, $\boldsymbol{P}_{\Delta y_{i,j}} := \{\Delta y_{i,j}, \Delta y_{i-1,j}, \Delta y_{i+1,j}, \Delta y_{i,j-1}, \Delta y_{i,j+1}\}$. Take Fig. 1 as an example. The CIs for the patches centered at pixel 1 to 5 correspond to $(\frac{1}{5} \times 3)^2$, $(\frac{1}{5} \times 2)^2$, $(\frac{1}{5} \times 2)^2$, 0, and $(\frac{1}{5} \times 1)^2$. It is obvious that the modification to a pixel affects not only the CI of the patch centered at itself, but also the CIs of the patches the pixel belongs to.

3   Solving the Problem

The optimization problem defined in Eq. (6) is complicated and non-convex. On one hand, it is difficult to solve the message constraint with a close-form solution. On the other hand, although the new defined distortion in Eq. (8) is in an additive form, the second term is defined on image patches and thus making the solution intricate to find. As a result, we adopt a compromising scheme to solve it in an approximal way. Similar to the steganographic schemes [2,15], the main idea is to divide the image $\boldsymbol{X}$ into sub-images and divide the message $\boldsymbol{m}$ into segments, and then embed each segment into the sub-image with updated auxiliary costs.

3.1   Division of Sub-images

We adopt a two-layer division approach to divide an image into 8 sub-images. In the first-layer division, two sub-images is generated from image $\boldsymbol{X}$ of size $M \times N$:

$$
\begin{aligned}
\boldsymbol{X}_a &= \left\{x_{i,j} \left| \lfloor \frac{i-1}{2} \rfloor + \lfloor \frac{j-1}{2} \rfloor \text{ is even} \right.\right\}, \\
\boldsymbol{X}_b &= \left\{x_{i,j} \left| \lfloor \frac{i-1}{2} \rfloor + \lfloor \frac{j-1}{2} \rfloor \text{ is odd} \right.\right\},
\end{aligned} \tag{10}
$$

where $\lfloor \cdot \rfloor$ is the rounding to floor operation, and the resultant image $\boldsymbol{X}_a$ and $\boldsymbol{X}_b$ are of size $M \times N/2$. In the second-layer division, $\boldsymbol{X}_a$ and $\boldsymbol{X}_b$ are respectively divided into four sub-images. Let $x_{a,i,j}$ and $x_{b,i,j}$ $(1 \leq i \leq M, 1 \leq j \leq N/2)$ be the (i, j)-th pixel of $\mathcal{X}_a$ and $\mathcal{X}_b$, respectively. Denote the resultant sub-images as $\mathcal{X}_{a,l,k}$ and $\mathcal{X}_{b,l,k}$ $(1 \le l, k \le 2)$, where

$$
\begin{aligned}
\mathcal{X}_{a,l,k} &= \left\{ x_{a,l+2m,k+2n} \,\middle|\, 1 \le l + 2m \le M, 1 \le k + 2n \le N/2 \right\}, \\
\mathcal{X}_{b,l,k} &= \left\{ x_{b,l+2m,k+2n} \,\middle|\, 1 \le l + 2m \le M, 1 \le k + 2n \le N/2 \right\}.
\end{aligned}
\tag{11}
$$

An example is shown in Fig. 2. Consider a 4×8 cover image (shown at the top of Fig. 2), two 4×4 first-layer sub-images are generated (shown in the middle of Fig. 2). The pixels in the original image circled by the same color (red or blue) belong to the same first-layer sub-image. Four 2×2 second-layer sub-images are formed from each first-layer sub-image, resulting in 8 second-layer sub-images in total (shown at the bottom of Fig. 2).

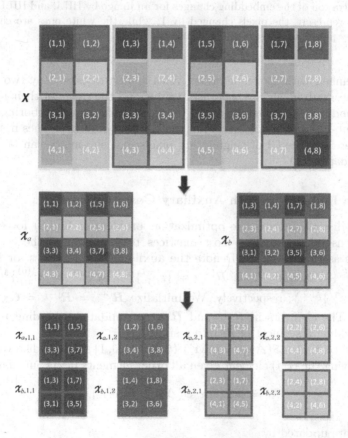

Fig. 2. The division procedure to generate 8 sub-images. Pixels with same color belong to the same second-layer sub-image. (Color figure online)

After such a division, we embed 8 segments of m with equal length into the corresponding 8 second-layer sub-images. The sub-images $\mathcal{X}_{a,l,k}$ are first embedded with order $(l, k) = (1, 1), (1, 2), (2, 1), (2, 2)$, and then the sub-images

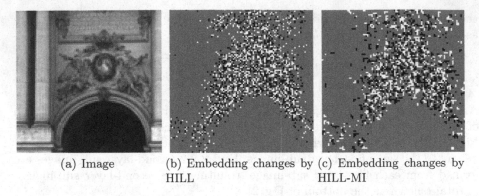

(a) Image   (b) Embedding changes by   (c) Embedding changes by
                        HILL   HILL-MI

Fig. 3. Illustration of the embedding changes for an image by HILL and HILL-MI. The black pixels represent the pixels changed by 1, while the white ones are changed by -1. The grey pixels are those without changes.

$\mathcal{I}_{b,l,k}$ are embed with the same order. With such a division, any two pixels in a second-layer sub-image are at a distance beyond the range of their individual neighborhood in the original image $\boldsymbol{X}$. In other words, two neighboring pixels in the same sub-image will not overlap in their corresponding patches in the input image. Therefore, the CI of neighboring pixels in a sub-image can be regarded as being independent.

3.2   Data Embedding with Auxiliary Costs Updating

Instead of directly solving the optimization problem of Eq. (8) for each sub-image, we use three auxiliary cost matrices to approximate the cost updating process as that in [2,15]. Denote the auxiliary cost matrices for the modification of +1, 0, and -1 as $\boldsymbol{R}^{(+)} = \{r_{i,j}^{(+)}\}^{M \times N}$, $\boldsymbol{R}^{(0)} = \{r_{i,j}^{(0)}\}^{M \times N}$, and $\boldsymbol{R}^{(-)} = \{r_{i,j}^{(-)}\}^{M \times N}$, respectively. We initialize $\boldsymbol{R}^{(+)} = \boldsymbol{R}^{(-)} = \boldsymbol{C_X}$ and set $\boldsymbol{R}^{(0)} = \boldsymbol{0}$. The elements in $\boldsymbol{R}^{(+)}$ and $\boldsymbol{R}^{(-)}$ are updated according to $\mathcal{S}(\varDelta \boldsymbol{Y})$ after embedding a segment of $\boldsymbol{m}$ into a sub-image.

To be specific, let $\mathcal{S}(\varDelta y_{i,j} = l | \varDelta \boldsymbol{Y})$ $(l \in \{-1,0,1\})$ be the distortion when only modifying the (i,j) element given all other elements in $\varDelta \boldsymbol{Y}$ unchanged. Let

$$t = \underset{l \in \{-1,0,1\}}{\arg\min} \ \mathcal{S}(\varDelta y_{i,j} = l | \varDelta \boldsymbol{Y}). \tag{12}$$

The costs are updated by

$$\begin{cases} r_{i,j}^{(+)} = c_{i,j}/\gamma, & \text{if } t = 1, \\ r_{i,j}^{(-)} = c_{i,j}/\gamma, & \text{if } t = -1, \end{cases} \tag{13}$$

where γ $(\gamma > 1)$ is an scaling factor. The updated costs $\boldsymbol{\rho} = [\boldsymbol{R}^{(+)}, \boldsymbol{R}^{(0)}, \boldsymbol{R}^{(-)}]$ are fed to a practical embedding scheme, such as STC [5]. By such a cost updating

---

Algorithm 1. Pseudo code of the proposed algorithm

Initiation:
Calculate the cost matrix C_X.
Initialize $R^{(+)} = R^{(-)} = C_X$ and $R^{(0)} = 0$.
Set $\Delta Y = 0$ and $Y = X$.
Divide m into 8 segments m_k with equal length.
Divide image into 8 sub-groups, $\mathcal{I}_k$, $k = 1, 2, ..., 8$, where k corresponds to the defined embedding order.

Embed:
1: **for** $k = 1$ to 8 **do**,
2:     **if** k==1 **then**
3:         Y_k=STC($\mathcal{I}_k, \rho, m_k$)
4:         Merge Y_k into Y
5:         $\Delta Y = Y - X$
6:     **else**
7:         **for** (i, j) in $\mathcal{I}_k$ **do**
8:             Compute $\mathcal{S}(\Delta y_{i,j} = l | \Delta Y)$ ($l \in \{-1, 0, 1\}$).
9:             Update $\rho = [R^{(+)}, R^{(0)}, R^{(-)}]$ according to (3).
10:        **end for**
11:        Y_k=STC($\mathcal{I}_k, \rho, m_k$)
12:        Merge Y_k into Y
13:        $\Delta Y = Y - X$
14:     **end if**
15: **end for**

Output: Y

---

scheme, the modification change of the pixel at (i, j) tends to be t since it is associated with a lower cost. The pseudo code in Algorithm 1 shows the details of the proposed algorithm. We name our algorithm as MI (modification interaction). In this paper, we use the cost function of HILL, given in (4), to obtain C_X. We name the scheme combining the MI algorithm with HILL as HILL-MI.

Figure 3 shows an image block of the "1013.pgm" image from BOSSBase [1] and the embedding changes respectively caused by HILL and HILL-MI under the same message payload. We can see that the embedding changes by HILL-MI has a higher clustering level than that by HILL.

4   Experiments

In this section, we show the experimental results. We used BOSSBase ver 1.01 image database [1], which contains 10000 grey-scale images of size 512×512. It is commonly used as the benchmark image source for steganographic and steganalytic experiments. The SRM [6] and its channel-aware version maxSRM [4] are used to extract features from both the cover and stego image set. The extracted features are then fed to the ensemble classifier [13] to obtain the classification results. During one classification process, 5000 pairs of cover and stego images are randomly selected and used as the train set, and the rest 5000 pairs form the testing set. The output testing error rate is defined as

$$P_e = \frac{1}{2}\left(P_{\text{FA}} + P_{\text{MD}}\right),\tag{14}$$

where P_{FA} is the false alarm rate (cover being classified as stego) while P_{MD} is the missed detection rate (stego being classified as cover). This training and testing process are repeated 10 times and the demonstrated result is the averaged value. The STC encoding scheme [5] with $h = 10$ is employed for all steganographic schemes.

First, we use SRM [6] to detect HILL-MI with payload 0.4 bpp (bit per pixel) under different combination of λ and γ. It can be observed from Table 1 that the selected parameter combinations do not affect the performance much. For all the

Table 1. Steganalytic performance under SRM detection with different parameters using payload 0.4 bpp.

γ	6	7	8	9
$\lambda = 5$	0.2821	**0.2838**	0.2825	0.2817
$\lambda = 7$	0.2832	**0.2839**	0.2809	0.2818
$\lambda = 9$	0.2810	**0.2832**	0.2817	0.2818
$\lambda = 11$	0.2822	**0.2850**	0.2805	0.2824
$\lambda = 13$	0.2817	**0.2836**	0.2812	0.2855
$\lambda = 15$	0.2823	**0.2840**	0.2811	0.2820
$\lambda = 17$	0.2820	**0.2821**	0.2820	0.2819
$\lambda = 19$	0.2828	**0.2820**	0.2829	0.2827

Table 2. Steganalytic performance of different steganographic schemes

	Scheme	0.1 bpp	0.2 bpp	0.3 bpp	0.4 bpp
SRM	HILL	0.4262	0.3471	0.2863	0.2346
	HILL-CMD	0.4465	0.3879	0.3343	0.2853
	HILL-MI	0.4458	0.3867	0.3302	0.2850
maxSRM	HILL	0.3879	0.3066	0.2412	0.2035
	HILL-CMD	0.4183	0.3474	0.2961	0.2555
	HILL-MI	0.4125	0.3457	0.2943	0.2503
PDAS-SRM	HILL	0.4230	0.3461	0.2830	0.2329
	HILL-CMD	0.4453	0.3826	0.3284	0.2782
	HILL-MI	0.4430	0.3807	0.3249	0.2759
PDAS-maxSRM	HILL	0.3854	0.2992	0.2393	0.1964
	HILL-CMD	0.4102	0.3386	0.2839	0.2456
	HILL-MI	0.4093	0.3375	0.2810	0.2380

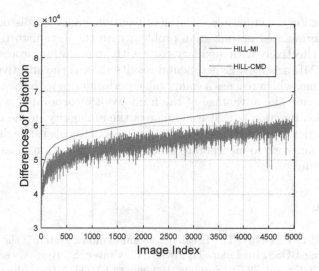

Fig. 4. The difference of distortion between HILL and HILL-MI (denoted by HILL-MI), and that between HILL and HILL-CMD (denoted by HILL-CMD).

experiments, we use $\lambda = 11$ and $\gamma = 7$ as default. Second, we compared the proposed scheme with the conventional HILL [14] and HILL-CMD [15]. We used SRM, maxSRM [4], and their PDAS (pixel-decimation-assisted steganalysis) version [21] to perform detection. From Table 2, it can be seen that HILL-MI and HILL-CMD are both superior to the original HILL with higher detection error rates. It is not surprised to observe that HILL-MI and HILL-CMD have comparable performance, since they are using a similar cost updating process. However, since the HILL-MI utilize an explicit term to model the modification interaction in the distortion function, it should have a lower distortion. In order to justify the claim, we conducted an experiment as follows. Firstly, we randomly select a number of 50 images from BOSSBase set. Then, we compute the distortion according to Eq. (8) for HILL, HILL-MI, and HILL-CMD. Finally, we compute the difference in distortion between HILL and HILL-MI (denoted by HILL-MI), and that between HILL and HILL-CMD (denoted by HILL-CMD). The distortion values are sorted in an ascending order for HILL-MI and the corresponding image index are sorted for HILL-CMD. The results are shown in Fig. 4. It can be observed that distortion differences for all test images are larger than 0, which implies that the distortion can be reduced by HILL-MI and HILL-CMD. The distortion difference between HILL and HILL-MI is larger than that between HILL and HILL-CMD, showing that the HILL-MI leads to a lower distortion.

5   Conclusion

In this paper, we propose a new distortion function for steganography with an explicit term to characterize the interaction of embedding changes. The proposed distortion function is compatible with the conventional additive distortion framework. The reformulated optimization problem with the new distortion function can be solved effectively with auxiliary costs with an updating process similar to the existing CMD schemes. Experimental results showed the effectiveness of the proposed scheme, which reaches a comparable performance with the state-of-the-art CMD scheme. The advantage of the framework incorporated with the proposed distortion function is that it eliminates the ambiguity in the definition of additive distortion caused by cost updating process. It is also straightforward to extend this framework to incorporate other effective distortion measures, which will be our future work.

References

1. Bas, P., Filler, T., Pevný, T.: "Break our steganographic system": the ins and outs of organizing BOSS. In: Filler, T., Pevný, T., Craver, S., Ker, A. (eds.) IH 2011. LNCS, vol. 6958, pp. 59–70. Springer, Heidelberg (2011). https://doi.org/10.1007/978-3-642-24178-9_5
2. Denemark, T., Fridrich, J.: Improving steganographic security by synchronizing the selection channel. In: Proceedings of the 3rd ACM Workshop on Information Hiding and Multimedia Security, pp. 5–14 (2015)
3. Denemark, T., Fridrich, J., Holub, V.: Further study on the security of S-UNIWARD. In: SPIE, Electronic Imaging, Media Watermarking, Security, and Forensics, pp. 902805-1–902805-13 (2014)
4. Denemark, T., Sedighi, V., Holub, V., Cogranne, R., Fridrich, J.: Selection-channel-aware rich model for steganalysis of digital images. In: Proceedings of IEEE International Workshop on Information Forensics and Security, pp. 48–53. IEEE (2014)
5. Filler, T., Judas, J., Fridrich, J.: Minimizing additive distortion in steganography using syndrome-trellis codes. IEEE Trans. Inf. Forensics Secur. 6(3–2), 920–935 (2011)
6. Fridrich, J., Kodovský, J.: Rich models for steganalysis of digital images. IEEE Trans. Inf. Forensics Secur. 7(3), 868–882 (2012)
7. Fridrich, J.: Minimizing the embedding impact in steganography. In: The Workshop on Multimedia and Security, pp. 2–10 (2006)
8. Fridrich, J.: Digital image steganography using universal distortion. In: ACM Workshop on Information Hiding and Multimedia Security, pp. 59–68 (2013)
9. Fridrich, J.J., Kodovský, J.: Multivariate Gaussian model for designing additive distortion for steganography. In: Proceedings of 2013 IEEE International Conference on Acoustics, Speech and Signal Processing, pp. 2949–2953 (2013)
10. Holub, V., Fridrich, J., Denemark, T.: Universal distortion function for steganography in an arbitrary domain. EURASIP J. Inf. Secur. 2014, 1–13 (2014)
11. Holub, V., Fridrich, J.: Designing steganographic distortion using directional filters. In: IEEE International Workshop on Information Forensics and Security, pp. 234–239 (2012)
12. Ker, A.D., et al.: Moving steganography and steganalysis from the laboratory into the real world. In: Proceedings of the first ACM Workshop on Information Hiding and Multimedia Security, pp. 45–58. ACM (2013)
13. Kodovsky, J., Fridrich, J., Holub, V.: Ensemble classifiers for steganalysis of digital media. IEEE Trans. Inf. Forensics Secur. 7(2), 432–444 (2012)

14. Li, B., Wang, M., Huang, J., Li, X.: A new cost function for spatial image steganography. In: Proceeding of IEEE International Conference on Image Processing, pp. 4026–4210 (2014)
15. Li, B., Wang, M., Li, X., Tan, S., Huang, J.: A strategy of clustering modification directions in spatial image steganography. IEEE Trans. Inf. Forensics Secur. 10(9), 1905–1917 (2015)
16. Li, B., He, J., Huang, J., Shi, Y.Q.: A survey on image steganography and steganalysis. Dep. Comput. 2(3), 288–289 (2011)
17. Li, B., Li, Z., Zhou, S., Tan, S., Zhang, X.: New steganalytic features for spatial image steganography based on derivative filters and threshold LBP operator. IEEE Trans. Inf. Forensics Secur. 13(5), 1242–1257 (2018)
18. Pan, F., Li, J., Li, X., Guo, Y.: Steganography based on minimizing embedding impact function and HVS. In: International Conference on Electronics, Communications and Control, pp. 490–493 (2011)
19. Pevny, T., Filler, T., Bas, P.: Using high-dimensional image models to perform highly undetectable steganography. In: Proceedings of International Workshop on Information Hiding, pp. 161–177 (2010)
20. Sedighi, V., Cogranne, R., Fridrich, J.: Content-adaptive steganography by minimizing statistical detectability. IEEE Trans. Inf. Forensics Secur. 11(2), 221–234 (2016)
21. Tan, S., Zhang, H., Li, B., Huang, J.: Pixel-decimation-assisted steganalysis of synchronize-embedding-changes steganography. IEEE Trans. Inf. Forensics Secur. 12(7), 1658–1670 (2017)
22. Tang, W., Li, H., Luo, W., Huang, J.: Adaptive steganalysis based on embedding probabilities of pixels. IEEE Trans. Inf. Forensics Secur. 11(4), 734–745 (2016)
23. Xu, G., Wu, H.Z., Shi, Y.Q.: Structural design of convolutional neural networks for steganalysis. IEEE Signal Process. Lett. 23(5), 708–712 (2016)
24. Zeng, J., Tan, S., Li, B., Huang, J.: Large-scale JPEG steganalysis using hybrid deep-learning framework. IEEE Trans. Inf. Forensics Secur. 13(5), 1200–1214 (2018)

A Novel Detection Method for Word-Based DGA

Luhui Yang[1(✉)], Guangjie Liu[1], Jiangtao Zhai[2], Yuewei Dai[2], Zhaozhi Yan[3], Yuguang Zou[3], and Wenchao Huang[3]

[1] Nanjing University of Science and Technology, Nanjing 210094, China
yangluhui005@foxmail.com
[2] Jiangsu University of Science and Technology, Zhenjiang 212003, China
[3] Nanjing Institute of Information Technology, Nanjing 210094, China

Abstract. As the existing DGA detection methods always don't take into account the problem of word-based DGA method, this will make it invalid. In this paper, a detection method against the word-based DGA has been proposed. Firstly, the word-based DGA methods are analyzed and three type features that the word feature, part-of-speech feature and word correlation feature are analyzed. Then 16 features are concluded from the above analysis and two typical word-based DGA methods Matsnu and Suppobox are chosen as the test object. Finally, the random forest classifier is used in detection. The comparison experimental results show that the proposed method has better performance than the existing ones.

Keywords: DGA detection · Random forest · Information security

1 Introduction

In network attacks, the malware that sneaked into the network requires a variety of covert communication methods which can improve their survivability to connect with the command and control server (C&C), of which the domain-fluxing is a common technique. This technology uses the Domain Generation Algorithm (DGA) to randomly generate a set of domain names and registers with the domain name service provider. In this way, Malware only need a random seed of built-in DGA algorithm, the available C & C server domain names are calculated and communicated. The existing DGA methods are based on a random combination of characters, however, now there are many methods that generate a domain name using random words, such as the famous Matsnu and Suppobox. The existing detection methods can effectively detect the DGA domain name of random characters, but poor in the DGA domain name composed of words. Detecting the word-based DGA domain name has attracted the researcher's attention.

For the detection method of DGA domain name, the early method mainly uses blacklist or fingerprint information for character matching. For example, Ref. [1] proposed to use the snort rules to detect the C&C domain name of the botnet. Subsequently, researchers began to study the characteristics of DGA domain names and

© Springer Nature Switzerland AG 2018
X. Sun et al. (Eds.): ICCCS 2018, LNCS 11064, pp. 472–483, 2018.
https://doi.org/10.1007/978-3-030-00009-7_43

classify them using machine learning [2–11]. In the past two years, some researchers have begun to detect DGA domain name using deep learning methods [12–14].

The feature-based and deep learning-based methods both have good detection performance on most DGA domain names composed of random characters. However, the detection of DGA domain names composed of words is still very poor.

Currently, there is no research on the detection of word-based DGA domain name. This paper firstly analyzed the features of word-based DGA domain names, then four common classifiers are used for detection, finally the results among the CNN-based algorithm, LSTM-based algorithm, previous-feature based algorithm and the algorithm proposed in this paper are compared.

2 Related Works

At present, the DGA detection methods mainly include fingerprint-based, feature-based and deep learning based method.

The first method is mainly used by various security software, such as Snort which is based on rules like character matching [1]. This method can accurately identify known malicious domain names, but the unknown domain name generated by DGA cannot be identified.

The second detection method is based on feature analysis of the domain name or the DNS traffic. Yadav et al. [2] analyzed the KL distance, Jaccard coefficient and edit distance of DGA domain names, Afterwards, more various features were analyzed in detail in [3], and linear regression classification algorithm was used for classification. This method can effectively detect part of the DGA domain name, however, it is limited by the features and the classifier is not efficient enough. Bilge [4] developed the EXPOSURE system on the basis of previous work, extracted 15 domain name features, used J48 decision tree for classification, and had performed well in practical application. This method achieved the best results in feature-based methods. However, all the methods above were against the DGA based on random characters, invalid for word-based DGA. After that, researchers began to introduce features other than domain names. Schiavoni et al. [5] considered that it is incomplete to analyze DGA domain names only. Based on the feature extraction of domain names, they add DNS traffic features, [6] is the deepening and optimization of this problem. Aiming at the problem that the detection on the unknown DGA domain was not effective, Mowbray et al. [7] studied a method based on the length distribution of DNS request domain name to detect unknown DGA. Raghuram [8] built a detection model on normal DNS domain names for rapid identification of abnormal domain names. Grill [9] studied a method only through NetFlow information over DNS traffic rather than domain names; Nguyen [10] used offline analysis to detect DGA botnets through whitelist filtering and clustering; Wang [11] proposed BotMeter, a tool that charts the DGAbot population landscapes in large-scale networks. [5–11] are all limited by the network environment and data. In actual networks, especially in large-scale networks, some features are difficult to collect. This paper believes that detecting domain names will be the fastest and most efficient method.

The third method uses deep learning algorithms for DGA detection. Woodbridge [12] used the LSTM model to detect DGA; Anderson [13] used Generative Adversarial Network and RNN for confrontational DGA generation and detection; Improved from [12], Yu et al. [14] used CNN and LSTM to detect DGA. Deep learning-based methods achieved better results than feature-based methods, but it still cannot solve the problem that word-based DGA detection is not effective.

The existing works all have poor performance in solving the problem of word-based DGA detection, thus, new features should be analyzed for this DGA method.

3   Feature Analysis

In this section, the multi-scale features of word-based DGA domain names are analyzed. As these domain names are composed of several words, thus, it is common to analyze their characteristics from the perspective of natural language processing (NLP). Its NLP characteristics are analyzed from three aspects: word frequency, part of speech and the correlation of words.

3.1   Word Frequency

To our best knowledge, a legitimate domain name often points to a meaningful website or application, especially when the domain name is composed of words. Some words are common in domain names, the top 1 million domain names are used as positive sample and the statistic result of the word frequency from Matsnu samples is given. The x-axis represents in Fig. 1 shows the word frequency ranking. It can be seen that most of words used in Matsnu gain a low ranking. Therefore, word frequency can be considered as a prominent feature of word-based DGA.

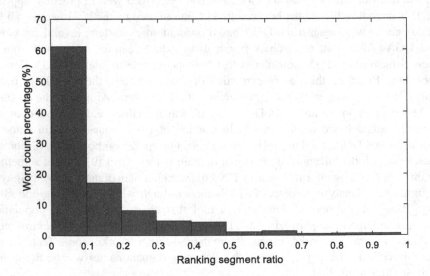

Fig. 1. Word frequency result

3.2   Part-of-Speech Analysis

The part-of-speech of a word represents the characteristics of the word. In domain names, some part-of-speech words are often used, and the most common part-of-speech is nouns. Some research was done on the frequency characteristics of the words' part-of-speech of the domain names. This paper counted top 1 million domain names and got the top part-of-speech as Fig. 2 shows. The union of two part-of-speech frequency was shown in Fig. 3. The part-of-speech was determined by NLTK [15].

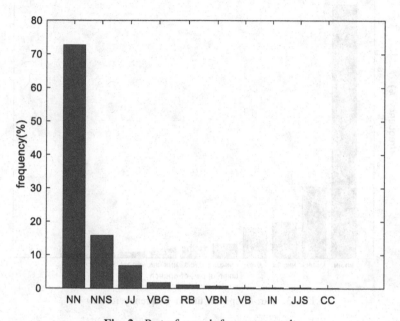

Fig. 2. Part-of-speech frequency result

As shown in the Fig. 3, the most common part-of-speech is nouns, and the most common part-of-speech composition is NN-NN, moreover, the top 10 part-of-speech compositions are all contains NN or NNS. Therefore, the part-of-speech and the union of part-of-speech can be considered as a distinctive feature of the word-based DGA.

3.3   Word Correlation Analysis

In our opinion, the normal domain names will be somewhat similar, especially when a certain word in the domain name is the same. With a sufficient number of normal domain names as samples, the anomaly can be judged by calculating the similarity among domain names.

This paper defines two word-correlations, the first one is Front-Word-Correlation (*FWC*) which means the similarity between the front words of two domain names when the last word is the same, the second one is Back-Word-Correlation (*BWC*) means the similarity of the back words of two domain names when the first word is the same.

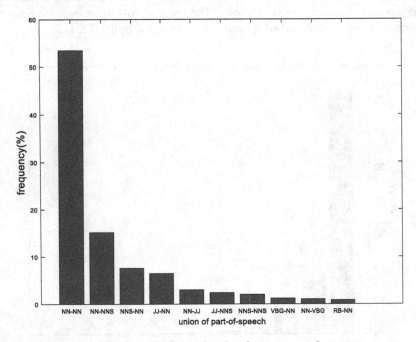

Fig. 3. Part-of-speech union frequency result

For a domain name *AB* composed of words *A* and *B*, the forward domain name list *ListF (CB, DB, ...)* and the backward domain name list *ListB (AE, AF, ...)* can be found from the sample of normal domain names, the relationship of *AB* with *ListF* and *ListB* can be calculated respectively, from what we can get two vectors *SimF* and *SimB* representing the correlation between *AB* and normal domain names. Google's word2vec [16] was used to calculate the similarity of two words.

$$SimF = Similarity(AB, ListF)$$
$$SimB = Similarity(AB, ListB)$$

(1)

Figure 4 shows a specific case of the word correlation defined in this paper. Obviously, normal domain names have a higher word-correlation with other normal domain names compared with DGA domain names.

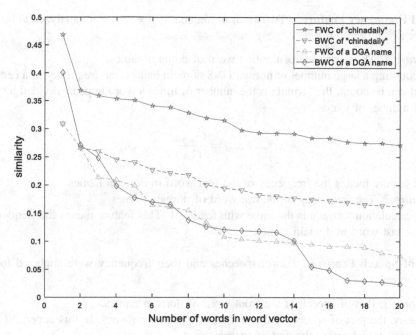

Fig. 4. An example of Word correlation

3.4 Characterization List

According to our analysis, some features of domain names were selected.

Table 1. Word-based DGA domain name features

	Word-based DGA domain name features
Word frequency aspect	The frequency of the first word of domain names The frequency of the last word of domain names
Part-of-speech aspect	Part-of-speech of the front word of domain names Part-of-speech of the back word of domain names part-of-speech union of words in domain names The frequency of part-of-speech of the front word in domain names The frequency of part-of-speech of the back word in domain names The frequency of part-of-speech union of the words in domain names
Word correlation aspect	Mean of *SimF* Mean of *SimB* Variance of *SimF* Variance of *SimB* Maximum of *SimF* Maximum of *SimB* Minimum of *SimF* Minimum of *SimB*

Word Frequency Features. Two kinds of frequency of words were analyzed to be the features.

Feature 1. The frequency of the first word of domain names.

By counting a large number of normal DNS domain names, the frequency of a certain word can be count, the formula is the number of times a word appears divided by the total number of words:

$$P_{word} = \frac{C_{appear}}{C_{total}} \tag{2}$$

This feature means the frequency of the first word in domain names.

Feature 2. The frequency of the last word of domain names.

The calculation formula is the same with feature 1. This feature means the frequency of the last word in domain names.

Part-of-Speech Features. Part-of-speeches and their frequency were analyzed to be the features.

Feature 3. Part-of-speech of the front word of domain names.

It means the part-of-speech of the first word in domain names. In this paper, NLTK was used to determine the part-of-speech.

Feature 4. Part-of-speech of the back word of domain names.

It means the part-of-speech of the last word in domain names.

Feature 5. Part-of-speech union of words in domain names.

It means the union of part-of-speech of all the words in domain names.

Feature 6. The frequency of part-of-speech of the front word in domain names.

It means the frequency of part-of-speech of the first word in domain names. The frequency calculation formula is the same with feature 1.

Feature 7. The frequency of part-of-speech of the back word in domain names.

It means the frequency of part-of-speech of the first word in domain names. The frequency calculation formula is the same with feature 1.

Feature 8. The frequency of part-of-speech union of the words in domain names.

It means the frequency of the union of part-of-speech of all the words in domain names. The frequency calculation formula is the same with feature 1.

Word Correlation Features. In the previous analysis, two vectors SimF and SimB can be counted, their statistical characteristics were selected to be the features. In this paper, word2vec was used to compute the similarity of the words.

Feature 9. Mean of SimF.

It means the average value of all values in vector SimF.

Feature 10. Mean of SimB.

It means the average value of all values in vector SimB.

Feature 11. The variance of SimF.

It means the variance of all values in vector SimF.

Feature 12. The variance of SimB.

It means the variance of all values in vector SimB.

Feature 13. The maximum value of SimF.

It means the maximum value of all values in vector SimF.

Feature 14. The maximum value of SimB.

It means the maximum value of all values in vector SimB.

Feature 15. Minimum of SimF.

It means the minimum value of all values in vector SimF.

Feature 16. Minimum of SimB.

It means the minimum value of all values in vector SimB.

4   Experimental Results and Analysis

4.1   Data Set

The normal domain name dataset used in this experiment comes from the world's top one million DNS request domain names collected by Cisco Umbrella (http://s3-us-west-1.amazonaws.com/umbrellastatic/index.html), the top 100,000 domain names that consist of two words were chosen as training samples.

The Matsnu and Suppobox were chosen as the DGA domain name samples, the data comes from 360lab: https://data.netlab.360.com/dga/. Our method focused on the two-word domain names. The 6876 domain names from Matsnu and 1190 domain names from Suppobox in 360lab were selected. As there is too little data on Matsnu and Suppobox, they were only used as a test sample and training samples were produced by ourselves. 100,000 domain names were generated randomly as training samples using Oxford 3000 words.

4.2   The Results and Analysis

This experiment used 100,000 normal domain names and 100,000 domain names we generated as training samples, and then the Matsnu and Suppobox data described above and 10000 normal domain names were used as test samples. Weka3.8 was used as the classification tool.

Several common classifiers were selected to test the validity of the feature model. They are Naive Bayes, SVM, J48 decision tree and Random Forest. The experiment results show that the Random Forest achieved the best performance, the classification accuracy of normal domain names is 85.2%, the accuracy of Matsnu domain names is 74.9% and the accuracy of Suppobox is 68.2%. Although the Naïve Bayes had better accuracy on Matsnu and Suppobox, the normal domain name accuracy of it is the lowest. On average, the Random Forest classification performance best (Table 2).

Table 2. Classification results of the proposed algorithm

	Normal domain names accuracy (%)	Matsnu domain names accuracy (%)	Suppobox domain names accuracy (%)
J48	83.6	73.5	68.9
Naive bayes	57.8	83.2	79.5
SVM	72.9	74.9	62.0
Random Forest	85.2	74.9	68.2

4.3 Comparative Experiments

In order to compare the work in this paper with previous algorithms, some comparative experiments have been done. Three typical algorithms were chosen. They were a previous feature-based algorithm, CNN-based algorithm, LSTM-based algorithm.

Previous Features. This algorithm selected 11 domain name structure features from other papers, as shown in Table 1. This experiment selects the Random Forest algorithm for classification and 10-fold cross validation for the training process (Table 3).

Table 3. The previous features summary

NO	Features
1	Domain Information Entropy
2	Average Jaccard index based on bigram
3	Average Jaccard index based on trigram
4	Domain readability
5	The ratio of words number and domain length
6	The ratio of words length and domain length
7	Domain length
8	Continuous consonant ratio
9	Digital ratio
10	Continuous digital ratio
11	Alphabet and digital switching ratio

LSTM Model. This model comes from [12]. The Keras model code is as follows.

```
model = Sequential()
model.add(Embedding(max_features, 128, input_length=maxlen))
model.add(LSTM(128))
model.add(Dropout(0.5))
model.add(Dense(1))
model.add(Activation('sigmoid'))
model.compile(loss='binary_crossentropy',optimizer='rmsprop')
```

CNN Model. This model is similar to the work in [14], but the parameters were adjusted for better performance. The Keras model code is as follows.

```
model = Sequential()
model.add(Embedding(max_features, 128, input_length=maxlen))
model.add(Conv1D(128, 5, strides=1, padding='valid'))
model.add(Activation('relu'))
model.add(MaxPooling1D(pool_size=4, strides=None,padding='valid'))
model.add(Dropout(0.5))
model.add(Flatten())
model.add(Dense(128))
model.add(Activation('relu'))
model.add(Dropout(0.5))
model.add(Dense(1))
model.add(Activation('sigmoid'))
model.compile(loss='binary_crossentropy', optimizer='rmsprop')
```

Results and Analysis. The comparison experimental results are shown in Table 4.

Table 4. Comparative results

	Normal domain names accuracy(%)	Matsnu domain names accuracy(%)	Suppobox domain names accuracy(%)
CNN	79.8	71.3	68.1
LSTM	75.2	66.2	50.0
Previous methods	67.6	59.5	53.7
Proposed algorithm	**85.2**	**74.9**	**68.2**

It can be seen from Table 4 that the experimental results that the algorithm proposed in this paper has better detection accuracy than the previous feature-based algorithm, CNN-based algorithm and LSTM-based algorithm.

5 Conclusions and Future Work

This paper focus on the research of word-based DGA domain names, it designed a novel algorithm against the word-based DGA. It analyzed the characteristics in terms of word frequency, part-of-speech, and word correlation, and extracted 16-dimensional features, then it generated a training set of word-based DGA and collect two typical word-based DGA domain names from the real world as the testing set. Four common classifiers were used for classification and Random Forest performed best. The comparative results were given among CNN-based algorithm, LSTM-based algorithm, previous-feature based algorithm and the algorithm proposed in this paper. The experimental results show that the proposed algorithm has better accuracy.

This paper only analyzed the word frequency, part-of-speech, and word correlation aspect features, more aspect can be analyzed. As to the word correlation aspect, this paper only considered the similarity as the correlation feature, more correlation ship can be tapped. Moreover, since the deep learning performed well in character-based DGA detection, feature analysis and deep learning can be combined for word-based DGA detection in the future.

Acknowledgment. This work was supported by the National Natural Science Foundation of China (Grants nos. 61702235, 61602247, 61472188, and U1636117), Natural Science Foundation of Jiangsu Province (Grants no. BK20160840 and BK20150472), CCF-VENUSTECH Foundation (Grant no. 2016011), and Fundamental Research Funds for the Central Universities (30920140121006 and 30915012208).

References

1. Chanthakoummane, Y., Saiyod, S., Benjamas, N., Khamphakdee, N.: Improving intrusion detection on Snort rules for Botnets detection. In: Kim, K., Joukov, N. (eds.) Information Science and Applications (ICISA) 2016. LNCS, vol. 376, pp. 765–779. Springer, Singapore (2016). https://doi.org/10.1007/978-981-10-0557-2_74
2. Yadav, S., Reddy, A.K.K., Reddy, A.L., Ranjan, S.: Detecting algorithmically generated malicious domain names. In: Proceedings of the 10th ACM SIGCOMM conference on Internet measurement, pp. 48–61. ACM (2010)
3. Yadav, S., Reddy, A.K.K., Reddy, A.N., Ranjan, S.: Detecting algorithmically generated domain-flux attacks with DNS traffic analysis. IEEE ACM Trans. Netw. **20**, 1663–1677 (2012)
4. Bilge, L., Sen, S., Balzarotti, D., Kirda, E., Kruegel, C.: Exposure: a passive DNS analysis service to detect and report malicious domains. ACM Trans. Inf. Syst. Secur. (TISSEC) **16**, 128 (2014)
5. Schiavoni, S., Maggi, F., Cavallaro, L., Zanero, S.: Tracking and characterizing Botnets using automatically generated domains. arXiv (2013)
6. Schiavoni, S., Maggi, F., Cavallaro, L., Zanero, S.: Phoenix: DGA-based botnet tracking and intelligence. In: Dietrich, S. (ed.) DIMVA 2014. LNCS, vol. 8550, pp. 192–211. Springer, Cham (2014). https://doi.org/10.1007/978-3-319-08509-8_11
7. Mowbray, M., Hagen, J.: Finding domain-generation algorithms by looking at length distribution. In: IEEE International Symposium on Software Reliability Engineering Workshops, pp. 395–400. IEEE (2014)
8. Raghuram, J., Miller, D.J., Kesidis, G.: Unsupervised, low latency anomaly detection of algorithmically generated domain names by generative probabilistic modeling. J. Adv. Res. **5**, 423–433 (2014)
9. Grill, M., Nikolaev, I., Valeros, V., Rehak, M.: Detecting DGA malware using NetFlow. In: 2015 IFIP/IEEE International Symposium on Integrated Network Management (IM), pp. 1304–1309. IEEE (2015)
10. Nguyen, T.D., Cao, T.D., Nguyen, L.G.: DGA botnet detection using collaborative filtering and density based clustering. In: Proceedings of the Sixth International Symposium on Information and Communication Technology, pp. 203–209. ACM (2015)

11. Wang, T., Hu, X., Jang, J., Ji, S., Stoecklin, M., Taylor, T.: BotMeter: charting DGA-botnet landscapes in large networks. In: 2016 IEEE 36th International Conference on Distributed Computing Systems (ICDCS), pp. 334–343. IEEE (2016)
12. Woodbridge, J., Anderson, H.S., Ahuja, A., Grant, D.: Predicting domain generation algorithms with long short-term memory networks. arXiv (2016)
13. Anderson, H.S., Woodbridge, J., Filar, B.: DeepDGA: adversarially-tuned domain generation and detection. In: Proceedings of the 2016 ACM Workshop on Artificial Intelligence and Security, pp. 13–21. ACM (2016)
14. Yu, B., Gray, D.L., Pan, J., De Cock, M., Nascimento, A.C.: Inline DGA detection with deep networks. In: 2017 IEEE International Conference on Data Mining Workshops (ICDMW), pp. 683–692. IEEE (2017)
15. Bird, S., Loper, E.: NLTK: the natural language Toolkit. In: Proceedings of the ACL 2004 on Interactive Poster and Demonstration Sessions, p. 31. Association for Computational Linguistics (2004)
16. Google: word2vec. https://code.google.com/archive/p/word2vec/. Accessed 12 May 2018

A Privacy Preserving Similarity Search Scheme over Encrypted High-Dimensional Data for Multiple Data Owners

Cheng Guo[1,2], Pengxu Tian[1,2(✉)], Yingmo Jie[1,2], and Xinyu Tang[1,2]

[1] School of Software Technology, Dalian University of Technology,
Dalian 116620, China
guocheng@dlut.edu.cn, tpx_dlut@163.com
[2] Key Laboratory for Ubiquitous Network and Service Software of Liaoning
Province, Dalian 116620, China

Abstract. Cloud computing has become increasingly popular because of the benefits it provides. However, the security of the data stored in a remote cloud has become a major concern. For privacy concerns, searchable encryption (SE), which supports searching over encrypted data, has been proposed and developed rapidly in secure Boolean search and similarity search. However, most SE schemes can only support single data owner which is opposite to the condition in the cloud environment. In this paper, we employed locality-sensitive hashing (LSH) and bilinear map to deal with a privacy preserving similarity search for multiple data owners. In our scheme, data users can encrypt their data using their own secret keys. And the data users can perform the similarity search without knowing any information about the secret keys which belong to the data owners. We formally analyzed the security strength of our scheme. Extensive experiments on actual datasets showed that our scheme is extremely effective and efficient.

Keywords: Searchable encryption · Multiple data owners · Similarity search

1 Introduction

Cloud computing has achieved great success in recent years. However, the security problem is deemed as the biggest challenge that hinders the development of cloud computing. Some schemes were proposed to preserve the privacy of the data [1, 2]. Once the data are outsourced to a remote cloud server, the data owner will lose direct control of the data. Some sensitive information in the data, such as e-mails, personal health records, photos, can be revealed. The cloud server provider may obtain the specific content of them. Encrypting the data before outsourcing seems like a straightforward way to solve the privacy preserving problem. Although encryption makes the data protected, it complicates the operation on the data such the fundamental search operation obviously. In general, it is very difficult that processing encrypted data without decrypting them. The problem is how the cloud can execute the search operation in the cipher-text domain while the data stored in the cloud won't be decrypted all the time. In fact, a large amount of algorithms have been proposed to

© Springer Nature Switzerland AG 2018
X. Sun et al. (Eds.): ICCCS 2018, LNCS 11064, pp. 484–495, 2018.
https://doi.org/10.1007/978-3-030-00009-7_44

support the task which are called searchable encryption scheme [3–16]. Traditionally, almost all of these schemes are proposed for exact keywords search, which means that they enable an exact query matching of the data in the cloud according to a specific feature.

In real word, however, it is more practical and natural to perform retrieval according to the similarity with the specific feature rather than an exact query matching, particularly for high-dimensional data. The k-Nearest Neighbor (kNN) is a state-of-the-art algorithm that deals with the similarity search for high-dimensional data. A result for a kNN problem consists of k points that are closest to the query point. The distances are usually evaluated by Euclidean distance. However, the compute-then-compare process with distances will cause a large amount computing overhead. To avoid this issue, a hash function called locality-sensitive hashing (LSH) is widely used as a solution for kNN problem. As known, LSH is an approximation algorithm that trades accuracy for efficiency. Unlike the traditional hash function which can perform a fast matching in a hash table by decreasing the collisions of hash values, LSH can leverage the collisions to evaluate the similarity and speed up the matching. Two similar data would be mapped into one bucket with a very high probability after computing by LSH. And two dissimilar data would be mapped into one bucket with a negligible probability. In other words, the LSH values of two similar data would be the same. Taking advantage of the characteristic of LSH, the similarity search problems over encrypted data can be solved easily by some searchable encryption schemes [17–20].

However, all these schemes are limited to a single-owner model, which means that there is only one data owner served in a cloud server. As a matter of fact, most cloud servers in practice support multiple data owners. Compared with the signal-owner schemes, it is challengeable to develop a full-fledged multi-owner scheme. In the multi-owner scenario, none of the data owners would be willing to share their secret keys to others. And each data owner would encrypt secret data using his/her owner secret key. Consequently, there is a large amount of redundant data in the cloud server that are encrypted by different secret keys. Besides, it is also difficult to perform a search operation in the cipher-text domain where the data are encrypted by different secret keys.

In light of these challenge, in this paper, we proposed secure indexes based on LSH and bilinear map to solve the aforementioned problems. The contributions of this paper are summarized as follows:

We proposed a secure searchable encryption scheme which can support similarity search in cipher-text domain for multiple data owners.

We transformed the indexes which are encrypted by different data owners into the form under another secret key.

We analyzed our scheme and proved that it is secure, and we performed extensive experiment on actual datasets to show our scheme is efficient and effective.

The rest of this paper is structured as follows. Section 2 introduces the related work, and the problem statement is presented in Sect. 3. And the entire scheme is demonstrated using an example in Sect. 4. The security of our scheme is analyzed in Sect. 5, the results of our experiments are presented in Sect. 6, and our conclusions concerning the scheme are presented in Sect. 7.

2 Related Work

Various protocols and security definitions have been proposed for searchable encryption. Traditional searchable encryption has been studied extensively as a cryptographic primitive. Song et al. [3] first proposed the concept of searchable encryption, and considered the first searchable symmetric encryption (SSE) scheme. Then, Goh et al. [4] proposed a Z-IDX construction which has linear search complexity and produces highly compact index via using the Bloom filter. And they proposed a definition of security for searchable symmetric encryption. Chang et al. [5] developed a per-file index design and introduced a simulation-based security definition, which was slightly stronger than the definition in [4]. However, these models are impractical for actual scenarios because of the heavy computation overhead.

Curtmola et al. [6] presented the first index-based SSE solution for single-keyword search which were achieved optimal search times. They also introduced the definition for adaptive security for SSE. Boneh et al. [7] proposed the first public key scheme for keyword search in encrypted data. According to the searchable public-key encryption model, a lot of search functions have been extended. The conjunctive keyword search was realized in [7, 8]. Boneh et al. [10] proposed a searchable encryption scheme that supports range search and Shi et al. [11] proposed a scheme that supports both range search and subset search.

Guo et al. [12] applied a single-keyword SSE scheme in the e-healthcare system. Cao et al. [13, 14], Sun et al. [15], Xia et al. [16], and Orencik et al. [17] extended the secure single-keyword approach for multi-keyword queries.

With the increasing of data volume and data dimensionality, finding similar records or nearest neighbors is much more common and practical. Fu et al. [18] proposed a similarity searchable encryption scheme based on sim-hash. In order to scale properly for large data sources, they also built a trie-based index to improve the performance of their scheme. Tao et al. [19] identified the nearest neighbor search problem in high-dimensional space in the plaintext domain. They took advantage of LSH in their scheme to achieve sub-linear search time. As an improvement, they also proposed an index called LSB-forest in their scheme, which consisted of a lot of LSB-trees. Wang et al. [20] proposed a secure searchable encryption scheme based on the wildcard to solve similar keyword search measured by the edit distance. Elmehdwi et al. [21] proposed a scheme that can solve the secure kNN problem. It was the first searchable encryption scheme that can protect access control in similarity search for high-dimensional data. Their scheme can compare two encrypted vectors without revealing any information. Based on the contribution of [19], lots of tasks have been completed using LSH. Yuan et al. [22] proposed a similar searchable encryption scheme that achieved a constant search time for large-scale data. They regarded the LSH values as keywords and used multiple choice hashing open addressing, and cuckoo hashing to get high performance. Wang et al. [23] utilized the R-tree structure to build an efficient index. To compare the location information, they used Order-Preserving Encryption (OPE) [24, 25] to encrypt the node of R-tree. Instead of generating a temporary circle in the kNN algorithm, they computed a temporary rectangle for easy encryption and comparisons.

Zhang et al. [26] proposed a scheme for multiple data owners that can support ranked multi-keyword search. Improved by [26], they further proposed another searchable encryption scheme [27] for multiple data owners. In their scheme, the different data owners encrypt their data using their own secret keys. After authentication, the data user can perform a multi-keyword search without knowing any of the secret keys of the data owners. However, for a search operation, it will cause a large number of computation costs such as exponentiation operations, multiplication operations and pairing operations. In addition, this scheme only support keyword search. Cui et al. [28] proposed a secure NDD scheme for multiple data owners that can support similarity search. They also used bilinear mapping to let users complete their queries without knowing any information about the data owners' secret keys. This paper pays close attention to an efficient similar searchable encryption scheme which aims to decrease the computation cost and communication cost.

3   Problem Statement

In this section, first, we introduce a system model which can achieve our goals. Then, we discuss the threat model according to the system model. Finally, we illustrate the design goals of our scheme.

3.1   System Model

There are three entities in a traditional searchable encryption system model. To support more data owners in a searchable encryption scheme, we add another cloud server in the model of the system, as shown in Fig. 1. The system model consists of data owners, data users, cloud server A, and cloud server B. Data owners have a collection of data D. To enable secure and efficient search operation on these data which will be encrypted, data owners extract secure searchable indexes I in advance. Then they submit I and secret messages Δ which include the information of their secret keys to cloud server B. What's more, data owners also encrypt their data collection D and outsourced them to cloud server A. As soon as receiving the index I and secret messages Δ, cloud server B re-encrypts the index and outsources the re-encrypted index to cloud server A. when a data user wants to perform a similarity search over encrypted data which are stored in cloud server A, he/she should generate a corresponding trapdoor T and submit it to cloud server B along with his/her secret message Δ. When receiving the trapdoor T and secret message Δ, cloud server B re-encrypts the trapdoor and outsources it to cloud server A. Cloud server A can match the re-encrypted index with the re-encrypted trapdoor and return the data user what he/she wants.

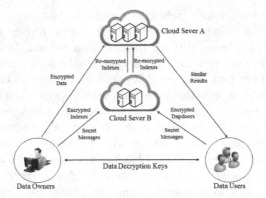

Fig. 1. System model

3.2   Threat Model

In our scheme, we assume that the authorization between data owners and data users is finished appropriately. And the data owners and data users who pass the authorization are trustworthy. Cloud servers deployed in untrusted cloud environment are deemed as 'curious but honest'. It means that the cloud servers are curious about obtaining the content of the encrypted data, but they follow the designed protocol exactly. Besides, we also assume that cloud server A will not collude with cloud server B.

3.3   Design Goals

Our scheme achieves both the performance goals and the safety goals, which will ensure secure similarity search for multiple data owners in a 'semi-honest' cloud environment.

Similarity search for multiple data owners: The cloud server A should return the similar data that are relevant to the search request. In addition, data users can generate their trapdoors without knowing any information about the secret keys of data owners which are used to encrypt their indexes.

Index and trapdoor privacy: Two aspects of index and trapdoor privacy should be protected, i.e., (1) since the index and trapdoor reflect the content of the data directly, the cloud servers cannot learn the content of them and (2) the cloud servers cannot deduce any content of the data by analyzing the encrypted index and trapdoor.

Secret message privacy: Since the re-encryption phase in our scheme needs the secret keys of data owners and users, any entities in the system model cannot obtain the exact values of these secret keys without utilizing a secure channel.

4 Our Proposed Scheme

In this section, we present the main scheme for secure similarity search where the data are encrypted by different secret keys. Our core design is to make the search operation more convenient and efficient. Below, we present the preliminary and our design rationale before providing the details.

4.1 Preliminary

Locality-Sensitive Hashing (LSH) [29]: Given a distance r, approximation ratio c, probability values p_1 and p_2 such that $p_1 > p_2$, a hash function $h()$ is (r, cr, p_1, p_2) local sensitive if it satisfies both conditions below:

1. If $\|o_1, o_2\| < r$, then $\Pr[h(o_1) = h(o_2)] \geq p_1$;
2. If $\|o_1, o_2\| > cr$, then $\Pr[h(o_1) = h(o_2)] \leq p_2$.

LSH functions are known for many distance metrics. For l_p norm, a popular LSH function is defined as follows:

$$h(o) = \left\lfloor \frac{\vec{a} \cdot \vec{o} + b}{w} \right\rfloor$$

Here, $\vec{o}$ represents the d-dimensional vector representation of a point o; $\vec{a}$ is another d-dimensional vector that each dimension is generated independently by a p-stable distribution; $\vec{a} \cdot \vec{o}$ denotes the dot product of two vectors. w is the width of a bucket. b is uniformly drawn from $[o, w)$.

Bilinear Map: Let G_1 and G_2 be multiplicative cyclic groups of prime order p, g_1 and g_2 be generators of G_1 and G_2, respectively. A bilinear map is a map $e : G_1 \times G_1 \to G_2$ that has the following properties:

1. Computability: there exists an efficiently computable algorithm for computing the map e.
2. Bilinear: for all $u, v \in G_1$ and $a, b \in Z_p^+$, $e(u^a, v^b) = e(u, v)^{ab}$.
3. Non-degeneracy: $e(g_1, g_1) \neq 1$.

Definition 1 (Bilinear Map Generation Algorithm): Bilinear map generation algorithm $Gen()$ is a probabilistic algorithm. $Gen()$ takes the security parameter k as input and outputs a five-tuple (p, g_1, G_1, G_2, e), where p is a k-bit prime number, g_1 is a generator of G_1 with the order p, and $e : G_1 \times G_1 \to G_2$ is a bilinear map.

4.2 Design Rationale

There will be a large amount of data owners served in a practical cloud application. Since the data are stored in a semi-trusted cloud environment, all the data owners will use their own secret key to encrypt their sensitive data. And they are not willing to share their secret keys to others. In this situation, it is challengeable to design a searchable encryption scheme. When performing a search operation, it is impractical for a data user to obtain the secret keys belonging to all the data owners. And the data user should be asked to generate only one trapdoor according to his/her retrieval which is as simple as the search request in the single-owner searchable encryption scheme. To address the above issues, we proposed a new scheme which can achieve the following three requirements: First, different data owners use their own secret keys to encrypt their data. Second, only one trapdoor should be generated for a search request by the data user and the data user does not need to know any information about the data owners' secret keys. Third, the cloud server can match the trapdoor with the indexes encrypted by different secret keys without obtain the actual values of the data and the trapdoor.

4.3   System Initialization

Our construction is based on the aforementioned bilinear map. With the security parameter k, (p, g_1, G_1, G_2, e) will be generated by calling $Gen(k)$. Given different secret parameters as input, a randomized key generation algorithm will output the private keys used in the system. $k_{o,i} \in Z_p^+$, $k_{u,j} \in Z_p^+$, $k_b \in Z_p^+ \leftarrow (0,1)^*$, where $k_{o,i}$ is the private key used to encrypt the index of data owner O_i, $k_{u,j}$ is the private key used to encrypt the trapdoor of data user U_j, k_b is the private key of cloud server B, respectively. Let LSH() be a public locality-sensitive hash function, its output locates in Z_p^+.

4.4   Details of Our Scheme

Each data owner O_i owns the original database (T_i) of n data items D. To compare the data items, our scheme should guarantee that these data items have the same number of dimensions. So, $D_{i,k}$ means the kth data item belonging to the data owner O_i. To enable efficient similarity search for multiple data owners, each data owner would build a secure searchable index I_i using his/her own secret key.

Algorithm 1

Input: the secret key: k, the data item: D
Output: the cipher-text data item: c
1: $v \leftarrow LSH(D)$ where $v = \{w_1, w_2, \cdots, w_l\}$
2: for all $w \in v$ do:
3:   $c_m = g^{k \cdot w}$
4:   $c.add(c_m)$
5: end for
6: send c to cloud server B

For Index Encryption: The data owner O_i first calls Algorithm 1. It should meet the requirement that different data owners use their own secret keys to encrypt the searchable index. The data owner first calls LSH function LSH() to compute the index of $D_{i,k}$ i.e. a vector of LSH value $v = \{w_1, w_2, \cdots, w_l\}$. Here the function LSH() can reduce the dimensionality of data items and evaluate the similarity more efficiently. In the next step, each $w \in v$ is protected by the key k_1 of the data owner O_i, i.e. $c_m = g_1^{k_{o,i} \cdot w_m}$ where g_1 is the generator of the multiplicative cyclic group G_1 in the bilinear operation. Consequently, the encrypted index is obtained as $c = \{c_1, c_2, \cdots, c_l\}$. Then the data owner O_i will send c to cloud server B. This scheme allows each authorized data owner and data user to generate his/he owner secret key for secure similarity search. In order to meet the aforementioned requirement, the encrypted index should be re-encrypted by cloud server B. For security, the data owner O_i will send the secret message $g_1^{1/k_{o,i}}$ denoted by Δ which includes the information of O_i's secret keys $k_{o,i}$ to cloud server B rather than plaintext through a secure channel. With the secret message $g_1^{1/k_{o,i}}$, cloud server B computes $g_1^{k_b/k_{o,i}} \in G_1$ without knowing the data owner's secret key $k_{o,i}$. And cloud server B can re-encrypt the index which is encrypted by the data owner's secret key into the form under cloud server B's secret key by computing $e\left(g_1^{k_{o,i} \cdot w}, g_1^{k_b/k_{o,i}}\right) = e(g_1, g_1)^{w \cdot k_b}$. Cloud server B further submits the re-encrypted index to cloud server A.

For Retrieval Phase: It should meet the requirement that each data user can generate the trapdoor without knowing any information about the data owners' secret keys. Same with the index encryption phase, the data user U_j will also call Algorithm 1 to generate his/her trapdoor T_j. For a query data item q, the data user calls LSH functions LSH() to process the query and encrypt the LSH value by computing $T_j = g_1^{k_{u,j} \cdot q}$. The data user submits the trapdoor and his/her secret message to cloud server B for further re-encryption. The cloud server B computes $g_1^{k_b/k_{u,j}} \in G_1$ and a re-encrypteds trapdoor $e(g_1, g_1)^{q \cdot k_b}$ and send them to cloud server A. Then, cloud server A can match the re-encrypted trapdoor with the re-encrypted indexes which are stored in the cloud.

5 Security Analysis

Our scheme can be used to conduct similarity search for multiple data owners by taking advantage of the technique about elliptic curve. In this section, we provide step-by-step description of the secure requirements have been satisfied.

5.1 Security of the Dataset

In our scheme, the datasets which belongs to different data owners are protect by symmetric encryption before they are outsourced to store in the cloud server A. As long as the symmetric cryptosystem is secure, the cloud server A cannot obtain the exact value of the data.

5.2 Security of the Index, Trapdoor and Secret Message

We formulate the security goals of the index, the trapdoor and the secret message achieved by our scheme with the following two theorems.

Theorem 1: (Decisional Bilinear Diffie-Hellman (DBDH) Assumption). Let $a, b, z \in Z_p^+$ be chosen at random. Given $g_1, g_1^a, g_1^b \in G_1$, the DBDH assumption states that no PPT algorithm A can distinguish the tuple $(g_1, g_1^a, g_1^b, e(g_1, g_1)^{ab})$ from the tuple $(g_1, g_1^a, g_1^b, e(g_1, g_1)^z)$ with non-negligible advantage.

Theorem 2: Given the DL (Discrete Logarithm) assumption, our scheme achieves secrecy in the random oracle model.

Proof: We use the following game played between an adversary A and a challenger C to prove the security of the index which is the same as the security of the trapdoor and secret message.

1. C first runs $Gen(k)$ to get (r, g, G), where g is the generator of cyclic group G with order p.
2. A freely chooses two values w_0 and w_1 where $w_0, w_1 \in Z_p^+$ and send them to C.
3. Upon receiving w_0 and w_1, C sets a bit $b = 0$ with probability 1/2 and sets $b = 1$ with probability 1/2. Then C sends $g^{k \cdot w_b}$ to A where k is the secret key of C and $k \in Z_p^+$
4. A tries to guess the value of b, and outputs its guess, b'.

If the probability of $|\Pr[b = b'] - 1/2|$ is negligible, then the above scheme is semantically secure against a chosen plain-text attack (CPA).

6 Performance Evaluation

In this section, we measure the efficiency of our proposed scheme. Due to the space limitation, we only present the experimental evaluation about some parameter that may affect the performance of our scheme.

First, we evaluate the performance of preparation cost by varying the number of data (n), the dimensionality of data (d) and the number of hash functions in LSH (h). Figure 2(a) shows the preparation time for different dimensionalities of data. The LSH function can map a high-dimensional data record into a LSH value with fixed dimensionality. The figure demonstrates that the preparation time has nothing to do with the dimensionality due to the employment of LSH function. And Fig. 2(b) shows that, for different numbers of data, the preparation time increases linearly with the number of hash functions in LSH.

Figure 3 shows the search time of our scheme. By employing the LSH function, the search operation is equal to search in a hash table and can be achieved in O(1) time. From the figure we can summarize that the search time has nothing to do with the number of data and the dimensionalities of data. And the search time increases sub-linear as the number of hash functions in LSH.

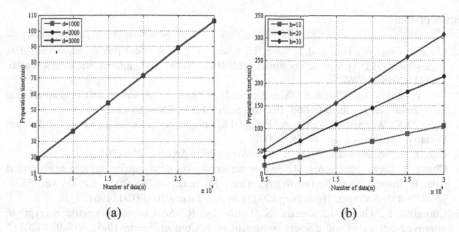

Fig. 2. Time cost for preparation

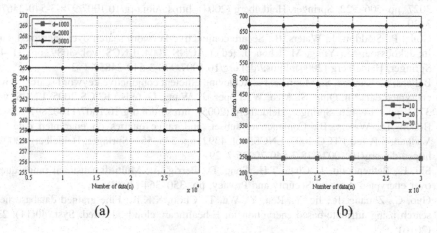

Fig. 3. Time cost for search

7 Conclusions

In this paper, we explored the problem of similarity search on over encrypted data for multiple data owners. And we proposed an effective searchable encryption scheme. In our scheme, the data owners can encrypt their data and indexes using their own secret keys. The data users can generate trapdoors without knowing any information about the secret keys of data owners. And the indexes and trapdoors encrypted by different keys would be re-encrypted into the form under another secret key. And the results of experiment show that our scheme is quite efficient in search operation.

References

1. Liu, Y., Guo, W., Fan, C.-I., Chang, L., Cheng, C.: A practical privacy-preserving data aggregation (3PDA) scheme for smart grid. IEEE Trans. Ind. Inform. https://doi.org/10.1109/TII2018.2809672

2. Liu, Y., Zhong, Q., Chang, L., Xia, Z., He, D., Cheng, C.: A secure data backup scheme using multi-factor authentication. IET Inf. Secur. **11**(5), 250–255 (2017)

3. Song, D.X., Wagner, D., Perrig, A.: Practical techniques for searches on encrypted data. In: Security and Privacy, pp. 44–55 (2000)

4. Goh, E.-J.: Secure indexes. IACR Cryptology ePrint Archive, 216 (2013)

5. Chang, Y.-C., Mitzenmacher, M.: Privacy preserving keyword searches on remote encrypted data. In: Ioannidis, J., Keromytis, A., Yung, M. (eds.) ACNS 2005. LNCS, vol. 3531, pp. 442–455. Springer, Heidelberg (2005). https://doi.org/10.1007/11496137_30

6. Curtmola, R., Garay, J., Kamara, S., Ostrovsky, R.: Searchable symmetric encryption: improved definitions and efficient constructions. J. Comput. Secur. **19**(5), 895–934 (2011)

7. Boneh, D., Di Crescenzo, G., Ostrovsky, R., Persiano, G.: Public key encryption with keyword search. In: Cachin, C., Camenisch, J.L. (eds.) EUROCRYPT 2004. LNCS, vol. 3027, pp. 506–522. Springer, Heidelberg (2004). https://doi.org/10.1007/978-3-540-24676-3_30

8. Golle, P., Staddon, J., Waters, B.: Secure conjunctive keyword search over encrypted data. In: Jakobsson, M., Yung, M., Zhou, J. (eds.) ACNS 2004. LNCS, vol. 3089, pp. 31–45. Springer, Heidelberg (2004). https://doi.org/10.1007/978-3-540-24852-1_3

9. Ballard, L., Kamara, S., Monrose, F.: Achieving efficient conjunctive keyword searches over encrypted data. In: Qing, S., Mao, W., López, J., Wang, G. (eds.) ICICS 2005. LNCS, vol. 3783, pp. 414–426. Springer, Heidelberg (2005). https://doi.org/10.1007/11602897_35

10. Boneh, D., Waters, B.: Conjunctive, subset, and range queries on encrypted data. In: Vadhan, S.P. (ed.) TCC 2007. LNCS, vol. 4392, pp. 535–554. Springer, Heidelberg (2007). https://doi.org/10.1007/978-3-540-70936-7_29

11. Shi, E., Bethencourt, J., Chan, T.H., Song, D., Perrig, A.: Multi-dimensional range query over encrypted data. In: Security and Privacy, pp. 350–364 (2007)

12. Guo, C., Zhuang, R., Jie, Y., Ren, Y., Wu, T., Choo, K.K.R.: Fine-grained database field search using attribute-based encryption for E-healthcare clouds. J. Med. Syst. **40**(11), 235 (2016)

13. Cao, N., Wang, C., Li, M., Ren, K., Lou, W.: Privacy preserving multi-keyword ranked search over encrypted cloud data. In: IEEE INFOCOM, pp. 829–837 (2011)

14. Cao, N., Wang, C., Li, M., Ren, K., Lou, W.: Privacy preserving multi-keyword ranked search over encrypted cloud data. IEEE Trans. Parallel Distrib. Syst. **25**(1), 222–233 (2014)

15. Sun, W., et al.: Privacy-preserving multi-keyword text search in the cloud supporting similarity-based ranking. IEEE Trans. Parallel Distrib. Syst. **25**(11), 3025–3035 (2014)

16. Xia, Z., Wang, X., Sun, X., Wang, Q.: A secure and dynamic multi-keyword ranked search scheme over encrypted cloud data. IEEE Trans. Parallel Distrib. Syst. **27**(2), 340–352 (2016)

17. Orencik, C., Kantarcioglu, M., Savas, E.: A practical and secure multi-keyword search method over encrypted cloud data. In: 6th International Conference on Cloud Computing. LNCS, vol. 8201, pp. 390–397. (2013)

18. Fu, Z.J., Shu, J.G., Wang, J., Liu, Y.L., Lee, S.Y.: Privacy-preserving smart similarity search based on simhash over encrypted data in cloud computing. J. Internet Technol. **16**(3), 453–460 (2015)

19. Tao, Y., Yi, K., Sheng, C., Kalnis, P.: Quality and efficiency in high dimensional nearest neighbor search. In: ACM SIGMOD International Conference on Management of Data, pp. 563–576 (2009)
20. Wang, C., Ren, K., Yu, S., Urs, K.M.R.: Achieving usable and privacy-assured similarity search over outsourced cloud data. In: IEEE International Conference on Computer Communications, pp. 451–459 (2012)
21. Elmehdwi, Y., Samanthula, B.K., Jiang, W.: Secure k-Nearest neighbor query over encrypted data in outsourced environments. In: IEEE ICDE, pp. 664–675 (2014)
22. Yuan, X., Cui, H., Wang, X., Wang, C.: Enabling privacy-assured similarity retrieval over millions of encrypted records. In: Pernul, G., Ryan, P.Y.A., Weippl, E. (eds.) ESORICS 2015. LNCS, vol. 9327, pp. 40–60. Springer, Cham (2015). https://doi.org/10.1007/978-3-319-24177-7_3
23. Wang, B., Hou, Y., Li, M.: Practical and secure nearest neighbor search on encrypted large-scale data. In: IEEE International Conference on Computer Communications, pp. 1–9 (2016)
24. Boldyreva, A., Chenette, N., Lee, Y., O'Neill, A.: Order-preserving symmetric encryption. In: Joux, A. (ed.) EUROCRYPT 2009. LNCS, vol. 5479, pp. 224–241. Springer, Heidelberg (2009). https://doi.org/10.1007/978-3-642-01001-9_13
25. Popa, R.A., Li, F.H., Zeldovich, N.: An ideal-security protocol for order-preserving encoding. In: IEEE Symposium on Security and Privacy, pp. 463–477 (2013)
26. Zhang, W., Xiao, Y., Lin, Y., Zhou, T., Zhou, S.: Secure ranked multi-keyword search for multiple data owners in cloud computing. In: 44th Annual IEEE/IFIP International Conference on Dependable System and Networks, Atlanta, USA, pp. 276–286 (2014)
27. Zhang, W., Lin, Y., Xiao, S., Wu, J., Zhou, S.: Privacy preserving ranked multi-keyword search for multiple data owners in cloud computing. IEEE Trans. Comput. 65(5), 1566–1577 (2015)
28. Cui, H., Yuan, X., Zheng, Y., Wang, C.: Enabling secure and effective near-duplicate detection over encrypted in-network storage. In: IEEE International Conference on Computer Communications, pp. 1–9 (2016)
29. Datar, M., Immorlica, N., Indyk, P., Mirrokni, V.S.: Locality-sensitive hashing scheme based on p-stable distributions. In: 20th Symposium on Computational Geometry, pp. 253–262 (2004)

A Privacy-Preserving Classifier in Statistic Pattern Recognition

Qi Wang[1], Dehua Zhou[1(✉)], Quanlong Guan[2], Yanling Li[1], and Jimian Yang[1]

[1] Department of Computer Science, Jinan University, Guangzhou, China
{wangqi,lynn0909}@stu2016.jnu.edu.cn, tzhoudh@jnu.edu.cn,
yangjimian@stu2017.jnu.edu.cn
[2] Network and Educational Technology Center, Jinan University, Guangzhou, China
gql@jnu.edu.cn

Abstract. Machine learning classification and pattern recognition are widely used in various scenarios nowadays, such as medical diagnosis and face recognition, both need to estimate the similarity measure between different samples. In such applications, it is critical to protect the privacy of both the private input data and the machine learning model. In this paper, we propose a privacy-preserving Mahalanobis distance scheme for the statistic pattern recognition, and construct a protocol for the privacy-preserving prediction phase by using the labeled-homomorphic encryption scheme, which combines linearly homomorphic encryption and pseudo-random function. And we consider an outsouring scenario, which most work to be outsourced to the cloud server. Our design goal is to ensure that the client's private data is permanently confidential and protect the secret model in cloud server. Most of the previous work proposed complex schemes with too many interactions between the clients and cloud server, and we propose an efficient scheme to minimal the complexity of the client side.

Keywords: Classification · Homomorphic encryption
Cloud computing

1 Introduction

With the development of artificial intelligence, machine learning and pattern recognition have made impressive success in a wide range of applications, such as medical, finance and industry. For example, predict the fracture parameters of high strength and ultra-high strength concrete beams [1] and predict the compressive strength of various SCC mixes [2], both are significant to the industry. Machine learning as a service (MLaas) is accessed by an increasing number of people, in order to do better service, the machine learning service provider would like to collect more data to train a more accurate model, so it will lead to serious security risks. In 2016, Rahman et al. [3] proposed the privacy challenges in mobile-based health (mHealth), as patients using mHealth

© Springer Nature Switzerland AG 2018
X. Sun et al. (Eds.): ICCCS 2018, LNCS 11064, pp. 496–507, 2018.
https://doi.org/10.1007/978-3-030-00009-7_45

sensors to record their daily activities, it may reveal sensitive information of them. It is necessary to encrypt our records in a variety of settings, such as secure cloud computing and encrypted database search. The privacy-preserving machine learning is a hot topic nowadays, there are many schemes to solve such secure multi-party computation problems, for example, some schemes [4,5] based on garbled circuit, which is a great tool to solve secure multi-party computation problems, but not so efficient to realistic scene. Another natural way to solve such problem is to rely on homomorphic encryption schemes, informally, these are encryption mechanisms that allow one to perform meaningful operations on the plaintexts (e.g., additions or multiplications) without needing to decrypt the corresponding ciphertexts, such as Goldwasser-Micali cryptosystem [6] and Paillier's cryptosystem [7]. In 2000, Lindell [8] first proposed the cryptography-based approach for learning the decision tree with the popular ID3 algorithm over horizontally partitioned data, which utilized Yao's secure two-party computation protocol. Then, an increasing number of different privacy-preserving machine learning schemes have been proposed, such as linear regression [9,10], logistic regression [11], decision tree [12] and deep learning [13,14]. Most existing work focuses on privacy-preserving training phase, few works address the prediction phase or consider a weaker security setting in which the model user learns the model [15]. We are interested in machine learning classification algorithms for the privacy-preserving prediction phase, which the user only receives the final classification result and no sensitive individual data will be revealed while the machine learning model in the cloud server undisclosed. The classification algorithms, for example, decision tree and logistic regression, both are good classifiers in most cases. And many classifiers also perform classification by similarity measure, such as clustering and k-Nearest Neighbor. Because the Euclidean distance does not consider the correlation between each feature, we prefer the Mahalanobis distance [16], which is a similarity measure technique considering the correlation between each feature, and widely used in statistical analysis and pattern recognition classification.

In different machine learning algorithms, there are different computations with various mathematical operations, such as addition, multiplication, exponentiation and natural logarithm. To deal with these operations, we need to construct secure and efficient privacy homomorphism techniques. However, most of the homomorphic encryption methods only support one operation: addition or multiplication. The existing fully homomorphic cryptosystem [17] and the somewhat-homomorphic encryption [18] already support both addition and multiplication, but both are not so efficient for constructing a privacy-preserving machine learning protocol. In 2015, a boosting linearly-homomorphic encryption scheme [19] has been proposed, which is capable of evaluating degree-2 computations on ciphertexts by utilizing linearly-homomorphic encryption scheme. And Barbosa et al. proposed a more interesting scheme named labeled-homomorphic encryption scheme [20], which modifies the former scheme with pseudo-random function to satisfy many machine learning scenarios in encrypted domain. Based on this cryptosystem, we propose a privacy-preserving Mahalanobis distance

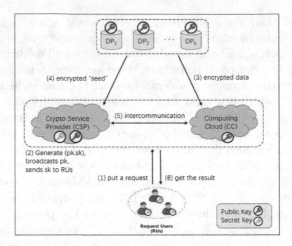

Fig. 1. System overview. The CSP initializes the encryption, RUs put a request so that DPs upload the encrypted data. Then the CC performs operations over ciphertexts. Finally, the RUs get the classification result without learning anything else.

classifier in this paper. Considering a scenario as shown in Fig. 1: assume request users (RUs) want to do classifications or statistics based on the data from data providers (DPs), but the DPs are not willing to disclose the sensitive data, then there are two non-collude servers, the crypto service provider (CSP) provides crypto service, and the computing cloud (CC) performs heavy computation, the two servers can calculate complex algorithms with the interactions, return the classification result to RUs in the end. Here, we can assume that the whole input data may from one or more providers, formally, it is a vertically partitioned data. In our scheme, it is easy to extend only one data provider to multiple providers. So for the sake of simplicity, we design the privacy-preserving protocol considering only one data provider.

The rest of this paper is organized as follows. In Sect. 2, we discuss the related work about the privacy-preserving machine learning and pattern recognition. Section 3 is dedicated to some preliminaries we will used in our work. Then the privacy-preserving system architecture is proposed in Sect. 4. Section 5 shows the security analysis. And the system evaluation will be given in Sect. 6. Followed by conclusion and future work in Sect. 7.

2   Related Work

Recently, many outsourced privacy-preserving machine learning schemes have been proposed. Grapel et al. [14] utilized a somewhat homomorphic encryption scheme to train several machine learning classifiers, but which is inefficient for the real application. And Nikolaenko et al. [10] presented a privacy-preserving ridge regression protocol, combines linearly-homomorphic encryption and Yao's garbled circuits, in their setting, the computations are outsourced to two non-collude

third parties, their scheme offers the practical advantage that the involvement
of data-owners is minimal: they just need to submit their private data and do
not participate in any further interaction. Our goal is also to minimal the work
of data providers, and outsourced most of the work to the third parties, but in
our scenario, we would like to do the privacy-preserving Mahalanobis distance
utilize only linearly-homomorphic encryption. Most of the privacy-preserving
machine learning algorithms can be simplified and then transfer to "ciphertext
multiplication": Given two ciphertexts $Enc(m_1)$ and $Enc(m_2)$, the goal is to
get the ciphertext $Enc(m_1 \cdot m_2)$. So as the Mahalanobis distance. The Mahalanobis distance is widely used in statistical analysis and pattern recognition
classification, we think it is meaningful to do some research on it. Zhu et al.
[21] proposed the privacy-preserving multiply to add protocol ($PPMtAP$), if
Alice and Bob respectively have private number x and y, and they share the
secret $s = x \cdot y$, using the $PPMtAP$, they can change the sharing form from
multiplying ($s = x \cdot y$) to adding ($s = u + v$). This protocol was applied to the
privacy-preserving ID3 data mining [22], but which is not efficient for practical
use because of the heavy communication. And there are some privacy-preserving
machine learning protocols constructed by using secret sharing [23] based on the
multiplication triplets, for this method, generating the desired shared multiplication triplets is a heavy work which is precomputed by two non-collude cloud
servers, but for the following machine learning protocol, it is also a drawback
because of too many times interactions. So we would like to construct a protocol
which reduces the communication between each parties. Stan et al. [24] apply the
basic Gaussian classifier to the smart cities by using the Paillier's cryptosystem
and BGV encryption scheme, but the main drawback of the former is the communication overhead induced by sending the quadratic terms from the client to
the server, for the latter, a Ring-LWE-based scheme which is more complex but
with more computing capabilities and quantum-safe. Both of these are not suitable for the real scene. In this paper, we propose an efficient privacy-preserving
Mahalanobis distance classifier using only linearly-homomorphic encryption that
needs less interactions between data providers and cloud services.

3 Preliminaries

3.1 Mahalanobis Distance

The Mahalanobis distance (MD) is the distance between two points in multivariate space, introduced by P.C.Mahalanobis in 1936. The MD takes into account
the correlation in the data, since it is calculated by using the inverse of the covariance matrix of the dataset. We consider a dataset X consisting of d-dimensional
feature vectors and a labeled vector, each sample is assumed characterized by a
Gaussian distribution with a mean μ_i and a covariance matrix S_i. In order to use
the Mahalanobis distance to classify a test point into one of N classes, one first
estimates the covariance matrix of each class, then computes the Mahalanobis
distance to each class, and classifies the test point to the class for which the
Mahalanobis distance is minimal.

The mean μ_i of a class C_i is a vector $\mu_i^T = [\mu_{i_1}, \mu_{i_2}, \mu_{i_3}, \cdots, \mu_{i_d}]$ with $\mu_i = \frac{\Sigma_{j=1}^k x(j)}{k}$, for the sample $x(j)$ belongs to class C_j.

The covariance matrix S of a class C_i is a $d \times d$ dimension matrix which is computed as: $S_{ij} = c(a, b)$ with $a, b \in \{1, 2, \cdots, d\}$, and $c(a, b)$ is the covariance between the features a and b.

The Mahalanobis distance of an observation $\boldsymbol{x} = (x_1, x_2, x_3, \ldots, x_N)^T$ from a set of observations with mean $\boldsymbol{\mu} = (\mu_1, \mu_2, \mu_3, \ldots, \mu_N)^T$ and covariance matrix S is defined as:

$$D_{\mathrm{M}}(\boldsymbol{x}) = \sqrt{(\boldsymbol{x} - \boldsymbol{\mu})^T S^{-1}(\boldsymbol{x} - \boldsymbol{\mu})}. \tag{1}$$

For convenience, we usually compute the following algorithm:

$$D_{\mathrm{M}}^2(\boldsymbol{x}) = (\boldsymbol{x} - \boldsymbol{\mu})^T S^{-1}(\boldsymbol{x} - \boldsymbol{\mu}). \tag{2}$$

So a feature vector $\boldsymbol{x}$ is thus classified by measuring a Mahalanobis distance from $\boldsymbol{x}$ to each of the classes and then select the minimal one. As you can see, while the covariance matrix is the identity matrix, the Mahalanobis distance equals to the Euclidean distance.

3.2 Labeled-Homomorphic Encryption

Barbosa et al. [20] introduced the new primitive "labeled-homomorphic encryption", which accelerates the computation over encrypted data. The cryptosystem encrypts a message $m \in \mathcal{M}$ via two-component ciphertext $(m - b, Enc(b))$, b is calculated by PRF under the corresponding label.

A general homomorphic encryption scheme often consists four algorithms: $KeyGen$, Enc, $Eval$ and Dec. Without loss of generality, we assume $Eval$ consists of two subroutines: one to perform homomorphic addition (Add) and another to perform homomorphic multiplication by known constants ($cMult$). We denote these operations with $\odot$ and $\cdot$. Namely, given two ciphertexts c_1 and c_2, $c = c_1 \odot c_2$ denotes homomorphic addition, and $c = a \cdot c_1$ denotes a multiplication by a constant a.

Here, we briefly recall the construction of the labeled-homomorphic encryption (labHE) cryptosystem for a quadratic functions by using linearly homomorphic encryption schemes, such as Paillier scheme [7].

$KeyGen(\kappa)$: Given the security parameter κ, outputs (pk, sk'), then chooses a random seed $K \in \{0, 1\}^k$ for the PRF, so the $sk = (sk', K)$, this algorithm outputs the key pair (pk, sk).

$labEnc(pk, K, m, \tau)$: To encrypt a message $m \in \mathcal{M}$ with label $\tau \in \{0, 1\}^*$, computes $b \leftarrow F(K, \tau)$ and outputs the ciphertext $C = (a, \beta) = (m - b, Enc_{\mathrm{pk}}(b))$.

$labEval$: This algorithm is composed of three different operations: Add, $cMult$ and $Mult$. Without loss of generality, we compactly denote the homomorphic addition with $\odot$, and denote the homomorphic multiplication by a known constant with $\cdot$.

Add: Input two ciphertexts $C_1 = (a_1, \beta_1), C_2 = (a_2, \beta_2)$, return a new ciphertext:

$$C = (a, \beta) = (a_1 + a_2, \beta_1 \odot \beta_2) = (a_1 + a_2, Enc_{\text{pk}}(b_1 + b_2)) .$$

cMult: Input a ciphertext $C = (a, \beta)$ and a known constant c, return a new ciphertext as follows:

$$C' = (a \cdot c, c \cdot \beta) = (a \cdot c, Enc_{\text{pk}}(c \cdot b)) .$$

Mult: Input two ciphertexts $C_1 = (a_1, \beta_1), C_2 = (a_2, \beta_2)$, return a "multiplication" ciphertext as follows:

$$C = Enc_{\text{pk}}(a_1 \cdot a_2) \odot cMult(a_1, \beta_2) \odot cMult(a_2, \beta_1)$$
$$= Enc_{\text{pk}}(m_1 \cdot m_2 - b_1 \cdot b_2).$$

labDec(sk, C): Input the general ciphertext C and sk, first decrypt the second component of the ciphertext $b \leftarrow Dec_{\text{sk}}(Enc_{\text{pk}}(b))$, then use the known b, the one can recover the correct message $m \leftarrow a + b$. For the "Add" ciphertext, one should first recover $b_1 + b_2$, then get the original plaintext. And for the "Mult" ciphertext, one should first recover $b_1 \cdot b_2$, then get the original plaintext.

4   Privacy-Preserving System Architecture

4.1   General Description

We propose the privacy-preserving minimum Mahalanobis distance from "distance metric learning", which is assumed that the model has already learned from the plaintext. The figure gives the detail description of our scenario, our goal is to privately get the classification result corresponds to x using this model. And we want to protect the data x from DPs, while also undisclose the information about model(S, μ) owned by CC. In the case of this classifier, each class C_j from the m classes defined during the training phase is assumed characterized by a Gaussian distribution with a mean μ_i and a covariance matrix S_i.

The goal of this classifier is to compute the following algorithm:

$$\begin{aligned} min(D_M^2(x, C_i)) &= (x - \mu_i)^T S_i^{-1}(x - \mu_i) \\ &= x^T S_i^{-1} x - 2\mu_i^T S_i^{-1} x + \mu_i^T S_i^{-1} \mu_i. \end{aligned} \tag{3}$$

In our scenario, the CC precomputes $S_i' = S_i^{-1}$, then $\mu_i^T S_i^{-1} \mu_i$ can be locally computed, the term $\mu_i^T S_i^{-1} x$ could be calculated by using additively homomorphic encryption. To calculate $x^T S_i^{-1} x$, we can simplify this term as follows:

$$x^T S_i' x = \sum_{i=1}^{n} \sum_{j=1}^{n} x_i x_j s_{ij}'. \tag{4}$$

Protocol 1. Privacy-preserving multiplication over two encrypted data
1. CSP generates (pk, sk), privately send sk to RU, and broadcast pk. In the meanwhile, share a PRF with DP.

1. CSP generates (pk, sk), privately send sk to RU, and broadcast pk. In the meanwhile, share a PRF with DP.
2. RU put a request to the CC, then CC will collects the distributed data from DP.
3. DP generates a random seed $s_i \in \{0, 1\}$, and then calculates $t_i = Enc_{pk}(s_i)$, send t_i to CSP.
4. For different plaintext m_i (here is the feature value), corresponds a different label τ_i, compute $b_i = PRF(s_i, \tau_i)$, then using the labeled homomorphic encryption, output the ciphertext $C_i = (m_i - b_i, Enc_{pk}(b_i))$.
5. When CC received the ciphertexts C_1 and C_2, he performs the labMul algorithm, gets the result $Enc_{pk}(m_1 \cdot m_2 - b_1 \cdot b_2)$.
6. When CSP received the t_i from DPs, he decrypts it to get s_i, then recovers the b_i, and computes $b_1 \cdot b_2$, encrypts it and sends to CC.
7. CC then calculates two ciphertexts to get the result $Enc_{pk}(m_1 \cdot m_2)$.

So the major problem is reduced to compute the $Enc(x_i \cdot x_j)$, there are two solutions: one is the DP first computes the $x_i \cdot x_j$, then encrypts it, sends all the encrypted data to cloud; another solution is DP provides the $Enc(x_i)$ and $Enc(x_j)$, then cloud performs calculations over encrypted data to get $Enc(x_i \cdot x_j)$. The former needs DP to do lots of computations, and will produce more communication, so we prefer the second solution, which the heavy computations are outsourced to cloud service. In next section, we will show how to apply the labHE scheme to solve this issue.

4.2 Computing the Mahalanobis Distance in the Encrypted-Domain

In this section, in order to compute the encrypted term $Enc(x_i \cdot x_j)$ by the given two ciphertexts $Enc(x_i)$ and $Enc(x_j)$, we construct a protocol for the multiplication over two encrypted data. In protocol 1, we assume the data all from the same data provider, but the whole data may from different data providers, so we just need to modify the step 3 in protocol 1: each of DPs generates different random seed, and sends to the CSP in encrypted form. While the labeled-homomorphic encryption is semantically-secure, then our protocol is secure.

By using the protocol 1 repeatedly, the CC will get all the ciphertexts of $x_i \cdot x_j$, then perform the $cMult$ algorithm and Add algorithm, the CC could get the final results of the Mahalanobis distance of each class, which are in encrypted form. To handle these encrypted data ($[\![d_1]\!], [\![d_2]\!], \cdots, [\![d_n]\!]$), then what we want to do is just finding out the minimum one from these ciphertexts. So in next section, we propose a protocol to find the minimal in encrypted data by modifying the protocol in [25].

4.3 Obtaining the Classification Result

Until now, there are many works about comparing encrypted data, like Bost et al. [25] and Veugen's protocol [26]. We describe a suitable building block

Protocol 2. argmin over encrypted data

Setup: CSP holds the secret key (SK_P, SK_{QR}), CC holds the public key (PK_P, PK_{QR}), RU only holds the SK_P

Input: CC input the ciphertext $(\llbracket d_1 \rrbracket, \llbracket d_2 \rrbracket, \cdots, \llbracket d_n \rrbracket)$

Output: the $argmin_i(\llbracket d_i \rrbracket)$

  1. CC: choose a random permutation π over $\{1, \cdots, n\}$, let $\llbracket min \rrbracket \leftarrow \llbracket d_{\pi(1)} \rrbracket$

  2. CSP: $m \leftarrow 1$

  3. for i = 2 to n do

  4.   Using the comparison protocol([25]), CSP gets the bit $b_i = (min \leq d_{\pi(i)})$

  5.   CC : choose two random integers r_i, s_i

  6.   CC : $\llbracket m_i' \rrbracket \leftarrow \llbracket min \rrbracket \cdot \llbracket r_i \llbracket$

  7.   CC : $\llbracket a_i' \rrbracket \leftarrow \llbracket d_{\pi(1)} \rrbracket \cdot \llbracket s_i \rrbracket$

  8.   CC sends $\llbracket m_i' \rrbracket$ and $\llbracket a_i' \rrbracket$ to CSP

  9.   if b_i is False then

10.   CSP : $m \leftarrow i$

11.   CSP : $\llbracket v_i \rrbracket \leftarrow Refresh\llbracket a_i' \rrbracket$

12.   else

13.   CSP : $\llbracket v_i \rrbracket \leftarrow Refresh\llbracket m_i' \rrbracket$

14.   end if

15.   CSP sends $\llbracket v_i \rrbracket$ and $\llbracket b_i \rrbracket$ to CC

16.   CC : $\llbracket min \rrbracket \leftarrow \llbracket v_i \rrbracket \cdot (g^{-1} \cdot \llbracket b_i \rrbracket)^{s_i} \cdot \llbracket b_i \rrbracket^{-r_i}$

17. end for

18. CSP sends $Enc(m)$ to RU

19. RU decrypt to recover m, then output $\pi^{-1}(m)$

referred to [25]: party A inputs $(PK_P, PK_{QR}, \llbracket a \rrbracket, \llbracket b \rrbracket)$ and party B inputs (SK_P, SK_{QR}), the protocol outputs A with $\llbracket a \leq b \rrbracket$ and B with $a \leq b$. We denote a bit b encrypted under the Quadratic Residuosity (QR) cryptosystem by $[b]$, and denote an integer m encrypted under Paillier's cryptosystem by $\llbracket m \rrbracket$.

We also modify the argmax protocol in [25] to appropriate our scenario, and construct the protocol 2. The main idea is: First, to prevent CSP from learning the order of these values, CC shares the permutation with RU, then CC and CSP perform the comparison protocol by interactions, at the end of this protocol, the CSP returns the result to RU in encrypted form, RU performs decryption and the inverse permutation to get the correct result. While all these parties are semi-honest, there are no extra information disclosed.

The correctness of protocol 2 is straightforward, so we argue the security: since CC applied a random permutation, CSP does not learn the ordering of the values, and at each iteration, CSP randomize the encryption of the minimum so that CC can not link this value to one of the values compared, and because CSP holds the SK_P, so CC add noise to $\llbracket a_i' \rrbracket$, thus, decryption at CSP yields random values. After the comparison of all values, CSP gets the encrypted "minimum index" (not the correct result), then sends it to RU, RU decrypts and performs the inverse permutation to get the final result. At the end of this protocol, each party learns no useful information.

5 Security Analysis

5.1 Security of the Encryption Scheme

In this section, we briefly describe the semantic security of labeled-homomorphic encryption scheme, for more details, please see the original paper [20].

The labeled-homomorphic encryption scheme is always semantic security, since the ciphertext $(m - b, Enc(b))$ contains two components, in which b is the pseudo-random number generated by PRF, it is computationally indistinguishable from the original one. Notice that

$$(m_0 - b_0, Enc(pk, b_0)) \approx (m_0 - b_0, Enc(pk, 0))$$
$$\equiv (m_1 - b_1, Enc(pk, 0)) \approx (m_1 - b_1, Enc(pk, b_1)).$$

where $\approx$ denotes computational indistinguishability by the semantic security of homomorphic encryption and $\equiv$ means that the distributions are identical.

5.2 Security of Our Protocol

Generally speaking, while the CSP and CC are semi-honest (honest but curious), they do not collude with each other, our scheme can guarantee privacy. But if the CSP and CC are malicious, the "two-server labeled-homomorphic encryption scheme" is not secure anymore, then all the encrypted input data will be recovered, so we emphasize that both servers are semi-honest is an important assumption in our scheme. For the security of our protocols, they are always secure as long as the labeled-homomorphic encryption is semantically-secure.

Then we analyze the privacy preserving in our scheme, since CC does not know the secret key, he cannot learn any useful information about the private input data from the original ciphertexts, and while interacting with the CSP, both parties are semi-honest, so he also learns nothing. For the CSP, even he holds the secret key, he has no channel to get the original encrypted data, for the DP uploads the data to CC by a secure channel (e.g. SSL/TLS), so he learns nothing about the input data. And we have analyzed the protocol 2 in Sect. 4.3, each of the parties only learns some useless information, and the RU will learn the correct classification result. For the security of PRF, you will not know the function result if you do not know the random seed, so only the CSP can recover the PRF result by decrypting the encrypted seed in our scheme, which will be used in the later calculations. After performing all the protocols, only the RU gets the correct classification result and learns no sensitive information. In conclusion, both the private input data and the machine learning model have been protected under the semi-honest setting. As for malicious scenario, we will consider it in our future work.

6 Evaluation

The main idea of our scheme is an outsourcing service, which most of the computation tasks are outsourced to the cloud server who has the unlimited computing and storage resources. In previous works, many schemes [12, 25] consider the setting that only one client inputs the data and one cloud server who holds the model to perform the machine learning prediction. In their prediction phase, the client needs to be online all the time, there are many interactions between the cloud server and the client. But in our "two-cloud servers" model, the client does not need to keep online, the only thing he needs to do is to encrypt and upload the private data, the later calculations and interactions will be transferred to the two cloud servers.

In our scheme, the data provider (DP) only does little work: first generates a random PRF seed and then encrypts and uploads the data. And for the request user (RU), all he needs to do is submit a request and wait for the encrypted classification result, then decrypts it. The two cloud servers afford nearly all of the computations and communications, this is the goal of our outsourcing system. In general, the non-cryptographic operations do not incur much computation overhead as compared to the cryptographic operations, so we are interested in comparing against cryptographic operations. In Table 1, we give the computation cost and communication cost for the data provider(s) in our scheme and some other schemes. We assume the input data consists of d features, and the model with m classes.

What is more, our scheme can be easily extended, while extending our scheme from one data provider to multiple data providers, only needs each data provider to send his encrypted random seed of PRF to CSP, the whole communication cost and computation cost only change a little, which nearly does no impact on overall performance.

Table 1. The costs of Data Provider(s)

	Computation cost	Communication cost
Our scheme	$\circ(d)$ encryption	$\circ(d)$ ciphertexts
[12, 25]	$\circ(d^2)$ encryption	$\circ(d^2)$ ciphertexts
	$\circ(m)$ homomorphic addition	$\circ(m)$ interactions

7   Conclusion and Future Work

In this paper, we present an efficient privacy-preserving scheme for the Mahalanobis distance which is widely used in machine learning classification and pattern recognition. Our scheme can protect the privacy of both the private input data and the machine learning model. Considering that the limited computation resources of clients, most of the works are outsourced to the cloud servers. We designed a protocol for only one data provider in this paper, but it is very easy to extend to multiple data providers, as we have explained before. The complexity analysis shows that our scheme is suitable for the outsourcing service.

Moreover, it is easy to extend our protocols to other privacy-preserving machine learning algorithms, as a future work, we will extend our research to more complex machine learning algorithms, such as k-means clustering and principal component analysis. And we are also working on other homomorphic cryptosystems and more efficient comparison protocols for a better performance.

Acknowledgements. This work is supported by NSFC (61602210), Science and Technology Project of Guangzhou City (No. 201707010320), Natural Science Foundation of Guangdong Province (No. 2014A030310156), the Fundamental Research Funds for the Central Universities (21617408), the Science and Technology Planning Project of Guangdong Province, China (2014A040401027, 2015A030401043, 2017A040405029).

References

1. Shah, V.S., Shah, H.R., Samui, P., Ramachandra Murthy, A.: Prediction of fracture parameters of high strength and ultra-high strength concrete beams using minimax probability machine regression and extreme learning machine. Comput. Mater. Continua **44**(2), 73–84 (2014)
2. Jayaprakash, G., Muthuraj, M.P.: Prediction of compressive strength of various SCC mixes using relevance vector machine. Comput. Mater. Continua **54**(1), 83–102 (2015)
3. Rahman, F., Addo, I.D., Ahamed, S.I., Yang, J.J., Wang, Q.: Privacy challenges and goals in mHealth systems. In: Advances in Computers (2016)
4. Yao, A.C.: Protocols for secure computations. In: Proceedings of the IEEE Symposium on Foundations of Computer Science, pp. 160–164 (1982)
5. Goldreich, O., Micali, S., Wigderson, A.: How to play any mental game. In: Nineteenth ACM Symposium on Theory of Computing, pp. 218–229 (1987)
6. Goldwasser, S., Micali, S.: Probabilistic encryption. J. Comput. Syst. Sci. **28**(2), 270–299 (1984)
7. Paillier, P.: Public-key cryptosystems based on composite degree residuosity classes. In: International Conference on Theory and Application of Cryptographic Techniques, pp. 223–238 (1999)
8. Lindell, Y., Pinkas, B.: Privacy preserving data mining. Adv. Cryptol. **15**(3), 177–206 (2000)
9. Gascn, A., et al.: Privacy-preserving distributed linear regression on high-dimensional data, vol. 2017, no. 4, pp. 345–364 (2017)
10. Nikolaenko, V., Weinsberg, U., Ioannidis, S., Joye, M., Dan, B., Taft, N.: Privacy-preserving ridge regression on hundreds of millions of records. In: Security and Privacy, pp. 334–348 (2013)
11. Aono, Y., Hayashi, T., Trieu Phong, L., Wang, L.: Scalable and secure logistic regression via homomorphic encryption, vol. 22, no. 1, pp. 142–144 (2016)
12. Wu, D.J., Feng, T., Naehrig, M., Lauter, K.: Privately evaluating decision trees and random forests. In: Proceedings on Privacy Enhancing Technologies 2016, no. 4 (2016)
13. Shokri, R., Shmatikov, V.: Privacy-preserving deep learning. In: ACM SIGSAC Conference on Computer and Communications Security, pp. 1310–1321 (2015)
14. Graepel, T., Lauter, K., Naehrig, M.: ML confidential: machine learning on encrypted data. In: Kwon, T., Lee, M.-K., Kwon, D. (eds.) ICISC 2012. LNCS, vol. 7839, pp. 1–21. Springer, Heidelberg (2013). https://doi.org/10.1007/978-3-642-37682-5_1

15. Bos, J.W., Lauter, K., Naehrig, M.: Private predictive analysis on encrypted medical data. J. Biomed. Inf. **50**(8), 234–243 (2014)
16. De Maesschalck, R., Jouan-Rimbaud, D., Massart, D.L.: The mahalanobis distance. Chemom. Intell. Lab. Syst. **50**(1), 1–18 (2000)
17. Gentry, C.: Fully homomorphic encryption using ideal lattices. In: ACM Symposium on Theory of Computing. STOC 2009, 31 May–June, Bethesda, MD, USA, pp. 169–178 (2009)
18. Brakerski, Z., Gentry, C., Vaikuntanathan, V.: (Leveled) fully homomorphic encryption without bootstrapping. In: Innovations in Theoretical Computer Science Conference, pp. 309–325 (2012)
19. Catalano, D., Fiore, D.: Using linearly-homomorphic encryption to evaluate degree-2 functions on encrypted data. In: ACM SIGSAC Conference on Computer and Communications Security, pp. 1518–1529 (2015)
20. Barbosa, M., Catalano, D., Fiore, D.: Labeled homomorphic encryption. In: Foley, S.N., Gollmann, D., Snekkenes, E. (eds.) ESORICS 2017. LNCS, vol. 10492, pp. 146–166. Springer, Cham (2017). https://doi.org/10.1007/978-3-319-66402-6_10
21. Zhu, Y., Huang, L., Yang, W., Li, D., Luo, Y., Dong, F.: Three new approaches to privacy-preserving add to multiply protocol and its application. In: Second International Workshop on Knowledge Discovery and Data Mining, pp. 554–558 (2009)
22. Li, Y., Jiang, Z.L., Wang, X., Yiu, S.M.: Privacy-preserving ID3 data mining over encrypted data in outsourced environments with multiple keys. In: IEEE International Conference on Computational Science and Engineering, pp. 548–555 (2017)
23. Mohassel, P., Zhang, Y.: SecureML: a system for scalable privacy-preserving machine learning. In: Security and Privacy, pp. 19–38 (2017)
24. Stan, O., Zayani, M.-H., Sirdey, R., Hamida, A.B., Leite, A.F., Mziou-Sallami, M.: A new crypto-classifier service for energy efficiency in smart cities. Cryptology ePrint Archive, Report 2017/1212 (2017). https://eprint.iacr.org/2017/1212
25. Bost, R., Popa, R.A., Tu, S., Goldwasser, S.: Machine learning classification over encrypted data. In: Network and Distributed System Security Symposium (2015)
26. Veugen, T.: Comparing encrypted data (2011)

A Robust Algorithm of Encrypted Face Recognition Based on DWT-DCT and Tent Map

Tong Xiao[1,2], Jingbing Li[1,2(✉)], Jing Liu[1,2], Jieren Cheng[1,2], and Uzair Aslam Bhatti[1,2]

[1] College of Information Science and Technology, Hainan University, Haikou 570228, China
xiaotong920923@sina.com, jingbingli2008@hotmail.com, jingliuhnu2016@hotmail.com, uzairaslambhatti@hotmail.com, cjr22@163.com
[2] State Key Laboratory of Marine Resource Utilization in the South China Sea, Hainan University, Haikou 570228, China

Abstract. With the progress of the Internet and the development of science and technology, face recognition technology is becoming more and more mature, has been paid more and more attention and application in the fields of monitoring, finance and information security. Compare with the traditional authentication methods, face recognition technology is more stable. However, the information data of face recognition system is still stored in the Internet, and may be attacked by hackers, resulting in the disclosure of personal privacy and data security issues. Therefore, this paper proposes a robust algorithm of encrypted face recognition based on DWT (Discrete Wavelet Transform) and DCT (Discrete Cosine Transform) and Tent Map. Firstly, by using Tent Map we generate pseudo-random sequences and encrypt face image in DWT-DCT domain. Then, combine PCA (Principal Component Analysis) and BP neural network to realize face recognition. Finally, we test the robustness by conventional attack and geometric attack and occlusion attack. The results of simulation experiment on ORL face database show that the recognition rate of this algorithm is higher than of unencrypted algorithm, at the same time, this algorithm can effectively protect the personal information security through encryption, and it has strong robustness and has wide application prospects.

Keywords: Face recognition · DWT-DCT encrypted domain · Tent Map
BP neural network · Robustness

1 Introduction

Face recognition technology mainly uses the uniqueness and discernibility of its biological features to complete the identification. Compared with the traditional authentication methods such as signature, secret key and document, face recognition technology is more secure and reliable. Therefore, it has broad application prospects in many fields like information security, surveillance and other field [1–3]. In recent years,

© Springer Nature Switzerland AG 2018
X. Sun et al. (Eds.): ICCCS 2018, LNCS 11064, pp. 508–518, 2018.
https://doi.org/10.1007/978-3-030-00009-7_46

the research on face recognition has achieved enormous results, but the corresponding research on the security and privacy of the original image data has not been accordingly developed. Once the original image is leaked, it is a permanent leak, which is more harmfulness than the traditional way of verification [4–6].

In the 1990s, Turk and Pentlad proposed the PCA algorithm, which transforms the original data into a set of linearly irrelevant representations of each dimension through linear transformation, PCA uses the features of less data to describe the samples to achieve the purpose of dimensionality reduction [7]. Rivest et al. proposed the idea of homomorphic encryption in 1978, and Gentry et al. proposed the first fully homo-morphic encryption scheme, which can operate on the encrypted data without leakage of the original data, and the decrypted data has the same result as the data before encryption. This ensures the security of raw data and is widely used in the storage of cloud data [8–12]. Paillier encryption is a homomorphic encryption that satisfies the homomorphisms of addition and multiplication. The DWT and DCT encryption domains are a secure signal processing technique based on Paillier encryption [13]. The artificial neural network has strong self-learning and self-adaptive ability, which is widely used in face recognition technology, but it can't recognize the encrypted images only by using neural network [14]. In this paper, we propose a robust face recognition algorithm based on DWT-DCT and Tent Map. This algorithm encrypts the image in DWT-DCT transform domain and then uses PCA to extract the encrypted image features combined with BP neural network to realize face recognition.

2 The Fundamental Theory

2.1 Discrete Wavelet Transform (DWT)

Discrete wavelet transform can decompose the wavelet at different scales. The low frequency part contains the main features of information, and the high frequency mainly contains the details of the information. Two-dimensional discrete wavelet transform (2D-DWT) decomposes the digital image into low frequency in horizontal and vertical directions (LL), low frequency in the horizontal and high frequency in the vertical direction (LH), high frequency in the horizontal and low frequency in the vertical direction (HL), and high frequency in horizontal and vertical directions (HH). The one-dimensional inverse discrete wavelet transform is carried out for each column of the decomposed result, and one-dimensional inverse discrete wavelet transform is performed on each row of the transform result to acquire a reconstructed image. To perform multilevel decomposition, it is repeatedly transformed on LL, the image of the first person in the ORL after two decomposition as shown in Fig. 1.

Mallat wavelet decomposition formula is defined as follows:

$$\begin{cases} c_{j+1,k} = \sum_{n \in Z} c_{j,n} \bar{h}_{n-2k} & k \in Z \\ d_{j+1,k} = \sum_{n \in Z} c_{j,n} \bar{g}_{n-2k} & k \in Z \end{cases} \tag{1}$$

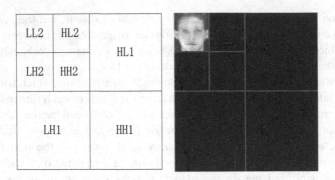

Fig. 1. Two decomposition of discrete wavelet

In order to reconstruct the signal f (t), the reconstruction formula is defined as follows:

$$c_{j,k} = \sum_{n \in Z} c_{j+1,n} h_{k-2n} + \sum_{n \in Z} d_{j+1,n} g_{k-2n} \qquad k \in Z \qquad (2)$$

In this paper, we adopt the 'db2' wavelet.

2.2 Discrete Cosine Transform (DCT)

Discrete cosine transform has a strong energy concentration characteristic, most of the signal energy after discrete cosine transform concentrated in the low frequency part. Two-dimensional Discrete cosine transform is widely used in image processing. If the size of the image is M × N, f (x, y) is the sampling value in the spatial domain and F (u, v) is the corresponding value in the frequency domain, the discrete cosine transform and inverse discrete cosine transform (IDCT) formulas are defined as follows:

$$F(u,v) = c(u)c(v) \sum_{x=0}^{M-1} \sum_{y=0}^{N-1} f(x,y) \cos \frac{(2x+1)u\pi}{2M} \cos \frac{(2y+1)v\pi}{2N} \qquad (3)$$

$$f(x,y) = \sum_{x=0}^{M-1} \sum_{y=0}^{N-1} c(u)c(v)F(u,v) \cos \frac{(2x+1)u\pi}{2M} \cos \frac{(2y+1)v\pi}{2N} \qquad (4)$$

$$c(u) = \begin{cases} \sqrt{1/M} & u = 0 \\ \sqrt{2/M} & u \neq 0 \end{cases} \quad c(v) = \begin{cases} \sqrt{1/N} & v = 0 \\ \sqrt{2/N} & v \neq 0 \end{cases}$$

Where x, y is the spatial domain sampling; μ, v is the frequency domain sampling value. x = 0, 1……M − 1, y = 0, 1……N − 1.

2.3 Tent Map

Tent mapping has the characteristics of good pseudo randomicity, sensitivity to the initial state and unpredictable orbits, which can be directly used to encrypt information [15]. The equation is defined as follows:

$$x_{k+1} = \begin{cases} \frac{x_k}{\alpha} & 0 \le x_k \le \alpha \\ \frac{1-x_k}{1-\alpha} & \alpha \le x_k \le 1 \end{cases} \tag{5}$$

When $\alpha \in (0, 1)$, Tent Map is in a chaotic state with a uniform distribution function on [0,1], and the chaotic sequence generated by the map had good statistical properties. When $\alpha = 1/2$, this is the famous triangle tent map, the corresponding equation is as follow:

$$x_k + 1 = \begin{cases} 2x_k & 0 \le x_k \le 1/2 \\ 2(1 - x_k) & 1/2 \le x_k \le 1 \end{cases} \tag{6}$$

The Tent Map at this time is topologically conjugated with the Logistic Map, and Tent Map has faster iteration speed and better ergodic uniformity than the Logistic Map [16].

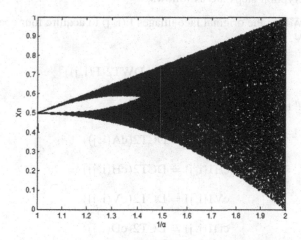

Fig. 2. Bifurcation plot of Tent Map

When $x_0 \in (0, 1)$, $1/2 \le \alpha < 1$, the Bifurcation plot of Tent Map as shown in Fig. 2.

2.4 Back Propagation (BP) Neural Network

BP neural network is widely used in the fields of data mining and pattern recognition. It is a kind of Multi-layered Feed forward network fashioned according to error back propagation algorithm. The back propagation is used to regulate the weight value and threshold value of the network in achieving the minimum error sum of square. The topological structure model as shown in Fig. 3, mainly includes the input layer, hidden layer and output layer.

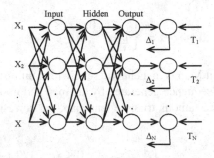

Fig. 3. BP neural network structure model

3   The Algorithm Process and Encryption Steps

In order to prevent the original image database from being leaked, we need to encrypt it. The main encryption steps are as follows:

(a) Perform DWT on the original face images F(i, j) to acquire four coefficient matrix [cA, cH, cV, cD];

$$[cA, cH, cV, cD] = DWT2(F(i,j)) \tag{7}$$

(b) Apply DCT to the four coefficient matrix;

$$cA1(i,j) = DCT2(cA(i,j)) \tag{8}$$

$$cH1(i,j) = DCT2(cH(i,j)) \tag{9}$$

$$cV1(i,j) = DCT2(cV(i,j)) \tag{10}$$

$$cD1(i,j) = DCT2(cD(i,j)) \tag{11}$$

(c) Set the original X0 = 0.225, Tent Map Chaotic system uses x0 to generate chaotic sequence b(j);

(d) Define a two value symbolic function Sign(i), and then construct a two valued matrix Sign(b(j)) according to the size of the image in the database, $1 \leq i \leq M, 1 \leq j \leq N$;

$$Sign(b(j)) = \begin{cases} 1 & b(j) \geq 0.5 \\ -1 & b(j) < 0.5 \end{cases} \tag{12}$$

(e) Do a dot multiplication operation with a binary matrix Sign(b(j));

$$cA2(i,j) = cA1(i,j). * Sign(b(j)) \tag{13}$$

$$cH2(i,j) = cH1(i,j). * Sign(b(j)) \tag{14}$$

$$cV2(i,j) = cV1(i,j). * Sign(b(j)) \tag{15}$$

$$cD2(i,j) = cD1(i,j). * Sign(b(j)) \tag{16}$$

(f) Perform inverse DCT (IDCT) on each sub-matrix;

$$cA3(i,j) = IDCT2(cA2(i,j)) \tag{17}$$

$$cH3(i,j) = IDCT2(cH2(i,j)) \tag{18}$$

$$cV3(i,j) = IDCT2(cV2(i,j)) \tag{19}$$

$$cD3(i,j) = IDCT2(cD2(i,j)) \tag{20}$$

(g) Perform inverse DWT(IDWT) on the reconstructed coefficients to acquire the encrypted face images E(i,j).

$$E(i,j) = IDWT2[cA3, cH3, cV3, cD3] \tag{21}$$

We used the first facial expression face of the first ten person in the ORL database as an example, before the encrypted images are shown in Fig. 4(a)–(j) and after the encrypted of the images are shown in Fig. 5(a)–(j).

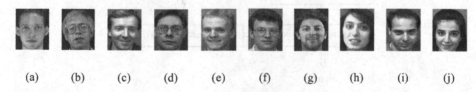

(a)   (b)   (c)   (d)   (e)   (f)   (g)   (h)   (i)   (j)

Fig. 4. The images are before encryption

From the Figs. 4 and 5, we can see that the image after encryption has a good quality, and we won't be able to distinguish the original image.

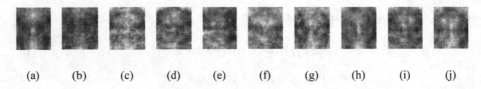

(a)   (b)   (c)   (d)   (e)   (f)   (g)   (h)   (i)   (j)

Fig. 5. The images are after encryption

The algorithm process described in detail as follows:

Step 1: Encrypt the original image database.
Step 2: Use PCA extract each encrypted image feature to acquire projection matrix.
Step 3: Create and train neural networks.
Step 4: Encrypt face image F(j) to acquire the encrypted face image E(j).
Step 5: Projecting E(j) onto the projection matrix to acquire feature matrix V(j).
Step 6: Put V(j) into the trained neural network to recognition.

The model of the complete algorithm system is shown in Fig. 6.

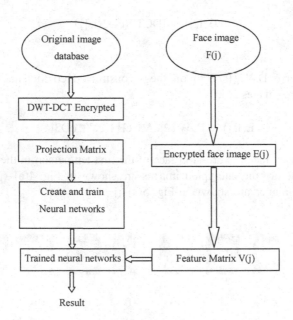

Fig. 6. The complete algorithm system model

4 Simulation Results

The recognition algorithm is implemented in Matlab 2015b platform to test and verify the effectiveness. The original image data is taken from the ORL face database, which contains 40 individuals, mark it as serial number. 1–40, each person has ten different facial expressions, the size of each image is 92(pix) × 112(pix), with 256 grey levels per pixel. We choose the first five facial expressions of each person as the training samples of BP neural network. The last five facial expressions of each person to test the neural network recognition rate. The neural network contains two hidden layers, and the numbers of hidden layer nodes are 60 and 15. The number of input layer nodes of BP neural network is 70, and the number of output nodes is 40. The experimental results of face recognition rate without encryption and encryption are shown in Table 1. As we can see from Table 1, the face recognition rate of the unencrypted algorithm is 81.5%, and the recognition rate of the encrypted which we proposed is 84%, the algorithm we proposed has a better recognition rate and can effectively protect the personal information security through encryption.

Table 1. Unencrypted and encrypted recognition rate

Identification method	Recognition rate (%)	Time(s)	Iterations
Unencrypted	81.5	10	1840
Encrypted	84	9	1780

In order to verify the robustness of the algorithm, we choose the first facial expression image of the first person as the experimental object. The face image is attacked by Gaussian noise, JEPG compression, median filtering, translation, rotation and occlusion. The original image under the attacks and the encrypted image are shown in Figs. 7, 8, 9, 10, 11, 12, 13, 14 and 15. The experimental data of unencrypted and encrypted images under the attacks are illustrated in Table 2. In Table 2, S, M, L indicate the relative size of occluded area and light intensity (L > M > S). Serial number 1 means that the recognition is correct, and the other serial numbers indicate the person whose error is identified as the corresponding serial number.

Fig. 7. Gaussion noise (10%) and the encrypted image

Fig. 8. JPEG compression (5%) and the encrypted image

Fig. 9. Median filtering [5 × 5] (10 times) and the encrypted image

Fig. 10. Anti-clockwise rotation (10°) and the encrypted image

Fig. 11. Horizontal right shift (10%) and the encrypted image

Fig. 12. Glass(M) and the encrypted image

Fig. 13. Mask(M) and the encrypted image

Fig. 14. Light(−L) and the encrypted image

Fig. 15. Light(L) and the encrypted image

From the Table 2, the PSNR value decreases when the attack intensity gradually increase, the image without encryption algorithm and the image after the proposed encryption algorithm can achieve accurate recognition under the conventional attack and light attack. For geometric attacks, the algorithm before encryption can't realize the face recognition when the image anti-clockwise rotation degree reaches 18° or the percentage of right shift to 10%, but the encrypted algorithm can always realize the face recognition accurately. As for occlusion attacks, the encryption algorithm can achieve face recognition only when the occluded size is large enough, this shows that the algorithm has a certain anti-occlusion attack ability. To sum up, the encryption algorithm our proposed has strong robustness.

Table 2. The experimental results of unencrypted and encrypted algorithm under the different attacks

Attacks	Parameters	PSNR (dB)	Unencrypted (serial number)	Encrypted (serial number)
Noise (%)	1	19.40	1	1
	10	10.68	1	1
	50	7.12	1	1
JPEG Compression (%)	5	25.13	1	1
	20	29.87	1	1
	50	32.86	1	1
Median filtering (10 Times)	[3 × 3]	29.11	1	1
	[5 × 5]	23.77	1	1
	[7 × 7]	20.01	1	1
Anti-clockwise rotation (°)	16	14.18	1	1
	17	14.00	1	1
	18	13.83	12	1
Horizontal right shift (%)	8	14.09	1	1
	9	13.52	1	1
	10	12.30	10	1
Occlusion (Glass)	S	18.78	1	1
	M	17.99	1	1
	L	15.77	1	40

(*continued*)

Table 2. (*continued*)

Attacks	Parameters	PSNR (dB)	Unencrypted (serial number)	Encrypted (serial number)
Occlusion (Mask)	S	18.32	1	1
	M	17.09	1	1
	L	15.15	1	30
Light	-L	11.53	1	1
	-M	14.92	1	1
	-S	22.31	1	1
	S	23.28	1	1
	M	15.00	1	1
	L	11.25	1	1

5 Conclusion

This algorithm combines the advantages of DWT and DCT, Tent Map and the BP neural network, encrypt image in the transform domain, compared with the traditional method of neural network, the recognition rate of our proposed algorithm is better. The experimental results show that the algorithm has strong robustness to Gaussian noise, JPEG compression, median filtering, anti-rotation, translation and occlusion attacks. Meanwhile, this algorithm can effectively protect the personal information security through encryption and has wide application prospects.

Acknowledgments. This work was supported by the Research Project of Hainan (ZDYF 2018129), and by the National Natural Science Foundation of China [No: 61762033] and The National Natural Science Foundation of Hainan [617048, 2018CXTD333].

References

1. Li, S.Z., Jain, A.K.: Handbook of Face Recognition, 2nd edn. Springer, London (2011). https://doi.org/10.1007/978-0-85729-932-1
2. Klare, B.F., Burge, M.J., Klontz, J.C., Vorder Bruegge, R.W., Jain, A.K.: Face recognition performance: role of demographic information. IEEE Trans. Inf. Forensics Secur. **7**(6), 1789–1801 (2012)
3. Hassaballah, M., Aly, S.: Face recognition: challenges, achievements and future directions. IET Comput. Vis. **9**(4), 616–626 (2015)
4. Bowyer, K.W.: Face recognition technology: security versus privacy. IEEE Technol. Soc. Mag. **23**(1), 9–20 (2004)
5. Ratha, N.K., Connell, J.H., Bolle, R.M.: Enhancing security and privacy in biometrics-based authentication systems. IBM Syst. J. **40**(3), 614–634 (2001)
6. Bhattasali, T., Saeed, K., Chaki, N., Chaki, R.: A survey of security and privacy issues for biometrics based remote authentication in cloud. In: Saeed, K., Snášel, V. (eds.) CISIM 2014. LNCS, vol. 8838, pp. 112–121. Springer, Heidelberg (2014). https://doi.org/10.1007/978-3-662-45237-0_12

7. Turk, M., Pentland, A.: Eigenfaces for recognition. J. Cogn. Neurosci. **3**(1), 71–86 (1991)
8. Rivest, R.L., Shamir, A., Adleman, L.: A method for obtaining digital signatures and public-key cryptosystems. Commun. ACM **21**(2), 120–126 (1978)
9. Goldwasser, S., Micali, S.: Probabilistic encryption. J. Comput. Syst. Sci. **28**(2), 270–299 (1984)
10. Dowlin, N., Gilad-Bachrach, R., Laine, K., Lauter, K., Naehring, M., Wernsing, J.: Manual for using homomorphic encryption for bioinformatics. Proc. IEEE **105**(3), 552–567 (2017)
11. Rivest, R.L., Adleman, L., Derlouzos, M.L.: On data banks and privacy homomorphisms. Found. Secure Comput. **4**(11), 169–180 (1978)
12. Beunardeau, M., Connolly, A., Geraud, R., Naccache, D.: Fully homomorphic encryption: computations with a blindfold. IEEE Secur. Priv. **14**(1), 63–67 (2016)
13. Paillier, P.: Public-key cryptosystems based on composite degree residuosity classes. In: Stern, J. (ed.) EUROCRYPT 1999. LNCS, vol. 1592, pp. 223–238. Springer, Heidelberg (1999). https://doi.org/10.1007/3-540-48910-X_16
14. Zhang, Y.Y., Zhao, D., Sun, J.D., Zou, G.F., Li, W.T.: Adaptive convolutional neural network and its application in face recognition. Neural Process. Lett. **43**(2), 389–399 (2016)
15. Masuda, N., Aihara, K.: Cryptosystems based on space discretization of chaotic maps. IEEE Trans. Circuits Syst. **49**(1), 28–40 (2002)
16. Feng, J.H., Zhang, J., Zhu, X.S., Lian, W.W.: A novel chaos optimization algorithm. Multimedia Tools Appl. **76**(16), 17405–17436 (2017)

A Secure Revocable Identity-Based Proxy Re-encryption Scheme for Cloud Storage

Wei Luo[✉] and Wenping Ma

State Key Laboratory of Integrated Service Networks, Xidian University,
Xi'an 710071, China
rovid008@163.com

Abstract. Identity-based encryption algorithm is applied to cloud storage to protect data security and provide a flexible access control scheme. However, in the existing schemes, the private key generator (PKG) knows secret keys of all users, which means that the PKG can decrypt all ciphertexts. In this paper, we propose a secure identity-based proxy re-encryption scheme, in which the PKG only generates partial secret keys for users. This can ensure users' data confidentiality and privacy security. Its security is based on the decision bilinear Diffie-Hellman (DBDH) assumption in the random oracle model. Besides, our scheme can resist collusion attacks and support user revocation. In addition, we compare our scheme with other existing schemes. The result demonstrates our scheme is comparable with other schemes in computation complexity.

Keywords: Cloud storage · Data security
Identity-based encryption · Proxy re-encryption · Access control

1 Introduction

Cloud storage has been rapidly used in recent years, which makes it possible that users can access and share their data anywhere and anytime just by using mobile devices jointing the Internet. But most of cloud storage systems simply store uploaded data without encryption, which brings a danger that users' data could be leaked due to a malicious attack or operational error by the cloud service provider. It is also desirable that some encryption algorithms and access policies are employed in cloud storage systems.

There are many encryption schemes proposed based on identity-based encryption for cloud storage systems. However, in most scenarios, the private key generator (PKG) issues the full secret keys for users. In this case, the PKG can decrypt all the ciphertext. What's the worse, data leaks can result if other users collude with the PKG or the PKG is compromised by an adversary.

This work was funded by National Key R&D Program of China under grant No. 2017YFB0802400, National Natural Science Foundation of China under grant No. 61373171 and 111 Project under grant No. B08038.

X. Sun et al. (Eds.): ICCCS 2018, LNCS 11064, pp. 519–530, 2018.
https://doi.org/10.1007/978-3-030-00009-7_47

1.1 Our Contribution

To solve this problem, we propose a novel identity-based proxy re-encryption (IB-PRE) scheme by splitting the private key [1]. The main contributions of this paper are the following:

1. In our proposed IB-PRE scheme, the PKG only generates the partial secret keys for users, which can provide the confidentiality of users' data and privacy security. Besides, the PKG does not participate in the generation of re-encryption keys.
2. Authentication is provided in the processes of secret key generation and data access. It ensures that authenticated users can obtain what data they want and that data cannot be intercepted by illegal users.
3. Even if the designated decryptor colluded with the proxy server, the data owner's secret key could not be obtained.

1.2 Organization

The remainder of this paper is organized as follows: Sect. 2 introduces related works on identity-based encryption schemes. The syntax of our identity-based proxy re-encryption scheme, security model and complexity assumption are detailed in Sect. 3. Our scheme is described in detail in Sect. 4. We make a security analysis for our proposed scheme in Sect. 5. Performance analysis is discussed in Sect. 6. Section 7 concludes this paper.

2 Related Work

In 1984, Shamir first proposes identity-based encryption (IBE) in order to achieve the purpose of the simplification of key management system [2]. IBE is an efficient cryptographic system, where the public key can be any string which can uniquely represent the user identity (such as id card number, telephone number and email address, etc.). The secret key is extracted from private key generator (PKG).

In [3], Green et al. propose the concept of IBE proxy re-encryption, which allows the proxy to translate a ciphertext encrypted by the sender's identity into one computed by the recipient's identity. But the size of its re-encrypted ciphertext is so large.

In [4], Matsuo proposes a proxy re-encryption system for IBE, which allows the proxy to translate ciphertext encrypted by the sender's public key (identity) into the re-encrypted ciphertext can be decrypted by using the recipient's secret key. A little disadvantage of this scheme is that there is no authentication (secret key verification, and the requester's identity verification).

In [5], Chu et al. propose two identity-based proxy re-encryption schemes, which are both proved secure in the standard model. One is efficient in both computation and ciphertext length, and the other achieves chosen ciphertext security. The scheme also has no authentication (secret key verification, and the requester's identity verification).

In [6, 9], Boldyreva et al. propose an IBE scheme with revocation mechanisms, which significantly improves key-update efficiency.

In [7], Tang et al. propose an inter-domain IBE proxy re-encryption scheme with low computation complexity. However, it is proved in [10] that the collusion attack against Tang's scheme. Then, Han et al. propose an identity-based data storage scheme supporting intra-domain and inter-domain queries, which is proved to be IND-sID-CPA secure and against the collusion attack. Also, Wang et al. propose two new identity-based proxy re-encryption schemes to prevent collusion attacks in [8], one of which is proved IND-PrID-CPA secure in the random oracle model, and the other of which achieves the IND-PrID-CCA security.

Liang et al. propose a cloud-based revocable identity-based proxy re-encryption scheme in [11]. However, Wang et al. show Liang's scheme has serious security problems and propose an improved scheme in [12], which not only achieves collusion resistance, but also takes lower decryption computation and achieves constant size re-encrypted ciphertext.

3 Background

In this section, we introduce the background of our proposed identity-based proxy re-encryption scheme.

3.1 Syntax of Our Secure Revocable IB-PRE Cloud Storage Scheme

There are four entities in our secure revocable identity-based proxy re-encryption cloud storage scheme as shown in Fig. 1: the private key generator (PKG), the proxy server (PS), the data owner (O) and the requester (R). The PKG is honest but curious, which issues secret keys for users. The proxy server stores the ciphertexts, re-encrypts the original ciphertexts and sends them to the requester who obtains access permission. The data owner encrypts data using public key (identity) and outsources them to the proxy server. The data owner authenticates the requester, generates the re-encryption keys independently and sends them to the PS. The requester obtaining the access permission can decrypt the re-encrypted ciphertexts.

Our secure revocable identity-based proxy re-encryption scheme is comprised 9 phases: Setup, KeyGen, IBEnc, Query, Permit, ReKeyGen, ReEnc, IBDec, Revoke.

Setup(k): This algorithm takes as inputs a security parameter k and outputs the public parameters $params$, the master secret key MSK for the PKG.

KeyGen($params$, O): This algorithm takes as inputs the public parameters $params$ and an identity O, and outputs a secret key SK'_O for the user with the identity O.

IBEnc($params$, O, m): This algorithm takes as inputs the public parameters $params$, the identity O and the message m, and outputs the ciphertext CT, which is sent to the proxy server PS.

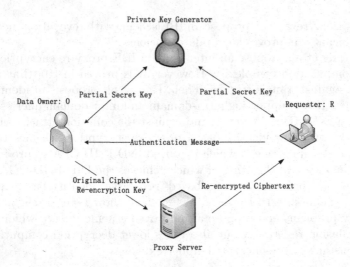

Fig. 1. System model

Query(R, SK'_R, CT): The requester R queries the data outsourced by the owner O. This algorithm takes as inputs the requester's identity R, secret key SK'_R and the ciphertext CT, and outputs an authentication information Ψ, which is sent to the proxy server PS.

Permit($params$, R, Ψ, $SK_{R,2}$): The data owner authenticates the requester by verifying the authentication information Ψ. If the requester is legal, continue to execute the next algorithm ReKeyGen($\bullet$). Otherwise, output $\bot$.

ReKeyGen(Ψ, R): This algorithm takes as inputs the authentication information Ψ and the identity R of the requester, and outputs the re-encryption key $RK_{O \to R}$, which is sent to the proxy server PS.

ReEnc(CT, $RK_{O \to R}$): This algorithm takes as inputs the original ciphertext CT and the re-encryption key $RK_{O \to R}$, and outputs the re-encrypted ciphertext CT'. The proxy server PS sends the re-encrypted ciphertext CT' to the requester R.

IBDec($\bullet$): The decryptor responses as follows with respect to the following two cases:

Case 1. IBDec(CT, SK'_O): This algorithm takes as inputs the original ciphertext CT and the secret key SK'_O of the data owner O, and outputs the message m.

Case 2. IBDec(CT', SK'_R): This algorithm takes as inputs the re-encrypted ciphertext CT' and the secret key SK'_R of the requester, and outputs the message m.

Revoke(id, RL): This algorithm takes as inputs the current revocation list RL and the identity id of the user to be revoked, and outputs the updated revocation list.

The correctness of an IB-PRE scheme is defined as follows: Given $params$, and two users' identities O and R, if

- $SK'_O \longleftarrow KeyGen(params, O)$,
- $SK'_R \longleftarrow KeyGen(params, R)$,
- $RK_{O \to R} \longleftarrow ReKeyGen(\Psi, R)$,

then the following results must hold:

1. $IBDec(CT, SK'_O) = m$,
2. $IBDec(CT', SK'_R) = m$.

3.2 Security Model

In this section, we present the security model of the chosen plaintext attacks (CPA) of an IB-PRE scheme. Before defining it, we make sure the following condition to be satisfied: given a challenge ciphertext CT^* for identity O^*, the adversary can make the following queries without knowing the secret key SK'_{O^*}, the secret key SK'_R and the proxy re-encryption key $RK_{O^* \to R}$. Let O^* be the target identity with which the adversary want to be challenged to the challenger.

Game CPA

Setup. The challenger $\mathbb{C}$ runs Setup(k) to generate the public parameters $params$, the master secret key MSK, and sends $params$ to adversary $\mathbb{A}$.

Phase 1. $\mathbb{A}$ can make the following queries:

1. Secret Key Query. $\mathbb{A}$ inputs the identity O, and $\mathbb{C}$ returns the SK'_O.
2. Proxy Re-encryption Key Query. $\mathbb{A}$ inputs the identity (O, R), and $\mathbb{C}$ returns the $RK_{O \to R}$.

Challenge. When $\mathbb{A}$ wants to end phase 1, it submits O^* and messages (m_0, m_1) of equal length. $\mathbb{C}$ flips a fair coin with $\{0, 1\}$ and obtains $\gamma \in \{0, 1\}$. It computes a challenge ciphertext CT^* for the message m_γ under the identity O^* and sends CT^* to $\mathbb{A}$.

Phase 2. $\mathbb{A}$ can adaptively make the following additional queries:

1. Secret Key Query. $\mathbb{A}$ inputs the identity O, where $O \neq O^*$, and $\mathbb{C}$ responds as in phase 1.
2. Proxy Re-encryption Key Query. $\mathbb{A}$ inputs the identity (Ψ, R), where $O \neq O^*$ and $R \neq O^*$, and $\mathbb{C}$ responds as in phase 1.

Guess. $\mathbb{A}$ outputs a guess γ' on γ.

Definition 1 (IND-PrID-CPA) [8]. In Game CPA, $\mathbb{A}$ wins the game if $\gamma' = \gamma$. An IB-PRE scheme is said to be indistinguishable against adaptively chosen an identity and chosen plaintext attacks (IND-PrID-CPA) if there is not any polynomial time algorithm with a non-negligible advantage in winning Game CPA.

3.3 Complexity Assumption

We describe the computation problems used within this work in this subsection.

Definition 2 (Bilinear Groups). Let $\mathbb{G}_1$ and $\mathbb{G}_2$ be two multiplicative groups with prime order p and g be a generator of group $\mathbb{G}_1$. A bilinear map e: $\mathbb{G}_1 \times \mathbb{G}_1 \longrightarrow \mathbb{G}_2$ is a map with between the groups $\mathbb{G}_1$ and $\mathbb{G}_2$ with the following properties:

- Bilinearity: $e(g_1^a, g_2^b) = e(g_1, g_2)^{ab}$ for $g_1, g_2 \in \mathbb{G}_1$ and two random numbers $a, b \in Z_p^*$.
- Non-degeneracy: $e(g, g) \neq 1$ where 1 is the identity element of the group $\mathbb{G}_1$.
- Computability: There is an efficient algorithm to compute $e(g_1, g_2)$ for all $g_1, g_2 \in \mathbb{G}_1$.

We say $(p, \mathbb{G}_1, \mathbb{G}_2, e, g)$ a bilinear groups.

Definition 3 (Decision Bilinear Diffie-Hellman (DBDH) Assumption) [9]. Given a bilinear groups $(p, \mathbb{G}_1, \mathbb{G}_2, e, g)$, define two distributions $D_0 = (A, B, C, Z) = (g^a, g^b, g^c, e(g, g)^{abc})$ and $D_1 = (A, B, C, Z) = (g^a, g^b, g^c, e(g, g)^z)$, where $a, b, c, z \in Z_p^*$. The DBDH problem in the bilinear group $(p, \mathbb{G}_1, \mathbb{G}_2, e, g)$ is to decide a bit γ from given D_γ, where $\gamma \in 0, 1$. The advantage of adversary $\mathbb{A}$ in soving the DBDH problem in the bilinear group $(p, \mathbb{G}_1, \mathbb{G}_2, e, g)$ is defined by

$$Adv_{\mathbb{A}}^{DBDH} = \left| Pr[\mathbb{A}(D_0) \longrightarrow 1] - Pr[\mathbb{A}(D_1) \longrightarrow 1] \right|.$$

4   Our Construction

In this section, we propose a secure revocable identity-based proxy re-encryption scheme, in which the PKG does not generate the full secret keys for users.

Based on the IB-PRE scheme [10], we propose a secure IB-PRE scheme with low computation complexity. The description of our secure IB-PRE scheme is as follows.

- Setup(k): The PKG takes a security parameter k as input, and returns a bilinear group $(p, \mathbb{G}_1, \mathbb{G}_2, e)$ with prime order p, where e: $\mathbb{G}_1 \times \mathbb{G}_1 \longrightarrow \mathbb{G}_2$. And choose cryptographic hash function H : $\{0, 1\}^* \rightarrow \mathbb{G}_1$. Let g, θ be the generators of $\mathbb{G}_1$. Then, the PKG sets $g_1 = g^\alpha$, $g_2 = g^\beta$, $\zeta = \theta^\alpha$, $\alpha, \beta \in Z_p^*$, and initializes a user list $UL = \Phi$ and a revocation list $RL = \Phi$. Finally, the PKG publishes the system parameters $params = (p, \mathbb{G}_1, \mathbb{G}_2, e, g, g_1, g_2, \theta, H)$ and keeps the master secret key $MSK = (\alpha, \beta, \zeta)$ secret.
- KeyGen($params$, O): The PKG takes the public parameters $params$ and an identity O as inputs, and outputs a partial secret key SK_O for the user with the identity O. The PKG randomly chooses $l_O \in Z_p^*$, and computes

$$SK_{O,1} = \theta^\alpha (H(O \oplus g_2))^{l_O}, \ SK_{O,2} = g^{l_O}.$$

The partial secret key for the user O is $SK_O = (SK_{O,1}, SK_{O,2})$. The PKG sends $\{SK_O, l_O\}$ to the user O through a secure channel such as email. The user O can verify the partial secret key by

$$e(SK_{O,1}, g) \stackrel{?}{=} e(g_1, \theta) \cdot e(H(O \oplus g_2), SK_{O,2})$$

The user O chooses $q \in Z_p^*$ and computes the secret key $SK_O' = (SK_{O,1}', SK_{O,2}')$.

$$SK_{O,1}' = \theta^\alpha (H(O \oplus g_2 \oplus q)^{l_O}, \ SK_{O,2}' = SK_{O,2}.$$

- IBEnc($params$, O, m): The data owner O takes the public parameters $params$, his/her identity O and the message m as inputs, and outputs the ciphertext CT, which is sent to the proxy server PS. The data owner O chooses $\varphi \in Z_p^*$ and computes the original ciphertext $CT = (C_1, C_2, C_3)$.

$$C_1 = m \cdot e(g, g_1)^\varphi, \ C_2 = g^\varphi, \ C_3 = (H(O \oplus g_2 \oplus q))^\varphi.$$

- Query(R, SK_R', CT): The requester R queries the data outsourced by the owner O. The requester R takes the identity R, secret key SK_R' and the ciphertext CT as inputs, and outputs an authentication information Ψ, which is sent to the data owner O. The requester R computes $F = g_2^l$ and $Q = F \cdot SK_{R,1}'$, and sends an authentication information $\Psi = \{H(R \oplus g_2 \oplus q'), R, C_2, Q, F\}$ to the data owner O.

- Permit($params$, R, Ψ, $SK_{R,2}$): The data owner authenticates the requester by verifying the authentication information Ψ. If the requester is legal, continue to execute the next algorithm (ReKeyGen($\bullet$)). Otherwise, output $\bot$. First, the data owner O queries the PKG on the partial secret key $SK_{R,2}$ of the requester R. The PKG search the identity of the requester in the revocation list RL. If the requester is a revoked user, the PKG responds the data owner $\bot$. Otherwise, respond with $SK_{R,2}$ of the requester. Receiving $SK_{R,2}$, the data owner O checks

$$e(Q, g) \overset{?}{=} e(g_1, g) \cdot e(H(R \oplus g_2 \oplus q'), SK_{R,2}) \cdot e(F, g)$$

- ReKeyGen(Ψ, R): The data owner takes the authentication information Ψ and the identity R of the requester as inputs, and outputs the re-encryption key $RK_{O \to R}$, which is sent to the proxy server PS. The data owner O computes the re-encryption key as

$$RK_{O \to R} = (\frac{H(R \oplus g_2 \oplus q')}{H(O \oplus g_2 \oplus q)})^\varphi.$$

- ReEnc(CT, $RK_{O \to R}$): The proxy server takes the original ciphertext CT and the re-encryption key $RK_{O \to R}$ as inputs, and outputs the re-encrypted ciphertext CT' which is sent to the requester R. The proxy server PS computes the re-encrypted ciphertext as

$$C_1' = C_1, \ C_2' = C_2, \ C_3' = RK_{O \to R} \cdot C_3.$$

The proxy server PS sends the re-encrypted ciphertext $CT' = (C_1', C_2', C_3')$ to the requester R.

- IBDec($\bullet$): The decryptor responses as follows with respect to the following two cases:

- Case 1. IBDec(CT, SK'_O): The data owner O takes the original ciphertext CT and his/her secret key SK'_O as inputs, and outputs the message m. The data owner O decrypts the original ciphertext as $m = C_1 \cdot \frac{e(SK'_{O,2}, C_3)}{e(SK'_{O,1}, C_2)}$.

- Case 2. IBDec(CT', SK'_R): The requester R takes the re-encrypted ciphertext CT' and his/her secret key SK'_R as inputs, and outputs the message m. The requester R decrypts the re-encrypted ciphertext as $m = C'_1 \cdot \frac{e(SK'_{R,2}, C'_3)}{e(SK'_{R,1}, C'_2)}$.

– Revoke(id, RL): The PKG updates the revocation list by $RL \leftarrow RL \bigcup \{id\}$, where id is the identity of the user to be revoked, and returns the updated revocation list.

Theorem 1 (Correction of Our Proposed IB-PRE Scheme). The proposed IB-PRE scheme is correct.

Proof. The correctness can be checked by the following equations.

– Correctness for case 1.

$$
\begin{aligned}
C_1 &\cdot \frac{e(SK'_{O,2}, C_3)}{e(SK'_{O,1}, C_2)} \\
&= m \cdot e(g, g_1)^\varphi \cdot \frac{e(g^{lo}, (H(O \oplus g_2 \oplus q))^\varphi)}{e(g_1(H(O \oplus g_2 \oplus q)^{lo}, g^\varphi)} \\
&= m \cdot e(g^\varphi, g_1) \cdot \frac{e(g^\varphi, (H(O \oplus g_2 \oplus q))^{lo})}{e(g_1(H(O \oplus g_2 \oplus q)^{lo}, g^\varphi)} \\
&= m \cdot \frac{e(g^\varphi, g_1(H(O \oplus g_2 \oplus q))^{lo})}{e(g_1(H(O \oplus g_2 \oplus q)^{lo}, g^\varphi)} \\
&= m
\end{aligned}
\tag{1}
$$

– Correctness for case 2.

$$
\begin{aligned}
C'_1 &\cdot \frac{e(SK'_{R,2}, C'_3)}{e(SK'_{R,1}, C'_2)} \\
&= C_1 \cdot \frac{e(SK'_{R,2}, RK_{O \to R} \cdot C_3)}{e(SK'_{R,1}, C_2)} \\
&= m \cdot e(g, g_1)^\varphi \cdot \frac{e(g^{l_R}, (\frac{H(R \oplus g_2 \oplus q')}{H(O \oplus g_2 \oplus q)})^\varphi \cdot (H(O \oplus g_2 \oplus q))^\varphi)}{e(g_1(H(R \oplus g_2 \oplus q')^{l_R}, g^\varphi)} \\
&= m \cdot e(g, g_1)^\varphi \cdot \frac{e(g^{l_R}, (H(R \oplus g_2 \oplus q'))^\varphi)}{e(g_1(H(R \oplus g_2 \oplus q')^{l_R}, g^\varphi)} \\
&= m \cdot e(g^\varphi, g_1) \cdot \frac{e(g^\varphi, (H(R \oplus g_2 \oplus q'))^{l_R})}{e(g_1(H(R \oplus g_2 \oplus q')^{l_R}, g^\varphi)} \\
&= m \cdot \frac{e(g^\varphi, g_1(H(R \oplus g_2 \oplus q'))^{l_R})}{e(g_1(H(R \oplus g_2 \oplus q')^{l_R}, g^\varphi)} \\
&= m
\end{aligned}
\tag{2}
$$

5   Security Analysis

Theorem 2 (IND-PrID-CPA of Our Proposed IB-PRE Scheme) [8].
Our proposed IB-PRE scheme is IND-PrID-CPA secure under the DBDH
assumption in the random oracle model. That is to say, if there is an adversary
that can break the IND-PrID-CPA security of our proposed IB-PRE scheme with
the non-negligible advantage ε within time t, then we can construct an algorithm
that can solve the DBDH problem in $\mathbb{G}_2$ with the non-negligible advantage ε'
within time t', such that

$$\varepsilon' \geq \frac{\varepsilon}{e \cdot (q_s + 2q_r)} \quad and \quad t' = t + \phi(t),$$

where e is the base of natural logarithm, $\phi(t)$ denotes the time required to
answer all queries, q_s and q_r are the numbers of secret key queries and proxy
re-encryption key queries, respectively.

Proof. The idea of proof is similar to the proof procedure in [8]. Due to space
limitations, we omit the complete proof of security here.

Theorem 3. Our scheme can resist the collusion attack.

Proof. Since the secure random number involved in the generation of the re-
encryption key in our scheme, the data owner's secret key can not be calculated
even if the designated decryptor can compromise the proxy server to obtain the
re-encryption key.

6   Performance Analysis

In this section, we compare our scheme with other existing schemes. First, we
make a comparison based on the security and features of all schemes as shown
in Table 1. The security of all schemes is based on the Decision Bilinear Diffie-
Hellman (DBDH) assumption. [7,11] are IND-CPA secure and others are IND-
sID-CPA or IND-PrID-CPA secure. [7] suffers from a collusion attack, which is
demonstrated in [10]. [10] and our scheme support the secret key verification
and the identity verification of the requester. [8] only supports the secret key
verification. Besides, [11,12] and our scheme support the user revocation.

Then, we compare our scheme with other scheme in term of efficiency. Here,
we suppose that the prime number p of all schemes is same. This suggests the
order of all the bilinear groups is equal. $|\mathbb{G}|/|\mathbb{G}_i|$ denotes one element in the group
$\mathbb{G}/\mathbb{G}_i$ and $|p|$ denotes the length of the binary representation. From Table 2, we
see that our scheme is the least in communication cost, and [7] is comparable
with other schemes. [11,12] have greater communication cost, where $|Path(\eta)|$
denotes the number of nodes in the path $Path(\eta)$ and l denotes the times of re-
encryption. Table 3 shows the comparison of computation complexity. We assume
that all operations are dyadic operation. T_E denotes one exponentiation and
$\tau_P/\tau_{\hat{P}}$ denotes one pairing operation. Obviously, our scheme has the advantages
compared with other schemes. [11,12] also have greater computation complexity.

Table 1. Security and features comparison of our scheme with other schemes

Schemes	Complexity assumption	Security	Authentication	User revocation
[4]	DBDH	IND-sID-CPA	No	No
[7]	DBDH	IND-CPA	No	No
[8]	DBDH	IND-PrID-CPA	Yes	No
[10]	DBDH	IND-sID-CPA	Yes	No
[11]	DBDH	IND-CPA	No	Yes
[12]	DBDH	IND-ID-CPA	No	Yes
Our scheme	DBDH	IND-PrID-CPA	Yes	Yes

Table 2. Communication cost comparison of our scheme with other schemes

Schemes	Secret key	Original ciphertext	Re-encryption key	Re-encrypted ciphertext
[4]	$2|\mathbb{G}|$	$2|\mathbb{G}| + |\mathbb{G}_1|$	$|p| + |\mathbb{G}|$	$2|\mathbb{G}| + |\mathbb{G}_1|$
[7]	$|\mathbb{G}|$	$|\mathbb{G}| + |\mathbb{G}_1|$	$2|\mathbb{G}| + |\mathbb{G}_1|$	$2|\mathbb{G}| + 3|\mathbb{G}_1|$
[8]	$2|\mathbb{G}_1|$	$3|\mathbb{G}_1| + |\mathbb{G}_2|$	$2|\mathbb{G}_1|$	$2|\mathbb{G}_1| + |\mathbb{G}_2|$
[10]	$3|\mathbb{G}|$	$2|\mathbb{G}| + |\mathbb{G}_\tau|$	$3|\mathbb{G}| + |\mathbb{G}_\tau|$	$5|\mathbb{G}| + |\mathbb{G}_\tau|$
[11]	$2|\mathbb{G}|$	$3|\mathbb{G}| + |\mathbb{G}_T|$	$9|\mathbb{G}| + 2|\mathbb{G}_T|$	$(l+3)|\mathbb{G}| + (2l+1)|\mathbb{G}_T|$
[12]	$2|Path(\eta)|||\mathbb{G}|$	$3|\mathbb{G}| + |\mathbb{G}_T|$	0	$6|\mathbb{G}| + |\mathbb{G}_T|$
Our scheme	$2|\mathbb{G}_1|$	$2|\mathbb{G}_1| + |\mathbb{G}_2|$	$|\mathbb{G}_1|$	$2|\mathbb{G}_1| + |\mathbb{G}_2|$

Table 3. Computation complexity comparison of our scheme with other schemes

Schemes	Encryption	Re-encryption key generation	Re-encryption	Decryption	Re-decryption
[4]	$4T_E + \tau_{\hat{P}}$	T_E	$T_E + \tau_{\hat{P}}$	$2\tau_{\hat{P}}$	$2\tau_{\hat{P}}$
[7]	$2T_E + \tau_{\hat{P}}$	$2T_E + \tau_{\hat{P}}$	$2T_E + 2\tau_{\hat{P}}$	$\tau_{\hat{P}}$	$4\tau_{\hat{P}}$
[8]	$4T_E + \tau_{\hat{P}}$	$3T_E$	$2\tau_{\hat{P}}$	$2\tau_{\hat{P}}$	$2\tau_{\hat{P}}$
[10]	$4T_E + \tau_P$	$6T_E + \tau_P$	0	$2\tau_P$	$2T_E + 2\tau_P$
[11]	$6T_E + \tau_P$	$12T_E + \tau_P$	$2l\tau_P$	$3\tau_P$	$2T_E + 4\tau_P/2lT_E + (l+3)\tau_P$
[12]	$4T_E + \tau_P$	0	$4T_E + \tau_P$	$3\tau_P$	$6\tau_P$
Our scheme	$3T_E + \tau_P$	T_E	0	$2\tau_P$	$2\tau_P$

In addition, we conducted experiments on our scheme using Pairing Based Cryptography (PBC) library [13]. Here, we use the Microsoft Visual C++ conversion pbc-0.4.7-vc. All algorithms were coded using C programming language and conducted on a system with Intel(R) Core(TM) i5-3470 CPU at 3.20 GHz and 3.20 GHz and 4.00 GB RAM in Windows 7. Type A pairings are used in the simulation, which are constructed on the curve $y^2 = x^3 + x$ over the field F_q for some prime $q = 3 \ mod \ 4$. This pairing is symmetric, where the order of groups is 160 bits, the base field size is 512 bits and the embedding degree is 2.

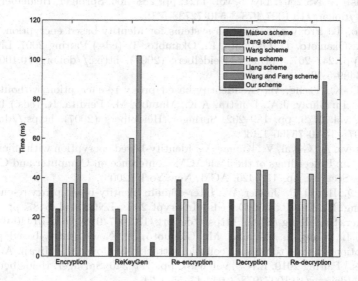

Fig. 2. Simulation results

The simulation results are shown in Fig. 2. We observe that our scheme has a significant advantage in ReKegGen, Re-encryption and Re-decryption. Although [7] has less runtime in Encryption and Decryption, it takes more time in Re-encryption and Re-decryption.

7 Conclusion

In this paper, we propose a secure revocable identity-based proxy re-encryption scheme for cloud storage, in which the PKG does not generate full secret keys for users. Therefore, the PKG can not decrypt the ciphertext without knowing the secret keys of users. Besides, the generation of re-encryption keys does not involve the participation of the PKG. Our proposed scheme is provably secure under the standard assumption (DBDH) in the random oracle model. In addition, our scheme is comparable with other schemes in computation complexity.

References

1. Al-Riyami, S.S., Paterson, K.G.: Certificateless public key cryptography. In: Laih, C.-S. (ed.) ASIACRYPT 2003. LNCS, vol. 2894, pp. 452–473. Springer, Heidelberg (2003). https://doi.org/10.1007/978-3-540-40061-5_29
2. Shamir, A.: Identity-based cryptosystems and signature schemes. In: Blakley, G.R., Chaum, D. (eds.) CRYPTO 1984. LNCS, vol. 196, pp. 47–53. Springer, Heidelberg (1985). https://doi.org/10.1007/3-540-39568-7_5
3. Green, M., Ateniese, G.: Identity-based proxy re-encryption. In: Katz, J., Yung, M. (eds.) ACNS 2007. LNCS, vol. 4521, pp. 288–306. Springer, Heidelberg (2007). https://doi.org/10.1007/978-3-540-72738-5_19
4. Matsuo, T.: Proxy re-encryption systems for identity-based encryption. In: Takagi, T., Okamoto, T., Okamoto, E., Okamoto, T. (eds.) Pairing 2007. LNCS, vol. 4575, pp. 247–267. Springer, Heidelberg (2007). https://doi.org/10.1007/978-3-540-73489-5_13
5. Chu, C.-K., Tzeng, W.-G.: Identity-based proxy re-encryption without random oracles. In: Garay, J.A., Lenstra, A.K., Mambo, M., Peralta, R. (eds.) ISC 2007. LNCS, vol. 4779, pp. 189–202. Springer, Heidelberg (2007). https://doi.org/10.1007/978-3-540-75496-1_13
6. Boldyreva, A., Goyal, V., Kumar, V.: Identity-based encryption with efficient revocation. In: Proceedings of the 15th ACM Conference on Computer and Communications Security, pp. 417–426. ACM, New York (2008)
7. Tang, Q., Hartel, P., Jonker, W.: Inter-domain identity-based proxy re-encryption. In: Yung, M., Liu, P., Lin, D. (eds.) Inscrypt 2008. LNCS, vol. 5487, pp. 332–347. Springer, Heidelberg (2009). https://doi.org/10.1007/978-3-642-01440-6_26
8. Wang, L., Wang, L., Mambo, M., Okamoto, E.: New identity-based proxy re-encryption schemes to prevent collusion attacks. In: Joye, M., Miyaji, A., Otsuka, A. (eds.) Pairing 2010. LNCS, vol. 6487, pp. 327–346. Springer, Heidelberg (2010). https://doi.org/10.1007/978-3-642-17455-1_21
9. Seo, J.H., Emura, K.: Revocable identity-based encryption revisited: security model and construction. In: Kurosawa, K., Hanaoka, G. (eds.) PKC 2013. LNCS, vol. 7778, pp. 216–234. Springer, Heidelberg (2013). https://doi.org/10.1007/978-3-642-36362-7_14
10. Han, J., Susilo, W., Mu, Y.: Identity-based data storage in cloud computing. Future Gener. Comput. Syst. **29**, 673–681 (2013)
11. Liang, K., Liu, J.K., Wong, D.S., Susilo, W.: An efficient cloud-based revocable identity-based proxy re-encryption scheme for public clouds data sharing. In: Kutyłowski, M., Vaidya, J. (eds.) ESORICS 2014. LNCS, vol. 8712, pp. 257–272. Springer, Cham (2014). https://doi.org/10.1007/978-3-319-11203-9_15
12. Wang, C., Fang, J., Li, Y.: An improved cloud-based revocable identity-based proxy re-encryption scheme. In: Niu, W., Li, G., Liu, J., Tan, J., Guo, L., Han, Z., Batten, L. (eds.) ATIS 2015. CCIS, vol. 557, pp. 14–26. Springer, Heidelberg (2015). https://doi.org/10.1007/978-3-662-48683-2_2
13. Lynn, B.: PBC library. http://crypto.stanford.edu/pbc

A Security Protocol for Access to Sensitive Data in Trusted Cloud Server

Mengmeng Yao(✉) ⓘ, Dongsheng Zhou(✉), Rui Deng(✉) ⓘ, and Mingda Liu(✉) ⓘ

Jiangnan Institute of Computing Technology, Wuxi, China
wellstudy@163.com

Abstract. For the purpose of enabling terminal users to access to sensitive data in cloud server, a security protocol TTAP (Trusted Terminal Access Protocol) is proposed for users, terminal, cloud server and attestation server based on TPM (Trusted Network Connect) and TNC (Trusted Network Connect). TTAP establishes a secure tunnel between cloud server and attestation server, which successfully proves the credibility of trusted terminal and the legitimacy of users. Moreover, strand space model is extended and new authentication tests theorem, namely signature test theorem and HMac (Hash Message Authentication Code) test theorem are proposed in this paper. The new theorems could be used to analysis complicated protocols with signature and HMac of algorithm complexity. TTPA proved by formal analysis method based on authentication tests is safe, so terminal users access to the cloud environment by TTPA are credible.

Keywords: TPM · TNC · Authentication tests · Formal analysis method

1 Introduction

With the continuous development of cloud computing technologies and network communications, users can be easy access to sensitive data in the trusted cloud server, this convenience also brings security threats. The sensitive data accessed by the user does not exist on the local but is stored on the cloud service platform. Similarly, the terminal used by the user can login to the cloud server by installing software that can login to the cloud service platform. For example, the user can log in through the web browser. Even if the cloud server is trustworthy, however, it cannot guarantee the other users can get the sensitive resources by some ways.

TNC and TPM, as the branches of the TCG (Trusted Computing Group), are responsible for the security of the access to trusted networks and the security of hardware and software environments. The trusted access technology based on trusted computing can verify the integrity of the system through interoperability and fine-grained approach [1]. In recent years, there are many scholars' researches on trusted network access to trusted computing cloud environments. OOAP (OIAP-OSAP-AACP) is designed based on OIAP, OSAP and AACP, and invokes TPM commands to run remote certification protocols on cloud computing platforms [2]. And OOAP protocol can prevent many types of malicious attacks. TNEAAP (Trusted Network

© Springer Nature Switzerland AG 2018
X. Sun et al. (Eds.): ICCCS 2018, LNCS 11064, pp. 531–542, 2018.
https://doi.org/10.1007/978-3-030-00009-7_48

Equipment Access Authentication Protocol) protocol is proposed in reference [3], which enables the network device to access the trusted network securely, and is analyzed the correctness of TNEAAP based on BAN logic. A protocol for mobile terminal access to trusted network is proposed in reference [4]. A security protocol for enabling trusted mobile terminals access to cloud server is proposed in reference [5]. C-TNC protocol is proposed in reference [6], which ensures the security of the cloud environment and prevents the various types of attacks caused by untrusted access terminals. Authentication module is designed based on the trusted mobile zone (TMZ) system [7].

Trusted access protocol is applied widely and plays a significant role in cloud computing environment. Formal analysis is an important method to ensure security of protocols. In recent years formal analysis based on strand space is applied more and more widely and relevant study is increasing. New concepts and theorems are proposed based on strand space in reference [8]. ISO/IEC9798-3 is analyzed via authentication test and flaws of the protocol are discovered [9]. In reference [10], re-defines authentication test theorems are proposed and Needham-Schroeder-Lowe is analyzed with improvement theorems. Reference [11] makes a study of security protocol's consistence of strand parameters. Strand space's algebra of messages and penetrator strand are extended and remote attestation protocol is analyzed based on strand space [12]. Reference [13] further extends strand space model and makes a successful analysis of fair exchange protocol through CPSA. Reference [14] raises a frame to describe state model and a mixed analysis method. Reference [15] makes a extension of strand space and authentication test theorem.

The contributions of this paper are as follows:

(1) A security protocol TTAP is proposed, which allows users, terminals, and trusted cloud sever to authenticate each other to ensure the security of the cloud computing environment. There are few interaction messages, and the cloud server does not need too many algorithm operations.
(2) The algebra of messages based on strand space is extended to analysis of the protocol using the signature algorithm.
(3) Based on the extended strand space theorems, the security of TTAP is analyzed. It is proved that TTAP is safe.

The structure of this paper is as follows:

The security threat of the trusted terminal accessing to the cloud server is introduced in Sect. 2. TTAP is designed in Sect. 3. The concept of strand space and new theorems are proposed in Sect. 4. Security of TTAP is analyzed based on authentication tests in Sect. 5.

2   Introduction to Trusted Terminal Security Access

2.1   Threats of Terminal Access to Cloud Server

Generally, users access to sensitive resources in cloud server by personal PCs and laptops, which are completely exposed to the Internet and are vulnerable to Trojan virus infection and malicious attacks. Attackers can use these insecure devices as springboards to access to trusted cloud and computing environments. These controlled springboard access to cloud resources, and cause data leakage, which bring a great security threats to the cloud server. Attackers can even listen to other user's communication and interrupt other users' normal accesses, and steal sensitive data. Similarly, users accessing to the cloud server with the user ID and password also pose a threat to the security of the cloud platform. The attacker can get passwords of users' by Password Attack or implanting Trojans on the terminals, and the virus obtain the legitimate user's ID and password. With IDs and passwords, an attacker can access to the cloud on any terminal. Although the user pays a service fee to the cloud provider, he does not know that the malicious user has accessed the cloud resource for free, and the cloud platform does not know whether the visitor is legitimate or not.

2.2 Security Attribute of Terminal Accessing to Cloud Server

(1) Identity attribute

If a trusted terminal, cloud server, or authentication server sends a message, it cannot be denied that the message had been sent already and the attacker cannot forge this message.

(2) Authentication attribute

Before the terminal connects to cloud server, the identity of the terminal required authentication. If the identity is certified, the terminal's status is measured. If the measurement result is trusted, the user's identity required authentication. If user's identity is certified, the terminal is allowed to connect to the cloud server.

(3) Integrity and confidentiality

When the ML (Measurement log) of terminal is transmitted on the internet, its integrity must be ensured and malicious attackers cannot tamper with the information. Confidential information such as the user's password cannot be leaked. Even if the attacker intercepts the information, he cannot restore the message. When attestation server transmits the measurement results on internet, the message must be encrypted with uncompromised key.

2.3 Access Model

The model shown in Fig. 1 references to literature [4, 5] is used in this paper.

When the user assesses to the cloud server, the platform measurement log is sent to the cloud server. The cloud server sends the message to the attestation server for authentication through the security tunnel. After the measurement log is certified, the results are sent back to the cloud server. The cloud server exchanges messages with the terminal user according to the measurement results. The model assumes that the terminal, cloud server, and attestation server have obtained the AIK certificate based on the TPM, which is issued by the private CA.

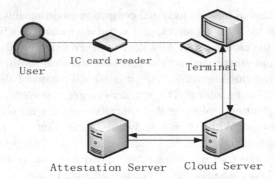

Fig. 1. Access model

3 TTAP

TTAP is divided into two parts, the establishment of the security tunnel between the cloud server and the attestation server (TTAP_1) and the interactive authentication of the terminal, user, and cloud server (TTAP_2).

3.1 Symbols

Italic characters indicate variables. The symbols are shown in following Table 1.

Table 1. Definitions of symbols

Symbols	Definitions
Cert(T,AIK)	AIK terminal certificate issued by private CA
Cert(C,AIK)	AIK cloud server certificate issued by private CA
Cert(A,AIK)	AIK attestation server certificate issued by private CA
T,A,C	Terminals, Attestation server, Cloud server
KEY_AC	Shared key between A and C
KEY_TC	Shared key between T and C
PK(T)	Private key of T
PK(A)	Private key of A
PK(C)	Private key of C
PUK(T)	Public key of T
PUK(A)	Public key of A
PUK(C)	Public key of C
N_1, N_2, N_3	Random numbers generated by trusted principal
$\{M\}_{Hash}$	Hash of message M
$\{M\}_{Sig\_K}$	Message M is signed with K
$\{M\}_K$	Message M is encrypted with K
g^x, g^y	Diffie-Hellman index

3.2 Process of TTAP_1

After the security tunnel is established between the cloud server and the attestation server, both parties generate the shared key *KEY_AC*. All messages transmitted over the security tunnel are encrypted with *KEY_AC*. There are four messages for *TTAP_1* to establish a security tunnel, which are as follows:

$$C \text{ to } A: \quad TTAP1\_M1 = \{g^x, N_1, \{g^x\}_{Sig\_PK(K)}, Cert(C, AIK)\};$$
$$A \text{ to } C: \quad TTAP1\_M2 = \{g^y, N_2, \{g^y\}_{Sig\_PK(C)}, Cert(C, AIK)\};$$
$$C \text{ to } A: \quad TTAP1\_M3 = \{N_2\}_{KEY\_AC};$$
$$A \text{ to } C: TTAP1\_M4 = \{N_1\}_{KEY\_AC}.$$

(1) *C* sends message *TTAP1_M1* to *A*.
(2) After receiving the message *TTAP1_M1*, *A* validates the *Cert(C, AIK)* and verifies the signature information firstly. If message *TTAP1_M1* passes validation, *A* sends *TTAP1_M2* to *C*.
(3) After receiving the message *TTAP1_M2*, *C* validates the *Cert(A, AIK)* and verifies the signature information. If message *TTAP1_M2* passes validation, *C* generates share key *KEY_AC* according to Diffie-Hellman algorithm and sends message *TTAP1_M3* to *A*.
(4) *A* receives the message *TTAP1_M3* and generates a shared key *KEY_AC* according to the Diffie-Hellman algorithm. Then *A* decrypts the message *TTAP1_M3* with *KEY_AC* and verifies the random number N_2. If N_2 passes validation, *A* sends message *TTAP1_M4* to *C*.
(5) *C* receives the message *TTAP1_M4* and decrypts the message. If the random number N_1 passes validation, After the random number is verified, the *TTAP_1* process is completed and the security tunnel between the cloud server and the attestation server is established successfully.

The *KEY_AC* can be updated according to a time period or other means. The messages encrypted with *KEY_AC* can be transmitted safely between *C* and *A*. The Diffie-Hellman algorithm is vulnerable to man-in-the-middle attacks when it exchange parameters without authentication identity of the other party [15]. In this paper, we use the PKI system to confirm the identity of the other party firstly and then perform Diffie-Hellman algorithm to protect it from man-in-the-middle attacks. N_1, N_2 are fresh value, which defend protocol from Dos and replay attacks. Message *TTAP1_M3* and message *TTAP1_M4* are for verifying that the shared private key of both side is the same.

If attackers tamper with g^x or g^y, the verification of the signature of g^x or g^y will be failed. Then *C* and *A* will not continue to perform Diffie-Hellman algorithm to ensure the privacy of the shared key.

3.3 Process of TTAP_2

Identity authentication are designed between terminals, users, and cloud server. We design six messages for *TTAP_2*. The messages are as follows:

T to $C : TTAP2\_M1 = \{ML, N_1, \{ML\}_{Hash}, \{\{ML\}_{Hash}\}_{Sig\_PK(T)}, Cert(A, AIK)\};$
C to $A : TTAP2\_M2 = \{ML, N_2, \{ML\}_{Hash}, \{\{ML\}_{Hash}\}_{Sig\_PK(T)}, Cert(A, AIK)\};$
A to $C : TTAP2\_M3 = \{Result\_plat, N_2\}_{KEY\_AC};$
C to $T : TTAP2\_M4 = \{Request\_plat, g^x, \{Request\_plat, gx\}_{Sig\_PK(C)}, N_3, Cert(C, AIK)\};$
T to $C : TTAP2\_M5 = \{g^y, \{g^y\}_{Sig\_PK(C)}, \{N_3, User\_ID, pwd\_info, IC\_info\}_{KEY\_TC}\};$
C to $T : TTAP2\_M6 = \{Result\_user\}_{KEY\_TC}.$

User_ID represents the user identity and *pwd_info* represents the user password. *IC_info* represents information in the Integrated Circuit Card, which are requested when a user is registered and login to the cloud server [4, 17, 18]. *Request_plat* represents that C requests the authentication of the user's information. *Result_plat* represents trusted authentication results of terminal, and *Result_user* represents trusted authentication results of the platform. The processes are as follows:

(1) When T connects to C, T sends message *TTAP2_M1* to C;
(2) After receiving *TTAP2_M1*, C sends *TTAP2_M2* to A.
(3) After receiving *TTAP2_M2*, A validates the *Cert(A, AIK)* and verifies the signature information. Then *ML* is measured. By the log, A judges whether the running state of T is trusted and generates measure results: *Result_plat*. At last, A sends message *TTAP2_M3* encrypted with *KEY_AC* which generated in *TTAP_1* to C.
(4) After receiving *TTAP2_M3*, C decrypts the message with *KEY_AC*. Then C verifies the random number *N2*. If *TTAP2_M3* passes validation, A sends message *TTAP2_M4* to T.
(5) After receiving *TTAP2_M4*, T verifies the validity of *Cert(C, AIK)* and verifies the correctness of the signature. If *TTAP2_M4* passes validation, T generates g^y. Then the shared private *KEY_TC* is calculated according to the Diffie-Hellman algorithm and message *TTAP2_M5* encrypted with *KEY_TC* is sent to C.
(6) After receiving the message 5, C verifies the signature. If the signature is verified, the shared private *KEY_TC* is calculated according to the Diffie-Hellman algorithm. Then C decrypts the message *TTAP2_M4* with *KEY_TC* and verifies consistent of fresh value *N3*. If the *User_ID*, *PWD*, and *IC_Infor* are consistently verified, C generates the result: *Result_user* encrypted with *KEY_TC* and sent it to T.

After receiving message *TTAP2_M5* and decrypting the message with *KEY_TC*, T responds to C according to *Result_user*.

In the phase of the authentication of the integrality, the hash value of the *ML* information is calculated, and then signed by private key of terminal, so as to prevent from being illegally tampered with. The cloud platform directly sends the information to the attestation server after generating the fresh value, which ensure that the consume of the cloud platform is minimized and the Dos attack will not work effectively. The fresh value also ensures that the attestation server can effectively defend against replay and Dos attacks. The verification of attestation server ensures that T is trusted. Strand space theorems.

3.4   Authentication Tests

The basic propositions in this paper are as follows [19, 20]:

Proposition 1 (Outgoing test theorem). Within a bundle of C, with n, $n' \in C$, $t = \{h\}_K$, $K^{-1} \notin P$, $a \subset t \subset term(n)$, t as a test component for a in node n, the edge $n \Rightarrow^+ n'$ consist of an outgoing test for a. Then:

(1) There is the general nodes m, $m' \in C$, and the edge $m \Rightarrow^+ m'$ is the transforming edge for a, $a \subset term(m)$; (2) Suppose the a just show on the $t0 = \{h0\}_{K0}$ of m', then $t0$ can't as a proper subterm of any general nodes of the components. Let $k_0^{-1} \notin P$, so the general negative node m'' exist in C, $t0$ is the component of this node.

Proposition 2 (Incoming test theorem). Within a bundle of C, with n, $n' \in C$, $t = \{h\}_K$, $a \subset t \subset term(n)$, $K \notin P$, t as a test component for a in node n, the edge $n \Rightarrow^+ n'$ consist of the incoming test for a, then there is the general nodes m, $m' \in C$, and $t \subset term(m')$, so the edge $m \Rightarrow^+ m'$ is the transforming edge for a.

Proposition 3 (Unsolicited test theorem). Within a bundle of C, with $t = \{h\}_K$, $K \notin P$, the negative node $n \in C$, n consist of the unsolicited test for t, so there is a regular node m, together with $t \subset term(m)$.

3.5   Capacity of Penetrator

Capacity of penetrator is defined in reference [21], which consists of 2 sets, sets of key grasped by penetrator and sets of penetrator strands.

3.6   Improved Theorems Based on Authentication Tests

Authentication tests are advanced rules based on strand space theorems, which make the authentication analysis of security protocols simple. The component $\{h\}_K$ indicates that the message h is encrypted with the key K, and the component information such as the signature/verification and HMac has no representation in the strand space and there is no correlation theorem. When the signature and Hmac algorithm are used in protocol, the formal analysis becomes somewhat complicated. In order to simplify the formal analysis of the protocol, signature test theorem and HMac test theorem are proposed in this paper.

Proposition 4 (Signature test theorem). Let n be a negative node of bundle C, and $t = \{h\}_{Sig\_k} \subset term(n)$ is a new component of n with $k \notin P$. Then, there must be a regular node $m \prec_c n$, and t and h are uniquely originating at m.

Prove. Let $D = \{n' \in C | t \subset term(n')\}$. D is a non-empty set, D exists $\prec_C$ minimum element denoted as m. The following uses the contradiction to prove correctness of Proposition 4. Suppose m is an unregular node. Since m is positive and a new component is generated, m cannot be in the penetrator strands: M-strand, K-strand, C-strand, S-strand, T-strand and F-strand. If m is in E-strand, D-strand, or SI-strand.

m is only possible on the third positive node of these three strands, and its key k is uniquely originating at the first negative node in the strand, which is contradicting with $k \notin P$. m must be a regular node. According to the principle of signature algorithm, t and h are uniquely originating at m.

Proposition 5 (HMac test theorem). Let n be a negative node of bundle C, and $t = \{h\}_{Hmac\_k} \subset term(n)$ is a new component of n with $k \notin P$. Then, there must be a regular node $m \prec_c n$, and t and h are uniquely originating at m.

The proof process of Proposition 5 is same as Proposition 4. Authentication tests has two security attributes, authentication attributes and confidentiality. The definition of attributes are as follows:

Definition 1 (authentication attributes). For all the bundles C and the strand s, if C-height of s in C is i, and some assumptions are true, then there must be a regular strand s' with C-height $t = j$ in the bundle C.

Definition 2 (confidentiality). For all the bundles C and the strand s, if C-height of s in C is i, and some of the assumptions are true, then there is no node $n \in C$ such that $term(n) = t$.

The general steps of analyzing the security of protocol is to propose a proposition according to Definition_1 or Definition_2 and then prove the proposition. If this proposition is correct, then the protocol is considered safe. By Definition 2, $PK(T)$, PK (A), $PK(C)$, KEY_TC and KEY_AC are uncompromised and confidentiality.

4 TTAP Security Analysis

4.1 TTAP_1 Protocol Formal Analysis

Figure 2 shows TTAP_1 protocol executive bundle, which contains 3 sets: cloud server strands, attestation server strands, penetrator strands. Trace of strands in TTAP_1 is in following Table 2. By Definition 2, it is assumed that bundle C is in space $\sum$ and strand $Scs \in cs[C, A, g^x, N_1, \text{AIK}]$ is in C with C-height = 4, KEY_AC, $PK(A)$, and $PK(C) \notin P$. Then there are must be a attestation server strand $S_{as} \in$ $as[C, A, g^y, N_2, \text{AIK}]$ in bundle C and C-height is 4 at least.

Proof. By Fig. 2, N_1 is uniquely originating at $< S_{cs}, 1 >$, $KEY\_AC \notin P$. It follows that edge $< S_{cs}, 1 > \Rightarrow^+ < S_{cs}, 4 >$ is a incoming test for N_1, and $\{N_1\}_{KEY\_AC}$ is the test component. By Proposition 2, there are must be two regular nodes (denoted as m, m') in bundle c and $m \Rightarrow^+ m'$ is transforming edge for N_1. And $\{N_1\}_{Kbs}$ is component of m'. By Fig. 2, m is the first node of some attestation server strand denoted as $S_{as}^* = as[C^*, A^*, g^{y*}, \text{AIK}^*]$ and m' is the fourth node of S_{as}^*.

Subterm $\{g^x\}_{Sig\_pk(A)}$ is received by $< S_{cs}, 2 >$, by theorem 4, there are must be a regular node (denoted as r) which is second node of some attestation server strand denoted as $S_{as}^{**} = as[C^{**}, A^{**}, g^{y**}, N_2^{**}, \text{AIK}^{**}]$. $< S_{cs}, 3 >$ sends message $\{N_2\}_{KEY\_AC}$ with $KEY\_AC \notin P$ and $< S_{cs}, 4 >$ receives $\{N_1\}_{KEY\_AC}$. By rule of KEY_AC generation [22] and the analysis above, we can get that: $S_{as}^{***} = S_{as}$, $S_{as}^{**} = S_{as}$, $S_{as}^* = S_{as}$, that is to say, there are must be a attestation server strand $S_{as} \in as[C, A, g^y, N_2, AIK]$ with *C-height* = 4.

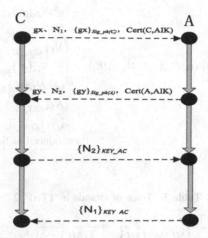

Fig. 2. Executive bundle of TTAP_1

4.2 TTAP_2 Protocol Formal Analysis

Executive bundle of TTAP_1 protocol is as shown in Fig. 3, which contains 4-type strands sets: terminal strands, cloud server strands, attestation server strands and penetrator strands. Trace of strands in TTAP_2 is in following Table 3.

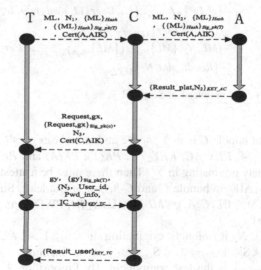

Fig. 3. Executive bundle of TTAP_2

Table 2. Trace of strands in TTAP_1

Sets of strands	Trace
Cloud server strands (cs[C, A, g^x, N_1, AIK])	$+\{g^x, N_1, \{g^x\}_{Sig\_pk(A)}, Cert(A, AIK)\}$
	$-\{g^y, N_2, \{g^x\}_{Sig\_pk(C)}, Cert(C, AIK)\}$
	$+\{N_2\}_{KEY\_AC}$
	$-\{N_1\}_{KEY\_AC}$
Attestation server strands (as[C, A, g^y, N_2, AIK])	$-\{g^x, N_1, \{g^x\}_{Sig\_pk(A)}, Cert(A, AIK)\}$
	$+\{g^y, N_2, \{g^x\}_{Sig\_pk(C)}, Cert(C, AIK)\}$
	$-\{N_2\}_{KEY\_AC}$
	$+\{N_1\}_{KEY\_AC}$
Penetrator strands (P)	Introduced in Sect. 4.2

Table 3. Trace of strands in TTAP_2

Sets of strands	Trace
Terminal strands (t[T, C, gx, ML, N_1, $User\_id$, pwd_info, IC_info, AIK])	$+\{ML, N_1, \{ML\}_{Hash}, \{\{ML\}_{Hash}\}_{Sig\_PK(T)}, Cert(A, AIK)\}$
	$-\{Request, g^x, \{Request, g^x\}_{Sig\_PK(c)}\}, N_3, Cert(C, AIK)\}$
	$+\{g^y, \{g^y\}_{Sig\_PK(c)}, \{N_3, User\_id, pwd\_info, Ic\_info\}_{KEY\_TC}$
	$-\{Result\_user\}_{KEY\_TC}$
Cloud server strands (cs[T, C, A, gy, N_2, N_3, AIK])	$-\{ML, N_1, \{ML\}_{Hash}, \{\{ML\}_{Hash}\}_{Sig\_pk(T)}, Cert(A, AIK)\}$
	$+\{ML, N_2, \{ML\}_{Hash}, \{\{ML\}_{Hash}\}_{Sig\_pk(T)}, Cert(A, AIK)\}$
	$-\{Result\_plat, N_2\}_{KEY\_AC}, +\{Request, g^x, \{Request, g^x\}_{Sig\_pk(c)}\}$
	$+\{Request, g^x, \{Request, g^x\}_{Sig\_pk(c)}\}$
	$-\{g^y, \{g^y\}_{Sig\_PK(c)}, \{N_3, User\_id, pwd\_info, Ic\_info\}_{KEY\_TC}$
	$+\{Result\_user\}_{KEY\_TC}$
Attestation server strands as[C, A, $Result\_plat$, AIK]	$-\{ML, N_2, \{ML\}_{Hash}, \{\{ML\}_{Hash}\}_{Sig\_pk(T)}, Cert(A, AIK)\}$
	$+\{Result\_plat, N_2\}_{KEY\_AC}$
Penetrator strands (P)	Introduced in Sect. 4.2

It is assumed that bundle C is in $\sum$ space and strand $Scs \in$ cs[C, A, g^x, N_1, AIK] is in C with *C-height* = 4, *KEY_AC*, *KEY_TC*, *PK(T)*, *PK(A)* and $PK(C) \notin P$. And N_1, N_2 and N_3 are uniquely originating in $\sum$. Then there must be a attestation server strand $S_{as} \in$ as[C, A, g^y, N_2, AIK] in bundle C and *C-height* is 2 at least. Similarly, there must be a terminal strand $St \in$ t[$T, C, A, g^x, ML, N_1, User\_ID$, PWD_*info*, IC_*info*, AIK] and *C-height* is 3 at least.

Proof. By Fig. 3, N_2 is uniquely originating at $<S_{cs}, 1>$, *KEY_AC* $\notin P$. It follows that edge $<S_{cs}, 1> \Rightarrow^+ <S_{cs}, 2>$ is a incoming test for N_2, and $\{Result\_plat, N_2\}_{KEY\_AC}$ is the test component. By Proposition 2, there are must be two regular nodes (denoted as m, m') in bundle C and $m \Rightarrow^+ m'$ is transforming edge for N_2. By Fig. 3, m is the first node of some attestation server strand denoted as $S_{as}^* = as[C^*, A^*, Result\_plat^*]$. And m' is the second node of S_{as}^*. By Proposition 4 and TTAP_1, it is known that $C^* = C, A^* = A$, $Result\_plat^* = Result\_plat$, that is to say, there must be a attestation server strand $S_{as} \in as[C, A, g^y, N_2, AIK]$ with $C\text{-}height = 2$.

$< S_{cs}, 1 >$ receives subterm $\{h\}_{Sig\_PK(T)}$, by Proposition 4, there must be a regular node (denoted as r) is the first node of some terminal strand demoted as $S_t^* = t[T^*, C^*, A^*, \ g^{x*}, ML^*, N_1^*, User\_id^*, pwd\_info^*, \text{IC\_info}^*, AIK^*]$. N_3 is uniquely originating at $< S_{cs}, 3 >$, $KEY\_AC \notin P$. It follows that the edge $< S_{cs}, 3 > \Rightarrow^+$ $< S_{cs}, 4 >$ is a incoming test for N_3, and $\{N^3, User\_ID, Pwd\_info, IC\_Infor\}_{KEY\_TC}$ is the test component. By Proposition 2, there are must be two regular nodes (denoted as d, d') are in bundle C. By Fig. 3, d is the second node of some terminal strand denoted as $S_t^{**} = t[T^{**}, C^{**}, g^{x**}, ML^{**}, N_1^{**}, \ User\_ID^{**}, PWD\_info^{**}, IC\_info^{**}, AIK^{**}]$ and d' is the three node of S_t^{**}. Because $PK(T)$ is private key of T and subterm of component of $< S_t^{**}, 1 >$ and $< S_t^*, 3 >$ is signed by $PK(T)$, $< S_t^*, 1 >$ and $< S_t^*, 3 >$ are in the same strand. It's concluded that $< S_t^{**}, 2 >$, $< S_t^{**}, 3 >$ and $< S_t^*, 1 >$ are in the same strand and $T^{**} = T^* = T$, so, there must be a terminal strand $St \in t[T, C, A, g^x, ML, N_1, User\_ID, pwd\_info, IC\_info, AIK]$ and $C\text{-}height$ is 3 at least.

Because $PK(T)$, $PK(A)$, $PK(C)$, KEY_TC, KEY_AC are uncompromised, so component encrypted with these keys are uncompromised.

5 Conclusion

TTAP protocol is designed in this paper, being suited to trusted terminal accesses to trusted cloud server, especially in some sensitive business environment. Strand space modal is extended in this paper. By analyzing TTAP protocol based on extended authentication tests, it is proved that authentication attribute is consistent and protocol is safe. In subsequent work, the focus is to continuously extend strand space, analyze sophisticated security protocol, and research on automatic formal analysis tool of safety protocol. Furthermore, we will focus on TNC and design the model and protocol of access to trusted cloud server.

References

1. Kong, G.: Advances on secure authentication and trusted admission protocols for cloud computing. J. Henan Univ. **47**(1), 62–64 (2017)
2. Luo, D., Wu, X., Zheng, X., Hu, Y.: OOAP: a novel authorization protocol for access to sensitive data in trusted cloud computing platforms. Int. J. Secur. Appl. **8**(6), 397–404 (2014)
3. Lai, Y., Chen, Y., Zou, Q., Liu, Z., Yang, Z.: Design and analysis on trusted network equipment access authentication protocol. Simul. Model. Pract. Theory **51**(51), 157–169 (2015)
4. Wang, J., Zhang, Z., Chang, Y.: A security protocol for trusted access to cloud environment. Recent Adv. Electr. Electron. Eng. **8**(2), 1–10 (2015)

5. Bo, Y., Guo, F.D., Yu, Q., Zhang, Y.J.: Secure access scheme of cloud services for trusted mobile terminals using trustzone. J. Softw. **27**(6), 1366–1383 (2016)
6. Bo, Z., Zhu, X., Shuang, X., Bing, Y.: C-TNC: trusted cloud access protocol for openstack. J. Huazhong Univ. Sci. Technol. **44**(3), 83–89 (2016)
7. Kim, G.L., Lim, J.D., Kim, J.N.: Secure user authentication based on the trusted platform for mobile devices. EURASIP J. Wirel. Commun. Netw. **2016**(1), 233 (2016)
8. Song, W.T., Bin, H.U.: One strong authentication test suitable for analysis of nested encryption protocols. Comput. Sci. **42**(1), 149–169 (2015)
9. Xiong, L., Peng, D.Y.: An improved authentication test for security protocol analysis. Commun. Technol. **47**(8), 951–954 (2014)
10. Muhammad, S.: Applying authentication tests to discover man-in-the-middle attack in security protocols. In: Eighth International Conference on Digital Information Management, pp. 35–40 (2013)
11. Lei, Y.U.: Analysis on properties for principals' keys on construction of test components. Comput. Eng. Appl. **49**(6), 114–117 (2013)
12. Wei, F., Feng, D.G.: Analyzing trusted computing protocol based on the strand spaces model. Chin. J. Comput. **38**(4), 701–716 (2015)
13. Guttman, J.D.: State and progress in strand spaces: Proving fair exchange. J. Autom. Reason. **48**(2), 159–195 (2012)
14. Ramsdell, J.D., Dougherty, D.J., Guttman, J.D., Rowe, P.D.: A hybrid analysis for security protocols with state. In: Albert, E., Sekerinski, E. (eds.) IFM 2014. LNCS, vol. 8739, pp. 272–287. Springer, Cham (2014). https://doi.org/10.1007/978-3-319-10181-1_17
15. Liu, J.: Automatic verification of security protocols with strand space theory. J. Comput. Appl. **35**(7), 1870–1876 (2015)
16. Khader, A.S., Lai, D.: Preventing man-in-the-middle attack in Diffie-Hellman key exchange protocol. In: International Conference on Telecommunications, pp. 204–208 (2015)
17. Xu, C., Jia, Z., Ma, Y.: Cryptanalysis and improvement of an enhanced smart card based remote user authentication scheme. J. Comput. Inf. Syst. **10**(5), 2035–2042 (2014)
18. Xu, C., Jia, Z., Wen, F., Ma, Y.: Cryptanalysis and improvement of a dynamic id based remote user authentication scheme using smart cards. J. Comput. Inf. Syst. **9**(14), 5513–5520 (2013)
19. Guttman, J.D., Thayer, F.J.: Authentication tests. In: Proceedings of 2000 IEEE Symposium on Security and Privacy, S&P 2000, pp. 96–109 (2000)
20. Guttman, J.D., Thayer, F.J.: Authentication tests and the structure of bundles. Theoret. Comput. Sci. **283**(2), 333–380 (2002)
21. Dolev, D., Yao, A.C.: On the security of public key protocols. IEEE Trans. Inf. Theory **29**(2), 198–208 (1983)
22. Diffie, W., Hellman, M.: New directions in cryptography. IEEE Trans. Inf. Theory **22**(6), 644–654 (1976)

A Study on Revenue Distribution of Information Sharing in the C2M Supply Chain

Chunxia Liu[1,2], Youyu Chen[2,3], Shu Tong[3(✉)], Wangdong Jiang[2], and Guang Sun[2]

[1] Changsha University of Science and Technology, Changsha 410114, China
[2] Hunan University of Finance and Economics, Changsha 410205, China
[3] Hunan University, Changsha 410082, China
leo.stone@qq.com

Abstract. There has been ongoing controversy among scholars as to whether the Customer to Manufactory (C2M) supply chain can generate revenue through information technology investment and how to distribute revenue obtained by information sharing. First, this dissertation constructs two kinds of revenue distribution models, namely models based on independent decision-making and collaborative decision-making. Then, according to the status differences between the manufacturer and the distribution enterprise in the supply chain, the C2M supply chain is divided into three situations for example analysis. The research revealed that under the condition of equal input level of information sharing, the revenue of information sharing is greater when the manufacturer and the distribution enterprise collaborate with each other. When manufacturers of equal status cooperate with distribution companies, their revenues of information sharing are directly proportional to their information sharing investment levels. However, when status is not equivalent, most of the revenues generated by information sharing are dominated by the dominant company. Therefore, there is insufficient motivation for cooperation between the two parties. Finally, this paper points out that a well-designed revenue redistribution mechanism can improve the efficiency of information sharing, achieve the rationality and effectiveness of supply chain profit distribution as well as maximize the value of C2M e-commerce supply chain information sharing.

Keywords: C2M · E-commerce supply chain · Information sharing Revenue · Distribution

1 Introduction

In January 2018, the "Statistical Report on China's Internet Development" released by the China Internet Network Information Center showed that by the end of 2017, the number of Chinese Internet users reached 772 million, and the Internet penetration rate was 55.8%. Under this background, in order to meet consumer demand for personalization in terms of price, quality, time, and convenience, companies have begun to use technologies such as big data, cloud computing, and mobile phone intelligence to

© Springer Nature Switzerland AG 2018
X. Sun et al. (Eds.): ICCCS 2018, LNCS 11064, pp. 543–552, 2018.
https://doi.org/10.1007/978-3-030-00009-7_49

launch a consumer-centered production model, which is called C2M (Customer to Manufacturer) mode. The successful operation of the C2M model is inseparable from the resource integration and information seamless connection between the companies in the supply chain. Whether or not C2M e-commerce supply chain can realize the value of information sharing through information technology investment and the size of the value creation are controversial.

Through empirical analysis Dan et al. (2016) found that information sharing can coordinate the competition among manufacturers. If and only if the competition intensity exceeds a certain threshold, information sharing can increase the expected profit of the system in the supply chain. Ha et al. (2011) revealed that in the Cournot competition environment, information sharing can increase the overall profit of the supply chain when the manufacturer's scale is not economically high. Through benchmark analysis, Zhou et al. (2017) found that horizontal competition and information incompletion were the two determinants of the low efficiency in a supply chain. Kim and Chai (2017) pointed out in their study that both information sharing and strategic sourcing play a positive role on improving supply chain agility. Yan and Pei (2011) conducted a comparative study on the pricing strategies of suppliers and retailers in the context of information asymmetry and information sharing, and found that information sharing can effectively improve the benefits of the entire supply chain. Yue and Liu (2006) studied the effect of information asymmetry under dual channels on manufacturers' pricing and performance in MTO (order-to-order model) and MTS (by-stock model), and research shows that information sharing can increase the revenue of manufacturers and retailers. However, the lack of a corresponding coordination mechanism for information sharing does not increase the overall profitability of the supply chain (Zhang 2012). The increased profit of information sharing is positively related to the accuracy and timeliness of information, and a matching information system can significantly increase the efficiency of information sharing and reduce inventory costs (Xiao 2014).

The e-commerce model has become an important sales model for supply chain node companies, the study on revenue distribution of information sharing in the C2M supply chain is very valuable and necessary.

2 Model Assumption

The C2M supply chain is mainly composed of manufacturers, platform operators, distribution enterprises, and consumers. The C2M e-commerce platform can be mainly divided into two modes: the manufacturer's self-built internet platform and the cooperation with the third-party e-commerce platform. The manufacturer's self-built internet platform model is the mainstream mode of the current C2M e-commerce platform. The successful operation of the C2M e-commerce model is closely related to the distribution business. It may be assumed that the C2M supply chain consists of the manufacturer 1 and the distribution enterprise 2. The manufacturer 1 sells goods directly to the customer through the e-commerce platform, and the distribution enterprise 2 is responsible for the distribution. And thus make further assumptions:

(1) Assume that the total information sharing benefit of the whole supply chain is W, and assume that the benefit sharing factors of manufacturers and the distribution enterprise (θ_1 and θ_2) satisfy $\theta_1 + \theta_2 = 1$ and $0 \leq \theta_1, \theta_2 \leq 1$;

(2) Assume that the total information sharing benefit mainly depends on the information sharing investment levels of the manufacturer 1 and the distribution enterprise 2, and assume that the more investment input, the more total benefit. If x_1 and x_2 show the information sharing investment levels of manufacturer and the distribution enterprise, the total revenue function can be expressed as:

$$W = \lambda x_1^\delta x_2^\gamma \tag{1}$$

among which δ and γ respectively represent the information sharing investment elasticity of the manufacturer 1 and the distribution enterprise 2, satisfying with $\delta + \gamma = 1$ and $0 \leq \delta, \gamma \leq 1$, while λ refers to environmental factors, facing the good environment, $\lambda \geq 1$, facing with bad environment $0 \leq \lambda \leq 1$;

(3) Suppose that total revenue function is also affected by information absorptive capacity of node enterprises. If ρ_1 and ρ_2 represent manufacturer and distribution enterprise's capacity to absorb shared information, i.e. absorptive capacity factor, then total revenue function can be expressed as:

$$W = \lambda x_1^\delta x_2^\gamma + \rho_1 x_2^2 + \rho_2 x_1^2 \tag{2}$$

$\rho_1 x_2^2$ represents benefits brought to the manufacturer by absorbing shared information of the other party, $\rho_2 x_1^2$ shows the benefit brought to the distribution enterprise by absorbing shared information of the other party.

(4) Suppose that the manufacturer and distribution enterprise all need to share the cost of information sharing, and assumes that it is directly proportional to the level of information sharing. If φ_1 and φ_2 refer to the cost impact factor of manufacturers and distribution enterprise, then the manufacturer's cost function C_1 and the distribution enterprise's cost function C_2 can be expressed as:

$$\begin{cases} C_1 = \varphi_1 x_1^2 \\ C_2 = \varphi_2 x_2^2 \end{cases} \tag{3}$$

At this point, it may be assumed that $\rho_1 < \varphi_2, \rho_2 < \varphi_1$.

Hence, the overall profit function of manufacturer, distribution enterprise and supply chain are respectively:

$$\begin{cases} \pi_1 = \theta_1 \lambda x_1^\delta x_2^\gamma + \rho_1 x_2^2 - \varphi_1 x_1^2 \\ \pi_2 = \theta_2 \lambda x_1^\delta x_2^\gamma + \rho_2 x_1^2 - \varphi_2 x_2^2 \\ \pi = \lambda x_1^\delta x_2^\gamma + \rho_1 x_2^2 + \rho_2 x_1^2 - \varphi_1 x_1^2 - \varphi_2 x_2^2 \end{cases} \tag{4}$$

3 Profit Distribution Model Based on Independent Decision-Making Between Enterprises

In the game model of Stackelberg, leading company make a decision first, and then following enterprises' decision afterwards. Assume that the manufacturer is the leading enterprise, and decision is first made by it. Since the method to solve the dynamic game is using backward induction, i.e. solving from the latter stage to the former stage or reaction is first made by distribution enterprise, and then the manufacturers make their optimization decision to response decision made by the distribution enterprise.

First phase: the distribution enterprise responds to the manufacturer's decision first, pursuing to maximize π_2, i.e. $\frac{\partial \pi_2}{\partial x_2} = 0$, then:

$$x_2 = (\frac{\gamma \lambda \theta_2}{2\varphi_2})^{\frac{1}{1+\delta}} x_1^{\frac{\delta}{1+\delta}} \tag{5}$$

Second phase: The manufacturer makes decision to reactions possibly made by the distribution enterprise, pursuing to the maximization of π_1, i.e. $\frac{\partial \pi_1}{\partial x_1} = 0$, then:

$$x_1 = \frac{\lambda}{2} (\frac{\delta(1-\delta)\theta_1\theta_2}{\varphi_1\varphi_2})^{\frac{1}{2}} (\frac{\delta\theta_1\varphi_2}{(1-\delta)\theta_2\varphi_1})^{\frac{\delta}{2}} \tag{6}$$

Substitute into the upper form, we can get:

$$x_2 = \frac{\lambda}{4} (\frac{\gamma(1-\gamma)\theta_1\theta_2}{\varphi_1\varphi_2})^{\frac{1}{2}} (\frac{\gamma\theta_2\varphi_1}{(1-\gamma)\theta_1\varphi_2})^{\frac{\gamma}{2}} \tag{7}$$

That is:

$$\begin{cases} x_1 = \frac{\lambda}{4} (\frac{\delta(1-\delta)\theta_1\theta_2}{\varphi_1\varphi_2})^{\frac{1}{2}} (\frac{\delta\theta_1\varphi_2}{(1-\delta)\theta_2\varphi_1})^{\frac{\delta}{2}} \\ x_2 = \frac{\lambda}{4} (\frac{\gamma(1-\gamma)\theta_1\theta_2}{\varphi_1\varphi_2})^{\frac{1}{2}} (\frac{\gamma\theta_2\varphi_1}{(1-\gamma)\theta_1\varphi_2})^{\frac{\gamma}{2}} \end{cases} \tag{8}$$

Proposition 1: Information sharing investment levels is directly proportional to the benefit sharing factors, i.e. the higher the information sharing investment levels, the higher the share of benefit level; meanwhile, information sharing investment levels of the other side is directly proportional to benefit sharing factors of their own side, i.e. the positive externalities exist.

By calculation, it can be obtained:

$$\begin{cases} \frac{\partial x_1}{\partial \theta_1} = \frac{\lambda(1+\delta)}{8} (\frac{\delta\gamma\theta_2}{\varphi_1\varphi_2})^{\frac{1}{2}} (\frac{\delta\varphi_2}{\gamma\theta_2\varphi_1})^{\frac{\delta}{2}} \theta_1^{\frac{\delta-1}{2}} > 0 \\ \frac{\partial x_1^2}{\partial \theta_1^2} = -\frac{\lambda(1-\delta^2)}{16} (\frac{\delta\gamma\theta_2}{\varphi_1\varphi_2})^{\frac{1}{2}} \times \theta_1^{\frac{\delta-3}{2}} < 0 \end{cases} \tag{9}$$

It shows that the information sharing investment level of the manufacturer is directly proportional to the profit sharing factor;

Further, there is also:

$$\begin{cases} \frac{\partial x_1}{\partial \theta_2} = \frac{\lambda(1-\delta)}{8}\left(\frac{\delta\gamma\theta_1}{\varphi_1\varphi_2}\right)^{\frac{1}{2}}\left(\frac{\delta\theta_1\varphi_2}{\gamma\varphi_1}\right)^{\frac{\delta}{2}}\theta_2^{-\frac{\delta+1}{2}} > 0 \\ \frac{\partial x_1^2}{\partial \theta_2^2} = -\frac{\lambda(1-\delta^2)}{16}\left(\frac{\delta\gamma\theta_1}{\varphi_1\varphi_2}\right)^{\frac{1}{2}}\left(\frac{\delta\theta_1\varphi_2}{\gamma\varphi_1}\right)^{\frac{\delta}{2}}\theta_2^{-\frac{\delta+3}{2}} < 0 \\ \frac{\partial x_1^2}{\partial \theta_2\theta_1} = \frac{\lambda(1-\delta^2)}{16}\left(\frac{\delta\gamma}{\varphi_1\varphi_2}\right)^{\frac{1}{2}}\left(\frac{\delta\varphi_2}{\gamma\varphi_1}\right)^{\frac{\delta}{2}}\theta_1^{\frac{\delta-1}{2}}\theta_2^{-\frac{\delta+1}{2}} > 0 \end{cases} \quad (10)$$

It shows that the information sharing investment level of the manufacturer is directly proportional to the profit sharing factor of the distribution enterprise, i.e. There are obvious positive externalities exist.

It can be calculated in a similar way: $\frac{\partial x_2}{\partial \theta_1} > 0, \frac{\partial x_2^2}{\partial \theta_1^2} < 0, \frac{\partial x_2}{\partial \theta_2} > 0, \frac{\partial x_2^2}{\partial \theta_2^2} < 0,$

$\frac{\partial x_2^2}{\partial \theta_2\theta_1} > 0$, i.e. It has a same conclusion to the distribution enterprise: the information sharing investment level of the distribution enterprise is directly proportional to the profit sharing factor, and the information sharing investment level of the manufacturer is directly proportional to the profit sharing factor of the manufacturer.

4 Profit Distribution Model Based on Collaborative Decision-Making

To enhance market competitiveness, each node enterprise on the supply chain establishes close cooperation, aiming at total profit maximization or the total cost minimization of the whole supply chain, forming a strategic alliance between manufacturers and distribution enterprises, strengthen the information sharing among the node companies in the supply chain and realize the value of information sharing to achieve a win-win goal. To differentiate profit distribution model that was based on independent decision-making, it is better to mark π as π', x_1 as x_1' and x_2 as x_2', i.e.:

$$\begin{cases} \frac{\partial \pi'}{\partial x_1} = \delta\theta_1\lambda x_1^{\delta-1}x_2^{\gamma} - 2\varphi_1 x_1 = 0 \\ \frac{\partial \pi'}{\partial x_2} = \gamma\theta_2\lambda x_1^{\delta}x_2^{\gamma-1} - 2\varphi_2 x_2 = 0 \end{cases} \quad (11)$$

Then x_1' and x_2' are as follows:

$$\begin{cases} x_1' = \frac{\lambda\gamma}{2(\varphi_2-\rho_1)}\left(\frac{\delta(\varphi_2-\rho_1)}{(1-\delta)(\varphi_1-\rho_2)}\right)^{\frac{1+\delta}{2}} \\ x_2' = \frac{\lambda\gamma}{2(\varphi_2-\rho_1)}\left(\frac{(1-\gamma)(\varphi_2-\rho_1)}{\gamma(\varphi_1-\rho_2)}\right)^{\frac{\delta}{2}} \end{cases} \quad (12)$$

Proposition 2: In cooperation, the information sharing investment level of the manufacturer and the distribution company is greater than that of information sharing at the time of independence.

Comparing the investment level of information sharing between the manufacturer's cooperation and independence, the following are available:

$$\frac{x_1^{/}}{x_1} = \theta_1^{-\frac{1+\delta}{2}} \theta_2^{-\frac{1-\delta}{2}} \left(\frac{\varphi_1}{\varphi_1 - \rho_2}\right)^{\frac{1+\delta}{2}} \left(\frac{\varphi_2}{\varphi_2 - \rho_1}\right)^{\frac{1-\delta}{2}} \tag{13}$$

Because $0 < \theta_1, \theta_2, \delta < 1$, and all are constants, so $\theta_1^{-\frac{1+\delta}{2}} \theta_2^{-\frac{1-\delta}{2}} > 1$; Because $\frac{\varphi_1}{\varphi_1 - \rho_2} > 1$, $\frac{\varphi_2}{\varphi_2 - \rho_1} > 1$, then $\left(\frac{\varphi_1}{\varphi_1 - \rho_2}\right)^{\frac{1+\delta}{2}} \left(\frac{\varphi_2}{\varphi_2 - \rho_1}\right)^{\frac{1-\delta}{2}} > 1$, so $\frac{x_1^{/}}{x_1} > 1$. It can be seen that when enterprises cooperate, manufacturers' information sharing investment level is higher than the information sharing investment level when the company is independent.

Comparing the investment level of information sharing between the distribution enterprise's cooperation and independence, the following are available:

$$\frac{x_2^{/}}{x_2} = \theta_1^{-\frac{1-\gamma}{2}} \theta_2^{-\frac{1+\gamma}{2}} \left(\frac{\varphi_1}{\varphi_1 - \rho_2}\right)^{\frac{1-\gamma}{2}} \left(\frac{\varphi_2}{\varphi_2 - \rho_1}\right)^{\frac{1-\delta}{2}} \tag{14}$$

In the same way, it can be proved that when enterprises cooperate, the distribution enterprise's information sharing investment level is higher than the information sharing investment level when the company is independent.

Proposition 3: The level of information sharing between manufacturers and distribution companies during cooperation is not related to the revenue-sharing factors of the company and the other company.

Because $\frac{\partial x_1}{\partial \theta_1} = 0, \frac{\partial x_1^2}{\partial \theta_1^2} = 0$, so manufacturer's level of information sharing investment has nothing to do with its revenue-sharing factors. Because $\frac{\partial x_1}{\partial \theta_2} = 0, \frac{\partial x_1^2}{\partial \theta_2^2} = 0, \frac{\partial x_1^2}{\partial \theta_2 \theta_1} = 0$, so manufacturer's level of information sharing investment has nothing to do with the distribution enterprise's revenue-sharing factors.

Similarly, it can be calculated $\frac{\partial x_2}{\partial \theta_1} = 0, \frac{\partial x_2^2}{\partial \theta_1^2} = 0, \frac{\partial x_2}{\partial \theta_2} = 0, \frac{\partial x_2^2}{\partial \theta_2^2} = 0, \frac{\partial x_2^2}{\partial \theta_2 \theta_1} = 0$, i.e. the same conclusion is for the distribution enterprise.

5 Numerical Experiments and Analysis

In order to make deeper analysis on the relationship among information sharing input level, information sharing benefits and benefits sharing factors, it may be further assumed that $\lambda = 1, \delta = \gamma = 0.5, \rho_1 = \rho_2 = 0.5, \varphi_1 = \varphi_2 = 1$, on the premise of satisfying the model's previous assumptions, and the following result can be got when the manufacturer and the distribution enterprise make decision independently:

$$\begin{cases} x_1 = \frac{1}{4}\theta_1^{\frac{3}{4}}\theta_2^{\frac{1}{4}} \\ x_2 = \frac{1}{4}\theta_2^{\frac{3}{4}}\theta_1^{\frac{1}{4}} \\ \pi = \frac{1}{32}\theta_1^{\frac{1}{2}}\theta_2^{\frac{1}{2}}(8 - \theta_1 - \theta_2) \\ \pi_1 = \frac{1}{32}\theta_1^{\frac{1}{2}}\theta_2^{\frac{1}{2}}(\theta_2 + 6\theta_1) \\ \pi_2 = \frac{1}{32}\theta_1^{\frac{1}{2}}\theta_2^{\frac{1}{2}}(\theta_1 + 6\theta_2) \end{cases} \tag{15}$$

Under the same assumptions, we can obtain the following when the manufacturer and the distribution enterprise cooperate in decision-making:

$$\begin{cases} x_1' = x_2' = \frac{1}{2} \\ \pi' = \frac{1}{4} \\ \pi_1' = \frac{1}{2}\theta_1 - \frac{1}{8} \\ \pi_2' = \frac{1}{2}\theta_2 - \frac{1}{8} \end{cases} \tag{16}$$

Companies in the supply chain have different resource endowments in key resources such as capital, technology, equipment, and information. They also have differences in control, trust, and special-purpose asset investment in the supply chain, resulting in an unequal power of the supply chain network. In different stages of the supply chain network development, the power position of each node enterprise is in a dynamic change. Therefore, according to the differences in the power status of each node's enterprises, the C2M supply chain is divided into three types: manufacturers and distributors are in a position of equal importance; manufacturers are core enterprises; distribution companies are supporting enterprises; manufacturers are supporting enterprises, and distributors are core companies.

When manufacturers and distributors are in a position of equal status, the revenue sharing factors of manufacturers and distributors are equal, that is, $\theta_1 = \theta_2 = 0.5$; If manufacturer 1 is in a core position, the revenue sharing factor of manufacturer 1 is greater than that of distributor 2, here suppose $\theta_1 = 0.64, \theta_2 = 0.36$; When the distributor 2 is at a core position, its revenue sharing factor is greater than that of the manufacturer 1, here suppose $\theta_2 = 0.64, \theta_1 = 0.36$. It is discussed in different situations as below:

(1) When manufacturers and retailers are in equal status, here suppose $\theta_1 = \theta_2 = 0.5$, it can be calculated as below:

If manufacturers and distributors make decision independently, then we can get: $x_1 = x_2 = 0.125, \pi = \frac{7}{64} \approx 0.1094, \pi_1 = \pi_2 = \frac{7}{128} = 0.0547$;
If manufacturers and distributors cooperate in decision-making, then: $x_1' = x_2' = 0.5, \pi' = 0.25, \pi_1' = \pi_2' = 0.125$.

As a conclusion, $\Delta x_1 = \Delta x_2 = 0.422, \Delta \pi_1 = \Delta \pi_2 = 0.0703, \Delta \pi = 0.1406$.

Conclusion 1: When manufacturer 1 and distributor 2 are in an equal status, the levels of information sharing input and revenues of cooperation are significantly higher than those when they are independent; The total revenue is also higher when they cooperate and the increased revenue is equally divided by manufacturer 1 and distributor 2; the increased information sharing input is half contributed by manufacturer 1 and distributor 2 respectively. Therefore, the cooperation at this time is fair and meaningful.

(2) When the manufacturer is in a core position, here suppose $\theta_1 = 0.64, \theta_2 = 0.36$, If manufacturers and distributors make decision independently, then we can get: $x_1 \approx 0.1386, x_2 \approx 0.1039, \pi = 0.105, \pi_1 = 0.063, \pi_2 = 0.0267$; If manufacturers and distributors cooperate in decision-making, then: $x_1' = x_2' = 0.5, \pi' = 0.25$, $\pi_1' = 0.195, \pi_2' = 0.055$.

As a conclusion, $\Delta x_1 = 0.3614, \Delta x_2 = 0.3961, \Delta \pi_1 = 0.132, \Delta x_2 = 0.0283, \Delta \pi = 0.145, \frac{\Delta \pi_1}{\Delta \pi} \approx 0.9103, \frac{\Delta \pi_2}{\Delta \pi} \approx 0.0897$.

Conclusion 2: When the manufacturer 1 is in the core position, and manufacturer 1 and distributor 2 cooperate in decision-making, then their information sharing input level and revenue are higher in compare with when they make decision independently. The total revenue during the cooperation is obviously higher than the total revenue during the independent period. Nearly 91% of the total increase revenue is occupied by the manufacturer 1, and the distributor 2 only shares 9% of the total revenue. In terms of input level of information sharing, the growth of information sharing investment in distributor 2 is higher than that of manufacturer 1. Therefore, at this time, cooperation is most beneficial to manufacturer 1. For distributor 2, the motivation for cooperation is insufficient.

(3) When the distribution enterprise is in a core position, suppose $\theta_2 = 0.64$, $\theta_1 = 0.36$, the formula mode is completely the same with that of (2), namely: $\Delta x_1 = 0.3961, \Delta x_2 = 0.3614$, $\Delta \pi_1 = 0.0283, \Delta x_2 = 0.132, \Delta \pi = 0.145, \frac{\Delta \pi_2}{\Delta \pi} \approx 0.9103, \frac{\Delta \pi_1}{\Delta \pi} \approx 0.0897$.

Conclusion 3: When distribution enterprise 2 are in a core position, information sharing investment levels and revenues of manufacturer 1 and distribution enterprise 2 are higher than those of independency; the total revenue of cooperation is significantly higher and nearly 91% of the total increase in revenue is occupied by distribution enterprise 2, and manufacturer 1 only shared 9% of them; in terms of information sharing input level, the increase in the level of information sharing investment of manufacturers 1 was higher than distribution enterprise 2. Therefore, the cooperation at this time is most beneficial to the distribution enterprise 2, and for the manufacturer 1, the motivation for cooperation is insufficient.

6   Conclusion

This article discusses the realization of the information sharing value of two-level supply chain composed of manufacturers and distribution companies under the mode of manufacturer's self-built Internet platform. Two Profit distribution model were constructed, one was based on collaborative decision-making and the other was based on independent decision-making between enterprises. The following conclusions were obtained through correlation analysis: Under the independent decision-making model, the input level of information sharing between manufacturers and distribution companies is directly proportional to the revenue-sharing factor. At the same time, the input level of one party's information sharing is proportional to the revenue-sharing factor of the other party, that is, there is a positive externality; In a mutually cooperative supply chain, the levels of information sharing input and revenues of cooperation are significantly higher than those when they are independent; the level of investment in information sharing has nothing to do with the profit-sharing factors of the company and its co-operatives.

According to the status differences between node companies, the C2M supply chain is divided into three situations for example analysis. The following conclusions were obtained: When manufacturers and distribution companies are in a position of equal importance, through cooperation, manufacturers and logistics and distribution companies can obtain equal revenue growth when they increase the amount of shared information, cooperation at this time can bring benefits to both parties, and both parties think it is fair; When the status of manufacturers and logistics and distribution companies is not equal, more than 90% of the increase in revenue brought about by cooperation is occupied by the core enterprises, while the information sharing input is mainly provided by supporting or non-core enterprises. The cooperation at this time is beneficial to the core enterprises. For supporting companies or non-core enterprises, they often find that the driving force for cooperation is insufficient because they feel unfair.

In the process of information sharing in the C2M supply chain, cooperation can effectively increase the profit level of the node companies, so cooperation should be encouraged. Due to the status differences between various companies in the supply chain, core enterprises may harm the interests of non-core enterprises; non-core enterprises will adjust information sharing inputs according to the benefits distribution of information sharing. This kind of cooperation, due to unfair distribution may lead to insufficient motivation for cooperation, and eventually lead to the breakdown of cooperation. The design of income redistribution mechanism is the core issue for the realization of information sharing value in the C2M supply chain. Only by constructing a good income redistribution mechanism can we ensure the rationality and effectiveness of the income distribution in the supply chain and improve the efficiency of information sharing in the supply chain and ensure the maximum value of the C2M supply chain sharing.

Acknowledgements. This paper is financially supported by the open Foundation for University Innovation Platform from Hunan Province (16K013); Hunan Philosophy and Social Science Fund (15YBA062); Hunan Natural Science Foundation (2017JJ3009); Hunan Provincial Social Science Achievement Appraisal Committee (GLX193, XSP17YBZC015, XSPYBZZ004); Postdoctoral Science Fund (2017M622562).

References

Dan, B., Zhou, M.S., Zhang, X.M.: Incentives for demand forecast sharing in group-purchasing supply chains with competing manufacturers. Chin. J. Manag. Sci. **24**(3), 41–51 (2016)

Ha, A.Y., Tong, S., Zhang, H.: Sharing demand information in competing supply chains with production diseconomies. Manag. Sci. **57**(3), 566–581 (2011)

Kim, M., Chai, S.: The impact of supplier innovativeness, information sharing and strategic sourcing on improving supply chain agility: global supply chain perspective. Int. J. Prod. Econ. **74**(187), 42–52 (2017)

Xiao, J.H., Wang, H.C., Xie, K.: The mechanism of value creation by supply chain information systems: a perspective of information sharing. Syst. Eng. Theory Pract. **34**(11), 2862–2871 (2014)

Yan, R., Pei, Z.: Information asymmetry, pricing strategy and firm's performance in the retailer-multi-channel manufacturer supply chain. J. Bus. Res. **64**(4), 377–384 (2011)

Yue, X., Liu, J.: Demand forecast sharing in a dual-channel supply chain. Eur. J. Oper. Res. **174**(1), 646–667 (2006)

Zhang, J.L., Zhang, X.S.: Information sharing in a supply chain with supplier and retailer's partial information. Chin. J. Manag. Sci. **20**(1), 109–116 (2012)

Zhou, M., Dan, B., Ma, S.: Supply chain coordination with information sharing: the informational advantage of GPOs. Eur. J. Oper. Res. **256**(3), 785–802 (2017)

A Tag-Based Protection Method
for Multi-tenant Data Security

Xin Lu$^{(\boxtimes)}$, Lifeng Cao, Xuehui Du, and Zhiyan Hu

State Key Laboratory of Mathematical Engineering and Advanced Computing,
Zhengzhou 450001, Henan, China
1209774364@qq.com

Abstract. Aiming at the security issues about isolation storage, access, and sharing of the multi-tenant data under cloud environment, based on the Hadoop storage architecture, this paper proposes a Tag-Based protection method for Multi-tenant data security. For the isolation storage and access security of the private data, by introducing security tag to participate in storage and authentication access of the data, a consistent hash improved algorithm on dual authentication of dynamic password and security tag is proposed, realizing efficient isolation storage and secure access of the multi-tenant private data. For the security of the sharing data, a tag-based proxy re-encryption data sharing scheme is proposed, completing data secret sharing under the security authentication of the tenant sharing tag. For proxy re-encryption, use sharing tag to replace sharing data. Through the analysis of the security and instantiation of the method, this method is proved to be reliable and feasible under the cloud environment.

Keywords: Cloud computing security · Consistent hash
Dynamic password authentication · Tag authentication · Proxy re-encryption

1 Introduction

In recent years, cloud computing [1] has become a major change in the Internet field in the 21st century. Cloud computing is a service mode that can obtain computer resources in a convenient and on-demand way [2]. It can improve usability with low cost, high reliability, dynamic scalability, and virtualization. Cloud computing can efficiently complete the security of storage, access, and sharing of the tenant massive data. But the resources under the cloud platform are shared by all tenants, making the cloud data in the uncontrollable domain of the tenants, producing large amounts cloud data's security issues [3]. Therefore, how to build a secure method for data storage, access, and sharing of multi-tenant data is a key hot issue to protect multi-tenant data security.

To guarantee the security of tenant private data, identity authentication is mostly used at present. Password authentication and digital certificates are widely used identity authentication methods. Dynamic password authentication is the main method of password authentication. The Lamport [4] method ensures security through a one-way hash function, and is of poor adaptability in the distributed application environment.

© Springer Nature Switzerland AG 2018
X. Sun et al. (Eds.): ICCCS 2018, LNCS 11064, pp. 553–565, 2018.
https://doi.org/10.1007/978-3-030-00009-7_50

The time-based authentication [5] method has higher requirement for time precision and is more difficult in technology. The traditional Challenge-Response [6] authentication method is simple and reliable, but the authentication process is one-way and vulnerable to server impersonation attacks. The certificate-based identity authentication method [7] only authenticate the tenant identity legality, ignoring the inspection of the source of the acquired access data and the isolation access, that is, it lacks the process of authentication of the acquired access data itself.

For the security of tenant sharing data, data encryption [8–10] is the basic way to solve the problem. Proxy re-encryption technology makes cloud data sharing easier and more secure. The proxy re-encrypted data sharing scheme was first proposed in [11]. The formal definition of a one-way proxy re-encryption data sharing scheme was given in [12]. But these two schemes cannot resist Chosen Ciphertext Attack (CCA). Multi-use CCA-secure proxy re-encryption data sharing scheme was proposed in [13], but there is a serious ciphertext expansion problem. The scheme is of poor adaptability in distributed cloud computing environment.

For the security of tenant data storage isolation and access, this paper proposes a consistent hash improved algorithm on dual authentication of dynamic password and security tag. By adding the uniqueness and confidentiality elements of tenant to the matching storage Hash value, the algorithm improves the singleness of the Hash value, achieves safe isolation storage and improves storage resource utilization and retrieval efficiency; By introducing dynamic password and security tag, the algorithm not only realizes two-way identity authentication of tenants and server, but also implements isolation access and authentication to the data itself, as well as the tag-encryption of the whole data access process. For the security of sharing data, this paper proposes a tag-based proxy re-encryption data sharing scheme. By introducing the concept of sharing tag and proxy re-encryption of fixed-length sharing tag, the scheme not only realizes the secure data sharing, but also reduces the waste of resources and security threats of directly re-encrypting the data. By authenticating the re-encryption process of the sharing tag, the integrity and security of the sharing data are guaranteed; Under the standard model, the scheme is proved to be CCA-secure, realizes the secure sharing of multi-party data and reduces the ciphertext expansion.

2   Relevant Basic Knowledge and Architecture Deployment

2.1   Relevant Basic Knowledge

1. **Bilinear Diffie-Hellman (BDH) parameter generator:** A randomized algorithm BS is a BDH parameter generator if BS: ① takes security parameter $K(K > 0)$, ② runs in polynomial time in K, and ③ outputs the description of groups G_1, G of prime order q and a pairing $e : G \times G \to G_1$. Formally, the output is $\langle G, G_1, e \rangle$.
2. **Decisional Bilinear Diffie-Hellman (DBDH) Problem:** Let $\langle G, G_1, e \rangle$ be the output of the algorithm BS and g be a generator of G. The DBDH in $\langle G, G_1, e \rangle$ is as follows: Given $\langle g, g^a, g^b, g^c, T \rangle \in G^4 \times G_1$ with uniformly random choices of

$a, b, c \in Z_q^*$ and $T \in G_1$. And determine whether the equation $(e(g, g)^{abc} = T)$ is true. If this equation holds, it is called a DBDH tuple.

2.2 Architecture Deployment

Hadoop [14] implements the infrastructure of cloud computing software including distributed file system HDFS [15] and MapReduce [16] framework. It is one of the widely used implementation of cloud platforms. HDFS is the basis of data storage management for Hadoop. HDFS adopts master/slave architecture with a NameNode and a set of DataNodes. The namenode is a central server that manages Datanodes and the client's access to the file data. The DataNodes in the cluster manage the data stored on the node. Data is stored in blocks.

Based on Hadoop platform, this paper proposes the tag-based data protection method. For the design of security storage access and sharing function of the tenant data, the method adds trusted third-party authentication serer (AS), key distribution server and proxy server in NameNode to complete authentication, key distribution and proxy re-encryption function. In addition, a back-end database server is added to provide secure storage support for tenant data management information. For the design of data processing and storage,DataNode is numbered for secure matching storage (Fig. 1).

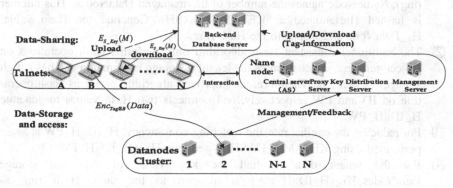

Fig. 1. Platform deployment diagram: the delivery of Tenant and server interaction information, security storage and access of tenant private encrypted data by tag, security sharing of tenant sharing data.

3 Formal Description of the Protection Method

3.1 Securely Isolation Storage and Access of Tenant Private Data

The Basic Idea

For secure and efficient storage isolation and access of private data, with the help of the consistent hash algorithm matching idea, by adding the tenant ID and password PW in the hash value, the algorithm completes efficient isolation storage and ensures the uniqueness and confidentiality of data matching storage. When the data is stored, the security tag is added to the data (tag-encryption). The tenant ID, password PW, the unique identifier serial number of the tenant and the data generated by the AS for the tenant are added to the tag to ensure safety isolation of data storage. For the private data access, two-way authentication of the tenant and the server is accomplished by improved two-way dynamic password authentication. Secondly, the AS completes second authentication of the tenant access data by calculating the security tag. During the entire storage and access process, the data is in a secure tag-encryption state. Tenants can perform the de-tag decryption operation and access private data only if the security tag is correctly calculated.

Formal Description of the Algorithm

Step 1 (Register): Tenants select the tenant ID and the security password to register on the server. The server generates the only secret serial number s for the tenant, encrypting s by the public key (PK) of the tenant, and sending $E_{PK}(s)$ to the tenant. After performing Hash (Instantiated as the algorithm SHA $-$ 256) operations on PW and s, the server saves $\{ID, H\_PW, H\_s\}$ to the back-end database server.

Step 2 (Isolated Storage):

① First construct an end-to-end integer ring of size 2^{32} (called a consistent Hash ring); NamcNode names the number of the managed DataNodes. This number is hashed (Instantiated as KETAMA_HASH). Generate the Hash value: $H_1\_DataNode$ and map it to the Hash ring.

② The traditional consistent Hash algorithm only performs Hash operations on Object numbers, which exposes the tenant's storage information and has a high storage conflict rate. Therefore, the improved algorithm performs Hash operation on ID and PW respectively, and connects two Hash values to generate $H\_ID\|H\_PW$;

③ For reducing the conflict rate and matching consistency, $H\_ID\|H\_PW$ is again performed using KETAMA_HASH to generate $H_1\_(H\_ID\|H\_PW)$;

④ For the tenant data to find the key value of the best storage DataNodes, $H_1\_(H\_ID\|H\_PW)$ is mapped to the same Hash ring as $H_1\_DataNode$. Then, find the DataNode's KEY value in a clockwise that is nearest to $H_1\_(H\_ID\|H\_PW)$ and can accommodate tenant data block. And the AS stores matching storage information $\{ID, DataNode, H\_ID\|H\_PW\}$ to facilitate data retrieval.

Matching storage instance is as follows:
   There are three storage DataNodes: $DataNode_1$, $DataNode_2$, $DataNode_3$. The size relationship of the DataNodes' KEY values is: $KEY_i = H_1\_DataNode_i, i = 1, 2, 3$ ($KEY_1 < KEY_2 < KEY_3$). Tenants T_1, T_2 and T_3 want to store data D_1, D_2 and D_3. Tenant ID numbers are ID_1, ID_2 and ID_3 and the passwords are PW_1, PW_2 and PW_3. After the Hash operation, the relation of the tenants' key value is: $key_i = H_1\_(H\_ID_i\|H\_PW_i), i = 1, 2, 3 (key_3 > key_2 > key_1)$.   Then,   the   tenant

clockwise finds the nearest storage node that can accommodate the tenant data. The distance relation is:key_1 is the closest to KEY_1, and $DataNode_1$ can store the data D_1; Both key_2 and key_3 are closest to $DataNode_2$, and the $DataNode_2$ can store the data D_2 and D_3 (Fig. 2).

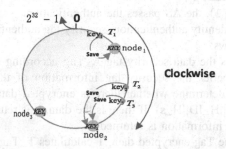

Fig. 2. Matching storage results: the data D_1 is stored in the $DataNode_1$, the data D_2 and D_3 are stored in the $DataNode_2$.

⑤ For refining data isolation and fast retrieval access, when a data is stored, the tenant generates a unique serial number **r** for the data, encrypted using the private key of AS and then transmitted to the AS. The tenant generates a unique security tag for the data with Tenant ID, PW, the serial number **r** and **s**. The tag-encryption data is uploaded to the DataNodes (Search for the best storage location based on ①–④). Format is: Tag = H_(H_r||H_PW||H_ID||H_s). The AS generates the same security tag. And the AS maintains security tag information, the format is: {ID, H_r, Tag}.

Step 3 (Dual authentication access): First, the improved two-way dynamic password authentication is as follows:

① T → AS: The tenant T inputs the account ID and uploads the data access request.

② AS $\xrightarrow{R}$ T: The AS queries the identity information of T. If there is no information of T, the request is rejected; otherwise T is required to upload authentication information and a random number R is transmitted to T.

③ T $\xrightarrow{V/H\_r}$ AS: T first calculates H_PW and H_R, generates a random number V, then connects H_PW and H_R, and performs a Hash operation again to generate X = (H_(H_PW||H_R)). X is XORed with V to generate S = (H_(H_PW ||H_R) ⊕ V). To ensure the integrity of V. S and H_S are passed to AS. In addition, H_r need to be transmitted to the AS to inform which data to be accessed.

④ $AS \xrightarrow{H\_(V+1)} T$: The AS calculates $X' = (H\_(H\_PW \| H\_R))$ and performs operation $V' = (X' \oplus S)$, and then calculates $S' = (H\_(H\_PW \| H\_R) \oplus V)$. If H_S is equal to H_S', T passes the authentication. Finally, the AS calculates $H\_(V'+1)$ as a response to T. Otherwise, the application is rejected.

⑤ $T \xrightarrow{\text{Reverse authentication}} AS$: The tenant calculates $H\_(V+1)$, if it is equal to the received $H\_(V'+1)$, the AS passes the authentication.

After successful identity authentication, security tag authentication of private data access is as follows:

⑥ The AS calculates the data security tag A_Tag according to ID, PW, H_r, and H_s; The AS queries the security tag information of the data and performs authentication to determine whether there is encrypted data of Tag = A_Tag = $H\_(H\_r \| H\_PW \| H\_ID \| H\_s)$. If there is the data, it is returned to T; otherwise, the access failure information is returned.

⑦ After receiving the Tag-encrypted data, T calculates T_Tag according to its own ID, PW, **r**, and **s**. If T_Tag = Tag, T can complete the de-tagged data decryption operation and achieve legal data access; otherwise, the data cannot be accessed normally.

3.2   A Tag-Based Proxy Re-encryption Data Sharing Scheme (Tag–PRE)

The Basic Idea

For the security of the sharing data, in the scheme, the sender A first encrypts the shared data with the symmetric key (S_Key), and then A encrypts S_Key using its own public key, and the ciphertext of S_Key is used as a sharing tag for proxy re-encryption. Then the sharing data ciphertext is uploaded to the Back-end database server. The AS sever completes the integrity authentication of the re-encryption transformation process and the semi-trusted proxy server authorized by AS re-encrypts the ciphertext tag. The proxy server sends the re-encrypted ciphertext tag to tenant B. B decrypts the re-encrypted ciphertext tag by its own private key to obtain the S_Key. After the ciphertext is downloaded, decryption is performed on the premise that the re-encrypted ciphertext tag authentication is valid, then the plaintext of the sharing data is obtained.

Formal Description of the Security Scheme

① Symmetric encryption sharing data M using private key **S_Key**:
   $Enc(m, S\_Key) \rightarrow C$: $C_m = E_{S\_Key}(M)$.

② Re-encryption of **S_Key**:

Setup(1^k): Input the security parameter K and select the bilinear pair mapping groups (G, G_T) with order prime $q > 2^K$. Assume that the discrete logarithm problem on G and G_T is difficult, and a symmetric bilinear mapping (q, g, h, G, G_T, e) is outputted, g and h are two different generators in G. $H: \{0,1\}^* \rightarrow \{0,1\}^k$ is defined as a one-way, collision-resistant Hash function. Combine the bilinear mapping and the hash function to get public parameters $(Param = (q, g, h, G, G_T, e, H, ID_A, ID_B))$.

GenKey(param) $\rightarrow$ **(sk_i, pk_i)**: By inputting the Param and selecting the random number $x \epsilon Z_q^*$, the system outputs the private key as $sk_i = x$, the public key as $pk_i = g^x$;

Enc_1(pk_i, param, $m = S\_Key$) $\rightarrow$ **C_i**: Input the param, pk_i and $m = S\_Key$, and obtain the first encrypted ciphertext tag C_i. Select the random number $r_i \epsilon Z_q^*$, calculate

$$C_1 = g^{r_i}, C_2 = me(h, pk_i)^{r_i}, C_3 = H\_(H\_C_1 || H\_C_2 || H\_ID_A); \tag{1}$$

Let $C_i = (C_1, C_2, C_3)$ and output C_i.

ReGenKey(sk_i, pk_j, param) $\rightarrow$ **$Rk_{i \rightarrow j}$**: A proxy re-encryption key $Rk_{i \rightarrow j}$ is generated. The proxy server uses the $Rk_{i \rightarrow j}$ to convert the cipher text encrypted by pk_i into the cipher text encrypted by pk_j. Select the random number $r_j \epsilon Z_q^*$, and calculate the $Rk_{i \rightarrow j}$.

$$Rk_1 = g^{r_j}, Rk_2 = h^{-sk_i} pk_j^{r_j}, Rk_3 = H\_(H\_Rk_1 || H\_Rk_2 || H\_ID_B). \tag{2}$$

The AS server authenticates Rk_3 to ensure the integrity of Rk_1 and Rk_2 and the reliability of the recipient identity. Let $Rk_{i \rightarrow j} = (Rk_1, Rk_2, Rk_3)$; then output $Rk_{i \rightarrow j}$.

ReEnc(C_i, $Rk_{i \rightarrow j}$, param) $\rightarrow$ **(C_j, $\perp$)**: The re-encryption process from the first encrypted ciphertext tag C_i to the re-encrypted ciphertext tag C_j is performed by an authorized proxy server. The process is as follows:

Before re-encrypting C_i, the AS authenticates C_3 and Rk_3, if any one of the equations does not hold, then output $\perp$. If all the equations are true, the AS authorizes the proxy server and re-encrypts C_i to obtain C_j:

$$C_1^j = C_1, C_2^j = C_2 e(C_1, Rk_2), C_3^j = Rk_1. \tag{3}$$

$$C_4^j = H\_\left(H\_C_1^j \middle\| H\_(C_1^j \middle\| C_2^j) \| H\_(C_2^j || C_3^j) || H\_ID_A\right), \quad C_j = \left(C_1^j, C_2^j, C_3^j, C_4^j\right). \tag{4}$$

Dec_1(param, sk_j, C_j) $\rightarrow$ **(m, $\perp$)**: There are two cases of decryption at this time:

Situation 1: The ciphertext m is decrypted by C_i, first authenticate the equation C_3, if the equation does not hold, then output $\perp$; Otherwise, the symmetric key is calculated:

$$S\_Key = m = C_2 / e\left(C_1, h^{sk_i}\right) \tag{5}$$

Situation2: After receiving the re-encrypted ciphertext tag, B first authenticates the equation C_4^j. If the equation does not hold, then output $\perp$; Otherwise, the symmetric key is calculated:

$$S\_Key = m = C_2^j / e\left(C_1^j, C_3^j\right)^{sk_j}. \tag{6}$$

③ Symmetric key **S_Key** decrypts sharing data M:

$$\textbf{Dec}(\textbf{S\_Key}, \textbf{C}) \rightarrow \textbf{M}: M = D_{S\_key}(C), \text{ output sharing data plaintext.}$$

4 Security Analysis

4.1 Security Analysis of Private Data Isolation Storage and Secure Access

① **Replay attack:** During the process of accessing the data, both the tenant and the AS use different random numbers to perform authentication, ensuring the non-relevance and unpredictability of the dynamic password. Therefore, even if an attacker intercepts a certain authentication interaction information, due to the dynamic nature of the password change, the information is invalid for the next authentication.

② **Server impersonation attacks:** Suppose the attacker counterfeit the authentication server to cheat the tenant. Because the attacker doesn't know the password information of the tenant, it can't decrypt the challenge value V of the tenant return, so it can't send the correct H_(V + 1) to the tenant.

③ **Data storage isolation security:** When the tenant data is stored, security tags with unique (**s**, **r**) and confidentiality (PW) elements are added to each tenant data, which fully guarantees the security and confidentiality of data storage.

④ **Dual authentication:** The tenant not only perform two-way identity authentication during data access, but also data is transmitted in the form of tag-encryption. Even if the malicious tenant hijacks other tenant data with security tags, the security tag also cannot be calculated because it includes secret information such as PW and **s**, thus the data cannot be deciphered correctly. When the tenant accesses malicious data, the data itself is authenticated by calculating the security tag to avoiding the malicious invasion.

4.2 Security Analysis of Sharing Data

Consistency Analysis

According to the nature of the bilinear pairing, do the following verification:

a. For the first-level ciphertext tag $C_i = (C_1, C_2, C_3)$, C_i only has the unique form:

$$C_1 = g^{r_i}, C_2 = me(h, pk_i)^{r_i}, C_3 = H\_(H\_C_1 || H\_C_2 || H\_ID_A). \tag{7}$$

If the authentication to C_3 is successful, it can be verified according to the formula:

$$\frac{C_2}{e(C_1, h^{sk_i})} = \frac{me(h, pk_i)^{r_i}}{e(g, h)^{r_i sk_i}} = m\frac{e(h, g^{sk_i})^{r_i}}{e(g, h)^{r_i sk_i}} = m\frac{e(g, h)^{sk_i r_i}}{e(g, h)^{r_i sk_i}} = m. \tag{8}$$

Therefore, the first-level ciphertext tag that can be re-encrypted is consistent.

b. For the re-encrypted ciphertext tag $C_j = \left(C_1^j, C_2^j, C_3^j, C_4^j\right)$, C_j only has the unique form:

$$C_1^j = C_1, C_2^j = C_2 e(C_1, Rk_2), C_3^j = Rk_1. \tag{9}$$

$$C_4^j = H_-\left(H\_C_1^j \| H\_(C_1^j \| C_2^j)\right) \| H\_(C_2^j \| C_3^j) \| H\_ID_A). \tag{10}$$

If the authentication to C_4^j is successful, it can be verified according to the formula:

$$\frac{C_2^j}{e\left(C_1^j, C_3^j\right)^{sk_j}} = m \frac{e(h, g)^{r_i sk_i} e(h, g)^{-r_i sk_i} e\left(g^{r_i}, pk_j^{r_j}\right)}{e(g^{r_i}, g^{r_j})^{sk_j}} = m \frac{e\left(g^{r_i}, g^{sk_j r_j}\right)}{e(g^{r_i}, g^{r_j sk_j})} = m. \tag{11}$$

Therefore, the re-encrypted ciphertext tag is consistent.

Security Analysis
The tag-based proxy re-encryption data sharing scheme in this paper is CCA-secure under the standard model. The security of the scheme is based on the DBDH problem assumption. The decision of this problem is difficult and the decision advantage is $negl(k)$. The size of $negl(k)$ can be ignored. That is, the following formula is satisfied:

$$\left|Pr\left[S(G, G_1, g, g^a, g^b, g^c, T = g^z) = 1\right] - Pr\left[S(G, G_1, g, g^a, g^b, g^c, T = g^{abc}) = 1\right]\right| \le negl(k). \tag{12}$$

$$pr[\text{Correct judgment}] \le \frac{1}{2} + negl(k). \tag{13}$$

Theorem 1: If adversary $\mathcal{A}$ can break the tag-based adaptive CCA-secure proxy re-encryption scheme with a non-negligible probability $\varepsilon(k)$ under a probabilistic polynomial time algorithm (PPT), then there must be a PPT algorithm B to solve the DBDH problem in bilinear groups with non-negligible probability. The proof is as follows:
Let Π represent the Tag-PRE scheme, $\mathcal{A}$ is a PPT algorithm and define as follow:

$$\varepsilon(k) \stackrel{\text{def}}{=} Pr\left[PubK_{\mathcal{A},\Pi}^{cca}(k) = 1\right]. \tag{14}$$

To prove that the scheme is indistinguishable under the condition of CCA, we need to prove that $\varepsilon(k) \le 1/2 + negl(k)$ is true with the size of $negl(k)$ is negligible.
Construct another PPT algorithm B according to algorithm A. Algorithm B generates the system parameters of the scheme to satisfy algorithm $\mathcal{A}$'s query, and gives a judgment based on algorithm $\mathcal{A}$'s guessing results. If algorithm B determines that the result is $T = g^{abc}$, then its output is 1; otherwise the output is 0. The entire simulation interaction process is divided into five phases, the process is as follows:

In the simulation process, B needs to maintain three tables C_{pk}, C_{sk} and C_{Rk}.

Stage 1 (selection): B randomly selects d from $\{0, 1\}$ and generates the system parameter (Param $= (q, g, h, G, G_T, e, H, ID)$);

Stage 2 (query): $\mathcal{A}$ makes queries to B, and each query corresponds to the following five query processes of oracles:

a. Public key generation oracle $[\delta_{pk}(i)]$:

$$B \xrightarrow{\text{GenKey(param),i}} (sk_i, pk_i) \; ; \; Send: B \xrightarrow{pk_i} \mathcal{A} \; ; \; (sk_i, pk_i) \xrightarrow{save} C_{pk} \; ;$$

b. Private key generation oracle $\left[\delta_{sk}\left(pk_j\right)\right]$:

$$\text{Quary the } C_{pk} \text{ to get } sk_j \colon B \xrightarrow{pk_j} C_{pk} \; ; \; Send: B \xrightarrow{sk_j} \mathcal{A} \; ; \; \left(pk_j, sk_j\right) \xrightarrow{save} C_{sk} \; ;$$

c. Proxy re-encryption key generation oracle $\left[\delta_{Rk_{i \to j}}\left(pk_i, pk_j\right)\right]$

$$B \xrightarrow{pk_i} C_{pk}; B \xrightarrow{\text{ReGenKey}(sk_i, pk_j, param)} Rk_{i \to j} \; ; B \xrightarrow{Rk_{i \to j}} \mathcal{A} \; ; \; Save: B \xrightarrow{(pk_i, pk_j, Rk_{i \to j})} C_{Rk};$$

d. Proxy re-encryption ciphertext generation oracle $\left[\delta_{ReEnc}\left(pk_i, pk_j, C_i\right)\right]$:

$$\text{Proxy re-encrypt}: B \xrightarrow{\text{ReEnc}\{C_i, \text{ReGenKey}(sk_i, pk_j, param), param\}} C_j,$$

Before generating C_j, B authenticates whether C_i is valid and $Rk_{i \to j}$ is a valid, if it is invalid, re-encryption is stopped. Otherwise, $B \xrightarrow{C_j} \mathcal{A}$ is executed;

e. Decryption oracle $\left[\delta_{Dec_1}\left(pk_j, param, C_j\right)\right]$:

$$\text{Quary } C_{pk} \text{ to get } sk_j \colon B \xrightarrow{pk_j} C_{pk}; B \xrightarrow{\text{Dec}_1(param, sk_j, C_j)} m.$$

Before decryption, B authenticates whether C_j is a valid re-encrypted ciphertext. If it is valid, perform $B \xrightarrow{m} \mathcal{A}$; the query process ends.

Stage 3 (challenge): After finishing the query, $\mathcal{A}$ selects two equal-length messages m_0, m_1, and selects a tenant whose public key is pk' (A has never queried the private key corresponding to pk'), and then submits (m_0, m_1, pk') to B;

Stage 4 (guess): $\mathcal{A}$ adaptively performs the stage 2 query process but is not allowed to query the private key of pk'; $\mathcal{A}$ is also not allowed to perform the query of $\delta_{Rk'_{\to i}}(pk', pk_i)$ while knowing the private key of pk_i; If $\mathcal{A}$ performs the query of $\delta_{Rk'_{\to i}}(pk', pk_i)$, and the challenge ciphertext C_i is equal to the ciphertext encrypted by the re-encryption key $Rk_{i \to i}$, the query of $\delta_{Dec_1}(pk_i, param, C_i)$ is not allowed. After the second round of query, $\mathcal{A}$ sends the guess $d' \in \{0, 1\}$ to B.

Stage 5 (decision): If $d' = d$, B outputs 1, which indicates that T is a DBDH tuple; otherwise, it outputs 0, and T is any element in G_1.

The following is proved by anti-evidence method: If $\mathcal{A}$ can distinguish the challenge ciphers in polynomial time with a probability of $\varepsilon(k)(\varepsilon(k) \geq 1/2 + negl(k))$, B can solve the DBDH problem in polynomial time.

a. When B outputs 0, T is a G_1 random element, that is:

$$\Pr[PubK_{\mathcal{A},\Pi}^{cca}(k) = 1|T = g^z] = \Pr[S(G, G_1, g, g^a, g^b, g^c, T = g^z) = 1] = 1/2; \quad (15)$$

b. When B receives a DBDH tuple, B outputs 1, then the challenge ciphertext must be the correct public key pk' encrypt the ciphertext of m_d, that is:

$$[PubK_{\mathcal{A},\Pi}^{cca}(k) = 1|T = g^{abc}] = \Pr[S(G, G_1, g, g^a, g^b, g^c, T = g^{abc}) = 1] = \varepsilon(k) \quad (16)$$

$$\therefore |\Pr[S(G, G_1, g, g^a, g^b, g^c, T = g^z) = 1] - \Pr[S(G, G_1, g, g^a, g^b, g^c, T = g^{abc}) = 1]| \\ = |1/2 - \varepsilon(k)|; \quad (17)$$

Suppose $\varepsilon(n) \geq 1/2 + negl(k)$, then $|1/2 - \varepsilon(k)| = |\varepsilon(k) - 1/2| \geq negl(k)$ is obtained. Finally, we get the following inequality:

$$|\Pr[S(G, G_1, g, g^a, g^b, g^c, T = g^z) = 1] - \Pr[S(G, G_1, g, g^a, g^b, g^c, T = g^{abc}) = 1]| \geq negl(k) \quad (18)$$

Obviously, this is contradictory to the difficult assumption of the DBDH problem. As a result, $\varepsilon(k) \leq 1/2 + negl(k)$, the size of $negl(k)$ is negligible.

To sum up, the Tag − PRE scheme in this paper is CCA-secure.

5 Application Example Analysis

The security system on this protection method can effectively protect the tenant data secure. This paper applies this method to concrete examples of solving medical information security issues as follows:

For ensuring the security of medical information, according to the method, a medical institution establishes a protection system, which includes clients (Attending Physicians) in various departments, AS server, medical information storage servers, and proxy servers, etc. Suppose the medical institution has an attending physician A and B in the orthopedic office, A has a new patient01 and a previous patient02, B has a previous patient03.

System processing: The attending physician should safely store the new medical records; The previous patients' medical records have been safely isolation stored; During the treatment of the patient, the attending physicians need to visit the medical records legally; In case of patient emergency or doctor's absence, other doctors can apply for safe sharing of medical record and achieve timely treatment.

Situation 1: Physician A stores and reads medical record of patient01

① Register: $A \xrightarrow{\{ID,PW\}} AS, AS \xrightarrow{H\_s_{01}} A$; Medical record storage process is as follow:

② Physician A sends a storage request to the AS server: $A \xrightarrow{\text{Storage request}} AS$;

According to the data storage algorithm in 3.1, the AS sever finds the most suitable storage location for the new medical record data. The Client$_A$ uploads the patient01's medical record encrypted by security tag and unique identification number **r**:

$Client_A \xrightarrow{Tag\_data} DataNodes; Client_A \xrightarrow{E_{SK_{AS}}(H\_r)} AS$;

Medical record access process:

③ First authentication: According to the two-way authentication in the 3.1, the system authenticates A and AS. Then, A uploads the relevant medical record identification information: $A \xrightarrow{H\_r, \ H\_s_{01}} AS$;

④ According to the security tag authentication in the 3.1, the AS calculates the security tag of the medical record, and then queries $\{ID, H\_r, Tag\}$ to inform DataNodes;

⑤ DataNodes $\xrightarrow{Tag\_medical\ record} Client_A$; The Client$_A$ calculates the corresponding security tag to decrypt the medical record.

Result: By applying this algorithm to the protection system, the storage and access of the patient01's medical record satisfies the above security in 4.1.

Situation 2: Physician A shares patient01's the medical record to physician B

① The physician B sends an medical record application to Client$_A$ and the AS sever;

② Client$_A$ submits the medical record encrypted by S_Key to the database storage server and submits $C_{A_{01}}$, $Rk_{A \to B}$ to the AS sever. AS authenticates the integrity and authenticity of $C_{A_{01}}$ and $Rk_{A \to B}$, if successful, go to ③;

③ The AS passes $C_{A_{01}}$ and $Rk_{A \to B}$ to the proxy server, and the proxy server re-encrypts $C_{A_{01}}$ to generate the medical record re-encrypted ciphertext flag $C_{B_{01}}$;

④ The proxy server passes $C_{B_{01}}$ to B. B downloads the medical record ciphertext from the database storage server, decrypts $C_{B_{01}}$, and then decrypts the medical record ciphertext to obtain the medical record, so that the patient01 can be timely treated.

Features: By applying the data sharing scheme to the system, sharing of the patient01's medical record satisfies the above security in 4.2

6   Conclusion

This paper proposes a Tag-Based protection method for Multi-Tenant data security. The method adds uniqueness and confidentiality to the Hash value in matching storage which achieves optimized and isolated tenant private data storage. By combining dynamic password authentication and security tag authentication, the method achieves the legality verification of tenant identity and the reliability authentication of the access data. By introducing sharing tag into proxy re-encryption data sharing scheme, a tag-based proxy re-encryption scheme is proposed, which realizes the demand of "small overhead and big data security sharing". The CCA-secure proof of the scheme is given based on the DBDH problem under the standard model. By the analysis of security and instantiation, this paper concludes that the method is of high feasibility, reliability and broad application prospects. In future, we will further optimize the method to improve the safety protection efficiency and implement the safety protection system in engineering based on the method.

Acknowledgements. This work is supported by the National Natural Science Foundation of China under grants No. 61502531.

References

1. Cui, Y., Song, J., Miao, C.C.: Mobile cloud computing research progress and trends. Chin. J. Comput. **40**(2), 273–295 (2017)
2. Mell, T., Grance, P.: The NIST definition of cloud computing (draft). National Institute of Standards and Technology, vol. 53, no. 6, p. 50 (2009)
3. Fang, J., Wu, H., Bai, S.L.: A Summary of the research on cloud computing security. Telecommun. Sci. **27**(4), 37–42 (2011)
4. Lamport, L.: Password authentication with insecure communication. Commun. ACM **24** (11), 770–772 (1981)
5. Liu, Y.C., Gong, P.: On the security of a dynamic identity-based remote user authentication scheme with verifiable password update. Int. J. Commun. Syst. **28**(5), 842–847 (2015)
6. Qu, X.: The research of SMS dynamic password identity authentication system based on challenge/response mechanism. Softw. Guide **14**(10), 134–137 (2015)
7. Han, S.L., Ma, M., Wang, T.: Design and implementation of digital certificate application system. Netinfo Secur. **9**, 43–45 (2012)
8. Wang, Q.F., Song, W.A.: Method for homomorphic encryption data security in cloud environment. Comput. Eng. Des. **38**(1), 42–46 (2017)
9. Wang, Z.H., Han, Z., Liu, J.Q.: File sharing scheme for multi-user in cloud environment. J. Comput. Res. Dev. **51**(12), 2614–2622 (2014)
10. Zhu, J., Chen, L.L., Zhu, X.: Certificateless proxy re-encryption scheme for cloud computing security. Comput. Eng. **43**(8), 8–14 (2017)
11. Blaze, M., Bleumer, G., Strauss, M.: Divertible protocols and atomic proxy cryptography. In: Nyberg, K. (ed.) EUROCRYPT 1998. LNCS, vol. 1403, pp. 127–144. Springer, Heidelberg (1998). https://doi.org/10.1007/BFb0054122
12. Ateniese, G.: Improved proxy re-encryption schemes with applications to secure distributed storage. ACM Trans. Inf. Syst. Secur. **9**(1), 1–30 (2006)
13. Shao, J., Cao, Z.F.: Multi-use unidirectional identity-based proxy re-encryption from hierarchical identity-based encryption. Inf. Sci. **206**(5), 83–95 (2012)
14. Fan, S.J., Tian, J.F.: Research and implementation of cloud computing platform based on hadoop. Comput. Technol. Dev. **26**(7), 127–132 (2016)
15. Gao, Y.Z., Li, B.L.: A forensic method for efficient file extraction in HDFS based on three-level mapping. Wuhan Univ. J. Nat. Sci. **22**(2), 114–126 (2017)
16. Dean, J., Ghemawat, S.: MapReduce: simplifier date processing on large clusters. Commun. ACM **51**(1), 107–113 (2008)

A Web Application Runtime Application Self-protection Scheme against Script Injection Attacks

Zhongxu Yin[1], Zhufeng Li[2(✉)], and Yan Cao[1]

[1] State Key Laboratory of Mathematical Engineering and Advanced Computing,
Zhengzhou 450001, China
yinzhxu@163.com
[2] Zhengzhou Information Science and Technology Institute,
Zhengzhou 450002, China
20086538@qq.com

Abstract. Script injection vulnerabilities are popular vulnerabilities in dynamic web applications. Necessary conditions were analyzed for the generation and exploitation of script injection vulnerabilities to provide protection against different injection types. Combined with the analysis of the host language and the object language, the statements were located with their types in the HTML statements. Based on the control flow graph, the data dependency relation subgraph containing source points and sink points was built. A filter insertion algorithm is designed for this sub-graph to define different input data type filtering strategies. Then a solution was implemented based on data flow analysis and automatic insertion of filters before relevant sink statements.

Keywords: Script injection · Program analyzing · Dataflow analyzing
Runtime application self-protection

1 Introduction

Social networking applications have become an important source of Internet services and traffic. It is generally based on dynamic page applications such as information sharing, interactive feedback, and service query provided by Web programs. Most cloud platforms and network device management interfaces also use Web interfaces. By arranging additional scripting statements in the user input, in the absence of reliable filtering methods, cross-site scripting can cause the effect of inserting redundant code into web applications pages, and violating the original page logic, causing the client to perform malicious actions.

Usually, cross-site scripting vulnerabilities can be avoided through secure programming methods such as user data filtering. Since Web applications are built on a high-level scripting language, developers are more concerned with the interface design with the Web 2.0 and front-end technologies become more complex. With the result of complicate the inter-flowing of variables. If it is lack of overall security design and development and there is no effective filtering and restrictions, as a vulnerabilities

© Springer Nature Switzerland AG 2018
X. Sun et al. (Eds.): ICCCS 2018, LNCS 11064, pp. 566–577, 2018.
https://doi.org/10.1007/978-3-030-00009-7_51

based on this kind of application architecture, cross-site vulnerabilities will inevitably exist, and thus become a current network security issue under the conditions of widely application.

Cross-site scripting vulnerabilities exist extensively in web applications in the OWASP top ten security vulnerability threat report (OWASP top 10), command injection and cross-site scripting remain important threats [1]. It can be detected both on the server side and the client side.

The server-side detection method is mainly to review the user's input content, filtering out untrusted contents, and make the malicious script code unable to reach the user's browser. In terms of server-side detection, representative methods is Browser-Enforced Embedded Policies (BEEP) [2], In order to prevent users from entering malicious script code into web applications, BEEP implements a white list of trusted scripts In this way, only the trusted script code created by the web developer can be executed on the client, and the rest are filtered out. However, BEEP has serious flaws when dealing with dynamically generated scripts. Especially when the current Web model framework allows procedural design, the problem is more obvious, and there have been more complex XSS attacks specifically targeting BEEP [3].

The detection method of Content Security Policy (CSP) [4] trusts the execution of the browser. It is considered that the cause of the XSS problem is a flaw in the Web application. For this reason, CSP attaches many attributes to the main part of each page generated on the server side. When generating a page, the reliability of scripts, pictures, or other content in the page is determined by these attributes. Thus, it provides a fault automatic protection function. Because the entire page is covered by this policy, untrusted content is constrained by the policy. However, because CSP imposes strict restrictions on the generated pages, it will cause serious performance problems in the face of large-scale web applications, and it also cannot adapt well to the web architecture of the procedural model design.

WAF (Web Application Firewall) [5], penetrates into the web protocol to filter and uses firewall technology to restrict connections. WAF is generally deployed at the front end of a web server cluster to protect websites, and uses a reverse proxy mode to perform bi-directional filtering on HTTP request packets [8]. If the firewall understands the protocol and parameter semantics of the application, it will lead to more accurate vulnerability detection. However, with the increase in the complexity of applications and the rapid emergence of new application types and technologies (such as JSON, REST, etc.), the ability of WAF to provide accurate vulnerability detection without artificial tuning has not yet been realized. Today, few people find WAF deployed in an unconditional blocking mode for any application, which proves the inherent inaccuracy of WAF technology. Some improved methods use machine learning to learn signature rules, and face the difficulty of data set acquisition and manual tagging workload [6].

Rathore proposed a method based on machine learning to detect XSS attacks against SNS [8]. In the method, the detection of XSS attacks is performed based on three characteristics: URL, Web page, and protocol of SNS. The disadvantage is that it can only protect the specific social network system.

The combination of server and client detection methods is mainly through the mandatory of client browser must parse the returned HTML document in the way specified by the server, so that malicious code can't be executed even if it reaches the client. Creating an end-to-end trusted path between the web application user and web server. Typical examples are Document Structure Integrity (DSI) [9].

The RASP (Runtime application self-protection) [10] technology is an improvement of the WAF. It injects protection code into the application program, integrates with the application program, and monitors and blocks attacks in real time, so that the program has its own protection capabilities. The protected application does not need to make any changes in the encoding, just with a simple configuration. This method is suitable for dynamic patch protection solutions for specific vulnerabilities. It cannot yet solve a certain type of security threat independently and comprehensively.

On one hand, the current security of web applications depends heavily on the programming habits of developers, but due to avoiding of the vulnerabilities needs to be restricted from different aspects. If the methods are not accurate enough, these measures will only increase the difficulty of exploiting the vulnerability, and it will be difficult to achieve the preventive effect. On the other hand, the overhead of reinforcement existing applications from source code is relatively large. At the same time, there is a lack of a unified and reliable solution for secure programming. We combines the automatic analyzing of the application, and inserting the filtering code during the interaction to implement the RASP method, and attaches the security module to the existing architecture to reduce the application security design cost as well as securing the existing application.

2   Script Injection Defense Based on Program Analysis

Our solution is to combine the analyzing of host program, script program, and target html statements, find all input variables using data flow analysis, and insert necessary check and filter statements between the variables' initialization and references. As there are many kinds of server-side scripting languages used in Web applications, such as ASP, JSP, and PHP. We take JSP as an example for researching the above methods.

As shown in the Fig. 1, the program introduces two reflected cross-site vulnerabilities by the input variable of "uname", and introduces a storage cross-site vulnerability through the "uid" and the query statement in the sixth line.

2.1   Taint Policy Definition and Data Dependency Analysis

Cross-site scripting is divided into reflected, stored and DOM-based XSS three categories. Among them, the storage type involves the taint data read from the database. For the former two, the analyzed target is the server-side script program. In the DOM-based XSS, the main taint data comes from the JavaScript variables, and the analysis target is the JavaScript program.

For the server-side script, the injected taint data passes through different input data sources such as GET, POST, and Session, Cookie, etc. to the Web, and in the storage-type XSS, taint data originate from the result of the database query and obtains the related taint source from the JSP. At the same time, the jump relationship between the pages determines the propagation logic of the taint. Among them, the ActionServlet

```
1.  <%
2.  request.setCharacterEncoding("UTF-8");
3.  String uname = request.getParameter("username");
4.  String uid = request.getParameter("id");
5.  Statement sm = conn.createStatement();
6.  ResultSet rs = sm.executeQuery("select CContext FROM Comments
    where CID='"+ uid +"'");
7.  if(rs.next()){
8.  String username = new String(uname.getBytes("ISO-8859-1"),"utf-8");
9.  out.print("the comments for user"+uname);
10. }
11. else{
12. throw new RuntimeException("Error condition!!!");
13. }
14. %>
15. String tips = "the comments for user"+username;
16. <td><%= tips %><%=rs.getString("CContext")%></td>
```

Fig. 1. Code fragment of JSP with three XSS vulnerability

decides which page process which action by parsing the configuration file. The relevant input variables were marked as source points for analysis.

For client-side scripts, the client needs to write large amounts of JavaScript code as part of the business logic. It mainly includes interfaces implemented by JavaScript and other Activex controls. In particular, in the AJAX-enabled code, JavaScript interacts with server side code dynamically, with the following taint sources and targets:

The sink points are statements using for converting variables to html elements for displaying. These statements are generally generated dynamically by the application. The script language used by the application program is called the host language, and the target html display statement and other statements inferencing objects such as flash and office objects are categorized as object languages. The location and type analysis of the sink points needs to be determined by a comprehensive analysis of the host language and the target language. Set related statements as key program points according to their related source points and sink points (Table 1).

For server-side scripts, depending on where the print statement is located. If the parameter to be printed is not a constant string, we set the relevant variable of parameter as a key point. For client-side scripts, the sink parameters listed in Fig. 2 are used as key points.

We make data flow analysis of the source code based on variables output to html. The control flow diagram in each process of the program and the inter-process call relations are constructed. The data between variables and input parameters are analyzed on the basis of the control flow and data flow analysis. Global data dependencies are established based on the data dependencies of the procedure. Figure 2 shows the data

Table 1. Sink points for client-side scripts

	The taint sink points	The taint source points
script injection	document.body.innerHtml document.cookie XMLHttpRequest.open(...,url,)	window.location. document.location. document.URL/
Request forgery	document.forms[0].action	document.URLUnencoded
Command injection	eval() window.setTimeout() window.execScript() window.setInterval() document.execCommand() window.attachEvent() document.attachEvent()	document.referrer. window.name event.data event.origin textbox.value forms.value
click hijacking	document.create() document.body.* document.write(...) document.writeln(...)	

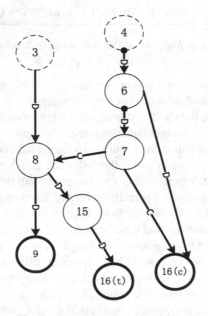

Fig. 2. Data dependencies of Fig. 1

dependency corresponding to the code fragment in Fig. 1. The node number indicates the line number, and the marked {C,D} on the edge indicates data dependency or control dependency. In the lexical analysis and its subsequent stages, the information of the nodes in the source program is preserved. 16(t) corresponds to the tips variable in line 16 and 16(c) corresponds to the CContext variable.

Static taint analysis is a code analysis method that directly analyzes source code. It mainly analyzes the control flow and data structure of source code and make use of lexical analysis, grammar analysis, key character research, and parameter filtering. The code performs taint marking and taint tracking, and finally checks the integrity of the code based on the taint propagation path.

2.2 Generation of Filtering Rules Based on Static Data Flow Analysis

The filter rules are related to source and sink points. For the sink point, according to the code location where the relevant variable is located, distinguish the program type to be analyzed as client or server script.

Filtered keywords are determined based on the relevant exploit feature. The latter has different utilization key points according to different sink points. For example, if the inserted code is between HTML tags, such as the vulnerability introduced in line 15 of Fig. 1, the exploit code will be directly inserted into the code. Otherwise if the code locates inside an HTML tag, the attacker need to close the original tag before inserting the script code. If it is located in the script code, the attacker need to close the original code with </script> and then insert the attack code. Table 2 described different exploit code according to different output points.

Table 2. Exploit code for different output points

The output point	The example statement	The exploit code
Between html tags	<body><%=request.getParameter("text")%></body>	<script>alert(1)<script> (inserting directly)
	<title><%=request.getParameter("text")%></title>	</title><script>alert(1)<script> (firstly enclosing the tag)
Insiding html tags	<input type=" text" value="<%=request.getParameter("text")%>"/>	"onclick = alert(1) x=" (firstly enclosing the attribute)
		"/><script>alert(1)<script> (firstly enclosing the tag)
Insiding the script code	<script>a=<%=request.getParameter("text")%>"; ...<script>	</script><script>alert(1)<script> (firstly enclosing the tag)
		"alert(1);

When exploiting cross-site scripting, the necessary condition is to enter a balance word in the string for inserting additional queries. Therefore, by filtering out the balance word in the input query keyword string variable, the type of injection can be blocked. For sink points whose output points are between HTML tags, the "<" symbol and its associated encoding can be directly filtered out. For sink points within an HTML tag, single and double quote characters need to be filtered out. For the sink point in the script code, we need to filter out the both the above characters.

Then, according to different types of source points, the corresponding statements are constructed with different decoder, which also judge and filter the balance words. According to the source location information obtained in the analysis, the statement is inserted after the statement that defines the input variable. Table 3 described different filtering rules according to different input source.

According to the type of the input keyword and the position of the output point, different types of vulnerability of script injection were distinguished and different checking and protecting sentences were inserted. The overall process and algorithm is as follows (Fig. 3):

Table 3. Filtering rules according to different input source

The input source	Between html tags	Inside html tags	Inside the script code
Database	Database decoding with <script> keyword filtering	Database decoding with quotation marks filtering	Database decoding with quotation marks and angle brackets filtering
Get	URL-Decoding with <script> keyword filtering	URL-Decoding with quotation marks filtering	URL-Decoding with quotation marks and angle brackets filtering
Post	Character-decoding with <script> keyword filtering	Character-decoding with quotation marks filtering	Character-decoding with quotation marks and angle brackets filtering
Session/application	Session decoding with <script> keyword filtering	Session decoding with quotation marks filtering	Session decoding with quotation marks and angle brackets filtering
Cookie	Cookie decoding with <script> keyword filtering	Cookie decoding with quotation marks filtering	cookie decoding with quotation marks and angle brackets filtering

On the whole, the first line of the algorithm extracts the sink points in the page, which includes output statements and dynamically generated html statements in the AJAX technology. For the extracted sink points, the flow-based slice analysis (second line) is performed on the program, and irrelevant statements are removed. On this basis, input statements that are not related to sink points are also filtered out (the third line). Then the data flow diagram for the sliced code (the fourth row) is generated. For each pair of input and output nodes, filter statements are automatically inserted (Fig. 4).

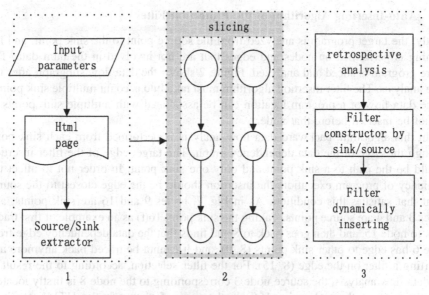

Fig. 3. Composition of the protection framework

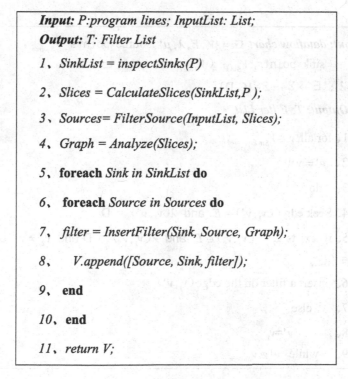

Fig. 4. Overall algorithm of the protection method

2.3   Auto-Inserting Algorithm of the Protection Filter

Firstly, the target program is analyzed from the source point to the sink point, and the pruning is performed on nodes and edges that are not involved in the taint data. The entire program is sliced and analyzed. Figure 2 shows the data flow subgraph after the slice analysis. The filter insertion algorithm must take into account multiple sink points. If the data flow of a program location can be associated with multiple sink points, it cannot be inserted before that node.

In this algorithm, backward data flow analysis is performed from each sink point through the edge of the data dependency graph. The target edge of the filter insertion should be the path to a sink point and only one sink point. In order not to affect the efficiency of program execution, the insertion should be the edge closest to the source point that satisfies this condition. As in Fig. 2, nodes 9 and 16 are sink points, and nodes 3 and 4 are source points. Taking the sink point 16(t) as an example, it first traces back to node 15, and then goes back to 8 and finds that the data dependency edge from node 6 has edge to other sink points (8, 9), and it cannot be traced back anymore and inserting a filter on the edge (8, 15). For the filter selection, according to the result of the data flow analysis, the source node 3 corresponding to the node 8 is firstly located, and the type of the sink point 16(t) is the type of "between the HTML tags". It generates the filter rule and inserts the corresponding filter statements (Fig. 5).

Input: dataflow chart $G = \{V, E, \lambda, \mu\}$, source points V_{Source},
   sink points, V_{Sink} ($V_{Source} \subset V$, $V_{Sink} \subset V$)

$\lambda : E \rightarrow \Sigma$, $\Sigma = \{C, D\}$

Output: T: Filter List

1、 for all $v \in V_{Sink}$

2、 $v' = v$

3、 do

4、 Seek edge $(v_1, v') \in E$ and $\lambda(v_1, v') = D$

5、 if exists v_2 , $(v_1, v_2) \in E$ and $\lambda(v_1, v') = D$ and $v_2 \neq v'$ or
$v_1 \in V_{Source}$

6、 insert a filter on the edge (v_1, v')

7、   else

8、 $v' = v_1$

9、 while $v' \notin V_{Source}$

Fig. 5. The protection filter insertion algorithm

3 Method Verification

3.1 Position and Type Analysis

The program analysis part of the automated tool is based on two open source tools of Soot and String [12]. The String tool can analyze all possible dependent variables of a particular string variable in a certain position in the java program. Then it can define the output statement as a tag, use the "StringAnalysis" class for analysis, and automatically analyze the variables based on the implementation of String to locate the sink point.

Soot is a tool for optimizing the Java bytecode. Because it analyzes the target program structure to the Java bytecode, and obtains the jimple intermediate description of the target program [13].

We use Soot to build a control flow graph for the target program, namely "UnitGraph", then we inherited the "BackwardFlowAnalysis" class from the Soot project and defines the data flow propagation strategy in the "flowThrough" function. We analyze data dependencies started from the sink point. Based on the Soot analysis results, the jimple statements are processed for liveness analysis, Alias Analysis, and data dependency analysis based on the target string variables, and only the data dependency related to the source and sink points are constructed.

According to the filter inserting algorithm described in Sect. 2.3, the corresponding filter code was inserted to deal with the input data type and query variable type separately. For example, the filter statement inserted on edge (6,16) in Fig. 1 is:

```
str=str.trim();
str = str.replace("\"", "");
str = str.replace("\'", "");
```

Only by replacing the quote character, we can prevent XSS while in most other methods need to replace a large number of keywords, which largely influences the efficiency, in contrast our method of setting filters on demand have much advantage.

3.2 Experimental Evaluation

We compare the method implemented here named "ODXSSA" with WAF, BEEP, CSP and other methods. For WAF we choose the open source JSP website firewall webcastellum [14]. The protection effect is tested by means of code substitutions including capital letter replacements, using stored XSS, using JavaScript pseudo-protocol methods, and using event handler functions. As shown in Table 4. The method of using the event function is combined with the return-to-libc method. The WAF method of webcastellum can't detect the abnormal behavior, and as the added event function code comes from the existing code, The BEEP method cannot prevent it. Both the CSP method and the ODXSSA can examine almost all test methods, but compared with ODXSSA, The cost of CSP is too expensive.

Table 5 described performance test result of ODXSSA. In terms of performance, four JSP projects were tested. The webgoat contained four XSS verification pages, and

Table 4. Tested protection methods

Method	encoding and confusion	Stored XSS	url pseudo protocol	Event handler + return to lib
webcastellum	√	√	√	×
BEEP	√	√	×	×
CSP	√	√	√	√
ODXSSA	√	√	√	√

the number of filters inserted was slightly higher than the number of sink points. The time spent for inserting and the number of filters are positive feedback relations, and the performance degradation brought by them is within 20%. With the increase of the code amount, the performance loss brought about by was in decrease.

Table 5. Performance test

Program	Sinks	Filters inserted	Time spent(s)	Performance loss
	;	$T(b) = T(a.f)$		
webgoat	4	4	8	19%
Pet Store	57	66	32	15%
focusSNS	429	486	115	13%
jspshop	341	382	86	14%

4 Conclusion

We proposed a scheme that automatically adds the injection filtering statement in the existing web program using code static analysis technology. By analyzing the server side script to determine the location of the relevant output points, the location attribute of sink point can be determined using data flow analysis. Then defense model was referenced to determine the prevention statement, which was ultimately inserted into the target program. We targeted JSP website for verification. The cost was reduced by means of inserting sink sensitive filters on demand and the method can effectively prevent common script injection attacks. In order to make this method effective, it is necessary to further solve the common problem of static analysis for other types of language, and improve analysis accuracy through inter-process data flow analysis. In addition, the prevention of DOM based XSS needs further research.

Acknowledgements. This work was supported by National Key Research And Development Plan (Grant Nos. 2016QY07X1404) and National Natural Science Foundation of China (Grant Nos. 61402526).

References

1. OWASP Top 10-2017. http://www.owasp.org.cn/owasp-project/OWASPTop102017v1.1. pdf. Accessed 17 Mar 2018
2. Chang, J., et al.: Analyzing and defending against web-based malware. ACM Comput. Surv. **45**(4), 49 (2013)
3. Engebretson, P.: Web-Based Exploitation. The Basics of Hacking and Penetration Testing (2013)
4. Weichselbaum, L., Spagnuolo, M., Janc, A.: Adopting strict content security policy for XSS protection. In: Cybersecurity Development. IEEE (2017)
5. Feng, G.L., Li, Z.-N.: Research on the application of web application firewall in university website system. In: Modern Computer (2017)
6. Appelt, D., et al.: A machine learning-driven evolutionary approach for testing web application firewalls. IEEE Trans. Reliab. **99**, 1–25 (2018)
7. Parvez, M., Zavarsky, P., Khoury, N.: Analysis of effectiveness of black-box web application scanners in detection of stored SQL injection and stored XSS vulnerabilities. In: Internet Technology and Secured Transactions, pp. 186–191. IEEE (2016)
8. Rathore, S., et al.: XSSClassifier: an efficient XSS attack detection approach based on machine learning classifier on SNSs. J. Inf. Process. Syst. **13**(4), 1014–1028 (2017)
9. Jong, K.D.: A new geodynamic model for the betic cordilleras based on P-T-t paths and structural data from the eastern betic. Física De La Tierra **4**, 77–108 (1992)
10. Čisar, P., Čisar, S.M.: The framework of runtime application self-protection technology. In: IEEE International Symposium on Computational Intelligence and Informatics, pp. 000081–000086. IEEE (2017)
11. Yan, M.M., et al.: The analysis of function calling path in java based on soot. Appl. Mech. Mater. **568–570**, 1479–1487 (2014)
12. Feldthaus, A., Møller, A.: The Big Manual for the Java String Analyzer. Department of Computer Science (2009)
13. WebCastellum. https://sourceforge.net/projects/webcastellum/. Accessed 17 Mar 2018

An Architecture of Secure Health Information Storage System Based on Blockchain Technology

Huirui Han[1], Mengxing Huang[1,2(✉)], Yu Zhang[1,2],
and Uzair Aslam Bhatti[1]

[1] State Key Laboratory of Marine Resource Utilization in South China Sea,
Hainan University, Haikou 570228, China
hanhr26@163.com, huangmx09@163.com
[2] College of Information Science and Technology,
Hainan University, Haikou 570228, China

Abstract. Most of medical institutions only store their medical data in their own system, which brought the problem of medical data isolated island. It makes secure medical data storage, privacy protection and data share in collaborative institutions difficult tasks. A novel blockchain architecture of secure health information storage system, which is decentralized, secure and trusted, tamper-resistant, is proposed to handle those difficult tasks. The proposed model combined consortium blockchain and fully private blockchain as a hybrid blockchain to improve the delay of data validation. Furthermore, some schemes were designed to improve the performance of blockchain technology in medical data storage. By comparing the existing problems in medical information storage, we analyzed the advantages and influence of the proposed model.

Keywords: Health information system · Blockchain · Secure storage
Data share

1 Introduction

WannaCry ransomware attack, using a kind of worm ransomware, is a May 2017 worldwide cyberattack, which was aimed at computers running Microsoft Windows operating system by encrypting data and ransomed payments in the Bitcoin [1]. With the attack of WannaCry, first time the national health system in United Kingdom was affected. On 12th May, computers from many British national hospitals were suffered from cyberattacks in a large scale, where at least 19 medical institutions including hospitals and clinics in England and Scotland was attacked by WannaCry. The hacker left a blackmail message in the attacked computer which claimed all data in the computer will be deleted if the hacker not gets payment. For a long time, the medical institution has been an important target of extorting worm attacks. In China, almost every hospital or clinic only store a copy of electric medical records of its visiting patients [2]. No matter hospitals or clinics suffer from cyberattack like WannaCry, they have to pay the ransom to the attackers. Therefore, constructing a more secure and

© Springer Nature Switzerland AG 2018
X. Sun et al. (Eds.): ICCCS 2018, LNCS 11064, pp. 578–588, 2018.
https://doi.org/10.1007/978-3-030-00009-7_52

reliable management mechanism for health information system is an urgent task for any medical institution.

Personal medical record is a kind of personal data which is owned by the individual. In order to protect personal privacy, a user can access a medical record only if he/she has the authorization. Protecting the privacy of personal medical records is not only a moral responsibility, but also a legal requirement. The traditional storage of electric medical records employs centralized scheme, which depends on reliable firewall, such as increasing factors of authentication or adopting more powerful encryption scheme and so on [3]. However, an attacker can access all medical data once he/she has entered the health information system, which means a single point of failure is existing. Meanwhile, patients need to trust the medical institutions storing medical records. How to protect the privacy of patients is a challenging to medical institutions.

With a creative design of data storage structure, transactions in Bitcoin network could be achieved without a centralized institution and the core technology is block chain, which was first proposed in 2008 and implemented in 2009 [4]. Block chain is a distributed database system [5], and also can be understood as a Distributed Ledger Technology (DLT) maintained by multiple nodes and has the key characteristics of decentralization, persistency anonymity and auditability [6]. The blockchain technology changed centralized medical data storage which needs specific institution to check permission and validate data. It shows a new mode which not needs middle institution, increases security of data and save time and costs.

Nowadays, Philips Medical and Tieron in the Netherlands are collaborating to accomplish authentication and privacy protection of medical records through blockchain technology. By setting complex and programmable authority protection, all data cannot be read and tamper with casually. It will not cause any problems even if some blocks in the blockchain system suffered from attack. Currently, there are a lot of research works about blockchain, while health information is considered in a few of them which can be divided into medical information protection, medical payment, medical data application, the storage and share of medical data and disease prediction etc. Do et al. [7] proposed a method of secure storage of medical records based on blockchain technology. Xiao et al. [8] constructed a model of health prediction crossing medical institutions by exploiting private blockchain technology. Ekblaw et al. [9] proposed a novel decentralized electric medical record management system. Some researches evaluated medical record storage systems using blockchain technology [9, 10]. In China, the researches integrating health domain and blockchain is few. Ying Mei proposed a scheme for secure storage of medical records based on block chain and cloud storage technology [11]. A creative medical data storage based on hybrid blockchain is proposed in this paper.

Inspired by the blockchain technology, a secure architecture aiming to management of health information based on blockchain technology is proposed. The main contributions of this paper are as follow:

- For medical institutions, a novel architecture of health information system is proposed to achieve more secure medical data storage, privacy protection and data share.

- Based on the flash network technology, consortium blockchain and fully private blockchain are combined as a hybrid blockchain to alleviate the delay of data validation. Furthermore, a novel mechanism of appending new block into the consortium chain is used to keep the increate of data size in consortium blockchain in a slower speed.
- In order to protect the privacy of patients, each medical data is encrypted by asymmetric encryption before it is appended into the hybrid blockchain.

The remainder of the paper is organized as follows. Section 2 presents some related works about blockchain and health information system. We describe proposed architecture in Sect. 3 and discussed the analysis of security in Sect. 4. Finally, Sect. 5 concludes the paper and gives an outlook on future works.

2   Blockchain Architecture

2.1   Blockchain

Blockchain is a sequence of blocks, which stores a complete list of transaction records [12]. Each block is linked to its previous block by hash value and shown as a block chain. The first block of blockchain is defined as *genesis block* which is the only one block without previous block. The basic data structure of blockchain consists of two parts, namely structure of block and chain structure among blocks. Figure 1 is shown a part of a blockchain. In general, the block header is made up of:

- Block version: the version number is used for tracking software or updating protocol.
- Merkle tree root hash: Merkle tree root hash is a 256-bit hash value of all transactions in the block.
- HashPreBlock: the previous block hash which is the value of hash function of the pervious block's block header
- Timestamp: A timestamp is a record of the current time.
- Bits: Bit indicates a hash value of current target.
- Nonce: Nonce denotes a 32-bit random value from 0.

Block body contains a transaction counter and available transactions during the period between producing the previous block and constructing the current block. The maximum number of transactions that a block can record depend on the size of block

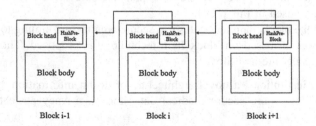

Fig. 1. The structure of a blockchain.

and the size of each transaction. Asymmetric cryptography is used by blockchain to generate the digital signatures of transaction [13]. Only the digital signatures in a block satisfy authentication, the block is able to pass verification.

2.2   Types of Blockchains

Currently, blockchain systems are categorized roughly into three types: public blockchain, consortium blockchain and fully private blockchain [14]. The comparison of different blockchain is listed in Table 1.

- Public blockchain is a blockchain which is opening up to anyone in the world. In the public blockchain, any node is free to join and quit the network, and anyone is allowed to read the block data and publish transactions. Furthermore, anyone can participate the consensus process of the public blockchain. Consensus process decides which block can be added into the blockchain.
- Consortium blockchain indicates a blockchain where consensus process is controlled by pre-selected set of nodes. For example, there is a consortium of 15 financial institutions, each of which operates a node and of which 10 institutions need to validate the new block to make it be valid. The authorization to read the blockchain maybe granted to public or restricted to participants. The design of authorization can also be hybrid. For example, the root hash and API (application programming interface) of the blockchain are opening to public to allow others to make a limited number of queries and get information about the state of blockchain. Those blockchains can be considered as "partially decentralized".
- Fully private blockchain is a blockchain where write permission is centralized in a specific institution, while read permission maybe opening to public or restricted to an arbitrary extent. The applications of fully private blockchain may include internal database management and auditing of a single company, where public readability may be unnecessary in many case though auditability is desired in a particular case.

Table 1. The Comparison of different blockchains

Property	Public blockchain	Consortium blockchain	Fully private blockchain
Consensus determination	All nodes	Selected nodes	A specific institution
Read Permission	Public	Could be public or restricted	Could be public or restricted
Efficiency	Low	High	High
Centralized	No	Partial	Yes

2.3   Digital Signature

Digital signature is string of figures that only the sender of information can generate and nobody can counterfeit. Digital signature is also an effective proof for the authenticity of information sent by the sender. The sender generates a digital abstract of a message by a Hash function, and then encrypts the digital abstract by its private key to generate a digital signature. The message and its digital signature are sent to a receiver together by the sender. At first, the receiver uses the same Hash function to compute the massage to get the validating digital abstract, then use the sender public key which is public to the network to decrypt the digital signature to get the original digital abstract. If the original digital abstract is same as the validating abstract, the receiver can ensure the digital signature is the miner. In other words, it is ensured that the message is sent by the sender because nobody can counterfeit the sender's signature and the massage is complete. One of digital signature algorithms used in blockchain is the elliptic curve digital signature algorithm (ECDSA) [15].

2.4 Digital Signature

Proof of work (PoW) is a computing result which is difficult to work out but easy for others to verify [16]. PoW uses Hash function to confuse the original data and make a pseudo random number, so as to ensure the reliability of the proven workload and avoid some irregular events. Assuming the initial number is Nonce and the average working difficulty coefficient is M, every node needs to carry out M hash operation at least to get the correct answer (for example, the hash value starting with several 0 is the correct answer). Obviously, the greater the average working difficulty coefficient M is, the larger the hash computation required by nodes. For the traditional Bitcoin system, a SHA-256 hash algorithm based PoW protocol was employed to select one out of miners to generate the next block.

2.5 Peer-to-Peer Network

Peer-to-peer network is a distributed application architecture which assigns tasks and workloads among peers. Peer-to-peer network is robust inherently due to its decentralized nature because it removes the single point of failure of a client-server based system. The system will be stable if some nodes or network suffers from network attack because services are decentralized into all nodes. The nodes in blockchain participate in the blockchain independently by applying P2P networking. Failure of a single node or network attack will not affect the blockchain system since every node is an individual.

3 Health Information Storage System Based on Blockchain

Inspired by blockchain technology, a novel scheme seeking to construct a more secure health information system is described in this section. This scheme uses 2 types of blockchains, namely consortium blockchain and private chain, to achieve secure storage and share of medical data. Therefore, the scheme is called hybrid health blockchain whose system architecture is shown in Fig. 2. In hybrid health blockchain, fully private blockchain is used as a traditional database in a medical institution and consortium blockchain used to store medical data submitted from all participant medical institutions. The medical data in hybrid health blockchain is public to participants which are authorized by healthcare supervision organization.

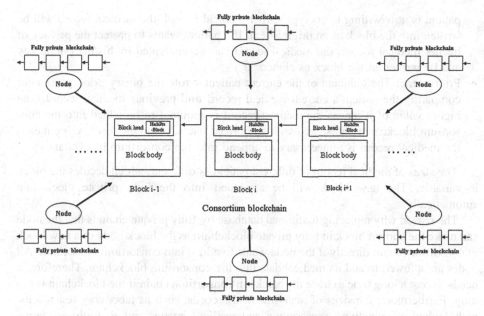

Fig. 2. The architecture of secure health information storage system based on hybrid blockchain architecture.

3.1 Medical Institutions and Patients

Generally, big medical data center is constructed in some important medical institutions. The number of visiting patients in a small-scaled medical institution is small, which means the size of medical data in such institution is small. In the background that important medical institutions are trusted by people, those medical institutions are acted as nodes in the Hybrid Health blockchain. Asymmetric cryptographic algorithm is applied to protect the privacy of patients and generate the signatures of nodes. As a result, every visiting patient has a public key and a private key. Similarly, every node in the Hybrid Health blockchain owns a public key and a private key.

3.2 Fully Private Blockchain in Hybrid Health Blockchain

Instead of storing medical records in traditional databased, fully private blockchain is applied to store medical records in every node. For any node, a medical record of a patient is mapping to a block in the fully private blockchain. The block is made up of block header and block body. The parameters of block header in fully private is set as that in normal blockchain. The structure of block body in the blockchain contains a public key of the current patient, the medical record of a patient and a priority tag.

- Public key of the current patient: A public key of the current patient is an identity of such patient because the public key is unique.
- Medical record: A patient's medical record contains medical information like a file of hospital record, a laboratory test result, a prescription and medical images. If a

patient is now willing to encrypt his/her medical record, the medical record will be written into the block as an original text. If a patient wants to protect the privacy of his/her medical record, the medical record can be encrypted by his/her public key and be written in the block as ciphertext.

- Priority tag: The clinician of the current patient wrote the binary priority tag after comparing the patient's current medical record and previous medical record. The higher value of it means the medical record is required to be added into the consortium blockchain and shared with authorized users, while the lower value means the medical record is unnecessary to append into the consortium blockchain.

The sizes of medical record of different patient is different, which decides the block is variable. The new block will be appended into the fully private blockchain automatically.

The reason why replacing traditional database by fully private chain is that the node can make the current block in fully private blockchain as the block body of a new block in consortium chain directly if the node wants to add it into consortium blockchain. All nodes are allowed to add its medical data into the consortium blockchain. Therefore, it needs to cost a long time to trace the blocks in consortium chain if the blockchain is too long. Furthermore, the sizes of many medical records, such as laboratory test results, pathological examinations, prescription and medical images and so forth, are large. With new blocks are produced continually, the size of medical data in consortium blockchain will be very large, which means every node needs to use a very large storage to keep the medical data in consortium blockchain. It is a storage burden for any node because it not only stores own medical data in fully private chain but also stores a much large shared medical data in consortium chain. For alleviating the storage burden of consortium chain, physician will decide whether the medical block of the current patient is necessary to be appended into the consortium blockchain. It reduces the increasing number of medical block in main chain and alleviates the storage burden of the nodes in the network to some extent. Thus, each node uses a queue to collect the numbers of candidate blocks selected to add into the consortium blockchain. The working procedures of processing a medical record is described as Algorithm 1.

Algorithm 1.

Step 1. A medical institution produces a medical record of a patient (M) with priority tag (PT).

Step 2. If the patient is not willing to publish his/her medical record, the medical record is encrypted by the patient's public key

Step 3. The node generates a new block according to the previous block and adds it into the fully private blockchain.

Step 4. The node check PT of the new block, if PT is equal to 1, the number of this block is appended into the candidate queue.

3.3   Consortium Blockchain in Hybrid Health Blockchain

Consortium blockchain technology is exploited to achieve the medical information share among the nodes. In the consortium blockchain, the data are only opening to authorized users and every node keeps a copy of data. All nodes are miners producing new blocks and appending them to consortium blockchain.

Similarly, the parameters of block header in consortium blockchain are set as that in normal blockchain, whereas the block body is made up of a candidate block in its private blockchain (called as private candidate block) and the digital signature of the node. The node's private key that ought to be kept in confidentiality is used to sign the private candidate block. The miner will make the private candidate block and its digital signature as the block body of the new block.

Proof of work is a mechanism to ensure the consistency of data in the blockchain. In order to compete appending a new block into the consortium chain, miners need to carry on a lot of computations, where the computing time depends on the difficulty coefficient of target and the operating speed. Instead of the difficulty coefficient of target increasing continually in Bitcoin system, the difficulty coefficient of target is set to keep stable in the consortium chain to reduce the time interval in appending new block. Once a miner finds the right answer in the first time, the miner is able to append the new block into the consortium blockchain broadcasts in the network. The working procedures of constructing consortium blockchain is described as Algorithm 2.

Algorithm 2.

Step 1. Every node writes a candidate block from its fully private chain and its digital signature into a new block,
Step 2. Every node calculates a random in its new block to find the correct answer.
Step 3. Once a node finds correct answer, it broadcasts the answer's mapping block to the network.
Step 4. Other nodes receive this block and validate its signature. The block is acceptable only if its signature passes validations.
Step 5. Every node uses the hash value of the block to carry out the computation of next block, which indicates nodes consider the block is valid.

It is possible two blocks are mined in the same time due to random hash computation and delay in the network. Then different miners continue to mine new block according to different previous blocks which leads to forks in blockchain, but the probability of this case is lower and lower. In the PoW network, people in the network will keep forks but miners just work in the longest blockchain. For example, some miners receive block A firstly, other miners receive block B. They mine new block according to their receiving blocks in fork A or fork B. Assuming a miner mines next block successfully in fork B and broadcasts to all nodes, miners in fork A will find fork B is longest and stop working in fork A to work in fork B. Thus, all miners will work in the same fork. Although the transactions in block A will be kept in transaction pool, they will still be written to new block in fork B later. For traditional Bitcoin system, a block in the longest chain followed by 5 blocks is consider that it is impossible to be forked. In this case, we consider any transaction in the block pass 6 validations. In terms of working difficulty coefficient, 6 is calculated from engineering computations. In hybrid blockchain, a block is appended into the consortium blockchain successfully only if it passes N validations. N is different from 6 in Bitcoin system because the working difficulty coefficient is different. Similarly, it is required to calculate N complex engineering computations. N maybe larger than 6 because working difficulty coefficient in consortium blockchain is smaller than that in Bitcoin system.

4 Security Analytics

This section presents a security analytics of hybrid health blockchain in the case of tamper proof and secure storage. Through comparing hybrid health chain and other strategies in existing researches, we analyzed the advantages of hybrid health chain.

4.1 Tamper Proof

Fully private blockchain of hybrid health blockchain is private to every node and only users with authorizations granted by the node can view medical information in it. Medical information in consortium blockchain of hybrid health blockchain is public and ordered by time sequence. Consortium blockchain applies consensus scheme to construct trusts in nodes without a centralized institution. After a block pass consensus and be appended into blockchain, it is recorded by all nodes and connects to the previous block using cryptology, which makes the difficulty and cost of tamper is very high. Digital abstract of digital signature technology is the hash value of the original data, any change of original data will change the hash value, which also ensure no one can tamper with the original data. Therefore, the risk of fraud is reduced, even if in the insecure network, by applying consortium blockchain to achieve medical data share in some medical institutions.

4.2 Reliable Storage

Storing complete information is one advantage of blockchain technology. Any participant is able to verify the data of any block in the blockchain by using encrypted hash value in any case. In a blockchain, all data blocks are serialized in chronological sequence to keep consistent data storage.

- Medical data are all stored in the hybrid health blockchain. They are public to authorized users and no one can tamper with them.
- In the hybrid health blockchain, any patient has the ownership of his/her medical information and the control of using the information. Medical node, such as a hospital or a centralized medical institution in a place, produces a medical record of a patient and add the ciphertext of the medical record encrypted by the patient's public key into its hybrid health blockchain. Only authorized users such as doctors is able to get the private keys from their patients. Then they can view the real medical records by decrypting the ciphertext using patients' private keys. No attacker can get the real medical information even if he/she acquired data from hybrid health blockchain, because both fully private blockchain of a node and consortium blockchain store medical records in ciphertext, which ensure the security of medical data in the hybrid health blockchain.

- Considering that a large amount of medical data affects the performance of consortium blockchain, a scheme is designed to make every node select important medical records to add into consortium blockchain. Therefore, the medical data in consortium blockchain of hybrid health blockchain are important medical data from all node, which are kept in every node. It overcomes the problem of single point of failure and prevents hijacked by unauthorized third party.

4.3   Evaluation

To evaluate the proposed blockchain architecture of secure health information storage system, we compared it with the existing system based on blockchain technology. Table 2 shows the differences among these models in 5 aspects, in which private blockchain includes fully private blockchain and consortium block-chain

Table 2. The comparison of different models.

	Based on blockchain	Consensus	Without the third party	Alleviating the size of data in blockchain	Private blockchain
Cloud-based EHR system [17]	No	No	No	No	No
MedRec [9]	Yes	PoW	Yes	No	No
Health blockchain [11]	Yes	PoW	No	No	No
ModelChain [8]	Yes	PoI	Yes	Yes	Yes
Hybrid health blockchain	Yes	PoW	Yes	Yes	Yes

5   Conclusion

A novel blockchain architecture of secure health information storage system is presented in this paper. For achieving secure medical information storage, privacy protection and medical data share, the proposed model combines fully private blockchain and consortium blockchain. Furthermore, some schemes are designed to overcome the shortcomings of blockchain technology.

However, a number of unknown problems may limit the implementation of the proposed model. The technologies of health information system need to be updated following by the advanced technologies. Another potential limitation is the cost for deploying the proposed model. Considering those limitations, we will continue to implement and improve the proposed model in our future works.

Acknowledgements. This research received financial support from the Natural Science Foundation of Hainan province (Grant#:617062 and Grant#: 20156235), Natural Science Foundation of China (Grant#: 61462022), the National Key Technology Support Program (Grant#: 2015BAH55F04, Grant#:2015BAH55F01), Major Science and Technology Project of Hainan province (Grant#: ZDKJ2016015), Scientific Research Staring Foundation of Hainan University (Grant#: kyqd1610).

References

1. WannaCry ransomware attack. https://en.wikipedia.org/wiki/WannaCry_ransomware_attack
2. Charles, D., Gabriel, M., Furukawa, M.: Adoption of electronic health record systems among U.S. non-federal acutecare hospitals: 2008-2012. ONC Data Brief, **9**, 1–9 (2013)
3. Weerasinghe, D., Rajarajan, M., Elmufti, K.: Patient privacy protection using anonymous access control techniques. Method. Inf. Med. **47**(3), 235 (2008)
4. Tsai, W., Blower, R., Zhu, Y.: A system view of financial blockchains. In: Service-Oriented System Engineering, pp. 450–457 (2016)
5. Christidis, K., Devetsikiotis, M.: Blockchains and smart contracts for the internet of things. IEEE Access **4**, 2292–2303 (2016)
6. Mainelli, M., Milne, A.: The Impact and Potential of Blockchain on Securities Transaction Lifecycle. Social Science Electronic Publishing (2016)
7. Do, H.G., Ng, W.K.: Blockchain-based system for secure data storage with private keyword search. In: IEEE Services, pp. 90–93(2017)
8. Xiao, Y., Wang, H., Jin, D.: Healthcare data gateways: found healthcare intelligence on blockchain with novel privacy risk control. J. Med. Syst. **40**(10), 1–8 (2016)
9. Ekblaw, A., Azaria, A., Halamka, J., Lippman, A.: A case study for blockchain in healthcare: "MedRec" prototype for electronic health records and medical research data. In: Proceedings of the 2016 IEEE of International Conference on Open and Big Data, pp. 25–30 (2016)
10. Baxendale, G.: Can blockchain revolutionise EPRs? ITNow **58**(1), 38–39 (2016)
11. Ying, M.: The utilizing blockchain-based method of the secure storage of medical records. J. Jiangxi Norm. Univ. **45**(5), 481–487 (2017)
12. Chuen, D.L.K.: Handbook of digital currency: bitcoin, innovation, financial instruments, and big data. J. Wealth Manag. **18**(2), 96–97 (2015)
13. Chen, Z., Zhu, Y.: Personal archive service system using blockchain technology: case study, promising and challenging. In: IEEE International Conference on Ai & Mobile Services, pp. 93–99 (2017)
14. Guegan, D.: Public Blockchain versus Private blockchain. Documents De Travail Du Centre Deconomie De La Sorbonne (2017)
15. Johnson, D., Menezes, A., Vanstone, S.: The elliptic curve digital signature algorithm (ecdsa). Int. J. Inf. Secur. **1**(1), 36–63 (2001)
16. Nakamoto, S.: Bitcoin: A peer-to-peer electronic cash system. Consulted (2008)
17. Xhafa, F., Li, J., Zhao, G.: Designing cloud-based electronic health record system with attribute-based encryption. Multimed. Tools Appl. **74**(10), 3441–3458 (2015)

An Evolutionary Algorithm Based on Multi-view and Prior Information for Community Detection

Xiaofeng Ma[1], Xiaofeng Song[2(✉)], Chao Fan[1], and Xi Wang[3]

[1] State Key Laboratory of Mathematical Engineering and Advanced Computing,
Zhengzhou 450001, China
[2] School of Information Communication,
National University of Defense Technology, Xi'an 710106, China
fengye_xty@163.com
[3] Chengdu Construction Engineering Quality Supervision Bureau,
Shuangliu Branch, Chengdu, China

Abstract. By fusing the follow, mention and retweet relationships between social network users and integrating the partial prior link information, a community detection method is proposed based on genetic optimization algorithm. The network modularity is taken as the optimization objective function, the user's follow, mention and retweet relationships are combined with genetic algorithm for network community detection. Furthermore, the prior information about the partial links between users is also fused into the detection algorithm to guide the evolutionary search process. The experimental results show that the fusion of multi-view information and prior information can improve the performance for network community detection.

Keywords: Social network · Community detection · Genetic algorithm
Multi-view learning · Prior information

1 Introduction

Community detection [1] is a very important task in social network analysis [2]. Through the community detection, we can tap the information about the organizational structure contained in the network and discover the social functions of the network [3]. Among so many network community detection methods [4, 5], the detection methods based on evolutionary optimization algorithm try to maximize the community division measurements such as modularity [6] and modularity density [7]. And this kind of methods can achieve the competitive detection performances because the powerful global optimization ability of evolutionary algorithm. However, the existing evolutionary detection methods only use the link relationships between network users for community detection, which in fact ignores the rich relationship information between network users. When users interact with each other through social networks, various interactions such as follow, mention, retweet [8] that can be discovered. These interactions reflect the closeness of users [9, 10] from different perspectives. Therefore, when using evolutionary optimization algorithm for community detection, the multi-view

X. Sun et al. (Eds.): ICCCS 2018, LNCS 11064, pp. 589–600, 2018.
https://doi.org/10.1007/978-3-030-00009-7_53

interactions should be fused at the same time to further improve the detection accuracy. In addition, some priori information also should be integrated into the optimal search process [11, 12].

Based on the above ideas, a network community detection method is proposed based on evolutionary optimization. The proposed method takes the network modularity as the optimization objective function and the multi-view information are fused to improve the detection accuracy. The prior information is also used to guide the evolutionary search process. In the following, the overall framework of the proposed community detection method is given firstly, and then the specific steps of the detection method are described in detail. Finally, the experimental results are presented.

2 Framework of the Proposed Community Detection Method

When the community detection is performed by evolutionary optimization, multi-view and prior information, the user relationship matrix is established according to the interactions among network users from different perspectives. The element values of the relationship matrix indicates the closeness relationship between users. Then, based on the user relationship matrix, genetic coding is used for individual coding, and the individual coding adopts the locus-based method [4]. That is, each gene location represents a user node, and the gene value is the order number of an adjacent user node in the network, and the individual decoding result corresponds to the result of the corresponding network community detection. Finally, based on the definition of individual code, the objective function, population initialization method, crossover operator, mutation operator, selection strategy and so on are determined. In addition, some prior information between users are used to direct the search process. The optimal individual is decoded as the final detection result. In summary, the overall framework of the proposed community detection method is shown as Fig. 1.

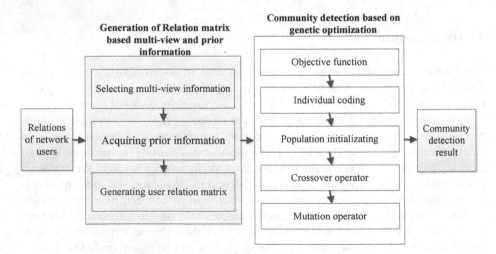

Fig. 1. Overall framework of the proposed evolutionary optimization method for community detection by multi-view and prior information.

As can be seen from Fig. 1, the proposed community detection methods mainly include two parts, the first part is the generation of user relationship matrix based on multi-view and prior information, and the second part is the division of community based on genetic algorithm. The former mainly uses the multi-view user interaction and priori link information to generate user relationship matrix; the latter is to find the optimal network community division based on the user relationship matrix. Compared with other community detection methods based on genetic algorithms, the main features of the proposed method lie in the utilization of the multi-view and prior information. In other words, the paper mainly explores how to integrate multi-view information and prior information into the community detection method based on genetic algorithms and study their impact on the community detection performance.

3   Implementation of the Proposed Detection Method

According to the overall framework of community detection algorithm shown in Fig. 1, the specific implementation process of the proposed detection method is described as follows.

3.1   Multi-view Information Fusion

Suppose the matrix $\mathbf{M}_f, \mathbf{M}_m, \mathbf{M}_r$ respectively represent the follow, mention and retweet relationships between network users. For the matrix $\mathbf{M}_f$, when the element $M_f(i,j)$ is 1, it indicates that user i has followed user j and $M_f(i,j)$ equal to 0 means no follow; For the matrix $\mathbf{M}_m$, the element $M_m(i,j)$ indicates that the number of mentions that user i mention user j when posting a tweet; and for the matrix $\mathbf{M}_r$, the element $M_r(i,j)$ indicates the number of retweets that user i has retweeted the tweet of user j. These three matrices actually represent the relationship of the network users from different views, and they can be used to get the relationship matrix which can reflect the closeness of users better.

For the fusion of different view relationship matrix, the single view matrix is transformed into symmetric matrix firstly. Then, the multi-view relationship matrix can be formed by weighted combination of the different view relationship matrices.

$$\mathbf{M} = \alpha \cdot \bar{\mathbf{M}}_f + \beta \cdot \bar{\mathbf{M}}_m + \gamma \cdot \bar{\mathbf{M}}_r \tag{1}$$

In the formula (1), α, β, γ represents the weight coefficient. The larger the value is, the larger the weight of the corresponding single view relationship matrix in the fused multi-view relation matrix, and the range of α, β, γ is [0, 1].

A multi-view relationship matrix reflecting the closeness among users from more aspect. The larger the matrix element value is, the closer the closeness between the users is and the more likely the two are divided into the same community.

3.2 Prior Information Fusion

For community detection, taking use of the prior information such as the link relationships between some known network users can improve the detection performance significantly. The use of these prior information is implemented by constraining the division among the users in the community detection process. For example, some users must be divided in one community (Must-Link), those users cannot be divided in one community (Cannot- Link).

Suppose a given network user connection diagram is $G = (\mathbf{V}, \mathbf{E})$, The division of community is $K = \{K_1, K_2, \cdots, K_k\}$, Given the ML collection $M = \{(x_i, x_j)\}$, CL collection $C = \{(x_i, x_j)\}$. Then, the relationship matrix $\mathbf{M}^p$ among users after the prior information being fused can be expressed as follows,

$$M_{ij}^p = \begin{cases} w, & i,j \ \ belongs\ to\ the\ same\ community \\ 0, & i,j \ \ belongs\ to\ the\ different\ community \\ M_{ij}, & others \end{cases} \tag{2}$$

In the above expression, w represents a weight, the greater the value is, the higher the probability of node i,j being divided into the same community. And $M_{ij}^p = 0$ means that nodes i and j cannot be divided into the same community.

Since the proposed detection method is based on genetic algorithm with locus-based coding. Therefore, if the nodes i and j must be connected, then the value of the gene location representing the node i in all individuals can only be the number of the node j. Conversely, if the node i and j cannot be connected, the value of the gene location representing node i in all individuals cannot be the node number of node j.

3.3 Optimization Objective Function

When genetic algorithm is used for community detection, the optimization objective function must be determined firstly. Here, the modularity proposed in [13] is chosen as the optimization target of community detection. Network modularity is a widely used for the measure of the community division. The basic idea is to judge whether there is a community structure in the network by comparing the difference between the real network and the random graph network. The concrete definition of network modularity is as follows:

$$Q = \frac{1}{2m} \sum_{ij} (A_{ij} - k_i k_j / 2m) \delta(x_i, x_j) \tag{3}$$

Here, m represents the total number of edges in the network, A_{ij} represents elements of the network adjacency matrix $\mathbf{A}$. When nodes x_i and x_j have adjacencies, $A_{ij} = 1$; otherwise $A_{ij} = 0$. k_i, k_j indicates node degree, When nodes x_i and x_j belong to the same community, $\delta(x_i, x_j) = 1$; otherwise $\delta(x_i, x_j) = 0$.

3.4 Encoding and Decoding Algorithm

For community detection with genetic algorithm, network division is represented by individuals of the population and each individual uses a locus-based coding scheme. Assuming there are N nodes in the network, an individual includes N genes $g_1, g_2, \cdots, g_N$, gene g_i represents the node i of the network, and its corresponding value is the order number of the any adjacent nodes in the network. The corresponding community division can be obtained by decoding the individuals with locus-based coding method. Figure 2 shows a network and its community detection process, and Fig. 2(a) shows the network connection, Fig. 2(b) shows the individual in the genetic algorithm, that is, a community division, Fig. 2(c) represents three communities acquired by decoding individual.

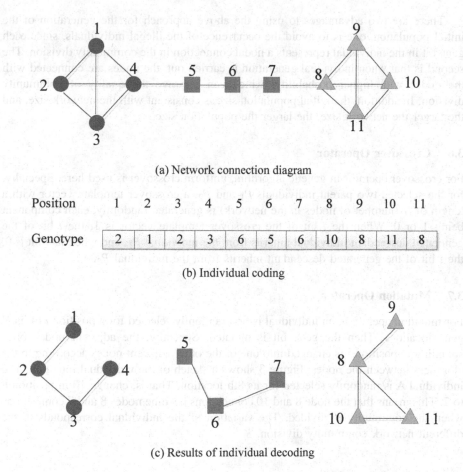

(a) Network connection diagram

Position	1	2	3	4	5	6	7	8	9	10	11
Genotype	2	1	2	3	6	5	6	10	8	11	8

(b) Individual coding

(c) Results of individual decoding

Fig. 2. Encoding and decoding process based on locus-based method.

3.5 Population Initialization

For genetic optimization, the initial population should be generated firstly. For each individual, the value of each gene location should be the order number of the node randomly selected according to the closeness with other nodes in the network. Specially, assuming that the node i has n adjacent nodes, $s_1, s_2, \cdots, s_n$ represent the closeness between node i and its n adjacent nodes, p_i represents the probability that the node will be selected. Then, the selection of the *i-th* gene bit is according to the probability value $(p_1, p_2, \cdots, p_n)$.

$$p_i = s_i \left/ \sum_{i=1}^{n} s_i \right. \tag{4}$$

There are two advantages to using the above approach for the generation of the initial population, one is to avoid the occurrence of the illegal individuals, since each gene bit in the individual represents a nodal connection in the community division. The second is that when individual generation is carried out, the nodes are connected with the nodes with higher probability, which can improve the quality of community division. In addition, the initial population size is consistent with the network size, and the larger the network size, the larger the population size.

3.6 Crossover Operator

For crossover operator in genetic algorithm, uniform crossover is used here. Specially, for the selected two parent individuals P_1 and P_2, a crossover template vector with a length of N (number of nodes in the network) is generated randomly, each component being 1 or 0. When the i bit of the crossover template vector is 1, the i bit of the generated descendant individual inherits from the individual P_1, and when its i bit is 0, the i bit of the generated descendant inherits from the individual P_2.

3.7 Mutation Operator

For mutation operation, an individual is first randomly selected for a position i of its N gene locations. Then the gene bit is mutated. Specially, the adjacent node corresponding to position i is changed into one of the other adjacent nodes according to the closeness between the nodes. Figure 3 shows a sketch of the individual mutation. The individual A is randomly selected for its 8th location. That is, change 10 in position 8 to 7. This means that the node 8 and 10 connections become nodes 8 and 7 connections when the community is divided. The variation of the individual corresponds to the different network community division.

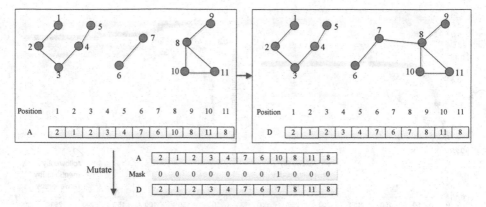

Fig. 3. Mutation operation of the individual.

4 Experimental Results and Analysis

4.1 Experimental Data Sets and Experiment Settings

The datasets used in the experiment include Football and Olympics, which were formed by web activity records of the organization members on Twitter [14]. Among them, the Football dataset is formed by the interactions of 248 Premier League players on Twitter, these players belong to 20 different clubs. The Olympics dataset was formed from Twitter interactions with 464 athletes who took part in the London Summer Olympics in 2012. These athletes belong to 28 different sport events. The above datasets contain the following kinds of interaction data: (1) followed by data. These data is an unauthorized graph. (2) mentioned by data. These data is directed weighted graph. (3) retweeted by dataset. These data is directed weighted graph.

The network modularity as shown in formula (3) is used to evaluate the community detection performances. The larger the modularity Q corresponding to the network community division, the better the network community detection accuracy is. Another evaluation measure is Normalized Mutual Information (NMI) [15].

4.2 Community Detection Performance Acquired by Genetic Optimization

For the proposed community detection algorithm, network modularity is used as the objective function of genetic optimization. Without considering the fusion of multi-view and prior information, the proposed method is similar with the existing community detection method based on genetic algorithm, the difference is that the objective function is modularity in this paper and is the community score in literature [4]. Figures 4 and 5 respectively show the variation of modularity and NMI value when the genetic algorithm is used to detect the community for two different datasets.

Figure 4 shows the change of modularity and NMI value with the iterations of genetic optimization on the Football dataset. Three different curves represents the modularity and NMI values according to the different relationship between the users.

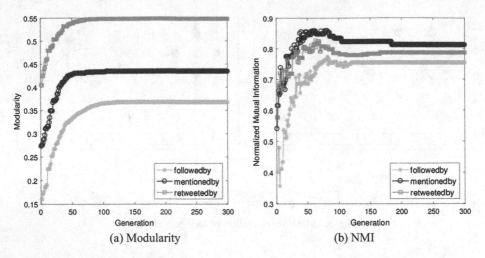

Fig. 4. Modularity and NMI change with the iterations of genetic optimization on football dataset.

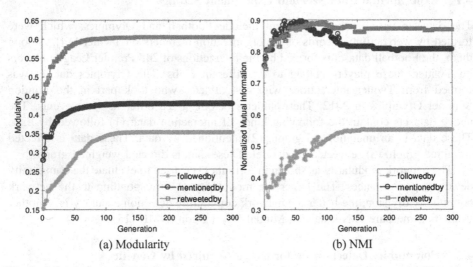

Fig. 5. Modularity and NMI change with the iteration of genetic optimization on the Olympics dataset

From Fig. 4, it can be seen that the modularity and NMI value is improved with the iteration of genetic optimization until them reach a steady state. Furthermore, it also can be seen that the modularity value are best when "retweetedby" relationship is used for community detection while the corresponding NMI value is not the best. This indicates that the different measures of community detection may be not consistent.

In Fig. 5, the variation of modularity and NMI value is given for Olympics dataset. It can be seen that the modularity and NMI value is best when "retweeted-by" relationship is used for community detection. However, for Football dataset, the "mentioned-by" relationship can get the best result. This indicates that the detection performance of the same view information may be not consistent for different datasets.

4.3 Community Detection Performance by Fusing Multi-view Information

In social networks, there are various interaction relationships between users, and these interactions reflect the relationships between users from the different views. Therefore, the community detection can be performed by fusing multi-view information to improve the detection performance.

In Table 1, modularity, NMI and community number are all given when the community detection is performed based on information with different views. From Table 1, it can be seen that the NMI value is the best one when "mentionedby" relationship is used for community detection for Football dataset. However, the corresponding modularity value is not the best. When the "followedby" relationship is used for community detection, the modularity and NMI value are all the worst.

Table 1. Detection performances for football dataset based on multi-view information (7 times)

Followed-by	0.3404	0.3763	0.3760	0.3684	0.3547	0.3731	0.3691
	0.6884	0.7814	0.7818	0.7623	0.6902	0.7618	0.7329
	9	11	11	10	9	10	9
Mentioned-by	0.4321	0.4328	0.4322	0.4348	0.4327	0.4349	0.4341
	0.8198	0.8187	0.8094	0.8176	0.8276	0.8207	0.8120
	13	13	13	13	13	13	13
Retweeted-by	0.5477	0.5486	0.5482	0.5475	0.5486	0.5473	0.5486
	0.7647	0.7924	0.7846	0.7677	0.7924	0.7930	0.7924
	26	27	27	27	27	28	27
Followed-by + mentioned-by	0.3506	0.3503	0.3500	0.3516	0.3521	0.3469	0.3513
	0.7949	0.8226	0.7598	0.8279	0.7970	0.7828	0.7947
	9	10	9	10	9	9	9
Followed-by + retweeted-by	0.3637	0.3721	0.3647	0.3655	0.3682	0.3688	0.3701
	0.7827	0.7597	0.7789	0.7353	0.7899	0.7590	0.7815
	10	10	11	10	11	9	11
Mentioned-by + retweeted-by	0.4336	0.4333	0.4330	0.4343	0.4333	0.4336	0.4313
	0.8237	0.8153	0.8173	0.8434	0.8153	0.8134	0.8250
	13	13	13	14	13	13	13
All	0.3517	0.3512	0.3518	0.3502	0.3508	0.3507	0.3486
	0.7970	0.7725	0.7872	0.7799	0.8014	0.7862	0.7921
	9	9	9	9	9	10	9

Table 1 also shows the detection performances when the "followedby", "mentionedby" and "retweetedby" are fused in different manners. For Football dataset, the fusion of "mentionedby" and "retweetedby" can obtain the relatively good results.

Although the fusion of "followedby" and other relationships cannot get better results. This may be the community relationship reflected by "followedby" relationship between the players is not obvious.

For the Olympics dataset, Table 2 shows the modularity, NMI and community number that are got based on different interaction relationships. As can be seen from Table 2, when "followedby", "mentionedby" and "retweetedby" interaction relations are used for community detection, the best NMI value is achieved by "mentionedby, and the second value is achieved by "retweetedby". The NMI value of "followedby" "relationship is worst. The same result is got for modularity value.

Table 2. Detection results for Olympics dataset based on multi-view information (7 times)

Followed-by	0.3876	0.3739	0.3686	0.3650	0.3552	0.3517	0.3968
	0.6479	0.5983	0.6770	0.6558	0.5907	0.6266	0.7042
	8	7	10	9	7	8	9
Mentioned-by	0.4296	0.4295	0.4294	0.4288	0.4301	0.4302	0.4253
	0.8167	0.8227	0.8261	0.8075	0.8304	0.8085	0.7962
	15	15	17	16	16	16	16
Retweeted-by	0.6062	0.6040	0.6070	0.6035	0.6069	0.6067	0.6054
	0.8686	0.8259	0.8601	0.8621	0.8517	0.8646	0.8553
	42	40	41	42	39	42	41
Followed-by + mentionedby	0.3536	0.3511	0.3566	0.3499	0.3494	0.3546	0.356
	0.7796	0.7804	0.7687	0.7773	0.7604	0.7633	0.7505
	11	11	10	12	10	11	10
Followed-by + retweeted-by	0.4024	0.3938	0.3876	0.4016	0.4024	0.4021	0.4010
	0.8217	0.7221	0.7456	0.7737	0.7950	0.7903	0.7481
	12	9	11	10	11	11	10
Mentioned-by + retweeted-by	0.4279	0.4276	0.4299	0.4284	0.4282	0.4299	0.4273
	0.8329	0.7869	0.8168	0.8223	0.8217	0.8115	0.8478
	16	15	16	17	16	16	17
All	0.3531	0.3562	0.3554	0.3536	0.3544	0.3530	0.3538
	0.7568	0.7750	0.7537	0.7658	0.7058	0.7264	0.7468
	11	10	10	11	8	9	10

For the fusion of different relationships, the fusion of "followedby" and other relationships has achieved higher modularity and NMI value than its own, but the result is not better than just using other relationships. This is probably because the community structure which "followedby" reflects is not clear. The fusion of "followedby" and other relationships can achieve a better result than the only use of "followedby".

From the above experiment results, it can be seen that the fusion of the interaction of network users with different views can improve the accuracy of network community detection. But it is important to note that the more network interactions not mean the higher community detection accuracy. It is because that some interactions reflect the obvious network community structure while some interactions are relatively chaotic. In addition, for different datasets, the same interaction may play different roles. This is because different network have different interaction characteristics.

4.4   Community Detection Result by Fusing Prior Information

In this section, the proposed detection algorithm is performed for Football datasets. There are two types of prior information, the Must-Link is for users of the same community, which selects a certain percentage of users to restrict them to be divided into one community; Cannot-Link is used for the users of different communities, and a certain percentage users are chosen to be restricted the connection. The percentage in the experiment from small to large were 0.05, 0.05, 0.1, 0.15 and 0.2. In addition, the relationship matrix is the fusion of "mentionedby" and "retweetedby". Table 3 gives modularity, NMI and community number after incorporating different proportions of prior information for the community detection on the Football.

Table 3.   Detection results for Olympics dataset by fusing prior information (7 times)

0.01	0.4342	0.4342	0.4315	0.4331	0.4343	0.4343	0.4333
	0.8138	0.8138	0.8111	0.8143	0.8120	0.8434	0.8551
	13	13	12	13	13	14	14
0.05	0.4202	0.4231	0.4248	0.4218	0.4207	0.4203	0.4226
	0.8930	0.8883	0.884	0.9037	0.8805	0.8916	0.9029
	19	19	19	20	18	19	19
0.1	0.4127	0.4093	0.4147	0.4209	0.4224	0.4225	0.4162
	0.9333	0.9402	0.9228	0.9268	0.9065	0.8859	0.8747
	21	21	20	20	20	20	20
0.15	0.4224	0.4268	0.4251	0.4255	0.4269	0.4228	0.4229
	0.9457	0.9281	0.9465	0.9334	0.9385	0.9706	0.9607
	21	20	21	20	21	20	21
0.2	0.4309	0.4326	0.4307	0.4287	0.4295	0.4333	0.4269
	0.9466	0.9385	0.9388	0.9639	0.9304	0.9324	0.9742
	20	20	20	21	21	20	21

From the experimental results shown in Table 3, it can be seen that the corresponding NMI value of community detection is also increasing with the increase of prior information. For example, when Must-Link and Cannot-Link ratio is 0.01, the mean value of NMI over seven times tests is 0.8, and when the ratio goes up to 0.2, the value is 0.94. This shows that the prior information can significantly improve the community detection performance, and the results from Table 3 also show that with the increase of prior information, the accuracy of community number is also getting better. For example, when the proportion of prior information reaches above 0.1, the community number is 20 or 21, which is the same or very similar to the actual number of player club. In addition, from Table 3, it can also be found that with the increase of prior information, the corresponding modularity value has not changed significantly. This indicates that the modularity and the NMI are not strictly relevant.

5 Conclusions

In this paper, a community detection method based on genetic algorithm is proposed by fusing multi-view information and prior information. For the proposed method, the network modularity is taken as the objective function. In order to improve the detection accuracy, multi-view information and prior information are integrated into the community detection process. Experimental results also show that the fusion of multi-view information and prior information can significantly improve the detection performance. It is important to note that, although this proposed method improves the community detection, however, the fusion method is relatively simple. How to integrate the information of different views to get more accurate detection results need to be studied further.

References

1. Fortunato, S.: Community detection in graphs. Phys. Rep. **486**(3–5), 75–174 (2010)
2. Mislovec, A., Marcon, M., Gummadi, K.P., et al.: Measurement and analysis of online social networks. In: Proceedings of the 7th ACM SIGCOMM Conference on Internet Measurement, pp. 29–42. ACM (2007)
3. Models and Methods in Social Network Analysis. Cambridge University Press (2005)
4. Pizzuti, C.: Community detection in social networks with genetic algorithms. In: Proceedings of the 10th Annual Conference on Genetic and Evolutionary Computation, pp. 1137–1138 (2008)
5. Guerrero, M., Montoya, F.G., Baños, R., et al.: Adaptive community detection in complex networks using genetic algorithms. Neurocomputing **266**, 101–113 (2017)
6. Duch, J., Arenas, A.: Community detection in complex networks using extremal optimization. Phys. Rev. E **72**(2), 027104 (2005)
7. Li, Z., Zhang, S., Wang, R.S., et al.: Quantitative function for community detection. Phys. Rev. E **77**(3), 036109 (2008)
8. Kwak, H., Lee, C., Park, H., et al.: What is Twitter, a social network or a news media? In: Proceedings of the 19th International Conference on World Wide Web, pp. 591–600. ACM (2010)
9. Yulong, P., Chakraborty,N., et al.: Nonnegative matrix tri-factorization with graph regularization for community detection in social networks. In: Proceedings of the International Joint Conference on Artificial Intelligence, pp. 2083–2089 (2015)
10. Nguyen, H.T., Dinh, T.N., Vu, T.: Community detection in multiplex social networks. In: Proceedings of Computer Communications Workshops, pp. 654–659 (2015)
11. Zhang, Z.Y.: Community structure detection in complex networks with partial background information. Europhys. Lett. **101**(4), 48005 (2013)
12. Silva, T.C., Zhao, L.: Semi-supervised learning guided by the modularity measure in complex networks. Neurocomputing **78**(1), 30–37 (2012)
13. Newman, M.E.J., Girvan, M.: Finding and evaluating community structure in networks. Phys. Rev. E **69**(2), 026113 (2004)
14. Greene, D., Cunningham, P.: Producing a unified graph representation from multiple social network views. In: Proceedings of the 5th Annual ACM Web Science Conference, pp. 118–121 (2013)
15. Danon, L., Díazguilera, A., Duch, J., et al.: Comparing community structure identification. J. Stat. Mech.: Theory Exp. **9**, 09008 (2005)

An Immunity-Based Security Threat Detection System for Cyberspace Digital Virtual Assets

Ping Lin[1], Tao Li[2(✉)], Xiaojie Liu[2], Hui Zhao[2], Jin Yang[2], and Fangdong Zhu[1]

[1] College of Computer Science, Sichuan University, Chengdu 610065, China
[2] College of Cybersecurity, Sichuan University, Chengdu 610065, China
litao@scu.edu.cn

Abstract. With a rapid accumulation of cyberspace digital virtual assets (CDVA), the serious security risks of CDVA appear since the lack of security protection methods for CDVA application systems. The present CDVA security systems mainly adopt the general network threat detection methods, do not deal with the specifics of CDVA, thus, they are not suitable for CDVA security threat detection. This paper presents an immune-based security threat detection system (IBSTDS) for CDVA. The system collects the data flow of fundamental infrastructure from Internet, extracts and formalizes the features to form antigens. The antigens are sequentially sent to the memory detectors and mature detectors for known and unknown threat detection. The immune detectors are optimized by detector dynamic evolution and immune feedback mechanism. The experiment proves that the system has the ability of threat-recognition and self-learning. Compared with the current CDVA security systems, IBSTDS supports adaptability, self-organization, robustness and self-learning, and provides a good solution to detect the security threat to digital virtual assets.

Keywords: Cyberspace digital virtual asset · CDVA
Artificial immunity · Threat detect

1 Introduction

Virtual asset, also known as virtual property, is a representation of currency in some environment or situation [1]. In this context, currency can be defined as either a medium of exchange or a property that has value in a specific environment, such as an online game, digital copyright, or a financial trading simulation exercise. From this perspective, it refers specially to the cyberspace digital virtual assets (or digital virtual assets). Nowadays, thanks to the prosperous development of global Internet economy, CDVA has become an important social asset, and the research on the protection of CDVA has drawn close attention from international academic frontiers.

© Springer Nature Switzerland AG 2018
X. Sun et al. (Eds.): ICCCS 2018, LNCS 11064, pp. 601–611, 2018.
https://doi.org/10.1007/978-3-030-00009-7_54

Since 2008, Goodman et al. [2] put forward a peer auditing scheme for cheat elimination in massively multiplayer online games(MMOG) to protect game assets. Denault et al. [3] proposed an online multiplayer fraud control protocol, and in 2013 Yahyavi et al. analyzed the peer-to-peer architectures for MMOG [4] and proposed a scalable cheat-resistant protocol for distributed multi-player online games [5]. Maguluri [6] put forward a multi-class classification method of textual data for detection and mitigation of cheating in massively multiplayer online role playing games. In 2014, Miller et al. [7] drew the blockchain into the protection of privacy in asset data and proposed a blockchain-based asset data security transaction model. In 2015, Dagher et al. [8] proposed a virtual currency protection program with privacy preservation based on private key segmentation, in which the user's private key was divided into different parts and stored in different carriers. In 2016, Peck [9] proposed a blockchain-based virtual currency protection scheme to realize the secure and private deals of digital virtual assets through zero-knowledge proof. As for protection for digital copyrights, Lazarovich et al. [10] built a platform that securely distributes encrypted user-sensitive data. It uses the Bitcoin blockchain to keep a trust-less audit trail for data interactions and to manage access to user data. Zyskind et al. [11] proposed a decentralized personal data management system and turned the blockchain into an automated access-control manager that does not require trust in a third party, which ensures users own and control their data. Kishigami et al. [12] put forward a blockchain-based digital content distribution system and Herbert et al. [13] proposed a method for decentralized peer-to-peer software license validation·using cryptocurrency blockchain technology to ameliorate software piracy, which provides a mechanism to protect copyrighted works. Moreover, Other research institutes such as Binghamton University [14], Carnegie Mellon University [15], Southern Methodist University [16], and Durham University [17] etc. have made certain researches on the risks in the development, certification, storage, extraction and transaction of virtual assets, and put forward a series of improved methods, including encryption, authentication, private key storage and fair trade agreement.

However, due to the networking, virtualization, openness, and vulnerability to attacks of CDVA, it is increasingly difficult to protect. Extance [18] analyzed the security of virtual assets and pointed out that, the current methods of property identification and protection based on game theory, advanced encryption and secret sharing are difficult to guarantee the security of virtual assets, and a more comprehensive and in-depth study in the security threat to the asset carriers and trading networks is urgently needed. Artificial Immune Systems (AIS) is another hotspot in the field of computing intelligence after neural networks, fuzzy systems and evolutionary computation. There are striking resemblances between digital virtual asset security issues and those encountered by human immune system, both of which maintain system stability in a constantly changing environment, and AIS supports adaptability, self-organizing, robustness, self-learning and immune memory. Therefore, it is a very important and meaningful research direction to introduce the related theories of AIS into the research of protection for CDVA.

In this work, we present an immune-based security threat detection system for CDVA. Our contributions in this paper can be summarized as follows:

- we analyze the relationship between digital virtual asset immune system and human immune system.
- we propose an immune-based detection system for protecting digital virtual assets, and give the basic definitions of *Ag, Self, Nonself* and *Detector* respectively.
- we define the architecture of immune-based detection method for CDVA, including dynamic evolution of immature detector, mature detector and memory detector respectively, and analyze the way to detect threat based on this method.

2 Relationship Between Digital Virtual Asset Immune System and Human Immune System

In this paper, artificial immune methods are applied in the detection of security threats to the digital virtual assets. The digital virtual asset data, operation behaviors and IP packets correspond to antigens, immune cells correspond to detectors in threat detection system, and the antibodies correspond to the relevant matchers. Therewithal, the digital virtual asset security threat discovery turns into to a process of classifying a set of input antigens into self and nonself through the immune detectors. Table 1 shows the relationship between the digital virtual asset immune system and human immune system.

Table 1. Relationship between digital virtual asset immune system and human immune system

Human immune system elements	Digital virtual assets immune system elements
Human immune system	Digital virtual asset immune system
Antigen	IP packet, data, and program
Immune cell	Detector
Antibody	Matcher
Antibody capture antigen	Find security threat
Body tissue	Digital virtual asset
Self	Legal behavior and data
Non-self	Illegal behavior and data

In the computer software system, all the information is finally reduced to a binary string. The detection of virtual asset security threat is actually a process of classifying binary strings according to certain rules and prior knowledge. Given the problem domain $\Omega = \bigcup_{i=1}^{\infty} \{0,1\}^i$, the set of IP packages and programs (or files) $Ag \subset \Omega$ as the antigen set, the normal network behavior and normal program set $Self \subset Ag$ as the self-set, and the illegal network activity and threat program set $Nonself \subset Ag$ as the non-self-set, where $Self \cup Nonself = Ag$, $Self \cap Nonself = \varphi$. The goal of threat detection system is to differentiate the patterns: Given an input pattern $x(x \in Ag)$, the system detects and determines whether the pattern is autologous $(Self)$ or non-autonomous $(Nonself)$. The $Self$ is normal network activity, and the $Nonself$ is the attack and security threat from network. For any element $x \in Ag$, given the Operator $\in_{APCs}$ and $\notin_{APCs}$ as $\begin{cases} x \in_{APCs} Self \; iff \quad x.a \in APCs(Self) \\ x \notin_{APCs} Self \; iff \quad x.a \notin APCs(Self) \end{cases}$, and detector set $B = \{<d, age, count, p> | d \in D, age, count \in N, p \in R\}$, where d is the antibody, age is the age of antibody, $count$ is the number of matches, p is the density of antibody, N is a natural number set, and R is a real number set. And $B = M \cup T$, $M \cap T = \varphi$ where M is the memory detector set and $M = \{x | x \in B, \forall y \in_{APCs} Self(< x, y > \notin Match \wedge x.count \geq \beta)\}$, β is the activation threshold. For the mature detector set $T = \{x | x \in B, \forall y \in_{APCs} Self(<x, y> \notin Match \wedge x.count < \beta)\}$, where $Match$ is the match function between B and Ag, and $Match = \{<x, y> | x \in B, y \in Ag, f_{match}(x.d, y.a) = 1\}$, and the value of $f_{match}(x, y)$ depends on the affinity of $x.d$ and $y.a$. If affinity is greater than a given threshold, the value equals to 1, otherwise it equals to 0. In this study, the affinity is defined as r-contiguous bites matching. Given the immature detector set $I = \{<d, age> | d \in D, age \in N\}$, which is mainly used to generate new mature detectors.

3   An Immunity-Based Security Threat Detection System for CDVA

The architecture of IBSTDS consists of two stages: data preprocessing and security threat discovery, as Fig. 1 shows.

- Stage 1 (data preprocessing): retrieving the data and application behaviors of the fundamental infrastructure connected to the Internet, the feature data is extracted for the self-set training and test sample at the stage of security threats discovery.
- Stage 2 (security threat discovery) includes six modules, namely feature space partitioning module, detector generation module, detector training module, clone and vaccine inoculation module, known threat detection module, and unknown threat detection module. Feature space partitioning module: analyze the representation of digital virtual assets, model the virtual assets and corresponding security threat features from data level and behavior level, make formal description on the heterogeneous multimodal data of digital virtual assets, and partition the feature space. The partitioned feature data is sent to the self for detector training. Detector generation module: generate the immature detectors based on the typical security threat genes, antibody gene library and random methods, and then sent to the marrow model for

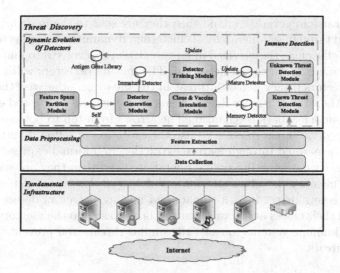

Fig. 1. The architecture of IBSTDS. The data from Internet is collected, the data feature is extracted and sent to the threat discovery unit for detector learning (dynamic evolution of detectors) and threat detection (immune detection stage).

training. Detector training module: execute immune tolerance training on the immature detectors through the self-dynamic evolution model, and narrow the training set by means of self-hierarchical clustering and others methods to improve the efficiency of detector tolerance. The immune detection module, including known threat detection module, and unknown threat detection module, performs immunoassay on the antigen extracted from the data preprocessing stage and updates the antibody gene library when the unknown threat is found (unknown threat detection module). Clone and vaccine inoculation module: the immature detectors, mature detectors and memory detectors dynamic evolve, which forms an adaptive, stable, feedback-based immune process; learn and evolve through immune mechanisms such as clonal selection algorithms; through distributed collaborative vaccines dissemination and updating, implement centralized training on the newly emerging threats of the distributed systems dynamically, update the self and antibody to enable systems to withstand similar threats to digital virtual assets. The detail of threat detection method will be described in the following section.

4   Immunity-Based Security Threat Detection Method for CDVA

Figure 2 describes the principle of immunity-based security threat detection method for CDVA. The arrows from the bottom to the top show the process of generation and evolutionary learning of the detectors. The immature detectors are generated according to the typical security threat genes, antibody gene library and random generation, and then they are sent to the marrow model for training, and through self-hierarchical clustering, dynamic autologous to improve the training efficiency; the survived immature detectors evolve into mature detectors and then engage in threat detection. The mature detectors will evolve into memory detectors if they detect a threat in the life cycle, otherwise they will be eliminated; the wrong memory detectors matching self will be cleared eventually through immune feedback mechanism. The arrows from top to bottom show the process of security threat discovery (also the evolution of self and antigen). The antigens are generated through feature extraction and formal expression of digital virtual asset data and behavioral operations, and then they are sequentially sent to the memory detectors and mature detectors for threat detection. The memory detectors detect known threats and mature detectors detect unknown threats, and their clones act as vaccines and broadcast into the memory detector set of other immune systems to resist the similar threats and prevent the spread of similar threats.

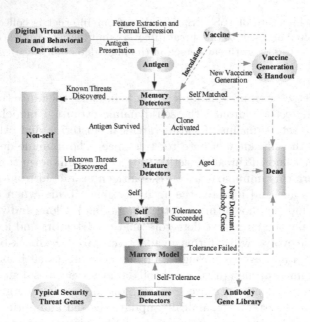

Fig. 2. The architecture of immune-based detection method for CDVA. The solid arrows indicate *Self* evolution, the long dashed arrows indicate *Detector* evolution while the short dashed arrows indicate threat-detection and vaccine-generation.

The Procedure of Immune detection is shown as Table 2, the main basis of which is to simulate the clonal selection mechanism of immune system. The clonal selection mechanism brings the learning ability to the evolution model and enables it to learn to detect unknown attacks or threats. The activation and cloning mechanism of memory detector simulates the secondary response of BIS, and the secondary response has no learning process and has the characteristics of quickly capturing the known security threats. The evolution of mature detectors simulates the BIS's initial response. After the detector gets mature, it must be integrated with the antigen within its lifetime and accumulate sufficient affinity (match enough amount of antigens), and then evolves into activated clone state, and evolve into a memory detector (to quickly capture the similar threat when it comes next time), otherwise it will die out and be replaced by newborn mature detectors. Immature detectors must pass through the tolerance and then enter the immune loop to participate in the security threat detection. The tolerance process simulates the growth of immature immune cells in the marrow (marrow model of the immune system). The detectors matching the self will be eliminated during the stipulated tolerance period to prevent the detector from attacking themselves.

Table 2. The Procedure of immune detection (POID)

POID(sAg,δ,β)
Input: sAg: the antigen to detect, δ:update cycle of the antigens,
$\quad\quad\beta$:the threshold of activating mature detectors
Output: memory detectors M, mature detectors T, $Self$
1. Detect the sAg using memory detectors M
2. Begin
3.   If the sAg matches, then delete the element, reset $memory.age$ to zero, goto step 14.
4.   If $memory.age$ equal to zero, then execute Memory aberrance.
5. End
6. Detect the sAg using mature detectors T.
7. Begin
8.   If the sAg matches, then delete the element; else goto step 12.
9.   If $custom.count >= \beta$, then add the mature detector into the memory detector;
$\quad\quad\quad$ else custom.count++.
10.   Goto step 14.
11. End
12. Insert the sAg into $Self$.
13. If $ab.age >= \delta$, then delete ab from $Noself$.
14. Output M, T and $Self$

5 Experiment and Analysis

5.1 Simulation and Experiment

To test the performance of the model, some simulation and experiment is run in real environment. The application scheme of IBSTDS is shown as Fig. 3. The self-set is defined as 200 important system files, and the detection objects include two parts: 50 attack samples files selected, including SQL injection, overflow attack, DOS, and worm; and 50 infected samples files, where 45 samples are used for learning and the other are used for test. Forest et al. [20] had proved that, for

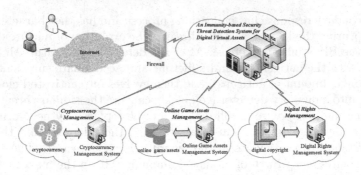

Fig. 3. The application scheme of IBSTDS. The system is deployed at the entrance and exit of the network, accesses the Internet through a firewall and filters the data from the internet (clarifying normal network flows and security threats).

r-contiguous bits matching rule, $P_m \approx 0.025625$. And referring to paper [19,20], parameter λ, age, ε, β is respectively set $\lambda = 5$, $age = 15$, $\varepsilon = 8$, $\beta = 0.6$. Since the mature detector evolves into the memory ones once it detects the antigens, the quantity variance of the memory detectors directly determines the detection of detectors to the antigens, including both the memory detectors and the mature detectors. Therefore, we just test relationship between the parameter M and the model performance.

As shown in Figs. 4 and 5, the size of M is positive correlative to the recognition ability of the model. Specially, when M equal to 0, the false-negative rate of the model is close to 100%. In other word, if there are not any detectors, the model has none recognition ability. When the size of M increases, the recognition ability increases. When the number of M is greater than 92, the model can recognize almost all threats, including the known threat and unknown threat. This indicates that the proposed model has a strong ability of self-learning.

5.2 Related Work Comparison

At present, IDS (intrusion detection system) is still the mainstream defense mechanism for digital virtual assets security threats protection internationally. The goal of digital virtual asset protection consists with intrusion detection's, except that the object of detection is not limited to the intrusion itself but also includes the threats to the digital virtual assets. Therefore, this paper takes six indicators of IDS Kim et al. [21] proposed into account, including distributed, multi-layer, self-organized, light-weight, diverse and disposable. This system is compared with some typical digital virtual asset protection systems (DVAPS), and the comparison results are shown in Table 3.

In view of the six features above, *Denault et al.* [3] (a massively multiplayer online games fraud control protocol) supports such features as distributed, multi-level, lightweight and does not have the characteristics of self-organization and diversification. And it's partially disposable (disposable in P2P model and not

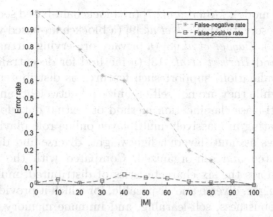

Fig. 4. The error rate of the system. The false-negative rate is the number of false-negative $Nonself$ element to total $Nonself$ element, the false-positive rate is the number of false positive $Self$ element to total $Self$ element. The false-negative rate and False-positive rate indicate the error rate of the system.

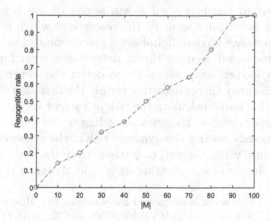

Fig. 5. The recognition ability of the system. The recognition rate is the number of true positive $Nonself$ element to total $Nonself$ element, and indicates the recognition ability of the system.

Table 3. IDS features for DVAPS

DVAPS	Distributed	Multi-layer	Self-organized	Lightweight	Diverse	Disposable
IBSTDS	Yes	Yes	Yes	Yes	Yes	Yes
Denault et al. [3]	Yes	Yes	No	Yes	No	Partial
Maguluri [6]	No	Yes	No	Yes	Yes	Yes
Miller et al. [7]	Yes	Yes	No	No	No	Yes
Peck et al. [9]	Yes	Yes	No	No	No	Yes
Dagher et al. [8]	Yes	Yes	No	No	No	Yes
Herbert et al. [13]	Yes	Yes	No	No	No	Yes

disposable in C/S mode); *Miller et al.* [7] (an blockchain-based secure transaction model for data preservation), *Peck et al.* [9] (a blockchain-based virtual currency protection scheme), *Dagher et al.* [8] (a privacy-preserving virtual currency protection scheme) and *Herbert et al.* [13] (a method for decentralize peer-to-peer software license validation) support such features as distributed, multi-layered and disposable, while they are not self-organized, lightweight, and diverse; *Maguluri* [6] (an multi-class classification method of textual data for detection and mitigation of cheating in massively multiplayer online role playing games) supports such features as multi-layered, lightweight, diverse and disposable, while it is not distributed and self-organized. Compared with the above DVAPS, the IBSTDS supports the six characteristics of distributed, multi-layered, self-organized, lightweight, diverse and disposable, for which it provides adaptability, self-organizing, robustness, self-learning, and immune memory and is a better solution to protect the digital virtual assets.

6 Conclusion

The security threat to digital virtual assets is one of the key issues to solve urgently in present cyberspace security, the research of which is profoundly significant to the cyberspace virtual digital asset protection technology. This paper presents an immune-based security threat detection system for digital virtual assets, which has good self-adaptive ability to detect the security threat to digital virtual assets. Security threat detection is only the first step of security threat management. On this basis, calculate the risk of current threat according to its variation, take proper defense strategies according to the current risk situation, and thence continuously control the dynamic risk of the system and improve its viability. In the future work, we need to further study the real-time quantitative calculation of the change of security threats and its dynamic risk control.

Acknowledgment. This work is supported by National Key Research and Development Program of China (Grant No. 2016YFB0800604 and No. 2016YFB0800605), Natural Science Foundation of China (Grant No. U1736212 and No. 61572334), and Sichuan Province Key Research and Development Project of China (Grant No. 2018GZ0183).

References

1. Rouse, M.: Definition of virtual asset (2018). http://searchfinancialsecurity. techtarget.com/definition/virtual-asset
2. Goodman, J., Verbrugge, C.: A peer auditing scheme for cheat elimination in MMOGs. In: Proceedings of the 7th ACM SIGCOMM Workshop on Network and System Support for Games, pp. 9–14 (2008)
3. Denault, A., Kienzle, J.: Journey: a massively multiplayer online game middleware. IEEE Softw. **28**(5), 38–44 (2011)
4. Yahyavi, A., Kemme, B.: Peer-to-peer architectures for massively multiplayer online games: a survey. ACM Comput. Surv. (CSUR) **46**(1), 1–51 (2013)

5. Yahyavi, A., Huguenin, K., Gascon-samson, J., Kienzle, J., Kemme, B.: Watchmen: scalable cheat-resistant support for distributed multi-player online games. In: IEEE International Conference on Distributed Computing Systems, pp. 134–144 (2013)
6. Maguluri, N.S.N.: Multi-class classification of textual data: detection and mitigation of cheating in massively multiplayer online role playing games (2017)
7. Miller, A., Juels, A., Shi, E., Parno, B., Katz, J.: Permacoin: repurposing bitcoin work for data preservation. In: 2014 IEEE Symposium on Security and Privacy (SP), pp. 475–490 (2014)
8. Dagher, G.G., Bünz, B., Bonneau, J., Clark, J., Boneh, D.: Provisions: privacy-preserving proofs of solvency for bitcoin exchanges. In: Proceedings of the 22nd ACM SIGSAC Conference on Computer and Communications Security, pp. 720–731 (2015)
9. Peck, M.: A blockchain currency that beat s bitcoin on privacy [news]. IEEE Spectr. 53(12), 11–13 (2016)
10. Lazarovich, A.: Invisible Ink: blockchain for data privacy. Ph.d. thesis, Massachusetts Institute of Technology (2015)
11. Zyskind, G., Nathan, O., et al.: Decentralizing privacy: Using blockchain to protect personal data. In: 2015 IEEE Security and Privacy Workshops (SPW), pp. 180–184 (2015)
12. Kishigami, J., Fujimura, S., Watanabe, H., Nakadaira, A., Akutsu, A.: The blockchain-based digital content distribution system. In: 2015 IEEE Fifth International Conference on Big Data and Cloud Computing (BDCloud), pp. 187–190 (2015)
13. Herbert, J., Litchfield, A.: A novel method for decentralised peer-to-peer software license validation using cryptocurrency blockchain technology. In: Proceedings of the 38th Australasian Computer Science Conference (ACSC 2015), vol. 27, p. 30 (2015)
14. Denemark, T.D., Boroumand, M., Fridrich, J.: Steganalysis features for content-adaptive JPEG steganography. IEEE Trans. Inf. Forensics Secur. 11(8), 1736–1746 (2016)
15. Akinwande, V.: Security assessment of blockchain-as-a-service (BaaS) platforms (2017)
16. Matters, M.: Bitcoins, block chains, and mining pools (2014)
17. Massacci, F., Ngo, C.-N., Williams, J.M.: Decentralized transaction clearing beyond blockchains (2016)
18. Extance, A.: The future of cryptocurrencies: bitcoin and beyond. Nat. News 526(7571), 21 (2015)
19. Li, T.: Dynamic detection for computer virus based on immune system. Sci. China Ser. F: Inf. Sci. 51(10), 1475–1486 (2008)
20. Glickman, M., Balthrop, J., Forrest, S.: A machine learning evaluation of an artificial immune system. Evolut. Comput. 13(2), 179–212 (2005)
21. Kim, J., Bentley, P.J., Aickelin, U., Greensmith, J., Tedesco, G., Twycross, J.: Immune system approaches to intrusion detection-a review. Nat. Comput. 6(4), 413–466 (2007)

Botnet Detection with Hybrid Analysis on Flow Based and Graph Based Features of Network Traffic

Yaoyao Shang[1,2], Shuangmao Yang[2], and Wei Wang[1,2(✉)]

[1] Beijing Key Laboratory of Security and Privacy in Intelligent Transportation,
Beijing Jiaotong University, 3 Shangyuancun, Beijing 100044, China
{16120335,wangwei1}@bjtu.edu.cn
[2] Science and Technology on Electronic Information Control Laboratory,
Chengdu 610036, China
ysm101@qq.com

Abstract. Botnets have become one of the most serious threats to cyber infrastructure. Many existing botnet detection approaches become invalid due to botnet structure sophistication or encryption of payload of the traffic. In this work, we propose an effective anomaly-based botnet detection method by hybrid analysis of flow based and graph-based features of network traffic. Frist, from network traffic we extract 15 statistical aggregated flow based features as well as 7 types of graph based features, such as in degree, out degree, in degree weight, out degree weight, node betweenness centrality, local clustering coefficient and PageRank. Second, we employ K-means, k-NN and One-class SVM to detect bots based on the hybrid analysis of these two types of features. Finally, we collect a large size of network traffic in real computing environment by implementing 5 different botnets including newly propagated Mirai and others like Athena and Black energy. The extensive experimental results show that our method based on the hybrid analysis is better than the method of individual analysis in terms of detection accuracy. It achieves the best performance with 96.62% of F-score. The experimental results also demonstrate the effectiveness of our method on the detection of novel botnets like Mirai, Athena and Black energy.

Keywords: Botnet detection · Network traffic · Network security

The work reported in this paper was supported in part by National Key R & D Program of China, under grant 2017YFB0802805, in part by Funds of Science and Technology on Electronic Information Control Laboratory, under Grant K16GY00040, in part by the Scientific Research Foundation through the Returned Overseas Chinese Scholars, Ministry of Education of China, under Grant K14C300020, in part by the Fundamental Research funds for the central Universities of China, under grant K17JB00060 and K17JB00020, and in part by Natural Science Foundation of China, under Grant U1736114 and 61672092.

X. Sun et al. (Eds.): ICCCS 2018, LNCS 11064, pp. 612–621, 2018.
https://doi.org/10.1007/978-3-030-00009-7_55

1   Introduction

A botnet is formed by a large number of hosts which are infected with zombie programs. Bots can be remotely controlled by attackers for Distributed Denial of Service (DDoS) attacks, spreading spam, conducting click fraud scams and stealing personal information. When botmaster commands a botnet, it requires a Command and Control (C&C) channel to accomplish such as scanning, binary download and other suspicious activities. The Internet Relay Chat (IRC) protocol was regarded as one of the most popular botnet communication protocols using the centralized topology. Later, a Hyper Text Transfer Protocol (HTTP) based botnet has emerged. HTTP-based botnet is more difficult to be detected as the http packets generated by the bots that can be flood in large amounts of web traffic records. Obviously there exist vulnerabilities in IRC and HTTP based botnet. Once C&C server is discovered and then closed, the entire botnet will be destroyed. In order to evade the identification, botmasters began to develop P2P (Peer to Peer) based botnet with strong concealment and robustness.

There exist related work on botnet detection. The signature-based approaches [7,22] are unable to detect unknown botnets and their variants, or even fail in case of encryption. The anomaly-based detection approaches [8,13,18,33] focus on the assumption that the communication pattern of botnets is different from those of benign hosts in the networks. The limitations of anomaly-based detection approaches are that bots may mimic the communication patterns of normal hosts to evade the detection. The detection approaches based on honeypot technology can only detect existing bots, and has poor real-time performance. Other specific protocol and structure based detection approaches [3,13,16,17,22] are unable to detect various types of other botnets. The community detection algorithms can accurately identify the botnets [10,15,20] when full communication graphs are available.

In order to effectively characterize bots and to detect unknown bots, in this work, we propose an anomaly-based botnet detection method by hybrid analysis of flow based and graph based features of network traffic. Our method is independent of botnet C&C protocols and structures and thus can be adopted to detect general botnets.

We make the following contributions:

(1) We collect a very large size of network traffic by simulating 5 newly propagated botnets, including Mirai, Black energy, Zeus, Athena and Ares in a real computing environment.
(2) We extract 15 statistical aggregated flow-based features as well as 7 types of graph-based features from network traffic. We employ K-means, k-NN and One-class SVM to detect bots and compare the detection performance with both types of features.
(3) We propose an effective anomaly-based botnet detection method by the hybrid analysis of flow based features and graph based features from network traffic. The extensive experimental results show that our method based on the hybrid analysis is better than the method of individual analysis. It achieves the best performance with 96.62% of F-score.

The rest of this paper is organized as follows. We review related work in Sect. 2. Section 3 introduces our framework for botnet detection. Section 4 describes the data sets and experiments. In Sect. 5, we introduce the limitations of the method. Conclusion follows in Sect. 6.

2   Related Work

Many botnet detection approaches have been proposed in recent years. Livadas et al. [14] proposed supervised machine learning based classification techniques on statistical flow characteristics to identify botnets. Samani et al. [18] proposed group exclusion and feature inclusion to select effective features. They employed C4.5 (decision tree) with reduced error pruning algorithm (REP) to classify the traffic flows. Gu et al. [8] designed a system called BotMiner that is independent of botnet C&C protocols and structures. By clustering similar communication flows and similar activities, they correlated hosts which exhibit both similar network characteristics and malicious activities to identify the presence of botnets. In our previous work, we also use machine learning methods for the detection of malicious Android Applications [27,29,31] or intrusions in computer networks [23,25,26,28] or in computer systems [24,30].

There also exist related work that employs graphs to identify the presence of botnets. Chowdhury et al. [4] proposed a method based on topological features of nodes within a graph. They enhanced the efficiency by removing inactive nodes. Lagraa et al. [12] developed a graph based models of NetFlow records which focused on modeling dependencies among flows, namely BotGM. Wang and Paschalidis [21] analyzed the social relationship between nodes by constructing SIG and SCG to distinguish botnet communities. Iliofotou et al. [9] proposed a graph based method that identified P2P flows by calculating the hosts ratio of in degree to out degree in protocol traffic graphs. Francois et al. [5] constructed node communication diagram and employed PageRank algorithm to detect botnet.

Previous work used either flow based method or graph based method to detect botnets. However, the bots always evolve. The individual detection method may be unable to detect complicated botnets. In this work, we propose an effective anomaly-based botnet detection method by hybrid analysis of flow based and graph based features of network traffic. It is more effective than any individual detection method.

3   Method

Figure 1 shows the framework of our botnet detection method. First, we collect a very large size of network traffic by simulating 5 newly propagated botnets. Second, we filter out irrelevant traffic flows. Third, we extract 15 aggregated flow based features as well as 7 types of graph based features. Fourth, we employ three anomaly detection models to evaluate the performance of our methods with both types of features. Finally, we combined the results of the two types of features and make a final decision on which hosts are bots.

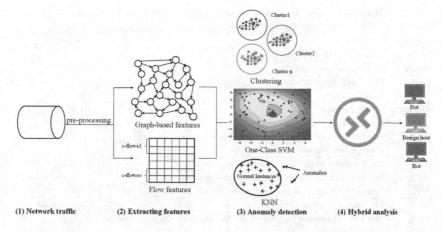

Fig. 1. The framework of our botnet detection method

3.1 Traffic Pre-processing

In order to reduce traffic workload and improve efficiency, we filter out irrelevant traffic flows. First, we filter out flows whose destinations are well known as legitimate servers (e.g., Google, Youtube) that will unlikely be botnet C&C servers. The white list is based on the top 1,000 popular websites from Alexa.com. Second, we filter out non-TCP protocol flows. Third, we filter out flows that are not completely established. We further reduce the traffic workload by aggregating related flows into C-flows [8].

3.2 Constructing Feature Vectors

Traffic-Based Features. The bots within the same botnet communication patterns may exhibit a more uniform behavior than normal hosts. In this work, we summarize more features based on the behavior of various botnets, including duration, the number of packets within an aggregated flow and other statistical characteristics. Table 1 describes these 15 statistical aggregated flow-based features in details, excluding the source and destination IP and port.

Graph-Based Features. We denote the network hosts with an undirected graph $G(V, E)$, where $V = \{v_1, v_2, \ldots, v_N\}$ is a set of unique vertices and $E = \{e_i = (v_i, v_j) | v_i, v_j \in V\}$ is a set of edges. We extract 7 feature vectors from network traffic: in degree, out degree, in degree weight, out degree weight, local clustering coefficient, node betweenness centrality and pageRank.

Bots make connection with C&C server frequently to receive and execute commands, thus high values of in/out degree for a particular node indicates that the node are the pivotal nodes (C&C servers or bots). In/Out degree weight can be described as the total number of data packets received/send by a particular node. The local clustering coefficient is a metric that represents the degree of closeness of a node to its neighbors. We calculate the coefficients through the

Table 1. Descriptions of traffic aggregated flow features.

Feature	Description	Reference
SrcIp	Flow source IP address	
SrcPort	Flow source port address	
DstIp	Flow destination IP address	
DstPort	Flow destination port address	
Duration	C-flow duration	[1,6]
PX	Total number of transmitted packets	[1,17–19,33]
NSP	Number of small packets (length of 63–400 bytes)	[1,13]
AIT	Average inter arrival time of packets	[17]
TBT	Total number of bytes e.g. fixed-length command	[1,6,13,17,19]
APL	Average payload packet length for time interval	[1,8,18,19,33]
PV	Standard deviation of payload packet length for time interval	[1,19,33]
FPS	The size of the first packet in the C-flow	[1,11,18,33]
DPL	The total of number of different packet size over the total number of packets in the C-flow	[18]
MPL	The maximum of packet length in the C-flow	[19]
MP	The number of maximum packets	[19]
MB	The total number of bytes transmitted by the largest packet	[19]
BPS	The average bits-per-second	[8,17,32]
PPS	The number of packets per second	[1,8,17,32]
FPH	The number of flows from this address per hour	[1,8,17]

number of neighbors of a node and the number of connected pairs between all neighbors of nodes.

The betweenness centrality of a node refers to the total number of node passing through all the shortest paths in the network. This feature can be used to characterize P2P botnets. The betweenness centrality [2] of node i is defined as

$$N_B(i) = \sum_{a \neq b \neq v \in V} \frac{\sigma_{ab}(i)}{\sigma_{ab}} \qquad (1)$$

where σ_{ab} is the total number of shortest paths from node a to b and $\sigma_{ab}(i)$ is total number of shortest paths that pass through node i.

The PageRank algorithm [5] is a link analysis algorithm used by the Google web search engine to weight the relative importance of web pages on the Internet. Intuitively, a frequently-connected node is important, and nodes connected to by few important nodes are also considered important. It corresponds to bots and C&C servers in the botnet detection. The definition for PageRank score of node u as

$$PR(u) = \frac{1-d}{N} + d \sum_{(v \in nb(u))} \frac{w(u,v) PR(v)}{d(v)} \qquad (2)$$

where d is the damping factor, N is the total number of nodes in the network. $nb(u)$ represents all the neighbor nodes of node u.

3.3   Detection Models

Based upon the two types of features, we build three anomaly detection models, including K-means, k-Nearest Neighbor(k-NN), and One-class Support Vector

Machine (One-class SVM). In order to find groups of hosts that share similar communication patterns, we apply K-means clustering algorithm. More specifically, we use K-means++ to initialize the centers of clusters in order to avoid the algorithm getting into the local optimum. K-NN is a typical distance-based anomaly detection classifier. We measure the outlier scores by calculating Euclidean distance between two C-flows. One-class SVM is a widely used classifier that attempts to find best hyper-plane decision boundary for normal samples.

3.4 Hybrid Analysis

The hybrid analysis overcomes the weaknesses and limitation of previous based aggregated flow features or graph based features of network traffic. Once we obtain the results of graph based features and flow features from network traffic, we perform hybrid analysis and make a final decision on which hosts are bots. P_f represents the prediction results based on aggregated-flow features. We also denote the results based on graph-based features as P_g. The hybrid detection results P_c are defined as Eq. 3

$$P_c = \alpha P_f + \beta P_g \tag{3}$$

where α and β represent the weights of aggregated flow method and graph based method, respectively. In this work, we assign $\alpha = 0.7$ and $\beta = 0.3$.

4 Evaluation

4.1 Data Sets

We have collected a very large size of network traffic by simulating 5 newly propagated botnets in a real computing environment, including Mirai, Zues, Athena, Black energy and Ares. The botnet data sets used in this work consist of TCP traffic starting at 18:47:09 on August 4, 2016. In these botnet traffic traces, the traffic of Mirai that was found first in 2016 was crawled for 16 days and its size is 5.1 G. Table 2 lists the basic information about these botnet traffic traces.

The background traffic is collected from a telecom company. There are about 200,000 hosts in background traffic. Table 3 lists the statistics for the 10 h of network traffic data we used to validate our method. We convert packets into C-flows as described in Sect. 3.1.

4.2 Experimental Results

The experiments were run on a 12-core Intel(R) Xeon(R) CPU E5-2650 v4 @ 2.20 GHz with 62 GB main memory with OS as Ubuntu 16.04.4 (GNU/Linux 4.4.0-98-generic x86_64). The performance of the proposed method has been evaluated with F-score. The F-score is defined as Eq. 4.

Table 2. Description of network traffic generated by five different types of botnets.

Trace	Bot	Protocol	Duration (hrs)	Size (G)	#Bots	#C&C	Notes
Trace-1	Mirai	Telnet	380	5.1	80	1	DDoS attacks
Trace-2	Zeus	HTTP	123	1.2	80	1	Steal banking information
Trace-3	Ares	HTTP	63	2.04	80	1	File download, screen monitor, keylogger
Trace-4	Athena	HTTP	90	3.2	5	1	DDoS attacks
Trace-5	Black energy	HTTP	140	0.99	60	1	Spaming

Table 3. Amount of data on each botnet trace.

Trace	#Pkts	#Flows	#botnet flows	#C&C flows	#C-flows	#Botnet C-flows	#C& C C-flows
Trace-1	96,558(0.21%)	160	80	80	160	80	80
Trace-2	59,748(0.13%)	6,458	3,229	3,229	3,309	80	3,229
Trace-3	81,217(0.18%)	23,629	16,443	7,186	7,266	80	7,186
Trace-4	18,971(0.04%)	3,654	1,827	1,827	1,832	5	1,827
Trace-5	386,786(0.84%)	73,366	35,183	35,183	35,243	60	35,183

$$F\text{-}score = \frac{2 \cdot Precision \cdot Recall}{Precision + Recall} \tag{4}$$

where Precision is the proportion of True Positive (TP) to all the positive results, and Recall is also called True Positive Rate (TPR) defined as the proportion of TP in all the positive instances.

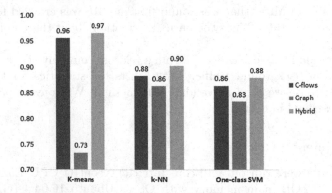

Fig. 2. Detection performance comparison with C-flow features, graph-based features and their hybrid analysis.

Table 4. Detection performance with different types of features.

Features	K-means	k-NN	One-class SVM
C-flows features	0.9569	0.8832	0.8642
Graph features	0.7342	0.8636	0.8332
Hybrid analysis	0.9662	0.9023	0.8794

We compare the detection performance with different types of features based on anomaly-based botnet detection method. Figure 2 presents the F-score values with different types of features based on the three detection models. It is observed that the aggregated flow features are more effective than graph-based features for botnet detection, as expected. However, the hybrid of C-flows features and graph-based features achieves the best performance with 96.62% of F-score. The final detection results are shown in Table 4. The extensive experimental results indicate that our hybrid analysis can identify botnets with no a priori knowledge of botnets.

5   Limitation

Botnets may try to utilize a legitimate website as their C&C communication to evade detection. In addition, botmasters can also randomize the communication patterns to invalidate the detection methods. For example, randomizing the number of packets per flow and the number of bytes per packet to evade detection. Furthermore, bots could use covert channels to hide their actual communications.

6   Conclusion

In this work, we propose an effective anomaly-based botnet detection method by hybrid analysis of flow based features and graph based features of network traffic. We employ three anomaly detection models, namely, K-means, k-NN and One-class SVM, with two types of features. The extensive experimental results show that the F-score of our method based on the hybrid analysis is better than the method based on individual type of features, achieving the best F-score as 96.62%. Our future work is to select more efficient flow features to characterize bots. In addition, analyzing social relationships between nodes to identify botnets is also a future research direction.

References

1. Alejandre, F.V., Cortés, N.C., Anaya, E.A.: Feature selection to detect botnets using machine learning algorithms. In: 2017 International Conference on Electronics, Communications and Computers, CONIELECOMP 2017, Cholula, Mexico, 22–24 February 2017, pp. 1–7 (2017)

2. Brandes, U.: A faster algorithm for betweenness centrality. J. Math. Sociol. **25**(2), 163–177 (2001)
3. Choi, H., Lee, H., Lee, H., Kim, H.: Botnet detection by monitoring group activities in DNS traffic. In: Seventh International Conference on Computer and Information Technology (CIT 2007), University of Aizu, Fukushima, Japan, 16–19 October 2007, pp. 715–720 (2007)
4. Chowdhury, S., et al.: Botnet detection using graph-based feature clustering. J. Big Data **4**, 14 (2017)
5. François, J., Wang, S., State, R., Engel, T.: BotTrack: tracking botnets using Net-Flow and PageRank. In: Domingo-Pascual, J., Manzoni, P., Palazzo, S., Pont, A., Scoglio, C. (eds.) NETWORKING 2011. LNCS, vol. 6640, pp. 1–14. Springer, Heidelberg (2011). https://doi.org/10.1007/978-3-642-20757-0_1
6. Garant, D., Lu, W.: Mining botnet behaviors on the large-scale web application community, pp. 185–190 (2013)
7. Goebel, J., Holz, T.: Rishi: identify bot contaminated hosts by IRC nickname evaluation. In: First Workshop on Hot Topics in Understanding Botnets, HotBots 2007, Cambridge, MA, USA, 10 April 2007 (2007)
8. Gu, G., Perdisci, R., Zhang, J., Lee, W.: BotMiner: clustering analysis of network traffic for protocol- and structure-independent botnet detection. In: Proceedings of the 17th USENIX Security Symposium, San Jose, CA, USA, 28 July–1 August 2008, pp. 139–154 (2008)
9. Iliofotou, M., Kim, H.C., Faloutsos, M., Mitzenmacher, M., Pappu, P., Varghese, G.: Graption: a graph-based P2P traffic classification framework for the internet backbone. Comput. Netw. **55**(8), 1909–1920 (2011)
10. Kheir, N., Wolley, C.: BotSuer: suing stealthy P2P bots in network traffic through netflow analysis. In: Abdalla, M., Nita-Rotaru, C., Dahab, R. (eds.) CANS 2013. LNCS, vol. 8257, pp. 162–178. Springer, Cham (2013). https://doi.org/10.1007/978-3-319-02937-5_9
11. Kirubavathi, G., Anitha, R.: Botnet detection via mining of traffic flow characteristics. Comput. Electr. Eng. **50**, 91–101 (2016)
12. Lagraa, S., François, J., Lahmadi, A., Miner, M., Hammerschmidt, C.A., State, R.: BotGM: unsupervised graph mining to detect botnets in traffic flows. In: 1st Cyber Security in Networking Conference, CSNet 2017, Rio de Janeiro, Brazil, 18–20 October 2017, pp. 1–8 (2017)
13. Liao, W.H., Chang, C.C.: Peer to peer botnet detection using data mining scheme. In: 2010 International Conference on Internet Technology and Applications, pp. 1–4, August 2010
14. Livadas, C., Walsh, R., Lapsley, D., Strayer, W.T.: Using machine learning techniques to identify botnet traffic. In: Proceedings of the 2006 31st IEEE Conference on Local Computer Networks, pp. 967–974, November 2006
15. Nagaraja, S., Mittal, P., Hong, C., Caesar, M., Borisov, N.: BotGrep: finding P2P bots with structured graph analysis. In: Proceedings of the 19th USENIX Security Symposium, Washington, DC, USA, 11–13 August 2010, pp. 95–110 (2010)
16. Rawat, R.S., Pilli, E.S., Joshi, R.C.: Survey of peer-to-peer botnets and detection frameworks. Int. J. Netw. Secur. **20**(3), 547–557 (2018)
17. Saad, S., et al.: Detecting P2P botnets through network behavior analysis and machine learning. In: Ninth Annual Conference on Privacy, Security and Trust, PST 2011, Montreal, Québec, Canada, 19–21 July, 2011, pp. 174–180 (2011)

18. Samani, E.B.B., Jazi, H.H., Stakhanova, N., Ghorbani, A.A.: Towards effective feature selection in machine learning-based botnet detection approaches. In: IEEE Conference on Communications and Network Security, CNS 2014, 29–31 October 2014, San Francisco, CA, USA, pp. 247–255 (2014)
19. Singh, K., Guntuku, S.C., Thakur, A., Hota, C.: Big data analytics framework for peer-to-peer botnet detection using random forests. Inf. Sci. **278**, 488–497 (2014)
20. Tegeler, F., Fu, X., Vigna, G., Kruegel, C.: BotFinder: finding bots in network traffic without deep packet inspection. In: Conference on emerging Networking Experiments and Technologies, CoNEXT 2012, Nice, France, 10–13 December 2012, pp. 349–360 (2012)
21. Wang, J., Paschalidis, I.C.: Botnet detection using social graph analysis. In: 52nd Annual Allerton Conference on Communication, Control, and Computing, Allerton 2014, Allerton Park & Retreat Center, Monticello, IL, 30 September–2 October 2014, pp. 393–400 (2014)
22. Wang, W., Fang, B., Zhang, Z., Li, C.: A novel approach to detect IRC-based botnets. In: 2009 International Conference on Networks Security, Wireless Communications and Trusted Computing, vol. 1, pp. 408–411, April 2009
23. Wang, W., Guan, X., Zhang, X.: Processing of massive audit data streams for real-time anomaly intrusion detection. Comput. Commun. **31**(1), 58–72 (2008)
24. Wang, W., Guan, X., Zhang, X., Yang, L.: Profiling program behavior for anomaly intrusion detection based on the transition and frequency property of computer audit data. Comput. Secur. **25**(7), 539–550 (2006)
25. Wang, W., Guyet, T., Quiniou, R., Cordier, M., Masseglia, F., Zhang, X.: Autonomic intrusion detection: adaptively detecting anomalies over unlabeled audit data streams in computer networks. Knowl.-Based Syst. **70**, 103–117 (2014)
26. Wang, W., He, Y., Liu, J., Gombault, S.: Constructing important features from massive network traffic for lightweight intrusion detection. IET Inf. Secur. **9**(6), 374–379 (2015)
27. Wang, W., Li, Y., Wang, X., Liu, J., Zhang, X.: Detecting android malicious apps and categorizing benign apps with ensemble of classifiers. Futur. Gener. Comput. Syst. **78**, 987–994 (2018)
28. Wang, W., Liu, J., Pitsilis, G., Zhang, X.: Abstracting massive data for lightweight intrusion detection in computer networks. Inf. Sci. **433–434**, 417–430 (2018)
29. Wang, W., Wang, X., Feng, D., Liu, J., Han, Z., Zhang, X.: Exploring permission-induced risk in android applications for malicious application detection. IEEE Trans. Inf. Forensics Secur. **9**(11), 1869–1882 (2014)
30. Wang, W., Zhang, X., Gombault, S.: Constructing attribute weights from computer audit data for effective intrusion detection. J. Syst. Softw. **82**(12), 1974–1981 (2009)
31. Wang, X., Wang, W., He, Y., Liu, J., Han, Z., Zhang, X.: Characterizing android apps behavior for effective detection of malapps at large scale. Futur. Gener. Comput. Syst. **75**, 30–45 (2017)
32. Yu, X., Dong, X., Yu, G., Qin, Y., Yue, D.: Data-adaptive clustering analysis for online botnet detection. In: 2010 Third International Joint Conference on Computational Science and Optimization, vol. 1, pp. 456–460, May 2010
33. Zhao, D., et al.: Botnet detection based on traffic behavior analysis and flow intervals. Comput. Secur. **39**, 2–16 (2013)

Clustering Algorithm for Privacy Preservation on MapReduce

Zheng Zhao[1], Tao Shang[2(✉)], Jianwei Liu[2], and Zhengyu Guan[2]

[1] School of Electronic and Information Engineering, Beihang University,
Beijing 100083, China
[2] School of Cyber Science and Technology, Beihang University,
Beijing 100083, China
shangtao@buaa.edu.cn

Abstract. Until now, a lot of clustering algorithms for differential privacy (DP) have been proposed. Practically, there still exist difficulties in implementing these algorithms in a big data platform. In this paper, we proposed a clustering algorithm for privacy preservation on MapReduce. The algorithm is implemented from two aspects. Firstly, the optimized Canopy algorithm is implemented to get the optimal number of clusters and the initial center points on MapReduce. Secondly, the DP K-means algorithm is implemented to get the final clusters on MapReduce. As a result, the proposed algorithm can generate the optimal clustering number that is same with the standard classified data set and can achieve better accuracy of the clusters with the suitable privacy budget ε.

Keywords: Clustering algorithm · MapReduce · Canopy
Differential privacy

1 Introduction

The rapid development of information technology has facilitated the widespread use of large databases. The vast amount of data in the databases has potential information that many companies and individuals are eagerly seeking. In response to the needs of data analysis, data mining emerged. As an important tool in data mining, clustering algorithms play an important role in daily life and work. The K-means algorithm is a typical clustering algorithm. The standard K-means algorithm was proposed by Hartigan and Wong [4]. The idea of the algorithm is simple and easily implemented by a variety of programming languages. The clustering performance obtained by the algorithm is also good. The algorithm has been recognized by the academic and has also developed a great deal of improved algorithms. Although the K-means algorithm is easily implemented, the selection of initial center points will have an important impact on clustering results. A lot of improvements have been made in the selection of initial center points to improve the clustering accuracy. Zhang et al. [14] proposed the method to select the initial clustering centers by using the mean of

© Springer Nature Switzerland AG 2018
X. Sun et al. (Eds.): ICCCS 2018, LNCS 11064, pp. 622–632, 2018.
https://doi.org/10.1007/978-3-030-00009-7_56

and the standard deviation of the sample data. Reddy et al. [11] constructed a voronoi diagram using Euclidean distance to select the initial cluster center. Hatamlou et al. [5] utilized the gravitational search algorithm (GSA) to optimize the clustering results to avoid low accuracy resulting from the random selection of initial cluster centers.

The clustering algorithms can provide valuable information, but it could cause the risk of privacy disclosure. In 2006, Dwork [2] first proposed differential privacy preservation to fundamentally solve this problem. Differential privacy preservation strictly defines the privacy preservation, defines reliable quantitative method and can resist a variety of new attacks. The method is widely used for data mining. Nissim et al. [10] proposed a PK-means algorithm to make K-means clustering satisfy differential privacy preservation, and also gave a way to calculate the sensitivity of query functions. Li et al. [7] proposed an IDP K-means algorithm. The algorithm improves the usability of clustering methods, also ensures the security by differential privacy. It also focuses on the accuracy of clusters and the privacy preservation. Shang et al. [12] proposed a theoretical DP Canopy K-Means algorithm. This algorithm uses the optimized Canopy algorithm based on the minimum and maximum to reduce the randomness of area radius selection, uses differential privacy to provide the security of clustering results and uses the K-means clustering based on the optimal clustering number generated by the optimized Canopy algorithm to implement the final clusters.

The traditional single-machine processing model cannot meet the needs of computing and storage while the big data with multiple attributes can be clustered. Replacing a serial algorithm with a parallel algorithm to improve the efficiency of a algorithm is currently the best solution. Hadoop platform provides a distributed computing environment with open-source scalability and high reliability and makes full use of cluster resources to store big data and perform extremely complex operations. MapReduce is an important part of the Hadoop platform and can greatly simplify the development of distributed programs [6]. The development involving the bottom layer has been well encapsulated. Users only need to design a parallel computing task that can be easily implemented by the MapReduce framework. Therefore MapReduce is currently the best computing model to improve the computing efficiency of big data sets. In this paper, we will implement the optimized Canopy K-means algorithm with the differential privacy preservation based on MapReduce, while improving the security, accuracy of the clustering and the efficiency of calculation.

2 Related Work

2.1 MapReduce Framework

Hadoop is composed of HDFS and MapReduce. HDFS provides distributed storage services for big data and MapReduce provides distributed computing services for big data based on distributed file systems. According to the principle of divide and conquer, MapReduce divides the input data set into separate chunks and processes data set in parallel.

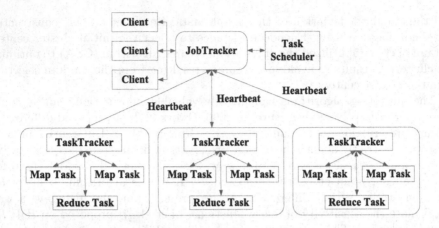

Fig. 1. MapReduce architecture

As shown in Fig. 1, the components of MapReduce include Client, Job-Tracker, TaskTracker and Task. Client submits the user-written programs to JobTracker, and the users can view the job status through the interface provided by the Client. JobTracker is responsible for resource monitoring and job scheduling. JobTracker monitors the status of TaskTracker and jobs. TaskTracker periodically reports resource usage and task progress to JobTracker, receives commands sent by JobTracker and performs corresponding operations. Task is composed of Map Task and Reduce Task. Map Task and Reduce Task are performed by TaskTracker. The input of Map Task is a number of file splits, and Map Task converts file splits to key-value pairs. Reduce Task reads the key-value pairs output by Map Task and sorts the key-value pairs according to the key.

2.2 DP Canopy K-Means Algorithm for Privacy Preservation

The key to the disclosure of privacy is the output center points by the traditional K-means algorithm, but the release of data sets do not require detailed data information. We can publish the approximate value of the final cluster centers which can provide privacy preservation and do not affect the accuracy of cluster results. The DP K-means algorithm adds Laplace noise to the center points and generate clusters with privacy preservation.

The implementation of the DP K-means algorithm focuses on the addition of Laplace noise to the sum of points (sum) and the number of points (num) in a data set D generated by the K-means algorithm. The next iteration of the center points can be calculated by sum' and num' added to Laplace noise. It is necessary to set a reasonable privacy budget ε and the allocation of the privacy budget ε. The rest of the algorithm is consistent with the traditional K-means algorithm.

The DP K-means algorithm provides the privacy preservation of information, but it still has some shortcomings in practical application.

(1) A lot of simulation experiments show that the DP K-means algorithm is more sensitive to the selection of the initial center points that are selected in a random way.

(2) There is no specific criterion for the optimal number of clusters K.

The optimized Canopy algorithm based on the minimum and maximum principle can solve the problem existing in the DP K-means algorithm and reduce the randomness of regional radiuses. In the optimized Canopy algorithm, we can assume that the first m points are known. The $m + 1$ center point of Canopy should be the maximum of the minimum distance between the candidate data points and the previous m centers. The process can be denoted by (1).

$$\begin{cases} DistCollect(m+1) = min\{d(x_{m+1}, x_r), r = 1, 2, ..., m\} \\ Dist_{min}(m+1) = max\{min[d(x_i, x_r)], i \neq 1, 2, ..., m, 1 \leq i \leq L\} \end{cases} \quad (1)$$

L is the amount of data in the current task. $DisCollect(m + 1)$ indicates the minimum distance between the $m + 1$ center point to be decided and the center points of the previous m-defined Canopy. $Dist_{min}$ indicates that the optimal x_{m+1} should be the largest of all shortest distances.

The optimized algorithm does not has the setting of regional radius T_2. It has the following characteristic by practical application. When the number of Canopy is close to or reaches the optimal value, the distance $Dist_{min}$ has a large mutation. $Depth(i)$ is introduced to represent the range of change in $Dist_{min}$ based on the characteristic. $Depth(i)$ can be defined as follows:

$$Depth(i) = |Dist_{min}(i) - Dist_{min}(i - 1)| + \\ |Dist_{min}(i + 1) - Dist_{min}(i)| \quad (2)$$

$Depth(i)$ reaches the maximum value when i is the optimal clustering number. If i is the optimal clustering number, the first i records of the center point sets are the optimal initial center points. Setting $T_1 = Dist_{min}(i)$ can make the final cluster center fall in the range of Canopy.

In fact, the first data point in the input data set that has the farthest initial distance can be replaced by the data point that distance from the origin of coordinates is the nearest or farthest.

3   Implemented Algorithm

The proposed algorithm is primarily implemented on MapReduce and combines the optimized Canopy with the DP K-means algorithm. It can be implemented from two aspects.

(1) The optimized Canopy algorithm on MapReduce is to get the optimal number of clusters and the initial center points.

(2) The DP K-means algorithm on MapReduce is to get the final clusters with differential privacy preservation.

3.1 Optimized Canopy Algorithm on MapReduce

The optimized Canopy algorithm [8] can be implemented in MapReduce, which can be divided into Mapper class and Reducer class. The input data set D needs to be normalized before the process of Mapper Class. The records in the data set are denoted as $x_i (1 \leq i \leq N)$ (N is the data set scale) and the dimension is d. Each dimension of the record in the data set D is normalized to the interval $[0,1]^d$ to get a new data set D_1.

Algorithm 1. Mapper - optimized Canopy

Require: The data records of current Mapper in the data set D_1: *value*
Ensure: A local center point set Q
1: Map function: $Q = null$.
   The Map function converts the input data string into the data object *value* and stores it in the array list *canClusters*.
2: Cleanup function: Set the number of iterations is $\sqrt{L}$. $L = Count(canClusters)$.
   for $i = 0$ to $\sqrt{L}$
   if$(Q = null)$
       Find the minimum distance between the data points and the origin of coordinates by Formula (1) and save the corresponding point q_0 to the set Q
     else
       Find the maximum of the minimum distance between the data points in *canClusters* and Q by Formula (1) and save the corresponding points q_i to the set Q
3: Output the set Q by *context.write* method.

Algorithm 2. Reducer - optimized Canopy

Require: The local center point sets output by each Mapper class $Q = \{Q_1, ..., Q_n\}$
Ensure: The final Canopy center point set U and radius T_1
1: Reduce function: Calculate $P = Count(Q)$. Set the number of iterations is $\sqrt{P}$.
   for $i = 0$ to $\sqrt{P}$
   if$(Q' = null)$
       Find the minimum distance between the data points and the origin of coordinates by Formula (1) and save the corresponding point q_0' to the set Q'.
     else
       Find the maximum of the minimum distance between the data points in Q' and Q by Formula (1) and save the corresponding points q_i' to the set Q.
2: Calculate $K = Count(Q')$.
   for $j = 0$ to $\sqrt{K}$
     Find the maximum of $Depth(j)$ by Formula (2).
3: Output $T_1 = Dist_{min}(j)$. Assign the first j points in Q' to the set U.
4: Output the set U by *context.write* method.

The optimized Canopy algorithm can output the final Canopy center point set U. Then the algorithm call the Mapper function again to calculate the Euclidean metric D between the data points in Mapper class and the center points in the set U. If $D \leq T_1$, the data point will be marked with the corresponding Canopy. Finally, the optimized algorithm outputs the center points set U and the marked data set D_2 by *context.write* method. The value of T_1 can make the final cluster center fall in the range of Canopy that can reduce the impact of noise data points.

3.2 DP K-Means Algorithm on MapReduce

The optimized Canopy algorithm can generate the optimal clustering by the maximum of $Depth(i)$. The DP K-means algorithm can reduce the number of iterations and improve the clustering accuracy. The DP K-means algorithm based on the optimized Canopy is designed as follows. The clustering number K is known.

Algorithm 3. Mapper and Reducer- DP K-means

Require: The marked data set D_2, the initial center set U, the number of iterations T and the threshold δ

Ensure: The final center points μ'

1: The task driver: Read the input set U as the initial center points.
2: MapReduce divides data records into several data chunks according to the input data set D_2.
3: **for** $i = 0$ to T

   Map function: Calculate and compare the distance between the marked input data point and the center points μ. Output the current data and its corresponding the nearest distance center point. Each record can get a $< key, value >$ pair where *key* represents the cluster center identity, and *value* represents the attribute vector of a record. The distance can be calculated by the Euclidean metric $d = \sqrt{\sum_{i=1}^{n} (\mu - x_i)^2}$.

   Reduce function: Read $< key, value >$ pair output by Mapper that belongs to the same center point. Calculate *sum* and *num*. Add the Laplace noise to them to get the center point with differential privacy property μ'. The task driver: Read the center points output by Reducer. Calculate whether the Euclidean metric d' between the current and the last round cluster center points.

   if$(d' < \delta$ or $i == T)$
      break;
4: Map function: Read the final center point set μ'. Calculate and compare the distance between the input data points and the final center point μ'. Mark the input data points to the nearest center point. Output the final cluster center points *clusters* and classified input data set *clusteredInstances* by *context.write* method.

The algorithm generates the final clustering center with differential privacy property by the optimized Canopy and the DP K-means algorithm.

4   Algorithm Analysis

4.1   Evaluation Index F-Measure

F-measure [9] can evaluate the availability of clustering results. F-measure can be calculated using the Precision (P) and Recall (R) commonly used in data mining results. F-measure represents the degree of the similarity of two clusters. The maximum value of F-measure is 1.

F-measure can be calculated as follows:

$$P_i = \frac{cover_i}{|D_i|} \tag{3}$$

$$R_i = \frac{cover_i}{|C_i|} \tag{4}$$

$$F_i = \frac{2P_i R_i}{P_i + R_i} \tag{5}$$

$$F = \sum_{i=1}^{K} \frac{|C_i|}{n} F_i \tag{6}$$

P_i and R_i ($1 \leq i \leq K$) are the precision and recall in the i-th set. K is the clustering number. C_i and D_i are the i-th cluster set of data sets C and D. $cover_i$ is the total number of the same data records in the data sets C_i and D_i. $|C_i|$ and $|D_i|$ are the total number of records in the data sets C_i and D_i. F_i is the F-measure of the i-th cluster set. n is the total number of the records in the data set.

4.2   Privacy Analysis

According to the characteristic of the differential privacy, the privacy budget of the whole algorithm is:

$$\varepsilon = \sum_{t=1}^{T} \varepsilon_t \tag{7}$$

T is the number of iterations in the DP K-means. In terms of budget allocation, the strategy is that each round iteration consumes half of the remaining private budgets. The privacy budget for the t th iteration is $\varepsilon_t = \varepsilon/2^t$.

The result is equivalent to the parallel combination of the Reducer operations because Reducer task performs the operations independently in each round iteration. If the algorithm satisfies the ε-differential privacy, each Reducer subtask in a distributed environment satisfies ε-differential privacy according to the characteristic of the differential privacy.

As can be seen from the definition of global sensitivity, the global sensitivity of num is $\triangle f_{num} = 1$. The global sensitivity of sum is $\triangle f_{sum} = d$ according to the number of attributes is d in the normalized data set D_1. The global sensitivity of the algorithm is $\triangle f = d + 1$. In the process of calculating the center points, the random Laplace noise $Lap(d+1)2^t/\varepsilon$ is added to num and sum at the t -th iteration.

4.3 Complexity Analysis

The traditional DP K-means algorithm randomly selects K data as the initial clustering centers. The whole algorithm runs until the center of gravity of the center set will no longer change. The traditional DP K-means computational complexity is $O(mKt)$. m is the number of documents, K is the number of classes, and t is the number of iterations. In the case of the DP K-means optimized by the Canopy algorithm, the division of Canopies is a division of points. Namely a point may belong to n Canopies. The clusters must be compared dKn^2t/c times, where c is the number of Canopies.

4.4 Experiment Analysis

The experimental setting is the Ubuntu 32-bit 14.04LTS version in the Linux operating system running on the virtual machine. Eclipse is used as IDE in the software environment, Hadoop 2.7.3 is used for the big data platform, and the algorithms is implemented by Java programming language.

The data sets used is the "Magic Gamma Telescope Data Set" and "Blood Transfusion Service Center Data Set" in the UCI Machine Learning Repository data set. Here the data sets are referred to as magic and blood. The details of magic and blood data sets are listed in Table 1.

Table 1. Data sets

Data set	Instances	Attributes	Data type	Classification
Magic	19020	11	Real	g:12332 h:6688
Blood	748	5	Real	0:579 1:178

The magic and blood data set are implemented by Algorithms 1, 2 and 3. Algorithm 1 is the optimized Canopy DP K-means algorithm in this paper. Algorithm 2 is the traditional DP K-means. Algorithm 3 is the IDP K-means proposed by [7]. These algorithms generate classified input data sets, respectively. We can observe the value of F-measure calculated by (6) in the process that ε is selected within the range of $[0, 2]$ and $[1, 0]$. Taking the average value of 10 clustering results is the final value of F-measure. The operating results in the magic and blood data set are shown in Figs. 2 and 3. We can know

(1) Random noise has less effect on the accuracy of the clustering results when the data set is larger. Namely the accuracy of the clustering is better under the same privacy preservation when the data set is larger. So the effect of the privacy preservation is better when the size of the data set is larger.
(2) Compared with traditional algorithms and IDP K-means, the optimized Canopy DP K-means under the same privacy budget improves the accuracy of the clustering results. And the optimal number generated by the optimized Canopy is the same with the standard data sets.

(3) The privacy budget ε is different when the performance of the algorithm is optimal for different data sets. In practical applications, lots of factors should be considered to determine the optimal privacy budget.

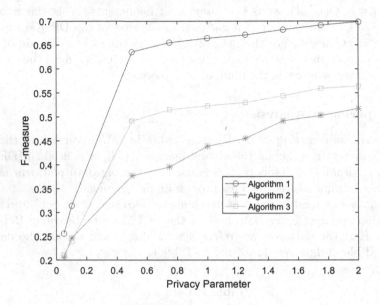

Fig. 2. Magic: F-measure

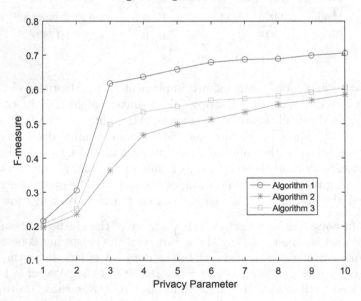

Fig. 3. Blood: F-measure

5 Conclusion

In this paper, we implemented an optimized Canopy differential privacy K-means algorithm. The algorithm takes into account the factors such as the number of clusters and the selection of initial center points. The clustering number generated by the proposed algorithm is the same with the classified data set in the UCI Machine Learning Repository by experiment so that the algorithm can generate the optimal clustering number. The proposed algorithm can improve the accuracy of clustering and provide privacy preservation for data set. In future research, we plan to improve the accuracy of clusters by optimizing the algorithm and apply the algorithm to more data sets for experiments.

Acknowledgment. Project supported by the National Key Research and Development Program of China (No. 2016YFC1000307) and the National Natural Science Foundation of China (No. 61571024) for valuable helps.

References

1. Blum, A., Dwork, C., Mcsherry, F., et al.: Practical privacy: the SuLQ framework. In: Proceedings of the 24th ACM SIGMOD-SIGACT-SIGART Symposium on Principles of Database Systems, pp. 128–138. ACM, New Work (2005)
2. Dwork, C.: Differential privacy. In: Bugliesi, M., Preneel, B., Sassone, V., Wegener, I. (eds.) ICALP 2006. LNCS, vol. 4052, pp. 1–12. Springer, Heidelberg (2006). https://doi.org/10.1007/11787006_1
3. Dwork, C.: A firm foundation for private data analysis. Commun. ACM **54**(1), 86–95 (2011)
4. Hartigan, J.A., Wong, M.A.: A K-means clustering algorithm. J. Roy. Stat. Soc. Ser. C. Appl. Stat. **28**(1), 100–108 (1979)
5. Hatamlou, A., Abdullah, S., Nezamabadi-pour, H.: A combined approach for clustering bases on K-means and gravitational search algorithm. Swarm. Evol. Comput. **6**, 47–52 (2012)
6. Hua, Y.H., Miao, K.X.: Understanding Big Data Processing and Programming, 1st edn. China Machine Press, Beijing (2014)
7. Li, Y., Hao, Z.F., Wen, W., Xie, G.Q.: Research on differential privacy preserving K-means clustering. Comput. Sci. **40**(3), 287–290 (2013)
8. Mccallum, A., Nigam, K., Ungar, L.H.: Efficient clustering of high-dimensional data sets with application to reference matching. In: Proceedings of the 6th ACM SIGKDD International Conference on Knowledge Discovery and Data Mining, pp. 169–178. ACM, New York (2000)
9. Mendes, R., Vilela, J.P.: Privacy-preserving data mining: methods, metrics, and applications. IEEE Access **5**(99), 10562–10582 (2017)
10. Nissim, K., Raskhodnikova, S., Smith, A.: Smooth sensitivity and sampling in private data analysis. In: Proceedings of the 39th Annual ACM Symposium on Theory of Computing, pp. 75–84. ACM, New York (2007)
11. Reddy, D., Jana, P.K.: Initialization for K-means clustering using Voronoi diagram. Procedia Technol. **4**(4), 395–400 (2012)

12. Shang, T., Zhao, Z., Guan, Z., Liu, J.: A DP canopy K-means algorithm for privacy preservation of hadoop platform. In: Wen, S., Wu, W., Castiglione, A. (eds.) CSS 2017. LNCS, vol. 10581, pp. 189–198. Springer, Cham (2017). https://doi.org/10.1007/978-3-319-69471-9_14
13. Xiong, P., Zhu, T.Q., Wang, X.F.: A survey on differential privacy and applications. Chin. J. Comput. **37**(1), 101–122 (2014)
14. Zhang, W.J., Gu, X.F., Chen, L.F.: A K-means initial clustering center selection algorithm based on mean-standard deviation. J. Remote Sens. **10**(5), 715–721 (2006)

Consistency Guarantee Method of Electronic Record Based on Blockchain in Cloud Storage

Yongjun Ren[1,2(✉)], Linhui Kong[1,2], Yepeng Liu[1,2], and Jin Wang[3]

[1] Jiangsu Collaborative Innovation Center of Atmospheric Environment and Equipment Technology (CICAEET), Nanjing University of Information Science and Technology, Nanjing, China
renyj100@126.com
[2] School of Computer and Software, Nanjing University of Information Science and Technology, Nanjing, China
[3] School of Information Engineering, Yangzhou University, Yangzhou, China

Abstract. Cloud storage is now a hot research topic in information technology, which has changed the technical architecture and implementation method of electronic record management. However, due to loss of physical control of the electronic record in cloud storage environment, it is more difficult to guarantee the consistency of record owner.

The blockchain is a distributed decentralized ledger, in which data cannot be forged or tampered. In the paper, the consistency guarantee method of electronic record based on Blockchain is proposed. To ensure the consistency of the electronic record in the cloud storage servers, this paper replaces the skip list to store the electronic record in the blockchain with the traditional Merkle tree. Moreover, we use the hash values generated by tags and array to ensure the integrity of the tags, reduce the computation and communication cost of update and to search for the electronic record.

Keywords: Cloud storage · Electronic record · Consistency

1 Introduction

Cloud storage is an information technology that is extended and developed by cloud computing. Cloud computing is a comprehensive application of traditional technologies such as grid computing distributed computing, parallel computing, utility computing, network technology, and virtual technology. It integrates the decentralized and individual resources to form a powerfully shared resource pool. Users can access this "capable" resource pool anytime and anywhere according to their own needs. Also, users do not need to build and maintain the platform personally but use the dynamic "pay as you go" method to obtain the robust services they provide. Users can also use various forms of terminals (such as computers, smartphones, smart TVs, and other mobile terminals) to access resource services through the Internet. Cloud computing saves users' money while also saving resources and energy for the society [1–3].

With the development of technology, cloud computing is gradually applied to the field of electronic record management. It provides support to electronic record

© Springer Nature Switzerland AG 2018
X. Sun et al. (Eds.): ICCCS 2018, LNCS 11064, pp. 633–642, 2018.
https://doi.org/10.1007/978-3-030-00009-7_57

management in various aspects, such as infrastructure, hardware, software, and platform. However, how to manage electronic records in a cloud environment presents challenges [4, 5]. In a cloud storage system, tens of thousands of servers make it reasonable for any component to have a transient or permanent fault. Network time delay, bandwidth, cost constraint, application to high performance, high availability, and high scalability, easy to manage requirements. All of these problems pose a challenge to the management of electronic records in the cloud storage environment. Moreover, how cloud services ensure the reliability, authenticity, integrity, reliability, effectiveness, and security of electronic records has become a significant consideration in the adoption of cloud services [6, 7]. In particular, the risk of security and confidentiality is a concern for stakeholders in the adoption of cloud services.

2 Related Work

2.1 Cloud Service and Its Features

Cloud service is referred to the resources calculated by the software, hardware, and data from the local migration to the cloud, the user anytime and anywhere through the lower cost of clients to connect to is in the clouds of software, hardware, and data resources. Its primary purpose is to realize the minimization of client computing cost and maximization of cloud benefits and to increase the core competitiveness of IT service providers [8, 9]. Cloud services enable companies to reduce IT operating costs by outsourcing hardware, software maintenance, and support services to service providers. In addition, since applications are centrally supplied, updates can be published immediately without requiring users to manually update or install new software. Users access the cloud service through a browser, desktop application, or mobile application. The service provider integrates a large number of resources for use by multiple users. The user can rent and adjust the resources at any time, releasing the unnecessary resources back to the entire architecture. Therefore, the user does not need to purchase a large number of resources due to short-term peak demand and only needs to increase the rent. When the demand decreases, the rent will be withdrawn. The main features are: (1) Supersize includes the number of servers, storage capacity, and computing power. (2) Virtualization. Cloud computing enables users to access application services at any location and various terminals. (3) Universality. Cloud computing is not targeted at specific applications. The same cloud can support different applications at the same time. (4) Easy sharing of data. Cloud computing can quickly realize the sharing of data and applications between different devices. (5) High scalability. The scale of "cloud" can scale dynamically to meet the needs of application and user scale growth. (6) "cloud" is a large pool of resources, which can be purchased on demand [10, 11].

2.2 Cloud Service Provider and Its Service Modes

Cloud computing has been emerging in China since 2009, including vertical industries, large enterprises, urban and public services, telecommunications and the cloud services provided by the Internet. Market power is arranged in the cloud service provider before including Alibaba, China Telecom, China Unicom, Microsoft, Kingsoft, Amazon, Capital Online, ChinaCache, and IBM. From IaaS to SaaS to PaaS, there are different types of services, which can be divided according to industry applications: government and institutions, to promote social governance and construction; Key industries and enterprises for accelerating informatization and intelligence; Personal and family, mainly for consumption and entertainment applications. From 2010 to 2013, China's cloud services market grew by more than 67%, and nearly 90% of the market remained in the infrastructure. At the SaaS level, which is close to 10%, the proportion of the PaaS layer is the smallest, but this piece of development is also going to be very fast. SaaS is the critical link between future cloud service application and the transformation direction of China's software industry [12, 13]. SaaS is a model of providing software over the Internet. Vendors deploy the application software on their own servers. Customers can order the required application software services through the Internet according to their actual needs. The number of services ordered and the time required Pay the fee to the manufacturer and obtain the service provided by the manufacturer through the Internet. Users no longer have to purchase software, but instead, rent Web-based software from providers to manage their business activities without the need to maintain the software.

2.3   Electronic Record Management in Cloud Service

Because of the convenience of cloud computing and the different types of services, it is increasingly used in electronic record management. According to the type of service provided, the primary cloud service type of electronic record management is as follows:

Infrastructure is the service (IaaS) model, which provides infrastructure for electronic record services and network resources management. The platform is the service (PaaS) mode, which provides the platform resources section of the infrastructure layer mainly for electronic record management. The service provides the necessary software platform resources for the electronic record application system, including operating system platform, software development environment, and various data storage environment. Electronic record application can be used to develop or deploy electronic records directly on the platform based on the service interface provided by the platform service. Software-as-a-service (SaaS) model, which is integrated with electronic record applications to deliver various electronic record applications to users in the form of services. End users can use not only electronic record resources through electronic record portals but also electronic record application services directly through the network or interface [14].

2.4   Challenge of Electronic Record Management in Cloud Storage

Cloud services are innovations in information and communication technology. It has also changed the environment for the formation and management of electronic records, and the content and form have also been affected. On the one hand, business activities in the cloud environment enable the formation and management of native electronic records in the cloud environment, and challenges from the aspects of technology, management, and justice. It requires the combination of the requirements of electronic record management and the characteristics of the cloud environment to form a relatively perfect management plan. On the other hand, cloud services provide new storage and management environments for electronic records. The electronic records formed in the non-cloud environment can be migrated to the cloud environment to use all kinds of hardware, platform, infrastructure, software and other cloud services. It also challenges the migration and even subsequent management. Given that application of electronic record management to cloud service in the United States and Australia, its challenge to electronic record management is presented in all aspects. Cloud applications may lack the ability to implement a record resolution plan. Cloud service providers have a limited understanding of record saving requirements. Different cloud organizations lack formal technical standards to know how data is stored and managed in a cloud environment. It is difficult to remove record or migrate records to another environment base on document management. Business operations of cloud service providers may disappear or terminate [15].

In China, cloud services are not only gradually applied in business activities but also used in the construction of digital archives. As in the United States and Australia, China also attaches importance to the impact of cloud services on the authenticity, readiness, credibility, integrity, availability, and security of electronic records. In particular, the laws and policies concerning cloud services are not perfect. Moreover, electronic record management for cloud service is just under the condition of limited application, how to use cloud storage services to ensure the safety of the electronic record is first put forward by the current challenge.

3 Problem Statement

According to the existing research, the security risks faced by electronic application cloud services are mainly reflected in technology and management. The types and specific performance of the risks are as follows (see Table 1). Moreover, cloud service providers are not taking into account the specific requirements of electronic record management. Alternatively, there is no requirement to specify the management of electronic records. More clearly is the management responsibility that the service provider can avoid. Is currently not in secrecy and safety requirements and has explicit provisions on the distribution of the parties' obligations. The absence of management and technical solutions to electronic record security and confidentiality, to ensure that electronic record credibility, authenticity, integrity, reliability, safety, and usability are all obstacles.

Table 1. Electronic record security and confidentiality risk in cloud environment

The serial number	Types of risk	The specific performance
1	The data that should be deleted has not been entirely deleted	Because cloud computing USES virtualization technology, the user deletes the data, only the logical deletion is realized, and the data in the particular storage space still exists. The formation of data residues may result in electronic record leakage [16]
2	Lose effective control of files	Cloud environment file owners and managers to access without control, the electronic record location knowledge is limited, weaken the control of the electronic record and its management system [17]
3	Network security affects the reliable storage of files	The cloud storage of electronic records is the online storage mode. Viruses, trojans, malicious code, and account theft can cause the electronic records that are hosted into the cloud to be attacked, and the contents are tampered with, resulting in the distortion of electronic records [18]
4	The cloud service underlying program has security holes	The virtualization software relied upon by cloud services can cause illegal operation and illegal access by users. If there are security holes in the underlying application, the criminals exploit these existing vulnerabilities. After the success of the invasion, they can steal the user's files [19]
5	Data isolation failure results in data leakage	If the isolation mechanism is weak or isolated, the data of different users will be mangled, resulting in file leakage [19]
6	Integrity damage caused by a data segmentation technical fault	If the data sharing technique fails, the data cannot be fully restored. This situation can cause partial data loss and destroy the integrity of electronic records [18, 19]
7	Encryption algorithms are cracked or lost	If the encryption algorithm of the cloud service provider is cracked, it will directly lead to the user's data leakage. Also, if lost the key, the file availability will be compromised [20]
8	File loss or distortion caused by an unauthorized intrusion	If the cloud computing service provider's authentication technology and access control technology have defects or security vulnerabilities, then the user's login account, the password may be copied or the user's unauthorized access. Thus the user's file or privacy disclosure [21]

4 Consistency Guarantee Method of Electronic Record Based on Blockchain in Cloud Storage

4.1 Blockchain

A blockchain is a data structure consisting of a similar chain table for data blocks in time order. Moreover, it is a cryptographic method to guarantee the unfalsifiable and unfalsifiable distributed decentralization of the ledger. The blockchain can safely store simple, sequential data that can be verified in the system [22]. The emergence of blockchain solves two significant problems of digital currency: double payment problem and Byzantine general problem [23–27]. The double payment problem is that the same sum of money has been used more than once, which is a fundamental avoidable problem in the traditional financial system based on the physical entity (paper money). Blockchain technology can solve the problem of double payment by consensus mechanism and distributed ledger without the need of a trusted third party, which is a breakthrough in the digital currency. Blockchain using proof of the work and proof of gaining or another agreement mechanism, combined with encryption technology, make an untrusted network into a trusted network. All participants can agree on some aspects without having to trust a single node.

The blockchain has the characteristics of decentralization, network robustness, flexibility, and security. First of all, the blockchain adopts the pure mathematics method to establish the trust relationship between distributed nodes and form a decentralized trusted distributed system. The activity of generating transactions, verifying transactions, recording transaction information and synchronizing is based on distributed network, which is entirely decentralized. Secondly, blockchain adopts unique economic incentive mechanism to attract node to complete the work (such as mining), prompting node provides force or other resources, ensure the smooth operation of the distributed network. The more nodes the entire distributed network holds, the stronger it is robustness. Unless more than half of the nodes have problems at the same time, the distributed network will always be safe to run. Once again, the blockchain provides a user-programmable script system, which significantly increases the flexibility of the application of the blockchain. In Bitcoin, the script is not very mature and it is mostly used for trading purposes. In the Ethereum, a more complete and robust script system intelligence contract enabled more sophisticated and advanced distributed applications to be implemented. Finally, the security of blockchain is guaranteed by encryption technology, and the computing power provided by the whole distributed network is awe-inspiring. It is not only theoretically possible to tamper with the data in the blockchain but also the cost of the power and equipment that spend on it is not worth it.

4.2 Consistency Guarantee Method of Electronic Record Based on Blockchain in Cloud Storage

This paper proposes to use blockchain to save electronic records. The non-modification of blockchain can guarantee the consistency of electronic records. Each block stores several corresponding electronic records. Traditional blockchain data storage uses

Merkle trees to ensure data integrity. When storing large amounts of data, the Merkle tree's query is very inefficient when searching data. For this reason, this paper proposes to solve this problem by using the Skip List structure, as described below.

Blockhead: the contents of the block header include the bulk hash value, time stamp, current PoW calculation difficulty value, the solution of the current block PoW problem (the random number to satisfy the requirement), and the Skip List structure generated by the electronic record. The blockhead design is one of the most critical rings in the overall blockchain design. The block header contains the information of the whole block, which can uniquely identify the location of a block in the chain and can also participate in the validation of transaction legality. At the same time, the volume is small (less than one-thousandth of the whole block), providing a basis for the implementation of the lightweight client.

Block body: the block body contains the complete transaction information of a block, which is organized in the form of Skip List. The build process of Skip List is a recursive calculation of hash values. Skip List is very extensible, regardless of the number of electronic records, and finally, Skip List can be generated. At the same time, the structure of Skip List guarantees the high efficiency of electronic record lookup. The advantage of being efficient in sizeable electronic record storage and queries is obvious. Skip List is used for generating the Hash value of a block (Fig. 1).

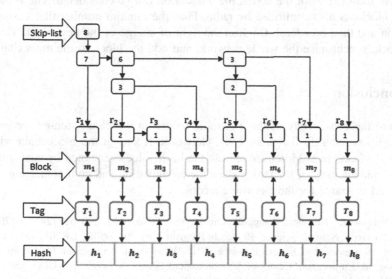

Fig. 1. Storage of electronic records based on Skip List

Chain structure: in addition to creating blocks, all blocks form a blockchain by means of a hash value containing the bulk of the upper area. At the same time, because of includes a timestamp, blockchain with scheduling. The more blocks that are linked behind, the longer time blocks, the more expensive it is to modify the block. When the blockchain increases the new block, there is a small probability that the "bifurcation" phenomenon occurs, that is, two blocks that meet the requirements are dug out at the same time. The solution to the bifurcation is to extend the time, wait for the next block to be generated, and select the longest chain to add to the master. The probability of bifurcation is tiny, and the probability of multiple bifurcations is negligible. "Bifurcation" is only a transient state, and the final blockchain must be the only determined most extended chain (Fig. 2).

Fig. 2. Storage of electronic records in blockchain

Broadcast mechanism: the way the blockchain network publishes transaction information is broadcast. The node that generates the transaction information broadcasts the information to the connected node. After passed the node verification, information will be broadcast again. Information is received swiftly by the nodes in the network. In fact, all nodes are not required to keep the transaction information. As long as receive most (51%) of the nodes, the transaction can be considered. The generation of new blocks is also confirmed by radio. Find the random number that satisfies the condition and then broadcast. Confirm the right of charge of the new block. Generate new block, synchronize the whole network, and add the block to the main chain.

5 Conclusion

To ensure the consistency of the electronic record in the cloud storage servers, this paper replaces the skip list to store the electronic record in the blockchain with the traditional Merkle tree. Moreover, we use the hash values generated by tags and array to ensure the integrity of the tags, reduce the computation and communication cost of update and to search for the electronic record.

Acknowledgment. This work is supported by the NSFC (No. 61772280, 61772454, 61702236), Jiangsu Province Natural Science Research Program (BK20130809, BK2012461), and the Project of six personnel in Jiangsu Province (2013-WLW-012), the research fund from Jiangsu Technology & Engineering Center of Meteorological Sensor Network in NUIST under Grant (No. KDXG1301), and the PAPD fund from NUIST. Prof. Jin Wang is the corresponding author.

References

1. Xie, L., Wang, J., Ma, L.: Trusting records: findings of team Asia InterPARES. Arch. Sci. Study **2017**(4), 8–13 (2017)
2. Ren, Y., Shen, J., Wang, J., Han, J., Lee, S.: Mutual verifiable provable data auditing in public cloud storage. J. Internet Technol. **16**(2), 317–323 (2015)

3. He, D., Kumar, N., Wang, H., Wang, L., Choo, K.: Privacy-preserving certificateless provable data possession scheme for big data storage on the cloud. Appl. Math. Comput. **314** (12), 31–43 (2017)
4. Shen, J., Zhou, T., Chen, X., Li, J., Susilo, W.: Anonymous and traceable group data sharing in cloud computing. IEEE Trans. Inf. Forensics Secur. (2017) https://doi.org/10.1109/tifs. 2017.2774439
5. Fu, Z., Huang, F., Ren, K., Weng, J., Wang, C.: Privacy-preserving smart semantic search based on conceptual graphs over encrypted outsourced data. IEEE Trans. Inf. Forensics Secur. **12**(8), 1874–1884 (2017)
6. Fu, Z., Wu, X., Guan, C., Sun, X., Ren, K.: Toward efficient multi-keyword fuzzy search over encrypted outsourced data with accuracy improvement. IEEE Trans. Inf. Forensics Secur. **11**(12), 2706–2716 (2016)
7. Wang, J., Cao, Y.Q., Li, B., Lee, S.Y., Kim, J.U.: A glowworm swarm optimization based clustering algorithm with mobile sink support for wireless sensor networks. J. Internet Technol. **16**(5), 825–832 (2015)
8. Wang, J., Ju, C., Kim, H.J., Sherratt, R.S., Lee, S.: A mobile assisted coverage hole patching scheme based on particle swarm optimization for WSNs. Cluster Comput. 1–9 (2017). http:// ssl1230a75e822c6f3334851117f8769a30e1c.vpn.nuist.edu.cn/10.1007/s10586-017-1586-9
9. Chao, L.: Research on electronic record migration model in cloud computing environment. Arch. Sci. Bull. **2013**(1), 53–56 (2013)
10. Chang, W., Guo, H.: The characteristics and application prospect of cloud computing. Digit. Technol. Appl. **2011**(4), 168–169 (2011)
11. Wang, J., Cao, J., Li, B., Lee, S., Sherratt, R.S.: Bio-inspired ant colony optimization based clustering algorithm with mobile sinks for applications in consumer home automation networks. IEEE Trans. Consum. Electron. **61**(4), 438–444 (2015)
12. Ge, C., Susilo, W., Wang, J., Huang, Z., Fang, L., Ren, Y.: A key-policy attribute-based proxy re-encryption without random oracles. Comput. J. **59**(7), 970–982 (2016)
13. Ge, C., Susilo, W., Wang, J., Fang, L.: Identity-based conditional proxy re-encryption with fine grain policy. Comput. Stand. Interfaces **52**(2), 1–9 (2017)
14. Niu, L., Han, X.: Study on information resources integration and service model of archives under the cloud computing environment. Arch. Sci. Study **2013**(5), 26–29 (2013)
15. Ren, Y., Shen, J., Liu, D., Wang, J., Kim, J.: Evidential quality preserving of electronic record in cloud storage. J. Internet Technol. **17**(6), 1125–1132 (2016)
16. Xiong, J., Li, F., Wang, Y., Ma, J., Yao, Z.: Research progress on cloud data assured deletion based on cryptography. J. Commun. **37**(8), 167–184 (2016)
17. Wang, J., Cao, J., Sherratt, R.S., Park, J.H.: An improved ant colony optimization-based approach with mobile sink for wireless sensor networks. J. Supercomput. 1–13 (2017). http://ssl1230a75e822c6f3334851117f8769a30e1c.vpn.nuist.edu.cn/10.1007/s11227-017-2115-6
18. Zhao, Y.: Opportunities and risks: electronic documents management under cloud computing environment. Arch. Constr. **2013**(10), 4–6 (2013)
19. Wei, F., Zhang, R., Ma, C.: A provably secure anonymous two-factor authenticated key exchange protocol for cloud computing. Fundam. Inform. **157**(1–2), 201–220 (2018)
20. Kang, S.: Risk assessment of cloud computing services for archival management. Zhejiang Arch. **2012**(5), 15–17 (2012)
21. Cui, H., Zhang, H.: The analysis of archives management system risk in cloud computing. Arch. Sci. Study **2013**(1), 56–60 (2013)
22. Yuan, Y., Wang, F.: Blockchain: the state of the art and future trends. Acta Automatica Sinica **42**(4), 481–494 (2016)

23. Qian, W., Shao, Q., Zhu, Y., Jin, C., Zhou, A.: Research problems and methods in blockchain and trusted data management. J. Softw. **29**(1), 150–159 (2018)
24. Li, X., Niu, J., Kumari, S., Wu, F., Sangaiah, A., Choo, K.: A three-factor anonymous authentication scheme for wireless sensor networks in internet of things environments. J. Netw. Comput. Appl. **103**(1), 194–204 (2018)
25. He, P., Yu, G., Zhang, Y., Bao, Y.: Survey on blockchain technology and its application prospect. Comput. Sci. **44**(4), 1–7 (2017)
26. Jiang, Q., Zeadally, S., Ma, J., He, D.: Lightweight three-factor authentication and key agreement protocol for internet-integrated wireless sensor networks. IEEE Access **5**, 3376–3392 (2017)
27. Zhu, L., et al.: Survey on privacy preserving techniques for blockchain technology. J. Comput. Res. Dev. **54**(10), 2170–2186 (2017)

Controlled Remote Preparation of an Arbitrary Two-Qubit State via the Brown State Under the Noisy Environment

Ting Dong[1], Song-Ya Ma[1,2,3(✉)], and Pei Zhang[1]

[1] School of Mathematics and Statics, Henan University, Kaifeng 475004, China
masongya0829@126.com
[2] Institute of Applied Mathematics, Henan University, Kaifeng 475004, China
[3] Science and Technology on Information Assurance Laboratory,
Beijing 100072, China

Abstract. Taking the controlled remote preparation of an arbitrary two-qubit state via the Brown state as an example, we investigate how the scheme is influenced by five-type noises, i.e., the bit flip, phase flip, bit-phase flip, amplitude-damping and phase-damping noise. The fidelity is adopted to describe how close the output state with the prepared state are. It can be seen that the fidelity is related to the coefficients of the prepared state and the noise parameter under five-type noises. Interestingly, the fidelity is connected with the participators' measurement results under the amplitude-damping noise, but it is not true under other noises.

1 Introduction

Information security is regarded as one of the most essential issues for network technology, especially when cloud computing technology is widely spreading. In order to solve this issue, quantum network is rapidly developing as the next generation network, in which the secure transmission of a quantum state has drawn much attention. The application of quantum entanglement provides some novel ways for the transmission of a quantum state. Quantum teleportation (QT) was first proposed by Bennett et al. [1] to securely transmit a quantum state by utilizing priorly shared entanglement and some classical communication. In QT, the sender owns the transmitted state but is ignorant of it's information. Under the assumption that the state is known to the sender, Lo [2] proposed another secure method called remote state preparation (RSP), which can be achieved with simpler measurement and less classical communication cost (CCC). So far, RSP has raised more and more concerns. Variable theoretical and experimental aspects of RSP have been reported [3–18].

In addition to two-party RSP, multi-party RSP [11–18] is investigated with the purpose of enhancing the security of information transmission. One branch of

© Springer Nature Switzerland AG 2018
X. Sun et al. (Eds.): ICCCS 2018, LNCS 11064, pp. 643–653, 2018.
https://doi.org/10.1007/978-3-030-00009-7_58

multi-party RSP is called joint remote state preparation (JRSP) [11–14]. JRSP requires at least two preparers who individually hold partial information of the original state. Only when those senders cooperate together, can they complete the task. The other branch of multi-party RSP is named as controlled remote state preparation (CRSP) [15–18]. In CRSP, one or several controllers are introduced in addition to the sender and the receiver. The receiver can't recover the original state without the assistance of the controlling party although he has nothing about the original state. At present, many researchers have studied CRSP using various entanglement resources. For instance, Chen et al. [16] used the Brown state to realize the CRSP of arbitrary two- and three- qubit states. But, these schemes have many restrictions on the prepared state. In order to make the application of the schemes more widely, Gao et al. [18] re-investigate the CRSP using the Brown state as the quantum channel. They proposed two schemes which have no restrictions about the prepared state and keep the same success probability 50%.

However, the above CRSP protocols are only considered in ideal environment. In fact, quantum noise is an inevitable factor in the process of information transmission. Hence, it is necessary to take the effect of quantum noises on the RSP into account. For example, Guan et al. [19] studied the JRSP of an arbitrary two-qubit state through the amplitude-damping and the phase-damping noisy environment. Liang et al. [20] came up with a JRSP scheme of a qubit in different noises by solving the master equation of Lindblad form. Ma et al. [21] proposed two deterministic RSP schemes via the Brown state and analyzed them in the amplitude-damping and phase-damping noisy environment. Wang et al. [22] studied the effect of four-type noises on the deterministic JRSP of an arbitrary two-qubit state. In this paper, we take the CRSP scheme of an arbitary two-qubit state in Ref. [18] as an example and investigate how the scheme is influenced by five-type noises, i.e., the bit flip, phase flip, bit-phase flip, amplitude-damping and phase-damping noise. The fidelity is used to show how close the output state with the prepared state are and describe how much information is lost.

The rest parts of the paper are organized as follows. In Sect. 2, we briefly describe the CRSP scheme of an arbitrary two-qubit state proposed by Gao et al. and the density operator representation of the scheme. In Sect. 3, we analyze the influence of five-type noises on the scheme. Some discussions and conclusions are given in the last section.

2   The CRSP Scheme in Ideal Environment

2.1   The CRSP Scheme of an Arbitrary Two-Qubit State

In the beginning, we present the CRSP scheme of an arbitrary two-qubit state via the Brown state in Ref. [18]. The sender Alice wishes to help the receiver Bob remotely prepare an arbitrary two-qubit state

$$|\varphi\rangle = a_0|00\rangle + a_1|01\rangle + a_2|10\rangle + a_3|11\rangle \tag{1}$$

under the supervision of the controller Charlie, where the complex coefficients a_j, $j = 0, \ldots, 3$ satisfy the normalization condition $\sum_{j=0}^{3} |a_j|^2 = 1$. Alice knows the parameters a_j completely, while either Bob or Charlie does not have any knowledge about them at all.

A Brown state

$$|Br\rangle_{12345} = \frac{1}{2}(|001\rangle|\phi_-\rangle + |010\rangle|\Phi_-\rangle + |100\rangle|\phi_+\rangle + |111\rangle|\Phi_+\rangle)_{12345} \quad (2)$$

is shared among the three participants, where

$$|\phi_\pm\rangle = \frac{1}{\sqrt{2}}(|00\rangle \pm |11\rangle), \quad |\Phi_\pm\rangle = \frac{1}{\sqrt{2}}(|01\rangle \pm |10\rangle). \quad (3)$$

In addition, Alice introduces an auxiliary qubit $|0\rangle_A$. The combined system is described as

$$|C_6\rangle = |Br\rangle_{12345}|0\rangle_A = \frac{1}{2}(|0001\rangle|\phi_-\rangle + |0010\rangle|\Phi_-\rangle + |0100\rangle|\phi_+\rangle + |0111\rangle|\Phi_+\rangle)_{A12345}, \quad (4)$$

where Alice holds qubits $(A, 1, 2)$, Charlie and Bob possess qubits 3 and $(4, 5)$, respectively.

The CRSP scheme of an arbitrary two-qubit state has three steps:

Step 1. The sender Alice performs a three-qubit projective measurement on her qubits $(A, 1, 2)$ under the basis $|\xi_0\rangle, \ldots, |\xi_7\rangle$ which is defined as

$$\begin{pmatrix} |\xi_0\rangle \\ |\xi_1\rangle \\ |\xi_2\rangle \\ |\xi_3\rangle \\ |\xi_4\rangle \\ |\xi_5\rangle \\ |\xi_6\rangle \\ |\xi_7\rangle \end{pmatrix} = \begin{pmatrix} F & F^* \\ F^* & -\frac{\mu^*}{\mu}F \end{pmatrix}^* \begin{pmatrix} |000\rangle \\ |001\rangle \\ |010\rangle \\ |011\rangle \\ |100\rangle \\ |101\rangle \\ |110\rangle \\ |111\rangle \end{pmatrix}, \quad (5)$$

where

$$F = \frac{1}{\sqrt{2}} \begin{pmatrix} b_0 & b_1 & b_2 & b_3 \\ -b_1 & b_0 & b_3 & -b_2 \\ -b_2 & -b_3 & b_0 & b_1 \\ -b_3 & b_2 & -b_1 & b_0 \end{pmatrix} \quad (6)$$

and $\mu = \sum_{j=0}^{3} b_j^2$ (the constant $-\frac{\mu^*}{\mu}$ is defined by 1 in the case that $\mu = 0$).

Here

$$b_0 = \frac{a_0 - a_3}{\sqrt{2}}, \quad b_1 = \frac{a_1 - a_2}{\sqrt{2}}, \quad b_2 = \frac{a_0 + a_3}{\sqrt{2}}, \quad b_3 = \frac{a_1 + a_2}{\sqrt{2}}. \quad (7)$$

After the measurement, Alice broadcasts the classical message m through a classical channel if the measurement result is $|\xi_m\rangle$, $m = 0, \ldots, 7$.

Step 2. The controller Charlie measures his qubit 3 under the Hadamard basis

$$|\pm\rangle = \frac{|0\rangle \pm |1\rangle}{\sqrt{2}} \tag{8}$$

and transmits the measurement result to Bob via a classical channel.

Step 3. The receiver Bob performs proper unitary operations to recover the prepared state. The recovery unitary operations relying on Alice's and Charlie's measurement results are listed in Table 1.

It is shown that Bob can recover the original state under the help of Charlie only if Alice's measurement result lies in $\{|\xi_m\rangle, m = 0, 1, 2, 3\}$. Therefore, the total success probability is 50%.

Table 1. The relation among Alice's and Charlie's measurement outcomes (ACMO), the collapsed state (CS) of the qubits (4, 5) after the measurements, and the receiver Bob's recovery unitary operation (BRUO) on the collapsed state. Here X, Y, Z denote the Pauli operations.

ACMO	CS	BRUO
$(|\xi_0\rangle, |+\rangle)$	$a_0|00\rangle + a_1|01\rangle + a_2|10\rangle + a_3|11\rangle$	$U_{0+} = I_4 I_5$
$(|\xi_0\rangle, |-\rangle)$	$a_3|00\rangle - a_2|01\rangle - a_1|10\rangle + a_0|11\rangle$	$U_{0-} = Y_4 Y_5$
$(|\xi_1\rangle, |+\rangle)$	$a_2|00\rangle - a_3|01\rangle - a_0|10\rangle + a_1|11\rangle$	$U_{1+} = Y_4 Z_5$
$(|\xi_1\rangle, |-\rangle)$	$a_1|00\rangle + a_0|01\rangle + a_3|10\rangle + a_2|11\rangle$	$U_{1-} = I_4 X_5$
$(|\xi_2\rangle, |+\rangle)$	$-a_3|00\rangle - a_2|01\rangle + a_1|10\rangle + a_0|11\rangle$	$U_{2+} = Y_4 X_5$
$(|\xi_2\rangle, |-\rangle)$	$a_0|00\rangle - a_1|01\rangle + a_2|10\rangle - a_3|11\rangle$	$U_{2-} = I_4 Z_5$
$(|\xi_3\rangle, |+\rangle)$	$-a_1|00\rangle + a_0|01\rangle - a_3|10\rangle + a_2|11\rangle$	$U_{3+} = I_4 Y_5$
$(|\xi_3\rangle, |-\rangle)$	$a_2|00\rangle + a_3|01\rangle - a_0|10\rangle - a_1|11\rangle$	$U_{3-} = Y_4 I_5$

2.2 Density Operator Representation of the CRSP Scheme

To analyze the effect of noise, we need to rewrite the scheme in the form of density operators. The prepared two-qubit state can be written as $|\varphi\rangle\langle\varphi|$. While the quantum channel is $\rho = |C_6\rangle\langle C_6|$. Alice's and Charlie's measurement operators are $M^A = \{|\xi_m\rangle\langle\xi_m|; m = 0, \ldots, 7\}$ and $M^C = \{|+\rangle\langle+|, |-\rangle\langle-|\}$, respectively. Then, the CRSP scheme can be rewritten as follows.

Step 1. Alice selects M^A as measurement operators for measuring her qubits $(A, 1, 2)$. Thus, the system of qubits $(3, 4, 5)$ becomes

$$\rho_1 = tr_{A12}\left(\frac{M_0^A \rho M_0^{A\dagger}}{tr(M_0^{A\dagger} M_0^A \rho)}\right). \tag{9}$$

Step 2. Charlie measures his qubit 3 by measurement operators M^C, the system of qubits $(4, 5)$ becomes

$$\rho_2 = tr_3 \left(\frac{M_+^C \rho_1 M_+^{C\dagger}}{tr(M_+^{C\dagger} M_+^C \rho_1)} \right). \tag{10}$$

Step 3. Bob performs a unitary operator U_{mn} ($m \in \{0, \ldots, 3\}, n \in \{+, -\}$) described in Table 1 to recover the prepared state. The output state is

$$\rho_{out} = U_{mn} \rho_2 U_{mn}^\dagger. \tag{11}$$

3 The CRSP in the Noisy Environment

In the entanglement-based quantum communication protocols, it is usually assumed that all participants have shared quantum entanglement in advance. But in real world, the generator need to send qubits to each participant via quantum channels. And each qubit will be affected inevitably by quantum noise. In the following, we study the influence of five-type noises (the bit flip, phase flip, bit-phase flip, amplitude-damping and phase-damping noise) on the CRSP scheme described in Sect. 2. Moreover, some analysis is made to show that in which noise channels more information is lost.

3.1 Five-Type Quantum Noises

3.1.1 The Bit Flip, Phase Flip, Bit-Phase Flip Noise

The bit flip noise turns the state of a qubit from $|0\rangle$ to $|1\rangle$ or from $|1\rangle$ to $|0\rangle$ with probability λ. The phase flip noise turns the phase of the qubit $|1\rangle$ to $-|1\rangle$ with probability λ. The bit-phase flip noise is the combination of the bit flip and phase flip noise. And their Kraus operators [23] are

$$E_0^{b-f} = \sqrt{1-\lambda}I, \quad E_1^{b-f} = \sqrt{\lambda}\sigma_x, \tag{12}$$

$$E_0^{p-f} = \sqrt{1-\lambda}I, \quad E_1^{p-f} = \sqrt{\lambda}\sigma_z, \tag{13}$$

$$E_0^{bp-f} = \sqrt{1-\lambda}I, \quad E_1^{bp-f} = \sqrt{\lambda}\sigma_y, \tag{14}$$

where $\lambda(0 \leq \lambda \leq 1)$ is the noise parameter, σ_x, σ_y, σ_z are Pauli operations.

3.1.2 The Phase-Damping Noise

The phase-damping noise describes the loss of quantum information without loss of energy which is also one of the important decoherence noise. The action of phase-damping noise is shown by a set of Kraus operators [23]

$$E_0^p = \sqrt{1-\lambda}I, \quad E_1^p = \sqrt{\lambda} \begin{pmatrix} 1 & 0 \\ 0 & 0 \end{pmatrix}, \quad E_2^p = \sqrt{\lambda} \begin{pmatrix} 0 & 0 \\ 0 & 1 \end{pmatrix}, \tag{15}$$

where $\lambda(0 \leq \lambda \leq 1)$ is the decoherence rate of the phase-damping noise.

3.1.3   The Amplitude-Damping Noise

The amplitude-damping noise is one of the most important decoherence noises that can be used to describe the energy dissipation effects due to loss of energy from a quantum system. The action of amplitude-damping noise is shown by a set of Kraus operators [23]

$$E_0^a = \begin{pmatrix} 1 & 0 \\ 0 & \sqrt{1-\lambda} \end{pmatrix}, \quad E_1^a = \begin{pmatrix} 0 & \sqrt{\lambda} \\ 0 & 0 \end{pmatrix}, \tag{16}$$

where $\lambda(0 \leq \lambda \leq 1)$ is the decoherence rate to indicate the error probability when the quantum state pass through the amplitude-damping noisy environment.

3.2   The Output State and the Fidelity in Noisy Environment

Suppose Alice has a quantum source generator in her laboratory and prepares the quantum channel $|C_6\rangle$, then she sends the qubit 3 to Charlie and the qubits $(4, 5)$ to Bob via the noisy environment. Assume that the noise effect on each channel is the same. Thus, the effect of noise on the shared channel ρ is

$$\varepsilon(\rho) = \sum_{j_1, j_2} E_{j_1}^3 E_{j_2}^4 E_{j_2}^5 \rho E_{j_1}^{3\dagger} E_{j_2}^{4\dagger} E_{j_2}^{5\dagger}, \tag{17}$$

where the subscripts j_1, j_2 represent which Kraus operators will be chosen to carry out, and the superscripts $3, 4, 5$ denote the operator E acts on which qubit.

In order to analyze the influence of noise on the CRSP scheme, we only need to replace ρ by $\varepsilon(\rho)$ into Eq. (9), and will get the output state from Eqs. (10) and (11). And the fidelity of the output state can be described as $F = \langle \varphi | \rho_{out} | \varphi \rangle$. Thus, we can calculate the output state and the corresponding fidelity in five-type noises. Here, we just need to consider the situation that the CRSP scheme is successful, i.e., Alice' measurement result lies in $\{|\xi_m\rangle, m = 0, 1, 2, 3\}$.

3.2.1   In the Bit Flip, Phase Flip, Bit-Phase Flip Noise

In the bit flip noisy environment, Bob will get the same output state

$$\begin{aligned} \rho_{out} = \ & \frac{1}{8P_{b-f}}[(1-\lambda)^2 (a_0|00\rangle + a_1|01\rangle + a_2|10\rangle + a_3|11\rangle) \\ & (a_0^*\langle 00| + a_1^*\langle 01| + a_2^*\langle 10| + a_3^*\langle 11|) \\ & \lambda^2 (a_3|00\rangle + a_2|01\rangle + a_1|10\rangle + a_0|11\rangle) \\ & (a_3^*\langle 00| + a_2^2\langle 01| + a_1^*\langle 10| + a_0^*\langle 11|)], \end{aligned} \tag{18}$$

where $P_{b-f} = \frac{1}{8}(2\lambda^2 - 2\lambda + 1)$ is the probability that Alice gets the measurement result $|\xi_m\rangle, m = 0, 1, 2, 3$.

And the fidelity can be described as

$$
\begin{aligned}
F_{b-f} = \ & \frac{1}{8P_{b-f}}\{|a_0|^2 c_1(a_0, a_1, a_2, a_3) + |a_1|^2 c_1(a_1, a_0, a_3, a_2) \\
& +|a_2|^2 c_1(a_2, a_3, a_0, a_1) + |a_3|^2 c_1(a_3, a_1, a_2, a_0) \\
& +\mathrm{Re}[a_1 a_0^* c_2(a_0, a_1, a_2, a_3) + a_2 a_0^* c_2(a_0, a_2, a_1, a_3) \\
& +a_1 a_3^* c_2(a_3, a_1, a_2, a_0) + a_3 a_2^* c_2(a_1, a_0, a_3, a_2) \\
& +a_3 a_0^* c_3(a_0, a_1, a_2, a_3) + a_2 a_1^* c_3(a_0, a_1, a_2, a_3)]\},
\end{aligned} \tag{19}
$$

where

$$
\begin{aligned}
c_1(a_0, a_1, a_2, a_3) &= (\lambda - 1)^2 |a_0|^2 + \lambda^2 |a_3|^2, \\
c_2(a_0, a_1, a_2, a_3) &= (\lambda - 1)^2 a_0 a_1^* + \lambda^2 a_3 a_2^*, \\
c_3(a_0, a_1, a_2, a_3) &= (\lambda - 1)^2 a_0 a_3^* + \lambda^2 a_3 a_0^*,
\end{aligned} \tag{20}
$$

$\mathrm{Re}(z)$ represents the real part of a complex number z.

Similar calculations can be made to get the fidelities in the other four-type noises. In the phase flip and bit-phase flip noise, the fidelities F_{p-f} and F_{bp-f} keeps unchanged whatever the measurement results are.

$$
\begin{aligned}
F_{p-f} = \ & \frac{1}{8P_{p-f}}\{|a_0|^2 d_1(a_0, a_1, a_2, a_3) + |a_1|^2 d_1(a_1, a_0, a_3, a_2) \\
& +|a_2|^2 d_1(a_2, a_3, a_0, a_1) + |a_3|^2 d_1(a_3, a_1, a_2, a_0) \\
& +\mathrm{Re}[a_1 a_0^* d_2(a_0, a_1, a_2, a_3) + a_2 a_0^* d_2(a_0, a_2, a_1, a_3) \\
& a_1 a_3^* d_2(a_3, a_1, a_2, a_0) + a_3 a_2^* d_2(a_1, a_0, a_3, a_2) \\
& +a_3 a_0^* d_3(a_0, a_1, a_2, a_3) + a_2 a_1^* d_3(a_1, a_0, a_3, a_2)]\},
\end{aligned} \tag{21}
$$

$$
\begin{aligned}
F_{bp-f} = \ & \frac{1}{8P_{bp-f}}\{|a_0|^2 e_1(a_0, a_1, a_2, a_3) + |a_1|^2 e_1(a_1, a_0, a_3, a_2) \\
& +|a_2|^2 e_1(a_2, a_3, a_0, a_1) + |a_3|^2 e_1(a_3, a_1, a_2, a_0) \\
& +\mathrm{Re}[a_1 a_0^* e_2(a_0, a_1, a_2, a_3) + a_2 a_0^* e_2(a_0, a_2, a_1, a_3) \\
& +a_1 a_3^* e_2(a_3, a_1, a_2, a_0) + a_3 a_2^* e_2(a_1, a_0, a_3, a_2) \\
& +a_3 a_0^* e_3(a_0, a_1, a_2, a_3) + a_2 a_1^* e_3(a_1, a_0, a_3, a_2)]\},
\end{aligned} \tag{22}
$$

where $P_{p-f} = P_{bp-f} = \frac{1}{8}(2\lambda^2 - 2\lambda + 1)$ is the probability that Alice gets the measurement result $|\xi_m\rangle$, $m = 0, 1, 2, 3$ and

$$
\begin{aligned}
d_1(a_0, a_1, a_2, a_3) &= (-2\lambda^3 + 4\lambda^2 - 3\lambda + 1)|a_0|^2 + (2\lambda^3 - 2\lambda^2 + \lambda)|a_3|^2, \\
d_2(a_0, a_1, a_2, a_3) &= (2\lambda - 1)[(\lambda - 1)a_0 a_1^* + \lambda a_3 a_2^*], \\
d_3(a_0, a_1, a_2, a_3) &= (-2\lambda^3 + 4\lambda^2 - 3\lambda + 1)a_0 a_3^* + (2\lambda^3 - 2\lambda^2 + \lambda)a_3 a_0^*, \\
e_1(a_0, a_1, a_2, a_3) &= (3\lambda^2 - 3\lambda + 1)|a_0|^2 + (\lambda - \lambda^2)|a_3|^2, \\
e_2(a_0, a_1, a_2, a_3) &= (3\lambda^2 - 3\lambda + 1)a_0 a_1^* - (\lambda - \lambda^2)a_3 a_2^*, \\
e_3(a_0, a_1, a_2, a_3) &= (3\lambda^2 - 3\lambda + 1)a_0 a_3^* + (\lambda - \lambda^2)a_3 a_0^*.
\end{aligned} \tag{23}
$$

3.2.2   In the Phase-Damping Noise

Under the phase-damping noise, we still get the same fidelity

$$
\begin{aligned}
F_p = \ & \frac{1}{16P_p}\{|a_0|^2 g_1(a_0, a_1, a_2, a_3) + |a_1|^2 g_2(a_0, a_1, a_2, a_3) \\
& + |a_2|^2 g_2(a_0, a_2, a_1, a_3) + |a_3|^2 g_1(a_3, a_1, a_2, a_0) \\
& + \mathrm{Re}[a_1 a_0^* g_3(a_0, a_1, a_2, a_3) + a_2 a_0^* g_3(a_0, a_2, a_1, a_3) \\
& + a_1 a_3^* g_3(a_3, a_1, a_2, a_0) + a_3 a_2^* g_3(a_1, a_0, a_3, a_2) \\
& + a_3 a_0^* g_4(a_0, a_1, a_2, a_3) + a_2 a_1^* g_4(a_1, a_0, a_3, a_2)]\},
\end{aligned}
\tag{24}
$$

where $P_p = \frac{1}{8}[\lambda^2 - 2\lambda + 1 + \lambda^2(|a_0|^2 + |a_3|^2)]$ is the probability that Alice gets the measurement result $|\xi_m\rangle, m = 0, 1, 2, 3$ and

$$
\begin{aligned}
g_1(a_0, a_1, a_2, a_3) &= (-2\lambda^3 + 4\lambda^2 - 3\lambda + 2)|a_0|^2 + (2\lambda^3 - \lambda)|a_3|^2, \\
g_2(a_0, a_1, a_2, a_3) &= (-\lambda^3 + 4\lambda^2 - 5\lambda + 2)|a_1|^2 + (\lambda^3 - 2\lambda^2 + \lambda)|a_2|^2, \\
g_3(a_0, a_1, a_2, a_3) &= (-\lambda^3 + 4\lambda^2 - 5\lambda + 2)a_0 a_1^* - (\lambda^3 - 2\lambda^2 + \lambda)a_3 a_2^*, \\
g_4(a_0, a_1, a_2, a_3) &= (-\lambda^3 + 4\lambda^2 - 5\lambda + 2)a_0 a_3^* + (\lambda^3 - 2\lambda^2 + \lambda)a_3 a_0^*.
\end{aligned}
\tag{25}
$$

3.2.3   In the Amplitude-Damping Noise

Under the amplitude-damping noise, one can get eight different fidelities based on Alice's and Charlie's measurement results. Here we just list the fidelity when the measurement result is $|\xi_0\rangle|+\rangle$.

$$
\begin{aligned}
F_a = \ & \frac{1}{16P_a}\{|a_0|^2 f_1(a_0, a_1, a_2, a_3) + |a_1|^2 f_2(a_0, a_1, a_2, a_3) \\
& + |a_2|^2 f_2(a_0, a_2, a_1, a_3) + (1 - \lambda)|a_3|^2 f_2(a_2, a_3, a_0, a_1) \\
& + \mathrm{Re}[a_1 a_0^* f_3(a_0, a_1, a_2, a_3) + a_2 a_0^* f_3(a_0, a_2, a_1, a_3) \\
& + (1 - \lambda)[a_1 a_3^* f_3(a_3, a_1, a_2, a_0) + a_3 a_0^* f_3(a_1, a_0, a_3, a_2)] \\
& + a_3 a_0^* f_4(a_0, a_1, a_2, a_3) + a_2 a_1^* f_4(a_1, a_0, a_3, a_2)]\},
\end{aligned}
\tag{26}
$$

where $P_a = \frac{1}{8}[(\lambda^2 - \lambda + 1)(|a_0|^2 + |a_3|^2) + (1 - \lambda)(|a_1|^2 + |a_2|^2)]$ is the probability that Alice gets the measurement result $|\xi_0\rangle$ and

$$
\begin{aligned}
f_1(a_0, a_1, a_2, a_3) &= (1 + \lambda^2)(|a_0|^2 + |a_3|^2) + \sqrt{1 - \lambda}(1 - \lambda^2)(|a_0|^2 - |a_3|^2), \\
f_2(a_0, a_1, a_2, a_3) &= (1 - \lambda)[|a_1|^2 + |a_2|^2 + \sqrt{1 - \lambda}(|a_1|^2 - |a_2|^2)], \\
f_3(a_0, a_1, a_2, a_3) &= (1 - \lambda)(a_0 a_1^* + a_3 a_2^*) + \sqrt{1 - \lambda}(a_0 a_1^* - a_3 a_2^*), \\
f_4(a_0, a_1, a_2, a_3) &= (1 - \lambda)[a_0 a_3^* + a_3 a_0^* + \sqrt{1 - \lambda}(a_0 a_3^* - a_3 a_0^*)].
\end{aligned}
\tag{27}
$$

3.3   Analysis

It can be seen that the fidelity is dependent on the coefficients of the prepared state and the noise parameter in five-type noises. And they are independent on Alice's and Charlie's measurement results in the four-type noises:

the bit flip, phase flip, bit-phase flip and phase-damping noise. However, in the amplitude-damping noise, there are eight kinds of fidelity according to different measurement results. When the prepared state are maximally entangled state $\frac{1}{2}|00\rangle + \frac{1}{2}|01\rangle + \frac{1}{2}|10\rangle + \frac{1}{2}|11\rangle$, the fidelities in five-type noisy environment are listed in Table 2. And the fidelities with the decoherence rate λ are plotted in Fig. 1. It can be seen that no matter how the noise parameter λ changes, the fidelity is always 1 in bit flip noise environment. However, it's interesting that the curves of fidelities are coincident under the phase flip and bit-phase flip noise. They first decrease and then increase with the increase of noise parameter λ. When $\lambda = 0$ or $\lambda = 1$, $F_{p-f}^* = F_{bp-f}^* = 1$, this result shows that there is no loss of information. While in the amplitude-damping and phase-damping noise, the fidelities reduce as the noise parameter λ increases, and when $\lambda = 1$, the fidelities reach minimum value $\frac{1}{4}$.

Table 2. The fidelity in five-type noisy environment when the prepared state is the maximally entangled state.

Noise	The fidelity F^*
Bit flip	1
Phase flip	$\frac{3}{2} - \frac{1}{4\lambda^2 - 4\lambda + 2}$
Bit-phase flip	$\frac{3}{2} - \frac{1}{4\lambda^2 - 4\lambda + 2}$
Phase-damping	$\frac{-4\lambda^3 + 17\lambda^2 - 20\lambda + 8}{12\lambda^2 - 16\lambda + 8}$
Amplitude-damping	$\frac{3\lambda^2 - 10\lambda + 8}{4(\lambda^2 - 2\lambda + 2)}$

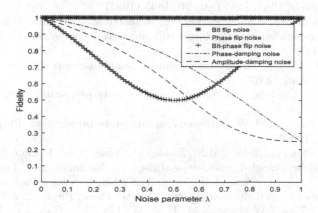

Fig. 1. The fidelity curves in five-type noisy environment when the prepared state is maximally entangled state.

4   Discussions and Conclusions

In this paper, we study the influence of five-type noises on the CRSP scheme of an arbitrary two-qubit state via the Brown state. It's found that the fidelity depends on the coefficients of the prepared state and the noise parameter in the five-type noises. And the fidelity in the amplitude-damping noise is related to Alice's and Charlie's measurement results. However, in the other four-type noises, fidelity is independent on measurement results. Moreover, we analyze the fidelity in the case that the prepared state is maximally entangled. In the bit flip noise, the fidelity is unit which means perfect communication. However, in the phase flip and bit-phase flip noise, the fidelities are coincident. It is worth mentioning that when $\lambda = 0$ or $\lambda = 1$, $F^*_{p-f} = F^*_{bp-f} = 1$, it shows that the noise has no effect on the CRSP scheme. In the amplitude-damping and phase-damping noise, the fidelity under the amplitude-damping noise is always larger than that in the phase-damping noise, which implies that more information is lost under the phase-damping noise. Similar analysis can be made for the CRSP of an arbitrary three-qubit state via the Brown state.

Acknowledgements. This work is supported by the National Natural Science Foundation of China (Nos. 61201253, 61572246), the program for science and technology innovation research team in universities of Henan province (No. 18IRTSTHN014), Foundation of Science and Technology on Information Assurance Laboratory (No. KJ-17-003)

References

1. Bennett, C.H., Brassard, G., Crepeau, C., Jozsa, R., Peres, A., Wootters, W.K.: Teleporting an unknown quantum state via dual classical and Einstein-Podolsky-Rosen channels. Phys. Rev. Lett. **70**, 1895 (1993)
2. Lo, H.K.: Classical communication cost in distributed quantum information processing - a generalization of quantum communication complexity. Phys. Rev. A **62**, 012313 (2000)
3. Devetak, I., Berger, T.: Low-entanglement remote state preparation. Phys. Rev. Lett. **87**, 197901 (2001)
4. Berry, D.W., Sanders, B.C.: Optimal remote state preparation. Phys. Rev. Lett. **90**, 057901 (2003)
5. Leung, D.W., Shor, P.W.: Oblivious remote state preparation. Phys. Rev. Lett. **90**, 127905 (2003)
6. Ma, S.Y., Chen, X.B., Luo, M.X., Zhang, R., Yang, Y.X.: Remote preparation of a four-particle entangled cluster-type state. Opt. Commun. **284**, 4088 (2011)
7. Ma, S.Y., Tang, P., Chen, X.B., Yang, Y.X.: Schemes for remotely preparing a six-particle entangled cluster-type state. Int. J. Theor. Phys. **52**, 968 (2013)
8. Peng, X.H., Zhu, X.W., Fang, X.M., Feng, M., Liu, M.L., Gao, K.L.: Experimental implementation of remote state preparation by nuclear magnetic resonance. Phys. Lett. A **306**, 271 (2003)
9. Erhard, M., Qassim, H., Mand, H., Karimi, E., Boyd, R.W.: Real-time imaging of spin-to-orbital angular momentum hybrid remote state preparation. Phys. Rev. A **92**, 022321 (2015)

10. Barreiro, J.T., Wei, T.C., Kwiat, P.G.: Remote preparation of single-photon "hybrid" entangled and vector-polarization states. Phys. Rev. Lett. **105**, 030407 (2010)

11. An, N.B.: Joint remote state preparation via W and W-type states. Opt. Commun. **283**, 4113 (2010)

12. An, N.B., Cao, T.B., Don, N.V.: Deterministic joint remote state preparation. Phys. Lett. A **375**, 3570 (2011)

13. Wang, D., Zha, X.W., Lan, Q.: Joint remote state preparation of arbitrary two-qubit state with six-qubit state. Opt. Commun. **284**, 5853 (2011)

14. Xia, Y., Chen, Q.Q., An, N.B.: Deterministic joint remote preparation of an arbitrary three-qubit state via EPR pairs. J. Phys. A Math. Theor. **45**, 055303 (2012)

15. Song, J.F., Wang, Z.Y.: Controlled remote preparation of a two-qubit state via positive operator-valued measure and two three-qubit entanglements. Int. J. Theor. Phys. **50**, 2410 (2011)

16. Chen, X.B., Ma, S.Y., Su, Y., Zhang, R., Yang, Y.X.: Controlled remote state preparation of arbitrary two and three qubit states via the Brown state. Quantum Inform. Process. **11**, 1653 (2012)

17. Wang, C., Zeng, Z., Li, X.H.: Controlled remote state preparation via partially entangled quantum channel. Quantum Inform. Process. **14**, 1077 (2015)

18. Gao, C., Ma, S.Y., Chen, W.L.: Controlled remote preparation via the Brown state with no restriction. Int. J. Theor. Phys. **55**, 2643 (2016)

19. Guan, X.W., Chen, X.B., Wang, L.C., Yang, Y.X.: Joint remote preparation of an arbitrary two-qubit state in noisy environments. Int. J. Theor. Phys. **53**, 2236 (2014)

20. Liang, H.Q., Liu, J.M., Feng, S.S., Chen, J.G., Xu, X.Y.: Effects of noises on joint remote state preparation via a GHZ-class channel. Quantum Inform. Process. **14**, 3857 (2015)

21. Ma, S.Y., Gao, C., Zhang, P., Qu, Z.G.: Deterministic remote preparation via the Brown state. Quantum Inform. Process. **16**, 93 (2017)

22. Wang, M.M., Qu, Z.G., Wang, W., Chen, J.G.: Effect of noise on deterministic joint remote preparation of an arbitrary two-qubit state. Quantum Inform. Process. **16**, 140 (2017)

23. Adepoju, A.G., Falaye, B.J., Sun, G.H., Camacho-Nieto, O., Dong, S.H.: Joint remote state preparation (JRSP) of two-qubit equatorial state in quantum noisy channels. Phys. Lett. A **381**, 581 (2017)

DDoS Attack Security Situation Assessment Model Using Fusion Feature Based on Fuzzy C-Means Clustering Algorithm

Ruizhi Zhang[1], Jieren Cheng[1,2], Xiangyan Tang[1(✉)], Qiang Liu[3], and Xiangfeng He[4]

[1] School of Information Science and Technology, Hainan University,
Haikou 570228, China
tangxy36@163.com
[2] State Key Laboratory of Marine Resource Utilization in South China Sea,
Haikou 570228, China
[3] College of Computer, National University of Defense Technology,
Changsha 410073, China
[4] Hainan Sub Center, National Computer Network Emergency Response
Coordination Center, Haikou 570206, China

Abstract. DDoS attacks have impaired the network availability seriously in the new network environment and the traditional network situation assessment methods cannot effectively evaluate the DDoS attack security situation. In this paper, a DDoS attack security situation assessment model using fusion feature based on Fuzzy C-means (FCM) clustering algorithm has been proposed. This model generates a fusion feature according to network flow changes in IP address of old and new users, and calculates the risk index of each network node on the basis of fusion feature and obtains the security situation information of the whole network by fusing the risk indexes of all network nodes, and clusters the fusion situation information with FCM into five security levels, so as to quantitatively evaluate the DDoS attack security situation of the whole network through the proposed situation risk degree recognition model. Experiments on real DDoS data show that the proposed model can assess the DDoS attack security situation reasonably and effectively and be more flexible than non-fuzzy methods.

Keywords: DDoS attack · DDoS attack security situation assessment
Fusion feature · FCM

1 Introduction

In recent years, along with the rapid development of Internet, security events of network happen frequently, which immeasurably impairs the trustworthiness of the Internet. The problem of network security has become a great threat to the application, management and development of computer network. And the frequent occurrence of network intrusion has caused great loss of people and our society. Among these security threats, DoS and DDoS attacks have gradually become the most serious ones,

© Springer Nature Switzerland AG 2018
X. Sun et al. (Eds.): ICCCS 2018, LNCS 11064, pp. 654–669, 2018.
https://doi.org/10.1007/978-3-030-00009-7_59

because they have potentially heavy damage and are not easy to be effectively prevented. In the wake of the rapid development of computing power and the arrival of the era of big data, DDoS attacks have more and more become a malicious tumor of the Internet and jeopardized the network security seriously.

In the light of the increasingly complex and perilous network environment, researchers have shown great interest in designing network security situation awareness system which consists of event detection, situation assessment and situation prediction. In order to ensure the important information is correctly understood by different levels decision makers and analysts by presenting them in an abstract visual format, the concept of Security Awareness (SA) was first introduced by Endsley [1]. Bass proposed Network Security Situation Awareness(NSSA) by applying the concept of SA into Network Security field [2]. As network security situation assessment is the most critical step in situation awareness, plenty of network situation assessment models have been proposed in recent years. Li et al. [3] have proposed a network evaluation model for adaptive situation assessment in the battle field by using a hierarchic multi-timescale bayesian network. A new network security situation assessment model based on T-S fuzzy neural network was proposed in [4]. Guang et al. [5] noticed that the previous network security situation assessment methods can't accurately reflect the features of large-scale, synergetic, multi-stage gradually shown by network attack behaviors, and proposed a network security situation evaluation method based on attack intention recognition from the angle of attacker by deeply analyzing the association between attack intention and network configuration information. Xiang et al. [6] improved the efficiency of the state transition matrix of the hidden Markov model by considering the defense efficiency in accordance with the game process between the security incidents and protect measures. A new assessment approach to determine the security situations of the all-optical network (AON) and a new quantification method of the security situation were developed in [7]. Wen and Tang fully considered the information fusion of multi-information sources and multi-level heterogeneous, and proposed a quantitative assessment model for network security situation based on weighted factors, which can display the current security situation of the overall network dynamically and reflect the network security situation accurately and quantitatively [8]. Li and Zhao utilized sliding time window mechanism to extract the observed value and hybrid multi-population genetic algorithm(MPGA) to train the HMM model parameters, so as to improve the reliability of parameters and the timeliness and accuracy of the evaluation results [9]. Jin et al. [10] presented a new network security situation assessment model based on random forest, and proved the proposed model is quicker and more accurate to evaluate the current network security situation compared with Bayesian Network. Wang [11] constructed a network situation awareness and estimation model based on Fuzzy Dynamic Bayesian network to better reflect the dynamic changes of network space operations. The authors in [12] novelly presented vulnerability, threat and basic operation as three dimensions at different levels, presented quantitative calculation method for each index, and used the multi-dimensional situation to accurately and intuitively depict the overall safety evolution process of network system. Zihao et al. [13] proposed a hierarchical network threat situation assessment method based on D-S evidence theory to effectively evaluate and vividly reflect the impact on network security situation under DDoS attacks. Jianwei et al. [14] proposed a quantitative assessment model for multi-node network security situation based on threat propagation in view of the complex network structure in the energy Internet. A network security situation assessment model and quantification method based on analytic hierarchy process (AHP) is proposed to solve the problems, such as subjective index weight factor, large evaluation index system, large amount of calculation and low efficiency in hierarchical network security situation assessment model [15]. Authors in [16] constructed the index system of network security risk assessment and optimized the Dempster synthesis rule, and determined the weights of each index system based on D-S evidence theory. They also synthesized the reliability distribution values of each index layer by the optimized Dempster synthesis rule to verify the reliability of the proposed method. Xu et al. [17] proposed a Quantitative Risk Assessment Model (QRAM) involving frequency and threat degree based on value at risk. They amended the influence coefficient of risk indexes in the network security situation assessment model to quantify the threat degree as an elementary intrusion effort and made use of multiple behavior information fusion so as to quantify threat frequency as intrusion trace effort, and they adapted the historical simulation method of value at risk under the influence of intrusion trace so as to dynamically access risk of Line-of-Business Services (LoBSs). Xi et al. [18] assessed the network threat situation more reasonably by combining raw alerts and contextual information. The approach in [19] offered methodology and tools, including data acquisition, processing and analysis, for a more accurate wireless security assessment. And the proposed methodology and tools are used for processing wireless scan results for the two capital cities, Hungary (Budapest) and Serbia (Belgrade). The study of Dai et al. [20] is capable of effectively identifying network security situations and assessing critical risk by presenting a risk flow attack graph (RFAG)-based risk assessment approach, which applied a RFAG to represent network and attack scenarios and then fed it to a network flow model for computing network risk flow. Rodriguez et al. [21] presented a Unified Modelling Language profile, named SecAM, which enables security assessment, through survivability analysis, of different security solutions before system deployment, to assess the survivability of the Saudi Arabia crude-oil network under two different attack scenarios and quantitatively estimate the minimization of attack damages on the crude-oil network with Generalized Stochastic Petri nets. The decision-aided situation awareness mechanism [22] is established based on multi-scale dynamic trust from the perspective of time and space, which regarded social network as the research object and carried out decision making assessment through trust authenticity test, logicality test, and feedback parameters to recognize misbehaviors and handle entity attacks relatively eclectic and realistic in aspect of trust determination.

Nevertheless, in the traditional network security situation assessment model, the detection information produced by traditional network security tools is pluralistic, individualized, and needs to be standardized. It is very difficult to standardize these detection information in the big data environment. Even if standardized, it usually comes at a significant cost and is not able to assess the network security situation effectively. In summary, the existing methods still have some problems.

(1) There is no appropriate network situation assessment model for DDoS attacks in a big data environment.

(2) The above situation assessment approaches give a fix value to represent the current network situation, which is not applicable for the real needs.

The main objective of DDoS attack security situation assessment is to evaluate the effects of real-time DDoS attack events on the security state of target assets in a specific time period. Therefore, the key is to find a appropriate value to indicate the network status. In this paper, we propose a characteristic value (risk value, RV) to distinguish attack network flow from normal network flow, so as to get the value of risk index to reflect the DDoS attack security situation. Moreover, the proposed fast IP address database is capable of reducing the rime complexity and space complexity effectively, just enough to meet the need of big data processing.

As for the second problem, the proposed network security assessment model is different from other approaches in introducing the concept of fuzzy clustering. The risk index obtained by risk value will be put into FCM clustering algorithm to generate five different network security levels. And the probability of a network node belonging to each security level can be calculated easily by the trained model, thus providing a more reasonable assessment data for network safety assessor. The main innovation of the proposed approach can be concluded as follows:

(1) The proposed DDoS attack security situation assessment model which uses fusion security situation information could cater to the evaluation work with massive attack data.
(2) The FCM clustering algorithm is introduced to classify network security levels and give a more reasonable and reliable assessment result.

The rest of the paper is organized as follows. The DDoS attack security situation evaluation model based on fusion feature and FCM is proposed in detail in the second section. In Sect. 2, a case study for assessing the security situation of network under DDoS attacks is given, and the performance of the proposed model is quantitatively analyzed. In Sect. 3, further exploration in the field of network situation awareness and the limitation of this study is discussed. Section 4 is a conclusion of this paper.

2   DDoS Attack Security Situation Assessment Model

The basic structure of the proposed model is shown in the following Fig. 1, we take normal network flow for training, and this process outputs the IP address database (IAD) which stores old users and parameters for the proposed model. Then the network flow can be detected by the proposed method and the IAD is inquired for checking whether an IP address is an old user or not. And we calculate the risk value of network node and use this value to generate the risk index. And then, the fusion risk index of the whole network is calculated on the basis of each risk index. Finally, the fusion risk index is clustered by FCM and standardized to five state types, namely, safe, mild risk, moderate risk, high risk and extreme risk.

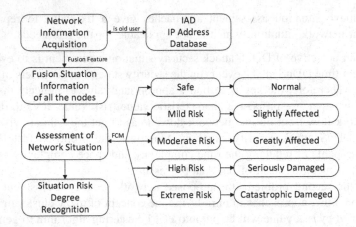

Fig. 1. A basic structure of the proposed model

2.1 Fusion Feature

Given a normal network flow U with n samples and a network flow V which requires detection with m samples, we define each sample as (T_i, S_i, D_i), where T_i is the arrival time of the packet i, S_i and D_i denotes its source IP and the destination IP respectively. We used the normal network flow U to generate a model which identifies and evaluates V, and we took a same Δt as a parameter for both training and detection algorithm. According to the above definition, in the training course, we collect a subgroup of samples G_k from normal network flow U within the k-th Δt. Once we've reached the end of every Δt, a filter is then applied to G_k to drop out all samples inside without a valid public IPv4 address of its S. The filtered sample group F_k is defined as

$$\forall G_{k_j} \in G_k$$
$$G_{k_j} \in F_k \quad if \ S_{G_{k_j}} \ is \ valid \ public \ IPv4 \ address \tag{1}$$

As the acquisition of each F_k, we incrementally built an IP address set O which denotes our old users. We union all S of group F_1 into O in the first time slice, $O = \{\} \cup \{S | S \in F_1\}$, and let $O_{max} = \|\{S | S \in F_1\}\|$. Then for each successive F_k, it's obviously that there are $\|F_k \cap O\|$ old users in the k-th time slice, and we update $O_{max} = \max(O_{max}, \|F_k \cap O\|)$.

$$\forall F_k$$
$$O_{max} = \begin{cases} \|F_1\| & if \ k = 1 \\ \max(O_{max}, \ \| \ F_k \cap O\|) & otherwise \end{cases} \tag{2}$$

After we calculated the O_{max}, we merges the F_k into O. By repeating these steps, we obtained an O_{max} which represents the maximum number of old user appeared in a certain time interval.

Along with the updating of $O_{\max}$, we computed an $N_k = ||F_k|| - ||F_k \cap O||$. We have defined that set $F_k \cap O$ denotes our old user, then correspondingly, the set $F_k \backslash O$ denotes new users, and N_k is the number of new user. By the time we get the final $O_{\max}$, we calculate our average number of new user over all the time slices as

$$\bar{N} = \frac{\sum_{i=1}^{k} N_i}{k} \tag{3}$$

When we acquired the four basic model parameters, namely, Δt, O, $O_{\max}$ and $\bar{N}$, the network detection process can be executed. We read the network flow V using the same Δt, and during each time slice k, we store all the source IP S in the dictionary W_k with S as key and the times it occurs as value, $W_k = [(S_{k,i}, o_{k,i})]$. Then we let set G_k equals to all the keys in W_k, and we define that $W_k[S_{k,i}]$ as the times of the corresponding source IP $S_{k,i}$ occurred in the k-th sample. At the end of each Δt, we calculate four features of the very time slice k

$$\begin{cases} R_k = \frac{||G_k \cap O|| - O_{\max}}{O_{\max}} \\ A_k = ||G_k \backslash O|| - \bar{N} \\ Z_k = \frac{||G_k \backslash O||}{O_{\max}} \\ E_k = \frac{\sum_i \{ W_k[S_{k,j}] \forall S_{s,j} \in (G_k \backslash O) \}}{||G_k \backslash O|| \Delta t} \end{cases} \tag{4}$$

where R_k denotes percentage of old user appeared in current k-th Δt over the maximum of our old user of some certain time slices, A_k suggests the changes of our new users in amount compared with the amount of the average new user $\bar{N}$, Z_k is the ratio of current new users to our maximum old users, and the last feature E_k represents current access rate of new users, to be specific, it denotes that there are E_k accessing requests per second per new user.

Definition 1. With the observation of real-life, during the normal time, our old users appear in a relatively fixed pattern. And we define a factor R as a measurement during DDoS attacks through this observation.

For instance, suppose we observed that $O_{\max} = 200$, and given a certain Δt in detection network flow, if $||G_k \cap O|| = 100$ old users, then R is calculated as R = (100 − 200)/200 = −0.5 = −50%. As R is a signed number, it can indicate both the increment and decrement of number of current old users compared with the amount of maximum old users in percentage.

Definition 2. Based on the definition of DDoS, we assume that if network of a network node is under a DDoS attack, there are supposed to be a large number of new users, therefore $||G_k \backslash O||$ is supposed to be much larger than the amount of average new users $\bar{N}$ in normal time. And we define a factor A, which is used as a quantity which represents the delta between the number of observed new users and the amount of average new users.

Definition 3. If a DDoS attack is in progress, it's reasonable to presume that the amount of current new users $||G_k \backslash O||$ is larger than the amount of current old users

$\|G_k \cap O\|$. However, timezone exists and new users may come from all over the world. Chances are that there are just a few old users and for whatever reason a small group of new users appears, in such case, if the amount of new users is larger than the old ones, using $\|G_k \backslash O\|/\|O\|$ will cause fluctuation. Thus we define a factor Z as the ratio of the amount of current new users to observed amount of maximum old users in training.

Definition 4. Based on assumptions A and Z, if there is a DDoS attack, then accessing rate from new users should be a pretty large value since they're sending flood packets. Nevertheless, if it is a normal network flow, because every normal user should obey the TCP/IP principles, thus the accessing rate should be a relatively small constant value. Therefore, a factor E is defined to denote the accessing rate of new users.

In the real-life DDoS flow, considering that attackers may fabricate IP address which could be an invalid public IP, we do not filter out invalid IP address in G_k. If we drop these invalid IP, we are actually shrinking the attack. However, when we calculate the old user set O from training network flow U, we do need to filter out all invalid IP addresses to ensure the correctness, which means that all old users come from valid public IP addresses.

And then we multiply them together as our fusion feature value RV_k, which could reflect the risk value of current time slice k,

$$RV_k = -R_k \times A_k \times Z_k \times E_k \tag{5}$$

Owing to we used a product of three aforementioned features, it is important to avoid 0 as factor in (5). Thus small changes have been made to the calculations of R_k and Z_k.

$$R_k = \begin{cases} \frac{\|G_k \cap O\| - O_{max}}{O_{max}} & if \|G_k \cap O\| - O_{max} \neq 0 \\ \frac{\|G_k \cap O\| - O_{max} - 1}{O_{max}} & otherwise \end{cases} \tag{6}$$

$$Z_k = \begin{cases} \frac{\|G_k \backslash O\|}{O_{max}} & if \|G_k \backslash O\| \neq 0 \\ \frac{\|G_k \backslash O\| - 1}{O_{max}} & otherwise \end{cases} \tag{7}$$

And to deal with the huge amount of the access and comparison of IP address, we designed a fast IP address database, which could flag, unflag and check for an IP address with O(1) time. In stark contrast, the original string format of IP comparison would take O(nm) time, as there are O(n) IP in our training set, and O(m) IP in our test set. Both n and m could be a pretty large number in real network environment, which makes it a pseudo polynomial time algorithm, especially when IPv6 is widely used. Even if we store the IPv4 address in raw format, i.e., unsigned 32 bit integer, that will take literally 4 GB space, let alone the storage of IPv6. However, we could use consecutive bits for our flag, which means it only requires 512 MB space for the whole IPv4. In the meantime, it is not only extensible for IPv6 if we use good hash algorithm to map the 128 bit IPv6 address to a 32 bit integer, but also practically works. As a result, the fast IP address database is capable of improving the performance of proposed model by time and space dimensions.

2.2 Fusion Situation Information Model

The risk value of the network security state of each network node can be calculated to determine the most likely security state of each network node in a specific time period. In order to express intuitively, qualitative description of the security state is replaced by the quantitative description, and the concept of risk index is presented at the same time, which quantitatively represents the value of risk of a network node under a certain situation. In the case that the risk value of network node in various DDoS attack security situation can be calculated, the following formula can be used to calculate the current risk index of network node:

$$RI_i = \frac{RV_i - RV_{\min}}{RV_{\max} - RV_{\min}} \tag{8}$$

In (8), RI_i is the risk index at the i-th time, RV_i is the risk value at the i-th time, and we assume that $RV_{\min}$ and $RV_{\max}$ is the minimum and maximum risk values obtained by the sample data set.

We introduce $x_1, x_2, \ldots, x_n$ to represent risk index of each network node at one point in time. And we define weight of these network nodes in the light of the their importance in the network assets as $\alpha_1, \alpha_2, \ldots, \alpha_n$.

$$\begin{aligned}
y_1 &= \alpha_1 x_{1,1} + \alpha_2 x_{2,1} + \ldots + \alpha_n x_{n,1} \\
y_2 &= \alpha_1 x_{1,2} + \alpha_2 x_{2,2} + \ldots + \alpha_n x_{n,2} \\
&\quad \cdots \cdots \\
y_m &= \alpha_1 x_{1,m} + \alpha_2 x_{2,m} + \ldots + \alpha_n x_{n,m}
\end{aligned} \tag{9}$$

In (9), y_i denote the weighted sum of risk index of all the network nodes at one point in time, namely, fusion risk index, the risk index of the whole network at some point of time can be calculated as below:

$$y_i = \alpha_1 x_{1,i} + \alpha_2 x_{2,i} + \ldots + \alpha_n x_{n,i}, i \in [1, \ldots m] \tag{10}$$

Because all the network nodes we have studied are ordinary hosts in the network, we could assume that the weights of all the network nodes are equal, which means

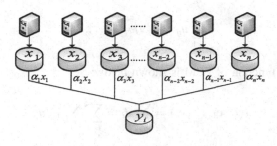

Fig. 2. Situation information fusion process

$\alpha_1 : \alpha_2 : \ldots : \alpha_n = 1 : 1 : \ldots : 1$, thus, the calculation of y_i is reduced to the following formula (Fig. 2).

$$y_i = x_{1,i} + x_{2,i} + \ldots + x_{n,i}, i \in [1, \ldots m] \tag{11}$$

2.3 DDoS Security Assessment Based on Fuzzy C-Means Clustering Algorithm

It is easy to see the Risk Index described in Sect. 2.2 is a number between 0 and 1, that is, Risk Index $\in [0, 1]$. And then the Fuzzy C-means clustering algorithm is used to cluster the values of Risk Index to different categories.

Fuzzy C-means clustering (FCM) Algorithm is one of the most widely used fuzzy clustering algorithms. Fuzzy c-means (FCM) clustering was developed by Dunn [23] in 1973, and improved by Bezdek [24] in 1981. Fuzzy C-means is one of the most efficient clustering algorithms which have been widely used in pattern recognition, data compression, image segmentation, computer vision and many other fields. FCM clustering algorithm plays an important role in dealing with massive data, and it can be both a modeling technique and a preprocessing step in plenty of data mining process implementations. Fuzzy clustering provides more flexibility than non fuzzy methods by allowing each data record to belong to more than one cluster to some degree. Some of the existing work has already verified the availability of FCM clustering algorithm in big data and distributed environments [25–28].

The fuzzy c-means algorithm is very similar to the k-means algorithm. It first chooses a number of clusters, then assigns coefficients randomly to each data point for being in the clusters, and finally, repeats until the coefficients' change between two iterations is no more than the given sensitivity threshold, which means the algorithm has converged. As a result, the centroid for each cluster and the coefficients of each data point of being in the clusters can be computed easily.

FCM algorithm divides n vector $x_i(i = 1, 2, \ldots N)$ into c fuzzy sets, and obtains the cluster center of each group while the value function of the non-similarity index reach the minimum. FCM uses membership degree between 0 and 1 to determine the degree of each sample data belonging to each group. In accordance with the introduction of fuzzy partition, the value of elements of membership matrix U is between 0 and 1. Besides, the sum of membership degrees of a sample data is equal to 1 according to the normalization rule:

$$\sum_{i=1}^{c} u_{ij} = 1, \forall j = 1, \ldots, n \tag{12}$$

The objective function of FCM is shown below:

$$J(U, c_1, \ldots, c_c) = \sum_{i=1}^{c} J_i = \sum_{i=1}^{c} \sum_{j}^{n} u_{ij}^m d_{ij}^2 \tag{13}$$

In (13), u_{ij} is between 0 and 1, c_i is cluster center of the i-th fuzzy group, d_{ij} is the Euclidean distance between the i-th cluster center and the j-th data point, that is $d_{ij} = \|c_i - x_j\|$. In order to obtain the minimum value of objective function (13), the following new objective function is constructed:

$$\bar{J}(U, c_1, \ldots, c_c, \lambda_1, \ldots, \lambda_n) = J(U, c_1, \ldots, c_c) + \sum_{j=1}^{n} \lambda_i \left(\sum_{i=1}^{c} u_{ij} - 1 \right)$$

$$= \sum_{i=1}^{c} \sum_{j}^{n} u_{ij}^m d_{ij}^2 + \sum_{j=1}^{n} \lambda_i \left(\sum_{i=1}^{c} u_{ij} - 1 \right) \tag{14}$$

In (14), λ_j (j = 1, 2, ... N) is the constrained Lagrange multipliers of (12). For all of the input parameters, the necessary conditions for reaching the minimization of the (13) are as follows:

$$c_i = \frac{\sum_{j=1}^{n} u_{ij}^m x_j}{\sum_{j=1}^{n} u_{ij}^m} \tag{15}$$

$$u_{ij} = \frac{1}{\sum_{k=1}^{c} \left(\frac{d_{ij}}{d_{kj}} \right)^{2/(m-1)}} \tag{16}$$

The fuzzy C mean clustering algorithm is a simple iterative process with the above two necessary conditions. In the course of the experiment, FCM uses the following steps to determine the cluster center c and the membership matrix U:

Step 1: Initialize the membership matrix U by random numbers between 0 and 1, and make sure the constraint condition in the formula (12) is satisfied at the same time.

Step 2: Use formula (15) to calculate the c-th cluster center c_i, i = 1, ..., c.

Step 3: Calculate the objective function according to the formula (13), and repeat this step constantly until the value of objective function is less than a certain threshold or the variation relative to the value of last objective function is less than a threshold.

Step 4: Calculate the new membership matrix U by (16). And return to step 2.

We set c = 5 according to the real-life network situation of a network node, namely, Normal, Slightly affected, Greatly affected, Seriously damaged and Catastrophic damaged. As m is a parameter that regulates the flexibility of FCM clustering algorithm, the clustering effect will be poor when m is too large, and the algorithm will be close to the Hard C Mean clustering algorithm when m is too small. Therefore, we determine the value of m by carrying out a set of experiments. The values of fusion risk index calculated above was clustered into five categories by processing the steps of FCM clustering algorithm, and the clustering results is shown in the following Fig. 3.

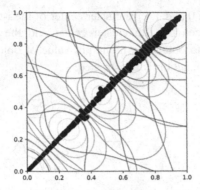

Fig. 3. Risk index clustered by FCM

We divided the network security into five levels in accordance with the five categories clustered by FCM clustering algorithm, so as to precisely characterize different DDoS attack security situations, which is shown in the following Table 1. And we presented Risk Degree on the basis of the cluster centers to denote different security levels, that is, Degree A, Degree B, Degree C, Degree D and Degree E represent Safe, Mild risk, Moderate risk, High risk and Extreme risk respectively.

Table 1. Network security status of the network

Risk degree	Security level	Network situation
A	Safe	Normal
B	Mild risk	Slightly affected
C	Moderate risk	Greatly affected
D	High risk	Seriously damaged
E	Extreme risk	Catastrophic damaged

2.4   Situation Risk Degree Recognition

After the processing of clustering, we could obtain the risk degree of network security at every moment. As Degree A, Degree B, Degree C, Degree D and Degree E are the five categories of clustering result, we define N_1, N_2, N_3, N_4, N_5 as the sum of number of each category in a period of time T, and the risk rate of network can be calculated as below:

$$P_i = \frac{N_i}{\sum\limits_{i=1}^{5} N_i}, \quad i \in [1, 2, 3, 4, 5] \tag{17}$$

In (17), P_i represent the proportion of different risk levels, that is, the risk rate of different DDoS attack security situations.

$$I = i, while \max(\theta_i P_i), \quad i \in [1, 2, 3, 4, 5]$$
$$Risk\,Degree = A, \; I = 1,$$
$$Risk\,Degree = B, \; I = 2,$$
$$Risk\,Degree = C, \; I = 3, \tag{18}$$
$$Risk\,Degree = D, \; I = 4,$$
$$Risk\,Degree = E, \; I = 5, \quad Risk\,Degree\,during\,T$$

In (18), θ_i is defined as the weight of different risk degrees, and we assume that θ_i is increasing proportionately in accordance with the increasing amount of susceptibility to DDoS attacks, that is, $\theta_i = i, i \in [1, 2, 3, 4, 5]$. Finally, we could get the risk degree of a network during a given time period T.

3 Experiment

Our experiment is based on the data set of CAIDA DDoS Attack 2007, we trained our model with different Δt = [0.05, 0.1, 0.5, 1.0, 2.0] s, and the proposed approach was able to calculate the risk index of network node swiftly and accurately. After calculating risk indexes of all the network nodes, we could get the fusion risk index of the whole network. Figure 4 vividly showed the trend of the DDoS attack security situation under different sample times.

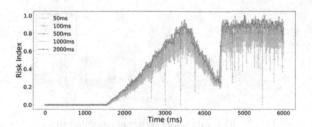

Fig. 4. Risk index of a network in 6000 ms

We put the fusion risk index of network into Fuzzy C-means clustering algorithm to get the security degree of the whole network. It can be educed from Fig. 4 that DDoS attack security situation of the network was relatively safe in the first 2000 ms and the network security was greatly affected in the following 2000 ms, and the network was under extreme risk continuously in the last 2000 ms. In addition, the following Table 2 shows the result of the experiment on some test data.

As seen from Table 2, the network security degree of test data T1 is C, showing about 1.12%, 0.33%, 96.84%, 1.59% and 0.12% of Degree A, Degree B, Degree C, Degree D and Degree E respectively, which means the network is under moderate risk and DDoS attack security situation of the network is likely to be greatly affected in some point of time. Similarly, we can say that the security level of T2 is extreme risk,

Table 2. Network security status of network node

Test data	A	B	C	D	E
T1	0.0111827	0.003282119	0.968440729	0.015897698	0.001196754
T2	0.000119084	0.001269601	0.000195053	0.000390926	0.998025336
T3	0.00232506	0.010395247	0.008099069	0.977258934	0.00192169
T4	0.920742534	0.004402337	0.061375304	0.011400754	0.002079071
T5	0.019409969	0.03174271	0.100824993	0.839842094	0.008180233

both T3 and T5 are under high risk, and the DDoS attack security situation of network of T4 is relatively safe.

In addition to the trend of fusion security situation, the risk rate of five different security levels under different sampling times is graphically illustrated, as shown in the figure below.

It can be seen from Fig. 5 that the result is not representative when the sampling time is 50 ms. Taking it by and large, Degree A, Degree B, Degree C, Degree D, Degree E roughly comprised 34%, 10%, 12%, 14% and 30% of status of the network in a period of time. Then, the value of $\theta_i P_i$ calculated by formula (18) reaches maximum while i = 5, thus, we could determine that the risk degree of the network is Degree E over the study time period.

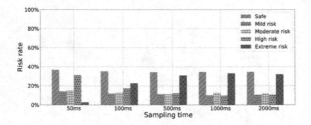

Fig. 5. Risk rate under different sampling times

Last but not least, in order to quantitatively evaluate the proposed algorithm, two indicators, namely, the number of error accumulating samples and average accuracy, have been presented.

(1) The number of error accumulating samples (EAS). This value represents the number of the total errors of accumulation, that is, the sum of the number of error accumulating samples in various categories. We define EAS_A, EAS_B, EAS_C, EAS_D and EAS_E represent the number of error accumulating samples in Degree A, Degree B, Degree C, Degree D and Degree E respectively.

$$EAS = EAS_A + EAS_B + EAS_C + EAS_D + EAS_E \qquad (19)$$

(2) Average accuracy (AA). Suppose the original dataset has k classes, C_i is used to represent class i, N_i is the number of samples in C_i, M_i is the correct number of clusters. Therefore, M_i/N_i is the accuracy of i class, and the average accuracy is as below (Table 3).

$$AA = \frac{1}{k} \sum_{i=1}^{k} M_i/N_i \tag{20}$$

Table 3. Algorithm performance under different sample times

Δt(ms)	EAS	AA
50	197	99.27%
100	56	99.40%
500	12	99.79%
1000	0	100%
2000	0	100%

4 Conclusion

In this paper, a DDoS attack security situation assessment model using fusion feature based on Fuzzy C-means clustering algorithm has been proposed. In order to quantitatively evaluate the DDoS attack security situation of the whole network, the proposed model generates risk value through network flow changes in IP address of old and new users to calculate the risk index of each network node, and fuses risk indexes of all the network nodes to get a fusion security situation information, and clusters the fusion situation information with FCM clustering algorithm to obtain different security levels, so as to characterize different DDoS attack security situations of the network. The whole situation of network is divided into five child situations by the proposed model: normal, slightly affected, greatly affected, seriously damaged and catastrophic damaged. And then the security status of network nodes are obtained by the trained model. After fusing the results of the five child situations, we could get the DDoS attack security situation of the whole network. With this approach, the DDoS attack security situation can be evaluated easily and quickly and demonstrated vividly and specifically. Experiments on DDoS dataset show that the proposed model is capable of assessing DDoS attack security situation in the new network environment accurately and effectively.

Acknowledgments. We thank all the anonymous reviewers and editors who helped to improve the quality of the paper. This work was supported by the National Natural Science Foundation of China [61762033, 61363071, 61702539]; The National Natural Science Foundation of Hainan [617048, 20 18CXTD333]; Hainan University Doctor Start Fund Project [kyqd1328]; Hainan University Youth Fund Project [qnjj1444].

References

1. Endsley, M. R.: Situation awareness global assessment technique (SAGAT). In: National Aerospace and Electronics Conference, vol. 3, pp. 789–795 (1988)
2. Bass, T.: Multisensor data fusion for next generation distributed intrusion detection systems. In: 1999 IRIS National Symposium on Sensor & Data Fusion, Proceedings of the Iris National Symposium on Sensor and Data Fusion, Baltimore, pp. 24–27 (1999)
3. Li, C., Cao, M., Tian, L.: Situation assessment approach based on a hierarchic multi-timescale Bayesian network. In: 2nd International Conference on Information Science and Control Engineering, pp. 911–915. IEEE, Shanghai (2015)
4. Chundong, W., Li, Y., Chenyang, D.: Situation assessment of network security based on T-S fuzzy neural network. J. Comput. Inf. Syst. 11(16), 5999–6006 (2015)
5. Guang, K., Guangming, T., Ding, X., Wang, S., Wang, K.: A network security situation assessment method based on attack intention perception. In: 2nd IEEE International Conference on Computer and Communications, pp. 1138–1142. IEEE, Chengdu (2016)
6. Xiang, S., Lv, Y., Xia, C., Li, Y., Wang, Z.: A method of network security situation assessment based on hidden Markov model. In: Li, K., Li, J., Liu, Y., Castiglione, A. (eds.) ISICA 2015. CCIS, vol. 575, pp. 631–639. Springer, Singapore (2016). https://doi.org/10.1007/978-981-10-0356-1_65
7. Zhao, Z.N., Qiao, P.L., Wang, J., Hu, G.Y.: Security situation assessment of all-optical network based on evidential reasoning rule. Math. Probl. Eng. 2016(4), 1–7 (2016)
8. Wen, Z., Tang, J.: Quantitative assessment for network security situation based on weighted factors. J. Comput. Methods Sci. Eng. 16(4), 821–833 (2016)
9. Li, X., Zhao, H.: Network security situation assessment based on HMM-MPGA. In: 2nd International Conference on Information Management, pp. 57–63. IEEE, London (2016)
10. Jin, Y., Shen, Y., Zhang, G., Zhi, H.: The model of network security situation assessment based on random forest. In: 8th IEEE International Conference on Software Engineering and Service Sciences, pp. 977–980. IEEE, Beijing (2017)
11. Wang, X.: Network information security situation assessment based on Bayesian network. Int. J. Secur. Appl. 10(5), 129–138 (2016)
12. Zhu, L., Xia, G., Zhang, Z., Li, J.: Multi-dimensional network security situation assessment. Int. J. Secur. Appl. 10(11), 153–164 (2016)
13. Zihao, L., Bin, Z., Ning, Z., Lixun, L.: Hierarchical network threat situation assessment method for DDoS based on D-S evidence theory. In: 2017 IEEE International Conference on Intelligence and Security Informatics, pp. 49–53. IEEE, Beijing (2017)
14. Jianwei, T., et al.: Threat propagation based security situation quantitative assessment in multi-node network. Comput. Res. Dev. 54(4), 731–741 (2017)
15. Wang, H., et al.: Research on network security situation assessment and quantification method based on analytic hierarchy process. Wirel. Pers. Commun. 2018(1), 1–20 (2018)
16. Yu, J., Hu, M., Wang, P.: Evaluation and reliability analysis of network security risk factors based on D-S evidence theory. J. Intell. Fuzzy Syst. 34(2), 861–869 (2018)
17. Xu, J., et al.: A quantitative risk assessment model involving frequency and threat degree under line-of-business services for infrastructure of emerging sensor networks. Sensors 17(3), 642 (2017)
18. Xi, R., Yun, X., Hao, Z., Zhang, Y.: Quantitative threat situation assessment based on alert verification. Secur. Commun. Netw. 9(13), 2135–2142 (2016)
19. Dobrilovic, D., Stojanov, Z., Jager, S., Rajnai, Z.: A method for comparing and analyzing wireless security situations in two capital cities. Acta Polytech. Hung. 13(6), 67–86 (2016)

20. Dai, F., Hu, Y., Zheng, K., Wu, B.: Exploring risk flow attack graph for security risk assessment. IET Inf. Secur. **9**(6), 344–353 (2015)
21. Rodriguez, R.J., Merseguer, J., Bernardi, S.: Modelling security of critical infrastructures: a survivability assessment. Comput. J. **58**(10), 2313–2327 (2015)
22. Li, F., Nie, Y., Zhu, J., Zhang, H.: A decision-aided situation awareness mechanism based on multiscale dynamic trust. Int. J. Distrib. Sensor Netw. **2015**, 1–14 (2015)
23. Dunn, J.C.: A fuzzy relative of the ISODATA process and its use in detecting compact well-separated clusters. J. Cybern. **3**(3), 32–57 (1974)
24. Bezdek, J.C.: Pattern Recognition with Fuzzy Objective Function Algorithms, vol. 22, no. 1171, pp. 203–239. Plenum Press, New York (1981)
25. Son, L.H., Tien, N.D.: Tune up fuzzy C-means for big data: some novel hybrid clustering algorithms based on initial selection and incremental clustering. Int. J. Fuzzy Syst. **19**(5), 1585–1602 (2017)
26. Vo, N.P., Dat, N.D., Tran, V.T.N., Chau, V.T.N., Nguyen, T.A.: Fuzzy C-means for english sentiment classification in a distributed system. Appl. Intell. **46**(3), 717–738 (2017)
27. Wu, J., Wu, Z., Cao, J., Liu, H., Chen, G.: Fuzzy consensus clustering with applications on big data. IEEE Trans. Fuzzy Syst. **25**(6), 1430–1445 (2017)
28. Li, Y., Yang, G., He, H., Jiao, L., Shang, R.: A study of large-scale data clustering based on fuzzy clustering. Soft. Comput. **20**(8), 3231–3242 (2016)

DDoS Attacks Detection and Traceback Method Based on Flow Entropy Algorithm and MPLS Principle

Xiaohui Yang[✉] and Yue Yu

Hebei University, Baoding 071002, China
yxh@hbu.edu.cn

Abstract. Distributed Denial of Service (DDoS) attacks on cloud computing platforms have become one of the key issues affecting cloud security. Single packet traceback technology against DDoS attacks has become the focus of research in the field of cloud security. Currently, single packet traceback technologies generally have problems of high cost and low accuracy. In this paper, an early warning mechanism is set up, the broadcast algorithm is improved, to avoid detecting the router is flooded with a large amount of redundant broadcast message, and the flow entropy is used to recognize the attack flow. A traceback method for the switching path generation theory based on MPLS (Multi-Protocol Label Switching) that establishing traceback marks on the traceable routers and reconstructing the DDoS attacks paths is proposed. This paper uses network probe to parallelize the establishment of traceback tables and estimate the load of traceback devices and so on to improve the processing speed and traceback accuracy of traceback routers. The simulation results show that the flow entropy method can recognize DDoS attacks when the strength of attack flow is nearly 2 times normal flow, and the probability of traceback can be reduced to 6%. After the establishment of traceback paths, the forwarding rate and traceback rate of IP packets are improved, the traceback accuracy than other methods to improve 30%, suitable for cloud computing large scale and high flow environment.

Keywords: Cloud computing security · DDoS attacks
Single packet traceback technology · Flow entropy algorithm
Attack flow recognition

1 Introduction

Cloud computing introduces a utility model to remotely supply extensible and measurable resources [1], so users store many resources on it, which also raises the concern of many illegal users outside the cloud and wants to use illegal means to obtain resources in the cloud for profit. Cloud security has become the focus of attention.

Distributed Denial of Service (DDoS) attacks are one of the major security threats to large scale networks and one of the security threats to cloud computing platforms [2]. DDoS attacks can paralyze the cloud computing platform, resulting in users can not use their services, and even reveal or lose users information, the damage caused is

© Springer Nature Switzerland AG 2018
X. Sun et al. (Eds.): ICCCS 2018, LNCS 11064, pp. 670–683, 2018.
https://doi.org/10.1007/978-3-030-00009-7_60

unpredictable [3]. In 2010, the Cloud Security Alliance viewed DDoS attacks as an important security issue facing cloud computing [4]. Therefore, the study of DDoS attacks on cloud environment is very necessary. In this paper, DDoS attacks are recognized and traced by improving the single packet traceback method and establishing the early warning mechanism.

2 Related Work

The key of entry filtering is to get the packet characteristics allowed or forbidden by the designated router ports. HCF constructs a mapping table IP2HC between IP and hop count by using the information about the number of hops between source and destination, and based on this table analyzes and evaluates the data packets [5]; RBF method based on the last hop routing information to recognize and delete the packets which forging the source IP address [6]; Ex-IDPF method is based on the key marking system, the packet header of each packet embedded security key, the forged source IP address packets are filtered by verifying that the source and target packets' keys match [7]. However, this method requires routers support and cooperation, so the update of the filtering rules is more difficult, scalability is poor, not suitable for cloud computing environment which flow is large. In addition, there is a DDoS attacks flow recognition and traceback method based on entropy change, which runs as a plug-in in the router, so there is no need to change the hardware and software environment of the router [8]. However, this method can recognize an attack only when the strength of the attack flow is much higher than the normal flow.

At present, most of the IP traceback methods are aimed at high speed DoS attacks [9], such as deterministic packets traceback method [10], traceback based on entropy evolution [11] and traceback method based on ICMP message transfer [12, 13] etc. However, there is relatively little research on single packet traceback technology for DDoS attacks.

A single packet traceback method based on packet feature extraction [14], the core of which is packet data feature extraction method. This method achieved automatic traceback. However, the packet memory occupied by the characteristic information is very large, and the cost of traceback processing is extremely high, it may construct the wrong paths of attacks, the traceback accuracy is low.

Single packet traceback based on packet abstract [15], the core of which is data compression algorithm. To a certain degree, this method reduces the storage overhead, but does not improve the traceback of low accuracy and high cost etc. In addition, it needs to send a large amount of request message during paths reconstruction, which further deteriorates the victim network.

Single packet traceback method based on router marking [16]. The core is the router re-identification algorithm, sign space coding strategy and algorithm of jumping path reconstruction, compared with the method of single packet traceback based on packet abstract, This method reduces traceback storage overhead to 1/3 of IP packet forwarding volume and the paths reconstruction time is reduced to half. However, with the increase of attack bandwidth, this method still does not get better improvement in terms of storage overhead, traceback overhead and accuracy.

Single package traceback method based on interface mark [17], this method requires only 320 KB of storage resources, and traceback accuracy up to 100%. however, it needs to be deployed on the entire network before it can operate normally, in addition, only one network device can be connected to each router interface in this system, which is obviously unreasonable in practical applications.

Single packet traceback method based on path marking [18], compared with the above methods, this method has the advantages of small memory overhead, short path reconstruction time, incremental deployment and easy to implement. but, it requires a larger traceback overhead, higher misdiagnosis rate and omissive judgement rate, and then influence the traceback accuracy.

Through the analysis of the above methods, early warning mechanism is first established, using flow entropy to recognize DDoS attacks flow, establishing traceback marks on the traceback routers based on the MPLS principle, tracebacking by reconstruct DDoS attacks paths, and the use of network probe to establish traceback tables, estimate the load of traceback devices and so on to improve the processing speed and traceback accuracy of traceback routers.

3 Early Warning Mechanism

The detection of DDoS attacks needs to be done by each router, so we use the Chord algorithm to organize them together to form a Chord ring. Hash the address of the routers and the address of the target servers, get the mapping values, all mapped in the Chord ring.

Each routing node in the traceback paths needs to undertake the task of DDoS attacks detection while forwarding data. The control node is set up, summarize and analyzed the message sent by the detection nodes, and respond to the attacks. The DDoS attacks detection mechanism structure shown in Fig. 1.

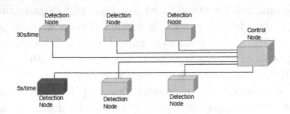

Fig. 1. DDoS attacks detection mechanism

(1) The whole idea of early warning mechanism

In this system, all nodes have two frequencies, detected once in 30 s and once in 5 s. In order to reduce the burden on the system caused by the data collection process, the initial detection frequency of the nodes is 30 s, use the method of flow entropy to detect the data flow, if a detection node detects an abnormal data flow suspected of being the DDoS attacks, it changes the detection interval to 5 s (in order to complete DDoS attacks detection and obtain attacks information in the shortest time) and send broadcast message to other detection nodes, the detection nodes that received the broadcast message also changed the interval to 5 s. The nodes that received the broadcast message do not detect the DDoS attacks within 30 s at the frequency of 5 s, indicating that has not been attacked and the frequency is changed back to 30 s.

In addition, the nodes that discover the DDoS attacks also need to send their attacks information to the control node. As the brief increase in network flow over certain periods of time, in order to avoid misdiagnosis, the control node receives the attacks information from the same node for three consecutive times, it can be determined that the node is subjected to the DDoS attacks and the control node sends the attacks information to the system administrators by mail for handling.

(2) Attack flow recognize

In order to recognize DDoS attacks in the low attack strength, flow entropy is used in early warning mechanism to recognize attack flow.

The following definitions are given:

Data flow f represents a set of packets with the same IP address and destination ports, cEntr represents the load entropy of data packets, fEntr represents the flow entropy, and sEntr represents the summation entropy.

$$sEntr = cEntr + fEntr$$

sEntr$^-$ represents the sEntr value without the attack, and sEntr$^+$ represents the sEntr value with the attack.

Let sEntr$^-$ be the average value of C, standard deviation be θ, since the number and size of network flows in a certain time interval are relatively stable (cloud computing centers often appear peak period of network services, making the flow changes dramatically, however, if it is divided into small time slices, then the flow changes can be considered stable), then there exists a threshold ψ such that formula (1) holds with a high probability:

$$|sEntr^- - C| \leq \psi \tag{1}$$

In order to adapt to the change of network flow, the average value of C and standard deviation θ are updated according to formula (2):

$$C[n] = \sum_{i=1}^{m} \alpha_i C[n-i], \quad \sum_{i=1}^{m} \alpha_i = 1$$
$$\theta[n] = \sum_{i=1}^{m} \beta_i \theta[n-i], \quad \sum_{i=1}^{m} \beta_i = 1 \tag{2}$$

Where C[n] represents the current average value of sEntr$^-$, C[n $-$ i] represents the average value of the i time sample nearest to the current sample, $\alpha_i (i = 1, 2, 3, \ldots, m)$ respectively represent the average values of the corresponding weight. In order to make the sampling that is short from the current moment has a greater impact on the current average value, here for any $i < j$, where $i, j \in Z$, $\alpha_i > \alpha_j$; $\theta[n]$, β_i are the same as those indicated by C[n] and α_i, respectively. If there is no DDoS attacks, then this module will observe and record the sEntr$^-$ value of flow, then stop the update until a DDoS attack is found.

If the attack flow is added to the data sampling that does not exist attack, then $sEntr^+$ will drop significantly, $sEntr^+$ changes more than $sEntr^-$, due to abnormal packets rate and load similarity is higher than normal flow, therefore, there is a threshold ψ such that formula (3) holds with a high probability:

$$|sEntr^+ - C| \geq \psi \tag{3}$$

If DDoS detection algorithm [18] proposed by H. Badis detects that the data flow contains DDoS attacks, then execute attack flow recognition and detecting the attack flow to obtain the information of its source address.

In summary, the attack flow recognition algorithm is as follows (with an attack flow):

Attack flow recognition algorithm

1. Input: average value of C, standard deviation θ, threshold ψ, set of data flow to be analyzed $(f_1, f_2, ..., f_n)$;
2. Output: attack flow source src.ip, source port information src.port.
3.   for i=1, i ≤ n, i++   For the flow f_i to be analyzed in the set, the sEntr value is
4.   sEntr.del.sEntr(F / f_i); // calculated after removing the flow information
5.   C' = update.c(C, θ, sEntr.del);
6. $sEntr^+$ =add.sEntr(F) ; // Represents the sEntr value after the join flow f_i is
7.   if (| $sEntr^+$-C' | ≥ψ) {   calculated
8.   print src.ip, src.port }   If f_i is added so that formula (3) holds, the data flow is
9.   else{   attack flow, otherwise it is normal flow, and so on,
10.   break;}   until each data flow is analyzed.
11. end for

The above algorithm does not need to mark the data packets and does not require ISP support, so it has a good adaptability and is easy to deploy.

(3) Improvement of broadcast algorithm

If the nodes detect DDoS attacks, then they will send broadcast message to other nodes, making the traceback paths full of broadcast message, the network load will be increased.

There are a limited number of node information stored in the pointer table of the detection node, which can only send broadcast message to a limited number of nodes. In order to enable all nodes in the traceback paths to receive broadcast message, the nodes that receive the message needs to continue broadcasting. Because the same node information may exist in the pointer table of each node, the same node will receive the same broadcast message sent by multiple nodes. A blocking message is added to the broadcast message to avoid the problem by limiting the range of receiving nodes.

As shown in Fig. 2, after receiving broadcast message, node S reads the node M of the item i from the pointer table, if the i + 1 item corresponding to the node N (no longer M) and the node M is between the S and the limit node L, the broadcast message is transmitted to the node M. In the next broadcast, read the pointer table i + 1 corresponding to the node N, M sends the broadcast message to node N, this prevents node N from receiving the same broadcast message from S and M.

Another case is that the node N is between S and the limit node L, as shown in Fig. 3, in order to prevent N from receiving the broadcast message from S, the limit node is changed to N. The broadcast message and the information of the limit node are then sent to the node M together. Finally read the next node in the pointer table, repeat the above operation, until the Chord ring is empty.

Fig. 2. Limit node before changing

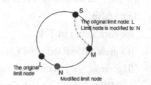

Fig. 3. Limit node after changing

4 Single Packet Traceback

First, by using the idea of forwarding equivalence classes in multi-protocol label switching networks, a set of data packets with the same destination address and routing path are collectively referred to as data equivalence class DEC, after that, the IP header field, which is not commonly used in the data packet, is used as a mark field, The mark field carries the router ID and label, the router ID is a routing identifier that replaces the redundant IP address, intermediate router ID can be stored directly into the packet's mark field, a label is an integer type identifier that distinguishes all data equivalence classes of common hosts but different origins. In addition, the router needs to establish a mapping table of the router ID and the corresponding IP address so that the routers can communicate normally, the router creates a traceback table according to the destination address, and records the marking information (including the router ID and the label) in the data packet into it.

4.1 The Process of Traceback Paths Establishment

When the IP packet arrives at the ingress router IR, first use the destination address of the IP packet to select the traceback child table, then assign the starting out label(can only be assigned by the ingress router) to the IP packet and mark [OOL, R1 ID] in it, finally it is forwarded to the downstream router R_i, R_i first assign a label to the IP packet, and then inserts the traceback mark [in label, out label, R_{i-1} ID] into the traceback child table related to the IP packet, at the same time [R_i ID, out label] marked into the IP packet, and forward it to the downstream, when the IP packet arrives at the destination host, the traceback path is established, all routing nodes then only need to traverse the traceback child table and mark the IP packet, it is unnecessary to insert traceback marks into the traceback child table.

The algorithm is as follows:

Traceback path establishment algorithm
1. Input: current router identifier d, arrived IP packet P, routing map table RMT, traceback table TT;
2. Output: the newly marked IP packet nP, the updated traceback table nTT.
3. for each P do   // For each IP packet arriving at the router
4.   if RMT conclude P.RID then
5.   use the P.destination address to get the subtable T from TT;
6.   flag:=false;
7.   for each item i in T do
8.   if i.prehopID=P.RID and i.inlabel=P.label then
9.   flag:=true;   //   Traceback marks have been established
10.   P.RID=d;   //   Mark new router IDs and labels to generate nP
11.   P.label:=i.outlabel;
12.   break;
13.   end for
14.   if flag=false then   //   Create a new traceback mark
15.   assign a new outlabel to L;
16.   generate a new item (P.RID, P.label, L) and insert it into T;
17.   P.RID:=d;
18.   P.label:=L;
19.   else
20.   P.RID:=d;
21.   P.label:= Original Out Label;
22. end for

4.2   Backtracking Process

After the attack, the IP packet is recognized by the flow entropy algorithm, then send a traceback request to the traceback manager, the traceback manager extracts the label information from the IP packets [upstream router ID, label], to determine the nearest traceback router from the victim, then [label, victim IP] is sent to upstream router R_i.

After receiving the request, R_i first selects a child table consistent with the IP address of the victim from the traceback table, and then match the out label, return the matching item. The RMT is used to convert the upstream router ID of the item into a router IP, so as to determine the upstream router R_{i-1} of R_i. Finally, send the [R_{i-1}, in label matching the item] to the traceback manager, and repeat the previous operation.

When the traceback manager finds that the in label of traceback respond is the starting out label, that is to say, the upstream router is the entrance to the attack paths, traceback process is over.

Algorithm is as follows:

Backtracking algorithm

1. Input: request (destination address D, label M), route mapping table RMT, traceback table TT;
2. Output: response (upstream router IP address ADR, label E).
3. use D to get the subtable T from TT;
4. for each item i in T do   //   By traversing, get the match item
5.   if i.outlabel=M.request then   //   Find the item matching the request label
6.   lasthopID=:i.lasthop;
7.   ADR.response =:RMT.getAddress(lasthopID);   //   Using RMT, convert router ID to
8.   E.response =:i.inlabel;   IP address
9.   return E.response;
10.   end if
11. end for
12. E.response=:NULL;   //   The traceback mark which is searched has been covered
13. return E.response;

4.3   Build Traceback Table

In order to improve the traceback table establishment rate and reduce the forwarding delay, the router needs the ability to process multiple data equivalence classes at the same time, therefore, it is possible to use the network probe (NP) with IP packet unpacking, traceback table query, and IP packet packing.

As shown in Fig. 4, there is a probe on both sides of the traceback router R_2, and each probe has a traceback table for storing path information through the corresponding interface. In other words, the access rate of the traceback table is equal to the rate of the packet arrival at the interface.

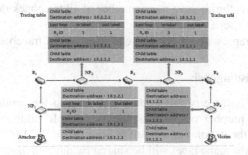

Fig. 4. Traceback network for deploying network probe

Because the NP is in accordance with the IP packet unpacking, traceback table query and IP packet packing sequential processing, and not each step requires all hardware participation, that is to say in the implementation of traceback table query, IP packet unpacking may have been free, can be used for the next IP packet processing, so that NP functions can be implemented using pipelining, reducing processing time.

4.4 Storage Resource Allocation

Due to the limited cost, ISP can provide limited resources and the number of traceback paths received by each interface of the router are different, which makes the load of the network probe unbalanced. If the traditional method of average allocation of resources is adopted, it will inevitably lead to a shortage of resources in the nodes with high load and the problem of the idle resources of the nodes with low load. In order to solve this problem, a resource estimation method can be used to allocate resources reasonably.

The method of resource estimation is as follows:

n is the total amount of storage resources that the ISP can provide, r is the number of traceback paths carried by each traceback device NP_i, and R is the traceback paths carried by the all links.

$$M(NP_i) = \frac{r}{R}$$

NP_i storage capacity that should be configured:

$$S(NP_i) = n \times M(NP_i)$$

If the traceback system has been deployed throughout the network, by introducing the node centrality theory of complex networks, then $M(NP_i)$ can be calculated as follows:

$$M(NP_i) = \frac{\sum\limits_{s \in \Omega user} \sum\limits_{t \in \Omega user} g_{NP_i}(s,t)}{\sum\limits_{NP_i \in \Omega NP} \sum\limits_{s \in \Omega user} \sum\limits_{t \in \Omega user} g_{NP_i}(s,t)}$$

$g_{NP_i}(s,t)$ represents the shortest route number of all traceback devices NP_i from the end user s to the end user t.

ΩNP and $\Omega user$ represents of NP and end user sets in traceback network.

4.5 Traceback Misdiagnosis

In this method, the shortage of label space will lead to the production of traceback misdiagnosis. If the number of paths of the victim's IP address as the destination address is more than the maximum amount of $|Z| = 2^{18} = 262144$ that can be borne by the label space, then the same label will be shared by multiple paths, resulting in errors in traceback marks.

In the ideal case of allocating all the labels to the attack paths, this method can construct 2^{18} attack paths with zero misdiagnosis rate. Only the number of attack paths is over 2^{18}, it may be misdiagnosis, however, such a large scale DDoS attacks is very rare, so this method can be traceback of the attack more accurately.

5   Simulation Experiment

Experimental setup: the network model is established using the network simulation tool OMNet ++ [19], and the attack scene is simulated by the IP network simulation INET and the DoS attacks simulation tool ReaSE [20].

Operating environment: Intel 2.50 GHz Core i5-3210 M CPU, 4 GB memory, Windows 7.

5.1   Attack Flow Recognize Experiment

The purpose of the experiment is to test the effectiveness of the attack flow recognition method.

(1) Poisson distribution and normal distribution data flow simulation experiment

In the pattern of network flow, Poisson distribution and normal distribution data flow are the most common, therefore, this experiment simulates these two data flow, observe the trend of sEntr without attacks when normal flow increases. First set the simulation flow for 5 min, the data packet transmission rate is 100 p/s, the time window is set to 3 s. As shown in Fig. 5:

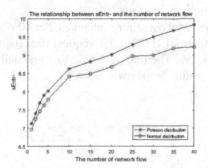

Fig. 5. The relationship between sEntr⁻ and the number of network flow

As the number of network flows increases, the overall trend of sEntr- rises, indicating that the value of sEntr⁻ is relatively stable in a relatively short period of time, in addition, this experiment simulated two kinds of flow patterns, and the changes of sEntr⁻ in both modes were stable, which showed that the flow recognition method described in this paper could recognize different distributed flow well.

(2) sEntr⁻ stability experiment when the flow fluctuates greatly

The purpose of this experiment is to verify the stability of sEntr⁻ when the flow rate fluctuates greatly. The flow sending rate is 100 p/s, two kinds of flow rate of standard deviation 25 p/s and 50 p/s are set up respectively. The experimental results shown in Fig. 6:

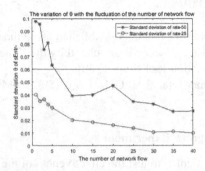

Fig. 6. The variation of θ with the fluctuation of the number of network flow

sEntr⁻ varies greatly at the beginning, but as the number of the network flow increases, the value of sEntr⁻ becomes gradually stable and the fluctuation range becomes smaller, indicating that when the variation of flow rate is large, the value of sEntr⁻ can be maintained in a more stable state.

Since the stable sEntr⁻ fluctuation range is within 0.06, we can specify a threshold $\psi = 0.06$ so that the DDoS attacks flow can be better recognized.

(3) Effect of attack strength on sEntr⁺

Add DDoS attack flow, analyze sEntr⁺ changes. Set 40 normal flow and an attack flow of a continuous sending of HTTP GET request packets, the rate of normal flow remains unchanged at 100 p/s. The rate of attack flow gradually increased from 0 to 7 times. The experimental results are shown in Fig. 7:

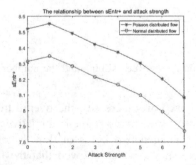

Fig. 7. The relationship between sEntr⁺ and attack strength

At first, sEntr$^+$ showed an upward trend due to the fact that the attack strength was so small that the overall distribution became disorganized. With the increasing attack strength, exceeds the normal flow rate, sEntr$^+$ began to decline, as can be seen from the above figure, if the threshold ψ is set to 0.06, the DDoS attack flow can be recognized when the attack flow strength is nearly 2 times normal flow.

5.2 Single Packet Traceback Experiment

Set the attacker host IP packets sending rate of 1 Kpps, the normal user packets sending rate in line with the normal distribution N (20 pps, 30 pps), each network probe packet processing rate is the same.

(1) Effect of attack time on the probabilities of traceback records

In order to verify the method described in this paper as the attack time goes by, the number of new traceback marks gradually reduced, by collecting the number of IP packets forwarded by the routers during each period of time and the number of traceback marks by the routers, calculate the ratio of the traceback marks number by the routers to the traceback marks number in the entire network.

As shown in Fig. 8, it is compared to a single packet traceback method based on packet abstract and router marks. At first, due to the fact that the attack path has not been established, the probability of traceback records of this method is higher than that of other methods. After the establishment of the attack paths, the recording probability will continue to decrease. After 3.5 s, the probability of traceback records of this method is lower than that based on routing marks, and has been reduced to 6%, far lower than other methods. Therefore, after the establishment of the traceback paths, the method in this paper only needs to execute the query operation, which improves the traceback and forwarding speed, the overhead is reduced.

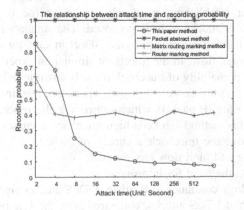

Fig. 8. The relationship between attack time and recording probability

(2) Effect of the number of attacks on the traceback accuracy

The purpose of this experiment is to verify that the traceback accuracy of this method remains high as the number of attacks increases. The attack time is set to 60 s.

As shown in Fig. 9, with the increase of the number of attacks, the traceback accuracy of other methods is reduced in varying degrees and is unstable. When the attacks ratio is over 75%, the traceback accuracy based on the packet abstract method is reduced to 0, the reason is that the attack flow rate is far greater than the normal packets sending volume, but the method of this paper has been able to maintain a high traceback accuracy, compared to other methods, this method can improve the traceback accuracy of 30%, so this method can adapt to the situation of larger attacks and ensure high traceback accuracy, which is suitable for large scale cloud computing and high flow environment.

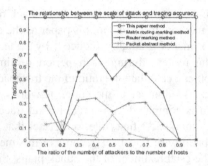

Fig. 9. The relationship between the scale of attack and traceback accuracy

6   Conclusion

In this paper, the early warning mechanism is established, the flow entropy is used to recognize the attack flow. A traceback method for the switching path generation theory based on MPLS that establishing traceback marks on the traceable routers and reconstructing the DDoS attacks paths is proposed. The simulation experiment shows that, the flow entropy method can recognize the DDoS attack flow when the attack flow is close to 2 times normal flow. In the traceback simulation experiment, the traceback method can make the probability of traceback records down to 6%, after the traceback paths are completed, can only execute the query operation, it is unnecessary to execute the insert operation to the IP packets which improving the processing rate of the IP packets. In addition, this method can keep high traceback accuracy, compared to other methods, it can improve the traceback accuracy of 30%, which is suitable for large scale cloud computing and high flow environment.

In the future work, the need for improvement:

As hacker technology continues to escalate, DDoS attacks are gradually evolving, for example, MDoS and LDoS attacks, compared with the traditional DDoS attacks, their low attack power, will make the server to maintain a low quality of service, which is difficult to be perceived and traced by the nodes, so in the future work, the attack flow recognition accuracy and traceback accuracy must be further improved to cope with the variations of DDoS attacks.

Acknowledgements. This work is supported by the National Key R&D Program of China under Grant 2017YFB0802300.

References

1. Erl, T., Mahmood, Z., Puttini, R.: Cloud Computing Concepts, Technology and Architecture, 1st edn., pp. 14–17. Mechanical Industry Press, Beijing (2014)
2. Gupta, B.B., Badve, O.P.: Taxonomy of DoS and DDoS attacks and desirable defense mechanism in a cloud computing environment. Neural Comput. Appl. **28**, 3655–3682 (2017)
3. Mahjabin, Tasnuva, Xiao, Yang, Sun, Guang: A survey of distributed denial of service attacks, prevention, and mitigation techniques. Int. J. Distrib. Sens. Netw. **13**(12), 1–33 (2017)
4. Cloud Security Alliance. Top threats to cloud computing. https://cloudsecurityalliance.org/group/top-threat (2018). Accessed 12 Mar 2018
5. Shiaeles, S.N., Papadaki, M.: FHSD: an improved IP spoof detection method for web DDoS attacks. Comput. J. **58**(4), 892–903 (2015)
6. Lee, Y.J., Baik, N.K., Kim, C., Yang, C.N.: Study of detection method for spoofed IP against DDoS attacks. Pers. Ubiquit. Comput. **22**(1), 35–44 (2018)
7. Xu, M.F., Li, X.H., Liu, H., Zhong, C., Ma, J.F.: Intrusion detection scheme based on semi supervised learning and information gain rate. Comput. Res. Dev. **54**(10), 2255–2267 (2017)
8. Wang, L.N., Tan, C., Yu, R.W., Yin, Z.G.: Malware detection against data leakage. J. Comput. Res. Dev. **54**(7), 1537–1548 (2017)
9. Li, H.W., Wu, J.Y., Cui, J.: A study of distributed denial of service attacks and IP traceback technology. Wireless Commun. Technol. **25**(2), 50–53 (2016)
10. Foroushani, V.A., Zincir, H.A.: Deterministic and authenticated flow marking for IP traceback. In: Proceedings of the 27th International Conference on Advanced Information Networking and Applications, pp. 397–404. IEEE, Barcelona (2013)
11. Singh, K.J., Thongam, K.: Entropy-based application layer DDoS attack detection using artificial neural networks. Entropy **18**(10), 412–425 (2016)
12. Saurabh, S., Sairam, A.S.: ICMP based on IP traceback with negligible overhead for highly distributed reflector attacks using bloom filters. Comput. Commun. **42**(2), 60–69 (2014)
13. Sun, S.X.: DDoS Attacks Traceability and Detection Methods. Liaoning University (2016)
14. Shuai, C.Y., Ouyang, X.: P-CCBFF: a lightweight cooperative detection and traceback framework of DDoS/DoS attacks. J. Internet Technol. **18**(5), 1147–1158 (2017)
15. Jeong, E., Lee, B.K.: An IP traceback protocol using a compressed hash table, a sinkhole router and data mining based on network forensics against network attacks. Future Gener. Comput. Syst. **33**(1), 42–52 (2014)
16. Nur, A.Y., Tozal, M.E.: Record route IP traceback: combating DoS attacks and the variants. Comput. Secur. **72**(1), 13–25 (2018)
17. Kamaldeep, Malik, M.: Implementation of single-packet hybrid IP traceback for IPv4 and IPv6 networks. IET Inf. Secur. **12**(1), 1–6 (2018)
18. Lu, N., Wang, Y.L., Su, S., Yang, F.C.: A novel path based on approach for single packet IP traceback. Secur. Commun. Netw. **7**(2), 309–321 (2013)
19. Zhao, Y.L., Zhang, J.: OMNeT++ and Network Simulation, 1st edn. People's Posts and Telecommunications Press, Beijing (2012)
20. Badis, H., Doyen, G.: A collaborative approach for a source based on detection of botclouds. In: Proceedings of the 2015 IFIP/IEEE International Symposium on Integrated Network Management, pp. 906–909. IEEE, Piscataway (2015)

Design and Application of Agricultural Product Traceability Management Platform

Bangguo Li, Pingzeng Liu$^{(\boxtimes)}$, Xiaotong Wu, Xue Wang,
and Rui Zhao

Shandong Agricultural University, Tai'an 271018, China
lpz8565@126.com

Abstract. Food traceability as an effective means to control food quality and safety has attracted increasing attention at home and abroad. In view of the construction requirements of the traceability system for different enterprises in China, in order to build a standardized Binzhou government traceability management platform, multiple traceability systems are integrated on the platform for unified management services, and the "Platform + System" application mode is constructed. Platform functions include retrospective tracing, system management, standard authentication, information service, traceability monitoring and other functions. The platform provides an effective way for the retrospective management construction of Binzhou's regulatory authorities and realizes the demonstration application of the integrated platform.

Keywords: Traceability management · Platform model
Government regulation

1 Introduction

With the continuous improvement of people's awareness of food safety, traceability system has become the popular direction of enterprise construction in recent years [6]. Through data collection and database management, it has an effective information record for every link of the whole circulation that includes product production, processing, testing, packaging, and transportation distribution [1]. The use of traceability system can reduce the risk of food quality, achieve the source of food, improve the recall efficiency of products and provide a strong guarantee for food safety [2–5].

Since the country proposed to implement the traceability system of agricultural products quality and safety, different regions and functional departments are carrying out quality traceability, then more and more local retrospective system and enterprise traceability system construction appears Due to the different quantitative basis of a traceability system, traceability standards, traceability function and traceability technology are different. The system cannot be compatible with each other, which makes it difficult to share information. These problems have weakened their ability greatly to provide information sources for government regulation.

This paper puts forward a solution of the municipal agricultural products traceability management platform, which can not only meet the construction of enterprise traceability system but also facilitate the government to manage different areas and

© Springer Nature Switzerland AG 2018
X. Sun et al. (Eds.): ICCCS 2018, LNCS 11064, pp. 684–693, 2018.
https://doi.org/10.1007/978-3-030-00009-7_61

different types of a traceability system. The construction of the platform can provide market dynamic, data analysis, market forecast, standard certification and other service modules for enterprises and government, and also provide more reliable support and guarantee for the quality and safety traceability of agricultural products.

2 Current Situation and Problems

2.1 The Construction of the Traceability System Is Repeated and Redundant

At present, agricultural products occupy a large market share in China, and the construction of quality and safety traceability system of agricultural products shows diversity. For example, the traceability system from various ministries such as the quality tracing network of planting products in Ministry of Agriculture, the national food safety traceability platform of NDRC and the ministry of Commerce's traceability system for meat and vegetables circulation; The Provincial Agricultural Committee platform such as the agricultural products quality and safety traceability management platform, the standard garden horticultural crops quality and safety traceability platform and the vegetable products quality and safety traceability platform in Jiangsu; The Agricultural committees of all levels and agricultural committees at county level (District) such as the agricultural products quality and safety supervision and management of geographic information platform and the meat and vegetables circulation platform and mobile supervision platform for quality and safety of agricultural products of Changzhou city [7].

These traceability systems are incompatible with each other and the overall operation efficiency of it is low, which causes the waste of information resources and easy to form "Information Island". It is not only difficult for consumers to search for traceability after the purchase of agricultural products, but also to increase the difficulty of supervision.

2.2 The Function Construction of the Platform Is Imperfect

With the development of market traceability system, consumers pay more attention to the information of agricultural products in the process of production and circulation. The increase of consumers' recognition degree of traceability products makes enterprises stricter in the control of information in the production process, and the requirements for the construction of the traceability system platform are more stringent [8]. At present, there is a large number of local retrospective platforms, but there is no emphasis on the function of management service in platform construction, and it also doesn't reflect the advantages and characteristics of retroactive platform integration.

2.3   The Construction Cost of the System Is High and the Government Cannot Participate Effectively

The promotion and application of the traceability management system of agricultural products is not only beneficial to the enterprises to improve the statistics and control of agricultural products production, processing, transportation and sales, to meet the information display of the key links of agricultural products, so that consumers can buy, but also for the relevant government departments to provide appropriate agricultural reference information data in order to allow the government to properly control the market economy and formulate corresponding economic policies. The construction, operation, and maintenance of agricultural product traceability system need a certain amount of manpower and material resources to support, so it is difficult for enterprises to obtain direct economic benefits from the retrospective product in the early stage of the construction of the retroactive system. Equipment upgrades, human input information, and other procedures increased costs, resulting in the use of enterprises to reduce the enthusiasm of the system. Equipment upgrades, human information input, and other procedures make the cost of enterprises increased, resulting in the use of the system to reduce enthusiasm. The construction of enterprise traceability system is not standard, and some enterprises give up the traceability system because of the high registration cost, which makes it difficult for the government to coordinate management.

2.4   The Low Level of Agricultural Organization Limits the Degree of Penetration of the Retroactive System

At present, the main models of agricultural production and management in China are mainly retail farmers, large farmers, cooperatives and other major situations, and large agricultural production enterprises are less distributed in China. So this leads to the low level of farmers' participation in agricultural production, the lacking of ability to operate computers and advanced equipment, the weak understanding of agricultural products traceability knowledge and information conversion ability, the low level scale of agricultural production, the inadequate guarantee of the quality of agricultural production supervision and the less information circulation between households and other issues. These problems seriously restrict the popularization and application of agricultural products quality and safety traceability in the agricultural production process.

3   Overall Design

3.1   The Significance of Constructing Platform

The construction of the quality and safety traceability management platform of agricultural products is based on the actual situation of the agricultural product retrospective management. We select the SOA analysis method which is process-oriented and integrated that combined with the "Platform + System" framework model to achieve [9]. The SOA architecture is a service-oriented architecture and a component model that links the service component of the application through interfaces and convention protocols. This interface is defined in a neutral way, independent of programming languages, operating systems, and hardware devices. Through interfaces, information can interact in a universal and unified way. By confirming the key starting point and the effective information point of the retroactive platform, the model can realize the effective management and maintenance of all the local retrospective enterprises by the government regulators, the code expansion and the interface development, so that it can track the data with the provincial and national level docking effectively and explore a suitable management of regional traceability system platform development direction [10].

3.2 Integrated Service

The construction of agricultural products quality and safety traceability platform in Binzhou City is committed to building a traceability system based on the Binzhou government as the core and combine the characteristic industries in Binzhou to achieve integrated management services. The construction of traceability platform based on the construction of "Platform + System" ideas, data resources covering various agricultural subsystems, including fruit and vegetable traceability system, traceability system of grain and oil, agricultural and sideline products traceability system, traceability system of livestock and poultry, aquatic product traceability system, forest product traceability system of six subsystems, platform construction and combined with the characteristics of the local agricultural products the development, based on the construction of the full coverage of agricultural products traceability system, to achieve the promotion of characteristic agricultural products in the construction of a series of advantages, such as Zhanhua jujube, Sanhe Lake leek, Yangxin pear and other characteristics of traceability system. For example, fruit and vegetable traceability system including the characteristics of Binzhou jujube traceability system, leek traceability system, traceability system, traceability system of apple pear and so on, the traceability system of different enterprise users, such as the Zhanhua Institute of Zhanhua jujube traceability system, traceability system of cooperatives jujube.

On the one hand is to improve the level of traceability management platform, the construction of many provincial and municipal platform to the enterprise as the main object, displayed on the system is arranged between the various enterprises, the Binzhou back platform construction through the reasonable distribution, with industry-driven enterprise, outstanding industrial structure adjustment. Through all kinds of traceability system of demonstrative promotion, the construction of traceability system covering the entire industry, thus promoting the traceability of scale expansion of Binzhou City, so the city's traceability system added to the platform management, realize the true sense of the category of traceability management, ensure the safety of consumers.

3.3 System Architecture

The Enterprise traceability management system uses GS1 coding to design traceability chain coding system for agricultural products [11]. By means of scanning the barcode on the product label, the system can obtain the data coding information of each node. The code encodes the participants, trade products, logistics orders, location, assets and service relationships of the system supply chain, thus solving the problem that information coding is not unique in the supply chain [12]. Besides, the coding has the global unity and scalability, which provides a reliable guarantee for data docking between platform and platform. The platform can not only meet the supervision department daily management and traceability of the application but also can realize five kinds of traceability system that include the computer query, SMS query, two-dimensional code query, telephone inquiry and touch screen query. It provides more efficient service to consumers and managers.

At the same time, The platform also controls the whole from four aspects: information acquisition, information processing, information service and information display. Information acquisition level is mainly to obtain the effective data of each block of each system, including data collection, key link data, production input and price benefit data, which provides data support for the overall analysis of the platform. The information processing level mainly through hand-held gun sweep code or two-dimensional code scanning to achieve the link between traceability code data transfer and the data back to the digital information interaction uses digital information technology to achieve quality and safety traceability management platform for information research and development. The information service layer provides the information service guarantee for the enterprise and the consumer through the development policy, the market dynamics, the analysis report, the agricultural guidance, the supply side information, the price quotation and so on. Consulting services and demand linkages enable producers and consumers to implement information interaction functions. The information display mainly through five query methods to facilitate consumers and regulators to query traceability related information. The four-layer frame diagram of the platform is shown as illustrated (Fig. 1).

3.4 The Design of System Function

The construction of the municipal traceability platform is different from the composition of the general enterprise traceability system. Enterprise traceability system is user-oriented enterprise, is through the analysis of enterprise internal supply chain, and establish traceability management system for the needs of the enterprise, the main function of the system is to realize the enterprise product traceability, the traceability system to improve the enterprise internal management and product quality and safety. Binzhou city agricultural product quality safety traceability platform for the operation of the object is Binzhou municipal government management, through the construction of a docking platform can realize the traceability system and platform, model to build "platform - multiple system", and the traceability system of Binzhou City, also through the construction of government macro-control of the municipal traceability system administrator the origin of the platform. By analyzing the data of agriculture, forestry, animal husbandry and fishery in every county of Binzhou City, we can provide accurate data for the whole analysis and location of Binzhou agricultural products and provide data support for the next development policy and decision.

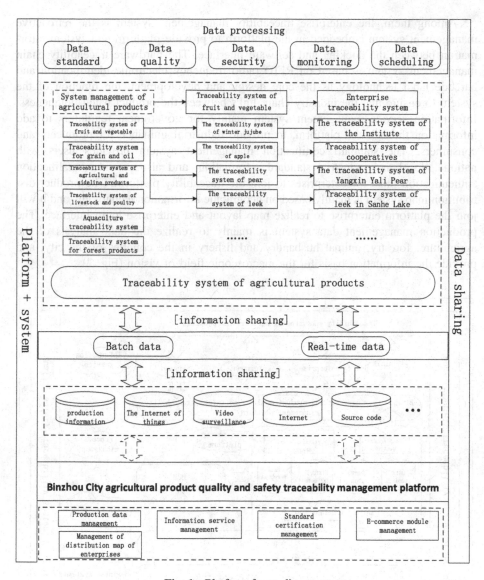

Fig. 1. Platform frame diagram

The management system of agricultural product quality and safety traceability includes agricultural product management subsystem, enterprise traceability management system, hardware traceability chain management system, information service management system, standard authentication management system, product distribution map system and production management data system. According to the classification standards of agricultural products by the Ministry of agriculture, the traceability system is divided into six types: fruits and vegetables, grain and oil, forestry, livestock, aquatic products and agricultural and sideline products.

Among them, the enterprise traceability management system is the retroactive management system embedded in the platform to provide platform and system information between the docking and software interface. The hardware traceability chain management system is based on RFID radio frequency electronic identification and barcode label technology as the core design and development, the function of the system to ensure that the industry chain links between the product batch uniqueness. Information service management system mainly for government regulators to add information through the platform, to provide industrial guidance for producers and consumers. The standard certification management system provides users with national, local and industrial standard information, and also provides qualification authentication links for enterprises to join the traceability platform. The product distribution map system is mainly based on geographic information technology, and it will join the platform enterprise to realize map layout and enterprise login interface. The production management data system is mainly to realize the data analysis of the agriculture, forestry, animal husbandry and fishery in the counties of the city, and provide the information basis for the macroscopic field of vision (Fig. 2).

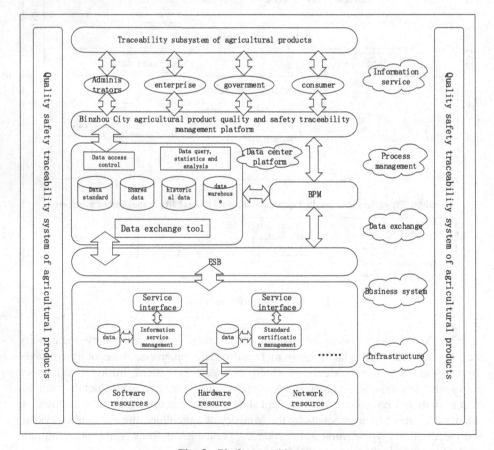

Fig. 2. Platform architecture

4 System Implementation

The system uses MyEclipse 10, MySQL, and Chrome browser as development tools based on the above platform traceability model. Based on Browser/Server (Browser/server) network structure model and SSH as the core web applications open source framework, we use the most general and best JAVA language as the foundation to develop the platform and the system to combine the whole industry chain process and the platform function of the enterprise agricultural product system. The producers and consumers can realize the comprehensive information about the market information and other relevant information through the platform. So that producers and consumers not only can achieve a comprehensive grasp of agricultural products traceability information but also through the platform to achieve a timely understanding of market information and other related information.

The construction of this project is based on the advantages of agricultural resources in Binzhou City, Focus on the development of local agricultural products with better characteristics through the construction of large-scale and intensive advantages. We will further expand the scale and output value, improve the visibility of regional products and build characteristics of agricultural products base. After the implementation of the project, while increasing the supply of high-quality agricultural products at the same time, it will have a positive impact in guiding farmers to learn science and technology, changing the traditional cultivation, farming methods, promoting agricultural restructuring, increasing farmers' income, improving the overall quality and competitiveness of agriculture and other aspect (Fig. 3).

Fig. 3. Platform interface

5 Conclusion

Takes Binzhou city agricultural products as an example:

(1) Analyzes the modeling process of the requirements definition of the Binzhou City retrospective platform through SOA and realizes the establishment of a "Platform + System" retrospective platform management model and analyzes the shortcomings of the current retrospective platform. The optimization of the platform model was optimized, and the respective functions of producer-consumer regulators were effectively integrated, and the Binzhou City agricultural product quality safety traceability management platform was established.

(2) The application of a number of companies in Binzhou City shows that the use of the platform can standardize the company's production level, improve the company's management capabilities, and optimize the product's entire industrial chain process to meet consumers' reliable understanding of the entire process of product information. And the government provides a platform for companies to build brands to increase product added value and increase revenue.

Acknowledgements. This work was financially supported by The Yellow River Delta (Binzhou) national agricultural science and Technology Park.

References

1. Yang, T.-H., Chu, B.-J.: "From farm to table" study on control system of food safety. Food Sci. **26**(3), 264–268 (2005). (in Chinese)
2. Dalvit, C., Marchi, M.D., Cassandro, M.: Genetic traceability of livestock products: a review. Meat Sci. **77**(4), 437–449 (2007)
3. Shanahan, C., Kernan, B., Ayalew, G.: A framework for beef traceability from farm to slaughter using global standards: an Irish perspective. Comput. Electron. Agric. **66**(1), 62–69 (2009)
4. Bevilacqua, M., Ciarapica, F.E., Giacchetta, G.: Business process reengineering of a supply chain and a traceability system: a case study. J. Food Eng. **93**(1), 13–22 (2009)
5. Ma, Y., Lin, J., Li, C.: Study on traceability system status information. Sci. Technol. Inf. **27**, 158 (2011) (in Chinese)
6. Yang, X.-T., Qian, J.-P., Sun, C.-H.: Research progress on key technologies of agricultural products and food quality and safety traceability system. Trans. Chin. Soc. Agric. Mach. **45**(11), 212–222 (2014). (in Chinese)
7. Qian, J.-P., Liu, X.-X., Yang, X.-T.: Establishment of traceability system traceability granularity evaluation index system. Trans. Chin. Soc. Agric. Eng. **1**, 98–104 (2014). (in Chinese)
8. Ma, H.-J.: Research and Implementation of the Vegetable Quality and Safety Traceability System Based on Supply Chain. Shandong Agricultural University (2014) (in Chinese)
9. Tounsi, I., Kacem, M.H., Kacem, A.H.: Transformation of compound SOA design patterns. Procedia Comput. Sci. **109**, 408–415 (2017)

10. Scheer, A.-W., Nüttgens, M.: ARIS Architecture and Reference Models for Business Process Management. In: van der Aalst, W., Desel, J., Oberweis, A. (eds.) Business Process Management. LNCS, vol. 1806, pp. 376–389. Springer, Heidelberg (2000). https://doi.org/10.1007/3-540-45594-9_24

11. Council U C.: Global Trade Item Number (2015)

12. Farmer, J.W., Farmer, J.G., Farmer, C.W.: Systems for accessing information related to an order of commodity: US, US 8407103 B2 (2013)

Design and Implementation of the Product Quality Traceability System for Winter Jujube

Bangguo Li, Pingzeng Liu$^{(\boxtimes)}$, Xiaotong Wu, and Jianyong Zhang

Shandong Agricultural University, Tai'an 271018, China
lpz8565@126.com

Abstract. In order to solve the industrial chain problem of winter jujube and improve the product quality and safety of winter jujube, proposes a traceability scheme based on the whole industry chain of winter jujube. Through the use of GS1 traceability coding, building a traceability information flow model, multiple identifications of information, modern database management and other technologies, the development of winter jujube product quality traceability system. The use of the system has improved the transparency of the production of winter jujube and provided an effective management tool for enterprises and governments. At present, it has been applied to the base of Zhanhua winter jujube research institute in Binzhou, China.

Keywords: Traceability system · Information flow model
Traceability technology

1 Introduction

The quality and safety of agricultural products are related to public health and the development of agricultural industry, which is an important part of the modernization of agriculture. With the improvement of living standards, people's consumption concept has changed from eating well to eating enough to eat healthily. With the increasing awareness of food safety, the problem of food quality and safety has attracted more and more attention from all sectors of society. Winter jujube is a significant source of Binzhou leading industry and farmers' income increase. The cultivation area and yield are the first in the National City [1]. But in recent years, the winter jujube industry in China has been declining. The quality of the winter jujube is not guaranteed [13]. With the increase of winter jujube consumption space, scattered issues, various aspects of jujube industry chain product information, product identification difficult no more important. At the same time, jujube quality and safety problems led to frequent consumers cannot really trust the product, the product problems are very difficult to recover the responsibility, which will affect the development of the winter jujube industry. Therefore, it is urgent to set up a traceability system that can cover the whole industry chain, so as to promote the transparency of production information, ensuring product quality and safety, and improve the competitiveness of agricultural products market.

Although the construction of traceability system is flourishing in recent years, some problems are still highlighted in the process of construction. The granularity of information in the traceability system is larger, neither complete nor rich, consumers

X. Sun et al. (Eds.): ICCCS 2018, LNCS 11064, pp. 694–705, 2018.
https://doi.org/10.1007/978-3-030-00009-7_62

are unable to understand the safety and quality of food; Lack of regulation of the truth and validity of information and the inability to truly "valid" food information traceability [9]; The scope of product traceability is relatively narrow, only for the product of the internal aspects of food information traceability, while ignoring the entire industry chain of information traceability [10]. To this end, many countries have asked for the establishment of traceability system based on the industrial chain of agricultural products and formulated relevant laws, which will lead the traceability system into the logistics system of agricultural products in the form of regulations. For example, Aung and Chang point out a traceability system for the design of the food supply chain by providing a complete trace of food information to ensure the quality and safety of the food [3]. Porto implements the traceability of the supply chain, the development of the external traceability and internal traceability system [2]. Regattieri points out that by integrating RFID technology into traceability system, enterprises can track products accurately along the industrial chain, and recall quickly if necessary [4]. Such as the traceability system of the developed aquaculture supply chain by Parreñomarchante [5] and Mainetti development based on RFID vegetable traceability system [6] and so on. To facilitate food information acquisition and quality supervision, Wang developed a food traceability system based on Google Zxing QR code [7]. The above research shows that the traceability system based on the industrial chain can effectively improve the quality and safety of agricultural products and promote the development of agricultural products industry.

Aiming at some existing problems, according to the demand of winter jujube enterprises in Binzhou, we constructed the information flow model based on winter jujube and designed the traceability system of winter jujube product quality. The system uses GS1 coding, radio frequency identification, one dimension code and QR code fusion, Internet of things technology, etc. Consumers can get the whole industry chain traceability information from the pre-production, planting, and sale to consumers through scanning the QR code or querying the system by the packaging source. This study provides product quality and safety guarantee for consumers to purchase winter jujube, and for enterprises to achieve scientific management and promote traceability of jujube products and e-commerce integration has played an exemplary role.

2 Demand

According to the actual requirements of Zhanhua winter jujube management, the analysis of decisive factors of jujube production, circulation and sales process affect the quality and safety of agricultural products and control points, to achieve traceability code identification, traceability information, multi-channel access to key industry chain of Zhanhua winter jujube traceability management, key technical problems from source information query, To establish the quality traceability system for the quality of winter jujube products for government, enterprises and consumers. Therefore, consider the following three aspects.

2.1   Enterprise Management

As the user of the traceability system, the traceability system can be used as an effective means to improve the level of the enterprise image. On the premise of ensuring the quality and safety of the winter jujube products, it will bring additional benefits to the enterprise by creating the trace of the winter jujube. On the premise of ensuring the quality and safety of the winter jujube products, it will bring additional benefits to the enterprise by creating the trace of the winter jujube. Optimize business management through traceability systems, we can input information such as planting information, testing information, sorting information, warehousing information transportation information and sales information conveniently and quickly, and achieve information dissemination and flow, to achieve the traceability management of the whole industrial chain of winter jujube.

2.2   Government Supervision

Government agencies as the information product traceability process supervisor, need all the key nodes of jujube production monitoring, supervision by video, pictures, key point description and other multimedia information, and through the winter jujube traceability system will test information provided to consumers, consumers are convinced that the quality and safety of products, to buy the rest assured.

2.3   Consumer Inquiries

The Consumer is a final buyer of the product, through the quality tracing system of winter jujube products, we can understand the traceability information of purchase products in a variety of ways, and get the accurate information in all links of winter jujube supply chain quickly and conveniently.

3   Design of Traceability Information Flow Model

Winter jujube traceability system from the perspective of enterprise management needs, the winter jujube production process of whole industry chain circulation system construction basis, through the realization of winter jujube industry base management, plant management, test management, sort management, warehouse management, distribution management, management service functions, determine the key points of information between the various modules, to achieve effective record and clear the main responsibility for implementation, ensure the reliability of each link in the chain of information flow continuity. The flow model diagram is designed as follows: W inter jujube traceability system from the perspective of enterprise management needs, the winter jujube production process of whole industry chain circulation system construction basis, through the realization of jujube industry base management, plant management, test management, sort management, warehouse management, distribution management, management service functions, determine the key points of information between the various modules, to achieve effective record and clear the main responsibility for implementation, ensure the reliability of each link in the chain of information flow continuity. The flow model diagram is designed as follows (Fig. 1):

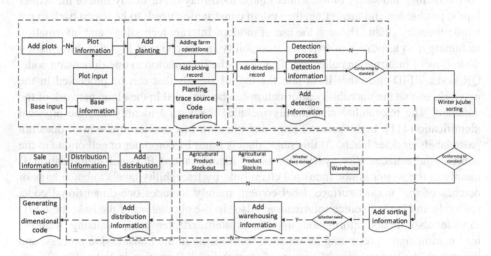

Fig. 1. Industrial chain process model of winter jujube

Base management mainly includes the basic management of the information of various bases by enterprises or farmers, mainly including the management of the base and the management of various plots. The main achievement of planting management is to record data of all planting management and farm operation during planting stage and supervise the operation of growers. The detection and management are mainly to detect and analyze the harvested winter jujube. The detection methods are divided into two kinds; one is self-examination, the other is the inspection of the quarantine technology center. After sorting out the winter jujube without any quality problems, the sorting way is classified according to the grade of winter jujube and the specification of winter jujube according to the NY/T2860-2015 issued by the Ministry of agriculture. Sometimes to meet the needs of the market, the harvested winter jujube needs to be kept fresh and stored in cold storage. In warehousing module, the winter jujube direct supply and marketing, otherwise, batch products will be added to the storage records and edited to add warehouse information according to the actual situation. A part of jujube products can achieve online sales, product sales and traceability system of data docking, the other part is ordered through the supermarkets, shopping malls and other enterprises, through the traceability system of direct recording of distribution data, finally achieved the traceability system of the whole industry chain traceability. In the distribution process, the administrator can print the QR code label of the batch product directly through the QR code printer, and consumers can scan the tracing information by mobile phone.

4 Key Point Analysis

4.1 Traceability Logo

As the quality and safety of the winter jujube food may occur in any link of the winter jujube production and marketing, the system construction needs to be traced back to the whole industry chain. Through the use of modern Internet technology and information technology, to achieve winter jujube traceability in the chain of logistics, information flow, flow of information collection. Transform the information in one-dimension code, QR code, RFID and other links into the digital signals that can be processed in the network, so that the traceability information can be included in the cloud network of the database. The traceability sign mainly includes the virtual identity and the physical identification [11]. In the prenatal stage and planting link, winter jujube itself does not paste labels or other labels. At this stage, data is input by computer or cell phone in the winter jujube traceability system for batch identification. Physical identification is mainly in the winter jujube industrial chain link, by traceability labels to batch bags or batches of the product surface, label content mainly includes one-dimensional code, QR code and tracing source information. Also, In the circulation of the link, the RFID module also inputs information into the system adapter card, realizing multiple information signs, preventing information from losing in the transmission process, and improving the transmission efficiency of traceability information in links (Fig. 2).

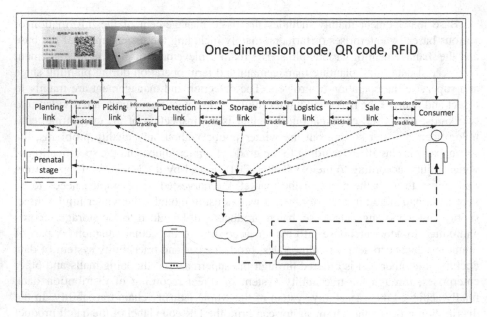

Fig. 2. Information transfer

4.2   Design of Traceability Database

The database is designed to require a reliable association of all information flows across the entire industry chain. In the design of the database, we use the traceability information flow model to design the design idea. From the antenatal, middle to postnatal, we set up the database table of key links and the composition of each staging table. The traceability code and external key table series and table information, ensure the effective storage and transmission of the information source. Below is the origin of the information flow part of the data in the information table (Fig. 3).

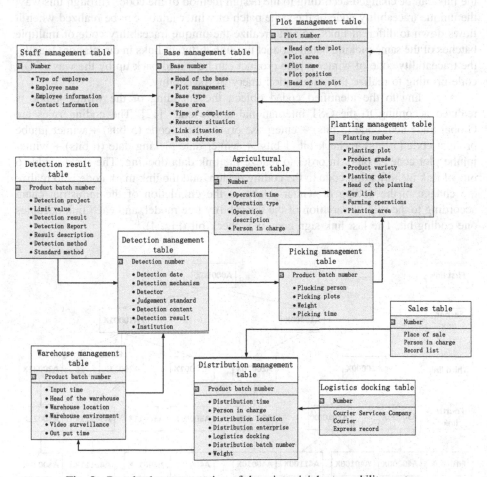

Fig. 3. Part database connection of the winter jujube traceability system

4.3   Traceability Code Design

The traceability code is the carrier of the traceability information of the winter jujube [14]. Through the analysis of the key points of the traceability of the winter jujube, the flexible industrial chain encoding for the traceability system is the key means of tracing back or tracing back to the [15]. In the face of the different business needs of the user and the enterprise, the system can finally show the scan-able QR code to the consumer through internal coding. The internal source code of the enterprise mainly solves the problem of the information flow docking between the winter jujube industry in picking, testing, warehousing, transportation and other links. In every link, the code number of the link can be changed according to the design method of the code. Through this way, the unique traceability code of the same batch of winter jujube can be realized when it flows down to different links, so as to realize the unique traceability code of multiple batches of the same picking batch product through different links in circulation. Finally, the traceability code of winter jujube product can be traced back up by the way of QR code printing to realize the information query of traceability.

According to the identified coded object, the encoding of the winter jujube is realized according to the GS1 international article code [12]. The coding rules are Global trade item code (3 bits) + enterprise organization code (5 bits) + winter jujube product code (5 bits) + check bit (1 bits) + winter date picking date (6 bits) + winter jujube plot code (5 bits). In order to realize the link data docking, The system adds 6 bits of link identification code to the coding design, and the link mark code is to realize the change of the coding of winter jujube in the circulation of the industrial chain according to the rule of variation of the traceability tree model, and each link occupies one coding bit. The last link sign code is a check bit (Fig. 4).

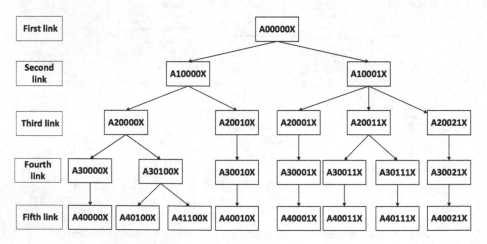

Fig. 4. Traceability code tree case diagram

The above picture is the tree model of the link identification code (6 bits) in the link between the links. The first part is the default batch picking jujube link, "A" stands for the traceability code before the link code, which will not change in the link. The first number indicates which link the product locate. The second number indicates in which batch the product is in the fifth link, the fifth number indicates in which batch the product is in the second link. The rule of change is: if the product branch occurs between the fourth ring section and the fifth link, the first node generated is 0, and then each node generates 1 on the second digit number. Similarly, the third bits indicate whether the third link to the fourth ring node produces a node branch. If the branch is added, the branch chain will add 1, and no branch will express the link's circulation with 0, and so on. The last bit check bit is used in data communication to ensure the validity of the data. Taking A40021X as an example, the traceability code indicates that in the same picking batch, the product is tested by the testing center and passes through the third-level sorting standard, and the batch only delivers a single order (Fig. 5).

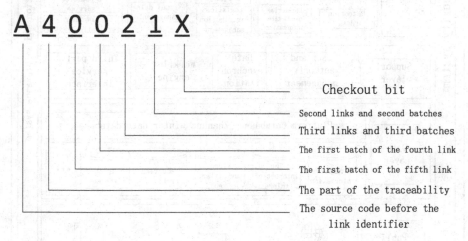

Fig. 5. An example diagram of the link coding of the winter jujube industry chain

5 System Architecture

The system construction of the government, enterprises and consumers to the three-party as the main body, with the whole process of winter jujube industry chain as the main process, realize the sensor information collection and manual input information, through the authority of product inspection and supervision by the government regulators, consumers through traceability information scanning QR code to get product.

The overall architecture of the system is shown as illustrated (Fig. 6).

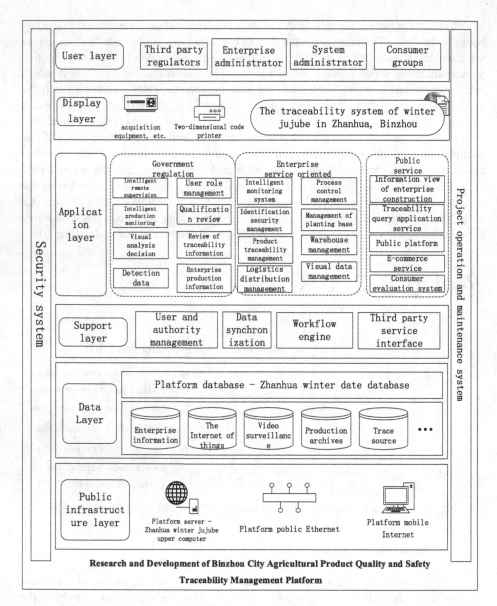

Fig. 6. System architecture

6   System Implementation

The traceability system of Binzhou Zhanhua winter jujube takes into account the diversity of users and the practicability of the system, system uses B/S architecture, Myeclipse 10 as development tool, MySQL as database management tools, Tomcat server, using SSH three layer architecture system, front-end development of traceability system is used in jQuery EasyUI, using JAVA as the development tool, using AJAX for asynchronous data processing, using JavaScript to transfer XHR objects the user interface of the data and return the results to the server, the server uses JSON unified format processing and transmitting data. The overall design of the system ensures the simplicity and ease of use. In the design of the system, it aims to facilitate the operation of users such as business owners (Figs. 7 and 8).

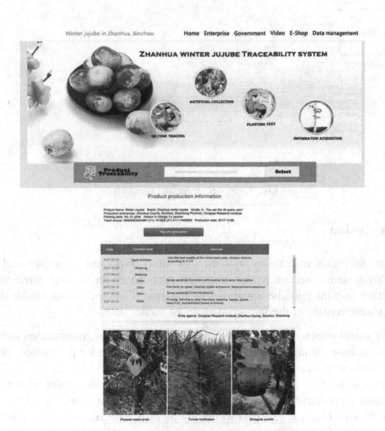

Fig. 7. Traceability information part display interface

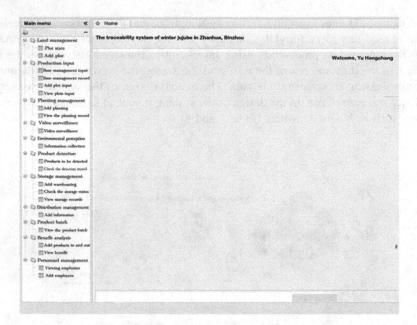

Fig. 8. System interface diagram

7 Conclusion

Based on the same traceability system, this study proposed a quality and safety traceability system based on winter jujube products based on the requirements of the construction of winter jujube enterprise in Binzhou, China, combined with the production characteristics of the industrial chain of winter date.

(1) This model uses technologies such as RFID, GS1 coding, information collection, and database management to build a traceability system for production, planting, and sales to the entire industry chain of winter jujube.

(2) The system has constructed a comprehensive traceable information stream including pre-harvest, mid-production, and post-harvest dates for winter jujube, which helps Binzhou Zhanhua winter jujube Institute achieve product information traceability. Consumers can scan the two-dimensional code or query the system according to the source code on the package. They can display the key link information, the entire industry chain information, and the geography environment information, etc., in the text, pictures or multimedia. Purchasing winter jujube provides product quality and safety protection, improves consumers' trust and purchasing power of traceable winter jujube products, thereby increasing corporate income and achieving higher prices for better quality.

(3) Enterprises can achieve standardization of production through the traceability system, which has guiding significance for improving the production management model, and also plays an exemplary role for enterprises to realize scientific management and promote the integration of winter jujube source products and e-commerce [8].

Acknowledgements. This work was financially supported by The Yellow River Delta (Binzhou) national agricultural science and Technology Park.

References

1. Guo, S.: Investigation and thinking on the production and management of winter jujube in Binzhou. Agric. Sci. Technol. Commun. **2**, 203–205 (2014)
2. Porto, S.M.C., Arcidiacono, C., Cascone, G.: Developing integrated computer-based information systems for certified plant traceability: case study of Italian citrus-plant nursery chain. Biosys. Eng. **109**(2), 120–129 (2011)
3. Aung, M.M., Chang, Y.S.: Traceability in a food supply chain: safety and quality perspectives. Food Control **39**(1), 172–184 (2014). (in Chinese with English abstract)
4. Regattieri, A., Gamberi, M., Manzini, R.: Traceability of food products: general framework and experimental evidence. J. Food Eng. **81**(2), 347–356 (2007)
5. Parreñomarchante, A., Alvarezmelcon, A., Trebar, M.: Advanced traceability system in aquaculture supply chain. J. Food Eng. **122**(1), 99–109 (2014)
6. Mainetti, L., Mele, F., Patrono, L.: An RFID-based tracing and tracking system for the fresh vegetables supply chain. Int. J. Antennas Propag. **2013**(2), 761–764 (2013)
7. Wang, Z.: Food Traceability system based on two-dimensional code. Agric. Eng. **7**(6), 29–32 (2017). (in Chinese with English abstract)
8. Bai, H., Sun, A., Chen, J.: Agricultural products traceability system for quality and safety based on internet of things. Jiangsu J. Agric. Sci. **29**(2), 415–420 (2013). (in Chinese with English abstract)
9. Yang, X., Wu, T., Sun, C.: Design and Application of Aquatic Enterprise Governance Traceability System Based on USB Key. Transactions of the Chinese Society for Agricultural Machinery **43**(8), 128–133 (2012). (in Chinese with English abstract)
10. Ma, H., Liu, P., Zhang, Y.: Design and implementation of vegetable supply chain traceability system. J. Chin. Agric. Mech. **36**(6), 230–234 (2015). (in Chinese with English abstract)
11. Chrysochou, P., Chryssochoidis, G., Kehagia, O.: Traceability information carriers. The technology backgrounds and consumers' perceptions of the technological solutions. Appetite **53**(3), 322–331 (2009)
12. Wang, D., Fu, F., Rao, X.: Fruit traceability system based on processing and grading line. Trans. Chin. Soc. Agric. Eng. (Transactions of the CSAE) **29**(7), 228–236 (2013). (in Chinese with English abstract)
13. Zhang, Y.: Requirements analysis and countermeasures of price fluctuation of Dongzao jujube. J. Anhui Agric. Sci. **38**(9), 4817–4818 (2010)
14. Mcmeekin, T.A., Baranyi, J., Dalgaard, P.: Information systems in food safety management. In: Book of Abstracts New Tools for Improving Microbial Food Safety & Quality, International ICFMH Symposium Food Micro. Ljubljana, September 2004

Design and Implementation of Web System Based on Blockchain

Ting Xiao[1,2] and Yongfeng Huang[1,2(✉)]

[1] Department of Electronic Engineering, Tsinghua University,
Beijing 100084, China
xtl5@mails.tsinghua.edu.cn, yfhuang@tsinghua.edu.cn
[2] Tsinghua National Laboratory for Information Science and Technology,
Beijing 100084, China

Abstract. The internet has a great development, but the cyber crimes are lack of effective supervision. Furthermore, the network congestion is still a common phenomenon in our daily life. This paper proposes a decentralized web system based on blockchain to solve the above problems. In this scheme, web content publisher uploads the web contents to the IPFS (InterPlanetary File System) net which is a peer to peer storage network, and gets the hashes of the web contents from IPFS system, then writes these hashes to the smart contract which has been deployed on the Ethereum blockchain; thousands of web users can read the hashes of these web contents on this smart contract on Ethereum blockchain, and browse the corresponding web contents by hashes on the decentralized IPFS network. The experimental results show that the decentralized web system based on Ethereum blockchain and IPFS network can provide faster access to web contents than the traditional HTTP web. Further more, this web system has strong ability to withstand large-scale concurrent based on IPFS network which is the decentralized web content storage system without centralized web server and can fight against the malicious tampering attack based on Ethereum blockchain which can resist 51% attack and record all transactions including tampering behaviors on the Ethereum blockchain with timestamp.

Keywords: Web · Blockchain · Ethereum · IPFS · Hash · Decentralized

1 Introduction

By June 2017, the total number of Internet [1] users worldwide had reached 3.89 billion, with a coverage rate of 51.7% [2]. As broad netizens use the WEB [3] deeply, they find the WEB has some fatal secure [4] problems, such as the WEB server [5, 6] can't be accessed because of malicious attacks [7], tampering [8] with or deleting WEB data maliciously and so on.

At present, the WEB data is transferred mainly based on HTTP [9, 10] protocol on which the Hypertext [11] is transferred from WWW [3, 12] server to local browser [13]. HTTP protocol has made very important contribution to the development of Internet, however it relies too heavily on the centralized server [14].

© Springer Nature Switzerland AG 2018
X. Sun et al. (Eds.): ICCCS 2018, LNCS 11064, pp. 706–717, 2018.
https://doi.org/10.1007/978-3-030-00009-7_63

The centralized server is vulnerable to DoS attack [15, 16], and it will result Internet users can't get the WEB data from centralized server normally. It is not enough reliable that the WEB data is stored in the centralized server, because the centralized server may break down due to various factors and the owner of the centralized server or the maintainer may tamper with and delete WEB data maliciously. Once the WEB data in the centralized server is tampered with or deleted purposefully, no one can recovery the data and find any change log left.

This paper proposes a IPFS (InterPlanetary File System) [17–20] decentralized web system infrastructure based on Ethereum [21–23] blockchain [24, 25]. This model takes advantage of IPFS which provides more reliable content storage and faster access to web content and Ethereum which guarantees that the data in the blockchain is stored permanently and can not be tampered with. It makes sure that the Internet users access web content more fluently and the web contents which can be against WEB tampering attacks are more trustworthy.

2 Related Works

Blockchain, originating from block chain [26], is a continuously growing list of records, called blocks, which are linked in chronological order and secured by cryptography [27]. It is a distributed ledger [28] which can not be tampered with. Ethereum provides a blockchain with a built-in fully fledged Turing-complete [29] programming language which can be used to create smart contracts [22, 30], which is a computer program that runs on a shared, replicated ledger and can process information, and receive, store and send value [31]. So, you can also consider Ethereum is an open-source, public, distributed computing platform and operating system where we can create any of the application.

The InterPlanetary File System (IPFS) is a peer-to-peer [32] distributed file system that seeks to connect all computing devices with the same system of files [18]. It is a protocol and network designed to create a content-addressable, peer-to-peer method of storing and sharing hypermedia in a distributed file system [33]. The files stored in the IPFS system can be accessed quickly all over the world through its excellent underlying protocols and the firewall can not prevent it [34]. The IPFS is based on content addressing, all content is uniquely identified by its multihash checksum [18, 35]. Therefore, all objects that have the same contents are equal and only stored once [18]. This deduplication technology can remove data redundancy.

3 Design and Implementation of the Web System

3.1 Constitution of the Web System

This paper proposes a decentralized web system based on blockchain. It contains web publisher, web users, Ethereum blockchain and IPFS Net. The system chart is showed in the Fig. 1 as below.

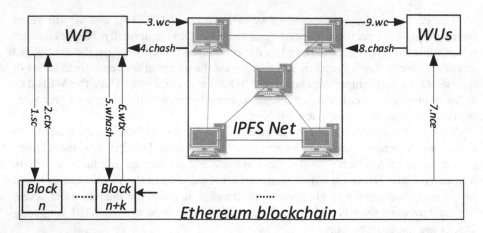

Fig. 1. System chart

For the convenience of writing, the meanings of the symbols at Fig. 1 are listed in the Table 1 as below.

Table 1. The meanings of symbols

Symbol	Meaning
WP	Web publisher
WU	Web user
WUs	Thousands of web users
sc	Smart contract on Ethereum blockchain
ctx	The transaction generated when WP deploys the smart contract on the Ethereum blockchain
wc	The web contents uploaded to the IPFS net by WP
chash	The hash of web content calculated by the IPFS system
whash	The whash function in the smart contract called by WP for writing hash into Ethereum blockchain
wtx	The transaction generated when WP calls the whash function
nce	The event generated when WP calls the whash function, which notifies the WUs that the new web content has been uploaded to the IPFS net

The functions of each part are described as below.

(1) Web publisher: He publishes the web contents on the IPFS Net, and get the hashes [18] of the web contents, then write the hashes into the smart contract on the Ethereum blockchain.

(2) IPFS Net: It stored the web contents from web publisher in decentralized way, and the web user can access the web contents by hashes.

(3) Ethereum blockchain: It stores the hashes of web contents and updates the events [36] which mean some new web contents have been uploaded to the IPFS net.

(4) Web users: They check the events on the smart contract and get the hashes of the web contents, then access the web contents on the IPFS net by the hashes.

3.2 Design of the Web System Workflow

This paper designs the workflow of the web system based on the Ethereum blockchain according to the Fig. 1. The detailed workflow is showed in the Fig. 2 as below.

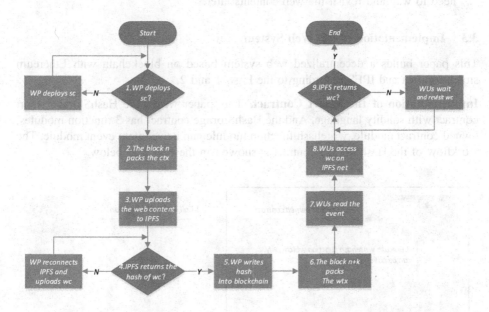

Fig. 2. Workflow of the web system based on blockchain

The workflow of the web system based on the Ethereum blockchain is described as below.

(1) WP deploys the smart contract on the Ethereum blockchain, it just needs to be done only once. If WP has deployed the contract, he can call the function in the contract repeatedly to write hashes [18].
(2) The block n packs the transaction at previous step, and this transaction includes the block height, smart contract ID, WP ID, timestamp [22], etc. Anyone can query the block information.
(3) WP uploads the web contents to the local IPFS node.
(4) The IPFS system returns the hashes of the web contents at previous step. If WP do not get the hashes, he should reconnect the IPFS net and upload the web contents again.
(5) WP calls the writehash function in the smart contract to write hashes of web contents at previous step.
(6) The block n + k packs the transaction at previous step, and this transaction includes the block height, WP ID, timestamp, hashes of web contents, etc.

Meanwhile, the smart contract updates the event which notifies the WUs that the new web content has been uploaded to the IPFS net.

(7) WUs check the event at smart contract, which includes the hashes of the web contents, WP ID, timestamp, etc.

(8) WUs access the web contents on the IPFS net by the hashes.

(9) IPFS returns the web contents to the WUs according to the hashes. If WUs do not get the web contents in time, it means the web contents are very big and the WUs need to wait and revisit the web contents later.

3.3   Implementation of the Web System

This paper builds a decentralized web system based on blockchain with Ethereum smart contract and IPFS according to the Figs. 1 and 2.

Implementation of the Smart Contract. This paper writes the HashStorage smart contract with solidity language. And the HashStorage contract has 3 function modules, owned contract module, writehash function module and newcontent event module. The workflow of the HashStorage contract is showed in the Fig. 3 as below.

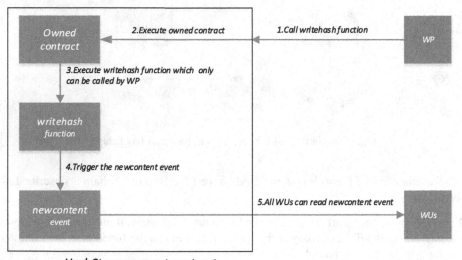

Fig. 3. Workflow of HashStorage smart contract

The workflow of the smart contract is described as below.

(1) WP submits the transaction and calls the writehash function at smart contract on the Ethereum blockchain.

(2) Owned contract restricts the writehash function which only can be called by the WP. This paper makes sure the owner is unique and anyone can track the ID of the

WP. When WP calls the writehash function, the owned contract will be executed at first.

(3) Writehash module is called by WP which can write the hashes of web contents to Ethereum blockchain. The block can store the hashes permanently which can not be tampered with.

(4) Newcontent module is triggered by the execution of writehash function, and it notifies the WUs that the new web content has been uploaded to the IPFS net

(5) WUs can check the newcontent event on the smart contract at any time.

Decentralized Storage on IPFS. This paper uses the IPFS (InterPlanetary File System) as the decentralized storage platform for web contents. It is a peer-to-peer distributed net which does not rely on the centralized server and can guarantee that the storage of the web contents is reliable. The workflow of decentralized storage on IPFS for web contents is showed in the Fig. 4 as below.

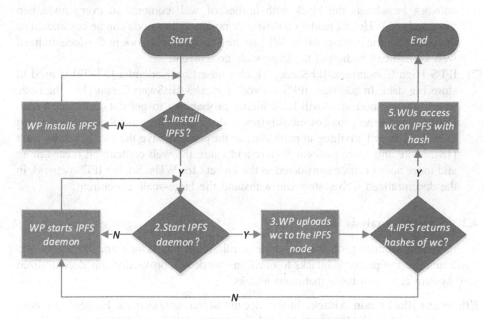

Fig. 4. Workflow of decentralized storage on IPFS for web content

The workflow of decentralized storage on IPFS for web contents is described as below.

(1) WP installs the IPFS which is the precondition for uploading the web contents.

(2) WP starts the IPFS daemon which can synchronize the web contents to the IPFS net. WP types ipfs daemon on the terminal that will start the IPFS server.

(3) WP uploads the web contents to the local IPFS node by typing ipfs add followed by file name on the terminal.

(4) IPFS system returns the hashes of web contents to the WP. If not, WP should restart the IPFS daemon and upload the web contents to the local IPFS node again.

(5) WUs access the web content by typing ipfs.io/ipfs/followed by the hash in the URL bar.

4 Reliability Analysis

4.1 High Concurrent Analysis

In this paper, the decentralized web system consists of Ethereum and IPFS network mainly. I will analyze it and prove that it has strong robust ability to adapt the high concurrent scenario.

(1) Ethereum High Concurrent: Ethereum based on Kademlia [37–39] is a peer-to-peer distributed network. There is no centralized server, every node gets data from neighbor nodes from its DHT [37]. In our system, the decentralized Ethereum network broadcasts the block with hashes of web contents to every node,then thousands of WUs just read it on their own nodes. Every node can be considered as the server for the corresponding WU, so the Ethereum network in the decentralized web system can withstand the large-scale concurrent.
(2) IPFS High Concurrent: IPFS network also based on Kademlia [37–39] is used to store big data. In addition, IPFS network includes BitSwap Credit [18], the node which shares more data will have higher probability to get data and vice versa. Further more, the protocol incentivizes nodes with Filecoin token to seed when they do not need anything in particular, as they might have the blocks others want [18]. More and more nodes will store and share the web contents, it means more and more nodes can be considered as the servers for WUs. So, the IPFS network in the decentralized web system can withstand the large-scale concurrent.

4.2 Security Analysis

In this paper, security problem may arise at Ethereum blockchain and IPFS network. I will analyze the probable attacks to our framework and prove that this decentralized web system can resist these malicious attacks.

Ethereum Blockchain Attack. In this decentralized web system, HashStorage contract is deployed on the Ethereum blockchain, so the malicious attacks can be analyzed at blockchain level and smart contract level.

(1) Blockchain attack: Ethereum is the second largest public blockchain beyond thousands of blockchains and has operated steadily for many years. Ethereum blockchain works with POW (proof of work) [22] and total Hash Rate is too high all over the world now that it is impossible for anyone to launch 51% attack [40]. So the data in the Ethereum blockchain is very hard to be tampered with. In addition, the blockchain can record all transactions including tampering behaviors with timestamp, it means any malicious behavior to the blockchain can be tracked.
(2) Smart contract attack: The malicious WPs may attack the HashStorage contract and publish some falsity information. In this paper, the owned contract [36] is designed

to protect the HashStorage contract, it makes the rule that only the owner who has deployed the HashStorage contract has right to write hashes on the smart contract.

IPFS Network Attack. In this decentralized web system, IPFS network based on S/Kademlia [18, 38] is used as the content storage system, and the main malicious attacks would be Sybil attack [18, 38] and eclipse attack [38].

(1) Sybil Attack: The IPFS system requires nodes to create PKI key pair, derive their identity from it, and sign their messages to each other [18]. This scheme has proof-of-work crypto puzzle to make generating Sybills expensive [18]. The IPFS scheme trusts the old nodes which have done well in the network more than the new nodes, it will increase the difficulty for Sybil attack.
(2) Eclipse Attack: The identity of IPFS node is generated from the 2048 bit RSA [41, 42] public key, the NodeId [18] is random. It is very hard to generate the specific node which has NodeId close to the target node and place many malicious nodes around the target node. Further more, the IPFS nodes lookup values over disjoint paths, in order to ensure honest nodes can connect to each other in the presence of a large fraction of adversaries in the network [18].

5 Experiment

5.1 Experimental Settings

In this paper, the decentralized web system based on the blockchain is tested on the home network by two normal private computers. WP uses the computer with 1.8 GHz Intel Core i5 CPU and 8 GB RAM. WP PC installs metamask wallet, truffle development framework, remix IDE, IPFS, create-react-app. WU uses the computer with 1.7 GHz Intel Core i3 CPU and 8 GB RAM. WU PC installs geth client and mist wallet.

WP writes and tests smart contract with truffle framework, then deploys the contract by remix IDE. WP should set up the metamask wallet to be in the Kovan Test Net and make sure the account has enough test ethers.

5.2 Experimental Results

In this paper, I have done some experiments to test this decentralized web system on the performance of upload, download. Both are very important technical indicators that will decide if this decentralized web system can be applied in practice and spread.

Web System Upload. WP uploads the same web contents in different sizes by decentralized web system and traditional HTTP web system respectively and compares the upload performance by time cost. In this experiment, the sizes of web content are from 1 M to 1.2G which can cover most of the web application. The experiment result is showed in the Fig. 5 as below.

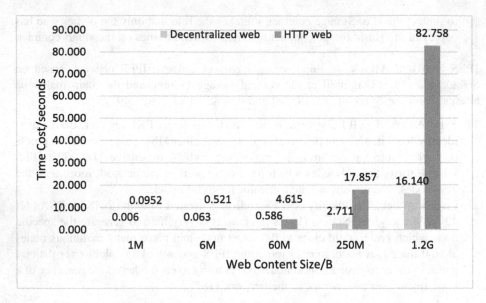

Fig. 5. Average time cost of web content upload

The values above are average with 10 repeated tests. According to experimental data, the upload speed of decentralized web system is faster than the traditional web system. Take 1.2 G web data for example, the upload speed of decentralized web system is 4.1 times faster than traditional web system. Certainly, the experimental data would be different when the network environment and computer configurations are different.

Web System Download. WU downloads the same web contents by this decentralized web system and traditional HTTP web system respectively and compares the download performance by time cost. In this experiment, the test web contents are the same as the upload experiment and the sizes are from 1 M to 1.2G. The experiment result is showed in the Fig. 6 as below.

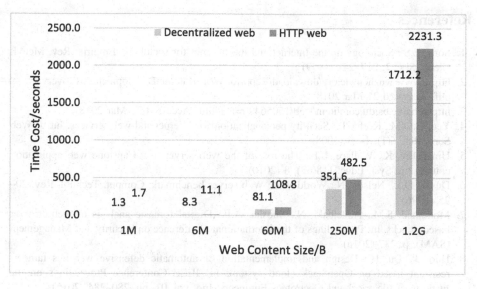

Fig. 6. Average time cost of web content download

The values above are average with 10 repeated tests. According to experimental data, the download speed of decentralized web system is faster than the traditional web system. Take 1.2 G web data for example, the download speed of decentralized web system is faster than traditional web system by 30.3%. Certainly, the experimental data would be different when the network environment and computer configurations are different.

6   Conclusion

This paper proposes the design of web system architecture based on the Ethererum and IPFS according to their decentralization characteristics, then establishes the corresponding execution flow and realization algorithm, and builds an experimental prototype system. Approved by the experimental tests, the decentralized web system based on Ethereum blockchain and IPFS network in this paper has better performance at upload and download than the traditional HTTP web system, it can meet the requirement of the application in practice for broad netizens. In addition, this decentralized web system has strong ability to withstand large-scale concurrent and can fight against the malicious tampering attack and record all transactions including tampering behaviors on the Ethereum blockchain with timestamp. I will add the web content encryption module for special WUs and web content comment module for all WUs in the future work.

Acknowledgements. I gratefully acknowledge Professor Huang for helpful technical discussions on this decentralized web system structure. This work is supported by the National Key Research and Development Program of China (No. 2016YFB0800402) and the National Natural Science Foundation of China (No. U1405254, No. U1536201 and No. U1705261).

References

1. Soro, E.S.: Sociology on the Internet and the Internet for sociology. Empiria: Rev. Metod. Cienc. Soc. **2**, 217–241 (1999)
2. http://www.wuzhenwic.org/download/ReportonWorldInternetDevelopment2017overview. pdf. Accessed 21 Mar 2018
3. https://baike.baidu.com/item/web/150564?fr=aladdin. Accessed 21 Mar 2018
4. Yee, G.O.M., Korba, L.: Security personalization for Internet and web services. Int. J. Web Serv. Res. **5**(1), 1–23 (2008)
5. Umapathy, K., Wallace, L.F.: The role of the web server in a Capstone web application course. Inf. Syst. Educ. J. **8**(62), 8 (2010)
6. Dusza, D.L., Nelson, N.: World Wide Web server benchmark. Comput. Technol. Rev. 20–25 (1996)
7. Mohamed, S.M., Abdelbaki, N., Shosha, A.F.: Digital forensic analysis of web-browser based attacks. In: Proceedings of the International Conference on Security and Management (SAM), p. 237 (2016)
8. Huo, J., Qu, H.: Design and implementation of automatic defensive websites tamper-resistant based on OpenStack cloud system. In: IEEE Conference Proceedings on the Institute of Electrical and Electronics Engineers, Inc. vol. 01, pp. 280–284 (2015)
9. https://baike.baidu.com/item/http. Accessed 21 Mar 2018
10. https://baike.baidu.com/item/https/285356. Accessed 21 Mar 2018
11. Aledhari, M., Saeed, F.: Design and implementation of network transfer protocol for big genomic data. In: IEEE Conferences, pp. 281–288 (2015)
12. Zhou, J.: The Internet, the World Wide Web, library web browsers, and library web servers. Inf. Technol. Libr. **19**(1), 50–52 (2000)
13. Awang, N.F., Ahmad, A., Ahmad, S.R.: Preventing web browser from cyber attack. GSTF J. Comput. (JoC) **2**(1), 164 (2012)
14. Sriraghav, K., et al.: Transaction overhead reduction by server localization in bank database management systems. Int. J. Comput. Appl. **158**(3), 11–16 (2017)
15. https://baike.baidu.com/item/dos%E6%94%BB%E5%87%BB/3792374?fr=aladdin. Accessed 21 Mar 2018
16. https://baike.baidu.com/item/%E5%88%86%E5%B8%83%E5%BC%8F%E6%8B%92% E7%BB%9D%E6%9C%8D%E5%8A%A1%E6%94%BB%E5%87%BB/3802159?fr= aladdin&fromid=177090&fromtitle=DDOS%E6%94%BB%E5%87%BB. Accessed 21 Mar 2018
17. Benet, J.: IPFS - Content Addressed, Versioned, P2P File System. Eprint Arxiv (2014)
18. https://gguoss.github.io/2017/05/28/ipfs/. Accessed 21 Mar 2018
19. http://ipfser.org/2018/01/25/r20/. Accessed 21 Mar 2018
20. https://www.cnblogs.com/fengzhiwu/p/5524324.html. Accessed 21 Mar 2018
21. http://www.8btc.com/how-does-ethereum-work-anyway. Accessed 21 Mar 2018
22. Buterin, V.: Ethereum: a next-generation smart contract and decentralized application platform. https://github.com/ethereum/wiki/wiki/White-Paper (2014)
23. https://baike.baidu.com/item/%E4%BB%A5%E5%A4%AA%E5%9D%8A/20865117?fr= aladdin. Accessed 21 Mar 2018
24. https://baike.baidu.com/item/%E5%8C%BA%E5%9D%97%E9%93%BE/13465666?fr= aladdin. Accessed 21 Mar 2018
25. https://baike.baidu.com/item/%E5%8C%BA%E5%9D%97%E9%93%BE2.0/22415327?fr= aladdin. Accessed 21 Mar 2018

26. https://baike.baidu.com/item/%E5%8C%BA%E5%9D%97%E9%93%BE1.0/22415324?fr=aladdin. Accessed 21 Mar 2018
27. Narayanan, A., et al.: Bitcoin and Cryptocurrency Technologies: A Comprehensive Introduction (2016)
28. Iansiti, M., Lakhani, K.R.: The truth about blockchain. Harv. Bus. Rev. **95**, 118–127 (2017)
29. Lauc, D.: Logical reconstruction of programming language paradigms. Int. J. Adv. Res. Comput. Sci. **4**(10), 17–20 (2013)
30. https://baike.baidu.com/item/%E6%99%BA%E8%83%BD%E5%90%88%E7%BA%A6/19770937?fr=aladdin. Accessed 21 Mar 2018
31. https://gendal.me/2015/02/10/a-simple-model-for-smart-contracts/. Accessed 21 Mar 2018
32. https://baike.baidu.com/item/%E5%AF%B9%E7%AD%89%E7%BD%91%E7%BB%9C/5482934?fr=aladdin. Accessed 21 Mar 2018
33. https://en.wikipedia.org/wiki/InterPlanetary_File_System. Accessed 21 Mar 2018
34. https://medium.com/@ConsenSys/an-introduction-to-ipfs-9bba4860abd0. Accessed 21 Mar 2018
35. https://www.jianshu.com/p/8da05084d9d7. Accessed 21 Mar 2018
36. https://media.readthedocs.org/pdf/solidity/v0.4.21/solidity.pdf. Accessed 21 Mar 2018
37. https://baike.baidu.com/item/DHT/1007999?fr=aladdin. Accessed 21 Mar 2018
38. Baumgart, I., Mies, S.: S/Kademlia: a practicable approach towards secure key-based routing. In: 2007 International Conference on Parallel and Distributed Systems, vol. 2, pp. 1–8. IEEE (2007)
39. https://baike.baidu.com/item/Kademlia/3106849?fr=aladdin. Accessed 21 Mar 2018
40. http://www.8btc.com/51attack. Accessed 21 Mar 2018
41. https://www.iplaysoft.com/encrypt-arithmetic.html. Accessed 21 Mar 2018
42. https://baike.baidu.com/item/%E5%8A%A0%E5%AF%86%E7%AE%97%E6%B3%95/2816213. Accessed 21 Mar 2018

Design and Verification of a Security Policy to Defense DDoS Attack for Cloud Robot

Boyi Liu[1,2], Xiangyan Tang[1(✉)], Jieren Cheng[1,4], and Jiquan Chen[1,3]

[1] School of Information Science and Technology, Hainan University,
Haikou 570228, China
Tangxy36@163.com
[2] University of Chinese Academy of Science, Beijing 100000, China
[3] School of Software and Microelectronics, Peking University,
Beijing 100000, China
[4] State Key Laboratory of Marine Resource Utilization in South China Sea,
Haikou 570228, China

Abstract. Cloud robot is becoming popular and security of cloud robot is important. However, the researches of cloud robot safety are a few. This work develops a security policy to defense DDoS attack of cloud robot. In this policy, complex, but accurate calculation models are deployed on the cloud, simple but efficient calculation models are deployed on the robot. In the cloud, there are master server and standby server. The master server transfers parameters of complex but accurate models to the standby server periodically and the master executes the start-stop backup policy. Specifically, this work proposes and proves an algorithm to dynamically adjust the interval of parameter transfer. According to a PDRA feature of Netflow, when DDoS attacks, the master server sends warning signals to the robot and standby server. The robot runs local models to avoid stopping work until it is connected to the standby server. Then, standby server provides service to the robot until the master server recover. Finally, this work implemented a gesture recognition cloud robot based on convolutional neural network, hidden Markov model and PDRA feature of Netflow to verify the policy. Experiment shows that the security policy to defense DDoS attack for cloud robot is effective.

Keywords: Cloud robotic · Security policy · DDoS

1 Introduction

Since the concept of the cloud robot was proposed by Dr. Kuffner of Carnegie Mellon University (now working at Google company) in 2010 [1], the research on cloud robots is rising gradually. Cloud robots are the combination of cloud computing and robotics. Like other network terminals, the robot itself does not need to store all the information or has a strong computing power. It only needs to demand from the cloud, and the cloud is responsive and satisfied. The idea of connecting a robot to an external computer appeared in 1990s. University of Tokyo Inaba proposed the concept of remote brain. Cloud robots will further explore this concept and explore the way to achieve cheaper computing and interconnect with ubiquitous networks. Since the concept of

© Springer Nature Switzerland AG 2018
X. Sun et al. (Eds.): ICCCS 2018, LNCS 11064, pp. 718–730, 2018.
https://doi.org/10.1007/978-3-030-00009-7_64

cloud robot was put forward, it has aroused the interest of many IT companies, scientific research institutions and researchers at home and abroad.

Cloud robot has become an important direction of research at home and abroad. The application of cloud robots is increasing with the research of cloud technology. At the beginning of 2011, the 4a study program of RoboEarth [2] was initiated by the Eindhoven university of Technology, Swiss Federal Institute of Technology Zurich, Technische Universitaet München, Saragossa university, Universität Stuttgart, and 35 scientists from Philips. Trying to get the robots to share information and store their discoveries helps the robots build their own Internet and Wikipedia. In early 2014, RoboEarth project was launched by scientists at the Eindhoven University of Technology. Four robots collaborated in a simulated hospital environment to take care of the patient through interaction with the cloud backend server, which enables them to share information and learn from each other. Google engineers have developed robot software based on the Android platform, which can be used for remote control based on the Lego mind-storms, iRobot Create and Vex Pro, etc. [3]. The ASORO lab in Singapore has built a cloud computing architecture that allows robots to build 3D maps of the current environment. In addition, its building speed is much faster than the robot's onboard computers [4]. Kehoe et al. of the university of California, Berkeley, based on cloud platform, used Willow Garage's PR2 robot and valley song target recognition engine to complete the 3D robot fetching task [5]. Researchers at France's Toulouse system analysis and structural laboratory created a "user manual" that can be stored in each target to help the robot complete its operational tasks [6]. In the children's hospital in Italy, the Nao robot of French Aldebaran relies on cloud architecture to perform speech recognition, face detection and other tasks, which facilitates the interaction between robots and patients [7]. Kamei et al. proposed a mall wheelchair robot, sharing map information through the cloud, positioning and navigation using cloud architecture, and helping disabled or disabled elderly people visit the mall [8].

Through the design of an autonomous low maintenance infrastructure in the cloud and can provide the resources based on supply and demand, and create an intelligent engine in cloud infrastructure, real-time resource scheduling and management of the robot, simplify the robot hardware facilities, robot knowledge sharing through the cloud, and ultimately the formation of the cloud robot system. The cloud robot becomes more and more popular, but few people consider its security. There are no papers about cloud robot security in google scholar or some other platforms. Most of cloud robots require accurate results from cloud to work. So, it will bring huge losses [9] if the cloud is attacked. When the cloud is attacked, the driverless cars will stop and cause traffic jams. It will even result in more serious consequences. If the cloud robot can play Go like AlphaGo Zero [10], it will lose the game when the cloud is attacked. If the cloud robot used in military [11], it is possible to stop working or even to attack the friendly army and lead to war failure.

There are many ways of cyber-attacks, DDoS is one of the most common. If DDoS attacks the server of the cloud robot, the robot will stop work. Which may cause great loss. Recently, there are a various of data on the network because of the development of big data. For years, Distributed Denial of Service (DDoS) attack has been one of the greatest threats to network security.

In recent years, the technologies that use cloud computing to protect network security tends to mature. Based on the consideration of the operation and maintenance costs of physical devices, more and more enterprises and organizations are using their global services provided by cloud computing technologies to migrate their enterprise applications to the cloud environment to effectively defense DDoS attacks. Reference [12] proposed to use the public cloud defense DDoS attack to classify the visiting data by historical records, thus filtering the malicious IP source address. Reference [13] used Netflow protocol to collect data traffic and detect DDoS attacks in a self-learning manner. Reference [14] presented the design, implementation, and evaluation of dynamic PID (D-PID), a framework that uses PIDs negotiated between the neighboring domains as inter-domain routing objects. The authors in [15] proposed a novel DDoS attack detection system based on Spark framework. The authors in [16] proposed a multi-queue SDN controller scheduling algorithm based on time slice allocation strategy.

Cloud robot has many challenges [17], safety is important. This work addresses the safety problem of the cloud robot by the example of DDoS attack. This work designed a security policy to defense DDoS attack for cloud robot and implemented a gesture recognition robot to verify.

2   Design of a Security Policy to Defense DDoS Attack for Cloud Robot

2.1   Cloud Robot System Design Matched with the Security Policy

As shown in Fig. 1, when there is no network attack, data will be collected by sensors of the robot. Then, it will be uploaded to the master server. Relying on powerful computing power, the master server drives complex models (such as Deep Learning Models) to get accurate results immediately. The master server sends the calculation results to the robot. As the system running, the master server transfer parameters of complex models to the standby server. What's more, the master server share knowledge with the cloud platform based on transfer learning or some other algorithms to improve

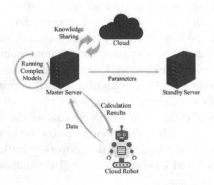

Fig. 1. Design of the cloud robot against DDoS attack

the performance of complex models. With the system running like this, the server gives a full play to the advantage of computing power. And the robot will make full use of the ability of information acquisition. Not only does the robot get accurate results, but also it removes heavy computing equipment.

The advantages of this scheme are as follows:

(1) Guaranteeing the advantage of the cloud robot: computing in the cloud. The computation speed is much faster than that is only in the robot. Heavy equipment removed from robots.
(2) Adding the knowledge sharing in the cloud. The math model does not only learn from the data collected by the robot, but also from the data from the cloud. With the development of transfer learning and some other machines learning method, this function module will play an increasingly important role.
(3) Adding the standby server. Instead of using "One server-robot" mode, the greatest degree of accuracy will be guaranteed when the DDoS attacks occur.

2.2 Dynamically Parameters Transfer Algorithm in the Security Policy

In the process of transferring, parameters will run in a reasonable cycle better. So, this work presents a setting method of the frequency of the parameters transfer from master server to the standby server in unit time. Firstly, this work proves that the frequency of DDoS attacks obeys the Poisson distribution. Then, stationary of this process are proved. Finally, according to the nature of stationary, this work presents the setting method of the frequency of the parameters transfer from master server to the standby server.

According to the characteristics of Poisson distribution, we first assume that the frequency of DDoS attacks obeys Poisson distribution [18]. Then we proved it: A random process $\{N(t), t \geq 0\}$ is called a counting process. $N(t)$ is random variable, representing the number of DDoS attacks. If it satisfies the following conditions, this counting process is called the Poisson process with the rate $\lambda(\lambda > 0)$ [19].

$N(0) = 0$;

$\{N(t)\}$ is an independent incremental process;

For any $t, s \geq 0, N(s, t+s]$ obey the Poisson distribution with parameter λt. That is:

$$P(N(s,t+s] = k) = \frac{\lambda t^k}{k!} e^{-\lambda t}; k = 0, 1, \ldots \tag{1}$$

Frequency of the occurrence of DDoS is regarded as random variety $N(t)$, among this, $t \geq 0$. When $t \geq 0$, $N(0) = 0$ obviously. So, the condition 1 is satisfied.

$N(t) - N(s)(0 \leq s < t)$ is the increment in $(s, t]$. The occurrence of DDoS attack is mutually independent. So, as for any positive integer n and any $0 \leq t_0 < t_1 < t_2 < \ldots < t_n$. There are n increments: $X_{(t_1)} - X_{(t_0)}, X_{(t_2)} - X_{(t_1)}, \ldots, X_{(t_n)} - X_{(t_{n-1})}$, which are interdependent. So, we can call $\{N(t), t \geq 0\}$ processes with independent increments and it is satisfied with condition (2). In a sufficient small-time interval h, only one DDoS attack event can occur. The probability of two or more occurrences is extremely low and negligible. That can be expressed as this:

$$P\{N(h) \geq 2\} = o(h); h > 0 \tag{2}$$

In a sufficient small-time interval h, it is assumed that the probability of 1 DDoS attack is proportional to the length of the time interval of h. That can be expressed as this:

$$P\{N(h) = 1\} = \lambda h + o(h); h > 0 \tag{3}$$

In the formula 3, $\lambda(\lambda > 0)$ is the rate of the counting process.

We can prove that the random variable N(t) obeys the Poisson distribution by simply verifying formulas (2) and (3) satisfy the formula (1).

This work makes the $P_n(t) = P\{N(t) = n\}$ and h > 0. Then we can get:

$$P_0(t+h) = P\{N(t+h) = 0\} = P\{N(t) = 0, N(t+h) - N(t) = 0\} =$$
$$P\{N(t) = 0, N(t+h) - N(t) = 0\}$$

From the Eqs. (2) and (3), we can get:

$$P_0(t+h) = P_0(t)[1 - \lambda h + o(h)] \tag{4}$$

Get:

$$\frac{P_0(t+h) - p_0(t)}{h} = -\lambda P_0(t) + \frac{O(h)}{h} \tag{5}$$

Let h $\rightarrow$ 0, take the limit and then we can get the differential equation:

$$P_0'(t) = -\lambda P_0(t) \tag{6}$$

From $p_0(0) = p\{N(0) = 0\} = 1$, we can get:

$$P_0'(t) = e^{-\lambda t} \tag{7}$$

Similarly, for n $\geq$ 1, a differential equation can be obtained:

$$P_n'(t) = -\lambda P_n(t) + \lambda P_{n-1} \tag{8}$$

When n = 1, from $P_0(t) = e^{-\lambda t}$ and $P_1(0) = 0$, we can get:

$$P_1(t) = \lambda t e^{-\lambda} t \tag{9}$$

According to mathematical induction and $P_n(0) = 0$, we can get:

$$P_n(t) = \frac{e^{-\lambda} t (\lambda^t)^n}{n!} \tag{10}$$

The formula (10) can prove that this random eligible constraint (3), so we can deem that the random N(t) obeys Poisson distribution. Therefore, the occurrence frequency of DDoS attacks obeys Poisson distribution. Then, we can easily draw the conclusion that the occurrence frequency of DDoS attacks and DDoS disappears are both obey Poisson distribution. Finally, we get that the frequency of the state of the server is overturned obeys Poisson distribution.

Now, we have known that the random process N(t) (The state of the server is overturned) obeys the Poisson distribution. Then, this work proves the stationary of the process.

We introduce s as a time point. So, $N \sim P(\lambda(t-s))$ in [s, t]. That is: $P(N=k) = \frac{(n(t-s))^k}{k!}$. We suppose:

$$p(x(0)=1) = p(x(0)=-1) = \frac{1}{2} \tag{11}$$

That is:

$$(n=k) = \frac{(\pi t - s)^k}{k!} \tag{12}$$

Then:

$$E(X(t)) = 1 \times P(N \text{ is even}) + (-1) \times P(N \text{ is odd})$$

$$P(N \text{ is even}) = \sum\nolimits_{k=0}^{\infty} \frac{(\pi(t-s))^{2k}}{(2k)!} e^{-(-\pi(t-s))} \tag{13}$$

$$P(N \text{ is odd}) = \sum\nolimits_{k=0}^{\infty} \frac{(\pi(t-s))^{2k+1}}{(2k+1)!} e^{-(-\pi(t-s))} \tag{14}$$

We know:

$$e^{(x)} = \sum\nolimits_{k=0}^{\infty} \frac{x^k}{k!} \tag{15}$$

We can get:

$$e^{(\lambda(t-s))} = \sum\nolimits_{k=0}^{\infty} \frac{(\lambda(t-s))^k}{k!} \tag{16}$$

$$e^{(-\lambda(t-s))} = \sum\nolimits_{k=0}^{\infty} \frac{(\lambda(t-s))^k}{k!} (-1)^k \tag{17}$$

From the above formulas, we can get:

$$E(x(t)) = e^{(-\pi t)} \tag{18}$$

Then we check second moment, and we can easily get:

$$E(x(t)x(s)) = 1 \cdot P(N\ (t-s)\text{is even}) - P(N(t-s)\text{is odd}) = e^{(-\pi|t-s|)} \tag{19}$$

Whether the first moment or the second moment, they are only dependent on the $|t - s|$, so the process is stationary. Because attacks and non-attacks always come in pairs, so the process of DDoS attack is stationary also. According to the feature of stationary: mathematical expectations in unit time remain unchanged. Then, we can get the reasonable parameters transfer cycle:

$$E_t = \frac{m(T_1) + m(T_2) + \ldots + m(Tn)}{nT} \tag{20}$$

$$T_{transfer} = \frac{T - T_{attack}}{E_t - Num_{attack}} \tag{21}$$

In the formula (19), E_t is the mathematical expectation of the DDoS attack frequency. T is a cycle time. n means the n cycle. m is the number of DDoS attacks in the N cycle. $T_{transfer}$ is the time required for the next parameter transfer. T_{attack} is the time of the last DDoS attack during the cycle. Num_{attack} is the number of DDoS attacks during this cycle. By this way, the system can transfer the parameters dynamically based on the frequency of DDoS attacks. The parameters can be transferred legitimately.

Periodically passing parameters is one of the policies. Another policy is start-stop backup. This policy makes backup from the master server to the standby server when the former start or stop work. Which can increase the robust of the security policy.

2.3   Cloud Robot System Running Process of the Security Policy

Running processes of the system designed for the cloud robot include the normal condition, the DDoS warning stage, the robot's own calculation stage, the service from standby server stage and the attack disappear stage (as illustrated in Fig. 2). When there is no DDoS attack, the system runs as normal. When there is DDoS attack, the robot turns to the DDoS warning stage. Then, the robot runs simple models with supports from the computing equipment of itself, that is the robot's own calculation stage. But it is not a permanent solution, so this work provides the service from the standby server to the robot in the next stage, that is the standby server stage. After the recovery of the master server, the master server sends safety signal to the robot and standby server, that is attack disappear stage. Run to this stage, the process of the robot defenses DDoS attack has completed. The cloud robot will turn to the normal condition finally. The process of every condition is illustrated in Table 1.

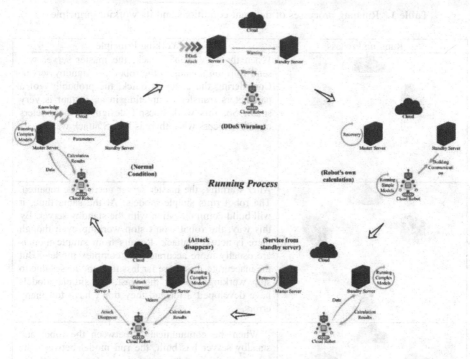

Fig. 2. Running processes of the cloud robot

3   Experiment

This work created a cloud gesture recognition robot against DDoS attack based on the scheme above. Considering we only need to verify the feasibility of the system. So, this work chose the simplest robot: manipulator. The robot control system runs in Jetson TX1. The complex model runs in master server is Deep CNN (Deep Convolutional Neural Network) [20]. The simple model runs is HMM (Hidden Markov Model) [21]. The DDoS detection method is "DDoS attack detection based on abnormal network flow with sliding window trending prediction" [22].

According to the experiment scheme above. This work carried out experiments in real conditions. The processes including normal condition where there is no DDoS attack and the condition when the DDoS attack occurs.

3.1   Gesture Recognition with Master Server in No DDoS Attack Condition in the Experiment

When there is no DDoS attack, the cloud robot runs the gesture recognition in the master server. We built deep CNN model in the master server. There are five gestures in the preinstall: nothing, OK, peace, punch and stop. The recognition results are very accuracy, as illustrated in Table 2. As shown in the Table 2 above. The first line in the table shows the real image from the camera. The second column in the table shows

Table 1. Running processes of different conditions and its working principle

Running Process	Working Principle
	When there is DDoS attack, the master server will send warning signals to the robot and standby server. Considering the attack is quick, the probability of a parameters transfer completing in an instant is very small. So, this work doesn't design the parameters transfer process when there is DDoS attack warning.
	After warning, the master server need to be repaired. The robot runs simple models. At the same time, it will build communication with the standby server. By this way, the robot won't stop working even though there is network attack. Results from simple models are usually more accurate than complex models. But the inaccurate losses are far less than the losses due to stop working. To say the least, the simple models have developed a lot and they don't have too many errors.
	When the communication between the robot and standby server has built, the run model between the robot and the standby server is the same as with the master server. The standby server will provide computing service for the robot when it has built communications with the robot. Relying on the parameters transferred timely from the master server, the standby server can set up an accurate model immediately. Then the robot can get real-time and accurate result.
	When the master server has been recovered, the master server sends the signal that there is no DDoS attack to the robot and the standby server. The priority of the master server is higher than that of the standby server. The robot transfer data to the master server when the master server provide service.

mask images of the real image based on image segmentation. The third column shows binary images and the last line is the recognition result present by bar. Considering the length of the paper, only some of the experimental results are shown here. From bars we can see that the recognition result of the deep CNN in the master server is accurate and positive. On the last row, I put a pen on the recognition area. From the mask image, the recognition is true and the result has high certainty.

Table 2. Gesture recognition results when there is no DDoS attac

Image of the video	Mask image	Binary image	Recognition result

3.2 Gesture Recognition in Robot Itself When No DDoS Attack Occurs in the Experiment

When there is DDoS attack, as illustrated in Fig. 2, the master server sends warning signal to the standby server. Then the standby server will build communication with the robot. In this period, the robot will run the HMM model to recognize gesture. This work builds HMM model in the cloud robot. There are six gestures in the preinstall of HMM model: OK, peace, punch and stop and one. There is one more gesture type which need to be recognized in HMM model. This reflect the advantage of the non-deep learning: The non-deep learning method requires much few sample images, so there are more types of gesture can be recognized by this way. However, there are also shortcomings of these models. The accuracy is not as high as the deep learning method. And the certainty is not enough. As illustrated in Table 3, it is the probabilities of each gesture in recognition results of HMM. Considering the length of the paper, only some of the experimental results are shown here. From the Table 3, we can see that the certainty is not so enough as deep CNN model. Despite the certainty is not so enough, we are still satisfied with this method. Because even the certainty is not enough, most of gesture recognition results are right. The correct rate is up to the level we can accept.

Table 3. Probabilities of each gesture in recognition results of HMM

"ONE"	"STOP"	"NOTHING"	"PEACE"

Table 3 shows the data of gesture recognition results. The results are right although the certainties of these results are not very high. So, when there is DDoS attack the HMM method can guarantee the right operation of robots.

3.3 DDoS Detection Experiment in the Master Server

To the DDoS detection method in the master server. We deploy the DDoS detection program proposed in Sect. 3.3 of the paper. in the master server. This work conducted experimental tests using network data with DDoS. Figure 3 is the detection effect of the proposed method compared with other popular methods. From this figure, we can see that the proposed method is excellent.

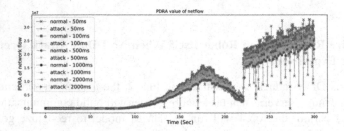

Fig. 3. (c). PDRA value of DDoS Attack 2007 dataset with different Δt

3.4 Realistic Test Scenario

As illustrated in Fig. 4, we took some pictures of realistic test scenario. The gesture of "Peace" makes the robot steer, the gesture of "Punch" makes the robot grab things, the gesture of "Stop" makes the robot stop grabbing etc.

Fig. 4. Realistic test scenario of gesture "Peace", "Punch" and "Stop"

From the results of the experiment. We can see that the method in this work is effective when there is DDoS attack. The gesture recognition robot gets accurate results from the master server. Even there is DDoS attack to the master server, the robot can work normally by running HMM in robot itself. This work also verified the DDoS detection method based on PDRA. It works pretty well in detect DDoS attack. So, the feasibility and effectiveness of the design of cloud robots against DDoS attack.

4 Conclusion

This work designed and implemented a cloud robot against DDoS attack. In particular, we proved DDoS attack obey Poisson distribution. The important parameter of backup interval is proposed in this work. Based on the scheme in this work, we used the deep CNN model, the HMM model and the PDRA feature of netflow to implement a safe gesture recognition robot. This robot proved that the security policy to defense DDoS attack for cloud robot is effective.

Acknowledgement. We thank all the anonymous reviewers and editors who helped to improve the quality of the paper. This work was supported by the National Natural Science Foundation of Hainan [617048, 20 18CXTD333]; The National Natural Science Foundation of China [61762033, 61363071, 61702539]; Hainan University Doctor Start Fund Project [kyqd1328]; Hainan University Youth Fund Project [qnjj1444].

References

1. Kuffner, J.J., Lavalle, S.M.: Space-filling trees: a new perspective on incremental search for motion planning. In: International Conference on Intelligent Robots and Systems, pp. 2199–2206. IEEE, San Francisco (2011)
2. Waibel, M., Beetz, M., Civera, J., et al.: RoboEarth - a world wide web for robots. IEEE Robot. Autom. Mag. **18**(2), 69–82 (2011)
3. Ravi, N., Mala, T., Srinivasan, M.K., et al.: Design and implementation of VOD (Video on Demand) SaaS framework for android platform on cloud environment. In: IEEE International Conference MDM 2, pp. 171–176. IEEE, Milan (2013)
4. Turnbull, L., Samanta, B.: Cloud robotics: formation control of a multi robot system utilizing cloud infrastructure, Southeastcon. In: 2013 Proceedings of IEEE, pp. 1–4. IEEE, Jacksonville (2013)
5. Kehoe, B., Matsukawa, A., Candido, S., et al.: Cloud-based robot grasping with the google object recognition engine. In: IEEE International Conference on Robotics and Automation. pp. 4263–4270. IEEE, Karlsruhe (2013)
6. Guizzo, E.: Robots with their heads in the clouds. IEEE Trans. Spectr. **48**(3), 16–18 (2011)
7. Furler, L., Nagrath, V., Malik, A.S., et al.: An auto-operated telepresence system for the Nao humanoid Robot. In: Communication Systems and Network Technologies (CSNT), pp. 262–267. IEEE, Gwalior (2013)
8. Kamei, K., Nishio, S., Hagita, N., et al.: Cloud networked robotics. IEEE Netw. **26**(3), 28–34 (2012)
9. Greene, J.: Our driverless dilemma. Science **352**(6293), 1514–1515 (2016)
10. Singh, S., Okun, A., Jackson, A.: Artificial intelligence: learning to play Go from scratch. Nature **550**(7676), 336 (2017)
11. Ranjan, N., Ghouse, Z., Hiwrale, N.: A multi-function robot for military application. Imp. J. Interdiscip. Res. **3**(3), 243–244 (2017)
12. Sahi, A., Lai, D., Li, Y., et al.: An efficient DDoS TCP flood attack detection and prevention system in a cloud environment. IEEE Access **5**(1), 6036–6048 (2017)
13. Rukavitsyn, A., Borisenko, K., Shorov, A.: Self-learning method for DDoS detection model in cloud computing. In: IEEE Young Researchers in Electrical and Electronic Engineering, pp. 544–547. IEEE, St. Petersburg (2017)

14. Luo, H., Chen, Z., Li, J., Vasilakos, A.V.: Preventing distributed denial-of-service flooding attacks with dynamic path identifiers. IEEE Trans. Inf. Forensics Secur. **12**(8), 1801–1815 (2017)
15. Han, D., Bi, K., Liu, H., Jia, J.: A ddos attack detection system based on spark framework. Comput. Sci. Inf. Syst. **14**(3), 769–788 (2017)
16. Yan, Q., Gong, Q., Yu, F.: Effective software-defied networking controller scheduling method to mitigate DDoS attacks. Electron. Lett. **53**(7), 469–471 (2017)
17. Kehoe, B., Patil, S., Abbeel, P., et al.: A survey of research on cloud robotics and automation. IEEE Trans. Autom. Sci. Eng. **12**(2), 398–409 (2015)
18. Haight, F.A.: Handbook of poisson distribution. J. R. Stat. Soc. **18**(4) (1967)
19. Sheldon, M.R.: Introduction to Probability Models, 11th edn. Academic Press, New York (2014)
20. Mohanty, A., Rambhatla, S.S., Sahay, R.R.: Deep gesture: static hand gesture recognition using CNN. In: Raman, B., Kumar, S., Roy, P.P., Sen, D. (eds.) Proceedings of International Conference on Computer Vision and Image Processing. AISC, vol. 460, pp. 449–461. Springer, Singapore (2017). https://doi.org/10.1007/978-981-10-2107-7_41
21. Lee, H.K., Kim, J.H.: An HMM-based threshold model approach for gesture recognition. IEEE Trans. Pattern Anal. Mach. Intell. **21**(10), 961–973 (1999)
22. Cheng, J., Xu, R., Tang, X., et al.: An abnormal network flow feature sequence prediction approach for DDoS attacks detection in big data environment. Comput. Mater. Contin. **55**(1), 95–119 (2018)

Detecting Inconsistency and Incompleteness in Access Control Policies

Hongbin Zhang[1,2]([✉]), Pengcheng Ma[1], and Meihua Wang[1]

[1] School of Information Science and Engineering,
Hebei University of Science and Technology, Shijiazhuang,
People's Republic of China
hbzhang@live.com
[2] Hebei Key Laboratory of Network and Information Security,
Hebei Normal University, Shijiazhuang 050024, China

Abstract. It is a key issue for detecting inconsistency and incompleteness in the management of access control policies. Traditionally the separate management of subjects and objects lead to the problem that the inconsistency and incompleteness detection is too complicated. In this paper, we use of partial order relationship between subjects and objects to constitute a directed acyclic graph (DAG) model. During the construction of the model, inconsistent and incomplete policies are detected. Finally, the experimental results verify the correctness and effectiveness of the method.

Keywords: Access control · Directed acyclic graph · Conflict detection

1 Introduction

There is large number of cloud users in the cloud computing environment. Users are dynamics, and their access to the cloud environment tends to be diversified. Security Mechanism for cloud computing systems is relatively lacking. The traditional access control model [1, 2] can no longer satisfy the need for fine-grained, dynamic authorization in cloud computing environments. It is known that the main purpose of the access control policy is to protect the system's data and resources from unauthorized access, these access control policies to identify the user's access rights to resources. As the core of system security management, the selection of appropriate system access control management methods is of particular importance for the detection of conflicts and incompleteness of access control security policies [3].

This paper proposes a Directed Acyclic Graph (DAG) model based on subject-object fusion, which transforms complex policy conflict and incomplete detection process into DAG construction process, and effectively simplifies design and management of access control policy. The rest of the paper is structured as follows. Section 2 presents the relating works, Sect. 3 introduces the preliminaries, Sect. 4 introduces the DAG's fusion construction algorithms and describes the policy detection process, Sect. 5 verify the feasibility of the proposed method by experiment and make a comparison of various types of other methods. Finally, we make the conclusion of the whole paper in Sect. 6.

© Springer Nature Switzerland AG 2018
X. Sun et al. (Eds.): ICCCS 2018, LNCS 11064, pp. 731–739, 2018.
https://doi.org/10.1007/978-3-030-00009-7_65

2 Related Works

Existing access control policy conflict detection methods focused on formal logic, description language, ontology reasoning, and directed acyclic graph model.

The literature [4] enumerates the applicability of the algorithms under the policy conflict based on time attributes, which verified for correctness. The literature [5] proposes a conflict redundancy detection and resolution algorithm, which maps the structure of the access control policy into a set of Venn diagrams, removes consistency and redundancies based on the association relationship between the sets. Such methods rely on the strong expression of the policy description language to perform policy conflict detection. The literature [6] inferred the if-then rules from the set of multi-attribute records through the data mining technology of association rules mining, built the attributes through the inference mechanism, and further built the rules with subsets of attributes. Literature [7] is based on binary decision tree coding to perform auto-mated feed-back state change information to construct an access control policy com-posed of fusion logic. Formal logic based access control policy, which is necessary to develop the corresponding tools to carry out the feasibility of verifing policy reasoning results in practical applications. The literature [8] is based on the method of opposing attribute inference. Shaikh et al. [9] proposed a policy detection method. First, the input data were normalized by the Boolean expression attribute sorting, and the decision tree was improved based on the proposed C4.5 algorithm, the result of the policy detection algorithm was presented to the policy administrator who will take remedial action. The limitation of this kind of method is that it needs to have the precondition of con-structing ontology, which is difficult to achieve. Literature [10] transforms the problem of conflict detection based on directed graphs into the problem of directed graph node relations, but it completely separates the subject directed graph from the object directed graph, which does not conform to the information system of the relationship between subject and object existence. Moreover, the detection of policy consistency is based on the DAG of assumption, which fails to provide a method for constructing DAG.

All methods mentioned above can solve policy conflict and incompleteness. The difference between them and the comparison with our method is shown in Table 1. This paper builds the DAG model to detect policy conflict and incompleteness based on access control policy. Construction of DAG model simplifies the detection process and increases the efficiency of detection.

3 Preliminaries

First, it is introduced the overall flow of access control policy inconsistency and incomplete detection. As showed in Fig. 1.

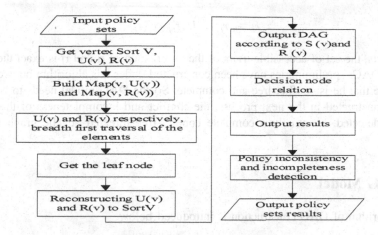

Fig. 1. Process of policy detection

According to the policy detection flow chart given in Fig. 1, We first define the policy detection set, which is expressed as U(v) and R(v), then map the set of policy (including the subject and the object), respectively expressed as Map(v,U(v)). Map(v,U (v)), we use the following algorithm to perform the preliminaries.

In turn, the hierarchical structure guarantees the correctness of access control relationships. Then the build process is as follows.

$U = \{u_1, u_2, \ldots\}$: set of system users;

$R = \{r_1, r_2, \ldots\}$: set of system resources;

Matrix $A = \{(u, r) \in U \times R\}$: the user can access the resource;

Defines the access control relationship between users and system resources;

The user u, R (u) $\in$ R: Represents the set of resources that u can access;

The resource r, U (r) $\in$ U: Represents the set of users that r can access;

Therefore, (u, r) $\in$ A is equivalent to r $\in$ R (u), is also equivalent to u $\in$ U (r).

Due to the assumption that the access relationship is explicitly defined in the system, any user u and resource r, R (u) and U (r) are all known.

$$u_i \leq_U u_j \rightleftarrows R(u_i) \subseteq R(u_j)$$

The resource that u_i can access is a subset of resources that u_j can access;

$$r_i \leq_R r_j \rightleftarrows U(r_j) \subseteq U(r_i)$$

That is, the user who can access r_i is a subset of the user who can access r_j;

$$u_i \equiv_U u_j \rightleftarrows R(u_i) = R(U_j)$$

That is, the resources that the two users can access and their access rights are exact the same.

$$r_i \equiv_R r_j \rightleftarrows U(r_j) = (r_i)$$

That is, the set of accessible users of the two resources ri and rj is exact the same.

The DAGs' preliminaries have been constructed under this algorithm but we fail to guarantee that he is conflict-free and complete. So the DAG model needs to be deep-rooted constructed in the next process, the conflict and incompleteness of the policy will be detected, eventually a complete conflict-free directed acyclic graph will be formed.

4 DAG Model

The algorithm of DAG construction is introduced below.

Input: The subject partial order structure $\leq U$, The object partial order structure $\leq R$;

Output: Hierarchical access control model $\leq V$;

(1) The subject partial order structure $\leq U$ is copied to form the partial order structure $\leq V$, that is, the initial state of $\leq V$ is $\leq U$;

(2) Select the node u_i according to the breadth-first traversal mode from the subject partial order structure $\leq U$, and press the node onto the stack SU;

(3) Select the node r_i according to the breadth-first traversal mode from the object partial order structure $\leq R$, and press the node onto the stack SR;

(4) Eject node r from SR; / / Prepare to insert data

(5) Eject node u from SU; / / Prepare to index data

(6) Find the node u in $\leq V$ and the direct successor node of this node u

If r $\in$ R (u) && r $\notin$ R (U ') Add r to the leaf node of the u in the $\leq$ V

Determine whether there is a direct successor to the r-node in the partial order structure $\leq R$ in the lower node of node r in $\leq V$, if there is, these successor nodes are linked to the r leaf nodes;

(7) if SU $\neq \emptyset$ GOTO (5); / / Determine the relationship between r and all nodes in U;

(8) if SR $\neq \emptyset$ GOTO (3); / / Reverse to breadth first traversal of all r$\in$ R;

(9) All r$\in$ R traversal in less than $\leq$ V, Determine whether there is u$\in$ U and has the same direct predecessor set and direct successor set, if such a r and u exist, the two nodes are merged into a node.

Figure 2 shows a complete DAG model constructed according to the algorithm.

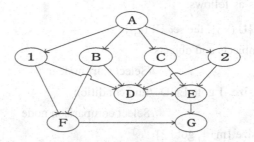

Fig. 2. Directed acyclic graph model

According to the algorithm, conflict and incompleteness of the policies can be found during the process of DAG construction. In the process of construction, it is the most important that the algorithm for equivalence node determination and parent-child node determination.

(1) Equivalence node determination algorithm

In the sort node set, vi and v_j was acquired, $v_i \equiv V\ v_i$ is equivalent, if and only if $U(v_i) \equiv U(v_j)$ and R (vi) $\equiv$ R (vj).
The decision algorithm is as follows:

Input: ordered node set SortV, set $\{U\ (v_i)\}$, and the set $\{R\ (v_j)\}$;
Output: Sorting node set SortV after merging equivalent nodes;

1.   i=0   //Get start node
2.   If i >= SortV. size goto END //End condition
3.   j = i +1   //select comparison node
4.   If j >= SortV. size {i++, goto 2}
5.   If $U(v_i) \equiv U(v_j)$ && $R(v_i) \equiv R(v_j)$ then $\{v_i=(v_i,v_j)$, SortV = SortV -$\{v_j\}\}$ // Comparing the subject and object sets of the two nodes and merging the equivalent nodes, vi= (vi, vj) indicates that a component element is added to the mul-ticomponent vi, that is, the node merges.
6.   j++   //Select the next node to be compared in the set SortV
7.   goto 4
8.   END

(2) Parent-child node determination algorithm

The parent-child relationship in the DAG can be determined directly by the subject-set inclusion relationship to form a pre-processed DAG. A node as an object needs to be added to the node set through a child node decision algorithm. The initial node set {v} is with only objects. If and only if S $(v_j) \subseteq$ S (v_i), v_j is the child node of v_i. The decision algorithm is as follows:

Input: set {v}, set {U (v_i)}, the set {R (v_j)}

Output: DAG of subjects and objects

1. m=0   //Select start node m

2. If m >= {v}. size -1 goto END //End condition

3. n = m +1   //Select comparison node

4. If n >= {v}. size {m++, goto 2}

5. If n $\notin$ DAG && U(m) $\subseteq$ U(n) then {add child nodes with n being m in DAG}

6. n++

7. goto 4

8. END

5 Experimental Verification and Results

Access control policies are described using the XACMIL language and are stored in XML format. The core idea of the experiment is to construct a directed acyclic graph (containing equivalent vertices), as showed in Fig. 2, and in turn, the hier-archical structure guarantees the correctness of access control relationships. The key issues of the experiment are to detect conflict and incompleteness in the policies. To confirm the correctness of our algorithm, a complete and correct access control policy set is given as showed in Fig. 3. Based on the preliminaries, DAG model of complete and conflict-free has been constructed. The following shows a detailed description of the detection of policy conflict and incompleteness.

Adding E -> H to construct an incomplete policy, who can clearly find by DAG model, only adding E -> H of node H, ignoring that the node above E can access H, resulting in an incomplete policy. Adding G -> D to form the loop policy D -> E -> G.

Add these two policies to the policy set and use the algorithm that constructs the DAG model given earlier to detect this policy set.

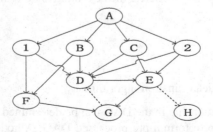

Fig. 3. DAG of incomplete strategy

After inconsistent and incomplete policies are inserted. Figure 3 are described as access control policies set, which are used for the experiment. DAG model and algorithm for equivalence node determination and parent-child node determination are used to verify the set.

The results for completeness is shown as:

```
policies completeness detection results
1[A] can access [A],[1],[B],[2],[C],[D],[E],[F],[G]
2[E]can access [E],[G],[H]
  You may omit the policy:[A]→[H]
1[1] can access [1],[D],[E],[F],[G]
2[E]can access [E],[G],[H]
  You may omit the policy:[1]→[H]
1[B] can access [B],[D],[E],[F],[G]
2[E]can access [E],[G],[H]
  You may omit the policy:[B]→[H]
1[C] can access [C],[D],[E],[F],[G]
2[E]can access [E],[G],[H]
  You may omit the policy:[C]→[H]
1[2] can access [2],[D],[E],[F],[G]
2[E]can access [E],[G],[H]
  You may omit the policy:[2]→[H]
1[D] can access[D],[E],[G]
2[E]can access [E],[G],[H]
  You may omit the policy:[D]→[H]
```

Fig. 4. Results of policy conflict detection

According to Fig. 3, we can clearly see that there is A, 1, B, 2, C, D above the H node. Figure 4 shows the algorithm detection results. The detection results are shown that the Penurious (Minssing) policy is A → H, 1 → H, B → H, 2 → H, C → H, and D → H. The missing policy displayed by the DAG model is consistent with the algorithm detection results.

```
Loop detection results
The subiect-set of [G] is: [A],[1],[B],[C],[2],[D],[E],[F],[G]
The object-set of [G] is [D],[E],[G]
The subiect-set of [E] is: [A],[1],[B],[C],[2],[D],[E],[F],[G]
The object-set of [E] is [D],[E],[G]
The subiect-set of [D] is: [A],[1],[B],[C],[2],[D],[E],[F],[G]
The object-set of [D] is [D],[E],[G]
loop conflict exist in the following nodes: [D],[E],[G]
```

Fig. 5. The results loop conflict detection

We can clearly see from Fig. 3 that $U(D) \equiv U(E) \equiv U(G)$ and $R(D) \equiv R(E) \equiv R$ (G). D, E, and G form a loop. According to the previous DAG model construction algorithm to verify the experimental results, Fig. 5 shows the detection results of policy loop conflict, and gives a set of nodes forming a loop. The verification results show that the detection results of the algorithm are consistent with the visual display of the DAG model.

Table 1 shows the comparison and analysis of related work and algorithm in this paper, and it can be found that DAG model is more practical and easy to find incomplete policies.

Table 1. Comparison of security policy conflict detection methods

Conflict detection category	Advantage	Disadvantage
Based on formal logic	Reasonable and accuracy	Difficult to achieve
Based on description language	Implementation is Simple	The scope of application is narrow and scalability is poor
Ontology-based technology	Include the above two points	Ontology-dependent
Based on DAG	Practical	Loop detection is complicated

6 Conclusion

The preliminary provides early preparations for the construction of the DAG model. During DAG model building, policy inconsistency and incompleteness are detected. It not only streamlines the process of policy management, but also improves the efficiency of policy detection. And the correctness of the results of DAG model decect was verified by our experiments. However, for inconsistent policies, the whole policies set should be verified for detection. And that is our work should be made in the future.

Acknowledgments. This research was supported in part by the National Natural Science Foundation of China under grant numbers 61672206, 61572170. Hongbin Zhang is the corresponding author of this article.

References

1. Sharma, M., Sural, S., Vaidya, J., Atluri, V.: An administrative model for temporal role-based access control. Comput. Secur. **8303**(39), 375–389 (2013)
2. Smari, W.W., Clemente, P., Lalande, J.F.: An extended attribute based access control model with trust and privacy: application to a collaborative crisis management system. Future Gener. Comput. Syst. **31**(1), 147–168 (2014)
3. Aqib, M., Shaikh, R.A.: Analysis and comparison of access control policies validation mechanisms. Int. J. Comput. Netw. Inf. Secur. **7**(1), 54–69 (2014)

4. St-Martin, M., Felty, A.P.: Verified algorithm for detecting conicts in XACML access control rules. ACM Sigplan Conf. Certif. Programs Proofs **25**(10), 166–175 (2016)
5. Lu, Q., Chen, J., Ma, H., Chen, W.: Optimization algorithm for extensible access control markup language policies. J. Comput. Sci. **44**(12), 110–113 (2017)
6. Bauer, L., Garriss, S., Reiter, M.K.: Detecting and resolving policy misconfigurations in access-control systems. ACM Trans. Inf. Syst. Secur. **14**(1), 1–28 (2008)
7. Cau, A., Janicke, H., Moszkowski, B.: Verification and enforcement of access control policies. Formal Methods Syst. Des. **43**(3), 450–492 (2013)
8. Calero, J.M., Pérez, J.M., Bernabé, J., et al.: Detection of semantic consistency in ontology and rule-based information systems. Data Know. Eng. **69**(11), 1117–1137 (2010)
9. Shaikh, R.A., Adi, K., Logrippo, L.: A data classification method for inconsistency and incompleteness detection in access control policy sets. Int. J. Inf. Secur. **16**(1), 91–113 (2017)
10. Li, T.: Research on checking and digesting policy consistency under multi-policy environments. Huazhong University of Science and Technology, pp. 16–27 (2011)

Author Index